T0189999

Communications
in Computer and Information Science   836

Commenced Publication in 2007
Founding and Former Series Editors:
Phoebe Chen, Alfredo Cuzzocrea, Xiaoyong Du, Orhun Kara, Ting Liu,
Dominik Ślęzak, and Xiaokang Yang

More information about this series at http://www.springer.com/series/7899

Jyotsna Kumar Mandal · Devadatta Sinha (Eds.)

Social Transformation – Digital Way

52nd Annual Convention
of the Computer Society of India, CSI 2017
Kolkata, India, January 19–21, 2018
Revised Selected Papers

 Springer

Editors
Jyotsna Kumar Mandal
Kalyani University
Kalyani
India

Devadatta Sinha
University of Calcutta
Kolkata
India

ISSN 1865-0929   ISSN 1865-0937   (electronic)
Communications in Computer and Information Science
ISBN 978-981-13-1342-4   ISBN 978-981-13-1343-1   (eBook)
https://doi.org/10.1007/978-981-13-1343-1

Library of Congress Control Number: 2018950770

This Springer imprint is published by the registered company Springer Nature Singapore Pte Ltd.
The registered company address is: 152 Beach Road, #21-01/04 Gateway East, Singapore 189721, Singapore

Foreword

The Computer Society of India organized its 52nd Annual Convention on the Theme "Social Transformation- Digital Way" during January 18–21, 2018 at Science City, Kolkata. Pre-Convention Tutorial was held on January 18. 2018. Over six hundred delegates, from all walks of lifle from academic institutions, government departments, industry houses and other stake holders *were* attend the Convention.

The Annual Convention of CSI is always an important and prestigious event of the Computer Society of India being held since the year 1966 when CSI-66 the first Annual Convention with the theme "An Ideal Computer Map for India" was held at Kolkata. Since then this annul mega event of the Society has been held at different cities having infrastructure facilities for organizing such events.

This year the event was organized at the Science City, Kolkata, India which provided, required infrastructure with. its ideal environment. As is followed every year, there were invited addresses and general speeches of interest, paper presentations, and panel discussions in multiple tracks/ sessions, covering diverse topics of interest. Proceedings of selected papers are being published by Springer in COS series indexed by SCIMago, Scopus. DBLP etc. The theme was on the social transformation through different digital ways. Connectivity, with governments, both at the central and state levels is using technology to make this transformation to achieve doorstep connectivity with its citizens. There were exhibition stalls where state-of- the- art and enlarging products and services were showcased and demonstrated to the interested delegates.

Extensive opportunities were there to encourage interaction and build everlasting relationship among all the participants in the Convention at all levels and also with the number of sponsors/partners at different levels. This Convention contributed actively towards the holistic development of the Society and makes the digital mission and social transformation in the years to come. This international conference connected face to face with 600+ professionals representing some of the top corporate in the country.

The CSI 2017 organized by Computer Society of India Kolkata Chapter is involving various International Researchers and Academicians, and industry Dignitaries. Dignitaries and eminent technical speakers from premier academic and research institutes in India namely, Indian institute of Science Bangalore, Indian Institute of Technology Kharagpur, Indian Statistical Institute Kolkata, Indian Institute of Management Bangalore, Jadavpur University, Calcutta University, TCS, Medical colleges, Kansas University etc. were participated. In addition, some leading academic and research luminaries representing Universities/Institutes of International repute from abroad have participated in the event.

This volume contains chapters like Signal Processing, Microwave and Communication Engineering, Circuits and Systems, Data Science and Data Analytics, Bio Computing, Social Computing, Mobile, Nano and Quantum Computing, Data Mining, Security and Forensics, Digital image Processing and Computational Intelligence.

Some papers in this volume are on Diabetes Mellitus risk factor prediction, eye tracking with evolutionary head movement for vision based rehabilitation, evaluation of bacterial blight in a rice plant, digital photo trichogram for hair fall diagnosis, identification of Benign and Malignant cells from cytological images. PV cell operated motor to drive fans and pumps in rural areas. Mobile governance using Sanskrit grammar etc.

Easy Chair scoring scheme has been adopted to select best 59 papers based on double blind reviews using Easy Chair. Papers were received from IITs, ISI, IIITs, JU, CU, KU along with some papers from USA and UK. Presented papers were modified as per suggestions of session judges and modified papers were uploaded into the Springer after checking similarities again. Springer scrutinized all uploaded papers and finally they have selected the papers for publication.

Hope this volume will be a very good value added material in the field of Computer Science, IT and transformation of social system into digital form. Researchers and academicians will he benefited from this volume as a state-of-the-art value added source of information.

Atal Chaudhuri

Preface

The Computer Society of India organized the 52nd Annual Convention on the theme "Social Transformation-Digital Way" during January 19–21, 2018, at Science City, Kolkata. The pre-convention tutorial was organized on January 18, 2018, at the Technology Campus of the University of Calcutta. The response was overwhelming and 370 enthusiastic participants came all the way from Gourbanga University, Malda and the colleges of Bankura, West Midnapur, Durgapur, Haldia, Kalyani, and Hooghly, in addition to various universities and institutes within the territory of Kolkata. Over 600 delegates, from all walks of life (academic institutions, government departments, industry houses, and other stake holders) attended the conference.

This is an important and prestigious event of the Society and has been held since 1966, when CSI-66, the first annual convention cum conference with the theme "An Ideal Computer Map for India," was held at Kolkata. Since then, this annual mega event of the Society has been held at different cities of India. The Kolkata Chapter has hosted this event eight times in 1966, 1978, 1986, 1990, 1994, 2001, 2006, and 2012. This was the ninth time that Kolkata hosted this conference.

The conference had an interesting combination of keynote addresses, motivational talk, invited talks, general speeches of interest, talks from industries, paper presentations, and panel discussions in multiple sessions, covering diverse topics of interest. The proceedings of the selected and presented papers was published in the CCIS series of Springer Nature, free of cost. We are thankful to the authority of Springer for their active association with CSI. Three best paper awards of 250 Euro, 200 Euro and 150 Euro in the form of eBook vouchers were also given by Springer.

The papers were checked for similarities multiple times through iThenticate, access of which was provided by Springer. The EasyChair scoring scheme was adopted to select the best papers (59 in all) out of 157 submissions based on reviews using EasyChair. We received papers from IITs, ISI, IIITs, JU, CU, KU, along with some papers from the USA and UK. The presented papers were modified as per the suggestions of the session judges and modified papers were uploaded to the Springer system after rechecking for similarities. We are grateful to the contributors and reviewers for their efforts.

The theme of the conference was well deliberated upon and the organizers unanimously decided on "Social Transformation" through different digital ways. This was primarily because the central and state governments at their respective levels were using technology to make this transformation possible by ensuring connectivity with its citizens. In line with the theme, the conference was organized in such a manner that participants could get extensive opportunities to explore and build everlasting networks at different levels.

We hope that this volume was useful and contributed extensively towards a holistic development of the Society, while fulfilling the digital mission of bringing on social transformation in the years to come. This volume aims to definitely be a value-addition for academicians, researchers, and budding engineers and scientists.

August 2018   Jyotsna Kumar Mandal
                                                                   Devadatta Sinha

Organization

Patrons

Taranjit Singh	JIS Group, India
Saikat Maitra	Maulana Abul Kalam Azad University of Technology, India
Subhansu Bandopadhyay	Brainware University, India
Dilip Kumar Sinha	Visva-Bharati, India
Rajat Bose	Kolkata Doordarshan Kendra, India
Manas Pratim Das	All India Radio, India
Dwijesh Dutta Majumder	Computer Society of India, India
Nirajit Kanta Roy	Computer Society of India, India
Debabrata Ghosh Dastidar	Computer Society of India, India
Shyam Sundar Aggarwal	Computer Society of India, India
Samir Kumar Bandopadhyay	Computer Society of India, India
Devaprasanna Sinha	Computer Society of India, India
Debesh Kumar Das	Computer Society of India, India
Subimal Kundu	Computer Society of India, India
Rabindra Nath Lahiri	Computer Society of India, India
Sibsankar Daspal	Computer Society of India, India
Devadatta Sinha	Computer Society of India, India
Dipti Prasad Mukherjee	Computer Society of India, India
Sanjay Mahapatra	Computer Society of India, India
Gautam Mahapatra	Computer Society of India, India
A. K. Nayak	Computer Society of India, India
Manas Ranjan Pattnaik	Computer Society of India, India
Anirban Basu	Computer Society of India, India

Advisory Board

Amiya Nayak	Ottawa University, Canada
Sajal Das	University of Texas at Arlington, USA
Santosh Mohanty	TCS, India
A. Damodaram	Jawaharlal Nehru Technological University, India
A. K. Nayek	Secretary, CSI, India
A. Kaykobad	Bangladesh University of Engineering and Technology, Bangladesh
Aditya Bagchi	RKM University, India
Anirban Basu	Immediate Past President, CSI, India
Arun Baran Samaddar	National Institute of Technology, Sikkim, India
Atal Chowdhury	Jadavpur University, India
Atulya Nagar	Liverpool Hope University, UK

Aynur Unal	Stanford University, USA
B. K. Panigrahi	Indian Institute of Technology Delhi, India
Barin Kumar De	Tripura University, India
Basabi Chakraborty	Iwate Prefectural University, Japan
Bidyut Baran Chaudhuri	Indian Statistical Institute Kolkata, India
Girijasankar Mallik	University of Western Sydney, Australia
Hyeona Lim	Mississippi State University, USA
K. V. Arya	Indian Institute of Information Technology and Management Gwalior, India
Kalyanmoy Deb	Michigan State University, USA
Millie Pant	Indian Institute of Technology Roorkee, India
Mrinal Kanti Naskar	Jadavpur University, India
Nandini Mukhopadhyay	Jadavpur University, India
Prith Banerjee	Schneider Electric, USA
R. N. Lahiri	CSI, Kolkata Chapter, India
Rahul Kala	Indian Institute of Information Technology Allahabad, India
Rajkumar Buyya	University of Melbourne, Australia
S. Bandopadhyay	Calcutta University, India
Shikharesh Majumdar	Carleton University, Canada
Siddhartha Bhattacharjee	RCC Institute of Information Technology, India
Somnath Mukhopadhay	Texas University, USA
Subarna Shakya	Tribhuvan University, Nepal
Subhansu Bandyopadhyay	Calcutta University, India
Ujjwal Maulik	Jadavpur University, India
Valentina E. Balas	Aurel Vlaicu University of Arad, Romania
Y. Narahari	Indian Institute of Science Bengaluru, India
Zbigniew Michalewicz	University of Adelaide, Australia
Manas Ranjan Pattnaik	Treasurer, CSI, India
Sanjay Mahapatra	President, CSI, India
Suresh Chandra Satapathy	PVPSIT, India

Conference Chair

| Goutam Mahapatra (Vice President) | CSI, India |

Convener

| Devaprasanna Sinha, (Regional Vice-President I) | CSI, India |

Editorial Board

| Jyotsna Kumar Mandal | University of Kalyani, India |
| Devadatta Sinha | University of Calcutta, India |

Organizing Committee

Phalguni Mukherjee (Chair)   CSI, India
Subir Lahiri (Co-chair)   CSI, India

Program Committee

Jyotsna Kumar Mandal (Chair)
Devadatta Sinha (Co-chair)

Exhibition Committee

Sib Daspal (Chair)
Gautam Hajra (Co-chair)

Finance Committee

Alakananda Rao
Sourav Chakraborty

Tutorial Committee

Amlan Chakrabarti
Debasish Dey
Somenath Mukhopadhyay

Event Committee

Samir Kr. Bandyopadhyay
Asish Kumar Mukhopadhyay

Registration Committee

Aniruddha Nag
Abhijit Sarkar

Hospitality Committee

Indranil Ghosh
Manas Kumar Sanyal
Subhranshu Roy

Publicity Committee

Subhobrata Roychaufhuri
Kaushik Roy

Souvenir Committee

Madhumita Sengupta

Technical Program Committee

Arindam Pal	TCS Innovation Lab, India
Anindita Roy	B. P. Poddar Institute of Management and Technology, India
A. C. Mondal	University of Burdwan, India
A. Chattopadhyay	Siliguri Institute of Technology, India
A. Bagchi	Swami Vivekananada University, India
A. M. Sudhakara	University of Mysore, India
Abhishek Bhattacharya	Institute of Engineering and Management, India
Ambar Dutta	Computer Society of India, Kolkata Chapter, India
Amiya Kumar Rath	Veer Surendra Sai University of Technology, India
Amlan Chakrabarti	Calcutta University, India
Andrew M. Lynn	Jawaharlal Nehru Technological University, India
Angshuman Bhttacharyya	National Institute of Technology Durgapur, India
Angsuman Sarkar	Kalyani Government Engineering College, India
Anirban Guha	Jadavpur University, India
Anupam Baliyan	Bharati Vidyapeeth's Institute of Computers Applications and Management, India
Anuradha Banerjee	Kalyani Government Engineering College, India
Arnab K. Laha	Indian Institute of Management Ahmedabad, India
Arpita Chakraborty	Techno India Salt Lake, India
Arun K. Pujari	University of Hyderabad, India
Arundhati Bagchi Misra	Saginaw Valley State University, USA
Asad A. M. Al-Salih	University of Bagdad, Iraq
Ashok Kumar Rai	Gujarat University, India
Asif Ekbal	Indian Institute of Technology Patna, India
Asok Kumar	MCKV Institute of Engineering, India
Atanu Kundu	Heritage institute of Technology, India
Ayan Datta	IACS, Kolkata, India
B. B. Pal	University of Kalyani, India
Balakrushna Tripathy	Vellore Institute of Technology, India
Banshidhar Majhi	National Institute of Technology Rourkela, India
Bhaba R. Sarker	Louisiana State University, USA
Bhabani P. Sinha	Indian Statistical Institute Kolkata, India
Bhagvati Chakravarthy	University of Hyderabad, India

Bhaskar Sardar	Jadavpur University, India
Bibhas Chandra Dhara	Jadavpur University, India
Biplab K. Sikdar	Indian Institute of Engineering Science and Technology Shibpur, India
Brojo Kishore Mishra	C. V. Raman College of Engineering, India
Buddhadeb Manna	University of Calcutta, India
C. K. Chanda	Indian Institute of Engineering Science and Technology, India
C. Srinivas	Kakatiya Institute of Technology and Science, India
Carlos A. Bana e Costa	Universidade de Lisboa, Portugal
Chandan Bhar	Indian School of Mines, India
Chandreyee Chowdhury	Jadavpur University, India
Chilukuri K. Mohan	Syracuse University, USA
Chintan Mandal	Jadavpur University, India
R. K. Samanta	Siliguri Institute of Technology, India
Dakshina Ranjan Kisku	National Institute of Technology Durgapur, India
Debashis De	Maulana Abul Kalam Azad University of Technology, India
Debasish Nandi	National Institute of Technology Durgapur, India
Debdatta Kandar	North East Hill University, India
Debesh Das	Jadavpur University, India
Debidas Ghosh	National Institute of Technology Durgapur, India
Debotosh Bhattacharjee	Jadavpur University, India
Deepak Khemani	Indian Institute of Technology Madras, India
Deepak Kumar	Amity University, India
Dhananjay Bhattacharyya	Saha Institute of Nuclear Physics, India
Dhananjay Kumar Singh	Global ICT Standardization Forum for India (GISFI), India
Diganta Goswami	Indian Institute of Technology Guwahati, India
Dilip Kumar Pratihar	Indian Institute of Technology Kharagpur, India
Dipanwita Roychowdhury	Indian Institute of Technology Kharagpur, India
Dulal Acharjee	Purushottam Institute of Engineering and Technology, India
Durgesh Kumar Mishra	Computer Society of India, India
Esteban Alfaro Cortés	University of Castilla-La Mancha, Spain
Ganapati Panda	Indian Institute of Technology Bhubaneswar, India
Goutam Sarker	National Institute of Technology Durgapur, India
Goutam Sanyal	National Institute of Technology Durgapur, India
Govinda K.	Vellore Institute of Technology, India
Gunamani Jena	Roland Institute of Technology, India
H. S. Lalliel	University of Derby, UK
Hirak Maity	College of Engineering and Management Kolaghat, India
Indrajit Bhattacharjee	Kalyani Government Engineering College, India
Indrajit Saha	National Institute of Technical Teachers' Training and Research Kolkata, India

J. V. R. Murthy	Jawaharlal Nehru Technological University Kakinada, India
Jimson Mathew	University of Bristol, UK
Jyoti Prakash Singh	National Institute of Technology Patna, India
K. K. Bagchi	University of Texas at El Paso, USA
K. Kannan	Nagaland University, India
K. Srujan Raju	CMR Group of Institutions, India
K. Suresh Basu	Jawaharlal Nehru Technological University, India
Kameswari Chebrolu	Indian Institute of Technology Bombay, India
Kandarpa Kumar Sarma	Gauhati University, India
Kartick Chandra Mandal	Jadavpur University, India
Kausik Dasgupta	Kalyani Government Engineering College, India
Koushik Majumder	Maulana Abul Kalam Azad University of Technology, India
Kui Yu	University of South Australia, Australia
Kunal Das	Narula Institute of Technology, India
Lothar Thiele	Swiss Federal Institute of Technology Zurich, Switzerland
M. Ali Akber Dewan	Athabasca University, Canada
M. S. Prasad Babu	Andhra University, India
M. Sandirigama	University of Peradenia, Sri Lanka
Malay Bhattacharyya	Indian Institute of Engineering Science and Technology, India
Malay Pakhira	Kalyani Government Engineering College, India
Manas Kumar Bera	Haldia Institute of Technology, India
Manas Ranjan Senapati	Centurion University of Technology and Management, India
Manish Kumar Kakhani	Mody University, India
Massimo Pollifroni	University of Turin, Italy
Md. Iftekhar Hussain	North East Hill University, India
Mohammad Ubadullah Bokhari	Aligarh Muslim University, India
Mohd Nazri Ismail	Universiti Pertahanan Nasional Malaysia, Malaysia
N. V. Ramana Rao	Jawaharlal Nehru Technological University, India
Nabendu Chaki	Calcutta University, India
Nibaran Das	Jadavpur University, India
Nilanjan Dey	Techno India College of Technology, India
P. Premchand	Osmania University Hyderabad, India
P. S. Neelakanta	Florida Atlantic University, India
Parag Kulkarni	iknowlation Research Labs Pvt. Ltd., India
Parama Bhaumik	Jadavpur University, India
Partha Pratim Sahu	Tezpur University, India
Pawan Kumar Jha	Purbanchal University, Nepal
Pawan Lingras	St. Mary's University, Canada
Pradosh K. Roy	Asia Pacific Institute of Information Technology, India
Pramod Kumar Meher	Nanyang Technological University, Singapore

Pranab K. Dan	Indian Institute of Technology Kharagpur, India
Prasanta K. Jana	Indian School of Mines Dhanbad, India
Prashant R. Nair	Computer Society of India, India
Pratyay Kuila	National Institute of Technology Sikkim, India
Priya Ranjan Sinha Mahapatra	University of Kalyani, India
R. K. Pal	University of Calcutta, India
Radha Krishna Bar	FIEM, India
R. DattaGupta	Jadavpur University, India
R. K. Jana	Indian Institute of Social Welfare and Business Management, India
R. N. Lahiri	Batanagar Institute of Engineering Management and Science, India
R. Sankararama Krishnan	Indian Institute of Technology Kanpur, India
Rajeeb Dey	National Institute of Technology Silchar, India
Ram Sarkar	Jadavpur University, India
Rameshwar Dubey	South University of Science and Technology of China, China
Ranjan Kumar Gupta	West Bengal State University, India
Ray Zhong	University of Auckland, New Zealand
Rober Hans	Tshwane University of Technology, South Africa
S. V. K. Bharathi	Symbiosis International University, India
S. D. Dewasurendra	University of Peradenia, Sri Lanka
S. G. Deshmukh	Indian Institute of Technology, Mumbai, India
S. K. Behera	National Institute of Technology Rourkela, India
S. P. Bhattacharyya	Texas A&M University, USA
Saikat Chakrabarti	CSIR-IICB, Kolkata, India
Samar Sen Sarma	University of Calcutta, India
Samiran Chattopadhyay	Jadavpur University, India
Sandip Rakshit	Kaziranga University, India
Sanjib K. Panda	Berkeley Education Alliance for Research in Singapore Limited, Singapore
Sankar Chakraborty	Jadavpur University, India
Sankar Duraikannan	Asia Pacific University of Technology and Innovation, Malaysia
Santi P. Maity	Indian Institute of Engineering Science and Technology Shibpur, India
Sarbani Roy	Jadavpur University, India
Satish Narayana Srirama	University of Tartu, Estonia
Saurabh Dutta	Dr. B.C. Roy Engineering College Durgapur, India
Seba Maity	College of Engineering and Management Kolaghat, India
Shangping Ren	Illinois Institute of Technology, USA
Soma Barman	University of Calcutta, India
Somdatta Chakraborty	MKAUT, India
Soumya Pandit	University of Calcutta, India
Sripati Mukhopadhyay	Burdwan University, India

Sruti Gan Chaudhuri	Jadavpur University, India
Subhadip Basu	Jadavpur University, India
Subho Chaudhuri	BIT Mesra Kolkata, India
Subhranil Som	Amity University Noida, India
Subir Sarkar	Jadavpur University, India
Subrata Banerjee	National Institute of Technology Durgapur, India
Sudhakar Sahoo	Institute of Mathematics and Applications, India
Sudhakar Tripathi	National Institute of Technology Patna, India
Sudip Kumar Adhikari	Cooch Behar Government Engineering College, India
Sudip Kumar Das	Calcutta University, India
Sudip Kundu	Calcutta University, India
Sudipta Roy	Assam University, India
Sukumar Nandi	Indian Institute of Technology Guwahati, India
Sumit Kundu	National Institute of Technology Durgapur, India
Sunirmal Khatua	Calcutta University, India
Supratim Sengupta	Indian Institute of Engineering Science and Technology, Shibpur, India
Sushmita Mitra	Indian Statistical Institute Kolkata, India
Suvamoy Changder	National Institute of Technology Durgapur, India
Swagatam Das	Indian Statistical Institute Kolkata, India
Swapan Kumar Mandal	Kalyani Government Engineering College, India
Syed Samsul Alam	Aliah University, India
T. K. Kaul	Sikkim University, India
Tamaghna Acharya	Indian Institute of Engineering, Science and Technology, India
Tandra Pal	National Institute of Technology, Durgapur, India
Tanushyam Chattopadhyay	TCS Innovation Lab, India
Tapan K. Ghosh	West Bengal University of Animal and Fishery Sciences, India
Tushar Kanti Bera	Yonsei University, South Korea
U. Dinesh Kumar	Indian Institute of Management Bangalore, India
Utpal Biswas	University of Kalyani, India
V. Prithiviraj	Pondicherry Engineering College, India
Vikrant Bhateja	Shri Ram Swaroop Memorial Group of Professional Colleges, India
Vladimir A. Oleshchuk	University of Agder, Norway
Yoshihiro Kilho Shin	University of Hyogo, Japan
Zaigham Mahmood	University of Derby, UK
Muheet Ahmed Butt	University of Kashmir, India
Arijit Chowdhury	TCS Innovation Lab, India
Hemanta Dey	Techno India College of Technology, India
Samir Malakar	Asutosh College, India
Snehasis Banerjee	TCS Innovation Lab, India

List of MC/NC 2017–2018 of Computer Society of India, Kolkata Chapter

Chairman

Subir Kumar Lahiri

Vice Chairman

Ambar Dutta

Secretary

Subho Chaudhuri

Treasurer

Madhumita Sengupta

Immediate Past Chairman

Jyotsna Kumar Mandal

MC Members

Sanjoy Kumar Saha   Ajanta Das
Nabendu Chaki   Abhik Mukherjee
Sumanta Bhattacharya   Manas Kumar Sanyal
Abhijit Sarkar   Asish Kumar Mukhopadhyay

NC Members

Indranil Ghosh
Radha Krishna Bar
Bidyut Chakrabort

Additional Reviewers

A. Bagchi	Swami Vivekananada University, India
A. C. Mondal	University of Burdwan, India
A. Chattopadhyay	Siliguri Institute of Technology, India
A. M. Sudhakara	University of Mysore, India
Abhishek Bhattacharya	Institute of Engineering and Management, India
Ambar Dutta	Computer Society of India Kolkata Chapter, India
Amiya Kumar Rath	Veer Surendra Sai University of Technology, India
Amlan Chakrabarti	Calcutta University, India
Andrew M. Lynn	Jawaharlal Nehru Technological University, India
Angshuman Bhttacharyya	National Institute of Technology Durgapur, India

Angsuman Sarkar   Kalyani Government Engineering College, India
Anindita Roy   B. P. Poddar Institute of Management
                            and Technology, India
Anirban Guha   Jadavpur University, India
Anupam Baliyan   Bharati Vidyapeeth's Institute of Computers
                            Applications and Management, India
Anuradha Banerjee   Kalyani Government Engineering College, India
Arindam Pal   TCS Innovation Lab, India
Arnab K. Laha   Indian Institute of Management Ahmedabad, India
Arpita Chakraborty   Techno India Salt Lake, India
Arun K. Pujari   University of Hyderabad, India
Arundhati Bagchi Misra   Saginaw Valley State University, USA
Asad A. M. Al-Salih   University of Bagdad, Iraq
Ashok Kumar Rai   Gujarat University, India
Asif Ekbal   Indian Institute of Technology Patna, India
Asok Kumar   MCKV Institute of Engineering, India
Atanu Kundu   Heritage institute of Technology, India
Ayan Datta   IACS, Kolkata, India
B. B. Pal   University of Kalyani, India
Balakrushna Tripathy   Vellore Institute of Technology, India
Banshidhar Majhi   National Institute of Technology Rourkela, India
Bhaba R. Sarker   Louisiana State University, USA
Bhabani P Sinha   Indian Statistical Institute Kolkata, India
Bhagvati Chakravarthy   University of Hyderabad, India
Bhaskar Sardar   Jadavpur University, India
Bibhas Chandra Dhara   Jadavpur University, India
Biplab K. Sikdar   Indian Institute of Engineering Science
                            and Technology Shibpur, India
Brojo Kishore Mishra   C. V. Raman College of Engineering, India
Buddhadeb Manna   University of Calcutta, India
C. K. Chanda   Indian Institute of Engineering Science
                            and Technology Shibpur, India
C. Srinivas   Kakatiya Institute of Technology and Science, India
Carlos A. Bana e Costa   Universidade de Lisboa, Portugal
Chandan Bhar   Indian School of Mines, India
Chandreyee Chowdhury   Jadavpur University, India
Chilukuri K. Mohan   Syracuse University, USA
Chintan Mandal   Jadavpur University, India
Dakshina Ranjan Kisku   National Institute of Technology Durgapur, India
Debashis De   Maulana Abul Kalam Azad University
                            of Technology, India
Debasish Nandi   National Institute of Technology Durgapur, India
Debdatta Kandar   North East Hill University, India
Debesh Das   Jadavpur University, India
Debidas Ghosh   National Institute of Technology Durgapur, India
Debotosh Bhattacharjee   Jadavpur University, India

Deepak Khemani	Indian Institute of Technology Madras, India
Deepak Kumar	Amity University, India
Dhananjay Bhattacharyya	Saha Institute of Nuclear Physics, Kolkata India
Dhananjay Kumar Singh	Global ICT Standardization Forum for India (GISFI), India
Diganta Goswami	Indian Institute of Technology Guwahati, India
Dilip Kumar Pratihar	Indian Institute of Technology Kharagpur, India
Dipanwita Roychowdhury	Indian Institute of Technology Kharagpur, India
Dulal Acharjee	Purushottam Institute of Engineering and Technology, India
Durgesh Kumar Mishra	Computer Society of India, India
Esteban Alfaro Cortés	University of Castilla-La Mancha, Spain,
Ganapati Panda	Indian Institute of Technology Bhubaneswar, India
Goutam Sanyal	National Institute of Technology Durgapur, India
Goutam Sarker	National Institute of Technology Durgapur, India
Govinda K.	Vellore Institute of Technology, India
Gunamani Jena	Roland Institute of Technology, India
H. S. Lalliel	University of Derby, UK
Hirak Maity	College of Engineering and Management Kolaghat, India
Indrajit Bhattacharjee	Kalyani Government Engineering College, India
Indrajit Saha	National Institute of Technical Teachers' Training and Research Kolkata, India
J. V. R. Murthy	Jawaharlal Nehru Technological University Kakinada, India
Jimson Mathew	University of Bristol, UK
Jyoti Prakash Singh	National Institute of Technology Patna, India
K. K. Bagchi	University of Texas at El Paso, USA
K. Kannan	Nagaland University, India
K. Srujan Raju	CMR Group of Institutions, India
K. Suresh Basu	Jawaharlal Nehru Technological University, India
Kameswari Chebrolu	Indian Institute of Technology Bombay, India
Kandarpa Kumar Sarma	Gauhati University, India
Kartick Chandra Mandal	Jadavpur University, India
Koushik Majumder	Maulana Abul Kalam Azad University of Technology, India
Kui Yu	University of South Australia, Australia
Kunal Das	Narula Institute of Technology, India
Lothar Thiele	Swiss Federal Institute of Technology Zurich, Switzerland
M. Ali Akber Dewan	Athabasca University, Canada
M. S. Prasad Babu	Andhra University, India
M. Sandirigama	University of Peradenia, Sri Lanka
Malay Bhattacharyya	Indian Institute of Engineering Science and Technology, India
Manas Kumar Bera	Haldia Institute of Technology, India

Manas Ranjan Senapati	Centurion University of Technology and Management, India
Manish Kumar Kakhani	Mody University, India
Massimo Pollifroni	University of Turin, Italy
Md. Iftekhar Hussain	North East Hill University, India
Mohd Nazri Ismail	University Pertahanan National Malaysia, Malaysia
N. V. Ramana Rao	Jawaharlal Nehru Technological University, India
Nabendu Chaki	Calcutta University, India
Nibaran Das	Jadavpur University, Kolkata, India
Nilanjan Dey	Techno India College of Technology, India
P. Premchand	Osmania University Hyderabad, India
P. S. Neelakanta	Florida Atlantic University, India
Parama Bhaumik	Jadavpur University, India
Partha Pratim Sahu	Tezpur University, India
Pawan Kumar Jha	Purbanchal University, Nepal
Pawan Lingras	St. Mary's University, Canada
Pradosh K. Roy	Asia Pacific Institute of Information Technology, India
Pramod Kumar Meher	Nanyang Technological University, Singapore
Pranab K. Dan	Indian Institute of Technology Kharagpur, India
Prasanta K. Jana	Indian School of Mines Dhanbad, India
Prashant R. Nair	Computer Society of India, India
Pratyay Kuila	National Institute of Technology Sikkim, India
Priya Ranjan Sinha Mahapatra	University of Kalyani, India
R. Datta Gupta	Jadavpur University, India
R. K. Pal	University of Calcutta, India
R. K. Jana	Indian Institute of Social Welfare and Business Management, India
R. N. Lahiri	Batanagar Institute of Engineering Management and Science, India
R. Sankararama Krishnan	Indian Institute of Technology Kanpur, India
R. K. Samanta	Siliguri Institute of Technology, India
Rajeeb Dey	National Institute of Technology Silchar, India
Ram Sarkar	Jadavpur University, India
Rameshwar Dubey	South University of Science and Technology of China, China
Ranjan Kumar Gupta	West Bengal State University, India
Ray Zhong	University of Auckland, New Zealand
Rober Hans	Tshwane University of Technology, South Africa
S. V. K. Bharathi	Symbiosis International University, India
S. D. Dewasurendra	University of Peradenia, Sri Lanka
S. G. Deshmukh	Indian Institute of Technology, Mumbai, India
S. K. Behera	National Institute of Technology Rourkela, India
S. P. Bhattacharyya	Texas A&M University, USA
Saikat Chakrabarti	CSIR-IICB, Kolkata, India
Samar Sen Sarma	University of Calcutta, India

Samiran Chattopadhyay	Jadavpur University, India
Sandip Rakshit	Kaziranga University, India
Sanjib K. Panda	Berkeley Education Alliance for Research in Singapore Limited, Singapore
Sankar Chakraborty	Jadavpur University, India
Sankar Duraikannan	Asia Pacific University of Technology and Innovation, Malaysia
Santi P. Maity	Indian Institute of Engineering Science and Technology Shibpur, India
Sarbani Roy	Jadavpur University, India
Satish Narayana	Srirama University of Tartu, Estonia
Saurabh Dutta	Dr. B.C. Roy Engineering College Durgapur, India
Seba Maity	College of Engineering and Management Kolaghat, India
Shangping Ren	Illinois Institute of Technology, USA
Soma Barman	University of Calcutta, India
Soumya Pandit	University of Calcutta, India
Sripati Mukhopadhyay	Burdwan University, India
Sruti Gan Chaudhuri	Jadavpur University, India
Subhadip Basu	Jadavpur University, India
Subho Chaudhuri	BIT Mesra Kolkata, India
Subhranil Som	Amity University Noida, India
Subir Sarkar	Jadavpur University, India
Subrata Banerjee	National Institute of Technology Durgapur, India
Sudhakar Sahoo	Institute of Mathematics and Applications, India
Sudhakar Tripathi	National Institute of Technology Patna, India
Sudip Kumar Adhikari	Cooch Behar Government Engineering College, India
Sudip Kumar Das	Calcutta University, India
Sudip Kundu	Calcutta University, India
Sudipta Roy	Assam University, India
Sukumar Nandi	Indian Institute of Technology Guwahati, India
Sumit Kundu	National Institute of Technology Durgapur, India
Sunirmal Khatua	Calcutta University, India
Sushmita Mitra	Indian Statistical Institute Kolkata, India
Swapan Kumar Mandal	Kalyani Government Engineering College, India
Syed Samsul Alam	Aliah University, India
T. K. Kaul	Sikkim University, India
Tamaghna Acharya	Indian Institute of Engineering, Science and Technology, India
Tandra Pal	National Institute of Technology, Durgapur, India
Tanushyam Chattopadhyay	Innovation Lab TCS Kolkata, India
Tapan K. Ghosh	West Bengal University of Animal and Fishery Sciences, India
Tushar Kanti Bera	Yonsei University, South Korea
U. Dinesh Kumar	Indian Institute of Management Bangalore, India

Contents

Circuits and Systems

Data Science and Data Analytics

Bio Computing

Social Computing

Mobile, Nano, Quantum Computing

Data Mining

Security and Forensics

Digital Image Processing

Computational Intelligence

Signal Processing, Microwave and Communication Engineering

Localization of Sensors in Wireless Sensor Networks

Pritee Parwekar$^{(\boxtimes)}$ and Anusha Vangala

Department of CSE, Anil Neerukonda Institute of Technology and Sciences,
Bheemunipatnam, India
{pritee.cse,anusha.cse}@anits.edu.in

Abstract. Deployment of Wireless Sensors encounter the first challenge of localization prior routing and networking. Localization can consume considerable energy of the already resource hungry sensors. Offloading the localization problem to the base station through a set of mobile sinks can facilitate high levels of computations which can enable localization as well as the routing protocol establishment. The paper brings out simple mathematical model of location estimation of the sensor nodes.

Keywords: Localization · Sensor · Sink · RSSI

1 Introduction

Wireless Sensor Networks are typically used in environments where laying of the network apriori is not feasible. This may be either due to the inhospitable environment or due to the real time requirement created due to an emerging situation. Such networks are therefore created out of a group of sensors which are deployed from a remote mechanism which may be terrestrial or aerial or aquatic (for underwater networks) into the area where they are required. Such region would be henceforth termed as region of interest (ROI). The sensors randomly take position in the region of interest. The sensors are autonomous having limited battery life and computation power. Thus the sensor on their own are not in a position to transmit the sensed data to the data collection and processing center which we will term as Base Station (BS). The sensors therefore are required to collaborate into a network and pass the data to and fro to the base station. This is achieved by establishing a routing protocol which helps routing the data.

Since the sensors are randomly placed in the region of interest, even to establish an efficient routing protocol, there is a need to know the location of these sensors in the region of interest with respect to a certain datum. This process of establishing the location of the deployed sensors in either two dimensional or three dimensional space is called localization. A considerable research is underway in the area of localization especially with more and more wireless devices being introduced in a variety of applications. The initial localization concepts were based on simple geometry and trigonometry. They have been used by seafarers since time immemorial. Coastal navigation saw the introduction of wireless technology in which coast based beacons were used to find the position of the ship near the coast by methods of triangulation.

© Springer Nature Singapore Pte Ltd. 2018
J. K. Mandal and D. Sinha (Eds.): CSI 2017, CCIS 836, pp. 3–10, 2018.
https://doi.org/10.1007/978-981-13-1343-1_1

Since the 1970s, initially with the NAVSTAR project and later on the GPS project, satellite based triangulation techniques have been used to find location of floating or flying objects which is even used till date. In the field of wireless sensor networks, the initial research was based on these age old techniques. Localization involves three distinct phases which are coordination phase, measurement phase and finally the position estimation phase. The coordination phase is about knowing about the sensors and their properties in the network. This can be controlled initially, prior deploying the sensors, or can be achieved by the sensors through mutual interaction. The idea is to know the synchronizing time up to microsecond accuracy when the measurement phase will begin. This is achieved either by the sinks broadcasting the message in the network which carry a time stamp, or in a clustered architecture the cluster head. In the measurement phase the signals are sensed and processed either by the nodes or the sinks in the network. The measurements techniques use one or combination of methods which may be range based or range free. Range free technique exchange only the connectivity information and require extra hardware. Further multi path fading or shadowing due to geographical structures may cause inaccuracy. Some of the promising algorithms are listed below.

- Centroid [1] – Centroid counts the beacon signals it has received from the pre-positioned beacon nodes and achieves localization by obtaining the centroid of received beacon generators.
- Appropriate point in triangle (APIT) [2] – requires a relatively higher ratio of beacons to nodes and longer range beacons for localization.
- DV-HOP [3] – uses position of beacon nodes, the hop count of beacon, and distance average per hop for localization.

Range based localization algorithms uses range (distance or angle) information from the beacon node to estimate a sensor node's location. They need at least three beacon nodes to estimate the position of a node. Several ranging techniques exist to estimate the distance of a node to three or more beacon nodes. Based on this information, location of a node is determined. Following are the range based localization algorithms.

- Received Signal Strength (RSS) profiling [4] – Distance apporximations are calculated from received signal strength indications (RSSI). However, due to non-uniform signal propagation, this is not precise and reliable.
- Time of Arrival (TOA) [5] – This method has better accuracy, but may require additional hardware at the nodes to receive a signal that has a smaller propagation speed than radio, such as ultrasound.
- Time Difference of Arrival (TDOA) [6] – This method estimates the gap between two communicating nodes. TDOA requires extensive hardware that is expensive and resource hungry and are hence not suitable for wireless sensor networks.
- Angle of Arrival (AOA) [7] – A technique that allows nodes to estimate and map relative angles between neighbors.
- Doppler Shift Method [8] – The nodes measure RF Doppler shift of the transmitted signal only when the locations of the sensors change.

The measured data is used for the final phase that is localization. Localization involves both direction finding and ranging. This is achieved using a combination of the following methods:

- Lateration [9] – uses ranges of landmarks and the dynamic node and provides the location data.
- Angulation [10] – uses anchor behaviour or angular spilt up between anchors and the mobile nodes to localize the nodes.
- Cellular Proximity [11] – It is a coarse grained approach where node is limited to the region in which it is identified.
- Dead Reckoning [12] has been used in a versatile but complex scenario in which both the anchor nodes and the normal sensors are mobile to get fine resolution localization.

With advances in data processing, two post processing techniques are also being utilized to capture the relevant information from noisy data

- Maximum likelihood estimation (MLE) – which estimates the values of the state based on measured data only, and no prior information about the state is used
- Sequential Bayesian estimation (SBE) – which estimates state values based on measurements, as well as prior information.

Whilst the above methods indicate the evolution of localization in sensor networks, no one method is applicable in all situations. Hybridization is the area of research which would be the next logical step to find a more globally applicable solution.

2   Assumptions and Initial Setup

In this paper the methods are implemented using simulations. The sensors were distributed randomly in the given region. All the sensors are of the same type and are assumed to have fully charged batteries prior deployment. The rate of change of RSSI vs distance is also assumed to be identical for all the sensors. The simulations and experimental studies have been done in TinyOS environment. The sensors broadcast their identity and receive messages from the neighbors for 10 s and then go into sleep mode. The identity is linked to the received signal strength and saved in the memory in a tabular form.

(a) The sensors wake up on receipt of beacon message from mobile sink and offload the saved data to the mobile sinks and again resume sleep mode.
(b) The mobile sinks offload sensors data to the base station where it is computed.
(c) The localization information and the routine protocol is synthesized by the base station using method 1 or method 2.
(d) The localization information and the routing protocol are transmitted to the network by the mobile sinks.

The real motes are used to see how the values changes with the distance. The change in the values of RSSI is recorded in outdoor. The nesC programming in TOSSIM with the real sensors is used for taking the RSSI values. The RSSI values with distance are shown in Table 1, Fig. 1.

Table 1. Values of RSSI with distance

Distance(m)	RSSI (db.)	Distance(m)	RSSI (db.)
2.5	−26	26	−41
5	−34	27	−41
6	−27	28	−42
7	−24	29	−39
8	−31	30	−43
9	−33	32	−43
10	−34	33	−42
11	−35	35	−43
12	−36	36	−44
14	−42	38	−44
15	−36	39	−44
16	−43	40	−43
17	−38	41	−44
18	−40	42	−42
19	−41	43	−43
20	−41	44	−42
21	−40	46	−43
22	−44	47	−44
23	−41	48	−39
25	−42	50	−44

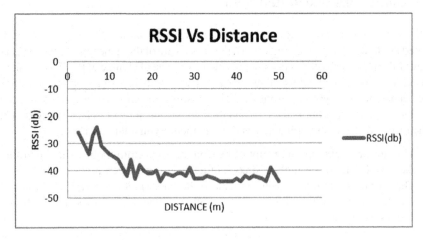

Fig. 1. RSSI Vs. Distance

3   Methods to Get the Coordinates

Method 1
Input: $d_i : i \varepsilon \{1, 2, 3, \ldots\ldots\ldots n\}$
where n is number of nodes
Output: $X_i Y_i i \varepsilon \{1, 2, 3, \ldots\ldots\ldots n\}$.

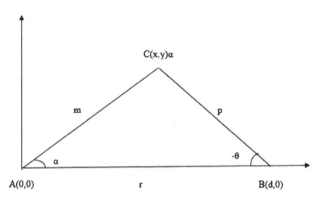

Fig. 2. Parametric method of location estimation of sensor

This method is explained with the three points the location of node C is unknown as shown in Fig. 2.

The location of A is (0, 0) and the distance of A to B is d.
By the Parametric method
At A

$$x = 0 + mcos\alpha \tag{1}$$

$$y = 0 + msin\alpha \tag{2}$$

At B

$$x = r + pcos\theta \tag{3}$$

$$y = 0 + psin\theta \tag{4}$$

Solving Eqs. (1), (2), (3) and (4)

$$x^2 + y^2 = m^2 \tag{5}$$

Solving Eqs. (3), (4) and (5)

$$cos\theta = \frac{(m^2 - (r^2 + p^2))}{2rp} \qquad sin\theta = \sqrt{1 - \left(m^2 - \frac{(r^2 + p^2)}{2rp}\right)^2}$$

Submitting the values of cosθ and sinθ in the equation we get

$$x = \frac{(m^2 + r^2 - p^2)}{2r}$$

&

$$y = \frac{\sqrt{(2m^2 r^2 + 2m^2 p^2 + 2r^2 p^2 - m^4 - r^4 - p^4)}}{2r}$$

Method 2
Finding the coordinates with the circle logic

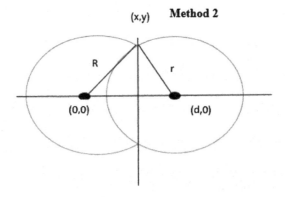

Fig. 3. Circle method

Since the locus of a fixed line is on a circle the point could be anywhere on the circle as shown in Fig. 3.

Consider the circle with the radius r and R with the center at (0, 0) and (d, 0). Then the first circle equation will be

$$x^2 + y^2 = R^2 \tag{6}$$

And the second circle equation will be

$$(x - d)^2 + y^2 = r^2 \tag{7}$$

Solving the equation we get

$$x = \frac{(R^2 - r^2 + d^2)}{2d}$$

And

$$y = \sqrt{\left(\frac{(4d^2R^2 - (d^2 - r^2 + R^2))}{2d} \right)}$$

Mean square error

$$MSE = \frac{1}{n} \sum_{i=1}^{n} (modeli - calculatedi)^2 \qquad (8)$$

To evaluate the accuracy mean square error is calculated with the model position and the calculated position.

4 Results and Discussion

The accuracy of the coordinates is calculated by mean square error as shown in Eq. (8). The calculations are done at the base station. The memory of the individual nodes are used only for the storage of the RSSI of the neighbors.

The experiment is tested with the different number of nodes from 1 to 25. The method 1 and method 2 is used to find the coordinates of the nodes. The results of method1 and method2 were compared the results with the fuzzy based range free algorithm [13]. The fuzzy based range free algorithm has calculated the coordinates of the sensors by designing rule based system using RSSI and LQI, this method has used anchor nodes. The proposed method in this paper has not used any anchor nodes. It's been found that the error factor is less using the proposed method. The results are shown in Fig. 4. The ranged based algorithm for localization performs better than the range free algorithms.

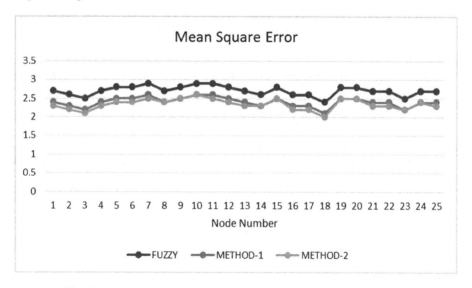

Fig. 4. Comparison of fuzzy based algorithm, method 1 and method 2

5 Conclusion

The paper has presented a parametric solution method for localization. The results have been compared with a fuzzy logic based localization. The results display better accuracy of the proposed method. Other benefits include reduced battery consumption and computational requirements as the same is offloaded to the Base Station. The future work would include use of better optimization techniques to reduce the Mean Square Error and making the localization process secure.

References

1. Bulusu, N., Heidemann, J., Estrin, D.: GPS-less low-cost outdoor localization for very small devices. IEEE Pers. Commun. 7(5), 28–34 (2000)
2. Li, X., Shi, H., Shang, Y.: A partial-range-aware localization algorithm for Ad-hoc wireless sensor networks. In: Proceedings of the 29th Annual IEEE International Conference on Local Computer Networks, LCN 2004, 16–18 November 2004, pp. 77–83
3. Wang, Y., Wang, X., Wang, D., Agrawal, D.P.: Range-free localization using expected hop progress in wireless sensor networks. In: IEEE Transactions on Parallel and Distributed Systems, vol. 20, no. 10, pp. 1540–1552, October 2009
4. Kmar, P., Reddy, L., Varma, S.: Distance measurement and error estimation scheme for RSSI based localization in wireless sensor networks. In: Fifth IEEE Conference on Wireless Communication and Sensor Networks (WCSN), Allahabad, India, pp. 1–4, December 2009
5. Voltz, P.J., Hernandez, D.: Maximum likelihood time of arrival estimation for real-time physical location tracking of 802.11a/g mobile stations in indoor environments. In: Position Location and Navigation Symposium (PLANS), California, USA, pp. 585–591, April 2004
6. Kovavisaruch, L., Ho, K.C.: Alternate source and receiver location estimation using TDOA with receiver position uncertainties. In: IEEE International Conference on Acoustics, Speech, and Signal Processing (ICASSP 2005), Pennsylvania, USA, pp. iv/1065–iv/1068, March 2005
7. Rong, P., Sichitiu, M.: Angle of arrival localization for wireless sensor networks. In: Annual IEEE Communication Society on Sensor Ad hoc Communication Networks, USA, vol. 1, pp. 374–382 (2006)
8. Kusy, B., Ledeczi, A., Koutsoukos, X.: Tracking mobile nodes using RF doppler shifts. In: Proceedings of the 5th International Conference on Embedded Networked Sensor Systems. ACM (2007)
9. Sichitiu, M.L., Ramadurai, V.: Localization of wireless sensor networks with a mobile beacon. In: 2004 IEEE International Conference on Mobile Ad-hoc and Sensor Systems. IEEE (2004)
10. Bal, M., et al.: Localization in cooperative wireless sensor networks: a review. In: 13th International Conference on Computer Supported Cooperative Work in Design, CSCWD 2009. IEEE (2009)
11. Kuriakose, J., Joshi, S., George, V.I.: Localization in wireless sensor networks: a survey (2014). arXiv preprint arXiv:1410.8713
12. Rashid, H., Turuk, A.K.: Dead reckoning localisation technique for mobile wireless sensor networks. IET Wirel. Sens. Syst. 5(2), 87–96 (2015)
13. Parwekar, P., Reddy R.: An efficient fuzzy localization approach in wireless sensor networks. IEEE International Conference on Fuzzy Systems (FUZZ). IEEE 2013 (2013)

Analytical Investigation of Tunneling Current in Nano-MOSFET Using BSIM4 Model for Low Power VLSI Applications

Anal Roy Chowdhury[1(✉)], Krishnendu Roy[1], Palak Saha[2], and Arpan Deyasi[2]

[1] Department of Electronic Science, A.P.C College, Kolkata, India
analroychowdhury084@gmail.com,
krishnendu.physics94@gmail.com
[2] Department of Electronics and Communication Engineering, RCC Institute of Information Technology, Kolkata, India
deyasi_arpan@yahoo.co.in

Abstract. In this paper, tunneling current in nanoscale MOSFET is analytically investigated using BSIM4 model for very low power VLSI applications. Simulation is carried out for low and high electric fields separately, and appropriate mathematical equations are formulated for that purpose by modifying the existing model proposed by Hu. Effect of dielectric thickness and internally generated electrical parameter variations are measured on tunneling current. Diode-like behavior under the application of high field speaks about the magnitude of critical field where thermionic current starts to dominate. Results are critically important for non-volatile memory applications.

Keywords: Tunneling current · Dielectric thickness · Flatband voltage
Auxiliary voltage · Nano MOSFET · Critical electric field

1 Introduction

Nanoelectronics is the domain of research where one can understand, explore and exploit the unique properties of low-dimensional devices compared to the bulk counterpart, and systems based on these devices offer novel features as contrary to the existing Si based VLSI technology. According to the ITRS [1], gate oxide thicknesses of 2–10 nm is required for sub-50 nm CMOS technology, But in this regime, direct tunnelling current increases exponentially with decreasing oxide thickness, which is of primary concern for CMOS scaling. Lai [2] showed that quantum mechanical tunnelling of electrical conduction in a thin insulating film (SiO$_2$/sub) is possible from the strongly inverted Si surface a decade ago. The impact of energy quantization on gate tunnelling current is studied by Chang [3] for double-gate and ultrathin body MOSFETs; where Hu [4] incorporated quantum correction model for ultrathin oxide MOSFET devices. Invoke of BSIM model in analytical calculation of tunnelling current starts with this novel literature [4].

© Springer Nature Singapore Pte Ltd. 2018
J. K. Mandal and D. Sinha (Eds.): CSI 2017, CCIS 836, pp. 11–18, 2018.
https://doi.org/10.1007/978-981-13-1343-1_2

Cassan's [5] theoretical work investigates some aspects of direct tunnelling gate current in ultra-thin gate MOSFET, as influence of bias, oxide thickness, and oxide thickness fluctuations. A semi-empirical model is proposed by Lee [4] to quantify the tunnelling currents through ultrathin gate oxides (1–3.6 nm). Explicit compact quantum model is presented for the gate tunnelling current in DG-MOSFETs [6]. Wann have established [7] the gate-induced drain leakage current due to band-to-band tunnelling which is a major component in off-state MOSFET. Chander shows [8] the impact of parameter optimization of n-type MOSFET for direct tunneling gate current using ultrathin Si_3N_4 and HfO_2 with Equivalent Oxide Thickness (EOT) of 1.0 nm, later verified by TCAD software. Qing [9] theoretically found gate-to-body tunnelling current model for SOI devices.

In last few years, compact models are employed by researchers [10] to evaluate tunnelling current at sub-100 nm range for logic devices. Tunnelling current is investigated for different MOSFET structures at lower applied field [11] and also by using multilayer dielectric [12] for non-volatile and flash memory applications respectively. BSIM 3 models are used for that purpose. In this paper, tunnelling current is calculated for nano-MOSFET using BSIM4 model, and separate formulations are presented for low and high electric fields. Existing model as presented by Hu [3, 4], are modified in order to include the effect of large electric field range, and also for the computation in nanometric range [below 10 nm]. Effect of oxide thickness is investigated along with a few internal electrical parameters, and band curvatures are also taken into account following Hu [4]. Simulated findings favour for use of the sub-10 nm device for digital applications.

2 Mathematical Formulation

The direct-tunneling current density for an oxide voltage V_{ox} smaller than the barrier height Φ_b is [4]:

$$J_n = A\left(\frac{\phi_b}{V_{ox}}\right)\left[\left(\frac{2\phi_b}{V_{ox}}\right) - 1\right]E_{ox}^2 \exp\left[-B\left(1 - \left(1 - \frac{V_{ox}}{\phi_b}\right)^{1.5}\right)\Big/E_{ox}\right] \quad (1)$$

where A and B are constants depending on material parameters; E_{ox} is the dielectric field, T_{ox} is dielectric thickness. This model is modified by Hu as following [4]:

$$J_n = \frac{q^3}{8\pi h\phi_b\varepsilon_{ox}}C(V_G, V_{ox}, T_{ox}, \phi_b)\exp\left[-8\pi\sqrt{2m_{ox}^*}\phi_b^{1.5}\left(1 - \left(1 - \frac{V_{ox}}{\phi_b}\right)^{1.5}\right)\Big/3hqE_{ox}\right]$$

$$(2)$$

where

$$C = \exp\left[\left(\frac{20}{\phi_b}\right)\left(\frac{(|V_{ox}| - \phi_b)}{\phi_{b0}} + 1\right)^\alpha\left(1 - \frac{V_{ox}}{\phi_b}\right)\right]\left(\frac{V_G}{T_{ox}}\right)N \tag{3}$$

$$N = \left(\frac{\varepsilon_{ox}}{T_{ox}}\right)\left[\eta_{inv}v_t\ln\left(1 + \exp\frac{V_{ge} - V_{th}}{\eta_{inv}v_t}\right) + \eta_{acc}v_t\ln\left(1 + \exp\frac{V_g - V_{FB}}{\eta_{acc}v_t}\right)\right] \tag{4}$$

where n_{inv} & n_{acc} are swing parameters; V_{th} is threshold voltage; V_{FB} is flatband voltage; V_t is thermal voltage; V_{ge} is gate voltage minus gate depletion voltage, ε_{Si} & ε_{ox} are dielectric constants of Si and SiO_2 respectively.

But the proposed model has a shortcoming that the function 'C' becomes a constant for a given range of electric field, and thus the variation of 'J' is very small. This is not true when nanometric dimensions are taken into account. Henceforth, we further propose another modification of the existing model as

$$C = \exp\left[\left(\frac{K}{\phi_b}\right)\left(\frac{(|V_{ox}| - \phi_b)}{\phi_{b0}} + 1\right)^\alpha\left(1 - \frac{V_{ox}}{\phi_b}\right)\right]\left(\frac{V_G}{T_{ox}}\right)N \tag{5}$$

where 'K' is an fitting array, depends on device parameters.

This modification helps to analyze the variation of tunneling current for low-dimensional device for both the regions of electric field.

3 Results and Discussion

BSIM4 model is invoked to calculate tunneling current in nano-MOSFET following the work of Lee and Hu, as mentioned in the mathematical modeling section. The calculation is made analytically, and gate current is obtained for a different range of structural parameters.

Figure: 1 shows the effect of the electric field on device current at higher range. The graph shows a typical diode like behavior which indicates the fact that the thermo-ionic current dominates over tunneling current. Result is plotted for 4 different dielectric thicknesses. Thermo-ionic injection reduces which modifies the parabolic behavior.

In Fig. 2, tunneling current is calculated w.r.t. electric field for different reference dielectric thickness. From the plot it is observed that increasing the thickness, the current is also increased. Again at very low electric field, current increases non-linearly, whereas it increases in log scale for moderator high field. Further, it may be observed from the graph, effect of dielectric material thickness in more pronounced for lower range of thickness. As compared with the data available for t_{ox} and t_{ox} reference, distance between the curves is higher in the case of t_{ox}, whereas the curves are condensed in t_{ox} reference plot.

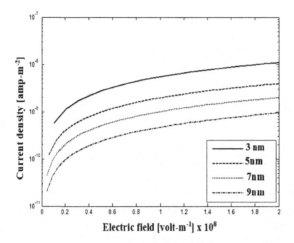

Fig. 1. Tunneling current density with electric field for different dielectric thicknesses

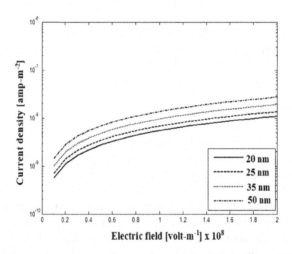

Fig. 2. Tunneling current density with electric field for different reference dielectric thicknesses

In Figs. 3 and 4, tunneling current is calculated as a function of electric field for the different value of flat-band voltages (V_{fb}) and auxiliary voltages (V_{aux}) respectively. From Fig. 3, it is observed that increasing the value of flat-band voltage (V_{fb}), current is also increased. Again at very low electric field, current increases non-linearly, whereas it increases in log scale for moderator high field. Further, it may be observed from the graph, effect of flat-band voltage (V_{fb}) in more pronounced for lower range of voltage. Similar variation is observed in Fig. 4 except the fact that magnitude of current is comparatively low than that obtained in Fig. 3.

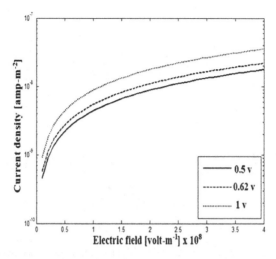

Fig. 3. Tunneling current density with electric field for different flatband voltages

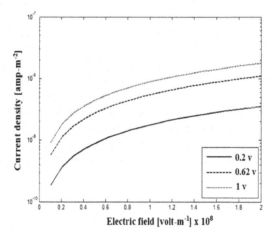

Fig. 4. Tunneling current density with electric field for different auxiliary voltages

Tunneling current is calculated at high electric field using WKB approximation based on the model of Lee and Hu where empirical fitting parameters are considered replacing the terms of electric field in the equations of Schuegraf. The low field currents are kept same as their variations are negligible w.r.t. different electrical and parameters, whereas the variations at high field are considered and simulated.

In Fig. 5, tunneling current is calculated as a function of electric field for different dielectric thickness. From the plot it is observed that increasing the thickness, current reduces. Again at very low electric field, current increases non-linearly, where as it increases in log scale for moderator high field. Further, it may be observed from the graph, effect of dielectric material thickness in more pronounced for lower range of thickness. Figure in inset shows the corresponding tunneling current at low field range.

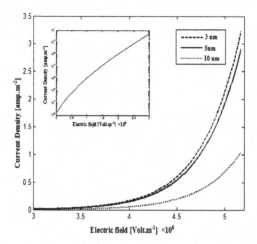

Fig. 5. Tunneling current at high electric field for different dielectric thicknesses

In Fig. 6, keeping the thickness of dielectric material constant, reference level is changed. Reverse trend is observed in this case. Higher reference thickness effectively reduces the normalized thickness value, (T_{ox}/T_{oxref}), which enhances the current density.

By increasing the flat band voltage, effective threshold voltage of the Nano-MOSFET reduces; which in turn enhance the current. According to BSIM4 model, auxiliary can be derived from square of the electric field. It is basically a fitting parameter, applicable for in all regions of operation. From the plot, it may be observed over a value of 0.6 V, rate of increasing current density reduces, and this reflects the fact that auxiliary voltage can't be sat at a very high value, because it adds no effect to current density over moderate range. Figure in inset shows the corresponding tunneling current at low field range.

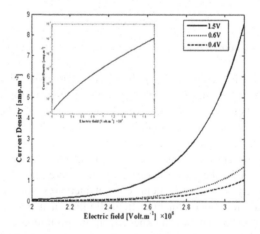

Fig. 6. Tunneling current at high electric field for different auxiliary voltages

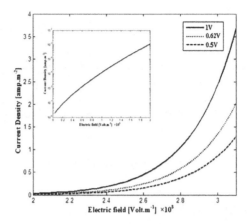

Fig. 7. Tunneling current at high electric field for different flatband voltages

In Fig. 7, tunneling current is calculated as a function of electric field for different value of flat-band voltage (V_{fb}). From the plot it is observed that increasing the value of flat-band voltage (V_{fb}), current increases. Again at very low electric field, current increases non-linearly, where as it increases in log scale for moderator high field. Further, it may be observed from the graph, effect of flat-band voltage (V_{fb}) in more pronounced for lower range of voltage. And the distance between three curves are almost same. Figure in inset shows the corresponding tunneling current at low field range.

In Fig. 8, tunneling current is calculated as a function of electric field for different value of α. The variation is similar to Fig. 7. Further, it may be observed from the graph, effect of α in more pronounced for lower range value. The curvature increases as "alpha" increases for silicon material.

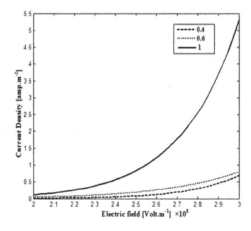

Fig. 8. Tunneling current at high electric field for different band curvatures

4 Conclusion

Variation of tunneling current is observed at very low and high electric field regions following BSIM4 model. Effect of fabrications parameters, electrical parameters and band curvature are studied analytically. Result shows that after critical electric field, tunneling current shows diode-like behavior which reveals the fact that dominance of thermionic effect starts after 2×10^8 V·m^{-1} value. The results are useful for application of the sub-10 nm device in memory applications.

References

1. ITRS Roadmap (2007)
2. Lai, P.T., Jingping, X., Liu, B.Y., Xu, Z.: New observation and improvement in GIDL of N-MOSFET's with various kinds of gate oxides under hot-carrier stress. In: IEEE International Conference on Semiconductor Electronics (1996)
3. Chang, L., Yang, K.J., Yeo, Y.C., Polishchuk, I., King, T.J., Hu, C.: Direct-tunneling gate leakage current in double-gate and ultrathin body MOSFETs. IEEE Trans. Electron Devices 49(12), 2288–2295 (2002)
4. Lee, W.C., Hu, C.: Modeling CMOS tunneling currents through ultrathin gate oxide due to conduction- and valence-band electron and hole tunneling. IEEE Trans. Electron Devices 48(7), 1366–1373 (2001)
5. Cassan, E., Dollfus, P., Galdin, S., Hesto, P.: Calculation of direct tunneling gate current through ultra-thin oxide and oxide/nitride stacks in MOSFETs and H-MOSFETs. Microelectron. Reliab. 40(4–5), 585–588 (2000)
6. Chaves, F.A., Jimenez, D., Sune, J.: Explicit model for the gate tunneling current in double-gate MOSFETs. Solid-State Electron. 68, 93–97 (2012)
7. Wann, H.J., Ko, P.K., Hu, C.: Gate-induced band-to-band tunneling leakage current in LDD MOSFETs. In: IEDM-92, pp. 147–150 (1992)
8. Chander, S., Singh, P., Baishya, S.: Optimization of direct tunneling gate leakage current in ultrathin gate oxide FET with high-K dielectrics. Int. J. Recent Dev. Eng. Tech. 1(1), 24–30 (2013)
9. Qing-Qing, W., Jing, C., et al.: Gate-to-body tunneling current model for silicon-on-insulator MOSFETs. Chin. Phys. B 22(10), 108501 (2013)
10. Gehring, A., Selberherr, S.: Modeling of tunneling current and gate dielectric reliability for nonvolatile memory devices. IEEE Trans. Device Mater. Reliab. 4(3), 306–319 (2004)
11. Govoreanu, B., Blomme, P., Houdt, J.V., De Meyer, K.: Enhanced tunneling current effect for nonvolatile memory applications. Jpn. J. Appl. Phys. 42(1-4B), 2020–2024 (2003)
12. Hong, S.H., Jang, J.H., Park, T.J., Jeong, D.S., Kim, M., Hwang, C.S.: Improvement of the current-voltage characteristics of a tunneling dielectric by adopting a $Si_3N_4/SiO_2/Si_3N_4$ multilayer for flash memory application. Appl. Phys. Lett. 87, 152106 (2005)

Optimization of InP HEMT Using Multilayered Cap and Asymmetric Gate Recess

Kumar Ankit$^{(\boxtimes)}$, Rohan Kumar$^{(\boxtimes)}$, Om Prakash$^{(\boxtimes)}$, and Aminul Islam$^{(\boxtimes)}$

Department of Electronics and Communication Engineering,
Birla Institute of Technology, Mesra, Ranchi, Jharkhand, India
ankitsfsj@gmail.com, rohan28kumar@gmail.com,
opabhi913@gmail.com, aminulislam@bitmesra.ac.in

Abstract. In this research article, we optimize the design metrics of InP (Indium Phosphate) HEMT (High Electron Mobility Transistor) using asymmetric gate recess and multi-layered cap. The device proposed in this paper possesses heavily doped Source/Drain (S/D) region, asymmetric gate recess, multi-layered cap region, InP layer between cap and buffer region. The proposed device incorporates the use of 'T' shaped gate and δ (delta) - doping technique. This paper analyzes the RF and DC performances of the device with an $In_{0.52}Al_{0.48}As$ supply layer, $In_{0.65}Ga_{0.35}As$ channel layer built on an InP substrate, with a delta doping of thickness 1 nm, cap layer with varying compositions of InGaAs and a heavily doped S/D region of $In_{0.52}Ga_{0.48}As$. Complete analysis of the device such as its output characteristics (Drain Current (I_D) – Drain Source Voltage (V_{DS})), transfer characteristics (I_D – Gate Source Voltage (V_{GS})), threshold voltage (from I_D - V_{GS} plot), transconductance and transition frequency (f_T) are obtained at room temperature (300 K) and the obtained values of these parameters are better as compared to the conventional HEMT because of the abatement of parasitics like S/D resistances. All simulations are performed using Silvaco ATLAS.

Keywords: InP HEMT · Threshold voltage · Transconductance
Multi-layered cap region · T-shaped gate · Asymmetric gate recess
Delta doping · Switching action · Heavily doped S/D region
Transition frequency (f_T)

1 Introduction

In today's modern era there has been an increase in the relentless push for higher wireless data rates along with the increasing limitations in the spectrum space and in these circumstances the new technologies are thankfully offering hope for the future. One obvious path forward is to continue to move more products and services into the higher frequencies where the bandwidth exists to support the higher data rates. This fertile wireless space is essentially untapped, mainly because there are not many devices capable of operating at these exalted frequencies. But things are changing, researches and developments in semiconductors are now making transistors and

© Springer Nature Singapore Pte Ltd. 2018
J. K. Mandal and D. Sinha (Eds.): CSI 2017, CCIS 836, pp. 19–28, 2018.
https://doi.org/10.1007/978-981-13-1343-1_3

integrated circuits for THz use. One of the result of the research work is the emergence of the device known as the high electron mobility transistor (HEMT).

Researches in the area of high electron mobility transistors (HEMT) is driven by applications requiring high gain and low noise figure combined with high efficiency when operated at microwave frequencies which makes them suitable for use in the field of RF circuit design. HEMTs have both military and commercial applications including operations in telecommunication, satellite, automotive and instrumentation. In recent years, it has proved to be a successful alternative to the existing devices used in millimeter-wave applications [1]. InP semiconductors provide higher average carrier throughout compared to the standard saturation velocity, which provides considerable benefits in terms of current gain, transition frequency (f_T), which is considered a major characteristic parameter of transistors.

InP HEMTs using InGaAs channel are much potent in its transconductance (g_m), drain current and f_T value making them superior in terms of their DC and RF performance in comparison to the conventional HEMTs and MOSFETs, constructed on Si, GaAs and GaN materials. Under high field conditions, InP HEMT exhibits higher saturation velocity. The free carriers in the quantum well form a 2-Dimensional Electron Gas (2-DEG) layer. In contrast to the MESFET technology, the 2-DEG layer has significantly less scattering in HEMT's, resulting in a very high mobility device.

The contributions of this paper are stated as follows:

- The proposed InP HEMT has been incorporated with an asymmetric gate recess for obtaining an improved breakdown voltage. The main motive of the asymmetric recess is to increase the gate-drain spacing so as to distribute the voltage drop over a wider region. This also contributes to reduce in the gate leakage current [2].
- The proposed InP HEMT has been analyzed by very high concentration of $In_{0.52}Ga_{0.48}As$ in S/D regions, which results in outstanding transconductance, drain current and transition frequency as compared to conventional HEMT devices. The main reason behind this is the abatement of parasitic capacitances (C_{GS} and C_{GD}), resistances (R_S and R_D) and reduction of device dimensions.
- The proposed InP HEMT possesses a heavily concentrated multi-layered cap region of $In_{0.52}Al_{0.48}As$ layer (4 nm thickness), $In_{0.53}Ga_{0.47}As$ layer (9 nm thickness) and $In_{0.7}Ga_{0.3}As$ layer (9 nm thickness), 4 nm InP layer sandwiched between barrier and the cap layer. This structural representation ensures minimization in the source and drain parasitic resistances.
- Authors in [3–12] have done advancements in basic InP HEMT structures and have attained enhancement in the device parameters and the device proposed in this paper achieves overall values better than those structures. Some of the authors in the recent past [14–20] have addressed the performance factors of InP based HEMT devices and have attained good results, but the device proposed in this paper proves to be more efficient than most of those structures in terms of device characteristics.

The remaining paper is divided into following sections. Section 2 describes the device architecture. Section 3 consists of the simulation results and discussions. Conclusion has been discussed in Sect. 4.

2   Device Architecture

The cross-sectional schematic of the simulated structure of InP HEMT with heavily doped Source/Drain region has been shown in Fig. 1. It consists of $In_{0.52}Al_{0.48}As$ of 500 nm thick buffer layer, $In_{0.65}Ga_{0.35}As$ of 15 nm thickness channel layer, 13 nm thick barrier layer consisting of 1 nm thick delta doping region.

The source and drain consist of an extended $In_{0.52}Ga_{0.48}As$ layer which are highly doped with a doping concentration of $5 \times 10^{19}/cm^3$ to improve the various device parameters by reduction in the parasitic capacitances. The cap layer also provides protection from oxidation for the sensitive InAlAs layer beneath. The cap region consists of multi-layer InGaAs of varying composition but with same concentrations in order to minimize the parasitic resistances. The multi-layer in the cap region consists of three layers which are $In_{0.7}Ga_{0.3}As$, $In_{0.53}Ga_{0.47}As$ and $In_{0.52}Ga_{0.48}As$ from top to bottom having doping concentration of $3.5 \times 10^{16}/cm^3$ each. The thickness and composition of the barrier layer ($In_{0.52}Al_{0.48}As$) highly determines the device transconductance, threshold voltage and access resistance (between channel and cap layer).

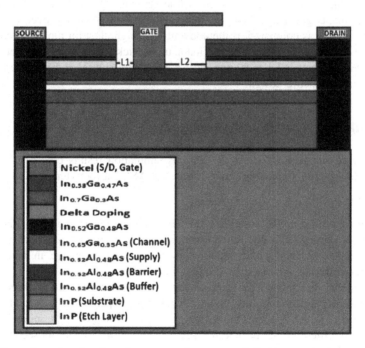

Fig. 1. The schematic showing the proposed structure InP HEMT device showing the composition of the various layers.

Table 1. Device structural parameters

Structural parameters	Values
Gate length (L_G)	0.13 µm
Source length (L_S)	0.004 µm
Drain length (L_D)	0.004 µm
Gate work function	5.13 eV
InAlAs supply doping concentration	1.0×10^{15}/cm^3
InGaAs channel doping concentration	1.0×10^{16}/cm^3
InAlAs buffer doping concentration	1.0×10^{13}/cm^3
InP substrate doping concentration	1.0×10^{10}/cm^3
Delta doping concentration	5.0×10^{15}/cm^3
InP between cap layer and buffer	3.5×10^{18}/cm^3
Extended S/D region concentration	5.0×10^{19}/cm^3

The device structural parameters are tabulated in Table 1. The proposed structure consists of a Nickel gate (work function = 5.13 eV). The reason for the gate being a 'T' shaped one is that the 'T' shape helps in achieving increased cross-sectional area and thus minimizes the resistance of gate while maintaining a small foot print and this results in a smaller gate length. The smaller gate length results in improved value of the device parameters as compared to the conventional high electron mobility transistors. The source and drain electrodes are also made up of Nickel. The separation between the cap layer and the gate is L1 = 50 nm and L2 = 130 nm and these difference in length owes to the asymmetric design.

3   Simulation Results and Discussions

The following sub-sections show the various simulation results concerned with the proposed device after simulating it in Silvaco ATLAS^{TM} at room temperature (300 K).

A. Meshing Profile

The meshing profile of the simulated InP HEMT structure is shown in Fig. 2. The denser mesh (see Fig. 2) at the junctions indicate the requirement of more number of iterations which ensures accuracy in result, owing to the change in band energy between the materials separated by the junctions.

The Parallel Electric Field Dependence model (Fldmob), which specifies the electric field dependent mobility and Concentration dependent Shockley-Read-Hall model (Consrh), which specifies the recombination occurring due to trapping using the minority carrier lifetimes has been utilized in the simulation of the proposed structure in Silvaco ATLAS^{TM}.

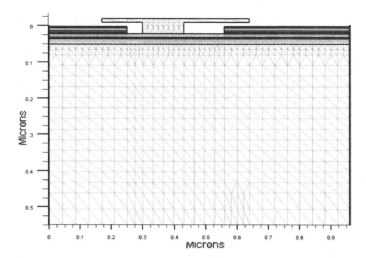

Fig. 2. Meshing profile for the proposed InP high electron mobility transistor (HEMT), simulated using Silvaco ATLAS^{TM}.

B. DC Analysis

This subsection analyses the DC parameters such as threshold voltage, transconductance and maximum drain current. The output characteristics resulted in a maximum drain current of 1650 mA/mm for a gate bias of $V_{GS} = 0.5$ V, optimum channel of 15 nm thickness and at a temperature of 300 K which is better than the maximum drain current obtained in [13] at 300 K which is ~ 450 mA/mm. The family of curves for the output characteristic (I_D - V_{DS} plot) for different gate voltages has been shown in Fig. 3 while the drain voltage is ramped from 0 V to 1 V.

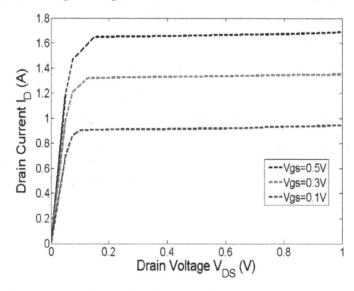

Fig. 3. Drain current versus drain voltage for the modeled InP HEMT, for various gate voltages.

The variation of I_D with V_{GS} to give the transfer characteristics of the device at the suitable physical conditions i.e. 300 K temperature is shown in Fig. 4. The threshold voltage of the proposed structure is observed to be equal to 0.2 V, whereas that of the device in [13] is ~ -0.3 V.

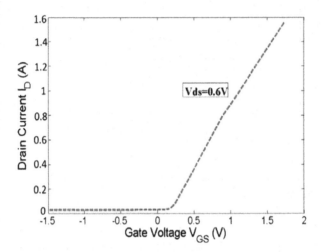

Fig. 4. Drain current as a function of gate voltage for the modelled InP high electron mobility transistor (HEMT), at drain bias voltage of 0.6 V.

The transconductance of the device affects the gain of the device. The higher the transconductance figure of the device, more is the gain delivering capability, holding all other factors constant.

The transconductance is given by the relation:

$$g_m = \left. \frac{\partial I_D}{\partial V_{GS}} \right|_{V_{DS}=Const.} \tag{1}$$

The plot showing the transconductance of the proposed structure is shown in Fig. 5. The peak transconductance observed is 2750 mS/mm. Thus, the proposed structure is capable of delivering higher gain and thus higher amplification.

In the work [13], variation of transconductance with the drain current is shown where the transconductance has a value of ~ 1600 mS/mm at 300 mA/mm which corresponds to gate voltage of 0.1 V. At nearly the same gate voltage transconductance of 2750 mS/mm was obtained.

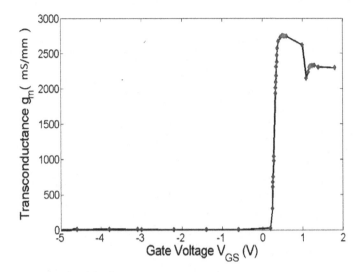

Fig. 5. Transconductance versus gate voltage for the modeled InP HEMT, for gate voltage ramp of −5 V to 2 V.

C. RF Analysis

The analysis of the current gain at radio frequency (RF) has been performed in this subsection.

The transition frequency (also known as unity gain frequency) is measured from the current gain and frequency plot (Fig. 6) as the frequency at which the current gain reduces to unity i.e. the frequency which corresponds to 0 dB current gain. For RF analysis of the device, the transition frequency (f_T) is obtained at $V_{GS} = -3.5$ V and $V_{DS} = 6.5$ V. The unity gain frequency is observed to be of the order of ~ 440 GHz and for the device in [13] it is equal to ~ 100 GHz. The greater value of transition frequency ensures better switching action. Transition frequency (f_T) is often used as indicators of the high-speed characteristics of transistors.

The transition frequency (f_T) is expressed by the expression given below

$$f_T = \frac{v}{2\pi L_G} \tag{2}$$

where v is the velocity of electron, L_G is the gate length. Thus, f_T depicts the velocity and traverse distance of the carriers inside the transistor.

It has been observed that the maximum current gain which can be depicted from the plot is equal to ~ 41 dB. Mathematically, current gain is expressed by (3).

$$Gain = 20 \log \frac{I_{DS}}{I_{INPUT}} dB \tag{3}$$

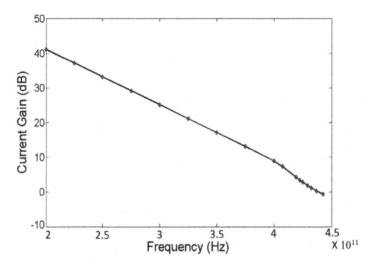

Fig. 6. Current gain (dB) versus frequency (Hz) for the modelled InP HEMT, for gate voltage −3.5 V and drain voltage 6.5 V.

Equation (3) implies that the output current (I_{DS}) is 112.2018 times the input current, which is quite a significant increase in the output current value (Tables 2 and 3).

Table 2. Comparitive study of the two structures

Features	Ref [13]	This paper
Heavily doped S/D region	Absent	Present
Multi-layered cap region	Absent	Present
InP layer between cap and buffer region	Absent	Present
Channel thickness	15 nm	15 nm

Table 3. Comparitive study of results obtained @300 k

Parameters	Ref [13]	This paper
Maximum drain current (I_D)	450 mA/mm	1650 mA/mm
Threshold voltage (V_{TH})	−0.3 V	0.2 V
Transconductance (gm)	1600 mS/mm	2750 mS/mm
Transition frequency (f_T)	100 GHz	440 GHz

4 Conclusion

The DC and RF performances of the proposed HEMT based on InP substrate with heavily concentrated S/D regions of $In_{0.52}Ga_{0.48}As$ having a doping concentration of 5×10^{19}/cm^3 was analyzed in this work. This structure shows a higher value of output current i.e. 1650 mA/mm and a very high transconductance value of 2750 mS/mm. The proposed device also has an improved switching action due to high value of the transition frequency (440 GHz). Due to the improved values of the parameters obtained from the proposed device it can be suitably used for a wide range of applications at elevated frequencies. This is in accordance with the fact that the bandwidths are getting occupied at a fast pace and InP HEMT is an apt solution for it.

References

1. Nguyen, L.D., Brown, A.S., Thompson, M.A., Jelloian, L.M., Larson, L.E., Matloubian, M.: 650-AA self-aligned-gate pseudomorphic Al/sub 0.48/In/sub 0.52/As/Ga/sub 0.2/In/sub 0.8/As high electron mobility transistors. IEEE Electron Device Lett. **13**(3), 143–145 (1992)
2. Robin, F., Meier, H., Homan, O.J., Bachtold, W.: A novel asymmetric gate recess process for InP HEMTs. In: Conference Proceedings 14th Indium Phosphide and Related Materials Conference (Cat. No. 02CH37307), pp. 221–224 (2002)
3. Takahashi, T., et al.: Enhancement of fmax to 910 GHz by adopting asymmetric gate recess and double-side-doped structure in 75-nm-gate InAlAs/InGaAs HEMTs. IEEE Trans. Electron Devices **64**(1), 89–95 (2017)
4. Cidronali, A., et al.: Ultralow DC power VCO based on InP-HEMT and heterojunction interband tunnel diode for wireless applications. IEEE Trans. Microw. Theory Tech. **50**(12), 2938–2946 (2002)
5. Rosenbaum, S.E., et al.: 155- and 213-GHz AlInAs/GaInAs/InP HEMT MMIC oscillators. IEEE Trans. Microw. Theory Tech. **43**(4), 927–932 (1995)
6. Endoh, A., Shinohara, K., Watanabe, I., Mimura, T., Matsui, T.: Low-voltage and high-speed operations of 30-nm-gate pseudomorphic In0.52Al0.48As/In0.7Ga0.3As HEMTs under cryogenic conditions. IEEE Electron Device Lett. **30**(10), 1024–1026 (2009)
7. Medjdoub, F., et al.: InP HEMT downscaling for power applications at W band. IEEE Trans. Electron Devices **52**(10), 2136–2143 (2005)
8. Roy, P., Jawanpuria, S., Vismita, S.P., Islam, A.: Characterization of AlGaN and GaN based HEMT with AlN interfacial spacer. In: 2015 Fifth International Conference on Communication Systems and Network Technologies, Gwalior, pp. 786–788 (2015)
9. Radisic, V., Leong, K.M.K.H., Mei, X., Sarkozy, S., Yoshida, W., Deal, W.R.: Power amplification at 0.65 THz using InP HEMTs. IEEE Trans. Microw. Theory Tech. **60**(3), 724–729 (2012)
10. Menozzi, R., Borgarino, M., Baeyens, Y., Van Hove, M., Fantini, F.: On the effects of hot electrons on the DC and RF characteristics of lattice-matched InAlAs/InGaAs/InP HEMTs. IEEE Microw. Guided Wave Lett. **7**(1), 3–5 (1997)
11. Miras, A., Legros, E.: Very high-frequency small-signal equivalent circuit for short gate-length InP HEMTs. IEEE Trans. Microw. Theory Tech. **45**(7), 1018–1026 (1997)
12. Smith, P.M., et al.: Advances in InP HEMT technology for high frequency applications. In: Conference Proceedings 2001 International Conference on Indium Phosphide and Related Materials 13th IPRM (Cat. No. 01CH37198), Nara, pp. 9–14 (2001)
13. Rodilla, H., Schleeh, J., Nilsson, P., Wadefalk, N., Mateos, J., Grahn, J.: Cryogenic performance of low-noise InP HEMTs: a Monte Carlo study. IEEE Trans. Electron Devices **60**(5), 1625–1631 (2013). https://doi.org/10.1109/TED.2013.2253469
14. Prasad, S., Dwivedi, A.K., Islam, A.: Characterization of AlGaN/GaN and AlGaN/AlN/GaN HEMTs in terms of mobility and subthreshold slope. J. Comput. Electron. **15**(1), 172–180 (2016)

15. Kumar, S., Kumar, V., Islam, A.: Characterisation of field plated high electron mobility transistor. In: 2016 International Conference on Microelectronics, Computing and Communications (MicroCom), Durgapur, pp. 1–3 (2016)
16. Chitransh, A., Moonka, S., Priya, A., Prasad, S., Sengupta, A. Islam, A.: Analysis of breakdown voltage of a field plated high electron mobility transistor. In: 2017 Devices for Integrated Circuit (DevIC), Kalyani, India, pp. 167–169 (2017). https://doi.org/10.1109/devic.2017.8073929
17. Sengupta, A., Islam, A.: Performance comparison of AlGaN/GaN HFET with sapphire and 4H-SiC substrate. In: 2017 Devices for Integrated Circuit (DevIC), Kalyani, India, pp. 190–195 (2017). https://doi.org/10.1109/devic.2017.8073934
18. Chatterjee, S., Sengupta, A., Kundu, S., Islam, A.: Analysis of AlGaN/GaN high electron mobility transistor for high frequency application. In: 2017 Devices for Integrated Circuit (DevIC), Kalyani, India, pp. 196–199 (2017). https://doi.org/10.1109/devic.2017.8073935
19. Moonka, S., Priya, A., Chitransh, A., Prasad, S., Sengupta, A., Islam, A.: Analysis of Al0.22Ga0.78As/In0.18Ga0.82As/GaAs pseudomorphic HEMT device with higher conductivity. In: 2017 Devices for Integrated Circuit (DevIC), Kalyani, India, pp. 360–363 (2017). https://doi.org/10.1109/devic.2017.8073969
20. Priya, A., Moonka, S., Chitransh, A., Prasad, S., Sengupta, A., Islam, A.: Development of HEMT device with surface passivation for a low leakage current and steep subthreshold slope. In: 2017 Devices for Integrated Circuit (DevIC), Kalyani, India, pp. 364–367 (2017). https://doi.org/10.1109/devic.2017.8073970

Phase Velocity Compensation in Compact Coupled-Line Bandpass Filter with Square Corrugations

Tarun Kumar Das[1]([✉]) and Sayan Chatterjee[2]

[1] Future Institute of Engineering and Management, Kolkata, India
tarunj1979@gmail.com
[2] Jadavpur University, Kolkata, India

Abstract. Present paper highlights the design of a compact coupled-line bandpass filter with extended stopband and improved second harmonic suppression. The proposed filter is designed at a center frequency of 2.5 GHz with 20% fractional bandwidth applicable in WLAN. The size of the ladder-type parallel-coupled line bandpass filter has been reduced to 44% and 62% by modifying it to folded and in-line structure. Accordingly, periodic square shaped corrugations are inserted to the coupled edges of the parallel lines. The second harmonic suppression of 60 dB with stopband rejection level of 62 dB and a size reduction of 52% have been achieved for folded filter with 6 periodic square corrugations. The in-line filter with four square corrugations gives the second harmonic suppression of 55 dB with a stopband rejection level of 58 dB and a size reduction of 70%.

Keywords: Bandpass filter · Coupled-line · Folded filter
Harmonic suppression · In-line filter · Square corrugations

1 Introduction

Modern wireless and microwave communication systems demand spurious harmonics free compact bandpass filters with sharp skirt characteristics and extended stopband. Parallel-coupled microstrip line bandpass filters have been employed for these purposes effectively owing to their variety of advantages [1]. However, due to asynchronous behavior of even-and odd-mode phase velocities of the propagating wave, spurious harmonics are generated at the multiples of the center frequency and the desired passband becomes asymmetrical in these types of filters [2]. This degrades the performance of the filter in mixer and frequency converter circuits. Moreover, these filters require much more space, restricting their applications in advanced communication systems. Numerous proposals have been made by the researchers to suppress the harmonics and reduce the filter size. In [3] a triple band parallel-coupled line bandpass filter with over-coupled and insufficient-coupled lines has been designed. Accordingly, low insertion losses, wide operating frequency bandwidths, and high out-of-band rejection levels have been obtained with center frequency of 1.8 GHz, 3.5 GHz and 5.2 GHz applicable for DCS, WIMAX and WLAN. In [4] a miniaturized bandpass

© Springer Nature Singapore Pte Ltd. 2018
J. K. Mandal and D. Sinha (Eds.): CSI 2017, CCIS 836, pp. 29–41, 2018.
https://doi.org/10.1007/978-981-13-1343-1_4

filter has been proposed by meandering the coupled-lines and second harmonic suppression of more than 50 dB with a significant size reduction have been reported. In [5] capacitive terminated and over-coupled coupled-lines have been employed to design a miniaturized bandpass filter. Accordingly, a size reduction of 25% with second and third harmonic suppression of 64 dB and 55 dB has been achieved experimentally. Periodic square and rectangular grooves are introduced to the coupled-edges of lines in [6] and a harmonic rejection level of more than 44 dB and a size reduction of more than 59% have been achieved. In [7] corrugated coupled microstrip lines have been proposed and more than 30 dB of second harmonic suppression level with 10% size reduction has been achieved. The work of [7] has been extended in [8] in which more than 30 dB of harmonic suppression is obtained upto $7f_0$ where f_0 is the center frequency. In [9] corrugated microstrip coupled lines are employed to design constant absolute bandwidth tunable filters by controlling the coupling coefficient. Triangular shaped corrugations have been introduced in a folded coupled line bandpass filter as reported in [10]. Accordingly, more than 62 dB rejection level with a size reduction of 63% has been reported. Fractal geometries are also considered in [11–13] to achieve the harmonic suppression in microstrip filters. The coupled-lines of the filter have been modified with Koch rectangular fractals in [11] and Koch triangular fractals in [12]. Accordingly, harmonic suppression levels of 42 dB and 60 dB have been achieved respectively. Koch rectangular fractals have been studied in [13] for both folded and in-line parallel-coupled lines bandpass filters. The second harmonic suppression of 36 dB and 34 dB along with a size reduction of 58% and 72% has been achieved respectively.

In present article, the study of second harmonic suppression has been carried out in a folded and in-line filter proposed in [13] centered at 2.5 GHz by introducing square shaped corrugations to the coupled-edges of parallel lines. This approach increases the odd-mode electrical length while that of even-mode remains unaltered. Accordingly, phase velocity compensation has been achieved between these modes and a second harmonic suppression of 60 dB and 54 dB along with a size reduction of 52% and 70% have been achieved respectively. The filters are designed over FR4 substrate with dielectric constant, $\varepsilon_r = 4.4$, thickness, $h = 1.6$ mm and loss tangent, $\tan\delta = 0.02$.

2 Filter Design Methodology

Table 1 provides the specifications of the proposed filter. The optimum dimensions of the filter are obtained by calculating the even-and odd-mode characteristic impedances [1]. Table 2 lists the design parameters of the bandpass filter. An open-end length correction (d) of 0.264 mm. is incorporated due to fringing fields. Figure 1 shows the layout of the proposed third-order parallel-coupled lines bandpass filter. The size of the conventional filter is 1291.53 mm^2 which restricts its use in wireless applications. Accordingly, the conventional filter structure is modified to folded and in-line structure as shown in Fig. 2 [13]. Thus, a size reduction of 44% and 62% has been achieved respectively. However, due to this folding mechanism offset gaps having width of 0.528 mm. have been introduced in both the filters with one for folded filter and three for in-line filter. This results additional capacitive coupling between the end-coupled in-line resonators.

Table 1. Specifications of the proposed bandpass filter

Parameters	Notations	Specifications
Order	n	3
Center frequency	f_c	2.5 GHz
3 dB bandwidth	BW	0.5 GHz
Fractional bandwidth	FBW	20%
Feed port characteristic impedance	Z_0	50 ohms
Insertion loss	IL	<3 dB
Return loss	RL	>10 dB
Passband ripple	L_{Ar}	0.01 dB
Filter type	-	Chebyshev type-I

Table 2. Filter design parameters.

j	$J_{j,j+1}/Y_0$	$(Z_{0e})_{j,j+1}$ (ohms)	$(Z_{0e})_{j,j+1}$ (ohms)	$w_{j,j+1}$ (mm.)	$s_{j,j+1}$ (mm.)	$l_{j,j+1}$ (mm.)
0	0.498	87.470	37.500	0.940	0.3	16.961
1	0.201	62.077	41.967	1.543	0.8	16.730
2	0.201	62.077	41.967	1.543	0.8	16.961
3	0.498	87.470	37.500	0.940	0.3	16.730

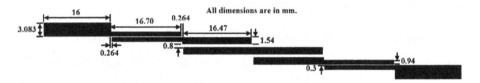

Fig. 1. Layout of third-order conventional parallel-coupled microstrip line bandpass filter centered at 2.5 GHz.

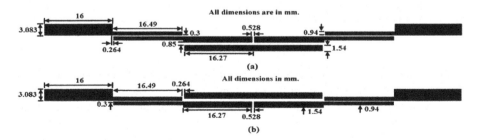

Fig. 2. Layout of third-order (a) folded and (b) in-line parallel-coupled microstrip line bandpass filter.

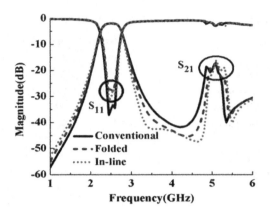

Fig. 3. Comparison of simulated S-parameters of conventional, folded and in-line parallel-coupled microstrip line bandpass filters.

Figure 3 compares the simulated S-parameters between the three filters, showing the presence of high second harmonic levels. It has been observed that both the folded and in-line filter exhibit improved passband symmetry and sharp stopband roll-off rate with upper stopband rejection level under 40 dB and minimum return loss less than of 25 dB in the passband. However, the second harmonic rejection level has not degraded by these folding mechanisms.

3   Harmonic Suppression by Corrugations

3.1   Study of Unit Parallel-Coupled Microstrip Line (PCML) Structure

Figure 4(a) shows the layout of a unit PCML structure. For the given filter specifications the values of width (w), line (l) and gap (s) can be determined by calculating the even-and odd-mode characteristic impedances Z_{0e} and Z_{0o} [1]. The inherent transmission zero of $|S_{21}|$ can be obtained by the condition [2]:

$$Z_{0e} \sin \theta_o - Z_{0o} \sin \theta_e = 0 \tag{1}$$

and hence, one of the possible solutions is

$$\theta_o = \theta_e = m\pi \tag{2}$$

Here, m = 1, 2, 3 ..., θ_e and θ_o are the electrical lengths of even-and odd-mode respectively. In a parallel-coupled lines structure due to the inhomogeneous dielectric medium of the microstrip structure, the odd-mode propagates faster with a higher phase velocity than the even-mode as the phase constant of odd-mode, β_o is less than that of even-mode, β_e [2]. Thus, by introducing corrugations to the coupled edges of the lines, the electrical length of the odd-mode has been extended keeping that of the even-mode almost unaltered. Accordingly, phase velocity compensation is achieved in coupled lines. Figure 4(b) shows the layout of unit PCML structure with 5 square shaped periodic corrugations in the coupled edges.

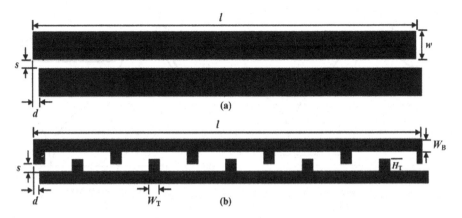

Fig. 4. Layout of unit PCML structure (a) $N = 0$, (b) $N = 5$ where N is the number of square corrugations.

In Fig. 4(b), W_T and H_T are the width and height of the corrugations respectively, s is the gap between two corrugated coupled lines, and $W_B = w - H_T$. Figures 5 and 6 illustrate the effects on $|S_{21}|$ and $|Z_{21}|$ for different number of periodic corrugations respectively for strong couplers ($s = 0.3$ mm.) and weak couplers ($s = 0.7$ mm.). The design specifications for the study are $l = 16.833$ mm., $w = 0.94$ mm., $W_B = H_T = W_T = w/2 = 0.47$ mm. From Fig. 5 it has been observed that the transmission zero of $|S_{21}|$ shifts to lower frequency as the number of corrugations increases and the resonant pole of $|Z_{21}|$ owing to the condition $\theta_o = \pi$ shifts to lower frequency more with compared to that for the condition $\theta_e = \pi$ as highlighted in Fig. 6. By properly choosing the dimensions of the corrugations, coupling gap between the corrugated lines and number of corrugations, the transmission zero of $|S_{21}|$ can be placed perfectly at the second harmonic frequency.

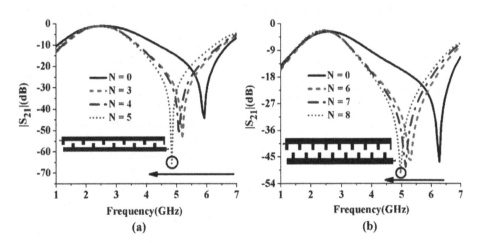

Fig. 5. Effects on $|S_{21}|$(dB) for different number of square corrugations, $l = 16.833$ mm., $w = 0.94$ mm., $W_T = H_T = W_B = w/2 = 0.47$ mm. (a) $s = 0.3$ mm. (b) $s = 0.7$ mm.

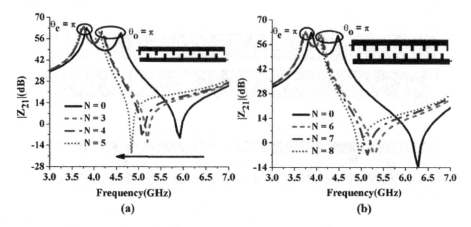

Fig. 6. Effects on $|Z_{21}|$(dB) for different number of square corrugations, l = 16.833 mm., w = 0.94 mm., $W_T = H_T = W_B = w/2$ = 0.47 mm. (a) s = 0.3 mm. (b) s = 0.7 mm.

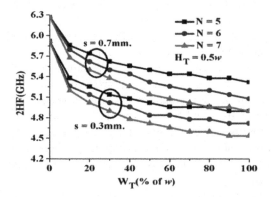

Fig. 7. Variation of transmission zero frequency (2HF) with different width of corrugations, W_T (% of w) with height, $H_T = w/2$ = 0.47 mm.

A study has been carried out by varying the width (W_T) of the corrugation as a proportion of w (%) with height (H_T) equals to $w/2$ for different number of corrugations in both strong and weak couplers as shown in Fig. 7. From Fig. 7 it has been observed that for strong couplers the transmission zero has been placed to second harmonic frequency of 5 GHz with W_T equals to 51%, 42% and 24% of w for N equals to 5, 6 and 7 respectively. As the number of corrugations increases, the electrical path of odd-mode increases more and hence lower dimensions of corrugations are required to place the transmission zero to 5 GHz. Moreover, for weak couplers W_T equals to 78% for N = 7 for the same purpose owing to reduction in coupling. Figure 8 describes the surface current distribution profile in a pair of parallel-coupled lines with and without corrugations at the center frequency of 2.5 GHz. It has been observed that current distribution is minimum at the peaks of the square corrugations and also at the open ends of the coupled resonators. This phenomenon justifies less accumulation of electromagnetic energy at the coupled edges of the lines compared to the outer edges.

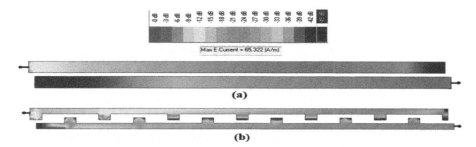

Fig. 8. Surface current distribution for a unit cell parallel-coupled line with corrugations.

3.2 Study of First-Order Folded PCML Filter with Corrugations

Figure 9(a) and (b) show the layout of a first-order folded PCML filter with and without corrugations. The effects on harmonic suppression due to different number of corrugations with $l = 16.833$ mm., $w = 0.94$ mm., $W_T = H_T = w/2 = 0.47$ mm. have been studied in Fig. 10 for both strong and weak coupling filters. It has been observed that the second harmonic is suppressed completely with $N = 5$ for strong coupling and $N = 9$ for weak coupling filters.

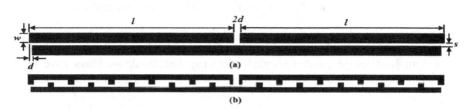

Fig. 9. Layout of first-order folded parallel-coupled microstrip line bandpass filter, (a) $N = 0$, (b) $N = 5$.

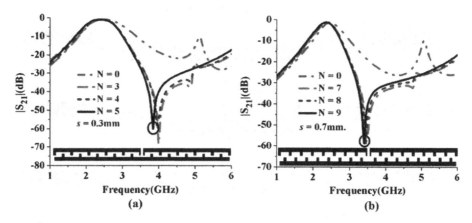

Fig. 10. Effects on second harmonic suppression in a first-order folded bandpass filter with square corrugations with (a) $s = 0.3$ mm. (b) $s = 0.7$ mm. $l = 16.833$ mm., $w = 0.94$ mm., $W_T = H_T = W_B = w/2 = 0.47$ mm.

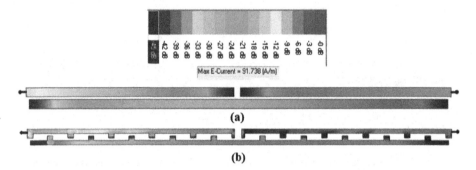

Fig. 11. Surface current distribution for a first-order parallel-coupled line folded bandpass filter with square corrugations.

As the coupling gap increases more number of corrugations are required for harmonic suppression as the wave travels faster through the coupled edge wiggles. The surface current distribution profile in a first-order folded bandpass filter with square corrugations is highlighted in Fig. 11.

3.3   Study of Third-Order Folded Bandpass Filter with Corrugations

The optimum value of the height and width of the corrugations have been obtained by parametric study as $w/2$ where w is the width of the coupled lines without corrugations. Three optimized folded parallel-coupled microstrip line bandpass filters have been designed with five, six and seven periodic square corrugations with the optimum dimensions as shown in Fig. 12(a)–(c) respectively. Comparison of simulated S-parameters of all designed folded filters has been plotted in Fig. 13. All the optimizations have been performed in IE3D EM wave simulator.

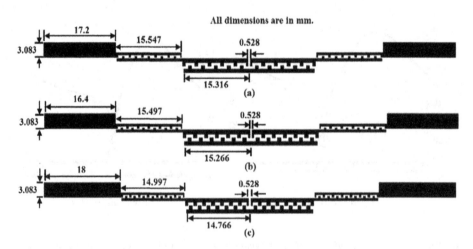

Fig. 12. Layout of optimized folded microstrip line bandpass filter with (a) $N = 5$, (b) $N = 6$ and (c) $N = 7$.

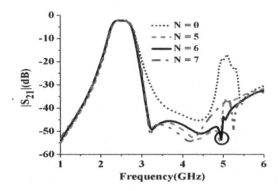

Fig. 13. Effects on second harmonic suppression in optimized third-order folded bandpass filters with square corrugations.

From Fig. 13 it has been observed that the folded parallel-coupled bandpass filter with six periodic square corrugations provides the maximum suppression of second harmonic to 54 dB compared to that of 16.85 dB for the folded filter without corrugations ($N = 0$).

3.4 Experimental Results and Analysis of Folded Filter with Corrugations

Figure 14 shows the photograph of the fabricated folded filter with six square corrugations and Fig. 15 compares the simulated vs. measures S-parameters plots.

Fig. 14. Photograph of fabricated third-order folded filter with six square corrugations.

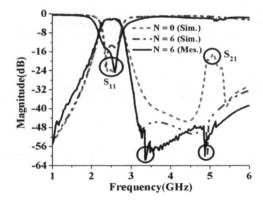

Fig. 15. Simulated vs. measured S-parameters comparison between third-order folded filters without and with corrugations.

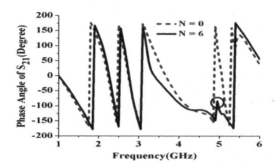

Fig. 16. Phase responses of S_{21}(Degree) comparison between folded bandpass filters with and without corrugations.

It has been observed from Fig. 15 that the second harmonic has been suppressed to 60 dB experimentally compared to folded filter without corrugations. Moreover, a sharp roll-off with maximum stopband rejection level of 62 dB has been achieved at 3.3 GHz. The insertion loss of 2.17 dB and return loss of 25 dB have been obtained within the desired passband. A wide stopband with rejection level below 48 dB has been achieved from 3.13 GHz to 5.21 GHz. Figure 16 compares the phase angle of S_{21} between simulated and measured results for $N = 6$ case. The phase response of S_{21} improves significantly within the passband and at the second harmonic frequency validating the effects of corrugations in harmonic suppression.

3.5   Study of Third-Order In-line Bandpass Filter with Corrugations

The study has been carried out for third-order in-line bandpass filter with the optimum dimensions of corrugations as $W_T = H_T = w/2$. Accordingly, three optimized in-line bandpass filters have been designed with three, four and five periodic square corrugations as shown in Fig. 17(a)–(c) respectively.

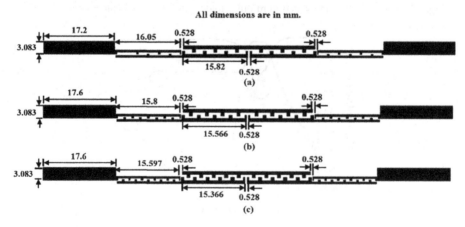

Fig. 17. Layouts of optimized third-order in-line microstrip line bandpass filter with square corrugations (a) $N = 3$, (b) $N = 4$ and (c) $N = 5$.

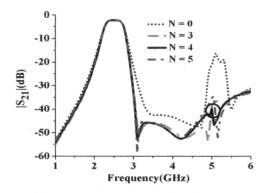

Fig. 18. Effects on second harmonic suppression in optimized third-order in-line bandpass filters with square corrugations.

Comparison of simulated S-parameters of all designed in-line filters with square corrugations has been plotted in Fig. 18. From Fig. 18 it has been observed that the in-line filter with five square corrugations gives the maximum suppression of second harmonic to 40 dB compared to 16.28 dB of in-line filter without corrugations.

3.6   Experimental Results and Analysis of In-line Filter with Corrugations

Figure 19 shows the photograph of the fabricated folded filter with four square corrugations and Fig. 20 compares the simulated vs. measures S-parameters plots.

Fig. 19. Photograph of fabricated third-order in-line filter with four square corrugations.

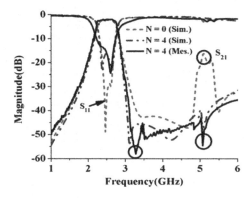

Fig. 20. Simulated vs. measured S-parameters comparison between third-order in-line filters without and with corrugations.

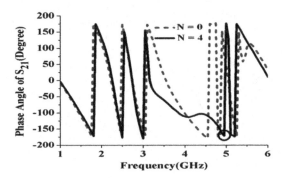

Fig. 21. Phase responses of S_{21}(Degree) comparison between in-line bandpass filters with and without corrugations.

It has been observed from Fig. 20 that the corrugated in-line filter gives more than 55 dB of second harmonic suppression compared to in-line filter without corrugations. Moreover, a sharp attenuation dip with rejection level of 58 dB has been achieved at 3.3 GHz. The insertion loss of 2.05 dB and return loss of 25 dB have been obtained within the desired passband. The stopband has been extended from 3.5 GHz to 5.17 GHz with rejection level below 45 dB. Figure 21 compares the phase angle of S_{21} between simulated and measured results for $N = 4$ case. The slope of phase response of S_{21} becomes steeper at the second harmonic frequency validating the effects of corrugations in harmonic suppression. Table 3 compares the performance of square corrugations on second harmonic suppression with the similar studies. Here, f_c = center frequency, *FBW* = fractional bandwidth, *2HIL* = second harmonic insertion loss.

Table 3. Performance comparison of different designs.

Designs	Structures used	f_c (GHz)	Order	FBW (%)	2HIL (dB)	Size reduction (%)
Proposed	Square corrugations	2.5	3	20	60 (Folded) 55 (In-line)	52 (Folded) 70 (In-line)
[4]	Meandered line	1.0	3	50	50	-
[5]	Capacitive termination	0.9	3	10	64	25
[7]	Square corrugations	2.45	3	10	30	10
[11]	Koch rectangular fractals	13	3	10	42	-
[12]	Koch triangular fractals	2	5	10	60	31

4 Conclusion

Present paper proposes the designs of a folded and in-line parallel-coupled microstrip band pass filters centered at 2.5 GHz with a fractional bandwidth of 20% and investigates the effects of periodic square corrugations around odd-mode region of coupled line for suppressing the harmonics. The folded bandpass filter with six square corrugations suppresses the second harmonic to 60 dB and gives a size reduction of 52% and those for in-line bandpass filter with four corrugations are 55 dB and 70% respectively. The performance of second harmonic suppression degrades in in-line filter compared to folded filter, but the in-line filter structure is more compact in size.

Acknowledgment. Authors are grateful to Mr. Arijit Majumder and Mrs. Souma Chatterjee for giving permission to use the facility of SAMEER Kolkata, India. One of the author Dr. Sayan Chatterjee is thankful to AICTE for the carrier award vide file no: 11-35/RIFD/CAYT/POL-1/2014-15.

References

1. Hong, J.S., Lancaster, M.J.: Microstrip Filters for RF/Microwave Applications. Willey, New York (2001)
2. Mattaei, G., Young, L., Jones, E.M.T.: Microwave Filters, Impedance-matching Networks, and Coupling Structures. Artech House, Norwood (1980)
3. Kung, C.Y., Chen, Y.C., Cheng, F.Y., Huang, C.Y.: Triple-band parallel coupled microstrip bandpass filter with dual coupled length input/output. Microw. Opt. Technol. Lett. **51**(4), 995–997 (2009)
4. Wang, S.M., Chi, C.H., Hsieh, M.Y., Chang, C.Y.: Miniaturized spurious passband suppression microstrip filter using meandered parallel coupled lines. IEEE Trans. Microw. Theory Tech. **53**(2), 747–753 (2005)
5. Cheong, P., Fok, S.W., Tam, K.W.: Miniaturized parallel coupled-line bandpass filter with spurious-response suppression. IEEE Trans. Microw. Theory Tech. **53**(5), 1810–1816 (2005)
6. Das, T.K., Chatterjee, S.: Performance of periodic grooves on harmonic rejection in C-band folded edge-coupled microstrip bandpass filters. In: Proceedings of ICCSE2016, Kolkata, India (2016)
7. Kuo, J.T., Hsu, W.H., Huang, W.T.: Parallel coupled microstrip filters with suppression of harmonic response. IEEE Microw. Wirel. Compon. Lett. **12**(10), 383–385 (2002)
8. Kuo, J.T., Hsu, W.H.: Corrugated parallel-coupled line bandpass filters with multispurious suppression. IET Microw. Antennas Propag. **1**(3), 718–722 (2007)
9. Tanani, M.A.E., Rebeiz, G.M.: Corrugated microstrip coupled lines for constant absolute bandwidth tunable filters. IEEE Trans. Microw. Theory Tech. **58**(4), 956–963 (2010)
10. Das, T.K., Chatterjee, S: Spurious harmonic suppression in a folded parallel-coupled microstrip bandpass filter by using triangular corrugations. In: Proceedings of DEVIC2017, Kalyani, India, pp. 391–395 (2017)
11. Kim, I.K., et al.: Fractal-shaped microstrip coupled-line bandpass filters for suppression of second harmonic. IEEE Trans. Microw. Theory Tech. **53**(9), 2943–2948 (2005)
12. Chen, W.L., Wang, G.M.: Effective design of novel compact fractal-shaped microstrip coupled-line bandpass filters for suppression of the second harmonic. IEEE Microw. Wirel. Compon. Lett. **19**(2), 74–76 (2009)
13. Das, T.K., Chatterjee, S.: 2nd harmonic suppression in parallel-coupled microstrip bandpass filter by using Koch fractals. In: Proceedings of INDICON2016, Bangalore, India (2016)

Segregation of Speech and Songs - A Precursor to Audio Interactive Applications

Himadri Mukherjee[1]([✉]), Santanu Phadikar[2], and Kaushik Roy[1]

[1] Department of Computer Science, West Bengal State University, Kolkata, India
himadrim027@gmail.com, kaushik.mrg@gmail.com
[2] Department of Computer Science and Engineering,
Maulana Abul Kalam Azad University of Technology, Kolkata, India
sphadikar@yahoo.com

Abstract. Audio interactive applications have eased our lives in numerous ways encompassing speech recognition to song identification. Such applications have helped the common people in using Information Technology by providing them a passage for skipping the complicated user interactivity procedures. Audio based search applications have become very popular nowadays especially for searching songs. A system which can distinguish between speech and songs can help to boost the performance of such applications by minimizing the search space and at the same time decide the method of recognition based on the type of audio. It can also help in music-speech separation from audio for karaoke development. In this paper, a system to segregate songs and speech has been proposed using Line Spectral Pair based features. The system has been tested on a database of 19374 clips and a highest accuracy of 99.88% has been obtained with Ensemble Learning based classification.

Keywords: Speech recognition · Audio based searching
Line Spectral Pair · Framing · Ensemble Learning

1 Introduction

Audio interactive applications have simplified the world of Information Technology (IT) for the people who find it difficult to interact with the IT enabled devices. It has enabled us to type without even touching the keys with the help of speech recognition based applications. Audio based searching of multimedia is another promising field of audio based applications which has gained popularity in the form of audio based searching of songs. Speech segments and songs are a bit different in terms of rhythm and presence of background music and noise. Thus processing these signals also require different techniques. Applications capable of processing both type of these signals that is which can recognize speech as well as search songs based on audio are really helpful. However, such a system when supplied with a song for audio based searching need not perform

J. K. Mandal and D. Sinha (Eds.): CSI 2017, CCIS 836, pp. 42–49, 2018.
https://doi.org/10.1007/978-981-13-1343-1_5

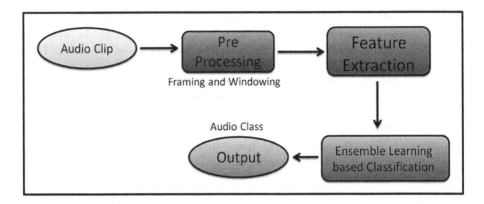

Fig. 1. Pictorial view of the system.

word level identification as in the case of speech recognition and when supplied with speech, it should not apply song searching techniques. A system which can distinguish speech from songs can in turn aid such systems by reducing their search space and improving their performance by helping them to invoke the specific modules based on input. It can also aid to separate background music from songs which can help in karaoke development as well. Prior to identification of speech segments from songs it is essential to distinguish songs and speech components in isolation. Here, a similar system is presented which works with Line Spectral Pair based features and Ensemble Learning based classification. The proposed system is pictorially presented in Fig. 1.

The rest of the paper is organised as follows: The related works are presented in Sect. 2 followed by the dataset details in Sect. 3. The proposed methodology, results and conclusion are presented in Sects. 4, 5 and 6 respectively.

2   Related Work

Various audio based works have been reported over time encompassing speech recognizers, audio based searching systems, speech and song separation, etc. Al-Shoshan [1] presented various frequency, time and time-frequency domain approaches for classifying and separating speech and music signals. They have talked about phoneme based representation of speech and differences between various languages in terms of the same. They have also presented mechanism of production and perception of speech as well as the production of sound by various musical instruments. A discussion about the various contrary factors and characteristics of both speech and music has also been discussed by them. Gao et al. [2] applied Deep Neural Network (DNN) for both feature extraction and classification on the Aurora4 noisy speech recognition task and achieved a word error rate of 10.3% by using multi condition training. Giri et al. [3] presented a system to recognize speech in reverberant conditions. They made use of the auxiliary information while training a DNN on the REVERB Challenge Corpus and obtained 7.8% WER. Ritter et al. [4] applied DNNs to recognize speech influenced by reverb and achieved a lowest WER of 41.9%. Wold et al. [5] presented an array of techniques for searching, retrieval and classification of audio. They have also presented different fields of applications of audio signal processing in the thick of audio editors, surveillance, sound separation, synthesis, etc. Rong used three type of features for the purpose of audio classification whose results are presented in [11]. Their datasets comprised of various general sounds and audio scenes which produced average accuracies of 0.876 and 0.863 respectively. Mazzoni et al. [6] performed content based music retrieval by generating continuous pitch contour instead of quantizing an audio signal provided as query. Foote [7] used MFCC based features for the task of content based music and audio retrieval by means of acoustic similarity. Prakash et al. [8] presented an audio separation technique which works for speech-speech as well as speech-music mixtures with the aid of wavelets. Gerhard had developed seventeen features to distinguish between singing and talking and tested them on a collected corpus. The corpus consisted of recordings in laboratory from volunteers as well as clips from various type of multimedia like movies, music, etc. A detailed account of the experiments is presented in [9] for the same. Ghosal et al. [10] designed a system for segregating speech and music with the aid of various signal based features. They further classified music as either song (voiced) or instrumental using MFCC based features. An accuracy of 97.11% was obtained for speech and music with the help of their proposed audio texture along with Random Sample and Consensus based classification. Saunders [12] presented a technique with the help of a multivariate-Gaussian classifier to distinguish music and speech from FM radio in real time and obtained an accuracy of 98%. Sadjadi et al. [13] presented an unsupervised clustering technique for distinguishing speech and music. They applied MFCC and perceptual features on a database of 40 min recorded from FM radio and obtained an accuracy of 98.75%. Thoshkahna et al. [14] proposed a system to distinguish speech and music with the aid of features based on Harmonics, Individual Lines and Noise. The system was tested on a database comprising of 66 files and an accuracy of 97% was obtained.

3   Dataset Development

Data is an important aspect of any experiment. The quality of data has a major impact on the final outcome of an experiment. In the current experiment, the top 3 spoken languages in India namely English, Hindi and Bangla were considered [15]. Speech segments as well as songs from Youtube in these three languages were used to engender the datasets. Audio clips were extracted from Youtube videos which were then used to generate 4 datasets (D_1, D_2, D_3 and D_4) comprising of audio clips of lengths 5, 10, 15 and 20 s respectively. Each of the clips were stored in .wav format at a bitrate of 1411 kbps in stereo mode. Noise suppression in the speech clips was avoided intentionally in order to simulate real world environment. The details of the prepared datasets is presented in Table 1.

Table 1. Number of clips in the datasets for each type of audio.

Dataset	Duration of clips (seconds)	Number of clips	
		Speech	Song
D_1	5	9703	9671
D_2	10	4841	4785
D_3	15	3219	3142
D_4	20	2413	2342

4 Proposed Method

4.1 Pre Processing

Framing: The spectral properties of an audio signal tend to show high deviations throughout its entire span. In order to analyse such signals, they are divided into smaller frames having pseudo stationary spectral property. In the current experiment the audios were framed in overlapping mode to ensure smoother transition in between two frames. The frame size was experimentally chosen to be of 256 sample points with an overlap of 100 points. A signal consisting of B sample points can be partitioned into C overlapping frames of size D with an overlap factor of E as shown in Eq. (1).

$$C = \left\lceil \frac{B - D}{E} + 1 \right\rceil \tag{1}$$

Windowing: Jitters may arise in frames which interfere during spectral analysis in the form of spectral leakage. In order to handle such components, the frames are multiplied with a Windowing function. In the current experiment, Hamming Window was chosen for this purpose based on experiment and its popularity [17].

4.2 Feature Extraction

In the present experiment, the input signals were characterized with the aid of Line Spectral Pair [18] based features. Line Spectral Pair is a unique technique of representing Linear Predictive Coefficients which ensures higher interpolation properties. In this technique, a signal is considered as the output of an all pole filter (H(z)) and the inverse filter is represented by (A(z)). A(z) is presented in Eq. (2) where $a_{1.....M}$ represents the Predictive coefficients up to the order (M).

$$A(z) = 1 + a_1 z^{-1} + a_2 z^{-2} + a_3 z^{-3} + \ldots\ldots + a_M z^{-M} \tag{2}$$

Such Line Spectral Pair (LSP) features of 10, 12, 15 and 20 dimensions were extracted for every frame. These values were used to find band wise sum of the LSP coefficients and then used to grade the bands in ascending order based on energy. This graded band sequences (for 10, 12, 15 and 20 dimensional LSPs) constituted the features of our experiment. A graphical representation of the average feature values of various dimensions for D_1 (since highest accuracy was obtained) is presented in Fig. 2.

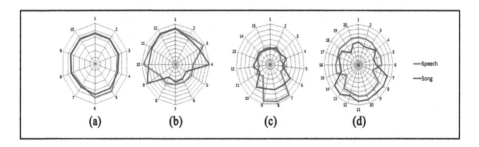

Fig. 2. Feature values for D_1 of (a) 10 dimensions, (b) 12 dimensions, (c) 15 dimensions, (d) 20 dimensions.

4.3 Ensemble Learning Based Classification

In the technique of Ensemble learning multiple learners are trained and combined to solve a problem. The learners generate a set of hypothesis during the training phase and take a decision by combining them in contrast to single hypothesis learning of various machine learning algorithms.

A Random Forest [19] based classifier was used in the current experiment which is an ensemble learner and consists of a set of decision trees. Random Forests efficiently estimate missing data and preserve the accuracy even in the absence of a proportion of data as often observed in real world scenarios. Moreover, Random Forests are fully parallelizable thereby making them an ideal choice for systems with parallel processing capability.

5 Result and Discussion

A 5 Fold Cross Validation technique was adopted for evaluating the proposed system. The obtained accuracies for the various feature sets across the various datasets is presented in Table 2 with the highest accuracy highlighted in Green which has been analysed in detail.

Correct classification rates of 99.86% and 99.91% were obtained for speech and song clips respectively for 10 dimensional features on D_1. One of the reasons for the slightly lower accuracy of the speech clips is due to the fact that most of the speech clips were accompanied with introductory as well as outro "music only sections" which led them to be confused as music clips. The correct classifications and misclassifications for the afore mentioned is presented in Figs. 3 and 4.

Table 2. Accuracies for various feature dimensions across the datasets.

Datasets	Feature Dimensions			
	10	12	15	20
D_1	99.88	97.54	94.30	99.63
D_2	99.58	99.31	99.00	99.68
D_3	88.35	99.28	99.53	99.04
D_4	87.57	99.83	99.12	99.58

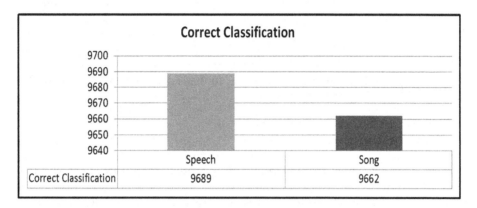

Fig. 3. Correct classifications out of 19374 instances for 10 dimensional features on D_1.

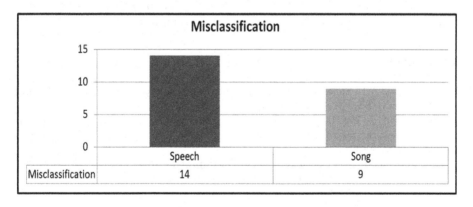

Fig. 4. Misclassifications out of 19374 instances for 10 dimensional features on D_1.

A few other classifiers which are popularly used in pattern recognition problems like LogitBoost, Naive Bayes, Bagging, J48, BayesNet, Simple Logistic and Multi Layered Perceptron from WEKA as used in [17] were also applied on the 10 dimensional D_1 whose results are presented in Fig. 5 with the highest accuracy shown in Red.

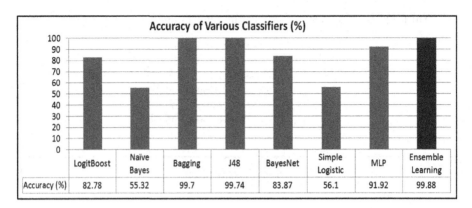

Fig. 5. Performance of various classifiers for 10 dimensional features on D_1. (Color figure online)

6   Conclusion

Here we have presented a technique for segregation of songs from speech. The same was subjected to real world data and we achieved a precision of 0.99. In future, we plan to use a bigger dataset of both real world and studio data as well as noisy data to test the robustness of the system. Experimentation with other features and classification techniques will also be performed. We also plan to integrate the proposed system with an audio based searching system and observe the performance of the same in various scenarios.

References

1. Al-Shoshan, A.I.: Speech and music classification and separation: a review. J. King Saud Univ. **19**(1), 95–133 (2006)
2. Gao, T., Du, J., Dai, L.R., Lee, C.H.: Joint training of front-end and back-end deep neural networks for robust speech recognition. In: Proceedings of ICASSP-2015, pp. 4375–4379 (2015)
3. Giri, R., Seltzer, M.L., Droppo, J., Yu, D.: Improving speech recognition in reverberation using a room-aware deep neural network and multitask learning. In: Proceedings of ICASSP-2015, pp. 5014–5018 (2015)
4. Ritter, M., Mueller, M., Stueker, S., Metze, F., Waibel, A.: Training deep neural networks for reverberation robust speech recognition. In: ITG Symposium on Speech Communication, pp. 1–5 (2016)
5. Wold, E., Blum, T., Keislar, D., Wheaten, J.: Content-based classification, search, and retrieval of audio. IEEE Multimedia **3**(3), 27–36 (1996)
6. Mazzoni, D., Dannenberg, R.B.: Melody matching directly from audio. In: Proceedings of ISMIR-2001, pp. 17–18 (2001)
7. Foote, J.T.: Content-based retrieval of music and audio. In: Multimedia Storage and Archiving Systems II, pp. 138–148 (1997)
8. Prakash, K., Hepzibha, R.D.: Blind source separation for speech music and speech speech mixtures. Int. J. Comput. Appl. **110**(12), 40–43 (2015)

9. Gerhard, D.B.: Computationally measurable differences between speech and song. Doctoral dissertation, School of Computing Science, Simon Fraser University (2003)
10. Ghosal, A., Chakraborty, R., Dhara, B.C., Saha, S.K.: A hierarchical approach for speech-instrumental-song classification. SpringerPlus **2**(1), 526 (2013)
11. Rong, F.: Audio classification method based on machine learning. In: Proceedings of ICITBS-2016, pp. 81–84 (2016)
12. Saunders, J.: Real-time discrimination of broadcast speech/music. In: Proceedings of ICASSP-1996, vol. 2, pp. 993–996 (1996)
13. Sadjadi, S.O., Ahadi, S.M., Hazrati, O.: Unsupervised speech/music classification using one-class support vector machines. In: Proceedings of ICICS-2007, pp. 1–5 (2007)
14. Thoshkahna, B., Sudha, V., Ramakrishnan, K.R.: A speech-music discriminator using HILN model based features. In: Proceedings of ICASSP-2006, vol. 5, pp. V 425-V 428 (2006)
15. Ethnologue. http://www.ethnologue.com. Accessed 1 Sept 2017
16. Youtube. http://www.youtube.com. Accessed 1 Sept 2017
17. Mukherjee, H., Rakshit, P., Phadikar, S., Roy, K.: REARC-a Bangla phoneme recognizer. In: Proceedings of ICADW-2016, pp. 177–180 (2016)
18. Paliwal, K.K.: On the use of line spectral frequency parameters for speech recognition. Digit. Signal Process. **2**(2), 80–87 (1992)
19. Breiman, L.: Random forests. Machine Learn. **45**(1), 5–32 (2001)

A Theoretical Framework of Lifetime Prediction of Wireless Sensor Networks

Sudakshina Dasgupta[1]([✉]) and Paramartha Dutta[2]

[1] Government College of Engineering and Textile Technology, Serampore, India
sudakshinadasgupta@yahoo.com
[2] Department of Computer and System Science, Visva Bharati University,
Santiniketan, India
paramartha.dutta@gmail.com

Abstract. Lifetime of a network induces a direct trade-off against the quality of service. Providing more energy can increase more quality of service but might decrease lifetime. Sensors in Wireless Sensor Networks have a variety of purposes, functions and capabilities with severe energy constraints. Due to the scarcity of energy resources, network organizational design imposes a challenging impact on energy consumption, which leads to an effect on operational lifetime of the entire network. Operational Lifetime becomes one of the precious context of merit of wireless sensor network which depends on the applications. Among different interpretations of the lifetime of sensor networks, it includes the time until the network is disconnected in two or more partitions. Hence, the application region might not be observed by one sensor node only. Therefore this observed region needs to partition into number of sub regions or clusters and instead of a single, a few number of sensors are required to cover the application area. In this paper we address one probabilistic prediction based approach for sensor network lifetime to determine in what situation this breaking into sub regions or clustering is required.

Keywords: Probabilistic lifetime prediction · Clustering
Wireless sensor network

1 Introduction

Recent technological improvements have made the deployment of low power hardware platforms that establish wireless communication capability by means of sensing, processing and transmitting information from or to be sent to the environment. These contrivances are called sensor nodes and grouped to from a wireless sensor networks (WSN). Sensors in WSNs have a variety of purposes, functions and activities. A limited amount of processing is done by each sensor node. But when receiving sensed information from numerous sensor nodes, they require to expense more energy to control the specified domain [4]. Therefore the active participation of sensor nodes depend on one of the main influencing factor i.e. energy consumption [5]. As sensor nodes are battery driven, they have very

© Springer Nature Singapore Pte Ltd. 2018
J. K. Mandal and D. Sinha (Eds.): CSI 2017, CCIS 836, pp. 50–57, 2018.
https://doi.org/10.1007/978-981-13-1343-1_6

low energy resource. This scarcity makes energy consumption most challenging in network because it involves in determination of survivability of sensor nodes by means of reduction of energy consumption. Therefore energy awareness is one of the crucial task of design and operation of sensor networks. Network architecture and protocols play vital roles in deploy and development of WSNs [6]. Due to power hungry property of the sensor nodes, network architecture design might be an decisive issue on the operational lifetime of any sensor network.

These physical limitations of sensor nodes and the restricted cost to supersede the non functional sensors in the network make energy a decisive issue to design and deploy a wireless sensor network [8] with extended life span. How to elongate the lifetime of such networks have been a topic of considerable interest in the research field of sensor network.

In the present work, a single hop network architecture of a WSN has been considered with thousand of nodes deployed across the application area. Base station has been positioned remotely outside the deployed region. Each sensor node send their collective information to the respective cluster head when cluster heads serve as relays for transmitting information to the Base station. This process can reduce in overall energy consumption of the network. It also helps to balance the network traffic which can in turn increase the scalability of the network [7]. Since all sensor nodes are homogeneous in nature and have the same transmission capability, clustering must be periodically performed to balance the traffic load over the network. As computational capacity is less in wireless sensor network, the energy requirement for sensing and processing is less than that for communication. Cluster head drained its energy very fast than other members of clusters [9]. Gradually whenever no more node be remain there to take the responsibility of the cluster then re-clustering is required. In this paper we address one probabilistic prediction based approach of sensor network lifetime to determine in what situation this breaking of sub regions or clustering is required. When energy level of most of the nodes of entire cluster fall below the threshold level, then this cluster don't have any communication capacity to maintain the surveillance. But when this type of situation has raised, it might be beneficial to predict the lifetime of sensor network earlier. This prediction leads to incorporate node scheduling approach among all sensor nodes of that cluster so that nodes can periodically change their mode of operation between active and sleep state. Therefore in each turn minimum number of nodes can cover the entire service area of clusters in scheduled basis [10]. As a result no more redundant information can be thrown to cluster head as well as Base Station and the survivability of the clustered WSNs will be maximized.

Rest of the paper is arranged in the following manner. Section 2 demonstrates the related work in suggested area. In Sect. 3, a novel probabilistic life time prediction technique of sensor nodes in WSN has been presented. Section 4 illustrates the theoretical analysis of the mathematical formulations and the last section concludes the work.

2   Related Work

Many recent research works in the area of Cluster-based Wireless Sensor Network have broadly addressed on energy efficiency, lifetime, stability and scalability [12,13,17]. Different clustering methods namely weighted clustering, hierarchical clustering and dynamic clustering algorithm have been reported to deploy sensor nodes in clusters to explore energy-efficient routing strategies [15,16,18]. Routing algorithms designed for WSN must address the power and resource constraints of the network nodes, the time-varying quality of the communication channel, and the chance for packet drop and delay. To encounter these design challenges different routing algorithms for wireless sensor network have been demonstrated in the literature [8,17]. To manage the tradeoff between optimality and efficiency of a WSN, the routing strategies must be introduced in an intelligent way in the targeted application [11]. Therefore the most important challenges in WSN are energy consumption of sensor nodes. Power consumptions of battery operated sensor nodes should be minimized in order to avoid recharging and replacing the nodes in harsh environment. Therefore lifetime prediction of a sensor node with respect to battery consumption is one of the major challenge in WSN. A few number of approaches has been proposed for the prediction of clustered sensor network lifetime to maintain a long survivability of the network [14]. In [1], author shows that due to high sleep rate of sensor node, it's lifetime will be longer and vice versa A sensor with higher transmission rate, lifetime will be shorter. But there is no significant idea about the changes of battery power from the initial energy level. In [2], AEON, a novel evaluation tool to predict the energy consumption of sensor nodes and to find which part of the operating System should be modified for further improvement of the network lifetime. AEON efficiently analyze the energy consumption of sensor nodes in various field of applications, it yet not support all node components. Sha and Shi Provide a set of formal models considering the remaining lifetime of each sensor as well as the remaining lifetime of whole sensor networks [3]. Here, two query protocols IQ and Traditional have been compared in terms of formal models by mathematical analysis where there is no consideration of sleep/active dynamics of sensor nodes.

3   Proposed Work

Let us assume a Wireless Sensor Network with n nodes with activation characteristics $P_1, P_2, P_3, ..., P_k$ respectively. The network will be crumbled when all the n nodes move into sleep state. Therefore the time to network failure is the maximum time of survival of a node among k nodes. All the sensor nodes are stationary after deployment having same initial energy and the Base Station is in a fixed position. The communication is in single hop. The objective of our work is to predict the lifetime of the sensor network to determine at what situation the breaking of sub regions or clustering is required. By clustering the responsibility of entire region space is reduced which lead to minimum energy consumption of sensor nodes again. With this probabilistic lifetime prediction technique of wireless sensor network unnecessary clustering can be prevented.

Let us assume

X = System collapse time

= Minimum time at which all nodes in the system fall asleep

It is a positive integer valued random variable. The Sleep-Active transition characteristic of the ith node is given by

$$\text{P}_i = \begin{array}{c} \\ \text{Active} \\ \text{Sleep} \end{array} \overset{\text{Active Sleep}}{\left(\begin{array}{cc} p_i & 1 - p_i \\ 0 & 1 \end{array} \right)}$$

Let X_i = Minimum time at which node i is falling asleep, $1 \leq i \leq N$ Note that

$$X = \underset{1 \leq i \leq N}{\text{Max}} \{X_i\}$$

$$= \text{Max}\{X_1, X_2, X_3, ...X_N\}$$

$$X_i \frown \text{geometric}(1 - p_i), p_i \in (0,1), 1 \leq i \leq N \tag{1}$$

$$P(X_i = k_i) = p_i^{k_i - 1}(1 - p_i), \ k_i \geq 1, 1 \leq i \leq N \tag{2}$$

$$P(X_i \leq k_i) = \bigcup_{r_i=1}^{k_i} P(X_i = r_i) = \sum_{r_i=1}^{k_i} p_i^{r_i-1}(1 - p_i)$$

$$= (1 - p_i) \sum_i^{k_i} p_i^{r_i-1}$$

$$= \frac{1 - p_i^{k_i}}{1 - p_i}(1 - p_i)$$

$$= 1 - p_i^{k_i}, \ k_i \geq 1, \ 1 \leq i \leq N$$

Therefore,

$$P(X_i \leq k_i) = 1 - p_i^{k_i}, \ k_i \geq 1, \ 1 \leq i \leq N \tag{3}$$

Naturally, $P(X_i > k_i) = p_i^{k_i}, \ k_i \geq 1, \ 1 \leq i \leq N$

Also note,

$$\{X \leq k\} = \bigcap_{i=1}^{N} \{x_i \leq k\}, \ k \geq 1$$

Therefore,

$$P(x \leq K) = P[\bigcap_{i=1}^{N} (x_i \leq k)]$$

$$= \prod_{i=1}^{N} P(x_i \leq k) \ (independence)$$

$$= \prod_{i=1}^{N}(1 - p_i^k), \ k \geq 1$$

Therefore,

$$P(x \leq K) = \prod_{i=1}^{N}(1 - p_i^k), \ k \geq 1 \tag{4}$$

$$P(X = k) = P(X \leq k) - P(X \leq k+1)$$
$$= \prod_{i=1}^{N}(1 - p_i^k) - \prod_{i=1}^{N}(1 - p_i^{k+1}), \ k \geq 1$$
$$= \prod_{i=1}^{N}(1 - p_i^k)[1 - (1 - p_i)], \ k \geq 1$$
$$= \prod_{i=1}^{N}(1 - p_i^k)p_i, \ k \geq 1$$
$$= [\prod_{i=1}^{N}(1 - p_i^k)] \prod_{i=1}^{N}p_i, \ k \geq 1$$

Therefore,

$$P(X = k) = [\prod_{i=1}^{N}(1 - p_i^k)] \prod_{i=1}^{N}p_i, \ k \geq 1 \tag{5}$$

$$E(X) = \sum_{k \geq 1} kP(X = k) = \sum_{k \geq 1}\prod_{i=1}^{N}p_i k[\prod_{i=1}^{N}(1 - p_i^k)]$$
$$= \prod_{i=1}^{N}p_i \sum_{k \geq 1} k \prod_{i=1}^{N}(1 - p_i^k)$$

Under identical node behavior, $p_i = p \ \forall i, 1 \leq i \leq n$. In that case,

$$E(X) = \prod_{i=1}^{N}p \sum_{k \geq 1} k \prod_{i=1}^{N}(1 - p^k)$$
$$= p^N \sum_{k \geq 1} k(1 - p^k)^N$$
$$= p^N \sum_{k \geq 1} k \sum_{r=0}^{N}\binom{N}{r}(-1)^r p^{k(N-r)}$$
$$= p^N \sum_{k \geq 1} k \sum_{r=0}^{N}\binom{N}{r}(-1)^r k \ p^{k(N-r)}$$

$$= p^N \sum_{r=0}^{N} \sum_{k \geq 1} k \binom{N}{r} (-1)^r k \, p^{k(N-r)}$$

$$= p^N \sum_{r=0}^{N} \binom{N}{r} (-1)^r \sum_{k \geq 1} k \, p^{k(N-r)}$$

$$= p^N \sum_{r=0}^{N} \binom{N}{r} (-1)^r \frac{p^{(N-r)}}{(1 - p^{(N-r)})^2}$$

$$= p^N \sum_{r=0}^{N} \binom{N}{r} (-1)^r p^{(N-r)} \sum_{l \geq 1} l \, (p^{(N-r)})^{l-1}$$

$$= p^N \sum_{r=0}^{N} \sum_{l \geq 1} l \binom{N}{r} (-1)^r (p^l)^{(N-r)}$$

$$= p^N \sum_{l \geq 1} \sum_{r=0}^{N} l \binom{N}{r} (-1)^r (p^l)^{(N-r)}$$

$$= p^N \sum_{l \geq 1} l \sum_{r=0}^{N} \binom{N}{r} (-1)^r (p^l)^{(N-r)}$$

$$= p^N \sum_{l \geq 1} l(1 - p^l)^N$$

Hence,

$$E(X) = p^N \sum_{l \geq 1} l(1 - p^l)^N \tag{6}$$

4   Theoretical Analysis

The previous section contains the derivation of the expected collapse time of a system of wireless sensor nodes, under the assumption of equiprobable transition characteristic, i.e., p_i being equal for node i. From this derivation it is evident that the expected collapse time is finite and bounded which technically means that such a network of wireless sensor nodes is bound to collapse within a finite amount of time. Moreover, it may be noted that the expected collapse time attains value zero in case of the homogeneous transition probability assuming value 0 or 1. This indicates that there exists at least one peak(s) of the expected collapse time for some value of the transition probability. In other words, for a given system of wireless sensor nodes, there is some choice of transition probability for which the expected collapse is delayed to the maximum level. What may be interesting an issue is to explore the influence of node density in the network on the expected collapse time.

5   Conclusion

In this article, a theoretical framework along with requisite derivation have been offered. The derivation formalized the dependence of the lifetime of the system on the node density and the transition probability.

References

1. Sharath Kumara, Y., Geetha, N.B., Rafi, M.: Prediction of sensor lifetime by using clustering-fuzzy logic in wireless sensor networks. In: 2014 IJCSMC, vol. 4, no. 4, pp. 835–841, April 2015
2. Landsiedel, O., Wehrle, K., Gotz, S.: Accurate prediction of power consumption in sensor networks. In: IEEE Xplore, 31 May 2005
3. Sha, K., Shi, W.: Modeling the lifetime of wireless sensor networks. Sens. Lett. **3**, 110 (2005)
4. Navimipour, N.J., Shabestari, S.H., Samacii, V.S.: Minimize energy consumption and improve the lifetime of heterogeneous wireless sensor networks by using monkey search algorithm. In: 2012 International Conference on Information and Knowledge Management. IPCSIT, vol. 45, pp. 42–47 (2012)
5. Nguyen, D., Minet, P., Kunz, T., Lamount, L.: On the selection of cluster heads in MANETS. Int. J. Comput. Sci. Issues **8**(2), 1–12 (2011)
6. Valli, R., Dananjayan, P.: Utility enhancement by power control in WSN with different topologies using game theoretic approach. In: CIT 2011 Proceedings of the 5th WSEAS International Conference on Communications and Information Technology, pp. 85–89 (2011). ISBN 978-1-61804-018-3
7. Koltsidas, G., Pavlidou, F.-N.: A game theoretical approach to clustering of ad-hoc and sensor networks. Telecommun. Syst. **47**(1–2), 81–93 (2011)
8. Katiyar, V., Chand, N., Soni, S.: A survey on clustering algorithms for heterogeneous wireless sensor networks. Int. J. Adv. Netw. Appl. **02**(04), 745–754 (2011)
9. Ramesh, K., Somasundaram, K.: A comparative study of clusterhead selection algorithm in wireless sensor networks. Int. J. Comput. Sci. Eng. Surv. (IJCSES) **2**(4), 153–164 (2011)
10. Maraiya, K., Kant, K., Gupta, N.: Efficient cluster head selection scheme for data aggregation in wireless sensor network (0975 - 8887). Int. J. Comput. Appl. **23**(9), 10–18 (2011)
11. Ralbi, J., Rajendran, G.: An enhanced LEACH protocol using fuzzy logic for wireless sensor network. Int. J. Comput. Sci. Inf. Secur. **8**(7), 189–194 (2010)
12. Gupta, I., Riordan, D., Sampalli, S.: Cluster head election using fuzzy logic for wireless sensor network. In: Communication Networks and Service Research Conference Publications, pp. 255–260, May 2005
13. Younis, O., Fahmy, S.: HEED: a hybrid, energy-efficient, distributed clustering approach for ad hoc sensor networks. IEEE Trans. Mob. Comput. **3**(4), 366–379 (2004)
14. Bandyopadhyay, S., Coyle, E.J.: An energy efficient hierarchical clustering algorithm for wireless sensor networks. In: IEEE INFOCOM, vol. 3, pp. 1713–1723, April 2003
15. Akyildiz, F., Su, W., Sankarasubramaniam, Y., Cayirci, E.: A survey on sensor netowrks. IEEE Commun. Mag. **40**(8), 102–114 (2002)

16. Manjeshwar, A., Agarwal, D.P.: APTEEN: a hybrid protocol for efficient routing An comprehensive information retrieval in wireless sensor networks. In: Proceedings of International Parallel and Distributed Processing Symposium. IPDPS 2002, pp. 195–202 (2002)
17. Heinzelman, W.B., Chandrakasan, A.P., Balakrishnan, H.: Application specific protocol architecture for wireless microsensor networks. IEEE Trans. Wirel. Netw. **1**(4), 660–670 (2002)
18. Heinzelman, W., Chandrakasan, A., Balakrishnan, H.: Energy-efficient communication protocol for wireless microsensor networks. In: 2000 Proceedings of the 33rd Annual Hawaii International Conference on System Sciences, vol. 2, no. 10, pp. 4–7, January 2000

Verification of OAuth 2.0 Using UPPAAL

K. S. Jayasri[1]([✉]), K. P. Jevitha[2], and B. Jayaraman[3]

[1] TIFAC-CORE in Cyber Security, Amrita Vishwa Vidyapeetham, Coimbatore, India
cb.en.p2cys16011@cb.students.amrita.edu
[2] Department of Computer Science and Engineering, Amrita Vishwa Vidyapeetham,
Coimbatore, India
kp_jevitha@cb.amrita.edu
[3] Department of Computer Science and Engineering,
State University of New York at Buffalo, Buffalo, USA
bharat@buffalo.edu

Abstract. Web services are software services that are accessible over the internet through a set of application program interfaces (APIs). The security of these APIs is a major concern because of their loose coupling, and protection mechanisms are needed to safeguard them from attacks. The simplest of these mechanisms are authentication and authorization. A client that requests access to a web API should be authorized by an end-user who has been authenticated by an authorization server. OAuth 2.0 can be used to achieve this protection. The security properties of a widely used protocol such as OAuth 2.0 should be verified, since many systems depend on this protocol for protection. This paper focuses on verifying three important classes of properties of OAuth 2.0, namely safety, liveness, and absence of deadlock. A model of the OAuth protocol was developed using UPPAAL, a tool used for modeling and verification. This model consists of four finite state machines, one representing each of the roles in OAuth 2.0, and the properties of interest were verified using this model.

Keywords: OAuth 2.0 · UPPAAL · Safety · Liveness
Formal methods

1 Introduction

Web services are a set of application program interfaces (APIs) that are accessed using HTTP. They have become an essential piece of the internet and, at the same time, have become subject to a wide range of attacks [1]. A protection mechanism is greatly needed in order to secure these web APIs from attacks. The protection mechanism should surpass the traditional password anti-pattern, since this approach is compromised by the user through password reuse [2]. Authentication and authorization are the most commonly used protection mechanisms. However, Basic Authentication and Digest Authentication [3] do not provide sufficient protection from attacks since they also follow the password anti-pattern, where the shared secret directly represents the party in question.

© Springer Nature Singapore Pte Ltd. 2018
J. K. Mandal and D. Sinha (Eds.): CSI 2017, CCIS 836, pp. 58–67, 2018.
https://doi.org/10.1007/978-981-13-1343-1_7

The latest and hitherto the most secure scheme for gaining access to web APIs is OAuth 2.0. It is a delegation protocol that facilitates an end-user to authorize a client to access the end-user's assets hosted on a resource server. Here, the user's credentials are not imparted to the client; instead, the client is issued a token that delegates restricted access to the user's assets. Given the importance of the OAuth 2.0 protocol, this paper addresses the question of how the security of this protocol can be formally verified.

Over the years, several authentication and communication protocols have been formally verified. Luo et al. [4] use formal methods to verify the correctness of Needham-Schroeder protocol. They use a symbolic model checker MCTK which uses ECKLn. The original Needham-Schroeder protocol as well as the Lowe's modified version have been verified. Diaz et al. [5] have verified the TLS handshake protocol using formal methods. SSL/TLS is the most widely used protocol to secure communication over HTTP. Their model verifies properties such as safety and liveness of the TLS handshake protocol. The authors use railway traffic as an analogy to explain each of the properties. The properties have been formulated and verified, and the model has been validated using UPPAAL. Yuan et al. [6] propose the formalization and verification of RESTful systems using CSP. Client, Server and Resources are modeled as CSP processes that communicate via CSP channels. The four HTTP methods, GET, PUT, POST and DELETE are taken into consideration while modeling these processes. Their model verifies the statelessness and hypertext-driven behavior in addition to defining the failure case for safety, idempotent and deadlock properties of HTTP methods. In [7] Yan et al. have used formal methods to discover three security weaknesses in the OAuth protocol. In [8], formal methods has been used to detect and address four possible attacks on the OAuth protocol. Pai et al. [9] use formal methods to prove the existence of a security vulnerability in OAuth, that allows an attacker to steal client's credentials from the client application.

The focus of our paper is the formal verification of safety, liveness and absence of deadlock properties of the authentication code mode of OAuth 2.0. The user-friendly nature of UPPAAL makes it an attractive tool for this experiment.

2 Overview of OAuth 2.0

OAuth 2.0 is an authorization framework that permits an end-user to authorize a client to access the end-user's resources at the resource server. OAuth 2.0 is not an extension to OAuth 1.0, but a different protocol. Henceforth, OAuth 2.0 and OAuth shall be used interchangeably in this document.

OAuth is widely used to protect web APIs that are accessed by client software. Traditionally, schemes such as Basic Authentication and Digest Authentication were used to provide security [3]. There are several advantages to using OAuth over traditional protection mechanisms for web APIs. First, end-users do not have to share their credentials with a third party client whose services they wish to use. Second, OAuth allows an end-user to restrict the scope of access granted to a third-party client. Third, compromise of third-party client does not expose the end-user's credentials, since the client never gets the end-user's credentials.

These along with modularity and extensibility offered by OAuth make it the obvious choice for securing web APIs [10]. The modularity and extensibility offered by OAuth can be attributed to the various modes of operations supported by OAuth. The four roles defined by OAuth and the four modes of operation of OAuth protocol are discussed in the following sections.

2.1   Roles

The four roles defined by OAuth [11] are as follows.

Resource Owner. It is the end-user or a system capable of authorizing a client to access a protected resource.

Client. It is an application that makes requests in the interest of the end-user. It redeems the authorization code for an access token at the authorization server and uses the same for gaining access to resources at the resource server.

Authorization Server. It validates the resource owner and provides an authorization code. The resource owner then redirects the client with this code to the authorization server. The client then redeems the authorization code for access token at the authorization server.

Resource Server. It is the server on which secured assets are hosted. This server accepts and responds to access tokens from a requesting client.

2.2   The OAuth Flow

We provide a brief explanation of the interaction among the roles described above. When the resource owner requests the services of a client, it receives an authorization request from the client. This request is either forwarded directly to the resource server or through the authorization server. To represent its authorization, the resource owner gives an authorization grant to the client. This grant is obtained by the resource owner from the authorization server by authenticating itself to the authorization server. The client then redeems this authorization grant for an access token at the authorization server or the resource server (if that is the only server involved). The client then proceeds to produce this access token at the resource server, so as to gain access to the resource owner's resources available at the resource server. It is favored to use the authorization server as an emissary while getting the authorization grant. A more detailed explanation of the OAuth flow can be found in [10,11].

2.3   Types of Authorization Grant

OAuth supports four modes or types of authorization grants. These modes along with other optional features provided by OAuth make it a flexible and modular framework [10].

Authorization code is the most generally utilized grant type. Here, the authorization server authenticates the resource owner, who then redirects the client to the authorization server with an authorization code. The client then redeems this code for an access token at the authorization server which is then produced at the resource server to gain access to resources. From a security perspective, the advantage of using this type is that the resource owner's credentials are never revealed to the client, and also the access token given to the client is never revealed to the resource owner. The focus of this paper is *authorization code* mode.

Implicit grant is a reduced version of the authorization code mode. This mode is used when the client is a part of the resource owner's user-agent, e.g., a JavaScript client in a browser that acts as the resource owner's user-agent. In this case, there is no advantage in implementing client redirection, since the client's operation is transparent to the user-agent and hence the client's access token cannot be protected from the user-agent. Therefore, the access token is delivered straight to the client without having to redeem an authorization code for access token.

Resource owner password credentials is used only when the resource owner and the client have high degree of confidence in each other or when none of the other modes can be used. Here, the resource owner gives its credentials to the client, who then uses it to get an access token from the authorization server. Since the resource owner's credentials are given to the client, this mode requires a high degree of trust.

Client credentials is used when the client is acting for itself, i.e., when the client is trying to access its own resources hosted on the resource server. A typical situation would involve two back-end systems trying to communicate with each other without involving a particular user. The client uses its credentials to gain an access token at the authorization server.

3   Methodology

Formal methods are mathematical verification techniques that are used to check whether a system conforms to a given specification. Traditionally, they have been used to develop a system specification or in the verification of embedded systems [12]. Today, formal methods are being applied to information systems and protocols as well [5]. Systems in development could use formal methods to guide their evolution from inception through conformance to a specification, whereas existing systems can make use of formal methods to identify and fix bugs.

3.1   UPPAAL

We show in this paper how the authorization code mode of OAuth 2.0 is verified using finite state automata designed in UPPAAL, a tool for formal verification of real-time systems using timed automata [13]. The tool comprises two parts, a graphical user-interface and a model-checker engine. The engine could be hosted on the same machine as the user interface or on a server with more capabilities. System behavior is modeled using finite state automata, for simulation and analysis [13].

Entities communicate using channels in UPPAAL. Some of the commonly used notations are as follows.

- ch? stands for a receive operation on channel ch
- ch! stands for a send operation on channel ch
- A state with a circle in it represents the start state
- A state with a c in it represents the commit state.

3.2 Modeling OAuth 2.0 in UPPAAL

Four finite-state automata were designed, one for each of the roles described earlier. The host or resource owner is a device or an end-user who initiates the process by requesting a service from the client. Figure 1 shows the states and transitions a host undergoes as the system evolves. Figures 2, 3, and 4 represent the client, the authentication server, and the resource server, respectively. A brief explanation of the working of this model is given below.

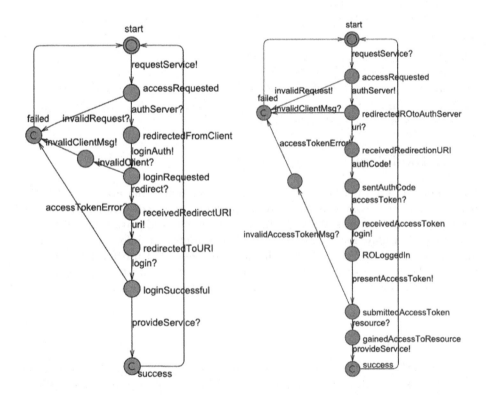

Fig. 1. Resource owner automaton   **Fig. 2.** Client automaton

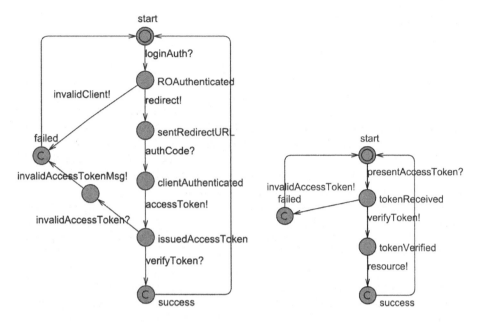

Fig. 3. Authentication server automaton   **Fig. 4.** Resource server automaton

The host requests access to a service offered by the client through the *request-Service* channel. It is then redirected to the authorization server of its choice. This choice is made available to the resource owner on the *authServer* channel. The resource owner authenticates itself by providing its credentials at the authorization server on channel *loginAuth*, and is then given an authorization code after which it is redirected to the client on channel *redirect*. The client receives the authorization code from the host on channel *uri*. The client submits the received authorization code to the authorization server on channel *authCode* and collects an access token from the authentication server on channel *accessToken*. Having received the access token, the client authenticates the resource owner on *login* channel. The client proceeds to submit the received access token to the resource server on channel *presentAccessToken*. The resource server communicates with the authorization server on channel *verifyToken* to check the legitimacy of the received access token. After successful validation, the resource server permits the client to access the requested asset on channel *resource*. Upon gaining access to the requested asset, the client offers the requested service to the end user on channel *provideService*.

Described above is the normal behavior of the system. There will, however, be situations where the system fails to evolve when the required conditions are unmet, such as failure to authenticate. These situations are modeled as transitions to the *failure* state. An example of failure scenario is when the access token produced by the client could be invalid, prompting the resource server to send an *invalidAccessToken* message to the authorization server who in turn informs the client of this error on the *invalidAccessTokenMsg* channel. The client then sends an *accessTokenError* message to the resource owner and denies service to the resource owner.

4 Results

The simulation feature of UPPAAL was used to carry out a basic sanity check that the designed model functions as expected and achieves the desired system behavior. This was done by interactively choosing at each step one of the enabled transitions in order to evolve the progress of the system. The normal flow of OAuth as captured by the UPPAAL simulator is shown in Fig. 5. This sequence diagram was generated by the UPPAAL simulator.

Three classes of properties were identified to be verified on the model. These properties, namely Safety, Liveness and Deadlock-Freedom were specified using propositional temporal logic [14]. A detailed explanation of these properties can be found in [15, 16].

Safety. A safety properties ensures that "something bad never happens" [15]. This can be done by verifying the conformance of the system to certain security restrictions.

- E<> not ResourceOwner.loginRequested imply Client.failed
- A<> (ResourceOwner.start imply Client.start) and
  (ResourceOwner.start imply AuthServer.start) and
  (ResourceOwner.start imply ResourceServer.start)

The first property ensures that the client cannot proceed further unless the resource owner provides its credentials. The second one verifies that the system can start functioning only if the resource owner demands a service from the client.

Deadlock-Freedom. This property is a special type of *safety* property that ensures the system never enters "a state of no progress".

- A[] not deadlock

Liveness. This property ensures that "something good eventually happens" [15]. It guarantees that the system is non-blocking.

- E<> (ResourceOwner.start imply ResourceServer.success) and
  (ResourceOwner.start imply Client.success) and
  (ResourceOwner.start imply AuthServer.success)
- A<> (ResourceOwner.start imply ResourceServer.success or
  ResourceServer.failed or ResourceServer.start) and
  (ResourceOwner.start imply Client.success or Client.failed or
  Client.start) and (ResourceOwner.start imply AuthServer.success
  or AuthServer.failed or AuthServer.start)

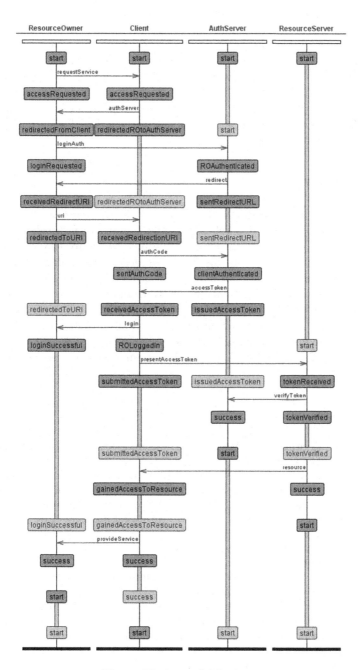

Fig. 5. Working of OAuth 2.0

The first property verifies that there exists at least one path in which the resource server enters the *final* state after the resource owner requests the client's service in *start* state. This essentially ensures that there is at least one path along which user authentication is successful. The second property verifies that the system functions as expected. When authentication succeeds, all components reach the *final* state, but when authentication fails, the components either reach *failed* state or return to *start* state.

The above properties were formulated using propositional temporal logic in UPPAAL's verifier and the designed model was checked for correctness with respect to these properties.

5   Conclusion

OAuth 2.0 is the most commonly used and by far the most secure authorization mechanism for protecting web APIs. The conformance of this widely used protocol to security standards needs to be verified to ensure that the API is as secure as it is assumed to be. In this paper, we designed a high level finite-state model of OAuth and checked three classes of properties, namely safety, liveness and absence of deadlock against this model. Both modeling and verification were carried out using UPPAAL, a state-of-the-art modeling, validation, and verification framework. As part of our future work, we plan to examine other modes of operation and optional features supported by OAuth 2.0 and enhance our model in order to verify them. We also plan to analyze real-world systems that use OAuth.

References

1. Mouli, V.R., Jevitha, K.: Web services attacks and security-a systematic literature review. Procedia Comput. Sci. **93**, 870–877 (2016)
2. Poornachandran, P., Nithun, M., Pal, S., Ashok, A., Ajayan, A.: Password reuse behavior: how massive online data breaches impacts personal data in web. In: Saini, H.S., Sayal, R., Rawat, S.S. (eds.) Innovations in Computer Science and Engineering. AISC, vol. 413, pp. 199–210. Springer, Singapore (2016). https://doi.org/10.1007/978-981-10-0419-3_24
3. Franks, J., et al.: HTTP authentication: basic and digest access authentication. Technical report (1999)
4. Luo, X., Chen, Y., Gu, M., Wu, L.: Model checking needham-schroeder security protocol based on temporal logic of knowledge. In: 2009 International Conference on Networks Security, Wireless Communications and Trusted Computing. NSWCTC 2009, vol. 2, pp. 551–554. IEEE (2009)
5. Díaz, G., Cuartero, F., Valero, V., Pelayo, F.: Automatic verification of the TLS handshake protocol. In: Proceedings of the 2004 ACM Symposium on Applied Computing, pp. 789–794. ACM (2004)
6. Yuan, T., et al.: Formalization and verification of REST on HTTP using CSP. Electron. Notes Theor. Comput. Sci. **309**, 75–93 (2014)

7. Yan, H., Fang, H., Kuka, C., Zhu, H.: Verification for OAuth using ASLan++. In: 2015 IEEE 16th International Symposium on High Assurance Systems Engineering (HASE), pp. 76–84. IEEE (2015)

8. Fett, D., Küsters, R., Schmitz, G.: A comprehensive formal security analysis of OAuth 2.0. In: Proceedings of the 2016 ACM SIGSAC Conference on Computer and Communications Security, pp. 1204–1215. ACM (2016)

9. Pai, S., Sharma, Y., Kumar, S., Pai, R.M., Singh, S.: Formal verification of OAuth 2.0 using alloy framework. In: 2011 International Conference on Communication Systems and Network Technologies (CSNT), pp. 655–659. IEEE (2011)

10. Richer, J., Sanso, A.: OAuth 2 in Action. Manning Publications, Shelter Island (2017)

11. Hardt, D.: The OAuth 2.0 authorization framework (2012)

12. Lodderstedt, T., McGloin, M., Hunt, P.: OAuth 2.0 threat model and security considerations (2013)

13. Behrmann, G., David, A., Larsen, K.G.: A tutorial on UPPAAL 4.0 (2006, 2014). URL http://www.it.uu.se/research/group/darts/papers/texts/new-tutorial.pdf

14. Larsen, K.G., Pettersson, P., Yi, W.: Uppaal in a nutshell. Int. J. Softw. Tools Technol. Transf. (STTT) **1**(1), 134–152 (1997)

15. Baier, C., Katoen, J.P., Larsen, K.G.: Principles of Model Checking. MIT Press, Cambridge (2008)

16. Sabnani, K.: An algorithmic technique for protocol verification. IEEE Trans. Commun. **36**(8), 924–931 (1988)

Utility of Data Aggregation Technique for Wireless Sensor Network: Detailed Survey Report

Kaustuv Sarangi[1]([⊠]) and Indrajit Bhattacharya[2]

[1] Department of Computer Science and Technology,
Women's Polytechnic Chandannagar, Hooghly, India
kaustuvsarangi@gmail.com
[2] Department of Computer Application,
Kalyani Government Engineering College, Kalyani, India
indra51276@gmail.com

Abstract. Small size sensor nodes form the ad hoc wireless sensor network (WSN). This network is generally used to collect and process data from different regions where the movement of human being are unusual in modern age. The sensor nodes are deployed in such position where fixed network is not being present. That location may be very remote or some disaster-prone area. In disaster-prone zone, after disaster, most often no fixed network remains active. In that scenario, one of the reliable sources to collect the data is the ad-hoc sensor network. As sensor nodes are very much battery hunger, an efficient power utilization is required for enhancing the network-lifetime by reducing data traffic in the WSN. For this reason, it is important to develop very efficient software and hardware solutions as well as managing different topological aspects to make the most efficient use of limited resources in terms of energy, computation and storage. One of the most suitable approaches is data aggregation protocol which can reduce the communication cost by extending the lifetime of sensor networks. The process on cost reduction of WSN techniques are developing in different aspects like intelligent cluster based and tree based approaches. These are used for most suitable data aggregation techniques. In this concern, many different approaches also be used for cluster formation and collecting data from different sensor nodes. This data may be aggregated after collection in sensor nodes (data fusion) or aggregated after collection in sink node/ cluster head. Our aim in the study paper is to visualize and analyze different approaches which are applicable to reduce the power consumption of the sensor node as well as to transfer data from source to destination in different unusual scenarios such as damage of sensor node or movability of nodes etc. efficiently. Our effort is to study, as much as possible, different types of data aggregation related techniques also. Achieving the concept, our findings will provide us with a new way-out for further development of sensor network as well as the efficient use of different techniques in specific applications of those networks in a suitable manner. At last our study is confined only in the case of various types of data aggregation techniques by giving special importance to the cluster based approach to increase the life time of different nodes used in WSN.

© Springer Nature Singapore Pte Ltd. 2018
J. K. Mandal and D. Sinha (Eds.): CSI 2017, CCIS 836, pp. 68–82, 2018.
https://doi.org/10.1007/978-981-13-1343-1_8

Keywords: Wireless sensor networks (WSN) · Data aggregation techniques
Tiny Aggregation (TAG) · Dominating set (DS) · Cluster formation
Distributed Source Coding (DSC) · Ant colony optimization (ACO)
Real-time Data Aggregation · Neural network

1 Introduction

The wireless sensor network is used to send data, may be in same or different types whatever collected by the sensor node and to broadcast the same in time interval. The main problem is raised in sending the data frequently. The sensor node is battery driven and for that reason the life span is limited [1–3]. By considering this important aspect various research works have been going on increasing the life span of sensor network in different manners for different application oriented scenarios. The data aggregation technique is a very important alternative of them.

The battery driven scenarios of sensor node are so important because the battery of the nodes placed in the remote regions, never be changed more than one times.

The nodes are deployed depending on the types of data which are required from the specified region. These are the fixed as well as movable nodes used to collect information from different locations. So different techniques and protocols are introduced for collecting and transferring the data from one region to destination region with the help of intermediate nodes which are only used to transmit data within the network. The main criteria of the protocol are energy consumption of the sensor node. Though the discussion about routine protocol is not the part of our paper but also it has been shared. Depending on the observed idea, the Multi-hopping communication is more energy-efficient than direct communication.

In WSN, the communicational cost is often higher than the computational cost. To optimize the communicational cost, data aggregation in WSN is one of the most efficient techniques which is computed in access point or sink/cluster head. The data are manipulated or aggregated in different ways depending on some specific applications. Total energy consumption in transporting the collected information from sensors to the sink/cluster head is to be defined as optimal aggregation if the topology of the network, resources and aggregation are optimized [4].

Various structured approaches [5, 6] have been proposed in data aggregation for sink or cluster head. The data gathering [7] occurs in the sink/cluster head after receiving the periodical reports from different application areas. After completion of aggregation, the collected data is transmitted to the destination. If the structure pattern remains unchanged, the structure aggregation techniques incur low maintenance overhead. If it is changed, new cluster formation technique can be introduced to collect the data. Simultaneously new aggregation technique is also being introduced.

In this paper, the first discussion is based on the challenging criteria for collecting data from the sensor node. These criteria are the key concept for the implementation of various sensor network applications. So, for implementing the applications, the criteria have to be maintained positively. Secondly, data must be collected depending on the topological aspect, that may be centralized or hierarchical, fixed structured or dynamic in unstructured format. In dynamic approach, the overhead depends on the mechanism of construction and the maintenance techniques of the structure. If the collected data signal is able to send the data to the center event due to perfect signal strength and in shorter distance, the optimal aggregation cannot be implemented. But obviously the benefits must be on data aggregation. So, data collection techniques from the assess point or the sink/cluster head is very much important. In this section, different types of data collection techniques are compared. Collection of data will play a vital role in implementing different applications in negative circumstances. Thirdly, the fusion and data aggregation techniques must be discussed in case of structured tree based as well as dynamic unstructured cluster oriented approach. In these approaches some theoretical aspects are there which cannot be directly related to the practical applications but helpful for the supporting concept. Fourthly, the various structure free scenarios are there which are used in various disaster management applications for sending redundant free information. Fifthly, for sending secured aggregated data by some intelligent, encoding approach can be introduced in situation dependent application.

Considering all the scenarios our goal is to find out the advantages and to implement the techniques in different applications which are basically situation based sensor network. The main technology may be based on neural network for implementing homogeneous or heterogeneous cluster based approach to reduce the overhead of sensor network and to optimize the data redundancy depending on coded intelligence based data aggregation techniques for collecting the pre- and post-disaster oriented data from the disaster-prone areas. ACO techniques or any other techniques can be used according to the demand of the characteristic of the situation.

Our finding demands that neural network for formation of cluster will be used and by using the structure the perfect data aggregation can be possible for disaster prone areas.

In the post disaster scenario, all fixed networks will become inactive and all predefined approaches will be collapsed and in some of the places the physical presence of device or human beings are impossible to reach. In that scenarios the collection of well-defined aggregated reliable data is required depending on past history if nature of disaster is known at that region.

In considering all aspects our proposal is to implement the intelligent based well secured data aggregation technique based approach in the disaster related application.

2 Related Work

Pottie and Kaiser [8] reported by giving an example that the cost of energy consumption for communication is often several orders larger in magnitude than the computation cost. So, data aggregation is very much essential to increase the network-lifetime. For that reason, some basic properties for implementing various protocols for data collection techniques have been introduced to route packets depending on the different structure for facilitating data aggregation techniques. First of all, the characteristic of protocol is defined.

1. Physical resource constraint,
2. Ad – hoc deployment,

3. Quality of service,
4. Scalability,
5. Fault tolerance,

To develop any kind of application of WSN the basic challenges must be used to overcome the problems for implementation of a sophisticated and unambiguous network system.

3 Basic Concept of Architectural Data Fusion Techniques in WSN

The collection technique can be implemented depending on various architectural point of view. Depending on that architecture the protocols for sending data can be changed. The efficiency of the network also depends on the characteristic or mechanism of the protocols and implementation can be done based on the topology. The efficiency of WSN can be measured by the utilisation of battery as well as by the technique of sending the secured irredundant information to the destination. The Architectural [9, 10] point of view of the network is classified in three parts such as (i) Centralized Architecture, (ii) Decentralized Architecture, (iii) Hierarchical Architecture [11]. Basically, the centralized and decentralized structure are grouped by the flat network and on the other hand hierarchical network is totally separate network configuration. All of the structures are utilized in different applications for particular scenario of implementing data aggregation. The structure can also be categorized into cluster-based and tree-based approaches. In this section, a brief structural characteristic is discussed based on the architectural point of view. Then the most suitable structure will be chosen for data aggregation depending on the situation based advantageous criteria.

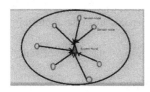

Fig. 1. For centralized architecture

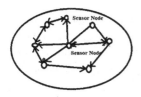

Fig. 2. Decentralized architecture

1: Centralized Architecture:- It is the very simple form of architecture. In the architecture the central processing node uses the fusion techniques with the data collected from different sensor nodes and takes the responsibility of whole network. The multi-hop style is cooperatively used in this type of network. The centralized nodes can easily detect the erroneous report. This is the basic advantage of this architecture. On the other hand, the dynamic approach is not applicable in centralized architecture (Fig. 1).

2: Decentralized Architecture:- In the decentralized WSN architecture the nodes are irregularly located in such a fashion that data fusion techniques perform locally at each node. The nodes locally share the information with neighboring nodes. The advantage is that it is expandable and tolerant to dynamic changes in the network (Fig. 2).

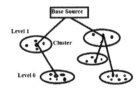

Fig. 3. Hierarchical architecture

3: Hierarchical Architecture:- This type of architecture consists of different levels of hierarchy and always make an important role in WSN. Normally simple sensor nodes are surrounded by an organized topological aspect to form the 0 level of this structure. One of the nodes is used as the access point in that level to transmit the fused data to higher-level access point. Using suitable routing algorithm, the base nodes transmit collected fused data from 0 level to higher-level accordingly. The advantageous part of the system is to balance the workload (Fig. 3).

In the continuation, another type of protocol hybrid protocol combined with reactive and proactive routing can be used. Hierarchical networks are classified in two types (a) cluster based where nodes are divided in groups called clusters and (b) location based which automatically select route to transfer data.

Here the data collection techniques are to be described in centralised and decentralised network (flat network) as well as hierarchical network. But whatever structure is used the basic concept is confined in the data aggregation characteristic. Firstly, the flat and hierarchical structures are to be classified. From the classification we can easily understand that 'in which aspect' and 'what type of structure' can be implemented for efficient data aggregation. Comparison of aggregation Techniques are (Table 1):

Table 1. For comparison of hierarchical and flat network aggregation techniques.

Hierarchical network	Flat network
Data aggregation occurs at cluster head or sink node	Data aggregation can be occurred in any of the node
Overhead is involved to form the cluster	Formed the regions depending upon the routes of data transmission
No effect will be there in failure of one cluster head	Entire system will collapse for the failure of sink node
Lower latency is involved	Higher latency is involved
Simple routing structure but not optimal	Optimal routing but generate extra overhead

On the other hand, the different types of tree based and the cluster based approaches motivate ourselves for working farther advancement of structures in clusters and related protocols. First of all, the focus will be on the working areas where the various tree and cluster structure [12] are used for making efficient data aggregation depending on the developing efficient protocols or mechanism. Then based on those approaches the further working areas will be exposed for future work.

A. Tree-based Approaches

The classical routing concept [13] are usually depend on a hierarchical organization of the nodes in the WSN. For that reason, the sink node is easily selected and used for data aggregation only because it is the higher region node. In concern with the fact the overhead is to be reduced for formation of structure during aggregation. The flow of data is directed through the elected nodes during transferring information from 0 level. The route may or may not be the shortest route but obviously situation based. The process may be election or selection [14] based. If the nodes are selected as a sink node the process must be static. The election based nodes must be dynamic in nature.

A node may be marked in this approach depending on the following special characteristics (i) data gathering tree [15], (ii) data resources, (iii) type of data stored in its queue [16], (iv) processing cost due to aggregation procedures [17]. In the aggregation tree the sink is selected first by using spanning tree and performed network aggregation along the tree by propagating the process level by level from its leaves to its root.

The same data may be reached to the sink at same time. Then the sink has to remove the duplicated data. This approach is perfectly static in nature. So, the total system may collapse totally in any unavoidable circumstances occurred in the structure.

In the case of dynamic approach this problem can be overcome and also the system will be robust in nature [18]. The optimal aggregation functions and efficient energy management characteristic can be achieved by using this mechanism. Through linear programming the residual energy of each node is utilized for aggregation in different topologies. In the method the required nodes for exploiting as an aggregation point for optimal performance can be determined by the investing factors.

Recently, tree-based approaches have been proposed for real time or time-constrained applications [19]. The scope of work is very much open in current situation based application, mainly disaster related approach.

Finally, the more efficient tree based aggregation is connected with dominating sets [20] approaches. It is very efficient techniques for energy balancing because the approaches cannot allow any node to sleep when the nodes are idle.

The study cannot be overlooked the Tiny Aggregation (TAG) [21] data centric protocol. It is based on aggregation trees and is designed for monitoring applications continuously. It can be classified for implementing the algorithms in two phases: (i) the distribution phase and (ii) the collection phase.

For the construction of tree based data aggregation algorithms related to the factor of minimum cost of energy efficient wireless sensor network is NP-completeness and approximation algorithm which are proposed for better solution.

B. Cluster-based Approaches

In the hierarchical organization [36] of WSN the cluster-based [22] schemes are most applicable in present scenarios. The routing protocol of the cluster based approach is mainly classified in (i) adaptive routing protocols for homogeneous cluster (ii) adaptive routing protocols for heterogeneous cluster. These two types of protocols can be designed based on the formation of two different types of cluster (i) homogeneous and (ii) heterogeneous. Actually, many work have been going on the formation as well as design of protocol based on the efficient data aggregation techniques in homogeneous cluster. Surveying all the aspect, it can be pointed out that the very open space for future work are there in the domain of heterogenous cluster formation and various challenging issues which will be open in that domain for preforming efficient aggregation techniques related to WSN.

The cluster–based approaches are used for the efficient utilization of power of sensors and increasing robustness in communication techniques to implement efficient data aggregation in WSN. The cluster formation techniques are used now a day in ad-hoc network scenario and the efficiency is higher than other approaches. The clustering of sensor nodes is formed into small groups and use an effective technique to achieve robustness, self-organization, power efficient, channel access, routing, etc.

To provide a secure distributed cluster formation protocols are to be used to organize the WSN into mutually disjoint cliques. This protocol can perform the operation depending upon some basic properties.

In large cluster based WSNs, the sensor nodes can be grouped into small clusters in such a way that the battery of the sensor node can be utilized for the physical proximity and each cluster may elect a cluster-head to coordinate the nodes in the cluster. It can be used in time-slotted scheduling techniques for accessing wireless channel to avoid the collision. On the other hand, a randomly deployed sensor node in WSN will form the new cluster for participating the node into the network.

The election of cluster head is an overhead for formation of cluster. The cluster heads required for the communication within the WSN can be classified into two formats (i) centralized, (ii) decentralized. Based on the leader election procedure. It also can be classified in (i) Leader-First (LF) approaches, (ii) Cluster-First (CF) approaches.

Several cluster formation protocols have been introduced for the selection criteria of cluster heads and the spatial case of problem which can be found by studying is the minimum dominating set (MDS) problem.

If the concentration is on the factors of Clustering Technique, it can be classified in three categories such as (i) Network Model, (ii) Clustering Objectives, (iii) Clustering Attributes.

Using this type of model, the dynamic network characteristic can be implemented in WSN. The basic objectives of that type of network formation are load balancing [23], fault tolerance and reducing the delay for the communication between the sensor nodes of inside or outside of cluster. The efficient cluster formation techniques consider the following objectives. These are (i) minimum cluster count, (ii) robust communication techniques, (iii) well formatted data transmission (iv) dynamic nature of cluster formation process. Following those maximum lifetime WSN can be formed using the clustering approach.

The communication between the clusters is also a challenging issue. The cluster formation techniques are different for different clusters which consist with in the WSN. The inter clustering attribute and factors are different which can be developed on the basis of different cluster formation algorithms. So, intra cluster communication is more complex and challenging. There are some sub factors in the formation of cluster:

- First consider that the network is dynamic in nature.
- Second is the in-network data processing.

- Third one is the node deployment and features of different nodes.

In comparing with others, in the first case the routes are predefined. Whereas for the case of random deployment the nodes are self-organized. So, the clustering process is complex and Intelligent mechanism. The nodes can have different characteristic so that the selection process for finding route can vary depending on the applications. The selection of cluster head is also an important challenging issue in the clustering process. The clustering objectives can vary for situation based applications.

Traditionally the aim of the algorithms is to generate a number of disjoint cluster depending and satisfying the different definitional criteria. In overlapping of clusters, one or more node(s) may belong to more than one clusters and it is the contrast of traditional clustering algorithms. Over lapping of clusters are useful in many sensor network applications, including inter-cluster routing node localization [24], and time synchronization protocols [25].

A homogeneous sensor network is commonly used in literature. The scope of implementation is also in designing the algorithm of heterogeneous cluster and set up the WSN using both of sensors and more powerful base stations in same fashion of homogeneous network. The main part of heterogeneous cluster is to transfer the information to the adjacent cluster using the cluster head by maintaining optimal principle graph representation. By this the boundary nodes can be represented as the gateway to transfer the information between the clusters. The NP-hard complexity problem may arise in that type of specific application. So here the randomized multi-hop heuristic algorithm must be introduced to reduce the of overlapping clusters in entire sensor network. In this concern the finite-state machine of the algorithm can be provided for high network coverage and connectivity.

The scope of work identified is a secure and distributed clique formation protocol that can be designed for the movable sensor nodes. Here characteristic of the network can be changed time to time and the cluster formation will be dynamic in nature.

Different algorithm complexities and properties of different clustering techniques can be classified in following manner (Table 2):

Table 2. For clustering attributes for clustering algorithms.

Clustering attributes / Clustering algorithms		LEACH [37]	HEED	FLOC	MOCA
Cluster properties	Cluster count	Variable	Variable	Variable	Variable
	Intra-cluster topology	Fixed (1-Hop)	Fixed (1-Hop)	Fixed (2-Unit)	Fixed (k-Hop)
	Intra-cluster connectivity	Direct link	Direct link/multi-hop	Direct link	Direct link/multi-hop
	Stability	Optional	Theoretically	Optional	Assumed
Cluster head capabilities	Mobility	Immobile	Immobile	Relocatable	Immobile
	Node type	Sensor	Sensor	Sensor	Sensor
	Role	Relaying	Aggregation and relaying	Aggregation and relaying	Aggregation and relaying

(continued)

Table 2. (*continued*)

Clustering attributes		LEACH [37]	HEED	FLOC	MOCA
Clustering algorithms					
Clustering process	Methodology	Distributed	Distributed	Distributed	Distributed
	Objective of node grouping	Save energy	Save energy	Scalability & fault tolerance	Overlapping & connectivity
	Selected head	Random	Random	Random	Random
	Algorithm complexity	Variable	Constant	Constant	Constant

4 Basic Comprising and Different Technique is Introduced to Collect Data

The Basic concept of data collecting system is most important concept of sensor networking. It can be classified in two types. The data is collected from sink/ cluster head or from access nodes. Actually, by this process the data mainly transmitted from rear location to the particular destination of performing or manipulating some activities. To be specific, for disaster management system, we are eagerly waiting for the information regarding the responsible element for collecting and transmitting the data. The approach is describing in distinguishing fashion (Table 3).

Table 3. The comparison of centralized and decentralized approach.

Centralized technique	Decentralized approach
The approaches are energy efficient for transmitting data from base to control station	It is not so much energy efficient for wireless sensor networks (WSNs)
The core components are clusters or sink tree. Aggregated data will be transferred from sink or cluster head	Rendezvous-based data collection approach is mainly used. Subset of nodes are used as the rendezvous points [26]. The nodes are used to buffer and to transfer organized aggregated data from sources to base station when the device arrives nearest to the node
Request is generated by an access point	It is used to balance the saving of energy and reducing delay of data collection due to control mobility of device
Multi-hop routing techniques are to be used for maintaining energy utilization with the help of fusion and data aggregation for transmission. For the further development this approach may be utilized	Mobility of specific node is used to collect data from rendezvous points at scheduled times. For that reason, disruption will be minimised and data will be delivered to the base station (BS) within time interval

5 Data Aggregation and Fusion Techniques in WSN

Now focus will be in the semantics of the aggregation process. Data aggregation and fusion techniques can be applied in two ways: (i) In each and every level of data from base level 0 to higher level can be fused depending on some parameter. (ii) Raw data can be collected and implemented aggregation technique in each node itself and there after the well formatted data is communicated to the sink/ cluster head. The advantages of the second one is that the overhead of sink node will be reduced due to the less traffic. In that case the distributed processing deals with data aggregation within the network.

The data aggregation techniques are used for transmitting the reduced number of packet. So, it has a significant impact on overall efficacy and emergency consumption. The techniques are tightly coupled. In-network data aggregation techniques can be considered a relatively complex functionality. In this concern our aim is to deal with the heterogeneous frame-format reducing the complexity of sink node for handling the complex format.

In-network aggregation process are of two types and that is described in distinguishing approach. The main objective is to reduce resource consumption and reducing traffic for increasing the lifetime of the network. Two different approaches are compared [26] here (Table 4).

Table 4. For comparison of In-network aggregation with or without size reduction.

Aggregation with size reduction	Aggregation without size reduction
• In this process the combined and compressed rescued data is coming from different sources • Collected information can be recovered at the sink	• The packets coming from different regions containing different physical quantities are merged into the same packet without data processing • Securely transmit heterogeneous data

Both of the strategies are used in concern with the data at different network layers. In-network aggregation techniques have some basic features: (i) suitable protocols for networking (ii) effective and efficient aggregation functions (iii) efficient data format inning strategy. Moreover, some synchronization is required among nodes for aggregation techniques in- networks. The main timing strategies [27] are (Table 5):

Table 5. For comparison of periodic simple or Pre-Hop aggregation.

Periodic simple aggregation	Periodic per-hop aggregation
Aggregated data received depending on pre-defined period of time and sent out as packet	After receiving the data from the children, the node transmitted the data depending on the time out session

The designing of routing protocol depends on the choice of the timing strategy. Our aim is to modify those strategies and combine them, as much as possible, into optimal format. The new approach must be applicable in many situations based applications and be able to transmit heterogeneous information with same frame-format by introducing Aggregation Functions [28].

The aggregation functions can be classified in several aspects and most of them are related to the specific WSN applications. The main classifications are lossy and lossless, duplicate sensitive and duplicate insensitive.

The characteristic of good aggregation functions in WSNs concerns with the very limited processing features and energy capabilities of sensor devices. The devices which are used in the network must be robust in nature. Modified routing protocols and efficient aggregation functions are used.

Several theoretical studies have some limitations in concern with the implementation of in-network data aggregation techniques and thus this can be used for assisting in the further design of suitable algorithms. The study also enriches our concepts for future implementation by changing the formation of the techniques.

In addition, the [29] opportunistic aggregation is also a concept that can be compared with the systematic aggregation in terms of cost ratio. The data aggregation techniques can also be implemented by using data centric and address centric routing heuristics [30]. But the optimal aggregation tree will be implemented using NP-hard algorithm in nature.

On the other hand, data fusion in WSN uses the limited resources in terms of power in shorter range of communication. The main difference is that data fusion techniques can be applied at a sensor node and the data aggregated used in multiple nodes. In the case of data processing, the data is processed after applying the fusion techniques and as a result the overhead of the transmission will reduce the cluster based hierarchical networking and data aggregation protocols. For this category some unconventional solution from the fields like computational intelligence (CI) are needed.

Before discussing the CI methods, the code system is described which is better to use in small scale aggregation techniques.

6   Distributed Source Coding

A recent development Distributed Source Coding (DSC) system is used for data aggregation. Based on the Slepian-Wolf theorem [31], the technique is used for joint coding of correlated data collecting from multiple sources without explicit communication. The data is not aggregated throughout the path to the sink. This is the disadvantage of the method.

On the other hand, the further savings of data can be achieved by utilizing in-network data fusion on the apex of compressed [32] per node distributed data. For this technique the loss of packet can be occurred. The scheme's inability is used to tolerate the lossless encoder techniques.

In summary, efficient DSC increases the complexity of computation and uses the statistic approaches for effective routing and coding [33] decisions independent of each other.

7 Computational Intelligence System for Data Aggregation WSN

CI based data aggregation techniques can be used to capable some intelligent tools for processing raw input sensory numerical data directly. It also capable to represent pipelining and parallelism problem. It has the power to generate reliability, timely respond capability and fault tolerance mechanism [6]. Neural networks, reinforcement learning, swarm intelligence, evolutionary algorithms, fuzzy logic and artificial immune systems are used by the CI paradigms. Neural network is also a part of CI.

Genetic algorithms (GA) has the parallelism characteristics. So, it can be used for implementing efficient data aggregation techniques for selecting suitable routes. In practical PSO is the suitable substitution of GA in WSN. In the same Ant colony optimization ACO is the effective technique for data aggregation due to its distributed characteristic. In implementation point of view the neural intelligent network system is one of the suitable techniques.

In continuation of the current scenario the ant colony optimization [34] is a meta-heuristic problem solving using combinatorial analysis optimization. ACO algorithms are inspired by real ant's colonies. For each component, ACO defines two parameters to calculate a probability for each component in selection process: (i) a heuristic value that representing a priori information about problem, and (ii) pheromone value that representing the frequentation of component. Based on parameters, best component will be selected in each constructional step.

In real-time [35] scenario most of them are very much appropriate and capable at the sensor level application but most of them are not suitable for complex and complicated situation. On the other hand, the artificial neural network techniques are to be flourished for solving different applications of sensor network. Back propagation-type NN is model based new structure. Though it depending on the past data the chance of accuracy for evaluating the solution is more specific and perfect. The application can be implemented by using the neural network approaches because for the disaster-prone zone the past history plays an important role to implement a suitable solution. The cluster formation using the sensor nodes can also be easily solvable (fixed and dynamic as well for homogeneous and the heterogeneous data collecting sensor nodes).

In this connection the Structure-free approaches can also be used for specific type of data aggregation using local information. The Real-time Data Aggregation Protocol concept is very promising for the further development.

8 Findings and Future Scope

After studying different types of data aggregation techniques, it is found that all the discussed techniques are very much situation specific. So, the usefulness of the algorithms or techniques will base specifically on the spatial data. All of the algorithms have some advantages or disadvantages depending on the characteristic of implementation scenarios.

From the study, the scope of future work is also found. In future a study can be done on the intelligent structure for data aggregation techniques suitable for implementing in different applications. Our proposed technique for data aggregation does not use any explicit structure. Based on that basic concept our suggestion is to build up the efficient data aggregation technique for disaster management using heterogenous cluster formation. The structure will be dynamic in nature. The proposed system can be implemented by the intelligent neural network. On the contrary, the simple data aggregation can also solve some problems. But that are only some special cases. For an exceptional case, like the disaster management systems, simple data aggregation will fail. So further implementation can be proceeded based on the heterogeneous dynamic cluster techniques for data aggregation.

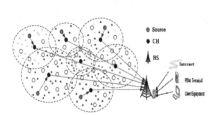

Fig. 4. Our proposed structure for data aggregation

The heterogenous cluster formation can be done by the neural network. The scope of the work is open because very less number of works have been done on the said matter. The nodes will be scattered in the disaster-prone area depending on the type of disaster occurred. In a domain, different types of disaster may occur. So, the heterogeneous information coming from the disaster area are to be sensed and sent for further processing. Now it is very challenging issue to send this data after aggregation. The sensor node may not be capable to send various types of data due to different sizes of data field and also may not broadcast various data format by single sink or cluster node. So, different cluster heads may be required for transmitting the various types of data (Fig. 4).

This type of data aggregation may also have some limitations but proposed structure will be generalized in nature. So, from the study it can be concluded that the future work can be proceeded based on the intelligent data aggregation techniques. Most specifically the heterogenous cluster formation using neural network have a great future aspect for developing various types of applications.

9   Conclusion

It can be concluded that all the aggregation techniques are situation dependent and useful in specific application oriented except the intelligent approaches. The neural network technology is one of the most appropriate concepts.

The new combination suggested is the wireless sensor networks implemented by using neural network technological aspects. By this study, we are capable to describe the experiences of constructing a combined system in order to resolve some of the long-standing issues in wireless sensor network technology.

References

1. Heinzelman, W., Chandrakasan, A., Balakrishnan, H.: Energy efficient communication protocol for wireless microsensor networks. In: Proceedings of the 33rd International Conference on System Sciences (HICSS 2000), vol. 2, Anchorage Alaska, pp. 1–10, January 2000
2. Chiasserini, C.-F., Chlamtac, I., Monti, P., Nucci, A.: Energy efficient design of wireless ad hoc networks. In: Gregori, E., Conti, M., Campbell, Andrew T., Omidyar, G., Zukerman, M. (eds.) NETWORKING 2002. LNCS, vol. 2345, pp. 376–386. Springer, Heidelberg (2002). https://doi.org/10.1007/3-540-47906-6_30
3. Demirbas, M., Arora, A., Mittal, V.: FLOC: a fast local clustering service for wireless sensor networks. In: Proceedings of First Workshop Dependability Issues in Wireless Ad Hoc Networks and Sensor Networks, June 2004
4. Hu, F., Xiaojun, C., May, C.: Optimized scheduling for data aggregation in wireless sensor networks. In: IEEE ITCC 2005, Las Vegas, NV, USA, April 2005
5. Heinzelman, W., Chandrakasan, A., Balakrishnan, H.: Energy efficient communication protocol for wireless microsensor networks. In: Proceedings of the 33rd Annual Hawaii International Conference on System Sciences, vol. 2, January 2000
6. Wong, J., Jafari, R., Potkonjak, M.: Gateway placement for latency and energy efficient data aggregation. In: 29th Annual IEEE International Conference on Local Computer Networks, pp. 490–497, November 2004
7. Cristescu, R., Beferull-Lozano, B., Vetterli, M.: On network correlated data gathering. In: IEEE INFOCOM 2004, Hong Kong, March 2004
8. Pottie, G.J., Kaiser, W.J.: Wireless integrated network sensors. Commun. ACM **43**, 51–58 (2000)
9. Bhatlavande, A.S., Phatak, A.A.: Data aggregation techniques in wireless sensor networks: literature survey (0975 - 8887). Int. J. Comput. Appl. **115**(10), 21–24 (2015)
10. Heinzelman, W.B., Chandrakasan, A.P., Balakrishnan, H.: An application specific protocol architecture for wireless microsensor networks. IEEE Trans. Wirel. Netw. **1**(4), 660–670 (2002)
11. Beal, J.: A robust amorphous hierarchy from persistent nodes, AI Memo, no. 11 (2003)
12. Tripathi, A., Gupta, S., Chourasiya, B.: Int. J. Adv. Res. Comput. Commun. Eng. **3**(7) (2014). ISSN 2319-5940
13. Akkaya, K., Younis, M.: A survey of routing protocols in wireless sensor networks. Elsevier Ad Hoc Netw. J. **3**(3), 325–349 (2005)
14. Tan, H.O., Korpeoglu, I.: Power efficient data gathering and aggregation in wireless sensor networks. ACM SIGMOD Rec. **32**(4), 66–71 (2003)
15. Solis, I., Obraczka, K.: Isolines: energy-efficient mapping in sensor networks. In: IEEE ISCC 2005, Cartagena, Spain, June 2005
16. Yu, Y., Krishnamachari, B., Prasanna, V.: Energy-latency tradeoffs for data gathering in wireless sensor networks. In: IEEE INFOCOM 2004, Hong Kong, March 2004
17. Luo, H., Luo, J., Liu, Y., Das, S.: Energy efficient routing with adaptive data fusion in sensor Networks. In: Third ACM/SIGMOBILE Workshop on Foundations of Mobile Computing, Cologne, Germany, August 2005
18. Manjhi, A., Nath, S., Gibbons, P.B.: Tributaries and deltas: efficient and robust aggregation in sensor network stream. In: ACM SIGMOD 2005, Baltimore, MD, USA, June 2005
19. Hu, Y., Yu, N., Jia, X.: Energy efficient real-time data aggregation in wireless sensor networks. In: ACM IWCCC 2006, Vancouver, British Columbia, Canada, July 2006

20. Han, B., Jia, W.: Clustering wireless ad hoc networks with weakly connected dominating set. J. Parallel Distrib. Comput. **67**, 727–737 (2007)

21. Madden, S., Franklin, M.J., Hellerstein, J.M., Hong, W.: TAG: a tiny aggregation service for ad-hoc sensor networks. In: OSDI 2002, Boston, MA, USA, December 2002

22. McDonald, A.B., Znati, T.: A mobility based framework for adaptive clustering in wireless ad-hoc networks. IEEE J. Sel. Areas Commun. **17**(8), 1466–1487 (1999)

23. Amis, A., Prakash, R.: Load-balancing clusters in wireless ad hoc networks. In: Proceedings of Symposium on Application-Specific Systems and Software Engineering (ASSET), March 2000

24. Ji, X.: Sensor positioning in wireless ad-hoc sensor networks with multidimensional scaling. In: Proceedings of IEEE INFOCOM, March 2004

25. Wu, T., Biswas, S.K.: A self-reorganizing slot allocation protocol for multi-cluster sensor networks. In: Proceedings of Fourth International Conference on Information Processing in Sensor Networks (IPSN 2005), pp. 309–316, April 2005

26. Jianbo, X., Siliang, Z., Fengjiao, Q.: A new in-network data aggregation technology of wireless sensor networks. In: IEEE SKG 2006, Guilin, China, November 2006

27. Krishnamachari, B., Estrin, D., Wicker, S.: The impact of data aggregation in wireless sensor networks. In: IEEE ICDCS 2002, Vienna, Austria, July 2002

28. Huang, L., Zhao, B., Joseph, A., Kubiatowicz, J.: Probabilistic data aggregation in distributed networks. Technical report, EECS Department, University of California, Berkeley. UCB/EECS-2006-11, 6 February 2006

29. Zhu, Y., Sundaresan, K., Sivakumar, R.: Practical limits on achievable energy improvements and useable delay tolerance in correlation aware data gathering in wireless sensor networks. In: IEEE SECON (2005)

30. Heinzelman, W.B., Chandrakasan, A.P., Balakrishnan, H.: Anapplication-specific protocol architecture for wireless microsensor networks. IEEE Trans. Wirel. Commun. **1**(4), 660–670 (2002)

31. Cover, T.M., Thomas, J.A.: Elements of Information Theory. Wiley, Hoboken (1991)

32. Pattem, S., Krishnamachari, B., Govindan, R.: The impact of spatial correlation on routing with compression in wireless sensor networks. In: ACM/IEEE IPSN 2004, Berkeley, CA, USA, April 2004

33. Sartipi, M., Fekri, F.: Source and channel coding in wireless sensor networks using LDPC codes. In: IEEE SECON 2004, Santa Clara, CA, USA, October 2004

34. He, T., Blum, B.M., Stankovic, J.A., Abdelzaher, T.: AIDA: adaptive application-independent data aggregation in wireless sensor networks. ACM Trans. Embed. Comput. Syst. **3**(2), 426–457 (2004)

35. Li, H.: Resource Management for Distributed Real-Time System, September 2006

36. Sabri, A., Al-Shqeerat, K.: Hierarchical cluster-based routing protocols for wireless sensor networks–a survey. IJCSI Int. J. Comput. Sci. Issues **11**(1), 93 (2014)

37. Dhand, G., Tyagi, S.S.: Data aggregation techniques in WSN: survey. Procedia Comput. Sci. **92**, 378–384 (2016)

A VDIBA Based Voltage-Mode Highpass and Bandpass Filter

Pallavi Singh, Vikash Kumar$^{(\boxtimes)}$, Lakshmi Pujitha Patnaik, and Aminul Islam

Department of Electronics and Communication Engineering,
Birla Institute of Technology, Mesra, Ranchi 835215, Jharkhand, India
pallavisingh21.ps@gmail.com, vikashkr@bitmesra.ac.in,
pujithapatnaik1997@gmail.com,
dr.aminul.islam@ieee.org

Abstract. A VDIBA based voltage-mode (VM) highpass and bandpass filter topology is presented. The topology utilizes two VDIBA blocks, two capacitors and one resistor. The topology has three voltage inputs, two voltage output and can realize highpass (HP) and bandpass (BP) filter operation from the similar structure. The corner frequency and quality factor of VDIBA based filter is electronically tuneable by virtue of bias current of the internal transconductance. The topology operates with very low supply voltage of ±600 mV and external DC bias current of 150 μA. The simulations are carried out at 45-nm CMOS technology using Virtuoso Analog design Environment of Cadence.

Keywords: VDIBA · Biquadratic filter · Voltage-mode · MISO

1 Introduction

Analog (continuous-time) active filters are the significant components for analog signal processing operations and are extensively used for applications such as communications, instrumentations, measurements, control systems, biomedical applications etc., [1]. Several kinds of active elements have been utilized in the recent past for implementing the analog filters [2]. Such active elements are categorized into two classes based on differential inputs. The active elements which operate with differential input currents are Current Differencing Buffered Amplifiers (CDBA) [3], Current Differencing Transconductance Amplifiers (CDTA) [4], etc., whereas the active elements which operate with differential input voltages are Voltage Differencing Transconductance Amplifier (VDTA) [5–7], Voltage Differencing Current Conveyor (VDCC) [8], Voltage Differencing Buffered Amplifier (VDBA) [9], etc. Voltage Differencing Inverting Buffered Amplifier (VDIBA) is a state-of-the-art active element which is introduced recently in [10]. VDIBA has gained popularity owing to its simpler structure, electronic tunability feature and has been utilized in a variety of applications [11].

This work proposes a VDIBA based voltage-mode (VM) highpass and bandpass filter topology. The filter topology contains three voltage inputs, two voltage output and incorporates two VDIBA blocks, two capacitors and one resistor for realizing filter

© Springer Nature Singapore Pte Ltd. 2018
J. K. Mandal and D. Sinha (Eds.): CSI 2017, CCIS 836, pp. 83–89, 2018.
https://doi.org/10.1007/978-981-13-1343-1_9

functions. With appropriate connections of input signals, highpass (HP) and bandpass (BP) filters can be implemented. The filter parameters of suggested filters especially the corner frequency (ω_C) and Q-factor or quality factor (Q) are electronically tunable via the bias currents of VDIBA.

The organization of the paper is done in the following way. Section 2 explains the concepts of VDIBA. In Sect. 3, the suggested VDIBA based filter topology is presented. Section 4 demonstrates the responses of the suggested VDIBA based filter topology. Eventually, the conclusion is drawn in Sect. 5.

2 Voltage Differencing Inverting Buffered Amplifier (VDIBA)

VDIBA is a 4-port active element. Its schematic representation is shown in Fig. 1. VDIBA consists of two input ports (p, n), one output port (z) and one inverting output port (w^-). The ports p, n and z are of high impedance whereas port w^- is of low impedance. The ports p, n and w^- are voltage ports whereas port z is a current port. The relation between the voltages and currents of VDIBA may be represented by the subsequent sequence of equations as

$$i_p = 0, \tag{1}$$

$$i_n = 0, \tag{2}$$

$$i_z = g_m(v_p - v_n), \tag{3}$$

$$v_{w-} = -\beta v_z. \tag{4}$$

Here, g_m and β stand for transconductance and parasitic voltage gain of VDIBA respectively. For ideal VDIBA, β is unity. Figure 2 depicts the transistor-level representation of conventional VDIBA.

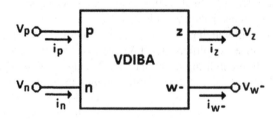

Fig. 1. Schematic representation of VDIBA.

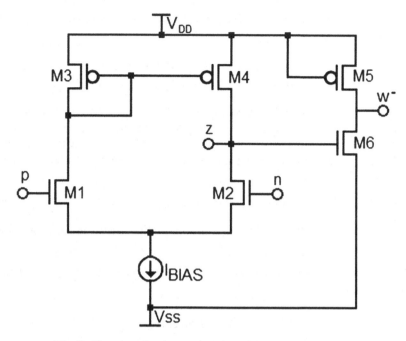

Fig. 2. Transistor-level representation of conventional VDIBA.

3 VDIBA Based Filter Topology

Figure 3 exhibits the suggested VDIBA based biquadratic filter topology. The filter topology comprises two VDIBA blocks, two capacitors (C_1, C_2) and one resistor (R). The filter is of multiple-input single-output (MISO) type and operates in voltage-mode (VM). The filter topology has three voltage inputs (v_{in1}, v_{in2}, v_{in3}) and one voltage output (v_{out}).

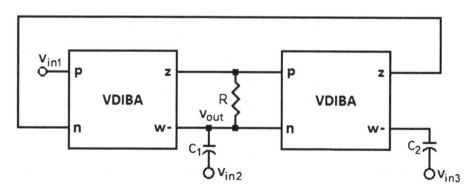

Fig. 3. VDIBA based filter topology.

Routine circuit analysis of the filter topology yields the subsequent expression of transfer function

$$v_{out} = \frac{s^2 C_1 C_2 R v_{in2} + s(C_2 R g_{m1} v_{in1} + \beta_2 C_2 R g_{m1} g_{m2} v_{in3})}{s^2 C_1 C_2 R + s(1 + \beta_1)C_2 + \beta_2(1 + \beta_1)g_{m1} g_{m2} R}. \tag{5}$$

where β_1 and β_2 are the parasitic voltage gain of the 1st and 2nd VDIBA respectively.

In order to realize the highpass and bandpass transfer function, the different combinations of voltage inputs (v_{in1}, v_{in2}, v_{in3}) are varied in such a way that they realize only one type of filter function (highpass or bandpass) at a time. The input combinations are given below:

(a) If $v_{in2} = v_{in}$ and $v_{in1} = v_{in3} = 0$, then highpass filter (HPF) transfer function is obtained.
(b) If $v_{in1} = v_{in3} = v_{in}$ and $v_{in2} = 0$, then bandpass filter (BPF) transfer function is obtained.

The filter parameters i.e. the corner frequency (ω_C) and Q-factor (Q) for the suggested filters can be obtained from (5) as

$$\omega_c = \sqrt{\frac{\beta_2(1 + \beta_1)g_{m1} g_{m2}}{C_1 C_2}}, \tag{6}$$

$$Q = R\sqrt{\frac{\beta_2}{(1 + \beta_1)}\frac{C_1}{C_2}g_{m1} g_{m2}}. \tag{7}$$

Considering $\beta_1 = \beta_2 = 1$, the transfer function can be re-written as

$$v_{out} = \frac{s^2 C_1 C_2 R v_2 + s(C_2 R g_{m1} v_1 + C_2 R g_{m1} g_{m2} v_3)}{s^2 C_1 C_2 R + 2s C_2 + 2g_{m1} g_{m2} R}, \tag{8}$$

Similarly, the filter parameters i.e. the corner frequency (ω_C) and Q-factor (Q) from (8) can be expressed as

$$\omega_c = \sqrt{\frac{2g_{m1} g_{m2}}{C_1 C_2}}, \tag{9}$$

$$Q = R\sqrt{\frac{C_1}{2C_2}g_{m1} g_{m2}}. \tag{10}$$

As observed from (6), (9) and (7), (10), that the corner frequency (ω_C) and Q-factor (Q) of the suggested filter are controllable through transconductances (g_{m1}, g_{m2}) of VDIBA. Since the transconductances of VDIBA depend on external DC bias current

(I_{BIAS}), the corner frequency (ω_C) and Q-factor (Q) are electronically controllable. Further, the Q-factor (Q) of the suggested filter may be independently controlled from the corner frequency (ω_C) through resistor (R).

4 Simulation Result

For justifying the speculative analyses obtained and discussed in the above sections, the filter is designed and simulated in Virtuoso Analog design Environment of Cadence at CMOS 45-nm CMOS process node. The suggested filter topology is biased with a supply voltage ($V_{DD} = -V_{SS}$) of ±600 mV. The bias current of VDIBA is taken as 150 μA. The gain response of the suggested highpass filter (HPF) and bandpass filter (BPF) is depicted in Fig. 4. Further, the transient response of the band-pass filter is also shown in Fig. 5. The transient response manifests that for 10 mV (peak-to-peak) input sinusoidal voltage, the filter produces 10 mV (peak-to-peak) output sinusoidal voltage, which validates the stability of the suggested filter.

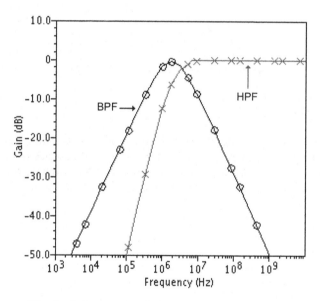

Fig. 4. Gain response of highpass and bandpass filter.

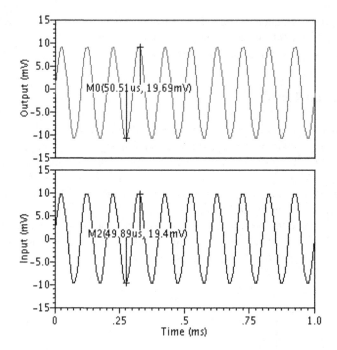

Fig. 5. Transient response of bandpass filter.

5   Conclusion

A VDIBA based voltage-mode (VM) highpass and bandpass filter topology is presented. The filter parameters of suggested filters i.e. corner frequency (ω_C) and Q-factor (Q) are electronically tunable via the bias currents of VDIBA. Both the filter parameters are also independently tunable through the resistor.

References

1. Dimopoulos, H.G.: Analog Electronic Filters: Theory, Design and Synthesis. Springer, USA (2012). https://doi.org/10.1007/978-94-007-2190-6
2. Biolek, D., Senani, R., Biolkova, V., Kolka, Z.: Active elements for analog signal processing: classification, review, and new proposals. Radioengineering 17(4), 15–32 (2008)
3. Acar, C., Ozoguz, S.: A new versatile building block: current differencing buffered amplifier suitable for analog signal processing filters. Microelectron. J. 30, 157–160 (1999)
4. Tangsrirat, W., Dumawipata, T., Surakampontorn, W.: Multiple-input single-output current-mode multifunction filter using current differencing transconductance amplifiers. Int. J. Electron. Commun. (AEU) 61, 209–214 (2007)
5. Kumar, V., Mehra, R., Islam, A.: A 2.5 GHz low power, high-Q, reliable design of active bandpass filter. IEEE Trans. Device Mater. Reliab. 17(1), 229–244 (2017)
6. Mehra, R., Kumar, V., Islam, A.: Floating active inductor based Class-C VCO with 8 digitally tuned sub-bands. AEU- Int. J. Electron. Commun. 83, 1–10 (2017)

7. Kumar, V., Mehra, R., Islam, A.: A CMOS active inductor based digital and analog dual tuned voltage-controlled oscillator. Microsyst. Technol. 1–13 (2017). https://doi.org/10.1007/s00542-017-3457-y
8. Chiu, W., Liu, S.I., Tsao, H.W., Chen, J.J.: CMOS differential difference current conveyors and their applications. IEE Proc. Circ. Dev. Syst. **143**, 91–96 (1996)
9. Kacar, F., Yesil, A., Noori, A.: New CMOS realization of voltage differencing buffered amplifier and its biquad filter applications. Radioengineering **21**(1), 333–339 (2012)
10. Herencsar, N., Cicekoglu, O., Sotner, R., Koton, J., Vrba, K.: New resistorless tunable voltage mode universal filter using single VDIBA. Analog Integr. Circ. Sig. Process **76**, 251–260 (2013)
11. Sotner, R., Jerabek, J., Herencsar, N.: Voltage differencing buffered/inverted amplifiers and their applications for signal generation. Radioengineering **22**(2), 490–504 (2013)

A Novel Solution for Controller Based Software Defined Network (SDN)

Parinita Dutta and Rajeev Chatterjee[(⊠)]

Department of Computer Science and Engineering,
National Institute of Technical Teachers' Training and Research, Kolkata,
Block-FC, Sec-III, Salt Lake City, Kolkata 700 106, India
mail2parinitadutta@gmail.com,
chatterjee.rajeev@gmail.com

Abstract. Software Defined Network (SDN) is the upcoming networking architecture where the data and control plane are separately handled by the system. This enhances the performance of the overall system including failover, back-up and recovery. SDN manages through dedicated controllers that take care of the control plane. Therefore, the data plane and the control plane work independent of each. However, a number of problems have been identified in the SDN architecture, including single point controller failure, controller placement problem and problems related to distributed or cluster controller environment. The authors in this research article proposed a framework with Backup and Restoration System (BRS) that minimizes the existing limitation of the SDN.

Keywords: Software defined network · SDN controller · Network topology

1 Introduction

SDN is a state of the art technology [1] which leads to an evolution of the Information and Communication Technology (ICT) by changing the traditional network architecture. SDN unlike conventional networking solution primarily segregate data and control plane and hence improve the overall performance of the architecture. Thus the control plane becomes centralized and the data plane remains distributed in a particular subnet or entire network. By decoupling the data plane and control plane the subnet or the network becomes more flexible and programmable. The overall management, administration and troubleshooting of the system becomes easier and more efficient. Today, the scope of the Computer Networks has grown beyond the conventional network architecture. This has further led the connectivity of mobile and handheld devices. The presence of mobile devices and their connectivity to the Internet has led to the ubiquitous computing environment. Therefore, the requirements have grown up leading to the new challenges and design issues. Speed, Quality of Services (QoS), Security, etc. are the new challenges that are hovering the minds of the network designers. Therefore, the goal of the designers is to provide flexible network architecture such as SDN architecture. SDN is in the developing stage and a number of issues related to QoS, Security and other parameters needs augmentation.

© Springer Nature Singapore Pte Ltd. 2018
J. K. Mandal and D. Sinha (Eds.): CSI 2017, CCIS 836, pp. 90–98, 2018.
https://doi.org/10.1007/978-981-13-1343-1_10

This paper is organized as follows. Section 2 provides the review works in the area of SDN. Section 3 discusses the existing model of SDN at a glance. Section 4 proposes architecture based on BRS. Section 5 deals with results. In Sect. 6 limitation of the proposed model is discussed. Conclusion and future scope is given in Sect. 7.

2 Review of Existing Works

In this section, the authors have studied issues related to SDN and its architecture, the controller and the role of controller in the SDN architecture. According to Sood and Nishtha [2] if entire SDN architecture for a particular network will be based on a single controller then it will be the cause of single point of failure. They proposed a cluster controller architecture. Marulanda and Esteban [3] proposed network using distributed cluster controller that reduces single point of failure which leads to more reliable, highly available, fault tolerant network. Berde et al. [4] evaluated a distributed SDN open network operating system and proposed that applying a distributed controller is more effective than applying a single controller in term of performance. Dixit et al. [5] proposed about ElastiCon which works as an elastic controller. This distributed controller can able to vary the performance according to traffic demand but did not comment on the number of controller and their placement in the network topology. Sallahi and St-Hilaire [6] used an expansion modal for determining the optimal number of the controller and their proper location. This expansion model explained how the network will expand according to its need. Bo et al. [7] proposed another way to solve controller placement problem using genetic algorithm and minimum delay algorithm, they did not comment on the implication of the sudden change of network traffic. Xiao et al. [8] highlighted controller placement problem for WAN, They used spectral clustering algorithm for partitioning the network and then calculated placement matrix for optimal placement of controller. But this cannot accommodate changes dynamically. Apart from this there is a lack of security issues, fault detection, and recovery issue. Huque et al. [9] presented an algorithm LiDy+ for large-scale dynamic controller placement problem. This algorithm is very effective, but security and failure and recovery management is absent. According to Hikichi et al. [10] in distributed cluster controller based SDN, unbalanced load is the main factor that causes bandwidth wastage. They proposed a load balancing technique that uses weighted round robin scheduling of load balancer. However, this architecture is more complex and having high computational overhead. Liu et al. [11] highlighted about two types of flow installation technique, proactive and reactive. However, they did not proposed the structure of packet and issues related to packet security. Aslan and Matrawy [12] proposed adaptive controller in SDN, proving that adaptive controller has better performance than their counter part. The authors did not mention about recovery methods from any failure of the controller. Khan et al. [13] proposed the mechanism of a controller based topology management that provides an abstract view of the entire network. This helps in better understanding of the topology of a subnet or the complete network. However, topology discovery in SDN is a complex and time consuming process along-with issues related to security. Gonzalez et al. [14] proposed a master-slave controller mechanism in which one controller works as a primary controller and another is working as a standby or high available controller. Whenever the primary controller fails the other controller replace the primary one which has consistent information about the network. Pashkov et al. [15] suggested a model of high availability controller by using master-slave configuration, which is reliable. This paper did not state the policy for high availability performance. Rao et al. [16] also use master slave controller policy for load balancing and high data availability. They use an election algorithm for choosing the master controller among the controllers. According to document of Open Networking Foundation (ONF) [17] SDN controller has various kinds of threats including spoofing, repudiation, information disclosure, denial of service (DoS) attack, etc. Qi et al. [18] suggested an architecture called Mcad-SA which proposes about the security of flow entries to identify a fake controller, and thus prevent attacks to the network. However, the paper lacks solutions to the issues related to information disclosure, DoS, spoofing of other peer level controller. Wilczewski [19] highlighted embedded based controller system and security.

3   Existing SDN Model at a Glance

In this section the authors have given brief information for existing SDN architecture. In today's environment it is found that Internet is omni-present. This provides the users the flair of ubiquitous computing over the Internet. There is a massive demand of high speed network connectivity over wired and wireless media. Mobile and hand held device connectivity including data connection over roaming is the requirement from a state of that network. QoS is also an important parameter for the network performance. From the aforesaid discussion, it is concluded that the existing networking solutions need substantial changes in its architecture and working. SDN may be a solution that can handle multidimensional problem related to traditional networks as SDN primarily overcome major limitations of traditional networking. It divides the networks into two planes, i.e. control plane and data plane. This makes SDN intelligent with centralized control with devices that perform on the basis of Controller. In the present era SDN depends on controllers and failure of controller can bring down the entire network. To reduce the single point of failure, implementation of cluster based controllers were adapted. Cluster controllers provide redundancy and failover protection mechanism. This is achieved with a cluster having at least three controllers. However, cluster controllers have their own limitations. One of the major limitation is controller placement problem. In SDN system there is an application layer which helps to see an abstract view of the whole system and make network programmable according to user's need. This layer also provides SDN with features like firewall, intrusion detection and protection mechanism, load balancing, QoS, etc. The control plane, creates an abstract view of the network which communicates to devices via Open-Flow protocol. An Open-Flow protocol is implemented by a collection of packets which are flowing between these two layers. Open-Flow protocol has some predefined rule which the data packets have to follow. The schematic diagram of SDN with multiple subnets and multiple controllers is given in Fig. 1. A subnet is a logical separation of a large network. A subnet is basically a group consisting of same type of device and networking equipment within a LAN.

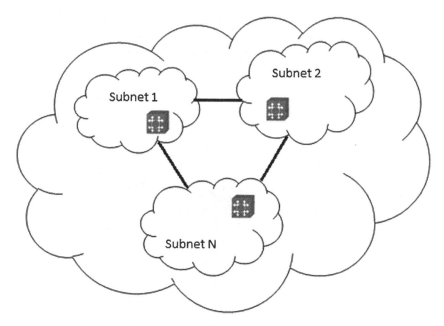

Fig. 1. Schematic diagram of SDN with multiple subnets

4 Proposed Architecture

In this research paper the authors have illustrated a system that consists of a number of subnets within a particular network. Each subnet is being managed by a dedicated SDN controller.

In Sect. 2, the authors discussed the various limitations in SDN architecture. SDN that are using a single controller; there is a single point of failure occurrence for that particular domain. For cluster controller based distributed system, there are problems related to controller placement, load balancing, failover management and recovery, availability and security issues.

In the proposed design each subnet has an identified controller that takes care of the control plane for that particular subnet. In due course of the implementation multiple VLANs for various subnets are provided and thus the segmentation of the entire network on the basis of subnet can be implemented. The authors are aware that a VLAN provides a segmentation service within a broadcast domain. VLAN creates multiple broadcast domains within a network. VLAN is normally implemented by switches at the core level. This increases huge management capabilities within a VLAN. When data are transmitted to one VLAN to other VLAN this process is called inter VLAN routing.

In the proposed design each SDN controller manages a particular subnet or VLAN. There are chances of failure of the SDN controller. In the event of the failure of the SDN controller the entire subnet may breakdown and the communication will be at stake. The authors propose a BRS that keep track of the current performance of each controller. BRS is proposed to be working as a centralized system that keeps track of all the SDN controllers with its scope. The BRS is supposed to be a system consisting of devices that are fault tolerant and consists of back management system. Figure 2, shows the proposed schematic architecture of SDN with BRS.

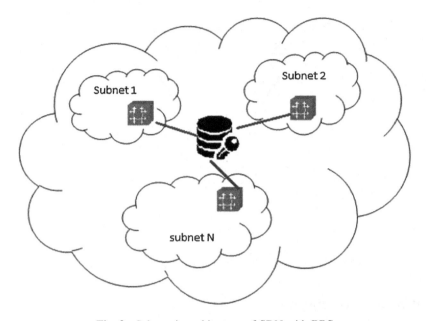

Fig. 2. Schematic architecture of SDN with BRS

In the event of failure of a particular controller the BRS will assign the job of the controller which is not working to a topologically adjacent controller. In this event the current state of the controller is required. This information will be fetched from the BRS to the assigned controller. Once the existing controller is revoked, the current state will be assigned to the existing controller by BRS again. Hence the controllers managing various subnets are required to update their current state to the BRS over a regular period of time. The proposed BRS help to achieve better reliability and performance.

4.1   Controller Failure Detection

In this proposed architecture the BRS will ping each controller on a regular time interval. Once the BRS detect a controller failure, it will send a request to the topologically adjacent controllers for management of the Control Plane of that subnet on ad-hoc basis. One of the adjacent controllers will be selected for management of an additional subnet. The assigned controller will be required to undergo an authentication process. Once the existing controller is recovered and start its normal function, the control plane management will be returned to the exiting controller.

4.2   Authentication Process

In this section, the authors use the arithmetic encoding technique for authentication between the BRS and the respective SDN Controller. The BRS will have Probability of Occurrence (PO) information shared with respective controller. The validity of this information is of fixed duration of time. Beyond this time, a new PO is shared suing the same mechanism. The algorithm for arithmetic encoding is given in Fig. 3.

```
//Algorithm for Arithmetic Encoding
Begin
   Step 1: Create interval range for each character based on PO
   Step 2: Take a string as a user input
   Step 3: Initialize n = string length
   Step 4: Initialized low value (L) =0, High value (H) =1
   Step 5: Take L & H of the first character. Determine the range
           R=H-L.
   Step 6: Calculate Low next (Lₙ) & High next (Hₙ) for next char-
           acters (string length <=n) using this bellow procedure
           and update the values of L & H.
           Repeat
           {
               Lₙ=L+R*lower interval
               Hₙ=L+R*higher interval
               Swap L=Lₙ
               Swap H=Hₙ
           }
           Proceed to step 5
End
```

Fig. 3. Arithmetic encoding algorithm

4.3   Controller Recovery Process

In this proposed architecture after recovery of the exiting controller for a particular subnet, the BRS will hand over the control plane to it. The same process of authentication using the exiting technique is followed for handing over process. Once handing over process will complete, the assigned controller is relieved from the additional load of management of a subnet.

4.4   Application of Proposed System

The proposed system can be used for large network with multiple subnet or VLAN. This system if implemented or deployed in the real time environment can support scalability without compromising performance of the system and its security. This is due to the reason that the BRS provides high availability of the other controllers to a subnet or VLAN in case of failure of the designated controller.

5 Results

The performance of the proposed system is discussed and is given in the Table 1. A good number of parameters are taken for analysis of the result. The criteria for comparison include back-up support, QoS, performance, reliability, data loss, maintenance, timeliness, cost, efficiency and adaptability. In most of the criteria, the proposed system is better and more effective. However, in case of cost i.e. most the installation cost and running cost the proposed system is on the higher side. The one-time cost of the proposed system can be justified when compared to the benefit it transfer to the overall system.

Table 1. Comparison of SDN architecture with and without BRS

Sl. No.	Criteria	Existing system (without BSR)	Proposed system (with BSR)	Remarks
1	Backup support	Within controller database	Centralized backup mechanism used	Better
2	Quality of service	Moderate	Have better QoS	Better
3	Performance	Lack of robustness	Robust architecture with centralized backup	Advanced
4	Reliability	Less	More	More reliable
5	Data loss	Present system may cause data loss	No loss even if controllers fail	Better
6	Maintenance	Require Instance Maintenance	Have time for maintenance	Spare time is available
7	Timeliness	If failure occur then processing stop	process every work within time	Time bound
8	Cost	Less costly	Cost more due to additional BRS system	One-time expense is more
9	Efficiency	Resources are not available in time of failure	System resources are highly available	More efficient
10	Adaptability	Not fault adaptive	Fault adaptive in a very intelligent way	Better adaptive

The proposed research work has been carried out as a pilot project with a prototype in a laboratory environment. Accurate quantitative measurement will be possible once the system is deployed in real world situation. The authors are carrying out the research activity to deploy the proposed solution in a large network environment.

6 Limitation of Proposed Model

This proposed solution has some limitations. In terms of cost there is a requirement of additional hardware and peripherals that may add-up system cost during the installation and deployment of the system. Apart from this there is an additional running cost for the system as maintenance of the BRS is an important parameter. Lastly cooling solutions, space and power requirements for BRS add up recurring cost to the system. There is a requirement of defining protocols and standards related to the security of the system. Elementary security issues using authentications and encryption are handled using the standard protocols available as of today.

7   Conclusion and Future Scopes

The authors in the research paper have proposed a system that is having a BRS for increasing the reliability of the overall system. This system will add more cost during the deployment, but the increased one-time cost may be justified with address reliability factor. In the future, the authors will propose the details implementation in the real-time environment that support state-of-the-art protocols like RIP, OSPF and BGP.

Acknowledgement. The authors of this article acknowledge research support provided by Department of Computer Science and Engineering, NITTTR, KOLKATA for their work. The authors sincerely thank each and every employee of Dept. of Computer Science and Engineering, of this institute for their immense support and inspiration.

References

1. Kreutz, D., Ramos, F., EstevesVerissimo, P., Esteve Rothenberg, C., Azodolmolky, S., Uhlig, S.: Software-defined networking: a comprehensive survey. Proc. IEEE **103**, 14–76 (2015)
2. Nishtha, Sood, M.: A survey on issues of concern in software defined networks. In: 2015 Third International Conference on Image Information Processing (ICIIP), pp 295–300 (2015)
3. Hernandez, E.: Implementation and performance of a SDN cluster-controller based on the open day light framework, pp 5–23 (2016). https://www.politesi.polimi.it/handle/10589/120563. Accessed 11 Nov 2017
4. Berde, P., et al.: ONOS. In: Proceedings of the Third Workshop on Hot Topics in Software Defined Networking - HotSDN 2014, pp 1–6 (2014)
5. Dixit, A., Hao, F., Mukherjee, S., Lakshman, T., Kompella, R.: Towards an elastic distributed SDN controller. In: ACM SIGCOMM Computer Communication Review, vol. 43. pp 7–12 (2013)
6. Sallahi, A., St-Hilaire, M.: Expansion model for the controller placement problem in software defined networks. IEEE Commun. Lett. **21**, 274–277 (2017)
7. Bo, H., Youke, W., Chuan'an, W., Ying, W.: The controller placement problem for software-defined networks. In: 2016 2nd IEEE International Conference on Computer and Communications (ICCC), pp 2435–2439 (2016)
8. Xiao, P., Qu, W., Qi, H., Li, Z., Xu, Y.: The SDN controller placement problem for WAN. In: 2014 IEEE/CIC International Conference on Communications in China (ICCC), pp 220–224 (2014)
9. UlHuque, M., Si, W., Jourjon, G., Gramoli, V.: Large-scale dynamic controller placement. IEEE Trans. Netw. Serv. Manag. **14**, 63–76 (2017)

10. Hikichi, K., Soumiya, T., Yamada, A.: Dynamic application load balancing in distributed SDN controller. In: 2016 18th Asia-Pacific Network Operations and Management Symposium (APNOMS) (2016)
11. Liu, R., et al.: Flow entries installation based on distributed SDN controller. In: 2015 IEEE/CIC International Conference on Communications in China (ICCC) (2015)
12. Aslan, M., Matrawy, A.: Adaptive consistency for distributed SDN controllers. In: 2016 17th International Telecommunications Network Strategy and Planning Symposium (Networks), pp 150–157 (2016)
13. Khan, S., Gani, A., Abdul Wahab, A., Guizani, M., Khan, M.: Topology discovery in software defined networks: threats, taxonomy, and state-of-the-art. IEEE Commun. Surv. Tutor. **19**, 303–324 (2017)
14. Gonzalez, A., Nencioni, G., Helvik, B., Kamisinski, A.: A fault-tolerant and consistent SDN controller. In: 2016 IEEE Global Communications Conference (GLOBECOM) (2016)
15. Pashkov, V., Shalimov, A., Smeliansky, R.: Controller failover for SDN enterprise networks. In: 2014 First International Science and Technology Conference (Modern Networking Technologies) (MoNeTeC) (2014)
16. Rao, A., Auti, S., Koul, A., Sabnis, G.: High availability and load balancing in SDN controllers. Int. J. Trend Res. Dev. **3**, 310–314 (2016). http://www.ijtrd.com/papers/IJTRD3636.pdf. Accessed 12 Nov 2017
17. https://www.opennetworking.org/wp-content/uploads/2014/10/Threat_Analysis_for_the_SDN_Architecture.pdf. Accessed 2 Nov 2017
18. Qi, C., Wu, J., Cheng, G., Ai, J., Zhao, S.: An aware-scheduling security architecture with priority-equal multi-controller for SDN. China Commun. **14**, 144–154 (2017)
19. Wilczewski, D.: Security considerations for equipment controllers and SDN. In: 2016 IEEE International Telecommunications Energy Conference (INTELEC) (2016)

A Novel Approach to Lossless Audio Compression (LAC)

Uttam Kr. Mondal[✉]

Department of Computer Science, Vidyasagar University, Midnapur, WB, India
uttam_ku_82@yahoo.co.in

Abstract. In this paper, an audio compression technique has been made based on Adaptive Differential Pulse-Code Modulation (ADPCM) and Run-Length Coding (RLC). The present technique has been developed in two phases-encoding phase signal and encoding amplitude signal respectively. Sampling the acquired audio succeeded by separating its phase and amplitude components. Phase signal is encoded by its height (magnitude value) and length (time) whereas, the amplitude signal is encoded by ADPCM expanding over different precession levels followed by RLC for generating more compressed pattern. The experimental results along with comparisons with existing techniques represent the compression ratio and efficiency of the present audio compression technique.

Keywords: Lossless audio compression · Audio compression ratio
Sampling audio · Separating phase and amplitude signals
Adaptive audio compression

1 Introduction

Audio compression is one of the challenging issues and it has huge necessities in modern world especially for social media. As audio carries multiple times information than that of image and it also consists of more sensitive data (as it is perceived by ears) than image – it has to be compressed in very precisely. Otherwise, audible quality will be changed and it will lose its importance. Compression of audio signals needs to be done in many ways. As lossy compression of audio is always matter of losing audio information/quality, lossless compression is essential for vital or serious applications like defense, forensic or medical treatment, etc.

In the present paper, a lossless audio compression technique has been proposed. Separating amplitude and phase components followed by encoding both the extracted audio components. As phase signal is the representation of magnitude value and time, it is easily encoded by the values of these two components. On the other hands, adaptive quantization method (with variable step values depending on signal neighboring amplitude values) is applied to encode the amplitude signal into stream of 0 and 1s. Further, applying Run-Length Coding (RLC) [5] is to produce more compressed representation of encoded values of audio signals. Therefore, the encoding values of phase and amplitude signals represent the total audio signal in less volume of data.

© Springer Nature Singapore Pte Ltd. 2018
J. K. Mandal and D. Sinha (Eds.): CSI 2017, CCIS 836, pp. 99–106, 2018.
https://doi.org/10.1007/978-981-13-1343-1_11

The organization of the paper is as follows. The techniques namely LAC – EPS, LAC – SAS, LAC – AM and LAC – SRS are presented in Sects. 2.1 to 2.4 respectively. Experimental results are given in Sect. 3. Conclusions are drawn in Sect. 4 that of references at end.

2   The Technique

The scheme fabricates the compressed audio signal with help of Adaptive Differential Pulse Code Modulation (ADPCM) and Run-Length Coding (RLC). Algorithms namely LAC – EPS, LAC – SAS, LAC – AM and LAC – SRS are fabricated the compression technique, the details of which are given in Sects. 2.1 to 2.4 respectively. In LAC - EPS, representing phase signal in term of its magnitude value and time, minimizes the volume of data for replacing normal representation of phase signal. Compressing amplitude signal is fabricated in Sects. 2.2 to 2.4 respectively. Applying ADPCM based encoding with variable step size (quantization level) for specific neighboring magnitude values of amplitude signal generated from original signal. The Run-Length Coding (RLC) is being applied over the output values of encoding to represent it in more compressed pattern. As the variable quantization levels minimize quantization error, the outputs of the technique represents an efficient lossless compression for audio signal.

2.1   Encoding of Phase Signal (LAC - EPS)

The exponential form of the Fourier series [2] is given in Eq. (1)

$$x_{p(t)} = \sum_{n=-\infty}^{\infty} x_n e^{j2\pi n f_0 t} \tag{1}$$

Equation 1 represents that $x_{p(t)}$ is combined of the frequency components at DC, fundamental and its higher harmonics. $|x_p|$ represents magnitude value at frequency $n f_0$ and φ_n (phase). The plot of $|x_p|$ vs. n (or $n f_0$) is known as the magnitude spectrum, and φ_n vs. n (or $n f_0$) represents the phase spectrum. The spectrum of a periodic signal only persists at discrete frequencies (at $n f_0$, $n = 0, \pm 1, \pm 2, \ldots$, etc.).

Therefore, in spite of sampled values of phase signal, values of $n, f_0, \emptyset$), $\emptyset =$ initial angle of phase signal and $n = 0, \pm 1, \pm 2, \ldots$, etc. will represent the phase component of audio signal.

2.2   Sampling Audio Signal (LAC-SAS)

Assigning near round off sampled values of audio to a certain level of fraction value as permitted by hardware (as commonly available systems) for all neighboring values of amplitude signal having same quantization level (adjusting with minimum error). Therefore, variable quantization levels are considered for the whole signal. The encoding technique has been outlined in Algorithm 1.

Algorithm 1: LAC – ASC

Input: Audio signal
Output: Encoded sampled values
Method: It produces sampled values of audio signal considering its neighboring magnitude values.

Step 1: Determine the similarity of values according to consider the neighboring magnitude values of the first magnitude position and continue to the next position. When it meets with a value whose magnitude value different from previous position more than the half of quantization step, new block or group has to be formed for the next neighboring values. Repeat the same procedure for whole amplitude signal for getting next set of magnitude values for next block and so on.

Step 2: Consider the precision level and the step difference are $16, \frac{1}{16}$ respectively for 1st group of neighboring magnitude values of amplitude signal. Therefore, ceiling values of each level are $0, \frac{1}{16}, \frac{2}{16}, \frac{3}{16}, \ldots, \frac{15}{16}$. In the similar way, assigning a sublevel within a step value, total ceiling values will be as follows $0, \frac{0.5}{16}, \frac{1}{16}, \frac{1.5}{16}, \ldots, \frac{15.5}{16}$(if required).

Step 3: Find sampled values of song for a particular position, and replace the value by its nearest quantization value (as shown in step 2 of Algorithm 1).

Step 4: Repeat step 2 for all 1st group neighboring sampled values of song.

Step 5: Repeat step 2 to 4 for all i^{th} group neighboring sampled values of song with considering appropriate quantization level for the particular group.

2.3   Amp-Modulating of Audio (LAC-AM)

Modulation of amplitude signal by using adaptive quantization technique with different quantization levels for different blocks of neighboring values (As discussed in step 1 of Algorithm 1). Let, the quantization level is Δ which is the average magnitude value in the 1st group of neighboring amplitude values, i.e., every position and its consecutive position the separation would be $\pm\Delta$ (Fig. 1). Therefore, the difference should be $\pm\Delta$ for each consecutive position. Find the ratio of phase and amplitude signal, generate the ratio signal R(n) which will represent the ratio of the phase and amplitude values (Fig. 2). Hence, the difference of two consecutive amplitude values is $\pm\Delta$, therefore, the difference between the maximum and the minimum would be lower for each group. The procedure of modulating amplitude signal is given in Algorithm 2.

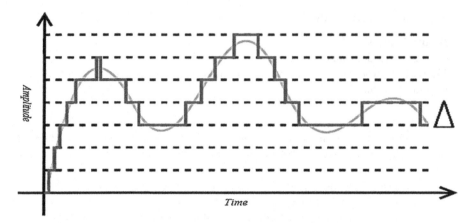

Fig. 1. Modulation of amplitude signal

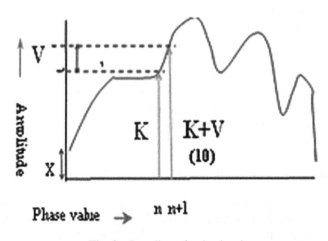

Fig. 2. Sampling of ratio signal

Algorithm 2: LAC - AM

Input: Sampled values of audio signal (generated by applying Algorithm 1).
Output: Ratio signal.
Method: Separating amplitude and phase from original signal and producing a ratio signal for its compression.

Step 1: Separate amplitude and phase from original signal produces two signals representing amplitude and phase characteristics respectively.
Step 2: Modulation of amplitude signal by using adaptive quantization technique with variable quantization steps for different blocks of neighboring values. Let, the quantization level is Δ which is the average magnitude value in the

1st group of neighboring amplitude values, i.e., every position and its consecutive position the separation would be $\pm\Delta$. Therefore, the difference should be $\pm\Delta$ for each consecutive position.

Step 3: Find the ratio of phase and amplitude signal, generate the ratio signal $R(n)$ which will represent the ratio of the phase and amplitude values. Hence, the difference of two consecutive amplitude values is $\pm\Delta$; therefore, the difference between the maximum and the minimum would be lower for each of these neighboring groups.

2.4   Sampling of Ratio Signal (LAC- SRS)

The encoding of ratio signal is to produce codes for representing signal into less number of bits. Let, X is the magnitude value of 1st position of block 1 of the generated ratio signal; Therefore, X value would be added to the output code. Though the amplitude variation for consecutive position of ratio signal is constant, therefore, it would be incremented or decremented by a fixed value V (say). Now, represent incremented V and decremented V by 1 and 0 respectively. Therefore, if the magnitude values of consecutive positions are K + V, K + V,V,V, K + V,V, K + V,V,V,V, K + V,V,V, K + V,V, K − V, V,V, K + V V,V, K + V, V, ... (where K is magnitude value of previous positions) (Fig. 2) then, it will be represented by 10, 10, 00, 00, 10, 00, 10, 00, 00, 00, 10, 00, 00, 10, 00, 01, ... respectively. [1] Representing more precisely and compressed way, Run-Length Coding (RLC) will be applied over encoded values of ratio signal for removing repeated number of symbols (0s or 1s). The technique is outlined in Algorithm 3.

Algorithm 3: LAC - SRS

Input: Sample values of ratio signal.
Output: Encoded values of ratio signal.
Method: The sampling of ratio signal and applying Run length coding produce the compressed pattern of audio signal.

Step 1: Find X (say) is the amplitude value of 1st position of the generated ratio signal.

Step 2: As the amplitude variation for consecutive position of ratio signal is constant, therefore, it would be incremented or decremented by a fixed value V (say). Now, represent incremented V and decremented V by 1 and 0 respectively. Therefore, if the amplitude values of consecutive positions are K + V, K + V,V,V, K + V,V, K + V,V,V,V, K + V,V,V, K + V,V, K − V, V,V, K + V V,V, K + V, V, ... (where K is amplitude value of previous positions) (Fig. 2) then, it will be represented by 10, 10, 00, 00, 10, 00, 10, 00, 00, 00, 10, 00, 00, 10, 00, 01, ... respectively.

Step 3: Apply Run-Length coding to represent the bit sequence into more compress way as given below

For the following sequence of output (As the example shown step 2 of Algorithm 3)

1010 00 0010 0010 0000001000001000 01

After applying RLC only for repeated symbol (0 or 1), the sequence would be **10150130170 1501401** (the number other than 0 or 1, say x, indicates the repetition of following symbol (0 or 1) of the x times).

3 Results and Analysis

Twenty five songs have been taken for analysis of the present technique and comparing with other existing algorithms. Two audio lossless compression techniques (Monkey's Audio [3] and Wavpack Lossless [4]) are used for comparison. Each song is of 10 s in

Table 1. Compression ratio (%) for 5 different types of songs for Monkey's Audio [3], WavPack Lossless [4] and LAC

Song type	Audio files (.wav) [10 s]	Compression ratio								
		Techniques								
		Monkey's Audio [3]			WavPack Lossless [4]			LAC		
		Individual (%)	Avg. (%)	Over all avg. (%)	Individual (%)	Avg. (%)	Over all avg. (%)	Individual (%)	Avg. (%)	Over all avg. (%)
Pop	pop_1	56.06	52.09	**46.88**	39.45	43.38	**48.67**	94.75	95.05	**94.91**
	pop_2	44.25			52.14			94.62		
	pop_3	60.07			34			94.72		
	pop_4	51.91			44.03			95.14		
	pop_5	48.16			47.28			96.01		
Rock	rock_1	60.48	62		33.88	34.2		94.62	96	
	rock_2	52.93			44.19			96.88		
	rock_3	65.43			29.93			95.65		
	rock_4	68.19			28.62			96.73		
	rock_5	62.98			34.35			96.13		
Ghazal/sufi	ghazal_1	40.62	44.64		54.2	50.24		93.31	95.02	
	ghazal_2	46.81			48.4			95.32		
	ghazal_3	46.98			46.45			94.15		
	ghazal_4	52.16			44.57			96.56		
	ghazal_5	36.6			57.59			95.77		
Rabindra Tagore	rabi_1	42.28	43.89		51.46	51.39		94.92	94.25	
	rabi_2	47.08			45.27			94.29		
	rabi_3	44.46			49.32			94.24		
	rabi_4	44.76			48.84			94.21		
	rabi_5	47.89			46.46			94.23		
Classical	classical_1	31.25	32.57		67.07	64.15		94.31	94.22	
	classical_2	29.15			66.86			94.57		
	classical_3	42.72			51.98			93.6		
	classical_4	35.44			62.76			94.95		
	classical_5	24.29			72.07			93.71		

length. There are five types of songs. These types are pop, rock, safi/ghazal, Rabindra Tagore's song (Rabindra Sangit) and classical. Five different songs are taken for each category, i.e., total twenty five different songs are taken for experimental results. The comparison is done by using compression ratio which is a statistical parameter and it is computed by Eq. (2) [6].

$$\text{Compression ratio} = \frac{\text{Number of bits before compression}}{\text{Number of bits after compression}} \quad (2)$$

Table 1 show the compression ration applying three audio lossless techniques (Monkey's Audio, Wavpack Lossless and LAC) over 25 different audio signals (five type of songs, five songs from each group of 10 s length). It is cleared from the statistical results of Table 1, LAC is efficient than that of other compression techniques considered here. It not only produce best overall compression ratio, it also shows best compressor ratio for each individual group (pop, rock, ghazal/safi, Rabindra sangit and classical respectively). The graphical representation of compression ratio (%) of 25 songs of five different categories including individual, each group and over all compression ratio are shown in Fig. 3. It shows the present compression technique (LAC) gives better results than other compression techniques.

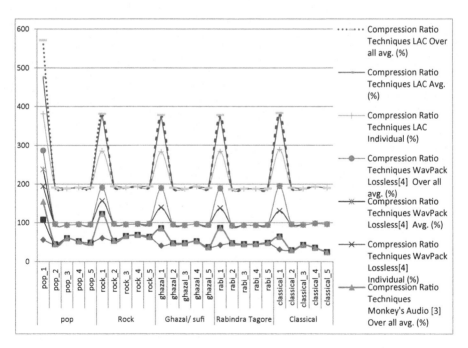

Fig. 3. Twenty five different songs with compression ratio (%) values for Monkey's Audio [3], WavPack Lossless [4] and LAC

4 Conclusions and Future Scope

Lossless compression of audio is required for crucial applications. The present technique is not only achieving overall good average compression ratio; it also maintains its audible quality without losing any information or data. In future, percentage of compression ratio will also be enhanced using any of the appropriate transform functions or searching better representation of audio signal with designing a better audio encoding technique.

References

1. Mondal, U.K., Mandal, J.K.: Songs authentication through embedding a self generated secure hidden signal (SAHS). In: Chaki, N., Cortesi, A. (eds.) CISIM 2011. CCIS, vol. 245, pp. 305–313. Springer, Heidelberg (2011). https://doi.org/10.1007/978-3-642-27245-5_36
2. http://nptel.ac.in/syllabus/117106090/. (Chap. 1). Accessed 30 Nov 2017
3. http://www.monkeysaudio.com/. Accessed 29 Nov 2017
4. http://www.wavpack.com/. Accessed 29 Nov 2017
5. https://en.wikipedia.org/wiki/Run-length_encoding. Accessed 30 Nov 2017
6. Li, Z.-N., Drew, M.S.: Fundamentals of Multimedia. Prentice Hall, Upper Saddle River (2004). Chap. 7. ISBN 0-13-127256-X

Extending Lifetime of a Network by Load Sharing in AODV Routing Protocol

Radha Krishna Bar[1(✉)], Jyotsna Kumar Mandal[2],
Tanmoy Kanti Halder[3], and Somnath Mukhopadhyay[4]

[1] Future Institute of Technology, Kolkata, West Bengal, India
rdhk_bar@yahoo.co.in
[2] University of Kalyani, Kalyani, West Bengal, India
[3] P.D. Women's College, Jalpaiguri, West Bengal, India
[4] Assam University, Silchar, Assam, India

Abstract. Sometime the nodes also have to perform some computation with the collected data and transfer it to the destination. Especially where the source of power of the nodes are consisting of limited power source or battery. This power is reducing at the cost of transferring data as well as for the internal computing purpose [1]. On exhaustion of power, eventually the nodes die. Then all the data computed by the node is also lost. Further data of that particular position where the sensor node was placed is also no more available. Gradually the number of nodes in the network also decreased. In this paper we use AODV routing protocol to transfer the data from the sensor node to the destination server. Generally in the shortest path is used to transfer the data from source to destination. We consider here two important metrics, one is residual power another is rate of power consumption for internal computing in the node. Considering these two factors for each node we make a rank and introduce a dynamic threshold value of rank. Now the node having rank less than the threshold is excluded from the internal computing, it can only transfer the collected data to its neighbor node which have sufficient power. Thus the life time of the node is extended eventually the average lifetime of the network is also extended. And as we determine the threshold value as dynamic, there is no sudden fall of power and maximum numbers of nodes will active towards the end.

Keywords: AODV · Life time of network · Load sharing

1 Introduction

Ad hoc On-Demand Distance Vector (AODV) Routing is one of the most popular routing protocols used to transfer data in wireless ad hoc networks and mobile ad hoc networks. In AODV protocol a path is established for data transfer from source to destination based on the minimum hop count [2]. The mobile nodes of the network have the limited source of power. The energy is drained for the transferring data as well as for the internal computation also [3]. The node which have less remaining power or the node whose rate of energy consumption is high will survive less. The remaining power of the node which takes part frequently in the rout establishment in AODV decreases sharply, eventually it will die. Thus the number of node in the network will

© Springer Nature Singapore Pte Ltd. 2018
J. K. Mandal and D. Sinha (Eds.): CSI 2017, CCIS 836, pp. 107–112, 2018.
https://doi.org/10.1007/978-981-13-1343-1_12

gradually decrease. On the other hand the computed data by the victim node will also be lost. In this paper we consider both remaining power and the rate of energy consumption for its internal computation in the path discovery of AODV routing protocol rather than hop count. When a node suffer from critical power then it transfer its computed data to its neighbor node which have sufficient remaining power, after transferring the data the victim node can only take part in the routing i.e. it is exempted from internal computation. Thus the victim node can survive more time in the network as well as we can recover the computed data.

2 Related Works

As lives of nodes of a sensor network depends on the limited power source, extending the lifetime of the sensor network become an important research perspective [4, 5]. For extending the life of a network several methods are proposed by researchers. Research objective is to choose the path to transfer data from source to destination where the minimum power is consumed. Another research objective is to balance the load throughout the network [6]. Daming Feng and Yanqin Zhu proposed I-AODV where remaining power is considered to chose the next hop [7]. In [8], the researchers considered the remaining power as well as the internal node in AODV routing protocol to enhance the lifetime of the network. Nisheeth Khanna and K. Krishna Naik proposed to enhance the lifetime of the network by distributing the routing load among the nodes in the network [9].

3 Proposed Works

Generally in AODV routing protocol the shortest path is established to transfer data from source to destination [10]. In this work we consider the residual power of nodes as a metric of the rout discovery process in AODV routing protocol. We introduce a dynamic threshold value of remaining power. This threshold value depends on the average remaining power of the last active nodes. The nodes which have the remaining power greater than the threshold value will take part in the rout discovery of the routing. But the nodes having the remaining power less than the threshold value are exempt from the rout discovery process in AODV. Thus we can choose a safe path to transfer the data from source to destination by avoiding low power nodes.

The power of a node is consumed for both data transferring as well as its internal computation work. Whenever a node is identified as the low power node, it transfer its computed data to its nearest node which have sufficient power. And we proposed to excuse this node from internal computing. Thus life time of the node is extended somewhat.

As the threshold value is calculated dynamically so its value will be decreased smoothly. Thus the nodes which were marked as low power node previously, may take part in rout discovery in next time. Thus maximum number of node will be alive up to the end.

4 Simulation

We have tested the we have used a popular extensible, modular, component-based C++ simulation library and framework, primarily for building network simulators. The simulator provides the required framework including the other common module like sensor networks, wireless ad-hoc networks, performance modelling, photonic networks, Internet protocols etc. We import INET which provides the network package of different routing protocols like AODV, DSR etc. The simulation is done through an Eclipse-based IDE interface of the simulator. We set the different parameters value as per our requirement to simulate our project. As different node may have different computing load we set value of energy consumption rate randomly for each node. The parameter and their values are described in the following table (Table 1).

Table 1.

Parameter name	Value	Parameter name	Value
Routing protocol	AODVUU	Start time	Uniform (1 s, 60 s, 1)
Application type	UDPBasicBurst	Route timeout	6000 ms
No. of application	1	Sending interval	0.25 s + uniform (−0.001 s, 0.001 s, 1)
Network interface card bit rate	54 Mbps	Limit of sending RREQ/RERR	1000
Covered area	800 m X 600 m battery	Nominal capacity	100 mAh
Maximum channel power	2.0 mW battery	Receive current	140 mA
Attenuation threshold	−110 dBm	Transmission current	160 mA
Mobility type	MassMobility	Idle current	100 mA
Mobility speed	50 mps radio	Sleep current	100 mA
Message length	512B # bytes	Sensitivity	−85 dBm
Battery capacity	1800 mAh	SNR threshold	4 dB
Battery voltage	3.7 V	Radio transmitter power	2.0 mW
Battery resolution	2 s	Local repair	True

5 Result Analysis

Using the above described parameter value we have simulated the proposed module with different number of nodes. We have measured the remaining power of each node of the network at several instances of the lifetime of the network and then the average remaining power is plotted against the time. We have done the same experiment again but without using our module. In Fig. 1 the solid line indicates the average remaining power of proposed our module and the dotted line indicates the average remaining power without using our power module.

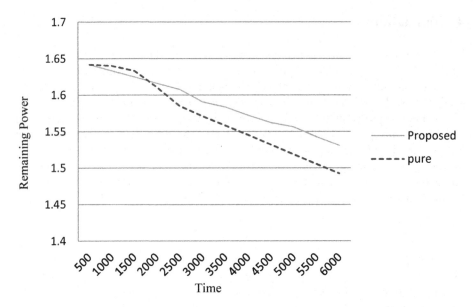

Fig. 1. Remaining power of our module vs pure AODV w.r.t. time for 20 nodes

From the above graph it is clear that after a certain time the average remaining power of our module is higher. Thus the lifetime of the network is also higher for our module. We have done the simulation with 25 nodes, 30 nodes, 35 nodes, and 40

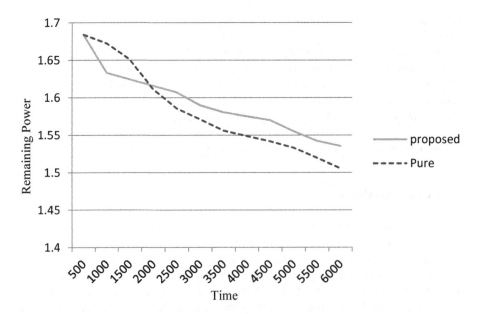

Fig. 2. Remaining power of our module vs pure AODV w.r.t. time for 40 nodes

nodes. In all the case the trend of the graphs are similar. Figure 2 is obtained from the experiment with 40 nodes. The solid line indicates the average remaining power of proposed our module and the dotted line indicates the average remaining power without using our power module.

We compared the remaining power of our module with the power module proposed in [8]. The following graph shows the comparing graph (Fig. 3) which clearly indicates that the average remaining power of our module is higher after a certain time of start.

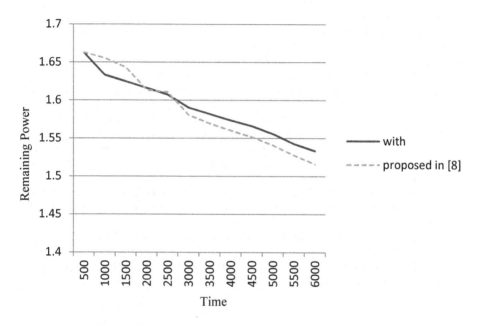

Fig. 3. Remaining power of our module vs proposed in [8]

6 Conclusion

In this work we exclude the low power nodes from the rout discovery in the AODV routing protocol, thus only the high power nodes take part in routing and threshold value is dynamically calculated from the average remaining power as well as the power drawn for its internal work. When a node marked as low power node, we stop its internal computing i.e. the power consumption for its internal work set to zero for that time, thus the average remaining power of the network is higher and it results a greater life time of the network. As the current threshold value depends on the previous remaining power so initially the remaining power proposed module lies below. But after certain time the average remaining power shows better values. The proposed power module is suitable for both small network and large network but it gives slide better result in larger network.

References

1. Perkins, C.: Adhoc On-demand Distance Vector (AODV) Routing, RFC3561[S] (2003)
2. Karthikeyan, N., Palanisamy, V., Duraiswamy, K.: A review of broadcasting methods for mobile ad hoc network. Int. J. Adv. Comput. Eng. (2012)
3. Rajaravivarma, V., Yang, Y., Yang, T.: System theory, 2003. In: Proceedings of the 35th Southeastern Symposium (2003)
4. Akyildiz, I.F., Su, W., Sankarasubramaniam, Y., Cayirci, E.: A survey on sensor networks. IEEE (2002). 0163-6804/02/$17.00
5. Zhang, R., Ingelrest, F., Barrenetxea, G., Thiran, P., Vetterli, M.: The beauty of the commons: optimal load sharing by base station hopping in wireless sensor networks. IEEE J. Sel. Areas Commun. 33(8), 1480–1491 (2015)
6. Feng, D., Zhu, Y.: An improved AODV routing protocol based on remaining power and fame. In: International Conference on Electronic Computer Technology (2009)
7. Halder, T.K., Chowdhury, C., Neogy, S.: Power aware AODV routing protocol for MANET. In: 2014 Fourth International Conference on Advances in Computing and Communications. IEEE (2014). 978-1-4799-4363-0/14 $31.00. https://doi.org/10.1109/icacc.2014.84
8. Khanna, N., Naik, K.K.: Design and implementation of an energy efficient routing approach based on existing AODV protocol in Mobile Adhoc networks for military. In: International Conference on IEEE Emerging Trends in Electrical Electronics & Sustainable Energy Systems (ICETEESES) (2016)
9. Amaresh, M., Usha, G.: Efficient malicious detection for AODV in mobile ad-hoc network. In: 2013 International Conference on Recent Trends in Information Technology (ICRTIT) (2013)
10. Chawda, K., Gorana, D.: A survey of energy efficient routing protocols in MANET. In: IEEE sponsored 2nd ICECS (2015)
11. Xiao, H.: Energy consumption in mobile Adhoc networks. In: National Conference on Recent Trend in Information, Telecommunication and Computing, pp. 23–27 (2010)

Circuits and Systems

An Electronically-Tuneable VDTA Based Sinusoidal Oscillator

Indrajit Pal, Vikash Kumar[✉], Sagnik Saha, Soham Banerjee,
and Aminul Islam

Department of Electronics and Communication Engineering,
Birla Institute of Technology, Mesra, Ranchi 835215, Jharkhand, India
pal.indrajit99@gmail.com, sahasagnik95@gmail.com,
banerjeesoham95@gmail.com, vikashkr@bitmesra.ac.in,
dr.aminul.islam@ieee.org

Abstract. This paper introduces an electronically-tuneable sinusoidal oscillator design utilizing VDTA as an active building block. The introduced design incorporates two VDTA blocks, two capacitors, one resistor and finds its suitability for fully integrated circuit applications. The condition for oscillation (CO) and frequency of oscillation (ω_{OSC}) of the proposed oscillator design are electronic tuneable by varying the DC bias currents of VDTA. The oscillator design operates at a low voltage of ± 1 V and consumes very low power of 2 mW. The frequency of oscillation of the proposed oscillator is evaluated to be 46 MHz. The simulation result confirms the theoretical prospects of the design. The oscillator design is analyzed using Virtuoso Analog design Environment of Cadence.

Keywords: Condition for oscillation VDTA · Sinusoidal oscillator
Analog integrated circuit · Frequency of oscillation

1 Introduction

Sinusoidal oscillator is a linear electronics circuit which is utilized in broad areas of electronics and computers to generate signals. An oscillator is a vital building block for several wireless transmitter, receiver, instrumentation, measurement, control and data monitoring systems [1–5]. In past decades or so, the designs of on-chip sinusoidal oscillators have become prominent. Such oscillators are based on different active elements and find their utility in fully integrated applications. Several active elements such as Opamp [6, 7], VDTA [8–12], Current Conveyors (CCII and CCIII) [13–16], etc., have been employed in recent past for the oscillator designs. Most recent oscillator designs emphasize on orthogonal or electronic control of condition for oscillation (CO) and frequency of oscillation (ω_{OSC}), which imparts extensive advantage to the range of applications of the oscillator. In recent past, the need for fully integrated oscillator designs has become much more prevalent.

In this research paper, a VDTA based sinusoidal oscillator has been presented which provides electronic control of CO and ω_{OSC}. Initially, a sinusoidal oscillator using passive inductor circuit has been designed. Later, the passive inductor is being

© Springer Nature Singapore Pte Ltd. 2018
J. K. Mandal and D. Sinha (Eds.): CSI 2017, CCIS 836, pp. 115–123, 2018.
https://doi.org/10.1007/978-981-13-1343-1_13

replaced by the active inductor equivalent. The CO and ω_{OSC} for both the oscillator designs has been provided. The introduced design comprises two VDTA blocks and all grounded passive components (resistor and capacitor), thereby, justifying its applicability for fully integrated circuit implementations.

This paper is organized in the following order. In Sect. 2, the circuit description of VDTA is discussed. Section 3 presents the proposed VDTA based sinusoidal oscillator design. In Sect. 4, the responses of the oscillator designs are given. Lastly, conclusions of the paper are deducted in Sect. 5.

2   Circuit Description of VDTA

VDTA (Voltage differencing transconductance amplifier) is a currently reported electronically controllable active building block. VDTA was initially introduced by the authors in [17]. Figure 1 illustrates the VDTA, which depicts its electrical (see Fig. 1 (a)) and behavior representation (see Fig. 1(b)). VDTA has two input terminals (p and n), one intermediate terminal (z) and two output terminals (x^+ and x^-). The output current at z terminal (i_z) is the function of voltage difference between p and n terminals (v_P and v_n) and the transconductance (g_{mF}). Similarly, the output currents at x^+ and x^- terminals are the function of voltage v_Z and transconductance (g_{mS}).

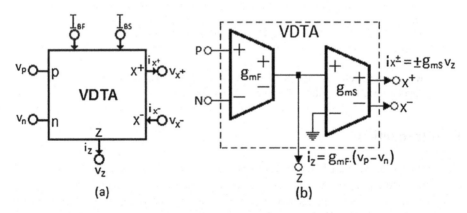

Fig. 1. (a) Electrical and (b) Behavioral level demonstration of VDTA.

The terminal relations of VDTA may be enumerated by the following equations [18]

$$i_p = 0, \tag{1}$$

$$i_n = 0, \tag{2}$$

$$i_z = g_{mF}(v_p - v_n), \tag{3}$$

$$i_{x+} = g_{mS}v_z,$$ (4)

$$i_{x-} = -g_{mS}v_z.$$ (5)

Here, g_{mF}, g_{mS} are the 1st and 2nd stage transconductances and are given as

$$g_{mf} \approx \frac{g_1g_2}{g_1+g_2} + \frac{g_3g_4}{g_3+g_4},$$ (6)

and

$$g_{ms} \approx \frac{g_5g_6}{g_5+g_6} + \frac{g_7g_8}{g_7+g_8}.$$ (7)

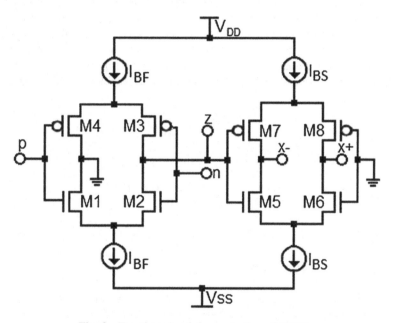

Fig. 2. Transistor level demonstration of VDTA.

The transconductances g_i (i = 1 to 4) and g_j (j = 5 to 8) are the function of VDTA bias currents I_{BF} and I_{BS} respectively. They are given as,

$$g_i = \sqrt{k_iI_{BF}},$$ (8)

$$g_j = \sqrt{k_jI_{BS}}$$ (9)

and

where,

$$k_{i,j} = \mu C_{ox} \left(\frac{W}{L}\right)_{i,j} \tag{10}$$

In (6), μ is carrier mobility; C_{ox} is the oxide capacitance, $W_{i,j}$ and $L_{i,j}$ is the width and length of ith or j^{th} MOS transistor respectively. Figure 2 shows the transistor-level demonstration of VDTA.

3 VDTA Based Sinusoidal Oscillator

Figure 3 displays the introduced VDTA based oscillator design. The oscillator design comprises one VDTA block, one grounded capacitor (C_1), one grounded resistor (R) and one grounded inductor (L). From the perspective of monolithic integration, employing grounding of passive elements allows compensation of parasitic stray elements at the respective nodes. The characteristic equation for the design is derived by utilizing the characteristics of VDTA terminals discussed previously. The characteristic equation is given by

$$s^2 LC_1 + s[RC_1 + g_{mF1}L(1 - g_{mS1}R)] + g_{mF1}R = 0, \tag{11}$$

From (11), the CO and ω_{OSC} can be evaluated as

$$RC_1 + g_{mF1}L(1 - g_{mS1}R) = 0, \tag{12}$$

and

$$\omega_{OSC} = \sqrt{\frac{g_{mF1}R}{LC_1}}. \tag{13}$$

Practically, for fully integrated circuit applications, inductors (passive or spiral) are difficult to implement. The active inductor implementation of grounded inductor using VDTA has been reported in [19] and has inductance value of

$$L = \frac{C_2}{g_{mF2}g_{mS2}}. \tag{14}$$

Replacing the inductor given in Fig. 3 with the active inductor, the modified oscillator design is shown in Fig. 4.

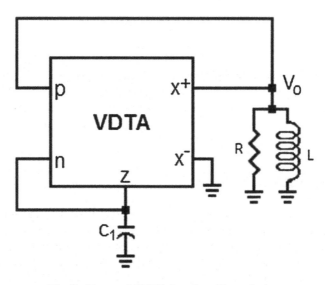

Fig. 3. Proposed VDTA based oscillator design.

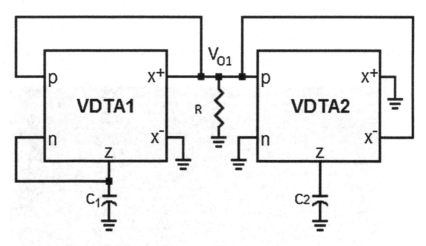

Fig. 4. Modified VDTA based oscillator design.

From Fig. 4, the characteristic equation for the design is modified as,

$$s^2 C_1 C_2 + s(g_{mF2}g_{mS2}RC_1 - g_{mF1}g_{mS1}RC_2 + g_{mF1}C_2) + g_{mF1}g_{mF2}g_{mS2}R = 0. \quad (15)$$

From (15), the CO and ω_{OSC} can be re-evaluated as

$$g_{mF2}g_{mS2}RC_1 - g_{mF1}g_{mS1}RC_2 + C_2 g_{mF1} = 0 \quad (16)$$

and

$$\omega_{OSC} = \sqrt{\frac{g_{mF1}g_{mF2}g_{mS2}R}{C_1C_2}}. \tag{17}$$

As observed from (16) and (17), the CO and ω_{OSC} of the proposed design may be varied by varying the transconductances (g_{mF} and g_{mS}) of the two VDTAs. The transconductances of VDTA are varied by adjusting the external DC bias currents (I_{BF}, I_{BS}) of VDTA (see (8) and (9)). This implies that the introduced oscillator design offers electronic tunability over the CO and ω_{OSC}.

4   Simulation Result

In order to elaborately support the proposal for VDTA based sinusoidal oscillator design; this section illustrates the various results obtained from examining the proposed circuit. The simulations are carried out in the Virtuoso Analog design Environment of Cadence. The MOS transistors (PMOS and NMOS) are simulated by utilizing the 45-nm CMOS technology node parameters. Supply voltage ($V_{DD} = -V_{SS}$) for the proposed oscillator design is considered as ±1 V. All the bias currents of VDTA are considered to be 250 µA. The total power consumption of the design results in 2 mW.

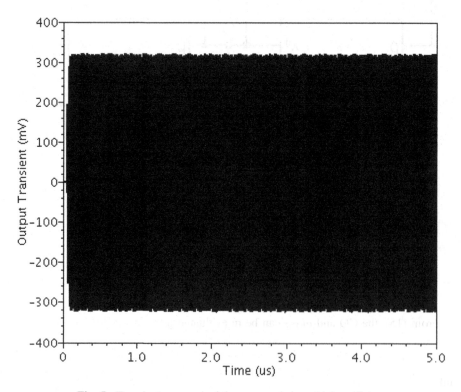

Fig. 5. Transient response of the proposed sinusoidal oscillator.

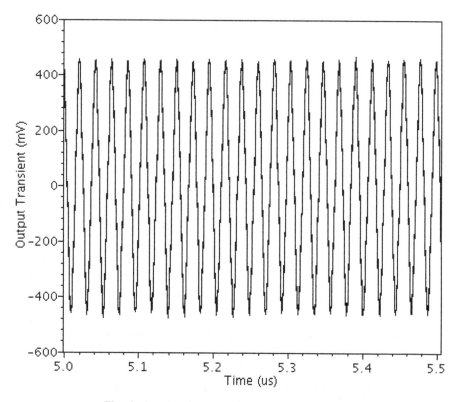

Fig. 6. Steady state response of proposed oscillator.

The transient and steady state sinusoidal waveforms are illustrated in Figs. 5 and 6 respectively, thereby justifying the validity of the proposed oscillator design. The oscillation frequency (ω_{osc}) is estimated as 46 MHz. Figure 7 displays the electronically tunable feature of proposed oscillator with external DC bias current. It shows ω_{osc} versus time plot for different DC bias currents. As shown, the frequency of oscillation (ω_{osc}) increases with increasing bias currents.

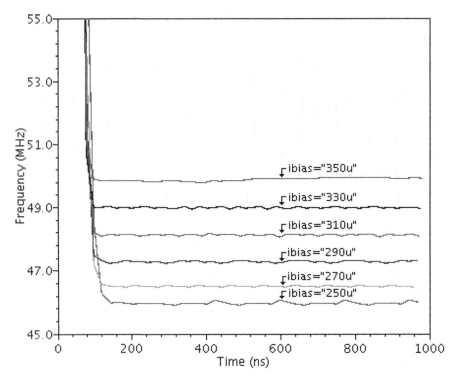

Fig. 7. Frequency versus time plot of proposed oscillator.

5 Conclusion

The proposed VDTA based oscillator design depicts sinusoidal oscillations with electronic control of the CO and ω_{OSC} which may be adjusted by varying the external DC bias currents of VDTA. The results illustrated in this paper validate the functionality of the proposed design. The theoretical analyses are in accord with simulated responses, thus strongly emphasizing on the appropriate functioning of the proposed design.

References

1. Toumazou, C., Lidgey, F.J., Haigh, D.G.: Analogue IC Design: The Current-mode Approach. Peter Peregrinus, London (1990)
2. Jantakun, A., Jaikla, W.: Current-mode quadrature oscillator based on CCCDTAs with noninteractive dual-current control for both condition of oscillation and frequency of oscillation. Turk. J. Electr. Eng. Comput. Sci. **21**, 81–89 (2013)
3. Biolek, D., Lahiri, A., Jaikla, W., Siripruchayanun, M., Bajer, J.: Realization of electronically tunable voltage-mode/current-mode quadrature sinusoidal oscillator using ZC-CG-CDBA. Microelectron. J. **42**, 1116–1123 (2011)

4. Šotner, R., Hrubos, Z., Slezak, J., Dostal, T.: Simply adjustable sinusoidal oscillator based on negative three-port current conveyors. Radioengineering **19**, 446–453 (2010)
5. Iqbal, A., Parveen, B., Muslim, T.A.: First order current mode filters and multiphase sinusoidal oscillator using CMOS MOCCIIs. Arab. J. Sci. Eng. **32**, 119–126 (2007)
6. Senani, R.: New types of sine wave oscillators. IEEE Trans. Instrum. Meas. **34**(3), 461–463 (1985)
7. Senani, R., Bhaskar, D.R.: Single op-amp sinusoidal oscillators suitable for generation of very low frequencies. IEEE Trans. Instrum. Meas. **40**(4), 777–779 (1991)
8. Chandee, S., Jaikla, W., Suwanjan, P., Pookrongtong, N., Kwawsibsam, A.: New quadrature sinusoidal oscillator with amplitude controllability. In: The 4th Joint International Conference on Information and Communication Technology, Electronic and Electrical Engineering (JICTEE), Chiang Rai, pp. 1–4 (2014)
9. Pourak, T., Suwanjan, P., Jaikla, W., Maneewan, S.: Simple quadrature sinusoidal oscillator with orthogonal control using sigle active element. In: 2012 IEEE International Conference on Electron Devices and Solid State Circuit (EDSSC), Bangkok, pp. 1–4 (2012)
10. Kumar, V., Mehra, R., Islam, A.: A CMOS active inductor based digital and analog dual tuned voltage-controlled oscillator. Microsyst. Technol. 1–13 (2017). https://doi.org/10.1007/s00542-017-3457-y
11. Tangsrirat, W.: Compact quadrature oscillator with voltage and current outputs using only single VDTA and grounded capacitors. Indian J. Pure Appl. Phys. **55**(4), 254–260 (2017)
12. Mehra, R., Kumar, V., Islam, A.: Floating active inductor based Class-C VCO with 8 digitally tuned sub-bands. AEU- Int. J. Electron. Commun. **83**, 1–10 (2017)
13. Horng, J.W., Hou, C.L., Chang, C.M., Chung, W.Y., Tang, H.W., Wen, Y.H.: Quadrature oscillator using CCIIs. Int. J. Electron. **92**(1), 21–31 (2005)
14. Horng, J.W.: Current/voltage-mode third order quadrature oscillator employing two multiple outputs CCIIs and grounded capacitors. Indian J. Pure Appl. Phys. **49**, 494–498 (2011)
15. Maheshwari, S., Khan, I.A.: Current controlled third order quadrature oscillator. IEEE Proc. Circuits Devices Syst. **152**(6), 605–607 (2005)
16. Maheshwari, S.: Current-mode third-order quadrature oscillator. IET Cricuits Devices Syst. **4**(3), 188–195 (2010)
17. Yesil, A., Kacar, F., Kuntman, H.: New simple CMOS realization of voltage differencing transconductance amplifier and its RF filter application. Radioengineering **20**(3), 632–637 (2011)
18. Mehra, R., Kumar, V., Islam, A., Kaushik, B.K.: Variation-aware widely tunable nanoscale design of CMOS active inductor-based RF bandpass filter. Int. J. Circ. Theor. Appl. **45**(12), 2181–2200 (2017). https://doi.org/10.1002/cta.2364
19. Kumar, V., Mehra, R., Islam, A.: A 2.5 GHz low power, high-Q, reliable design of active bandpass filter. IEEE Trans. Device Mater. Reliab. **17**(1), 229–244 (2017)

Multi-functional Active Filter Design Using Three VDTAs

Anushka Gon, Vikash Kumar[(✉)], Saumya Pandey, and Aminul Islam

Department of ECE, BIT, Mesra, Ranchi 835215, Jharkhand, India
anushkagon11@gmail.com, vikashkr@bitmesra.ac.in,
saumya181197@gmail.com, dr.aminul.islam@ieee.org

Abstract. This paper suggests a single-input multi-output (SIMO) multi-function current mode active filter design using three voltage differencing transconductance amplifiers (VDTAs) as an active element. The filter is realized in current-mode (CM) and delivers several filter operations such as HP, LP, BP, BR and AP filter functions with appropriate connections of input signal. The filter consists of three VDTAs and two capacitors, which are grounded. The significance of the suggested filter is that it provides electronic and independent controllability of filter parameters i.e. pole frequency (ω_p) and Q-factor (Q). The filter design is analyzed using Virtuoso Analog Design Environment of Cadence.

Keywords: VDTA · Current-mode · Universal filter · SIMO

1 Introduction

Over the last few decades or so, the design of multi-functional active filters has evolved enormously in areas of communication, electronics, instrumentation systems, etc. Multi-function filter is the filter that can implement multiple filter operations such as low-pass (LP), high-pass (HP), band-pass (BP), band-reject (BR) and all-pass (AP) filters from one configuration with appropriate connections of input signal. Several multi-functional active filters based on distinct active elements for example operational transresistance amplifier [1], current-conveyor [2], OTA [3], etc., have been suggested. Either of these filters is of voltage-mode (VM) filters or of current-mode (CM) filters. Current-mode filters are preferred over the voltage-mode filters due to their lower cost, simpler circuitry, lower power consumption and wider bandwidth [4]. Further, the filters are also classified as single input multiple output (SIMO) [5], multiple input single output (MISO) [6] and multiple input multiple output (MIMO) [7] filters, based on the number of input and outputs.

This paper introduces a multi-functional single-input multi-output (SIMO) filter based on current-mode (CM) and is using voltage differencing transconductance amplifier (VDTA). VDTA is a fairly new active element with the capability of operation in both VM and CM [8]. In this paper, the multi-function active filter is designed with three VDTAs and two grounded capacitors. Using only one input signal, five

© Springer Nature Singapore Pte Ltd. 2018
J. K. Mandal and D. Sinha (Eds.): CSI 2017, CCIS 836, pp. 124–130, 2018.
https://doi.org/10.1007/978-981-13-1343-1_14

different functions i.e. LP, HP, BP, BR and AP filters are realized. Electronic and independent controllability of filter specifications i.e. the pole frequency (ω_p) and Q-factor (Q) are provided through the DC bias currents of VDTA. The filter configuration is absolutely resistor-less and finds its suitability in fully integrated circuit operations.

The arrangement of the paper is described below. In Sect. 2, the description of VDTA is discussed. Section 3 presents the suggested multi-functional active filter configuration. In Sect. 4, the simulation results are provided. Lastly, in Sect. 4, conclusion is drawn.

2 Description of VDTA

The modern active element, VDTA has been recommended by Biolek in [9]. Several applications of VDTA have been reported, most notably the filters [10] and oscillators [11]. VDTA is a two-stage transconductance amplifier, which contains two Arbel-Goldminz transconductances (g_{mf} and g_{mf}). The first stage transforms the differential voltages from input ports "p" and "n" into output current at intermediate port "z" with first transconductance (g_{mf}). While, the second stage transforms the voltage at intermediate port "z" into output currents at output ports "$x-$" and "$x+$" with second transconductance (g_{ms}). The block level representation of VDTA showing the associated port voltages and currents is depicted in Fig. 1. The various port voltages and currents of VDTA are related as

$$\begin{bmatrix} i_z \\ i_{x+} \\ i_{x-} \end{bmatrix} = \begin{bmatrix} g_{m1} & -g_{m1} & 0 \\ 0 & 0 & g_{m2} \\ 0 & 0 & -g_{m2} \end{bmatrix} \begin{bmatrix} v_p \\ v_n \\ v_z \end{bmatrix}, \tag{1}$$

where, the Arbel-Goldminz transconductances (g_{mf} and g_{ms}) are defined as [12]

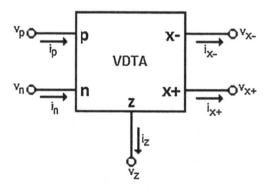

Fig. 1. Block level representation of VDTA.

$$g_{mf} = \frac{g_1 g_2}{g_1 + g_2} + \frac{g_3 g_4}{g_3 + g_4}, \tag{2}$$

$$g_{ms} = \frac{g_5 g_6}{g_5 + g_6} + \frac{g_7 g_8}{g_7 + g_8}. \tag{3}$$

$$\text{where, } g_j = \sqrt{\mu C_{ox}(W/L)_j I_{bias}} \tag{4}$$

is the transconductance and $(W/L)_j$ is the aspect ratio of jth MOS transistor. The value of j varies from 1 to 6. μ is carrier mobility; C_{ox} is the gate oxide capacitance and I_{bias} is external DC bias current of VDTA. Figure 2 represents the transistor level representation of VDTA and is displayed below.

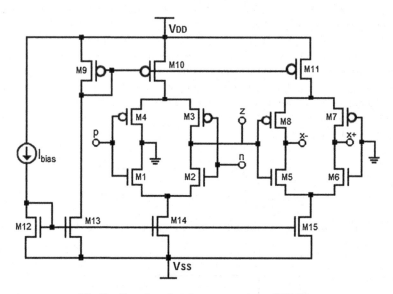

Fig. 2. Transistor level representation of VDTA.

3 Suggested Filter Configuration

The suggested VDTA based multi-functional current-mode (CM) single-input multi-output (SIMO) active filter configuration is shown in Fig. 3. The configuration comprises three VDTAs and two grounded capacitors (C_1 and C_2). The filter operates in current-mode (CM) and has one input current (i_{in}) and five corresponding output currents (i_{LP}, i_{HP}, i_{BP}, i_{BR} and i_{AP}). Routine analysis of the filter configuration using (1) yields the following current transfer functions

$$\frac{i_{LP}}{i_{in}} = \frac{g_{ms2} g_{ms3} g_{mf3}}{D(s)}, \tag{5}$$

$$\frac{i_{HP}}{i_{in}} = \frac{s^2 C_1 C_2 g_{mf2}}{D(s)}, \tag{6}$$

$$\frac{i_{BP}}{i_{in}} = \frac{s C_2 g_{ms2} g_{mf2}}{D(s)}. \tag{7}$$

The band-reject (BR) filter current transfer function is achieved by addition of output currents of HP and LP filter i.e. $i_{BR} = i_{HP} + i_{LP}$. The filter's current transfer function is achieved as

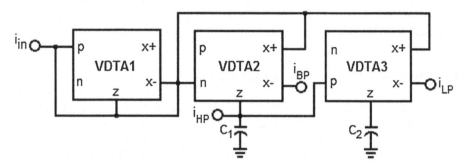

Fig. 3. Suggested filter configuration.

$$\frac{i_{BR}}{i_{in}} = \frac{s^2 C_1 C_2 g_{mf2} + g_{ms2} g_{ms3} g_{mf3}}{D(s)}. \tag{8}$$

The all-pass (AP) filter current transfer function is achieved by addition of output currents of HP, LP filter and inverted BP filter i.e. $i_{AP} = i_{HP} + i_{LP} - i_{BP}$. The filter's current transfer function is achieved as

$$\frac{i_{AP}}{i_{in}} = \frac{s^2 C_1 C_2 g_{mf2} + g_{ms2} g_{ms3} g_{mf3} - s C_2 g_{ms2} g_{mf2}}{D(s)}, \tag{9}$$

where,

$$D(s) = s^2 C_1 C_2 (g_{mf1} + g_{ms1}) + s C_2 g_{mf2} g_{ms2} + g_{mf2} g_{mf3} g_{ms3}. \tag{10}$$

Here g_{mf1}, g_{mf2}, g_{mf3} and g_{ms1}, g_{ms2}, g_{ms3} are the first stage and second stage transconductances of first, second and third VDTA respectively.

Therefore, from (5)–(9), it is observed that the designed multi-functional filter realizes LP, HP, BP, BR and AP filters with appropriate connection of input signals. The filter parameters i.e. the pole frequency (ω_p) and Q-factor (Q) for the suggested filter can be obtained from (10) as

$$\omega_0 = \sqrt{\frac{g_{mf2}g_{mf3}g_{ms3}}{(g_{mf1} + g_{ms1})C_1C_2}}, \tag{11}$$

$$Q = \frac{1}{g_{ms2}} \sqrt{\frac{g_{mf3}g_{ms3}(g_{mf1} + g_{ms1})C_1}{g_{mf2}C_2}}. \tag{12}$$

It can be observed from (11) and (12) that the pole frequency (ω_0) and Q-factor (Q) of the designed filter are controllable through transconductances of VDTA. Since the transconductances of VDTA depend on external DC bias current from (4). Therefore, the pole frequency (ω_p) and Q-factor (Q) are electronically controllable via external DC bias current. Moreover, the Q-factor (Q) of the designed filter can be self-controlled from the pole frequency (ω_p) through transconductance g_{ms2}.

4   Simulation Results and Discussion

The functionality of the designed multi-functional CM SIMO active filter using VDTA is investigated through Virtuoso Analog design Environment of Cadence. The simulations are performed at 45-nm technology node. The supply voltage is taken as V_{DD} (or $-V_{SS}$) = ± 900 mV. The bias currents are selected as I_{BIAS} = 150 μA. The overall power dissipation of the designed configuration is 1.8 mW. The following filter outputs realizing LP, HP, BP, BR and AP filter are achieved and is shown in Fig. 4. All the filters have the same pole frequency (ω_p) of 1 MHz. The transient response of the current-mode filter is shown in Fig. 5. The output sinusoidal current (i_{out}) as obtained by applying a input sinusoidal current having a total amplitude of 20 mA and frequency of 1 MHz. As shown in Fig. 5, the output transient waveform need some clock cycles to settle down and then after produces a stable current waveform. The table of comparison of the suggested filter configuration with other filter configuration is presented in Table 1.

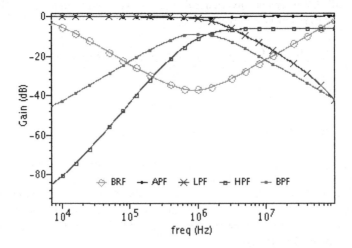

Fig. 4. Gain response of current-mode filters.

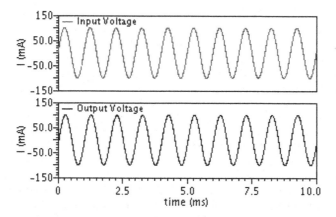

Fig. 5. Transient response of the suggested current-mode filter.

Table 1. Performance comparison with other reported works

Ref.	Standard filter functions	Passive components	Supply voltage	ω_0
[8]	LP, HP, BP (VM and CM mode)	Three C and One R	±0.9 V	1 MHz
[13]	LP, HP, BP, BR, AP	Two C and Two R	±2 V	3.03 MHz
[14]	LP, HP, BP (in VM mode) and LP, HP, BP, BR, AP (in TA mode)	Two C	±1.25 V	3.04 MHz
This work	LP, HP, BP, BR, AP (in CM mode)	Two C	±0.9 V	1 MHz

5 Conclusion

In the suggested paper, we have shown CM SIMO multi-functional active filter consisting of three VDTAs and two capacitors, which are grounded. The presented filter configuration realizes LP, HP, BP, BR and AP filters with relevant connections of input currents. The electronic and independent controllability pole frequency (ω_p) and Q-factor (Q) is provided depending upon the DC bias currents of VDTA. The suggested filter can be employed in communication, electronics, and instrumentation systems.

References

1. Kilinc, S., Keskin, A.U., Cam, U.: Cascadable voltage-mode multifunction biquad employing single OTRA. Frequenz **61**, 84–86 (2007)
2. Shah, N.A., Quadri, M., Iqbal, S.Z.: CDTA based universal trans-admittance filter. Analog Integr. Circ. Sig. Process. **52**, 65–69 (2007)
3. Horng, J.W.: Voltage-mode universal bi-quadratic filter using two OTAs and two capacitors. IEICE Trans. Fundam. Electron. Commun. Comput. Sci. **E86A**, 411–413 (2003)

4. Tangsrirat, W., Jetsdaporn, S.: Compact VDTA-based current-mode electronically tunable universal filters using grounded capacitors. Microelectron. J. **45**, 613–618 (2014)
5. Pandey, N., Paul, S.K.: SIMO trans-admittance-mode active-C universal filter. J. Circ. Syst. **1**, 54–58 (2010)
6. Chen, H.P.: Universal voltage-mode filter using only plus-type DDCC's. Analog Integr. Circ. Sig. Process. **50**(2), 137–139 (2007)
7. Horng, J.W.: High-input impedance voltage-mode universal biquadratic filter using three plus-type CCIIs. IEEE Trans. Circ. Syst. II: Analog Digit. Sig. Process. **48**, 996–997 (2001)
8. Pandey, R., Pandey, N., Singhal, N.: Single VDTA based dual mode single input multioutput biquad filter. J. Eng. **2016**, 1–10 (2016)
9. Biolek, D., Senani, R., Biolkova, V., Kolka, Z.: Active elements for analog signal processing: classification, review, and new proposals. Radioengineering **17**(4), 15–32 (2008)
10. Kumar, V., Mehra, R., Islam, A.: A 2.5 GHz low power, high-Q, reliable design of active bandpass filter. IEEE Trans. Device Mater. Reliab. **17**(1), 229–244 (2017)
11. Mehra, R., Kumar, V., Islam, A.: Floating active inductor based Class-C VCO with 8 digitally tuned sub-bands. AEU-Int. J. Electron. Commun. **83**, 1–10 (2017)
12. Arbel, A.F., Goldminz, L.: Output stage for current-mode feedback amplifiers, theory and applications. Analog Integr. Circ. Sig. Process. **2**(3), 243–255 (1992)
13. Satansup, J., Pukkalanun, T., Tangsrirat, W.: Electronically tunable single-input five-output voltage-mode universal filter using VDTAs and grounded passive elements. Circ. Syst. Sig. Process. **32**(3), 945–957 (2013)
14. Chamnanphai, V., Sa-ngiamvibool, W.: Electronically tunable SIMO mixed-mode universal filter using VDTAs. Przegląd Elektrotechniczny **1**(3), 209–213 (2017)

Robustness Study of Muller C-element

Komal Agrawal, Sneha Chowdhury, Shashank Kumar Dubey[(✉)],
and Aminul Islam

Department of Electronics and Communication Engineering,
Birla Institute of Technology, Mesra, Ranchi, Jharkhand, India
k.ag.gumla@gmail.com, dubey.shashank1991@gmail.com,
aminulislam@bitmesra.ac.in

Abstract. This paper analyses the static implementation of Muller C-element based on CNFET and MOSFET. Muller C-element is a state holding circuit in which the output is equal to that of input if both the inputs are similar else it holds the previous state [1]. We are comparing the performance of CNFET based circuit to that of MOSFET based circuit because of the known fact that CNFET has high channel capacity and better gate capacitance versus voltage characteristics. PVT variation of the circuit is done by using Monte Carlo analysis at 32-nm technology node for CNFET whereas MOSFET at 22-nm technology node on HSPICE [2]. The Muller C-element is simulated at nominal supply voltage 0.95 V with a $\pm 10\%$ variation in it [3]. Impact of temperature variation on ON-current (ON-current variability) is analyzed by varying the temperature from -50 °C to 80 °C (-50 °C to 150 °C) [4].

Keywords: CNFET · MOSFET · CNT

1 Introduction

Carbon nanotube field effect transistor (CNFET) is widely growing as it has many advantages over MOSFET. In this paper, a state holding circuit known as Muller C-element circuit is implemented. Muller C-element is also well known as C–gate or coincident flip flop. It is generally used in asynchronous circuits for data storage. Muller C-element is an essential component of virtually any handshaking module used in transceiver. Muller C-element circuit is named after American mathematician and computer scientist David E Muller who proposed it in 1955 [5]. Muller C-element is similar to S-R latch which is also a state holding circuit. Table 1 shows the output of S-R latch and the circuit diagram of S-R latch is shown in Fig. 1. But the limitation of SR latch is that it gives an invalid state when both the inputs are 1. Muller C-element overcomes this limitation as it gives output same as input when both the inputs are same [6].

Table 1. S-R latch

Input 1 (S)	Input 2 (R)	Output (Q_{n+1})
0	0	Q_n
0	1	0
1	0	1
1	1	Invalid

J. K. Mandal and D. Sinha (Eds.): CSI 2017, CCIS 836, pp. 131–139, 2018.
https://doi.org/10.1007/978-981-13-1343-1_15

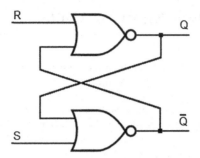

Fig. 1. S-R latch.

The static implementation of Muller C-element shows a better performance in terms of average power, current, PDP, EDP when CNFET technology is used. For static implementation, the basic parameters like voltage and temperature are varied and its effect on design metrics (average Power, PDP, EDP) using both CNFET and MOSFET is observed. This shows that the design metrics have higher values for MOSFET than for CNFET and variations is high in MOSFET implementation than in CNFET implementation, exhibiting the robustness of the circuit if realized with CNFET.

CNFET is more robust than MOSFET against PVT variation. With the technology scaling, the variability is playing a significant role in the analysis of circuits. The robustness is shown by low variability in CNFET as compared to MOSFET. CNFET being the stable one, has low deviation in PDP, EDP, average power and current from its mean values. This reduces the overall value of variability.

2 Carbon Nanotube Field Effect Transistor: An Emerging Device

With the passage of time the technical world is changing. The smaller the technology, the better it is. Presently the era of nanotechnology is going on which uses nanoscale MOSFETs for realizing circuits and systems. However, due to aggressive scaling of MOSFET devices, designing robust circuits has become a challenging task for a circuit designer. Carbon nanotube field effect transistors are a new device with better future [7]. There is a possibility that the coming era will use CNFET rather than MOSFET. The fabrication process is difficult but similar to MOSFET. However, CNFET offers low losses in the circuit. N-type and P- type CNFET are different from N-type and P-type MOSFET. In CNFET N-type and P-type have same mobility and driving current, this is not the case with MOSFET.

CNTs are the hollow cylindrical rolled sheets of Graphene. The CNTs are two types [8]. Single-walled CNT (SWCNT) contains a single Graphene sheet. The multi-walled CNT (MWCNT) contains multiple number of Graphene sheets rolled in a concentric manner. More or less the SWCNT are similar to that of MWCNT. The advantage with MWCNT is that they are more resistant to chemical [9].

Chirality (a, b) is an important parameter in CNFETs [8]. Diameter of CNTs can be calculated using chirality. The condition when a = b or a − b = 3n, where n is an integer, the material acts as a metal. For conditions other than this it is a semiconductor. Threshold voltage (Vt), chirality (C) and diameter (D) of CNTs can be calculated using following equations [10].

$$D_{CNT} = \frac{a}{\pi} \sqrt{n_1^2 + n_2^2 + n_1 n_2} \tag{1}$$

$$V_t \approx \frac{E_g}{2q} = \frac{aV_\pi}{\sqrt{3} \times qD_{CNT}} \tag{2}$$

where, E_g is energy gap, q is electronic charge. V_π = 3.033 eV is the carbon π–to–π bond energy in the tight bonding model. a = $\sqrt{3}$d = 2.49 Å is the lattice constant (where d = 1.44 Å is inter carbon atom distance).

3 Operation of Muller C-element

Muller C-element circuit forms the fundamental element for asynchronous circuits. The output of Muller C-element circuit alters to 1 if all the inputs are 1 and to 0 if all the inputs are 0. So, it can be regarded as a non-inverting buffer. For other combinations of input, it retains the previous state of the output [6]. This nature of Muller C-element circuit is used for synchronization of many inputs. In flip flops, clock edge decides the reference for output. On the contrary, in case of Muller C-element, reference is based on output change. So, it is used in asynchronous circuits. The transitions in Muller C-element will only take place if both the inputs are high i.e., output will produce a rising transition. If both the inputs are low, the output will produce a falling edge [11]. This circuit is also used for designing self-timing circuits' i.e., it makes every transition in asynchronous circuit meaningful in absence of the clock [12]. C-elements show resemblance to AND-OR-INVERT logic or OR- AND-INVERT gate logic. After simulation in HSPICE the plot of Muller C-element obtained is shown in Fig. 2. Muller C-element circuit is shown in Fig. 3. In the circuit X and Y are the input for the Muller C-element and Z_{n+1} is the output of the circuit. The circuit uses P type CNFET named as CP1, CP2, CP3, CP4, CP5 and CP6. N type CNFET named as CN1, CN2, CN3, CN4, CN5 and CN6 are also used in the circuit.

In this article, static realization of Muller C-element is analyzed. In static implementation, capacitors are substituted by transistor logic. The number of gate transistors should be as less as possible to nullify the internal delay in the circuit. The static implementation of Muller C-element shows the presence of two cross coupled inverters at the output [13]. These inverters help to give required output by allowing the input to control the output. Also, this circuit has a feedback loop to pass the output to all the input states. This is how the function of state holding in Muller C-element is implemented. It holds the previous state without driving any other output when '0 and 1' or '1 and 0' is given as input. The output of the Muller C-element circuit is shown in Table 2.

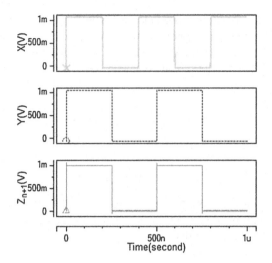

Fig. 2. Plot of Muller-C-element.

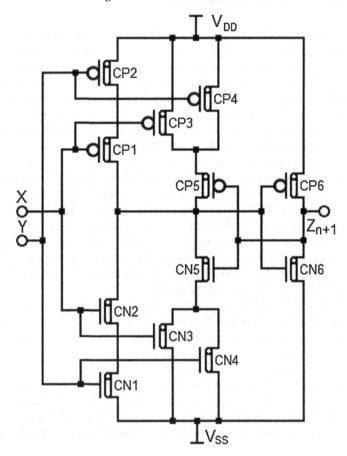

Fig. 3. Diagram of Muller-C-element.

Table 2. Truth table of Muller-C-element

Input 1 (X)	Input 2 (Y)	Output (Z_{n+1})
0	0	0
0	1	Z_n
1	0	Z_n
1	1	1

The state logic function of Muller C-element is identified as a combination of AND gates given by

$$Z_{n+1} = XY + (X + Y)Z_n \tag{3}$$

Where, X and Y are inputs and Z_{n+1} is the output.

4 Simulation Results and Discussion

In the aggressively scaled devices, circuit parameters are not robust and they are prone to process, voltage and temperature (PVT) variations [4]. In this paper, we have analyzed the effect of variations in change in voltage. Voltage is varied from 0.9 V to 1.0 V. There is a significant change in the circuit parameters. The increase is seen in the average power, EDP and PDP. At the same time variability in the circuit decreases with increase in voltage in CNFETs whereas there is significant increase in the variability with increase in voltage in MOSFETs. The change in temperature has its own effect in the circuit parameters. ON-current, EDP and PDP increases with the increase in temperature.

4.1 Average Power Estimation and Its Variability Analysis

The Muller C-element is analyzed by varying the nominal supply voltage of 0.98 V by 10% and observing its effect on the average power of the circuit. Average power ($P_{AVG} = P_{STATIC} + P_{DYNAMIC}$) for a given period T has two components: static power (P_{STATIC}) and dynamic power ($P_{DYNAMIC}$), which are expressed as shown below:

$$P_{STATIC} = I_{OFF} \times V_{DD} \tag{4}$$

$$P_{DYNAMIC} = \frac{1}{T} \int_0^T I_{ON}(t) V_{DD} dt \tag{5}$$

where I_{OFF} is the leakage current, which includes subthreshold leakage current, gate leakage current, junction leakage current and gate-induced drain leakage current and I_{ON} is the ON current of the devices.

Muller C-element is implemented both using CNFET and MOSFET and the results are compared [3]. Figure 4 is the plot of average power versus supply voltage which shows the variation in average power with change in supply voltage for both CNFET and MOSFET. The dynamic power is also expressed as.

$$P_{DYNAMIC} = V_{DD}^2 \times f \times C_L \times \alpha \qquad (6)$$

where, f is the switching frequency, C_L is the capacitive load α is the switching activity factor $(0.4 < \alpha < 1)$.

It can be observed from the above equations that the average power increases as the supply voltage increases. Observing the case of CNFET, identical results are obtained i.e., average power increases with increase in the supply voltage but in case of CNFET the increase is not so large as in case of MOSFET. So, comparatively, there is low power consumption in CNFET for the same supply voltage. This is mainly because of lower leakage currents in CNFET.

We have also performed variability analysis of average power. It can be observed from Fig. 5 that the CNFET-based Muller C-element exhibits narrower spread in average power as compared to its MOSFET counterpart. This implies that the CNFET-based Muller C-element is more robust as compared to MOSFET based Muller C-element. So, it can be concluded that CNFET based circuit is highly applicable for cases where low power is to be dissipated [14] and circuit need to be robust.

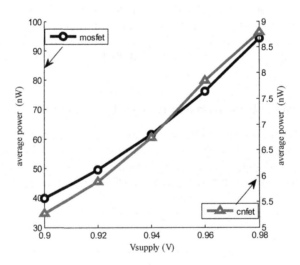

Fig. 4. Plot of average power (nW) vs. voltage (V).

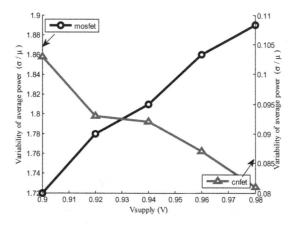

Fig. 5. Plot of variability of average power vs. voltage (V).

4.2 ON-current Estimation and Its Variability Analysis

It is the current flowing between the drain and source when a device in the circuit is in ON state. Temperature is varied from −50 °C to 150 °C [4]. ON-current increases with the increase in temperature as shown in the plot and in the table. This is due to the fact that there is a significant vibration in the circuit with the increase in voltage which leads to the overall increase in mobility of charge carrier of the devices in the circuit. As mobility increases the current in the circuit increases which clearly justify our observation [15]. Plot of ON-current versus temperature is shown in Fig. 6.

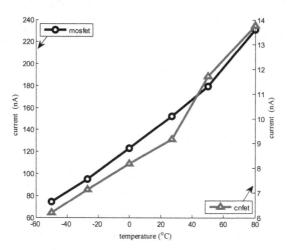

Fig. 6. Plot of current vs. temperature.

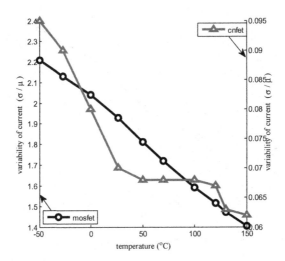

Fig. 7. Plot of variability of current vs. temperature.

Variability analysis is an important part of the analysis of a nanoscale circuit [9, 4]. Variability being the ratio of sigma (σ) by mean (μ) value of the parameter, gives the measure of variation in design metrics. As can be observed from Fig. 7, the CNFET-based Muller C-element exhibit tighter spread in current variability as compared to its CMOS counterpart. Being more robust has low variability as compared to MOSFET. From the observation it is clear that CNEFTs have low variability than MOSFET [2]. It is interesting to note that the variability decreases with increase in temperature due to the continuous increase in the mean value in the case of MOSFET. For CNFET the variability decreases from −50 °C to 50 °C and then becomes constant for 50 °C to 100 °C and again decreases for temperature 100 °C to 150 °C [15] as shown in the Fig. 7.

5 Conclusion

The main objective of this paper is to compare the performance of state holding circuit, Muller C-element when it is statically implemented by CNFET and CMOS using Monte Carlo simulations. The circuit is subjected to voltage and temperature variation. The observed results show that for given value of voltage, CNFET based model dissipates very low average power compared to MOSFET-based Muller C-element. Hence, it can be stated that CNFET based Muller C-element is more power efficient. As far as temperature variation is concerned, estimated values of ON-current for CNFET circuit is less than that of its CMOS counterpart. These results show that CNFET-based design exhibits lower variability in average power and ON-current as compared to MOSFET-based design. So, it is concluded that CNFET based Muller C-element is more robust against variations in environmental parameters such as supply voltage and operating temperature.

References

1. Nguyen, N.P.D., Kuwahara, H., Myers, C.J., Keener, J.P.: The design of a genetic Muller C-element. In: 13th IEEE International Symposium on Asynchronous Circuits and Systems (ASYNC 2007), Berkeley, CA, pp. 95–104 (2007)
2. Sedra, A., Smith, K.C.: A second generation current conveyor and its applications. IEEE Trans. Circ. Theory **CT-17**, 132–134 (1970)
3. Sedra, A., Smith, K.C.: A second-generation current conveyor and its applications. IEEE Trans. Circ. Theory **17**(1), 132–134 (1970)
4. Sedra, A., Smith, K.C.: Microelectronic Circuits. Oxford University Press, New York (1999)
5. Antoniou, A.: Realisation of gyrators using operational amplifiers, and their use in RC-active-network synthesis. In: Proceedings of the Institution of Electrical Engineers, pp. 1838–1850 (1969)
6. Pal, K.: Floating inductance and FDNR using positive polarity current conveyors. Act. Passive Electron. Comp. J. **33**(21), 81–83 (2004)
7. Madian, A.H., Mahmoud, S.A., Soliman, A.M.: New 1.5 V CMOS second generation current conveyor based on wide range transcondutor. Analog Integr. Circ. Sig. Process. **49**, 267–297 (2006)
8. Ferri, G., Guerrini, N.C.: Low Voltage Low Power CMOS Current Conveyors. Springer, New York (2003). https://doi.org/10.1007/b105853
9. Chatterjee, A., Fakhfakh, M., Siarry, P.: Design of second-generation current conveyors employing bacterial foraging optimization. Microelectron. J. **41**(10), 616–626 (2010)
10. Sagbas, M., Ayten, U.E., Sedef, H., Koksal, M.: Floating immittance function simulator and its applications. Circ. Syst. Sig. Process. **28**(1), 55–63 (2009)
11. Kiranon, W., Pawarangkoon, P.: Floating inductance simulation based on current conveyors. Electron. Lett. **33**(21), 1748–1749 (1997)
12. Sedaf, H., Acar, C.: Simulation of resistively LC ladder filters using a new basic cell involving current conveyors. Microelectron. J. **30**(1), 63–86 (1999)
13. Pal, K.: Novel floating inductance using current conveyors. Electron. Lett. **17**(18), 638 (1981)
14. Surakampontorn, W., Riewruja, V., Kumwachara, K., Dejhan, K.: Accurate CMOS-based current conveyors. IEEE Trans. Instrum. Meas. **40**(4), 699–702 (1991)
15. Nguyen, V.H., Song, H.: Impact of temperature variation on performance of carbon nanotube field-effect transistor-based on chaotic oscillator: a quantum simulation study. Chin. Phys. Lett. **32**(3), 038201 (2015)

Automated Cobb Angle Computation
from Scoliosis Radiograph

Raka Kundu[1]([⊠]), Amlan Chakrabarti[1], and Prasanna Lenka[2]

[1] Department of A. K. Choudhury School of Information Technology,
University of Calcutta, Kolkata, India
kundu.raka@gmail.com, acakcs@caluniv.ac.in
[2] Department of Rehab Engineering,
National Institute for the Orthopaedically Handicapped, Kolkata, India
lenka_pk@yahoo.co.uk

Abstract. In this paper we propose a fully automatic technique for Cobb angle computation from Scoliosis radiograph image where the objectives are to have no user intervention and to increase the reliability of spinal curvature magnitude quantification. The automatic technique mainly comprises of four steps, namely: Preprocessing, ROI identification, Object centerline extraction and Cobb angle computation from the extracted spine centerline. Bilateral image denoising is considered as the preprocessing step. Support Vector Machine classifier is used for object identification. We have assumed that the spine is a continuous contour rather than a series of discrete vertebral bodies with individual orientations. Morphological operation, Gaussian blurring, spine centerline approximation and polynomial fit are used to extract the centerline of spine. The tangent at every point of the extracted centerline is taken and Cobb angle is evaluated from these tangent values. To analyze the automated diagnosis technique, the proposed approach was evaluated on a set of 21 coronal radiograph images. Identification of ROI based on Support Vector Machine classifier is effective enough with a sensitivity and specificity of 100% and the center line extraction from this ROI gave correct results for 57.14% subjects with very less or negligible angular variability. As the vertebral endplates in radiograph images have poor contrast due to reduced radiation dose, the continuous contour based approach gives better reliability.

Keywords: Spine radiograph (X-ray) image · Scoliosis · Cobb's method
Support Vector Machine · Gabor feature
Automated Computer Aided Detection and Diagnosis

1 Introduction

Scoliosis [7] a 3-dimensional deformity of spine is normally characterized by lateral curvature and often accompanied by rotation of individual vertebrae. The magnitude of scoliosis is determined by lateral curvature computation from medical image. This paper has selected the widely practiced Cobb's method [7] for realizing the spine curve magnitude. Manual Cobb's method from printed medical image includes identification of extreme vertebrae of the curve, which incline more severely towards the curve

© Springer Nature Singapore Pte Ltd. 2018
J. K. Mandal and D. Sinha (Eds.): CSI 2017, CCIS 836, pp. 140–155, 2018.
https://doi.org/10.1007/978-981-13-1343-1_16

coactivity. One line is drawn following slope of upper extreme vertebrae and another line is drawn through slope of lower extreme vertebrae. Finally the interior angle formed by intersection of these two lines is the Cobb's angle which gives the curve magnitude. An example is given in Fig. 1.

Radiograph imaging is common non-invasive form of diagnosis. This Cobb angle computation using radiograph image is standardized by the Scoliosis Research Society [12]. Cobb's method is widely preferred because of its easier application and proper management of large spinal curvature angles. Many times there is not enough number of doctors or trained technicians to interpret the medical information from the image. So, a fully automatic Computer Aided Detection and Diagnosis (CADx) plays a significant role in medical treatment. Object recognition and segmentation are challenging tasks in radiograph image due to low radiation dose and anatomical overlap property. Such object recognition algorithm and segmentation techniques must accomplish its tasks in accurate and robust manner, because false results of CADx will break interpretation confidence and will reduce its clinical practice acceptability.

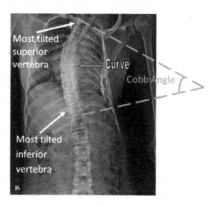

Fig. 1. The figure shows a coronal radiograph image of Scoliosis curve and the traditional manual Cobb angle computation method

2 Related Works

In past years many digital techniques have been put forward for spine curve magnitude computation. The proposed work in this paper uses image processing techniques to develop an automated Cobb angle computation method for spinal curvature. The motivation of the proposed research is discussed in Sect. 3. "Our Approach" is followed by Sect. 4, "Automated Cobb Angle Computation" that explains the process for Cobb angle evaluation. In Sect. 5 "Results and Discussion" possess visual and experimental results with discussion. Conclusion and future work are discussed in Sect. 6.

Jeifries et al. [10] put a pair of points on every vertebra to approximate the center between each pair of points. Lines were taken parallel to vertebral body for calculating the Cobb angle. The method required much user intervention. Wever et al. [21]

proposed a technique for Cobb method. The technique required six manual landmarks on every vertebra of the anterior-posterior input radiograph image. The coordinate values of landmarks helped in computing the midpoint of vertebral bodies. The lateral tilts of upper and lower endplates of every vertebra were computed by the computer algorithm. Huang et al. [9] proposed a fully automatic technique for Cobb method. The algorithm contains preprocessing, image segmentation and automatic Cobb angle measurement. The first step includes removing noise by Gaussian smoothing and histogram equalization to improve image quality. The second step possesses segmentation of vertebral column including ribs from the whole body bone scan. The Cobb angle is measured in the final step. The validation of the technique was performed on 11 random selected whole body bone scan image. The CADx results were compared with results obtained from experienced physician and a mean difference of 4.14 degree was obtained. We expect to have more experiments to validate the technique. Allen et al. [2] put forward a reliable Cobb angle computation technique using active shape model. Training set of radiograph images was taken that represented the scoliosis curve. The training set helped in recognition of vertebrae. The drawback of the technique was that active shape models could only produce shapes similar to the training set. At the time of training the boundary of the object is created by manual digitized landmark points on the perimeter of the region of interest. Zhang et al. [23] proposed a technique on Cobb angle measurement with prior vertebral shape. The extreme vertebrae of the curve which tilt more toward the curve coactivity were selected. Edge detection and Fuzzy Hough transform were performed to find the slope of the endplates of the two ROI. Cobb angle was computed from the obtained slopes. The technique is not user intervention free. Duong et al. [5] proposed a technique for detection of spinal curves from posterior-anterior radiograph image. Region of interest (ROI) was extracted. The region possesses 17 bounding boxes indicating T1 to L5 vertebral level. Texture descriptors for every block are computed and taken for training with support vector machines. Then vertebral regions are predicted and curve is fitted through the centers of predicted vertebral regions. A computer aided technique was proposed by Abuzaghleh and Barkana [1] where the ROI (spine) was cropped from the whole image. Sobel edge detection and image binarization helps in segmentation of the spine. The segmented spine was divided into blocks followed by contrast enhancement. Finally the Hough transform detected the slopes of the curvature. The number of experiments for establishing the reliability was very less. Besides this the technique need a prior selection of ROI. Anitha and Prabhu [3] put forward a technique for quantification of spinal curve in Scoliosis radiology image. The digital computation is done on a cropped ROI. Anisotropic diffusion denoising, Active Contour based vertebrae segmentation, morphological operations and Hough transform were used to compute the Cobb angle from the input radiograph. The proposed technique was validated on 250 radiograph image and shows reduced intra-observer and inter-observer error. These errors occurred due to selection of different end vertebrae. The major drawback of the technique is performing the CADx on a ROI. So, it can be said that the digital computation is not totally free from user interaction. There lies a scope of improvement to make the computation intervention free. Shaw et al. [17] put forward a technique for Cobb angle measurement in scoliosis using iPhone. Smartphone Cobb measurements were done using Apple iPhone, and a Tiltmeter software. The software was downloaded from Apple iTunes store. The Tiltmeter software required printed X-ray image and position the X-ray image on X-ray reader box. However the technique is not totally automated and requires printed X-ray images. Samuval et al. [14] proposed a mask-based segmentation algorithm for computation of Cobb angle from radiograph image. A manual landmark on center of each vertebra was taken. The mask was placed on the landmark and was resized to get the best match. So, one drawback is the technique needed user interaction. Sardjona et al. [15] proposed a technique for Cobb angle computation. A modified Charged Particle Model (CPM) has been developed and used to determine the spinal curvature. The radiograph image was charged negatively depending on the gradient-magnitude image, where the particles were attracted towards the object contour. The Cobb angle was computed from the spine contour. Yildiz [22] proposed a Computer-assisted Cobb angle measurement technique from posterior-anterior radiographs by curve fitting. Inaccurate selection of end vertebrae of a Scoliosis curve causes measurement errors in Cobb method. In this paper such subjectivity problem has been minimized by using a curve fitting method. Midpoints defined by user on digital posterior-anterior radiograph image denote the midpoints of the vertebrae. The midpoints were used to fit the polynomial equation. The end vertebrae locations were calculated using first order derivative of the polynomial equation and the Cobb angle was obtained. Small angle deviation proved that subjectivity was minimized. The drawback of the method is that it required user intervention.

3 Our Approach

The major contributions of our work are emphasized as follows:

1. The proposed approach automatically identifies the region of interest (ROI), the spinal column. We have used Support Vector Machine classifier and Gabor feature to fit our purpose. The classification method was followed by morphological operation and outlier rejection of ROI. We have achieved a sensitivity and specificity of 100% for our identification method.
2. Some Scoliosis involves deformation of vertebrae where the end plate and edges of vertebrae are not properly visible in radiograph image. This deformation of vertebrae is also the source of error in the selection of extreme vertebrae in traditional Cobb method. This problem is overcome by our technique where the spine is considered as a continuous structure.
3. As our technique has assumed the spine as a continuous structure, our technique works well for low radiation dose radiograph image where the vertebral endplates are not properly visible. Thus reducing the affect of ionization.
4. No manual intervention is required for the total process. The paper proposes a totally automated CADx for Cobb angle determination.
5. Cobb angle is the final result of the automated diagnosis. Our results were validated on 21 radiograph images and we have achieved reliable Cobb angle magnitude for 57.14% cases.

This paper proposes a first of its kind CADx approach for automated Cobb angle determination from digital radiograph image and shows reduced variability for estimating angle value. The method is based on supervised learning and no manual input was taken for the computation.

4 Automated Cobb Angle Computation

To perform Cobb method, the most tilted end vertebral bodies of the Scoliosis curve must be first selected. The vertebrae that have greatest tilt with respect to the horizontal baseline are the end vertebrae of the Scoliosis curvature. From literature review it can be revealed that segmentation of vertebral bodies and then decision about most tilted end vertebrae of curvature are another source of errors.

Most segmentation depends on edge information. Objects possessing prominent and continuous edges are comparatively easier for segmentation. Coronal radiograph image of spine have weak edges due to its accusation at low X-ray radiation. Low X-ray radiation is always preferred because X-ray is ionized in nature. It is always taken care to have an X-ray image that serve the diagnosis with use of minimum radiation dose. X-ray image also have anatomical overlap property where one structure overlap other. This increases the difficulty for segmentation. Besides this object shape variation is natural property in medical images. The spine is required to be isolated from undesired details like, the ribs, pelvic girdle, lungs and other organs. To overcome this we have considered the spine as a continuous structure which runs from top to bottom instead of number of isolated vertebral bodies. This assumption will help us to overcome the erroneous result that can occur due to segmentation. We have directly obtained the centerline of spine.

Slope at every point of the centerline are computed. Due to unavailability of enough number of double curvature (S-shaped) cases, we have showed our automated computation results for single curvature (C-shaped) Scoliosis. The longest adjacent positive and negative slope series were taken into account and the maximum positive slope and the minimum negative slope were added to get the Cobb angle. The pointing out of center points having maximum positive and minimum negative slopes of longest series is equivalent to the decision about most tilted end vertebrae of the scoliosis curve. So, this step further reduces the computation error.

Figure 2 presents the workflow of the proposed CADx. The process mainly comprise of four steps: Preprocessing, ROI identification, Object centerline extraction and Cobb angle computation from the centerline.

4.1 Preprocessing Using Bilateral Filter

Presence of noise in image will disturb image processing steps. In our proposed supervised technique the radiograph training-set and the input test radiograph image are preprocessed by Bilateral filter [19]. The filter preserves edges and features while removing noise from the image.

4.2 ROI Identification Using Support Vector Machine and Gabor Feature

Support Vector Machine (SVM) classifier using Gabor features is used for vertebral column recognition from coronal spine radiograph image.

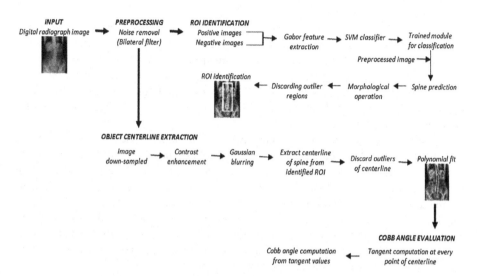

Fig. 2. Sequential steps of automated Cobb angle detection

In digital image processing, Gabor filter [Wikipedia] is a linear filter for edge detection. Frequency and orientation description of Gabor filters has high resemblance to that of human visual system, and they are found to be particularly proper for texture representation and distinction. Simple cells present in visual cortex of mammalian brains can be sculpted by Gabor functions. So, image analysis using Gabor filters is expected to be alike to perception in human visual system.

SVM [4, 13, 20] is associated with supervised classification which analysis data and recognizes pattern for regression and classification problem. SVM tries to maximize the decision boundary between two classes that helps in better classification. It is also efficient in classifying the object which is not linearly separable. The input data set is mapped to higher dimensional space where the data is separable by hyper-plane. It gives less over fitting. A set of feature vectors of radiograph vertebrae images were taken for designing the classifier. The training set possessed 506 numbers of positive images and 641 numbers of negative images. We took vertebra as positive image and other regions of spine radiograph as negative images. A generalized tool [16] using SVM classifier and Gabor feature was optimized for our classification implementation. We have prepared the positive and negative image database using spine radiograph images. The radiograph images were obtained from National Institute for the Orthopaedically Handicapped (NIOH).

Obtaining ROI

The resultant image from classification was converted to binary image. ***Morphological operation*** like *hole filling* [6] was performed to fill holes of binary image. A hole is a region of dark pixels (considered as background) surrounded by white pixels (foreground) in the binary image. Hole filling in digital image is accomplished based on dilation, complementation and intersection. In our CADx, the hole filling operation was performed on the identified regions.

Due to low contrast, structure overlapping property of radiograph image, variation of shape and size of vertebrae, some small isolated regions other than vertebral column were identified. Vertebral column lies in the center of the image. So, ***rejecting regions*** from extreme left and right portion would not create any disturbance in the next steps. To avoid the isolated regions the width of the coronal radiograph was divided into 5 segments. The regions that were in the first and last segment were not considered for the later computation.

Centroid of every region was computed. The centroid possessed two values, the X-coordinate and the Y-coordinate. The vertebral column has the central position in the radiograph image. So, the mean value of Y is taken which gives the estimated vertebral column central position along the width of the image. A 90 pixels length was considered as the width of ROI for a radiograph image having size 304×250. A width of length 45 pixels was subtracted from the central position and a width of length 45 pixels was added to the central position. This gave the width of the ROI. The height of ROI was considered along the minimum X-coordinate and maximum X-coordinate value. Figure 3 represents outputs from this section.

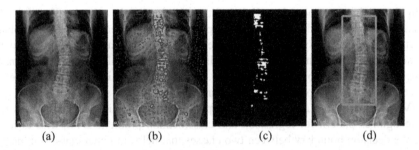

(a)	(b)	(c)	(d)

Fig. 3. (a) Input image (b) Output of SVM classification using Gabor feature (c) Output obtained after morphological operation and rejection of regions (d) Identified ROI from centroid values

Object Centerline Extraction

Obtaining Continuous Structure

If we observe the vertebral column from up-down position, it appears as a continuous structure. The endplate in the radiograph image partitions the structure into segments. Down-sampling the radiograph will reduce the information of endplate which is not required in our next computational steps of the proposed CADx. Down-sampling will simultaneously reduce the vertical edge information of the spine. This edge makes the vertebral column appear like a canal. The vertebral column which is hard tissue has higher intensity value in comparison to the regions that lie on the left and right side of the vertebral column. So, even after down-sampling, the vertical lines of the vertebrae can be distinguished from its background. The radiograph image in the experiment is down-sampled to 213 × 175. Histogram equalization is performed on the down-sampled image to get better contrast. Matlab function "histeq" is used for this operation. As only centerline of spine is required for our automated Cobb computation, we are interested with only the spine. High Gaussian blurring was performed on the radiograph image that made the spine centerline and contour more prominent like a continuous structure, reducing other information of the spine. The next operation for centerline extraction was performed on this blurred image considering only the pre-determined ROI. Figure 4 shows the results from this section.

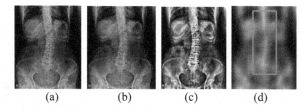

(a)   (b)   (c)   (d)

Fig. 4. (a) Original image (b) Down-sampled image (c) Contrast enhanced image (d) Output after high Gaussian blurring where the spine in radiograph image appears like a continuous structure. The bounding box shows the ROI superimposed on the blurred image where it encapsulates the continuous structured spinal column

Centerline Extraction
Center point is considered as a single point along a row of the ROI. The pixel having maximum intensity along a row is selected as the center point of the spine for that particular row. The center point determination starts from the first row and continues till the end row of the ROI. For every row we have an approximated center point. As the vertebral column is of hard tissue, it has higher intensity in comparison to its surrounding soft tissue region. It is observed that in most cases after high Gaussian blur ring the center of the spine for any particular row of the ROI has highest intensity value in that row. Figure 5 shows an intensity plot of rows in the ROI. Center points esti-mated from up down position of the spine gives the vertebral column centerline. We have selected three subjects for the illustration.

Outlier Rejection
Some outliers if present after extraction of centerline were rejected based on the median value of the Y-coordinate of the centerline. The variation of the centerline was in Y-direction of the spine. Center points having Y-coordinates within the range median −15 pixels and median +15 pixels was observed to be a suitable range to consider the real center points and reject the outliers that lie far from the center of the spine.

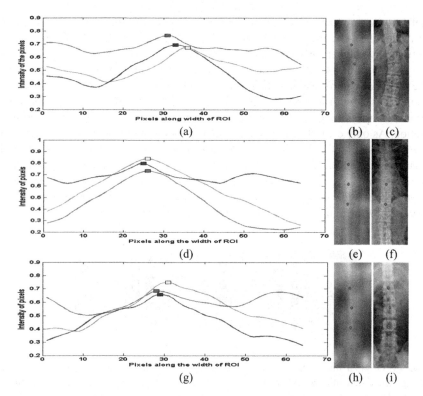

Fig. 5. (a), (d), (g), shows the intensity plot of 40th, 70th and 100th row from the three respective radiograph subjects, where the highest intensity value of the row represent the center-point of the vertebral column. (b), (e), (h) are the superimposed center points on the respective Gaussian blurred image. (c), (f), (i) are the superimposed center points on original input image

Polynomial Fit

A polynomial fit (curve fitting) was performed based on Y-coordinate. The operation involved interpolation that was performed on the pixel coordinated of the extracted spine centerline. A 3rd order polynomial was considered for the polynomial fit which means that the polynomial will fit through 4 points of the obtained centerline. In MATLAB for polynomial fit there is polynomial function. The "polyfit" function of order 3 was used to determine the polynomials. "polyval" function was followed to evaluate the new Y-coordinated of the polynomial curve. Figure 6 shows outputs from this section.

Cobb Angle Computation from the Centerline

Tangent

After polynomial fit on the extracted centerline, tangent was computed at every center point to get slope value. Slope value can be positive, negative or zero. For concave down graph, slopes of a tangent are decreasing as travelled from left to right and slope value increases when traveled right to left for concave up graph. Positive and negative slopes are explained in Fig. 7.

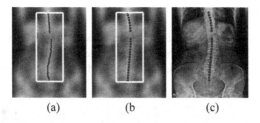

(a)   (b   (c)

Fig. 6. (a) Center points estimated from blurred ROI. Center points of this radiograph image have some outliers. (b) Shows polynomial fit from center points after outlier rejection. (c) Center points on original input image

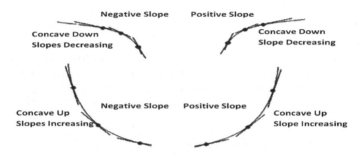

Fig. 7. Representing positive and negative slopes of a curve

Cobb Angle Evaluation from Tangent
After calculating slope of every center point, the longest consecutive positive and negative slope series was selected as the curvature for computing the Cobb angle of the Scoliosis spine. The maximum positive slope and the minimum negative slope of the series represented the slope of the extreme vertebrae of the Scoliosis curve that tilt more severely w.r.t. the horizontal axis. The maximum positive slope and minimum negative slope values were summed together to generate the Cobb angle.

5   Results and Discussion

Radiograph images are taken from National Institute for the Orthopaedically Handi-capped (Ministry of Social Justice and Empowerment) medical database. The experiments were validated on 21 digital radiograph images. For implementation of our CADx, MATLAB 2014a software was used. For every experiment of the paper, we have adjusted the input radiograph image size to 304×250 to get the best classification result from the used tool [16]. The supervised classification result is dependent on size of the positive and negative image database and size of the input test image. A machine specification of Intel (R) Core (TM) i3 CPU, 1.7 GHz, 4 GB RAM, 64 bit OS, Windows 7 was used. In practical a high specification RAM can speed up the CADx process. Aim of this paper was to develop a user intervention independent, reliable CADx technique.

5.1 ROI Identification Results

A series of results from our automated technique based on SVM classifier are shown in Fig. 8. The given results show the respective identified region of interest from posterior-anterior spine radiograph image. The ROI possess the vertebral column.

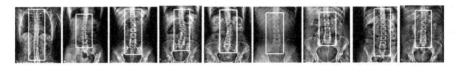

Fig. 8. ROI (vertebral column) identification results from radiograph images

Classification

Sensitivity and Specificity
Performance verification metrics for classification are sensitivity and specificity. In classification 'positive' means 'detected' and 'negative' means 'not detected'. Sensitivity verifies the positives that are in real detected and specificity verifies the real negatives. In our test, true positive, true negative, false positive and false negative are regarded as follows:

True Positive (TP) = correctly classified as spinal column
True Negative (TN) = correctly detected as background
False Positive (FP) = wrongly classified as spinal column
False Negative (FN) = wrongly detected as background

The equations of sensitivity and specificity are shown as follows:

$$Sensitivity = \frac{TruePositive}{TruePositive + FalseNegative} \tag{1}$$

$$Specificity = \frac{TrueNegative}{TrueNegative + FalsePositive} \tag{2}$$

The sensitivity and specificity was performed on 21 radiograph image. The image was classified into two groups the vertebral column (ROI) and the background possessing the other regions of the radiograph image. A sensitivity of 100% and specificity of 100% was obtained from our experiment.

Precision and Recall
Another metric for classification are precision and recall. Precision is the ratio of cases that are correctly classified as spinal column to the sum of cases correctly classified as spinal column and number of cases wrongly classified as spinal column. Equation of precision is expressed as follows:

$$\Pr ecision = \frac{TruePositive}{TruePositive + FalsePositive} \tag{3}$$

Whereas recall is the ratio of cases correctly classified as spinal column to the total number of cases correctly classified as spinal column and cases wrongly classified as spinal column. The equation is illustrated as follows:

$$Recall = \frac{TruePositive}{TruePositive + FalsePositive} \tag{4}$$

We have achieved a value of 100% for precision and have obtained a percentage of 100% for recall from 21 radiograph images.

5.2   Results from Object Centerline Extraction

The radiograph image is blurred to reduce unwanted information and obtain the spine as a continuous structure. Figure 9 shows a number of outputs after high Gaussian blur.

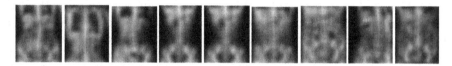

Fig. 9. The figure shows outputs from high Gaussian blurring where the spine appears as a single continuous structure

Output of centerline extractions are shown in Fig. 10. The Cobb angle is computed from the slopes of this extracted centerline.

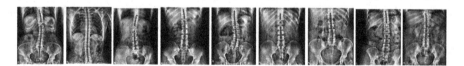

Fig. 10. Results showing 3rd order polynomial fit center points. Center points are superimposed on radiograph image

A selection of polynomial fit for order 3 was taken instead of order 2 and order 4. It was observed that radiograph images gave better result for order 3 which is shown in Table 1. We have selected seven subjects for this experiment. The Cobb angle values from different polynomials are verified with the manual Cobb angle technique and it is observed that 3rd order polynomial gave most similar and consistent results considering manual as the standard Cobb angle value.

Table 1. Cobb angle from our CADx for different order polynomials (2nd, 3rd and 4th order)

Subject ID	Manual	2nd order	3rd order	4th order
Sub 1	21	19.18	**22.64**	20.07
Sub 2	14	8.13	**13.64**	14.39
Sub 3	16	16.08	**16.1**	12.37
Sub 4	29	20.41	**29.47**	24.13
Sub 5	11.53	4.27	**11.57**	18.47
Sub 6	9	No value	**10.04**	7.16
Sub 7	38.12	32.52	**39.90**	32.52

5.3   Angle Evaluation

Analysis tests were carried out for our automated Cobb angle (Lateral curvature angle from posterior-anterior) computation from 2D digital radiograph image. For every subject the analysis was performed by 3 observers on 2 different occasions. The tests were performed by Doctor, Radiologist and Researcher. It was noticed that the Cobb angle value generated from our automated CADx gave same value on a particular image for every experiment. For experimental verification, manual and digital comparison was done where manual is considered as the standard value for our verification. But in practical Manual Cobb angle measurement may itself be subject to error many times. We have taken care so that an accurate Manual Cobb angle is measured. For this we have tried to cross the line for angle computation exactly through correct corners of the endplate. Every observer for every subject performed the angle computation twice, one for manual Cobb computation and other for automated Cobb computation. The automated Cobb angles that were quite similar to the manual angle values were considered as true angles from our automated technique. $\pm 5°$ changes of Cobb angle value in radiographs w.r.t. manual value are regarded to be clinically significant [12]. From our test results out of 21, 12 subjects gave significant Cobb angle values.

Relative Difference

Cobb angle assessment based on relative difference is shown in Table 2 where the Cobb angle assessment was done between automated Cobb value and manual Cobb value. The minimum and maximum relative difference values for every observer on 12 radiograph subjects (whose angle deviation is between $\pm 5°$) are given for observation (Observation 1, Observation 2).

Table 2. Cobb angle analysis based on relative difference

Observer	Relative difference (Observation 1)	Relative difference (Observation 2)
Observer 1	0.0154 (Minimum)	0.0235 (Minimum)
	0.5308 (Maximum)	0.4518 (Maximum)
Observer 2	0.0189 (Minimum)	0.0020 (Minimum)
	0.2686 (Maximum)	0.3836 (Maximum)
Observer 3	0.0480 (Minimum)	0.0043 (Minimum)
	0.3598 (Maximum)	0.2565 (Maximum)

Mean Absolute Deviation

Mean Absolute Deviation (MAD) was used as another metric for realizing the angle variation. The experiment was performed only on the subjects that gave significant results ($\pm 5°$ difference). An Intra-observer and inter-observer angle variation analysis based on MAD is shown in Tables 3 and 4 respectively. The tabulated results show the mean value on 12 subjects that have acceptable variance ($\pm 5°$) [12] for angle computation with respect to manual computation.

Table 3. Intra-observer variability analysis based on MAD

Image	Observer 1		Observer 2		Observer 3	
	Manual	Digital	Manual	Digital	Manual	Digital
12	1.633	0	1.065	0	1.424	0

Table 4. Inter-observer variability analysis based on MAD

Image	Manual	Digital
12	1.45	0

Thus the results of the proposed method reflect good influence with less Cobb angle measurement variability.

6 Conclusions and Future Work

This paper presented Cobb angle evaluation from radiograph image which was based on supervised classification and centerline extraction. From the point of view some previous computerized Cobb angle computations yield good results, but still the research prefers a method that will require no user intervention at all and will give significant results for every spine radiograph image. The advantage of this approach is to have no user intervention for the total process. It was a challenging task to extract the centerline from radiograph images having low contrast, anatomical overlap and object shape variation of radiograph images. The ROI identification based on traditional SVM classifier was efficient to establish the automated CADx. And the center line extraction from this ROI gave correct results for 57.14% subjects with very less or negligible angular variability. The results and findings of this automated research is an effective step in CADx for clinical application. Future study will focus on to perform Cobb angle computation with more adaptive supervised technique and get more information from Scoliosis spine radiograph image.

References

1. Abuzaghleh, T., Barkana, B.: Computer-aided technique for the measurement of the Cobb angle. In: Proceedings of the WorldCom 2012 (2012)
2. Allen, S., Parent, E., Khorasani, M., Hill, D.L., Lou, E., Raso, J.V.: Validity and reliability of active shape models for the estimation of Cobb angle in patients with adolescent idiopathic scoliosis. J. Digit. Imaging **21**(2), 208–218 (2008)
3. Anitha, H., Prabhu, G.K.: Automatic quantification of spinal curvature in scoliotic radiograph using image processing. J. Med. Syst. **36**, 1943–1951 (2012)
4. Cortes, C., Vapnik, V.: Support-vector networks. Mach. Learn. **20**(3), 273–297 (1995). https://doi.org/10.1007/BF00994018
5. Duong, L., Cheriet, F., Labelle, H.: Automatic detection of scoliotic curves in posteroanterior radiographs. IEEE Trans. Biomed. Eng. **57**(7), 1143–1151 (2010)
6. Gonzalez, R.C.: Digital Image Processing. Prentice Hall, Upper Saddle River (2008). ISBN 9780131687288
7. Greiner, K.A.: Adolescent idiopathic scoliosis: radiologic decision-making. Am. Fam. Phys. **65**(9), 1817–1822 (2002)
8. Grigorescu, S.E., Petkov, N., Kruizinga, P.: Comparison of texture features based on gabor filters. IEEE Trans. Image Process. **11**(10), 1160–1167 (2002)
9. Huang, J.Y., Kao, P.F., Chen, Y.S.: Automatic Cobb angle measurement system by using nuclear medicine whole body bone scan. In: MVA2007 IAPR Conference on Machine Vision Applications, Tokyo, pp. 16–18 (2007)
10. Jeifries, B.F., Tarlton, M., De Smet, A.A., Dwyer, S.J., Brower, A.C.: Computerized measurement and analysis of scoliosis: a more accurate representation of the shape of the curve. Radiology **134**, 381–385 (1980)
11. Li, Y., Savvides, M.: An automatic iris occlusion estimation method based on high-dimensional density estimation. IEEE Trans. Pattern Anal. Mach. Intell. **35**(4), 784–796 (2013)
12. Morrissy, M., Goldsmith, G., Hall, E., Kehl, D., Cowie, G.: Measurement of the Cobb angle on radiographs of patients who have scoliosis. Evaluation of intrinsic error. J. Bone Joint Surg. **72**, 320–327 (1999)
13. Murty, M.N., Raghava, R.: Support Vector Machines and Perceptrons. Springer, Berlin (2016). https://doi.org/10.1007/978-3-319-41063-0
14. Samuvel, B., Thomas, V., Mini, M.G.: A mask based segmentation algorithm for automatic measurement of Cobb angle from scoliosis x-ray image. Paper presented at: Proceedings of the International Conference on Advances in Computing, Communications and Informatics, Chennai, pp. 110–113 (2012)
15. Sardjono, T.A., Wilkinson, M.H.F., Veldhuizen, A.G., Van Ooijen, P.M.A., Purnama, K.E., Verkerke, G.J.: Automatic Cobb angle determination from radiographic images. SPINE **38**(20), E1256–E1262 (2013)
16. Sakhi, O.: Face Detection using Support Vector Machine (SVM) (2010). http://in.mathworks.com/matlabcentral/fileexchange/29834-face-detection-using-support-vector-machine-svm/content/fdsvm11/main.m
17. Shaw, M., Adam, C.J., Izatt, M.T., Licina, P., Askin, G.N.: Use of the iPhone for Cobb angle measurement in scoliosis. Eur. Spine J. **21**, 1062–1068 (2012)
18. Tanure, M.C., Pinheiro, A.P., Oliveria, A.S.: Reliability assessment of Cobb angle measurements using manual and digital methods. Spine J. **10**, 769–774 (2010)
19. Tomasi, C., Manduchi, R.: Bilateral filtering for gray and color images. In: Proceedings of the IEEE International Conference on Computer Vision, Bombay (1998)

20. Tzotsos, A., Argialas, D.: Support vector machine classification for object-based image analysis. In: Blaschke, T., Lang, S., Hay, G.J. (eds.) Object-Based Image Analysis. Springer, Berlin (2008). https://doi.org/10.1007/978-3-540-77058-9_36

21. Wever, D.J., Tonseth, K.A., Veldhuizen, A.G., Cool, J.C., Van, H.J.R.: Curve progression and spinal growth in brace treated idiopathic scoliosis. Clinic Orthop. Relat. Res. **377**, 169–179 (2000)

22. Yildiz, I.: Computer-assisted Cobb angle measurement from posteroanterior radiographs by a curve fitting method. Turk. J. Electr. Eng. Comput. Sci. **24**, 4604–4610 (2015)

23. Zhang, J., Lou, E., Le, L.H., Hill, D.L., Raso, J.V., Wang, Y.: Automatic Cobb measurement of scoliosis based on fuzzy Hough transform with vertebral shape prior. J. Digit. Imaging **22** (5), 463–472 (2009)

Nonvolatile Write Driver for Spin Transfer Torque Memory and Logic Design

Sagnik Saha[✉], Shashank Kumar Dubey, Soham Banerjee,
Indrajit Pal, and Aminul Islam

Department of Electronics and Communication Engineering,
Birla Institute of Technology, Mesra, Ranchi, Jharkhand, India
sahasagnik95@gmail.com, dubey.shashank1991@gmail.com,
banerjeesoham95@gmail.com, pal.indrajit99@gmail.com,
aminulislam@bitmesra.ac.in

Abstract. This paper proposes a compact model of STT-MTJ being operated in the sub-volume (MTJ lateral diameter less than 40 nm) region. The model is found to have lower switching currents as well as higher thermal stability factor as compared to the conventional MTJ models being used. This paper mainly deals with the description of the static behavior of the model. This includes the critical current calculations, thermal stability calculations, TMR and MTJ resistance dependence on bias voltage. This paper also proposes a new READ and WRITE circuitry to facilitate an easier read and write operation. The paper illustrates a transmission gate based 2T1M MRAM bit cell which uses MTJ as a memory element.

Keywords: Spintronics · Magnetic Tunnel Junction (MTJ) compact model
TMR · Static behaviors · Sub-volume · Thermal stability

1 Introduction

Traditional electronic devices such as MOSFETs, FinFETs, etc. have the flow of charge through them as the controlling principle in their operations. Spintronics devices however, work on the principle of the up or down spin of an electron rather than electrons or holes as in traditional semiconductor devices. Large scale nonvolatile memories (e.g., hard disk drives or HDDs) exploit ferromagnetism to store information by altering the spin alignment of large number of electrons. Spintronics has made it possible for scientific research and microelectronic industry to build innovative magnetic/electronic devices with added perks of nonvolatility and improved area efficiency.

Contemporary CMOS technologies possess numerous weaknesses such as long reboot latency of programmable circuits, volatile nature of the data stored and high leakage currents which result in a large increase of stand-by power consumption. In order to mitigate the above problems in nanoscale devices such as carbon nanotubes, nanowires, heterojunction HEMTs, spintronics devices etc. are considered as future prospects. However, despite having several weaknesses, CMOS technology is still predicted to play a pivotal role in circuit design and fabrication over the next few years.

© Springer Nature Singapore Pte Ltd. 2018
J. K. Mandal and D. Sinha (Eds.): CSI 2017, CCIS 836, pp. 156–166, 2018.
https://doi.org/10.1007/978-981-13-1343-1_17

Therefore, proper interfacing capability with CMOS transistors is an advantageous factor for these nanodevices which can be employed and commercialized in the near future. The Magnetic Tunnel Junction (MTJ) is one of those commercially feasible candidates which satisfy most of the aforementioned benefits while providing adequate interfacing capability with CMOS technology. It's nonvolatile property, scalability potential and compatibility with the MOS technology make it an attractive device for the future. The scalability of MTJ leads to efficient switching operation provided by spin transfer torque in nanoscale MTJs. Moreover, thermal stability is ensured by perpendicular anisotropy materials due to less dependence on shape anisotropy [1].

2 MTJ Technologies and Modeling

MTJ is a nonvolatile device with a fixed magnetic layer or pinned layer (PL) and a free magnetic layer (FL) with an oxide barrier separating them (see Fig. 1). It is a device with varying electrical resistance depending on the orientation of the free layer with respect to the permanent layer owing to the tunnel magnetoresistance (TMR) effect. The MTJ offers high resistance (logic 1) when the magnetization free layer direction is anti-parallel to that of the fixed layer while it provides low resistance (logic 0) in parallel orientation. The MTJ's magnetic state can be electrically controlled by the Voltage Controlled Magnetic Anisotropy (VCMA) or Spin Transfer Torque (STT) effect or through a combination of both.

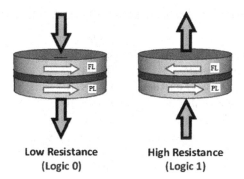

Low Resistance
(Logic 0)
       High Resistance
(Logic 1)

Fig. 1. Structure of magnetic tunnel junction (MTJ). Low resistance is exhibited when both FL and PL are in parallel and high resistance is exhibited when FL is in antiparallel with PL.

TMR allows for simple and stable sense amplifiers in the process improving the reading accuracy. Write operation involves use of magnetic fields or spin polarized current depending on the MTJ technology [2–4]:

- Field induced magnetic switching
- Toggle switching
- Thermally assisted switching
- Current induced magnetic switching

The magnetization layers are made of CoFeB and the oxide separating them is MgO [5]. On the basis of three STT-MTJ mathematical models (Brinkman Physical model of MTJ conductance, Voltage dependent TMR effect model and Slonczewski model of critical switching current), we proposed a new SPICE model. These models describe their static behavior and described below:

2.1   Static Model

The critical current density, resistances and TMR calculations are explained by the static behavior of the model.

Critical Current Calculations

The expression for deriving the intrinsic switching current density of the MTJ is given by [6]

$$J_{C0} = \frac{\alpha 4\pi e}{g\hbar} M_S^2 d^{eff} \tag{1}$$

$$I_{C0} = J_{C0} \times A \tag{2}$$

where d^{eff} is effective thickness of free layer = $k.d^n$, k being the fitting parameter and n being the exponent of the thickness d. k lies in the range from 0 to 1. In this model, d^{eff} is taken to be 0.77d. Other parameters used in the equation are described in Table 1.

Table 1. Parameters and constants used in MTJ model

Parameters	Description	Value
Shape	Shape of MTJ device	Cylindrical
a	Lateral diameter	30 nm
d	MTJ free layer thickness	0.85×10^{-7} cm
t_{ox}	Oxide layer thickness	0.85×10^{-7} cm
Area	Surface area	$\pi \times 15^2$ nm^2
Ferromagnetic material	Both free and fixed layer material	$Co_{0.60}Fe_{0.20}B_{0.20}$
Insulating barrier	Tunneling barrier material	MgO
RA	Resistance area product	5 k$\Omega\mu$m^2
H_K	Anisotropy field	4.5×10^3Oe
M_S	Saturation magnetization	800 emu/cm^3
α	Gilbert damping constant	0.036
e	Elementary charge	1.6×10^{-19}C
μ_B	Bohr magneton	9.27×10^{-24} J/T
μ_0	Permeability in free space	1.25×10^{-6} H/m
g	Spin polarization efficiency factor	0.57

(continued)

Table 1. (*continued*)

Parameters	Description	Value
θ	Magnetization angle of free and pinned layer	$\theta = 0$ for parallel magnetization and $\theta = \pi$ for anti-parallel magnetization
TMR(0)	TMR with 0 voltage bias	100%
V_{BIAS}	Biasing voltage	0.85 V
R_P	Parallel state resistance	7.16 kΩ
R_{AP}	Anti-parallel state resistance	14.32 kΩ (0 bias voltage) 9 kΩ(V_{BIAS} = 0.85)
I_{PtoAP}	Parallel to anti-parallel switching current	$\approx$88.85 µA
I_{APtoP}	Anti-parallel to parallel switching current	$\approx$−35.64 µA

The term d^{eff} is used to take care of the interfacial effects occurring in ferromagnetic material and oxide interface, with the factors being varied for distinct MTJ structures and accuracy prerequisites. Since macro-spin region does not offer the large spin torque efficiency, thus it challenges the MTJ's internal switching mechanisms that had been observed below the 40-nm region.

Thermal Stability Calculations

It is a measure of the retention of magnetization state of MTJ. A high thermal stability guarantees MTJ's state immunity to thermal fluctuations. The thermal stability factor considering shape-dependent demagnetization field energy can be given by [7].

$$E_b = \frac{M_Z H_K}{2} V + 2\pi M_S^2 V \frac{3}{2} [1 - N_Z(\psi)] \tag{3}$$

Assuming N_Z to be a fixed function of ψ and ψ to be sufficiently limited so that the curve is a continuous, three-order approximation of adequate accuracy 1776, −338.7, $N_Z(\psi) = \sigma\psi^3 + \beta\psi^2 + \gamma\psi + \delta$, where σ, β, γ and δ are the fitting coefficients having values 9.8 and 0.9 respectively. The variation of demagnetization with MTJ diameter is plotted in Fig. 2. It can be observed that as the MTJ size scales down, demagnetization also reduces.

In Fig. 3, we observe that the thermal stability factor goes down with the decreasing MTJ diameter but the decrease of demagnetization with size as illustrated in Fig. 2 makes it suitable for retention.

Modeling the Brinkman Physical Model of MTJ Conductance: The model describes MTJ resistance which consists of oxide barrier interfacing with ferromagnetic layer. In this model tunnel barrier's height and the interfacing effect is important parameter of the resistance. The parallel MTJ resistance is given by [8],

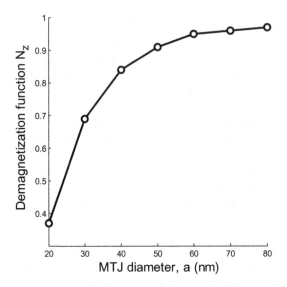

Fig. 2. Demagnetization function N_z versus the MTJ diameter.

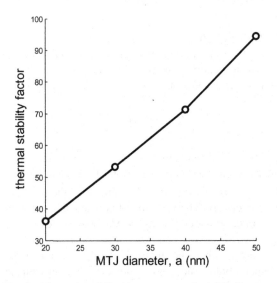

Fig. 3. Thermal Stability factor versus the MTJ diameter.

$$R_P(0) = \frac{t_{ox}}{FA.\varphi^{-1/2}.\pi a^2/4} \exp(0.01025.t_{ox}.\varphi^{-1/2}) \times 10^{-2} \qquad (4)$$

Here, FA is equal to '3322.53/RA', R_P and t_{ox} units are Ω and cm respectively. The resistance value is dependent on the bias voltage. The dependence is shown by the following relation:

$$R(V) = \frac{R_P}{1 + \left(\frac{t_{ox}^2 \times e^2 \times m}{4 \times \hbar^2 \times \phi}\right) \times V^2} \tag{5}$$

The resistance at the anti-parallel state is given by the addition of R_P (V) and R_a (V), where R_a (V) is given by:

$$R_a(V) = R_p(V).TMR(V) \tag{6}$$

$$R_{AP}(V) = R_a(V) + R_P(V) = R_P(V)[TMR(V) + 1] \tag{7}$$

Here, TMR (V) = tunnel magnetoresistance as a function of the biasing voltage.

TMR Dependence on Bias Voltage: The Tunnel Magnetoresistance (TMR) of an MTJ is a measure of evaluating the overall efficiency of the MTJ's spintronic operation [9]. TMR is given by

$$TMR(0) = \frac{R_{AP} - R_P}{R_P} \tag{8}$$

Here, R_{AP} & R_P defines resistance in anti-parallel and parallel state respectively.

The TMR value reduces with the increase in bias voltage (due to increasing barrier height), the relation being given by:

$$TMR(V_{BIAS}) = \frac{TMR(0)}{1 + \frac{V_{BIAS}^2}{V_{HALF}^2}} \tag{9}$$

Here, TMR (0) is the TMR value when no bias voltage is applied, V_{BIAS} being the bias voltage and V_{HALF} is the bias voltage corresponding to which TMR value is half of the value of TMR (0).

The variation of Resistance in parallel and antiparallel state is plotted in Fig. 4(a). The corresponding change in TMR (in %) is shown in Fig. 4(b).

Slonczewski Model of Static STT Switching: This model portrays the switching magnetization characteristics of the free ferromagnetic layer when the current density J exceeds the critical current density J_{C0}. Having calculated the critical current density from Eq. (1) individual currents for parallel and anti-parallel states can be given using the Slonczewski model and by using the known relation V = I * R [10]:

$$I_P = \frac{V_{BIAS}}{R_P(V)} \tag{10}$$

$$I_{AP} = \frac{V_{BIAS}}{R_P(V) + R_a(V)} \tag{11}$$

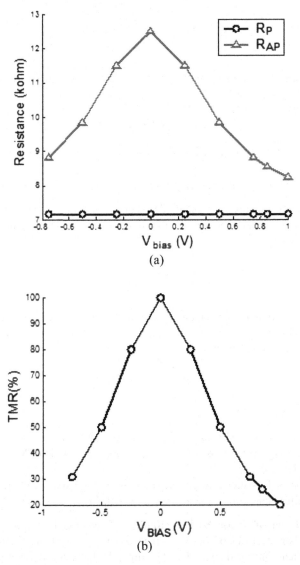

Fig. 4. (a) Variation of the parallel and anti-parallel state resistance with the bias voltage. (b) Variation of TMR with the bias voltage.

Figure 5 shows the variation of the MTJ current in its parallel and anti-parallel state with respect to bias voltage. As the bias voltage is increased, the current flowing through it also increases in both cases.

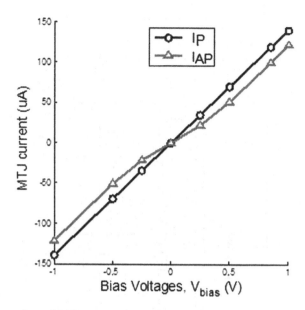

Fig. 5. Representation of MTJ current in parallel and anti-parallel state while varying bias voltage.

3 Proposed Read and Write Circuitry Using Write Driver

In the proposed circuitry (shown in Fig. 6) the MTJ along with the access transistors MP1 & MN1 act as MRAM cell. The proposed circuitry consists of the write driver, which consists of the MN3, MN4, MN5, MN6, MN8, MP3, MP4, MP5, MP6 and MP8 (not MN7 and MP7). The write driver ensures that when the write enable (WEN) is high, BL and BLB get driven to complement of DX and DXB respectively, where DX represents the data to be written in the MRAM cell and the low value of WEN makes the supply terminals of MN3, MN4, MP3 and MP4 to float resulting in floating BL and BLB, thereby isolating rest of the circuitry from the write driver.

The read circuitry consists of MN2, MN9, MP9, MP2 and R_1 that creates current path for the current to flow through the MRAM cell. The voltage developed at BL depends mainly on the resistance of the MTJ because the equivalent resistance offered by MN1/2, MP1/2 and R_1 remains unchanged (the only change in the resistance value is the value of the resistance of MTJ in the path from V_{DD} to GND through MTJ). Therefore, we measure the voltage at BL to read the data stored in MTJ which is given by the following equation:

$$V_{BL} = V_{DD} \frac{R_{EQ}}{R_{EQ} + R_{MP2}} \qquad (12)$$

where, $R_{EQ} = R_{TG} + R_{MTJ} + R_{MN2} + R_1$ and, $R_{TG} = R_{MN1} || R_{MP1}$.

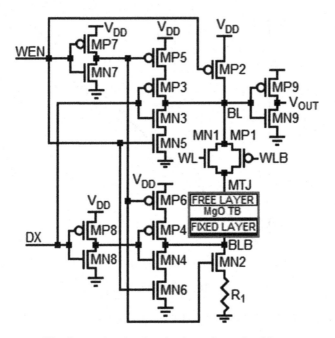

Fig. 6. Read and write circuitry using write driver.

4 Simulation Results and Discussion

The proposed MTJ model has been implemented in Verilog-AMS and simulated in HSPICE. The model has two electrical terminals, two resistances R_P and R_{AP} and a switch. The switch is in ON condition in parallel state providing a low resistance path through the switch between the two terminals. In anti-parallel state, the switch remains off thus cutting off the low resistance path and in the process giving an equivalent resistance equal to $R_P + R_{AP}$. The model operates below sub-volume limit (diameter less than 40 nm). We measured various MTJ electrical parameters including the critical switching current, resistance values in parallel and anti-parallel states, thermal stability factor, TMR and resistance dependence on the bias voltage. We obtained the critical current value for anti-parallel to parallel switching and the value for parallel to anti-parallel switching equal to 88.85 μA and −35.64 μA respectively. These current values are lower as compared to the conventional models following the macro-spin theory due to the modulation of the anisotropy energy arising from the edge effects. Low switching current results in reduced power consumption, low self-heating effect and less temperature rise within the cell [11]. It was also observed that the thermal stability factor decreases with size but as observed from Fig. 3, the demagnetization also decreases, thereby the barrier height increases resulting in the MTJ having high stability and longer holding time. The given model attained a thermal stability factor, $\Delta = 53.26$. This value is sufficiently high for the MTJ to retain its state. This attribute makes an MTJ nonvolatile and hence an MTJ finds its application in various memory and logic

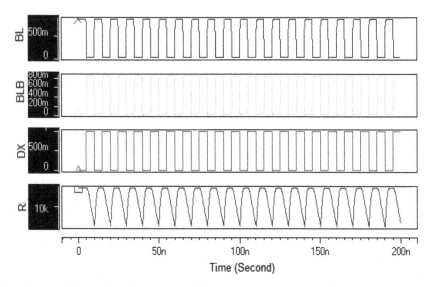

Fig. 7. Plot of voltages at DX, BL, BLB and the MTJ resistance versus time.

circuits. The resistance hysteresis curve was also obtained showing the obvious voltage-resistance dependence.

Figure 7 shows the variation of voltages at DX, BL, BLB and the MTJ resistance, R with time. As can be observed from the plot, the data to be written is given as input at the DX terminal. This voltage is and its complement is replicated in the BL/BLB rail. Accordingly, the MTJ resistance (R) also varies with the input present at DX terminal. When the input at DX terminal is high, the MTJ is in anti-parallel state. When the input is reversed, the MTJ switches states and exhibits lower resistance. The difference in resistance leads to a difference in the current flowing through the MTJ. This difference in current is measured by a sense amplifier which then is used to read the current status of BL and BLB rails. The presence of STT-MTJ in the design makes it nonvolatile and ensures that data can be stored even if the power supply is cut off.

5 Conclusion

A compact SPICE modeling of STT-MTJ is done using the contemporary mathematical models. The MTJ is made to operate in the sub-volume region (MTJ lateral diameter less than 40 nm). The model is found to have satisfactory values for the switching current (close to 88.85 μA) and thermal stability factor (close to 53.26). The results obtained in simulation are found to be matching with the experimental values found in the literature. The STT-MTJ has been integrated with a conventional write driver circuit which provides nonvolatility as well as has higher scope in improving write error rates and the area efficiency.

References

1. Wolf, S.A., et al.: The promise of nanomagnetics and spintronics for future logic and universal memory. Proc. IEEE **98**(12), 2155–2168 (2010)
2. Azevedo, J., et al.: Dynamic compact model of self-referenced magnetic tunnel junction. IEEE Trans. Electron Dev. **61**(11), 3877–3882 (2014)
3. Sugahara, S., Nitta, J.: Spin-transistor electronics: an overview and outlook. Proc. IEEE **98** (12), 2124–2154 (2010)
4. Ikeda, S., et al.: Magnetic tunnel junctions for spintronic memories and beyond. IEEE Trans. Electron Dev. **54**(5), 991–999 (2007)
5. Liu, X., et al.: Ferromagnetic resonance and damping properties of CoFeB thin films as free layers in MgO-based magnetic tunnel junctions. J. Appl. Phys. **110**, 033910 (2011)
6. Dorrance, R., Ren, F., Toriyama, Y., Hafez, A.A., Yang, C.K.K., Markovic, D.: Scalability and design-space analysis of a 1T-1MTJ memory cell for STT-RAMs. IEEE Trans. Electron Dev. **59**(4), 878–887 (2012)
7. Zhang, Y., et al.: Compact model of subvolume MTJ and its design application at nanoscale technology nodes. IEEE Trans. Electron Dev. **62**(6), 2048–2055 (2015)
8. Yee, C.J., Hatem, F.O., Kumar, T.N., Almurib, H.A.F.: Compact SPICE modeling of STT-MTJ device. In: 2015 IEEE Student Conference on Research and Development (SCOReD), Kuala Lumpur, pp. 625–628 (2015)
9. Lu, Y., et al.: Bias voltage and temperature dependence of magnetotunneling effect. J. Appl. Phys. **83**(11), 6515–6517 (1998)
10. Xu, Z., Sutaria, K.B., Yang, C., Chakrabarti, C., Cao, Y.: Compact modeling of STT-MTJ for SPICE simulation. In: 2013 Proceedings of the European Solid-State Device Research Conference (ESSDERC), Bucharest, pp. 338–341 (2013)
11. Chatterjee, S., et al.: Impact of self-heating on reliability of a spin-torque-transfer RAM cell. IEEE Trans. Electron Dev. **59**(3), 791–799 (2012)

Optimal Equipment Positioning and Technology Selection for RFID Enabled Warehouses

Sandeep Kumar Singh$^{(\boxtimes)}$, Arun Kumar Biswal, Sonu Kumar, Tanya Singh, and Mamata Jenamani

Department of Industrial and Systems Engineering, IIT Kharagpur, Kharagpur 721302, India
sandeep.singh@iitkgp.ac.in,
{akb,mj}@iem.iitkgp.ernet.in,
kumar.sonoo@gmail.com, tanyaa43@gmail.com

Abstract. The paper presents two models for selecting optimal number of RFID readers and antennas to cover the designated storage area in a warehouse containing tagged items so as to minimize the equipment cost. While the first model considers the case where the equipment and the tags are technically compatible, the second one handles a situation where all of them may not be. Inputs to the model are potential positions for placing the RFID equipment in the warehouse, their physical characteristics and the cost. The output is the optimal locations of the equipment. We demonstrate the application of the model to the warehouse layouts approved by the Food Corporation of India (FCI).

Keywords: RFID · Food security · Facility location · Warehouse

1 Introduction

Radio Frequency Identification (RFID) technology is one of the most popular solutions for real-time item level visibility and inventory data management [1]. The main benefits of RFID adoption in a warehouse are improvement in product location strategy, visibility of real time information and cost saving [2]. The selection of right RFID equipment and their positioning in a warehouse depends on the prior experience of the implementing agency. The agencies mostly focus on coverage of storage location of tagged items, not on minimizing the cost. The cost of the RFID technology though is decreasing over the years, is still not within the reach of many [3, 4]. Hence, mathematical models are developed to minimize the RFID implementation cost in various domains such as healthcare, manufacturing etc. However, such models in the context of warehouse are limited [5].

The work presents mathematical models to find the optimal position of RFID equipment such as readers and antennas, in a warehouse with an objective to reduce total cost while ensuring the coverage of the tagged items. Present work is influenced by Jimenez et al. [6] and Drezner and Wesolowsky [7] to a large extent. Jimenez et al. consider optimal positioning of RFID equipment in an aircraft for coverage of tagged

© Springer Nature Singapore Pte Ltd. 2018
J. K. Mandal and D. Sinha (Eds.): CSI 2017, CCIS 836, pp. 167–182, 2018.
https://doi.org/10.1007/978-981-13-1343-1_18

components with permissible amount of weight on board [6]. However, their model is not appropriate for a warehouse setting for three reasons. First, the number of items in a warehouse being much larger can make the model monolithic by incorporating one constraint for each tagged item. Second, the exact location of the items cannot be precisely entered as the constraint. Third, the items kept in the warehouse are in transit and are stored for a limited period. The models proposed in this paper overcome this problem by demarcating the storage area in a warehouse, gridding them and finding the potential positions for readers and antennas; then, modeling it as a facility location problem. Our attempt to find the potential position for the readers and their antennas for maximum coverage in a facility is influenced by Drezner and Wesolowsky [7]. They consider the facility location problem in a feasible region covering some parts of network links within a given radius. While their model is generic for any kind of network location problem, our model is for the network of RFID reader antenna where the corresponding physical constraints play a major role. We apply the proposed model to study the equipment positioning in the warehouse layouts approved by Food Corporation of India (FCI).

In summary, this paper aims to reduce the total equipment cost of RFID implementation in a warehouse, using optimal number of readers and antennas by proposing two models considering: (1) a single technology, where the tags and RFID equipment are compatible, and (2) multiple technologies, where inherent incompatibility issues are taken care of. The constraints we use to govern this minimization problem for both the models are; (1) each tagged item is read by at least one reader antenna, (2) each reader has certain number of ports available, (3) the antenna connected to one reader cannot be connected to any other reader, and additionally, for the second model we ensure that (4) the RFID components are compatible with each other, to avoid any connection error during their communication. To our understanding, this paper is the first of its kind for optimal positioning of RFID equipment in a warehouse setting with three specific contributions. First, consideration of physical constraints due to existing layout of a warehouse makes its application versatile. Second, gridding of storage area makes the antenna coverage constraint linear; which in practice is elliptical in nature. Third, in case of multiple technologies, the constraints are designed to consider compatibility issue.

The rest of the paper is organized as follows. Section 2 presents the literature review. Section 3 introduces the mathematical model. Section 4 shows the application of the model to a real case. The last section concludes the paper.

2 Literature Review

While extensive research has been performed on the positioning of wireless sensor network for indoor locations [8], such attempts in the context of RFID network is limited. As suggested by Luo et al. [9], high communication cost and deployment cost associated with RFID equipment requires developing models for optimal positioning of equipment in a warehouse. Literature on traditional facility location models especially in the context of warehouse design can form the basis of such models. Hence, we review some traditional facility models related to warehouses and supply chain organizations. The main features of these models are always same: space including metric, customers whose locations in the given space are known and facilities whose locations have to be determined in possible places according to some objective functions [10]. Our model falls under the category of discrete model. The methodologies we concern are RFID tags, readers, and reader antennas as discrete elements, and goes for determining the optimal positions and appropriate technology of the RFID system components.

Facility location problems are to locate the new facilities from a given set of potential sites so as to minimize the total cost while satisfying the customer demands [11]. As cost is the primary factor in RFID implementation, so in the objective function, cost minimization has been considered to provide decision support for the customers. Most of the papers in the literature feature a cost minimization objective [12]. The covering problem models are mainly used when profit based objective or a cost based objective is required [13]. In our RFID location model, the coverage of all the demand nodes is mandatory which covers all the tags within this region for collecting the data through reading modules.

Facility location is a critical decision that impacts a lot of operational and logistical decisions. Therefore, facility location decisions are frequently fixed and difficult to modify even in the halfway [14]. In FCI warehouses, decision makers must select the locations for implementing the RFID systems that will not only perform well according to the current scenario but will also be profitable during the warehouse's lifetime. When modelling a RFID system, the warehouse configuration (position and location of storage area) is not easy to change or modify because it needs certification [15]. Thus, RFID location decisions are long-term decisions. Inefficient locations, as well as an inadequate technological selection of the deployment of RFID systems in a warehouse, will result in excessive cost throughout the lifetime of the warehouse.

3   Problem Formulation

Two mathematical models are formulated in this section: (1) single technology model and (2) multiple technologies model. In the first model the tags, readers and antennas are assumed to be technologically compatible; whereas, in the second model, they are not. The objective in both the models is to minimize the total equipment cost which includes the cost of RFID reader and reader antenna. The cost of the RF cable is negligible as compared to the cost of the RFID readers and antennas, so it is not considered during cost evaluation. The constraints for both the models include ensuring that (1) each tagged item is read by at least one reader antenna, (2) the number of antennas connected to the readers is less than the ports available, (3) the antenna connected to one reader cannot be connected to any other reader, and (4) the distance between the antenna and the reader does not exceed length of the RF cable. An additional constraint for the second model is to ensure that RFID components are compatible with each other to avoid any connection error during their communication. The notations for the proposed models are given in Table 1. We now describe the constraints common to both the models. We first explain the physical and design principles behind each constraint and subsequently represent them mathematically.

3.1   Storage Area Coverage Constraints Based on Technical Characteristics of the RFID Equipment

A typical warehouse consists of mainly three sections: Storage, office, and weighing area [16, 17]. The storage area is usually separated from the others, and the stacks are arranged such that they resemble grids of the same size. The problem here is to cover the storage area with RF signals from reader antennas. In this formulation, we consider a directional antenna with high gain to maximize the read range of the reader as shown in Fig. 1. If the antenna is fixed on the ceiling, it will work like a circularly polarized antenna which has two benefits: First, it maximizes the coverage area; second, it will have least obstacles with compared to fixing on the ground. With this motivation, in our formulation we consider that RFID readers and antennas are installed on the ceiling of the storage area to read the tagged items in the stacks below them. Therefore, the signal coverage area can be treated as circular. Thus, the constraint corresponding to coverage of the entire storage area becomes non-linear. In order to get an equivalent linear model we grid the storage area and then assume that circular signal cover them. The intersections of these grids are considered as the *potential reader antenna positions*.

The tags which are under the read range of a reader antenna can only be tracked. As discussed earlier, including one constraint to check whether each of the tag is covered like earlier literature is not a computationally feasible proposition in case of a warehouse setting because of three reasons: first, the number of items are very large in a warehouse; second, the items keep coming and going from the warehouse; third, the position of the items within the warehouse may change. But the position of the reader and antenna need to be installed in a *potential position* to cover the entire area. To ensure this, we further divide the grid in the storage area in a manner so that each block of the smaller grid can be under the coverage region of a reader antenna placed in one of the *potential positions*. The corner points of these smaller grids are called as the *covering positions*. Here, the intuition is, if all the covering positions are under signal covering area of at least one reader antenna then all the items stacked in the storage area can be tracked.

To demonstrate the concept of *covering* and *potential positions*, considering a typical warehouse layout as shown in Fig. 2, we distinguish points on the stack grids in the storage area into two types: Covering positions (Fig. 3) and potential positions (Fig. 4). The covering positions (red and yellow points) are the locations, which have to be covered by the antenna signal so that the tagged items within the rectangle are also ensured to be covered by the corresponding reader antenna. The potential positions (red points) are the possible available positions for the readers and their antennas. The number of readers and antennas to be placed at these potential positions can be optimized based on the signal radius (Fig. 5) of the RFID antenna read range while ensuring full coverage of the stacks in the storage area by minimizing the cost of the RFID components to be installed in the warehouse.

Fig. 1. Radiation pattern of directional antenna

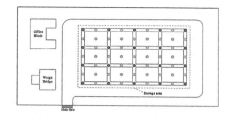

Fig. 2. Typical warehouse layout with covering positions (yellow) and potential antenna positions (red) (Color figure online)

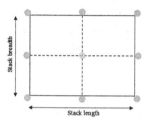

Fig. 3. Covering positions in a stack (Color figure online)

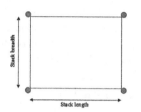

Fig. 4. Potential reader antenna positions in a stack (Color figure online)

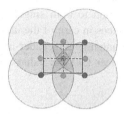

Fig. 5. Stack covered by the 4 circles (antenna signal) (Color figure online)

Storage area Coverage Constraints is based on technical characteristics of the equipment. The read range of the reader antenna varies according to the amount of power required by the tag for the respective operation, and is ideally 100% up to a certain distance and is null beyond that. The capability of a tag to receive a signal from the reader antenna depends on the impedance match of its antenna and the sensitivity of the microchip. The signal power transmitted from the reader antenna must be such that it activates the tag within its read range, i.e. it must be equal to or more than the tag's threshold power [18]. This read range is now used to create a binary matrix called, *the covering matrix*. The columns in the matrix corresponds to the equipment, in this case the reader antenna and rows of this matrix corresponds to the covering positions in the physical storage area of the warehouse. For example, for the storage area in Fig. 2, the covering matrix would be of 15 columns (Red dots) and 63 rows (red and yellow dots). This kind of data structure not only helps avoiding the non-linear constraint posed by the antenna coverage equation, but also helps reducing the number of constraints by accommodating all the antenna constrantaints within the same data structure. To design this constraint, we first determine a matrix of distances between the antenna covering positions and potential positions. This distance matrix is used to construct the coverage matrix (a_{ij}), where elements are assigned the value 1 only when the respective distance matrix element is within the read range of the reader antenna. The coverage matrix is used for mathematically represent the coverage constraint as shown in the Eq. (2) below.

3.2   Equipment Connectivity and Compatibility Constraints

As the energy travels through the antenna cable connecting the RFID antenna to the RFID reader, power is lost. Longer the cable more is the power loss. To ensure minimal power loss for generating the strong RF field, we assume antenna cable length to be 15 m in our model as suggested in the literature. If the antenna cable length is 15 m then the power loss is about 0.6mW for LMR-400 cable [19]. To implement *RF cable constraint*, we use another matrix called the rectilinear distance matrix (d_{jk}). d_{jk} obtains the value 1 when rectilinear distance between the antenna and the reader potential position is less than the RF cable length.

Each antenna is connected to only one reader. Similarly, the number of antennas to be connected to a reader is limited by the number of ports available in the reader. These constraints are also need to be taken care of. Besides above constraints which are common to both single and multiple technologies RFID systems, another constraint surfaces in case of the latter. We use two binary matrices Q_{ij} and T_{jk} to take care of the tag-antenna and reader-antenna compatibilities respectively. Both the matrix elements matrices take the value 1 in case technologies are compatible otherwise they are zero.

Table 1. Notations

Decision variable	
Y_j	Positioning choice of reader antenna for a single technology
	$Y_j = \begin{cases} 1, & \text{if potential position } j \text{ is chosen for the antenna} \\ 0, & \text{otherwise} \end{cases}$
R_k	Positioning choice of reader for a single technology
	$R_k = \begin{cases} 1, & \text{if potential position } k \text{ is chosen for the reader} \\ 0, & \text{otherwise} \end{cases}$
$Y_j^{t_a}$	Positioning choice of reader antenna for technology t_a
	$Y_j^{t_a} = \begin{cases} 1, & \text{if antenna type } t_a \text{ is chosen at potential position } j \\ 0, & \text{otherwise} \end{cases}$
$R_k^{t_r}$	Positioning choice of reader for technology t_r
	$R_k^{t_r} = \begin{cases} 1, & \text{if reader type } t_r \text{ is chosen at potential position } k \\ 0, & \text{otherwise} \end{cases}$
Parameter	
a_{ij}	Tag covering variable (Covering matrix)
	$a_{ij} = \begin{cases} 1, & \text{if } i^{th} \text{ covering position is within the read range} \\ & \text{of reader antenna, which is at potential position } j \\ 0, & \text{otherwise} \end{cases}$
d_{jk}	Reader antenna-reader connecting variable (Rectilinear distance)
	$d_{jk} = \begin{cases} 1, & \text{if antenna at } j \text{ is connected to reader at } k \\ 0, & \text{otherwise} \end{cases}$
$a_{ij}^{t_a}$	Tag covering variable for reader antenna type t_a
	$a_{ij}^{t_a} = \begin{cases} 1, & \text{if } i^{th} \text{covering position is within the read range of} \\ & \text{reader antenna } (t_a), \text{ which is at potential position } j \\ 0, & \text{otherwise} \end{cases}$

(continued)

Table 1. (*continued*)

Q_{ij}	Tag-reader antenna compatibility variable for multiple technologies
	$Q_{ij} = \begin{cases} 1, & \text{if the tag located within } i^{th} \text{ covering position is compatible} \\ & \text{with the reader antenna}(t_a), \text{which is at potential position } j \\ 0, & \text{otherwise} \end{cases}$
T_{jk}	Reader antenna-reader compatibility variable for multiple technologies
	$T_{jk} = \begin{cases} 1, & \text{if reader antenna at position } j \text{ is compatible with reader at position } k \\ 0, & \text{otherwise} \end{cases}$
C_a	Cost of reader antenna
C_r	Cost of reader
N	Number of covering positions
M	Number of potential positions
G_T	Linear gain of the transmitting reader antenna
G_R	Linear gain of the receiving tag antenna
λ	Transmission wavelength
L	Attenuation constant
$P_{T(antenna)}$	Transmitted power of the emission reader antenna
s_{ij}	Distance between transmitting and receiving antennas
$P_{th(tag)}$	Threshold power of the tag antenna

3.3 Binary Integer Linear Programming Model for a Single Technology RFID System

Incorporating the constraints as discussed above the proposed model aims to minimize the total fixed cost associated with readers and antennas in a RFID enabled warehouse setup by choosing the optimal locations for the equipment. The decision variables $Y_j = 1$ if the potential position j is chosen for the reader antenna and $R_k = 1$ if the potential position k is chosen for the reader, and both are 0 otherwise. The binary integer linear programming model for the single technology RFID system design in the warehouse can be written as follows:

$$\min C_a \sum_j Y_j + C_r \sum_k R_k \tag{1}$$

Subject to:

$$\sum_j a_{ij} Y_j \geq 1, \, i = 1, \ldots, N \tag{2}$$

$$\sum_k d_{jk} R_k \geq Y_j, \, j = 1, \ldots, M \tag{3}$$

$$\sum_j d_{jk} Y_j \leq n, \, k = 1, \ldots, M \tag{4}$$

$$a_{ij} = \begin{cases} 1, & \text{if } i^{th} \text{ covering position is within the read range } (r) \text{ of antenna,} \\ & \text{which is at the potential position } j \\ 0, & \text{otherwise} \end{cases} \quad (5)$$

$$d_{jk} = \begin{cases} 1, & \text{if rectlinear distance between reader antenna and reader} \leq \text{cable length} \\ 0, & \text{otherwise} \end{cases}$$

$$\hspace{12cm} (6)$$

$$a_{ij} \in \{0, 1\}, i = 1, \ldots, N; j = 1, \ldots, M \quad (7)$$

$$d_{jk} \in \{0, 1\}, j = 1, \ldots, M; k = 1, \ldots, M \quad (8)$$

$$Y_j \in \{0, 1\}, j = 1, \ldots, M \quad (9)$$

$$R_k \in \{0, 1\}, k = 1, \ldots, M \quad (10)$$

The objective function (Eq. 1) minimizes the total cost of reader and antennas. Constraint 1 Eq. (2) ensures each tagged item is read by at least one reader antenna. Here, the covering matrix (a_{ij}) is obtained from the technical characteristics of the equipment as discussed in Sect. 3.1 and shown in Eq. 5. In the covering matrix $a_{ij} = 1$ if the antenna at position j covers the tag at covering position at i. There are N such constraint one for each reader. Constraint 2 Eq. (3) depicts that each reader antenna is connected to at exactly one reader. The matrix d_{jk} is a binary matrix. The rectilinear distance (d_{jk}) is the state variables and $d_{jk} = 1$ if the antenna at position j can be connected to the reader at position k, and are otherwise 0. Constraint in Eq. (6) depicts that the distance between the reader and the reader antenna has to be less than the available RF cable length as discussed in Sect. 3.2. Please note that, this constraint ensures that a reader is selected if at least one antenna is connected to it. Constraint 3 (Eq. 4) ensures the number of antennas connected to the readers is less than the ports available.

3.4   Binary Integer Linear Programming Model for Multiple Technologies RFID System

The multiple-technology model extends the single technology model with the additional consideration that we have t_a and t_r types of technologies for antennas and readers respectively. The decision variables $Y_j^{t_a} = 1$ if potential position j is chosen for the antenna type t_a, and $R_k^{t_r} = 1$ if potential position k is chosen for the reader type t_r, and are 0 otherwise. The covering matrix $a_{ij}^{t_a} = 1$ if the antenna at potential position j covers the tag t_t within the ith covering position, and $d_{jk} = 1$ if the antenna type t_a at potential position j is connected to the reader type t_r at potential position k, and are 0 otherwise. The binary integer linear program for the multiple technologies of the RFID system design in the warehouse can be written as follows:

$$\min C_a \sum_j \sum_{t_a} Y_j^{t_a} + C_r \sum_k \sum_{t_r} R_k^{t_r} \qquad (11)$$

Subject to:

$$\sum_{t_a} \sum_j a_{ij}^{t_a} Y_j^{t_a} \geq 1, \; i = 1, \ldots, N \qquad (12)$$

$$\sum_{t_r} \sum_k d_{jk}^{t_r} R_k^{t_r} \geq \sum_{t_a} Y_j^{t_a}, \; j = 1, \ldots, M_a \qquad (13)$$

$$\sum_{t_a} \sum_j d_{jk}^{t_a} Y_j^{t_a} \leq n, \; k = 1, \ldots, M_r \qquad (14)$$

$$\sum_{t_a} Y_j^{t_a} \leq 1 \qquad (15)$$

$$\sum_{t_r} R_k^{t_r} \leq 1 \qquad (16)$$

$$a_{ij}^{t_a} = \begin{cases} 1, & \text{if } Q_{ij} = 1 \text{ and } i^{th} \text{ covering position is within the read range } (r) \\ & \text{of reader antenna}(t_a), \text{ which is at the potential position } j. \\ 0, & \text{otherwise} \end{cases} \qquad (17)$$

$$d_{jk} = \begin{cases} T_{jk}, & \text{if rectilinear distance between antenna and reader} \leq \text{cable length} \\ 0, & \text{otherwise} \end{cases} \qquad (18)$$

$$Q_{ij} = \begin{cases} 1, & \text{if the tag } (t_t) \text{ located within } i^{th} \text{ covering position is compatible} \\ & \text{with the reader antenna, which is at potential position } j. \\ 0, & \text{otherwise} \end{cases} \qquad (19)$$

$$T_{jk} = \begin{cases} 1, & \text{if the reader antenna at potential position } j \text{ is compatible with} \\ & \text{the reader at potential position } k. \\ 0, & \text{otherwise} \end{cases} \qquad (20)$$

$$a_{ij}^{t_a} \in \{0,1\}, \; i = 1, \ldots, N; j = 1, \ldots, M \qquad (21)$$

$$d_{jk} \in \{0,1\}, \; j = 1, \ldots, M; k = 1, \ldots, M \qquad (22)$$

$$Y_j^{t_a} \in \{0,1\}, \; j = 1, \ldots, M \qquad (23)$$

$$R_k^{t_r} \in \{0,1\}, \; k = 1, \ldots, M \qquad (24)$$

$$Q_{ij} \in \{0,1\}, \; i = 1, \ldots, N; j = 1, \ldots, M \qquad (25)$$

$$T_{jk} \in \{0,1\}, \; j = 1, \ldots, M; k = 1, \ldots, M \qquad (26)$$

One additional constraint for this model is to ensure that RFID components are compatible with each other. The compatibility variables $Q_{ij} = 1$ if the tag (t_t) at i is compatible with antenna at j, and $T_{jk} = 1$ if the antenna at j is compatible with reader at

k, and are 0 otherwise. Constraint in Eqs. (19) and (20) depict the compatibility of the tag and reader antenna, and the reader antenna and reader, respectively.

4 Case Study

To illustrate the application of this model we consider the warehouse layout prescribed by Food Corporation of India (FCI). FCI was set up in 1965 under the Food Corporation Act 1964 to achieve the objective of the National Food Policy of the Government of India. The primary functions of the FCI are procurement, storage, movement, transportation, distribution and sale of foodgrains on behalf of Government of India (GOI) [20]. Since its inception, FCI has played a key role towards making the nation food secured, and today with sufficient amount of buffer stock, it has completely ruled out the possibility of feminine in the country [20, 21]. It is the backbone for delivering foodgrains to the most vulnerable section of the society through the Targeted Public Distribution System.

However, the system is plagued with inefficiencies. It is suffering from problems like resource wastage, corruption, leakage, non-accountability and non-transparency to name a few [21]. The inefficiency at the FCI warehouse is a major cause of concern. Rotting of food grains, stealing, quality degradation, poor utilization of storage spaces, and mismanagement are some of the many malaises at the warehouse level. Item level RFID implementation could be a possible solution to address the problems in FCI warehouses as it would enable to track the stocks on real time basis. However, because of high implementation cost, it has not gained acceptance in the system [22]. In the recent years, RFID tag cost is decreasing due to rapid advancement in microelectronics. Optimising the number of Readers and Antennas required to cover a warehouse by using this mathematical model could substantially reduce the initial investment cost. We propose to use Ultra High Frequency (UHF) tags in the study for two reasons; the allowed RF range for operation in India is 865–877 MHz, and the UHF tags are the most popular ones being used globally. The UHF tags have the longest reading distance, which makes them advantageous and relevant for the case scenario. The readers considered in the case study work similar to UHF range and their ports are used as mono-static, i.e. each port behaves like a transceiver. The cost of the tags, readers and antennas vary with the technologies used.

As discussed in Sects. 3.3 and 3.4 and illustrated below, we consider two technology settings. First, tag, reader and reader antenna are compatible with each other, and, second, where they are not. While first scenario is very likely in FCI due to independence of each warehouse, the second scenario may arise due to different technology decisions at individual warehouses and inter warehouse exchange of grain packets.

4.1   Prescribed Layouts of FCI

FCI gives a general description of the layout of the warehouse with capacities starting from 1670 Metric Tons (MT) to 50,000 MT [16]. Let's consider a warehouse of 5000 MT capacity. The centre to centre length of the warehouse is (125.55 × 21.80) m. It has three compartments each of capacity 1670 MT. Each Compartment has 12 stacks of size (6.10 × 9.15) m. The intersection of these stacks is considered as potential positions. There are some pillars at the potential positions in the FCI warehouse, where we cannot allocate any RFID reader or reader antenna. We assume these potential positions as invalid positions and rest are valid positions. The top view of the potential and optimal positions in 1670 MT capacity warehouse are shown in Fig. 7. The number of tags in the warehouse would vary from time to time. In the case study, we assume that the coverage of the storage area of the warehouse is approximated by dividing it into small sections of positions ensuring the complete coverage of the warehouse (Fig. 6).

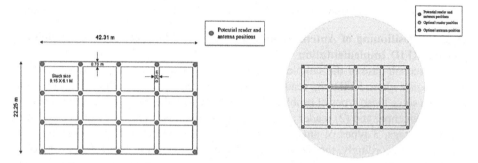

Fig. 6. Top view of the potential positions in the 1670 MT warehouse

Fig. 7. Top view of the optimal positions in the 1670 MT warehouse

4.2 Illustration of the Proposed Model

Two binary integer linear programming models using single and multiple technologies are illustrated below for this study using MATLAB 2014a. The inputs to the model are the dimension of the warehouse layout and parameters associated with RFID equipment. The output of the model is the optimal positions for the reader and reader antenna in the form of two-dimensional (x, y) co-ordinates.

Optimal Positioning of Antennas and Readers with Single Technology for RFID Implementation

The first case of the sample solutions is evaluated with a single set of RFID technology where RFID tag, reader and reader antenna are all compatible. Using the physical parameter values of the RFID system, the read range turns out to be 34.87 m [23]. The results of the optimum number of readers and the reader antennas in three warehouses of capacity 1670, 5000, and 10,000 metric tons (MT) are shown in Table 2. As suggested, by layout plan the stacks for storing food grains are of 3 rows and 4 columns, 3 rows and 12 columns, and 6 rows and 12 columns respectively for the aforesaid warehouse capacities. Solving the single technology model for a warehouse with 3 rows and 4 columns of stacks leads to 40 decision variables and 103 constraints. The optimization results suggest one reader and one reader antenna at a specific position as shown in Fig. 7 out of 20 potential positions (valid and invalid) for warehouse of 1670 MT capacity consisting of 3 rows and 4 columns of stacks. Please note that, the invalid positions refers to the places where the equipment cannot be positioned due to some physical obstacles.

Similarly, for a warehouse with 3 rows and 12 columns of stacks, the formulation leads to 104 decision variables and 279 constraints. The optimization results in 52 potential positions (valid and invalid), and it suggests the two antennas and two readers, respectively. The problem of a warehouse with 6 rows and 12 columns of stacks, the formulation leads to 182 decision variables and 507 constraints. The optimization results suggest two readers and four antennas out of 91 potential positions (valid and invalid), respectively. Now, we can observe from Table 2 that even though the capacity of the warehouse is double (5000 MT to 10,000 MT) but the cost is not.

Optimal Positioning of Antennas and Readers with Multiple Types of Technologies for RFID Implementation

The second case of the sample solutions is evaluated with multiple types of RFID technologies where RFID tag, reader and reader antenna are not compatible with each other. To solve these types of problems we need to check the compatibility of (1) reader & reader antenna, and (2) reader antenna & tag. In this case study, we have considered 2 types of tags, 3 types of antennas and 2 types of readers for implementation in a warehouse. Accordingly, these components have different physical parameters and cost as given in Table 3. As explained in Sect. 3.1, to take care of the compatibility issues we introduce the two more matrices in the formulation considering their frequency range of operation. We obtain different read ranges according to the tag antenna and the reader antennas parameters. The different combinations of read ranges are given in Table 4.

Table 2. Optimal positions of reader and antenna

Warehouse capacity (in MT)	(row-by-column) of stacks	RFID component	No. of optimal positions	X co-ordinate (in m)	Y co-ordinate (in m)	Total cost (in ₹)
1670	3-by-4	Reader	1	10.4	6.86	1,28,910.96
		Antenna	1	20.8	6.86	
5000	3-by-12	Reader	2	41.6	6.86	2,57,821.92
				83.2	6.86	
		Antenna	2	31.2	6.86	
				93.6	6.86	
10,000	6-by-12	Reader	2	31.2	27.44	3,00,399.84
				104	20.58	
		Antenna	4	20.8	27.44	
				41.6	27.44	
				93.6	20.58	
				114.4	20.58	

The inclusion of multiple technological choices further increases the problem complexity. The results of the optimum number of readers and the reader antennas in warehouses with 3 rows and 4 columns, and 3 rows and 12 columns of stacks are shown in Table 5. The optimization results suggest only one reader and one antenna at specific positions out of 20 potential positions for warehouse with 3 rows and 4 columns of stacks of 1670 MT capacity, the formulation leads to 100 decision variables and 203 constraints. Similarly, in case of the warehouse with 3 rows and 12 columns of stacks, the formulation leads to 260 decision variables and 539 constraints. The optimization model results in 52 potential (valid and invalid) positions, and it gives the two reader antennas and the two readers, respectively. Now, from the Tables 2 and 5 we can observe that the total equipment cost in 1670 MT capacity and 5000 MT capacity warehouse is lower in multiple types of technology as compared to the single type of technology for RFID implementation. This is because the reader selected as a solution in the second model is a four port reader which costs less as compared to that in the first model which is an eight port reader.

Table 3. Physical parameters of RFID

	Type	Cost (in ₹)		Threshold power, P_{th} (in W)
Tags	1	15.39		.000014
	2	29.75		.00001
	Type	Cost (in ₹)		Transmission gain, G_T (in W/m)
Reader antenna types	1	21,288.96		7.079
	2	28,916.95		5.02
	3	30,274.80		5.623
	Type	Cost (in ₹)	Frequency range	No. of monostatic ports
Reader types	1	34.866	29.337 MHz	31.074
	2	41.254	34.712 MHz	36.767

Table 4. Read range (in m)

		Antenna type		
		1	2	3
Tag type	1	34.866	29.337	31.074
	2	41.254	34.712	36.767

Table 5. Optimal positions of available multiple types of readers and antennas

Warehouse capacity (in MT)	(row-by-column) of tacks	Tag type	RFID component	Type	No. of optimal positions	X co-ordinate (in m)	Y co-ordinate (in m)	Total cost (in ₹)
1670	3-by-4	1	Reader	2	1	20.8	13.72	1,06,343.69
			Antenna	1	1	20.8	0.0	
5000	3-by-12	1	Reader	2	2	31.2	0.0	2,12,687.38
						104.0	13.72	
			Antenna	1	2	31.2	6.86	
						93.6	13.72	

5   Conclusions and Perspectives

In this paper, we present two models considering the physical characteristics of RFID readers and antennas to minimize the fixed cost by optimally positioning equipment for full coverage of the tags in the warehouses. We apply the model to the real warehouse specifications provided by Food Corporation of India. We make two important observations. First, equipment cost does not increase proportionally as the warehouse size increase. Therefore, at least in large warehouse where problems like resource wastage, corruption, leakage, non-accountability and non-transparency are more acute may be considered to be RFID enabled for real time tracking. Second, use of versatile reader and antenna that can track tags with multiple technologies lowers the cost further for large warehouses, hence, may be preferred compared to single technology solutions. Specifically, the warehouses which acts as the hub and connect many small warehouses must go for such solution so as to avoid multiple tag types coming from individual smaller warehouses.

Our model can be extended in many ways. First, many other parameters related to physical characteristic of the equipment may be studied. Examples include, studying the effect of attenuation factor, and the angular power drop in the wave propagation on the coverage matrix. The directions propagation and the polarization of the antennas are the various factors which could be included using appropriate equations in the physical model to obtain more accurate results from the optimization model. The current model does not consider the losses caused due to the metallic environment and other surrounding materials. Though the case study presented here does not require such a constraint, other types of warehouses may require them. Hence, the formulation in such situations needs to be modified accordingly. The constraint of tag collision needs to be included in the model to make it more realistic. Meta heuristic methods may be used to solve the problem for bigger warehouses. Besides, problem specific heuristics may be designed. For example, in case of multiple technologies, the problems may be simplified by categorizing the items with the similar type of tags and put them together in a specified area. Then, the optimal solution can obtain by applying the single technology formulation in that specified area.

References

1. Ngai, E.W.T., Moon, K.K.L., Riggins, F.J., Yi, C.Y.: RFID research: an academic literature review (1995–2005) and future research directions. Int. J. Prod. Econ. **112**, 510–520 (2008)
2. Lim, M.K., Bahr, W., Leung, S.C.H.: RFID in the warehouse: a literature analysis (1995–2010) of its applications, benefits, challenges and future trends. Int. J. Prod. Econ. **145**, 409–430 (2013)
3. Biswal, A.K., Jenamani, M., Kumar, S.K.: Warehouse efficiency improvement using RFID in a humanitarian supply chain: implications for Indian food security system. Transp. Res. Part E Logist. Transp. Rev. **109**, 205–224 (2018)
4. Osyk, B.A.: RFID adoption and implementation in warehousing. Manag. Res. Rev. **35**, 904–926 (2012)
5. Pacciarelli, D., D'Ariano, A., Scotto, M.: Applying RFID in warehouse operations of an Italian courier express company. NETNOMICS Econ. Res. Electron. Netw. **12**, 209–222 (2011)
6. Jimenez, C., Dauzère-Pérès, S., Feuillebois, C., Pauly, E.: Optimizing the positioning and technological choices of RFID elements for aircraft part identification. Eur. J. Oper. Res. **227**, 350–357 (2013)
7. Drezner, Z., Wesolowsky, G.O.: Covering part of a planar network. Netw. Spat. Econ. **14**, 629–646 (2014)
8. Halder, S., Ghosal, A.: A survey on mobility-assisted localization techniques in wireless sensor networks. J. Netw. Comput. Appl. **60**, 82–94 (2016)
9. Luo, J., Zhou, S., Cheng, H., Liao, Y., Guo, B.: The design and implementation of a cost-effective RFID indoor localization system. In: Proceedings of the 1st Workshop on Context Sensing and Activity Recognition, pp. 1–6 (2015)
10. Revelle, C.: The maximum capture or sphere of influence location problem - Hotelling revisited on a network. J. Reg. Sci. **26**, 343–358 (1986)
11. Farahani, R.Z., Asgari, N., Heidari, N., Hosseininia, M., Goh, M.: Covering problems in facility location: a review. Comput. Ind. Eng. **62**, 368–407 (2012)
12. Tragantalerngsak, S., Holt, J., Rönnqvist, M.: An exact method for the two-echelon, single-source, capacitated facility location problem. Eur. J. Oper. Res. **123**, 473–489 (2000)
13. Church, Velle: The maximal covering location problem. Pap. Reg. Sci. **32**, 101–118 (1974)
14. Melo, M.T., Nickel, S., Saldanha-da-Gama, F.: Facility location and supply chain management – a review. Eur. J. Oper. Res. **196**, 401–412 (2009)
15. FCI: Depot Online System Detailed Project Report (2015)
16. FCI: Engineering Specification of the Godown. http://www.fci.gov.in/engineerings.php?view=7
17. Baker, P., Canessa, M.: Warehouse design: a structured approach. Eur. J. Oper. Res. **193**, 425–436 (2009)
18. Zhang, Z., Lu, Z., Saakian, V., Qin, X., Chen, Q., Zheng, L.R.: Item-level indoor localization with passive UHF RFID based on tag interaction analysis. IEEE Trans. Ind. Electron. **61**, 2122–2135 (2014)
19. Armstrong, S.: RFID Antenna Cables: Getting the Highest Performance Possible. http://blog.atlasrfidstore.com/rfid-antenna-cables-getting-the-highest-performance-possible
20. CAG: Storage Management and Movement of Food Grains in Food Corporation of India (2013)

21. Kumar, S.: Report of the High Level Committee on Reorienting the Role and Restructuring of the Food Corporation of India (2015)
22. Wadhwa, J.D.: Report on the State of Delhi, Central Vigilance Committee on Public Distribution System (2007)
23. MTI Wireless Edge: MT-242027/NRH/K 865 - 870 MHz, 8.5dBic RHCP Reader Antenna. http://www.mtiwe.com/?CategoryID=278&ArticleID=56

Data Science and Data Analytics

Comparative Study Between Classification Algorithms Based on Prediction Performance

A. G. Hari Narayanan[1,2], Megha Prabhakar[2(✉)],
B. Lakshmi Priya[2(✉)], and J. Amar Pratap Singh[3(✉)]

[1] Department of Computer Application,
Noorul Isalm Centre for Higher Education, Kumaracoil, Thucklay,
Kanyakumari 629 180, Tamilnadu, India
hariag2002@gmail.com
[2] Department of Computer Science and IT, Amrita School of Arts and Sciences,
Kochi Amrita Vishwa Vidyapeetham, Kochi, India
meghal2@live.com,
lakshmipriyab007@gmail.com
[3] Department of Computer Science and Engineering,
Noorul Isalm Centre for Higher Education, Kumaracoil, Thucklay,
Kanyakumari 629 180, Tamilnadu, India
japsindia@yahoo.com

Abstract. In todays "data-centric" world, the prevalence of vast and immeasurable amount of data pertaining to various fields of study has led to the need for properly analyzing and apprehending this information to yield knowledge that becomes useful in decision making. Among the many procedures for handling this multitude of data, "classification" is the one that aids in making decisions based on categorization of data and "feature selection" is the process of picking out attributes relevant to the study. Keeping classification as the central idea of our study, we aim at presenting a comparative analysis of prediction accuracies obtained by two chosen classification algorithms, namely, SVM and RBFN. We proceed to introduce feature selection using both filter and wrapper methods along with SVM and RBFN to showcase a detailed analytical report on variations in performance when using classification algorithms alone, and with application of feature selection. The four approaches used for feature selection in our study are; Information Gain, Correlation, Particle Swarm Optimization (PSO) and Greedy method. Performance of the algorithms under study is evaluated based on time, accuracy of prediction and area under ROC curve. Although time and accuracy are effective parameters for comparison, we propose to consider ROC area as the criterion for performance evaluation. An optimal solution will have the area under ROC curve value approaching 1.

Keywords: Classification · Feature selection · SVM · RBFN
KNN · ROC curve

1 Introduction

We live in a data age. All around us and in every field of work like medicine, engineering, science, business etc., bulk amount of data is generated at an explosive rate. This growth can be attributed to computerization of our society and also the

J. K. Mandal and D. Sinha (Eds.): CSI 2017, CCIS 836, pp. 185–196, 2018.
https://doi.org/10.1007/978-981-13-1343-1_19

development of data management tools and storage mechanisms. It is common knowledge that businesses use this tremendous and widely available data to procreate meaningful information by understanding, analyzing and manipulating this data based on their requirements. This has essentially led to the development of "data mining", a hugely popular field of study today that deals with churning out useful information or knowledge from raw, unprocessed data using many data mining methods and techniques.

Following are the main functions in the process of mining data:

- Characterization: Summarization of general features of a target class
- Discrimination: comparing features of a target class against other conflicting classes
- Mining frequent patterns, associations and correlation: Extract usual and frequent patterns
- Classification: procedure of building a model to interpret and ascertain object classes
- Prediction: process of deducing class labels for objects whose labels are unknown
- Clustering: Congregating similar objects in groups
- Outlier Analysis: process of analyzing incompatible objects or outliers

The process of mining data is realized through a number of steps, were a combination of more than one these steps usually yields better results in terms of performance to the end user. These are:

- Cleaning and assimilating data from different sources
- Selecting data applicable to the analysis task
- Fine tune data to a form that supports the task in hand
- Extract desired results using mining methods
- Evaluate the result
- Deliver the result in a meaningful and useful manner

Realization of each of these steps or functions is possible through certain methods, techniques and algorithms available with various data management tools. A detailed discussion on all the above steps and functions is out of scope of our study as we focus mainly on classification, prediction and feature selection. The classification algorithms used here are Support Vector Machine (using SMO) and Radial Basis Function Network (RBFN). Along with classification, feature selection concept is also experimented to improve that performance of the algorithms under study. We chose two filter methods using Information Gain and Correlation, and two wrapper methods using PSO and Greedy method.

A. Classification

Data objects may be associated with a class or a category and the objects may fall into one or more classes. In data mining terms, "classification" refers to the process of sculpting a model that identifies and distinguishes the classes among objects. Classification process is associated with a "training set" which refers to the original data that is used to generate the model using a classification algorithm. Once a successful model is created, a "test set" can be run on the model to predict the class labels of unclassified objects in the test set. For example, a data collection describing features of emails received in an inbox can have them fall into any of the two categories; spam or not-spam. A model can be created using an available training data and the generated model can be used to determine whether a new email in the inbox is a spam or not.

Support Vector Machines

SVM is a highly accurate algorithm that categorizes objects by trying to compute a maximum margin hyper plane. This hyper plane would enhance the training data to a high dimension by separating objects that belong to different classes. SVMs can assort classes to objects that are linearly or non-linearly separable, making it even more acceptable. The separating hyper plane is calculated using the following formulae;

$$W.X + b = 0$$

where W is a weight vector and $W = \{w_1, w_2, w_3, w_4, \ldots, w_n\}$ and b or "bias" is a scalar value.

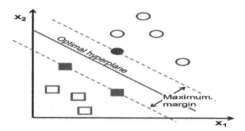

Fig. 1. Support vector machine (Color figure online)

There may be in most conditions infinite number of hyper planes available and SVM algorithm has to find out the best one out of them. The best hyper plane is estimated as the one having the largest margin so that it can precisely categorize future objects than the hyper planes with smaller margins (as shown in Fig. 1). The colored objects in Fig. 1 represents the "support vectors" and are equally close to the optimal dividing hyper plane. We chose to use the SMO package in WEKA to implement SVM based classification.

Radial Basis Function Network

RBFN is a neural networks based algorithm that uses radial functions to realize its calculations. It is associated basically with three layers, namely, the input layer, hidden layer and the output layer. In terms of classification process, the input layer represents all the attribute input units of the task. The hidden layer consists of nodes were each node represents a radial function. Each input node is connected to each of the nodes in the hidden layer. The output layer gives you the "class" of an object and is a weighted sum of all the outputs from the hidden layer. A general representation of the RBFN algorithm is depicted in Fig. 2.

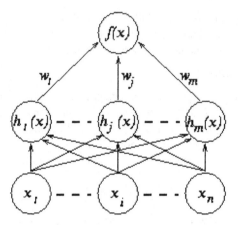

Fig. 2. Radial basis function network

Here, x represents the n input attributes or nodes that are dispatched forward to each of the hidden layer nodes. The hidden layer nodes are represented as the function h(x) and the output as f(x). The radial function h(x) at each hidden node is represented as,

$$h(x) = \exp\left(-\frac{(x-c)^2}{r^2}\right)$$

where r is the radius or standard deviation, c is the center and can be calculated using any clustering method like the K-Means. The output function f(x) takes the following form,

$$f(x) = \sum_{j=1}^{m} w_j h_j(x)$$

The initial step is the calculation of the centers c and the number of centers will represent the total number of nodes in the hidden layer. The second step attaches a weight w to the output of the hidden layer nodes in order to calculate the sum and give out the final output. Although neural networks are generally disregarded for their relatively larger time consumption for training and poor interpretability, they are well received and acknowledged for their ability to tolerate noisy data and classify objects into categories they are unaware of. In WEKA, RBFNetwork package is used to perform a radial basis function network based classification.

B. Feature Selection

A realistic data set may contain huge amount of tuples represented using comparatively larger number of attributes or features. And all these attributes may not prove to be appropriate or relevant to the analysis task in hand and should be ignored based on some statistical conditions. Feature Selection or Attribute Subset Selection is a data preprocessing step that aims at discarding attributes that are irrelevant and not applicable to the analysis task in hand. This elimination of irrelevant features is done such that the results attained are proximately similar or better than those achieved by considering all the attributes. This process is intended at ignoring all the insignificant features thus prompting better accuracy, performance and reduced time and complexity. The two approaches to feature selection are using filter and wrapper methods. Filter methods aspire to rank or score the attributes in a way independent to the classifier used. Thus, they provide you with a more generalized result than that of wrapper methods which tries to score attributes and generate a subset by exploring the feature set by means of a classification model. Each new subspace of attributes are tested against the model and accordingly scored based on performance. Wrapper approach of feature subset selection is thus considered better than filter methods as they furnish the optimal feature subset.

Feature Ranking Based on Information Gain

Information Gain is a measure used for choosing attributes that have the most information required to perform a task like classification. It removes ambiguity by recognizing only those features that holds the highest value among others. An attribute with the highest information gain is considered as the "splitting attribute" where the feature set gets split or divided. The expected average information required to classify an object is given by,

$$\text{Info(D)} = -\sum\nolimits_{i=1}^{m} p_i log_2(p_i)$$

where p_i is the probability that a tuple belongs to class C_i and Info(D) is also called the entropy of D. Now, if the feature set is split at attribute A, then the amount of expected information required further to achieve an efficient classification is given as,

$$\text{Info}_A(D) = \sum\nolimits_{j=1}^{v} \frac{|D_j|}{|D|} \times Info(D_j)$$

Information Gain is given as,

$$\text{Gain(A)} = Info(D) - Info_A(D)$$

The attributes with the highest gain value is chosen as the next splitting attribute so that the overall information required to classify an object or tuple is kept at minimum. The final output offered by this measure will be a ranked list of attributes of a feature set starting from the ones that hold highest value (information gain) or information. In WEKA, feature selection using Information Gain is realized using the InfoGainAttributeEval method

Feature Ranking Based on Correlation

Correlation among attributes in a feature set illustrates the dependency between attributes or how strongly on feature entails another. Correlation for a numeric data goes by the following formulae,

$$r_{A,B} = \frac{\sum_{i=1}^{n}(a_i b_i) - n\bar{A}\bar{B}}{n\sigma_A \sigma_B}$$

where r represents the correlation coefficient, n is the number of tuples, a_i and b_i are the values of A and B in tuple i, $\bar{A}$ and $\bar{B}$ are mean values of attributes A and B and σ_A and σ_B are the standard deviations of A and B. The principle followed for ranking and selecting features based on correlation is that the attributes remain highly correlated to the class and minimally correlated to each other. It is implemented in WEKA using CorrelationAttributeEval method.

Particle Swarm Optimization

PSO is a type of meta-heuristic optimization algorithm inspired from the social behavior of birds or fish. It was developed in the year 1995 with the objective of creating a model to express the social behavior of animals like a flock of birds or school of fish and later on came to be used as an optimization algorithm in various branches of science and engineering like machine learning, data mining, image processing etc. The main task of an optimization problem is to find the "best" solution and for this, it uses the concepts of communication and learning. PSO works similarly by enabling the swarm (search space) members to communicate learn about each other and achieve the global best solution. Each swarm member i have a position denoted by X_i, a velocity V_i that describes the movement of a particle and a personal best experience denoted by $Pbest_i$ as in Fig. 3.

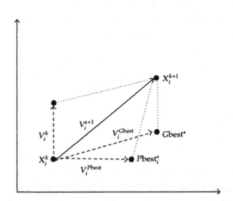

Fig. 3. PSO working

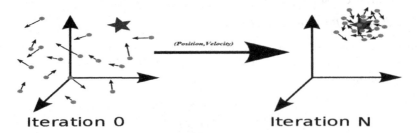

Fig. 4. Swarm movement

In advance to position, velocity and personal best, there is a global best value common to all swarm members and is not specific to any swarm member denoted by Gbest as in Fig. 4. With each iteration, the swarm members co-operate to achieve this global best solution by updating their position and velocity accordingly in each iteration. In Fig. 3, the particle X_i^k has velocity V_i^k and personal best value Pbest$_i$. In the next iteration k + 1, the particle moves parallel to its velocity vector, personal best vector and the global best vector to achieve the new position X_i^{k+1} which could be a better position for the particle i. Hence in every iteration, particles move closer to the global best solution in the swarm. The formulae for updating particle position in the swarm is given by,

$$X_i^{k+1} = X_i^k + V_i^{k+1}$$

$$V_i^{k+1} = wV_i^k + C_1\left(V_i^{Pbest}\right) + C_2\left(V_i^{Gbest}\right)$$

where w, c1 and c_2 are real valued coefficients, $V_i^{Pbest} = \left(Pbest_i^k - X_i^k\right)$ and $V_i^{Gbest} = \left(Gbest_i^k - X_i^k\right)$. This optimization capability of PSO makes it highly efficient and suitable for feature subset selection applications. It is implemented in WEKA using the PSOSearch algorithm.

Greedy Method

Greedy methods can be employed in algorithms to look for an optimum solution in every step. In WEKA, it is implemented using the GreedyStepwise algorithm along with an evaluator. The algorithm can start from any position in the search space with no/all attributes under consideration. It then moves forward/backwards by adding/removing attributes at every step. The evaluator algorithm verifies the performance of the subspace and if a decrease in evaluation if encountered, the algorithm terminates.

2   Related Works

To support our study, we have analyzed various research works done in the same context. Iain Brown and Christophe Mues in their study [1] have proposed a comparative study between traditional classification algorithms like logistic regression, neural networks and decisions trees while also exploring the possibilities of least square support vector machines, gradient boosting and random forests. Performance was measured based on the Area under the curve (AUC) value. Their study was carried out on a credit score feature set prone to imbalanced data. The implementation and analysis of the problem offered a result that favors random forests and gradient boosting classifiers which were found to have better performance than the other classifiers as they were found to have better tolerance to imbalanced data.

Yet another analysis study [2] offers a collative study between the Naïve Bayesian and Decision Tree algorithm. These were applied on a collection of crime information to predict the type of crime in different states of The United States of America. The analysis was implemented in WEKA tool and evaluated based on accuracy value. The authors found that Decision Tree algorithm for classification surpasses Naïve Bayesian classifier by offering an accuracy of 83.9519%.

Kotsiantis has successfully and clearly explained some of the best supervised learning approaches [3]. This survey provides an in-depth analysis of some of the most popular algorithms under the categories of logic-based, perceptron-based, statistical and instance-based. Decision tree algorithm is chosen for analysis under logic-based approach, Single layered perceptron, multi layered perceptron and radial basis function networks are reviewed under the perceptron-based category, Naïve Bayesian and Bayesian networks are explored under the statistical category and K-nearest neighbor classifier is examined under the instance-based method. Further, the study proceeds to analyze Support Vector Machines which is one of the recent and popular classification algorithms used. The analytical survey offered by the author provides adequate prior knowledge about various supervised learning methods.

A comparative study [4] done on a feature set having information regarding a car manufacturer's product characteristics proposed the usage of classification algorithms like CHAID, C&R and QUEST belonging to tree category algorithms. Along with these, neural networks, Bayesian, logistic regression and SVM classifiers were also tested on the data for fault prediction. Support Vector Machines were found to have the overall better accuracy level compared to all the other classifiers chosen. The output of the study also suggests that even though the tree algorithms consume more time to build the model for classification, they offer good accuracy levels.

A survey report presented by Dash and Liu [5] illustrates in detail the use of feature selection in classification. Feature selection has become popular in the recent times as it reduces the time, complexity and is found to improve performance of a classifier. The authors in their study provides an extensive analysis on the types of feature selection methods and identifies four steps in feature selection namely, generation procedure, evaluation function, stopping criterion, and validation procedure. It is found that surprisingly, many feature selection methods do not perform or attempt the first two steps.

Some other notable study references are also discussed briefly. In [6], the author makes an analysis on comparative approach of study, proposes a recommended approach, and also offers a list of pitfalls to avoid while making a comparative study. [7] provides an insight into the evolutionary optimization algorithm known as Particle Swarm Optimization(PSO). PSO is applied on an SVM classifier to address prevalent classification problems and found that PSO-SVM hybrid approach gives better accuracy than other feature selection approaches. Instance-Based or Memory-Based Learning, Error back propagation, (k-NN) k-Nearest Neighbor algorithm and (MLP) multilayer perceptron algorithms are implemented in [8] on a data set using WEKA tool and the results favors kNN classifier that achieved 73.33% accuracy.

3 Experiment

In the experiment study, we chose to compare the predictive classification performances of two algorithms namely, SVM (using SMO) and RBFN taken individually and also with each of the feature selection methods. This gives us the following different algorithms for comparison; SMO, InfoGainAttributeEval - SMO, CorrelationAttributeEval - SMO, PSO - SMO, GreedyStepwise - SMO, RBFN, InfoGain AttributeEval - RBFN, CorrelationAttributeEval - RBFN, PSO – RBFN and GreedyStepwise - RBFN. We chose to work in WEKA platform as it is a simple, easy-to-use and powerful tool that offers surplus amount of algorithms, methods and solutions to realize data mining tasks. A model is build using a chosen classifier from the above list on the training set. Using this model, a test data set is evaluated in order to study the performance of the algorithm and to analyze which feature selection approach provides better evaluation results for each classifier. The collative study is done based on three values obtained after prediction; time to predict, accuracy and ROC area. The experiment results are depicted in Table 1.

A. Time to Predict

This value corresponds to the time taken by a classifier to predict the class labels for a test set based on a predictive model. An efficient algorithm will always take the least amount of time for classification.

B. Accuracy

In WEKA, the classification result parameter "Correctly classified instances" is regarded as the accuracy for that classifier. It represents in number and percentage the amount of test tuples that were correctly classified against the prediction model. This value directly reflects the accuracy of the classifier used for the process.

C. ROC curve

Receiver Operating Characteristics curve plots the trade-off between true positive rates (TPR) and false positive rates (FPR). TPR corresponds to the magnitude of positive tuples that are correctly labeled and FPR represents the magnitude of negative tuples that are incorrectly labeled as positive. The area under the ROC curve exemplifies the accuracy of the classification algorithm used. A proficient and compelling classifier will have the average ROC curve value approaching 1 while any value less that 0.5 is equal to random guessing. ROC curve representations for the best two classifiers among SMO and RBFN are depicted in Figs. 5 and 6, where the X-axis represents true positives and the Y-axis depicts false positives.

D. Database

All the algorithms under consideration were run on a data set representing types of forests based on their spectral characteristics. There are 27 attributes that describe the spectral characteristics in wavelengths captured from satellite images. The feature set provides a training set having a total of 198 instances and a test set with 325 instances. The four class labels are described as s, h, o and d attributing to the four different forest types.

Table 1. Predictive analysis results for forest type's data

Prediction algorithm		Time to test (in seconds)	Accuracy (%)	Avg. ROC area
SMO	SMO	0.04	84	0.917
	InfoGain-SMO	0.04	84.3077	0.921
	Correlation-SMO	0.02	83.3846	0.913
	PSO-SMO	0.01	83.0769	0.914
	GreedyStewise-SMO	0.03	83.0769	0.912
RBFN	RBFN	0.03	13.5385	0.495
	InfoGain-RBFN	0.01	50.4615	0.744
	Correlation-RBFN	0.01	49.8462	0.738
	PSO-RBFN	0.01	48	0.749
	GreedyStewise-RBFN	0.01	53.5385	0.700

4 Experiment Results

From the results of the experiment study presented in Table 1, it is clearly specific that Support Vector Machines using SMO provides better prediction results than Radial Basis Function network classifier. SMO achieves better accuracy and average area under ROC curve that are indications of an efficient classifier. It is also found that feature selection in general has a positive effect on prediction results of both the classifiers. The finest performance is achieved by InfoGain-SMO classifier with an accuracy of 84.3077% and ROC area of 0.921, which is closer to 1. The least performance is displayed by the RBFN classifier without the use of any feature selection mechanism. Also, the results rank information gain and Particle Swarm Optimization as the best feature subset selection methods. Taking into consideration the time taken to

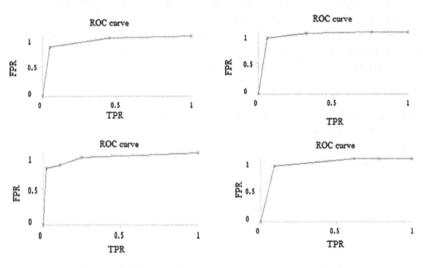

Fig. 5. ROC curve for classes d, h, o and s using SMO

predict the classes for tuples, it is found that RBFN holds a better stand when compared to SMO. This suggests that SMO, while being the better classifier than RBFN in terms of accuracy and ROC area, consumes more time to realize its output.

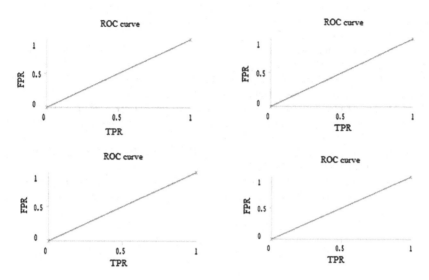

Fig. 6. ROC curve for classes d, h, o and s using RBFN

5 Conclusion

Classification is an important task in data mining that can provide efficient solutions to categorization problems in the real world. It is therefore of the utmost importance that classifiers of the highest efficiency in terms of performance are identified to reduce complexity, consumption of time and errors. The proposed study precisely aims at addressing this need by presenting a comparative study between two different classification algorithms and a combination of feature selection approaches along with them. It is found that Support Vector Machine classifier using SMO generally offers better prediction performance than RBFN classifier and feature selection used along with classification algorithms proves to provide better prediction results. These results are achieved on a numerical data set and may vary depending on the type of data used for the task.

For future works, more data sets or corpuses containing different types of data like numeric, nominal, mixed, etc. could be used for a similar kind of analytical experiment using different classification algorithms. Further, more evolutionary and genetic algorithms (GA) for feature selection besides PSO could be studied as they are highly efficient, popular and usually used along with classification algorithms to obtain better results.

References

1. Brown, I., Mues, C.: An experimental comparison of classification algorithms for imbalanced credit scoring data sets. Expert Syst. Appl. **39**(3), 3446–3453 (2012)
2. Iqbal, R., Murad, M.A.A., Mustapha, A., Panahy, P.H.S., Khanahmadliravi, N.: An experimental study of classification algorithms for crime prediction. Indian J. Sci. Technol. **6** (3), 4219–4225 (2013)
3. Kotsiantis, S.B.: Supervised machine learning: a review of classification techniques. Informatica **31**, 249–268 (2007)
4. Amooee, G., Minaei-Bidgoli, B., Bagheri-Dehnavi, M.: A comparison between data mining prediction algorithms for fault detection. IJCSI Int. J. Comput. Sci. **8**(6(3)) (2011)
5. Dash, M., Liu, H.: Feature selection for classification. Intell. Data Anal. **1**, 131–156 (1997)
6. SalzBerg, S.L.: On comparing classifiers: pitfalls to avoid and a recommended approach. Data Mining Knowl. Discov. **1**, 317–327 (1997)
7. Tu, C.-J., Chuang, L.-Y., Chang, J.-Y., Yang, C.-H.: Feature selection using PSO-SVM. IAENG Int. J. Comput. Sci. **33**(1), IJCS_33_1_18
8. Stylios, I.C., Vlachos, V., Androulidakis, I.: Performance comparison of machine learning algorithms for diagnosis of cardiotocograms with class inequality. In: International IEEE Conference on TELFOR 2014 (2014)

Determination of Connectivity Using Minimum Connected Dominating Set Based on the Measure of Eigen Centrality in a Heterogeneous IoT Network

Partha Sarathi Banerjee[1(✉)], Satyendra Nath Mandal[1], and Biswajit Maiti[2]

[1] Kalyani Government Engineering College, Kalyani, India
psbanerjee.kgec@gmail.com, satyen_kgec@rediffmail.com
[2] Government General Degree College Khargapur, Khargapur, India
bmkgec@gmail.com

Abstract. Ubiquitous connectivity, irrespective of technology, is one of the main challenges that have to be conquered to make the things speak among themselves and to make a successful IoT (Internet of Things) framework. The problem of IoT, at present, lies in the intercommunication among devices having different kinds of connection interface. As a result, percolation of message is blocked even between two neighbors of same kind within close proximity because of the presence of large number of other devices having mismatched communication interface in the neighborhood. Hence, a seemingly connected network may become disconnected.

In this paper, effort has been made to overcome the communication bottleneck that may arise due to co-located sensing and/or actuating nodes with different network interfaces. To investigate the problem mathematically, the network is taken as a graph consisting of randomly deployed nodes of different interface types. Minimum Connected Dominating Set (MCDS) algorithm is used to find out the optimal positions of nodes where Special-Purpose-Multiple-Interface nodes (SPMIN) capable to communicate with different types of connection interfaces are to be placed. Extensive simulation of this arrangement has been done and is found to improve the path finding probability, packet-delivery-ratio and reliability in the network.

Keywords: Internet of Things (IoT) · Heterogeneous network
Ubiquitous connectivity · Minimum connected dominating set
Multiple-interface nodes

1 Introduction

Internet of Things (IoT) has ushered in a revolution in the wireless communication by means of large scale deployment of spatially distributed devices with embedded identification, sensing and/or actuating capabilities. It is envisioned to wipe out the conceptual barrier between physical and virtual world to a maximum possible extent. IoT can be instrumental in achieving this long nourished dream of network engineers

© Springer Nature Singapore Pte Ltd. 2018
J. K. Mandal and D. Sinha (Eds.): CSI 2017, CCIS 836, pp. 197–211, 2018.
https://doi.org/10.1007/978-981-13-1343-1_20

all over the world [1–3]. IoT resembles a pervasive network infrastructure consisting of RFID embedded objects, sensors, mobile phones etc. Successful operation of this infrastructure depends on percolation probability of information/data from source to sink. It is envisioned that trillions of devices should communicate among each other to provide a seamless connectivity irrespective of any infrastructural constraints [4–6].

Smart services like Smart city, Smart health, Smart home etc. are the demand of the day. IoT is the only way to achieve these goals. Several challenges have been identified in addressing different features of IoT [7]. Communication blockage due to inherent heterogeneity in real life IoT network has been considered to be one of the most prominent problem to be overcome, though few proposals have been made so far to resolve this problem [8–17]. Actually, IoT, in real sense, can be considered as a network of closely collaborated objects those have the ability to communicate among themselves. But, communication is possible only among the peers, equipped with similar type of identifier as well as connection interface. It is quite impossible to make one type of node, viz., Wireless Sensors to exchange data with a different type of node like RFID embedded devices.

WSN have been considered for long as the basic building block of IoT. Usually WSN consists of homogeneous devices to form isolated clusters of a kind or other those cannot interoperate with each other having varied connection interfaces. So, different WSN (Wireless Sensor Network) nodes cannot make a session if they have mismatched connection interface. In spite of these limitations, WSN nodes are indispensible part of IoT architecture. A smart network by principle should be event driven and sensor nodes are the only interfaces through which environmental data can be read. Keeping these nodes intact, some solutions need to be devised so that seamless percolation of data/information within a network, consisting of heterogeneous nodes, is possible. With this problem in view, effort has been made to tackle the issue by optimal distribution of SPMIN in the network.

2 Related Work

Heterogeneous IoT framework has recently been very popular in network research. There are two domains in which the total set of works has been divided. One is homogeneous domain where the nodes are of similar type and hence the gateways are placed in a fixed optimal position without taking care of technology mismatch among the nodes. The other domain is heterogeneous IoT, where nodes with different technologies try to communicate with each other. The latter is tested in this work. Heterogeneity has been explored in IoT related literatures in different aspects. Shih et al. [8] has proposed a new middleware for integrating the IoT nodes of different types. Multiple Protocol Transport Network (MPTN) gateway is implemented for distribution of messages among multiple networks. Service oriented heterogeneity has been explored by De Poorter in [9] and Gama et al. in [10]. In [9], a new architecture IDRA has been devised to take care of interconnectivity of resource-hungry heterogeneous IoT nodes. A middleware for the IoT has been developed using the concepts of Service Oriented Computing [10]. The authors in [11] have presented a technique for strategic use of gateways to minimize message loss and hence optimize energy consumption in heterogeneous IoT network. Multi-functional Special-purpose-Gateway placement has been proposed as a solution to the problem of communication bottleneck in [12]. The authors of [13] have suggested an agent based framework 'iotSilo' to address the problem of connectivity in IoT framework consisting of heterogeneous nodes. Parallel opportunistic routing has been used as a technique to interconnect the technically varied devices through the Solution Specific Gate-Ways (SSGW) which are optimally deployed in a heterogeneous IoT network [14]. Optimal gateway placement in heterogeneous WSN has been discussed in [15, 16]. An ILP based cost-optimized solution framework has been developed to place the gateways. Penumalli and Palanichamy [17] have devised an optimal CDS construction algorithm for activity scheduling in MANET. Sheu et al. has devised an energy efficient probabilistic coverage criterion for WSN [18] which is one of the most important factors for optimal placement of gateways.

In this paper a novel solution to the communication problem among the heterogeneous IoT nodes has been proposed through the determination of minimum connected dominating set. The algorithm, discussed in this paper, suggests an optimal number of special-purpose multi-interface nodes and their optimal positioning, so that, the connectivity and throughput of the ensuing network is increased.

3 System Description

A small network resembling simple IoT situation is shown in Fig. 1 below. Here, a Bluetooth enabled node communicates with other Bluetooth enabled nodes but can not communicate with WiFi enabled nodes. The same problem occurs with other types of nodes also.

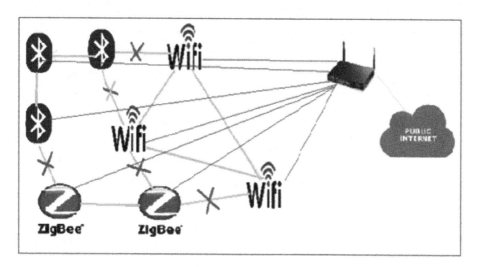

Fig. 1. Sample IoT network with heterogeneous nodes.

Usual way to connect all these nodes to Internet, they are arranged to remain connected to a common Gateway. This may cause excessive power dissipation in these nodes and hence affect the life span of the network. This problem is addressed to some extent by introduction of agent nodes which can be deployed in close proximity of the network nodes. These agent nodes will then represent a particular technology and communicate with the gateway. Then the network is subjected to a single-point-failure as excessive engagement of these agent nodes will make them dissipate energy at a faster rate and die. Our suggestion to get rid of the communication bottleneck problem is to deploy special purpose multi-interface nodes at some strategic locations as shown in Fig. 2(a). In Fig. 2(b) the same is represented as graph of nodes for the sake of mathematical analysis. These special nodes would communicate with all other types of nodes in the network and remove the communication impairment. This arrangement would result in an increased lifetime of the network as the power consumption due to transmission is lesser than the previous arrangement.

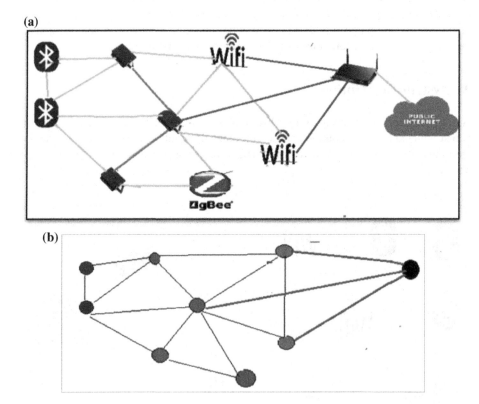

Fig. 2. (a) Network with Special-Purpose-Multi-Interface (SPMIN) nodes to improve commu-nication among heterogeneous nodes. (b) Graph corresponding to the network of (a). Red nodes are the SPINs capable of communicating with any node within their range. (Color figure online)

4 System Model

4.1 Network that Resembles Random Geometric Graph

The standard configuration model of wireless network may be thought of as an ensemble of random graphs, in which network connectivity is specified only by the degree distribution of different kinds of nodes and the available amount of connectivity among these nodes. In a densely populated region, nodes should have higher degree than in a sparse region. Random geometric graph [18, 19] has always been a natural choice when there is a need to represent a wireless network. V is assumed to be the set of nodes or vertices. A geometric graph G = (V, r) can be similar to a graph G_1 = (V, E), in which V is the set of all vertices and E = $\{(u, v)|\forall u, v \in V, \|u - v\| \leq r\}$, where 'r' denotes the uniform transmission range of all the nodes. A random geometric graph (G) consists of nodes that are independent and identically distributed (i.i.d). In this paper, nodes are assumed to be dispersed randomly in a square area. The nodes in the network can make links/edges with neighbor nodes those fall within its transmission range r. But, presence of nodes with different kinds of interfaces should reduce the amount of links/edges as one kind of node cannot directly communicate with other kind though found within its range.

A simple network has been considered with only two types of nodes as shown in Fig. 3. Neighborhood of a node is usually formed purely on the basis of transmission range. Effective neighborhood of a node in a network, consisting of different types of nodes, is formed when the edge set E is filtered according to the types of the nodes. Therefore, modified E becomes $E_{mod} = \{(u, v)|\forall u, v \in V, type(u) = type(v), \|u - v\| \leq r\}$. Two nodes will be able to communicate through an edge that is a member of E_{mod}.

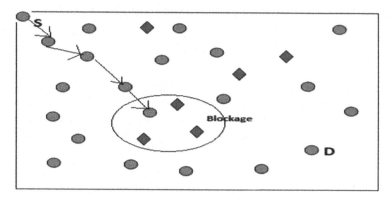

Fig. 3. Network consisting of two different types of nodes: Blue and Red. S is source and D is the destination. (Color figure online)

A good network is characterized by reliable communication between any pair of source and destination. To achieve this, introduction of SPMINs can be thought of as interpreter between two different technologies as is shown in Fig. 2. Strategic deployment of optimal number of these SPMINs is expected to solve the problem to the maximum extent. From obvious reasons, the strategic locations will be the points where maximum bottleneck occurs and these points are determined using MCDS algorithm. Since these nodes are costly, their deployment density should well planned. The MCDS algorithm is used here to determine the optimum number of multi-interface nodes and their optimum placement in the network.

5 Definitions

5.1 Random Geometric Graph

A Random Geometric Graph [19], as already discussed in previous section, closely resembles a wireless network. The neighbours of a node are defined to be the set of nodes of same interface type those are located within the minimum transmission range of a node. Then it is necessary to filter the neighborhood on the basis of type of node and the following algorithm based on Jaccard Dissimilarity criterion is used to take care of this.

5.2 Jaccard Dissimilarity Based Eigen Centrality [20]

Jaccard Similarity is described as the proportion of shared neighbors between two adjacent nodes in a network and is defined in the following way

$$S = \frac{|V^+(i) \bigcap V^+(j)|}{|V^+(i) \bigcup V^+(j)|} \tag{1}$$

where $V^+(i)$ represents the neighbors of i those lie in the transmission region of i and $V^+(j)$ represents the neighbors of j those lie in the transmission region of j.

Then, Dissimilarity is defined as the neighbor nodes those are not shared by i and j, i.e., the nodes those are not common neighbors of i and j. Therefore, it can be expressed as

$$D_{ij} = 1 - \frac{|V^+(i) \bigcap V^+(j)|}{|V^+(i) \bigcup V^+(j)|} \tag{2}$$

This kind of dissimilarity measure is not sufficient to describe the effective influence of a node in the network as it should depend on the relative dissimilarity of its neighbors. Therefore, Eigen centrality which is a measure of relative dissimilarity of a node is defined as the following manner to account for the effective dissimilarity

$$C_i = \frac{1}{N} \sum_{j=1}^{N} W_{ij} C_j, \tag{3}$$

where N is the number of nodes, C is the centrality index of every node in the network and $W_{ij} = A_{ij} D_{ij}$; A_{ij} is the adjacency matrix of the network-graph.

5.3 Minimum Connected Dominating Set (MCDS) [21]

A Connected Dominating Set (CDS) of a graph G represents a set of connected nodes which are adjacent to other nodes of the network. There may be more than one connected dominating sets of a graph.

A Minimum Connected Dominating Set (MCDS) of a graph is a Connected Dominating Set which has the least possible cardinality among all the connected dominating sets of the graph. In this work members of MCDS are chosen based on two criteria: number of neighbors and dissimilarity index of the nodes. Symbolically, a random geometric graph can be represented as G (V, r) where V is the set of nodes and r is the transmission range of a node. Edge set E can be expressed as

$$E = \{(u, v) | \forall u, v \in V, \|u - v\| \leq r\} \tag{4}$$

Minimum Connected Dominating Set (MCDS) is determined in terms of degree of a node, d(u) and is given by

$$MCDS = \{i | i \in V, d(i) \text{ is maximum, } C(i) \text{ has the maximum value}\} \tag{5}$$

where C is the set of centrality indices of the nodes.

6 Algorithm

A number of application specific sensors of common communication technology in near vicinity are grouped into a cluster. Every such cluster is represented by a cluster-head that may be referred to as collector node. These collector nodes collect data from

Table 1. Algorithm for finding out the dissimilarity based centrality index for each of the sink nodes according to jaccard dissimilarity measure

ALGORITHM A :
Inputs:
Set of sink nodes S=$\{s_{11}, s_{12}, s_{13}, \ldots \ldots s_{1(n-m)}, s_{21}, s_{22}, s_{23}, \ldots s_{2m}\}$, with cardinality n. S contains two types of nodes type 1 and type 2. There are (n-m) number of type 1 nodes and m number of type 2 nodes. The nodes are assumed to form a graph G(N.E), where N is the set of vertices and E is the set of edges
Transmission range between each pair of S is r. s_i and s_j are neighbor to each other if {distance $(s_i, s_j) \leq r$}
1. *Create A_{ij} (adjacency matrix) for the given network G(N,E)*
2. *Calculate dissimilarity index D_{ij} for each node i with respect to all its neighbors j.* $$D_{ij} = 1 - \frac{|V^+(i) \cap V^+(j)|}{|V^+(i) \cup V^+(j)|}, \text{ where } V^+(i) \text{ represents the neighbors of i who lies in}$$ *the transmission region of i and are homogeneous to i. $V^+(j)$ represents the neighbors of j who lies in the transmission region of j and are homogeneous to j. If i and j are of same type, $|V^+(i) \cap V^+(j)|$ is maximum*
3. *Find $W_{ij} = A_{ij} D_{ij}$, where i,jϵ\{1,2,3,......,N\}*
4. *Calculate $C_i = \frac{1}{N} \sum_{j=1}^{N} W_{ij} C_j$, where i=1,2,3.....,N*
5. *Create an ordered set of nodes $K = \{k_1, k_2, k_3, \ldots k_N\}$ and $C = \{C(k_1), C(k_2) \ldots .. C(k_N)\}$, where dissimilarity based centrality index $C(k_1) > C(k_2) > C(k_3) > \cdots .. > C(k_N)$*
6. *Return K and C*

the respective cluster members and send the collected data to the cloud through the gateway. Every collector node has to reach the Gateway in a single hop. In order to introduce a cooperative multi-hop data-carriage by the collector-nodes, SPMINs are placed in such a way that all the collector nodes are connected to the SPMINs via single hop. Connected SPMINs further enhance the reliability of the network. Effort has been made to find out the minimum connected set of SPMINs that enhances the connectivity of the network with optimal deployment cost. The algorithms ALGORITHM A (Table 1) and ALGORITHM B (Table 2) have been used to find out the strategic positions of the SPMINs.

MCDS contains the nodes which can be replaced by the SPMINs or the SPMINs can be placed in the close vicinity of the nodes in MCDS such that the SPMINs are within the minimum transmission range of the nodes in MCDS.

Table 2. Algorithm for finding out the optimal positions of the SPMINs

---

ALGORITHM B:

Inputs:

Graph G(N,E) with N={$node_1$, $node_2$, ... $node_{|N|}$}, Adjacency matrix A_{ij} corresponding to G(N,E), Ordered set C of dissimilarity index obtained in algorithm A

1. *Create a bipartite graph from the adjacency matrix A_{ij} corresponding to G(N,E). Two sets are created 'dominitee' and 'dominated'. 'dominitee' contains all the nodes of G(N,E) and 'dominated' contains the neighbors of the members of the set 'dominitee'. There is an edge 'e' from every member of 'dominitee' to respective neighbors listed in the set 'dominated'.*

2. *Create a set actual_nb={$node_j$| $A_{ij} = 1 \forall i \neq j, i,j \in N$} which contains the neighbors of each node*

3. *While |dominitee| > 0*
    a. *Given condition 1: dominitee(i) has the maximal number of neighbors in 'dominated'*
    b. *Given Condition 2: dominitee(i) has the largest value in C*
    c. *Given Condition 3: Node ID of dominitee(i) is minimum*
            If (more than one dominitee(i) satisfy 1)
                If (more than one dominitee(i) satisfy 2)
                    Select dominitee(i) that satisfy 1 ∩ 2 ∩ 3
                Else select dominitee(i) that satisfy 1 ∩ 2
            Else select dominitee(i) that satisfy 1
        MCDS=MCDS ∪ dominitee(i)
        dominitee = dominitee − dominitee(i)
        dominated = dominated − actual_nb(dominitee(i))
        actual_nb = actual_nb − actual_nb(dominitee(i))
        End of While loop
4. *Return MCDS*

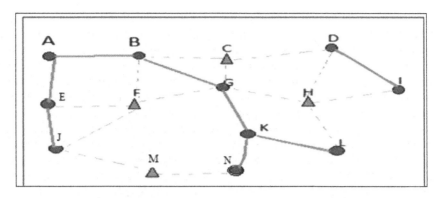

Fig. 4. Sample network with 14 nodes (node A to node N)

Figure 4 shows a sample network with 14 nodes (A to N). Among the 14 nodes A, B, E, J, D, G, I, K, L and N are of similar type. Nodes C, F, H and M belong to another type. Here, it is assume that the nodes differ according to the nature of communication interface. Jaccard Dissimilarity technique (Algorithm A) has been applied on the network to find out the dissimilarity based Eigen-centrality (C) of all the nodes.

Table 3 shows the required values of the parameters obtained after simulation of the sample network. From Table 3 it is found that centrality C is the maximum for the node H and minimum for nodes A and K. Following the algorithm shown in Table 2, the MCDS has been found to be H, G, F, E, J, M, N.

Table 3. Values of different parameters after simulation performed in the sample network

Node	1	2	3	4	5	6	7	8	9	10	11	12	13	14
Eff. mismatch	0	2	3	2	1	4	3	4	1	2	0	1	2	1
$\sum W_{ij}$	0	24.46	32.58	24.66	12.26	44.67	36.51	43.75	12.45	25.06	0	11.72	23.52	12.46
C	0	0.23	0.35	0.23	0.11	0.48	0.35	0.48	0.12	0.25	0	0.12	0.27	0.12
MCDS	H, G, F, E, J, M, N													

7 Simulation

The simulation of the proposed algorithm has been done with the following parameters (Table 4).

Table 4. Simulation parameters

Parameters	Area of the network	Transmission range (r) (uniform for all nodes)	Number of nodes (randomly deployed)	Types of nodes	% of different types of nodes
Value	50 × 50 sq. unit	20 unit	20, 30, 50, 60, 80, 100, 150	2	5% to 70%

The nodes are so deployed that they form a connected network such that any node is in the transmission range of one or the other. Coordinates of the nodes are randomly generated so that they are randomly placed in the network area. Care has been taken such that the source and destination nodes will be the ones those are at the furthest corners of the network, i.e., the distance between source and destination is the maximum among all the node-pair distances. For a particular session, percentage of mismatched type of nodes has been increased starting from 5% to 70% of the total number of nodes. In order to keep the number of nodes fixed, some of the nodes are randomly chosen to be converted to another type. For example, suppose there are N number of Type-1 nodes in the network. Now M number of Type-2 nodes are introduced in the network such that M < N and Type-1 nodes + Type-2 nodes = N, i.e., M number of Type-1 nodes are randomly selected and converted to Type-2. Care must be taken so that the source and destination are of same type. M is gradually increased from 5% to 70% of N. All the results correspond to the average of 100 simulations run for every set of nodes.

8 Results and Analysis

The simulation is performed to determine average number of paths between a pair of source and destination and mean all pair cost involved in generating the paths. Here, cost indicates the Euclidian distance between a pair of randomly deployed nodes. These network parameters are important in regard to connectivity and longevity of a network. These parameters have been investigated as a function of heterogeneity in the network and have also tried to see the variation as the network dimension (node concentration) is increased. For obvious reason, average number of paths decreases and mean cost increases with increasing heterogeneity, but this decrease in case of path and increase in case of cost is slowed down when SPMINs are deployed at the strategic locations as determined by the proposed MCDS algorithm. Even at higher percentage of heterogeneity (above 50%) when number of paths goes down to zero in an unmodified network, some mean paths have always been found to be present in the network with SPMINs and the mean cost of link is also reduced appreciably. These are shown in Figs. 5 and 6 for a representative network with N = 70 nodes randomly placed in a network of area A = 50 × 50 square unit having mean transmission range r = 20 unit. Another way to study the network connectivity is by means of percolation limit (removal of edge leading to no connectivity) and as heterogeneity in the network is increased little amount of removal of edges should lead to no connection state. However, as SPMINs are incorporated, the percolation limit improves a lot and is shown in Fig. 7.

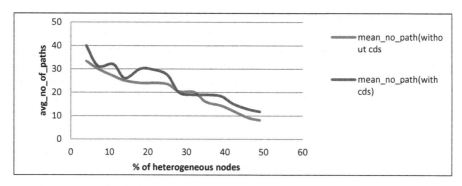

Fig. 5. Comparison plot of average number of paths between a pair of source and destination as a function of amount of heterogeneity in the network for a network dimension of 70 nodes with and without considering MCDS

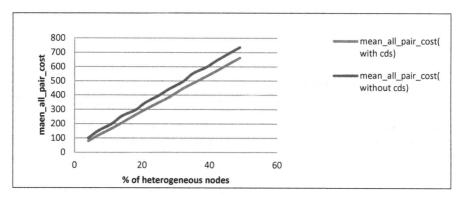

Fig. 6. Comparison plot of mean-all- pair-cost of a network of 70 nodes as a function of amount of heterogeneity in the network with and without considering MCDS

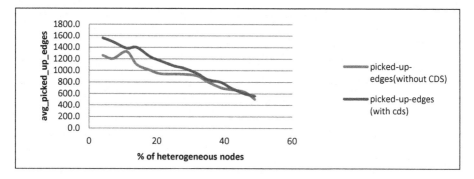

Fig. 7. Comparison plot of percolation threshold in terms of average picked up nodes for initiating no connection in a network of 70 nodes as a function of amount of heterogeneity in the network with and without considering MCDS

As the node density in the network is increased the probability of finding a path between a pair of source and destination involving neighbor nodes should increase and the difference between the presence of SPMINs or no SPMINs is reduced. This is presented in Figs. 8, 9 and 10 where it is observed that need of deployment of SPMINs is less at higher node concentrations in the network. This is quite obvious as the probability of finding a neighbor node of same kind is higher as the node density in the network is increased.

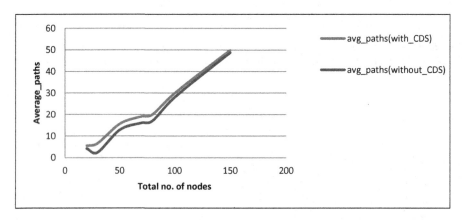

Fig. 8. Comparison plot of average number of paths between a pair of source and destination as a function of density of nodes for a fixed heterogeneity in the network with and without considering MCDS

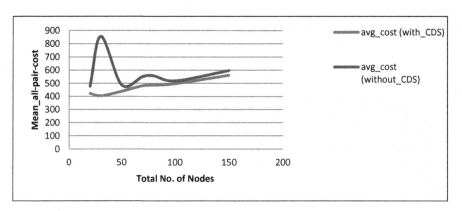

Fig. 9. Comparison plot of mean all pair cost of networks of varied dimension (density of nodes) for a fixed of heterogeneity in the network with and without considering MCDS

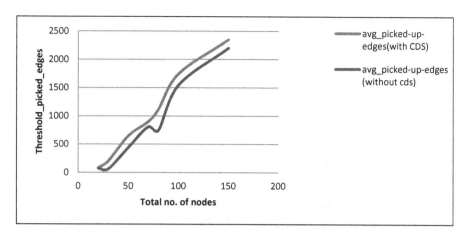

Fig. 10. Comparison plot of percolation threshold in terms of average picked up nodes for initiating no connection in networks of varied dimension (density of nodes) for a fixed amount of heterogeneity in the network with and without considering MCDS

9   Conclusion and Future Scope

Primary thing in a heterogeneous network resembling IoT is to establish connectivity in the network with minimum network cost and to increase the life span of the network. Heterogeneity which is a must in IoT has the detrimental effect in terms of decreasing connectivity as well as longevity of a network. To overcome this, it is proposed to use Special-Purpose-Multiple-Interface nodes (SPMIN) capable of communicating with any kind of interface. But, these devices being costly, their judicious deployment is necessary. A Minimum Connected Dominating Set (MCDS) algorithm is proposed to determine the optimal number of SPMINs and their strategic locations in the network. The algorithm is found to improve well the network connectivity in terms higher average number of paths, percolation threshold and decreased network cost in presence of heterogeneity. The algorithm is tested with only two types of nodes while a real network may contain several types of nodes. It is further observed that MCDS algorithm shows little improvement at higher node densities in determining network connectivity. The algorithm has a very simple consideration of taking equal connection probability for all the nodes irrespective of their position or neighbours, it is to some extent effective for low heterogeneity, but should pose crucial limitation while considering large degree of heterogeneity.

Though MCDS algorithm shows its resilience against connectivity bottleneck problem in case of not too high node density in a heterogeneous network, it may be further improved to accommodate larger heterogeneity with identification tagging of different kinds of nodes, consideration of different connection probability for nodes depending on their position in the network, visualization and insertion of directional dependence of connection path from a source to destination. Also, it is required to introduce node dynamicity in the MCDS algorithm to analyze a real heterogeneous network. Another consideration is the dynamic adaptation depending on the traffic situation and its time management. These factors will be introduced in future course of study of heterogeneous network.

Acknowledgements. The authors would like to thank to the Department of Science & Technology, Government of West Bengal (Memo No.-20(Sanc.)/ST/P/S&T/Misc-9/2014 dated 16/05/2017) for funding this research work.

References

1. Ng, J.K.: Ubiquitous healthcare: healthcare systems and application enabled by mobile and wireless technologies. J. Converg. **3**(2), 15–20 (2012)
2. Bandyopadhyay, D., Sen, J.: Internet of things: applications and challenges in technology and standardization. Wirel. Pers. Commun. **58**(1), 49–69 (2011)
3. Regina, T.R., Tome, T., Rothenberg, C.E.: Scenario of evolution for a future internet architecture. In: Tronco, T. (ed.) New Network Architectures, pp. 57–77. Springer, Heidelberg (2010). https://doi.org/10.1007/978-3-642-13247-6_4
4. Sundmaeker, H., Guillemin, P., Friess, P., Woelffle, S.: Vision and challenges for realizing the internet of things. In: Cluster of European Research Projects on the Internet of Things. European Commission (2010)
5. Augusto, J.C., Callaghan, V., Cook, D., Kameas, A., Satoh, I.: Intelligent environments: a manifesto. Hum.-Centric Comput. Inf. Sci. **3**, Article 12 (2013)
6. Atzori, L., Iera, A., Morabito, G.: The internet of things: a survey. Comput. Netw. **54**(15), 2787–2805 (2010)
7. Miorandi, D., et al.: Internet of things: vision, applications and research challenges. Ad Hoc Netw. **10**(7), 1497–1516 (2012)
8. Shih, C.-S., Wu, G.-F.: Meta-routing over heterogeneous networks in M2M systems. In: Proceedings of the 2014 Conference on Research in Adaptive and Convergent Systems. ACM (2014)
9. De Poorter, E., Moerman, I., Demeester, P.: Enabling direct connectivity between heterogeneous objects in the internet of things through a network-service-oriented architecture. EURASIP J. Wirel. Commun. Netw. **2011**, 61 (2011). https://doi.org/10.1186/1687-1499-2011-6
10. Gama, K., Touseau, L., Donsez, D.: Combining heterogeneous service technologies for building an Internet of Things middleware. Comput. Commun. **35**(4), 405–417 (2012)
11. Altamimi, A.B., Ramadan, R.A.: Towards internet of things modeling: a gateway approach. Complex Adapt. Syst. Model. **4**(1), 25 (2016)
12. Li, J., et al.: Connectivity, coverage and placement in wireless sensor networks. Sensors **9**(10), 7664–7693 (2009)
13. Jung, E., Cho, I., Kang, S.M.: iotSilo: the agent service platform supporting dynamic behavior assembly for resolving the heterogeneity of IoT. Int. J. Distrib. Sensor Netw. **10**(1), 608972 (2014)
14. Singh, F., Vijeth, J.K., Siva Ram Murthy, C.: Parallel opportunistic routing in IoT networks. In: 2016 IEEE Wireless Communications and Networking Conference (WCNC) (2016)
15. Capone, A., Cesana, M., De Donno, D., Filippini, I.: Optimal placement of multiple interconnected gateways in heterogeneous wireless sensor networks. In: Fratta, L., Schulzrinne, H., Takahashi, Y., Spaniol, O. (eds.) NETWORKING 2009. LNCS, vol. 5550, pp. 442–455. Springer, Heidelberg (2009). https://doi.org/10.1007/978-3-642-01399-7_35

16. Rehena, Z., et al.: Multiple sink placement in partitioned wireless sensor networks. Int. J. Next-Gen. Comput. **6**(2), 79–95 (2015)
17. Penumalli, C., Palanichamy, Y.: An optimal CDS construction algorithm with activity scheduling in ad hoc networks. Sci. World J. **2015**, Article ID 842346, 12 p. (2015). https://doi.org/10.1155/2015/842346
18. Sheu, J.-P., Lin, H.-F.: Probabilistic coverage preserving protocol with energy efficiency in wireless sensor networks. In: 2007 IEEE Wireless Communications and Networking Conference, WCNC 2007 (2007)
19. Penrose, M.D.: Random Geometric Graphs. Oxford University Press, Oxford (2003)
20. Alvarez-Socorro, A., Herrera-Almarza, G., Gonzalez-Diaz, L.: Eigencentrality based on dissimilarity measures reveals central nodes in complex networks. Sci. Rep. **5**. (2015). https://doi.org/10.1038/srep17095
21. Scholartica Channel: Connected Dominating Sets and its Applications: Part 2 - Greedy Algorithm, online video clip, YouTube, 17 September 2015, Web 2 September 2017

Diabetes Mellitus Risk Factor Prediction Through Resampling and Cost Analysis on Classifiers

S. Poonkuzhali, J. Jeyalakshmi[(⊠)], and S. Sreesubha

Department of Information Technology, Rajalakshmi Engineering College,
Chennai, Tamil Nadu, India
poonkuzhali.s@rajalakshmi.edu.in,
balajeyalakshmi@gmail.com

Abstract. With increasing change in sedentary life style and food habits, diabetes is greatly becoming a bane. It is becoming very critical disease in India with more than 62 million diabetic individuals currently diagnosed with the disease. It is also a growing issue throughout the world. But with modern techniques for analysis, it is very much possible to predict the disease very early and control it by pervasive care. Data Mining techniques and Predictive Analysis are focussed in the proposed system. When select techniques are used for classification after pre-processing the data, along with attribute selection and, it is found that the performance of the classifiers is good. The system presents correlation and correspondence analysis over the attributes in the dataset, a comparative analysis amid several classifiers under the experimental environment in order to propose an efficient hybrid classifier to provide precise prediction over the disease.

Keywords: Data mining · Diabetes · Hybrid classifier · Predictive analytics
Pervasive healthcare

1 Introduction

Clinical data mining has become more prominent in the present data age. In the abundance of clinical data, clinical data mining has been an area of deep interest, in order to interpret of useful and unknown information from data and perform appropriate timely decisions for healthcare professionals in order to save patients lives. And ever since data analytics has become a life boat for healthcare industry. The abundance of patient health records, the data analytics options and the range of diagnosis and therapeutic options make it a more suitable weapon for clinical data analysis [2–4].

In present days, pervasive healthcare with cheaper diagnostic tools and sensors at the patient's premises most of the time has proven to be a supplier for the abundant database of clinical patient records, also providing personalized healthcare. It has catered to continuous and long term monitoring of the patients and timely medical help has been possible henceforth. This has created avenues for incident management, addressing emergency scenarios and hence decreasing the mortality rates. This prevents adversities of the disease conditions [11].

© Springer Nature Singapore Pte Ltd. 2018
J. K. Mandal and D. Sinha (Eds.): CSI 2017, CCIS 836, pp. 212–225, 2018.
https://doi.org/10.1007/978-981-13-1343-1_21

Predictive analysis [13, 14] is the heart and brain of clinical data mining wherein, based on the dataset available, range of techniques are used to use the pattern that prevails in the data and find future values. It involves the correlation of several independent attributes in the dataset towards the change of the dependent attribute. The available data points are classified and the available classification is used in order to predict the possible future values for similar values. But artificial intelligence and machine learning also bring other techniques of learning knowledge from the training dataset and then using them over the test data and hence uncovering new knowledge therein.

A review of the epidemiology of diabetes in rural India was conducted by Smita [1]. In the study, they have done the analysis and concluded that the males have high incidence of diabetes disease. They have found demographical prevalence pattern and the prevalence of risk factors. Off late, diabetes mellitus has been also a serious issue round the world [1].

1.1 Machine Learning

It is found that using efficient hybrid prediction with Data Mining and Analytics, more precise findings can be made leading to eradication of adverse effects of diabetes. Deepika and Poonkuzhali [16] designed an hybrid classifier using ensemble learning technique to predict diabetes. The hybrid model developed using the voting ensemble technique produced the maximum accuracy rate of 100% in predicting the Diabetic disease from the Pima diabetes data set. The predictions of the ensemble learning techniques can be entwined with pervasive monitoring leading to reducing the impact of the disease.

Hashi et al. illustrates about various mining algorithms to find the trend of the disease using various comparisons among few machine learning algorithms the study uses. The study goes with accuracy as the base parameter for comparison. Vaishali et al. suggest their findings on the hyperglycaemic condition of patients in countries like India. The work proposes the Fuzzy Classifier gives a better result on accuracy with feature selection, using evolutionary model. Further genetic algorithms are used to improve the accuracy [20, 21].

Negi et al. in their work on Diabetes suggest the need for a global method for data curation and processing. The results can be improved at prediction with validated training set and then moving on to applying the knowledge gained towards the test set to enhance the functional nature of expertise gained from the machine learning algorithms. Jung et al. suggest their work on hypoglycaemia, where prediction is performed from data collected from mobile applications which are designed for use by patients themselves. The work was performed to educate the patient and improve the condition and probably reverse the same. Jankovic et al. present an existing system, with deep learning frameworks and thereby improve on the edge of the processing time. But only use a network which has only two layers. They suggest one layer for prediction and other for correction. The work improves the accuracy of the algorithm hereby [22–24].

Botros et al. suggest their work on foot ulcer and gangrene which is very common in Diabetic condition. Clinical evaluation was performed using various classification and prediction algorithms and application of specialized footwear for the patients.

LaPierre et al. use instance learning algorithms and apply machine learning over genomic data acquired from Type 2 - Diabetes patients. Later clustering and feature extraction happen in the work. Clusters are formed and risk factors are characterized for every cluster [25, 26].

1.2 Resampling

Yousefi et al. have analysed the comorbidities of Diabetes like hypertension and lipid profile and the incidental influence on the patients. The existing work uses, Dynamic Bayesian Networks and cohort analysis. The results are based on clinical trials. The occurrence or negative evaluation of the same is done via case control analysis [19]. Sheng et al. suggest in their work about resampling but with an enhanced adaptive framework. The authors concentrate on the under sampling and over sampling issue. Using density peaks and minority instance checks over the subclasses the inference is made [28].

Resampling come handy when information from huge datasets can be inferred by applying new hybrid techniques by combining resampling, filtering and subset evaluation incorporated with due attribute selection techniques. The experiments outperform the others at a much lower cost. Classification is a useful analytical technique, and when active learning is involved, the labeling task is exhaustive. But by the application of techniques like resampling the size of the labels needed will decrease significantly and also achieves higher rate of accuracy. So manual intervention by domain experts can also be reduced a lot.

Wang et al. state that online class imbalance learning is a tedious learning problem that indicated need for innovative techniques. If the imbalance status can be identified dynamically using computer aids, the learning can be improved. The techniques like resampling and time decaying metrics, may help in recognizing the minority classes. These also show higher OOB and UOB towards contribution of better accuracy [17].

1.3 Kappa Statistic

Salekin et al. perform classification work over kidney disease data of 400 patients. Accuracy is detected and cost accuracy tradeoff is discussed in the work. The authors analyse the predictability of the content and provide a fuzzy ranking. Further evaluation is done over the findings with ground truth [27].

Viera et al. [29] state that sometimes there is a chance factor that can influence the classifiers that has to take into account that the subjects values of agreement and disagreement may happen by chance. Kappa statistic close to 0 states the algorithm is having this chance factor, and a kappa value of 1 says chance factor does not influence the algorithm.

There are previous works that state kappa statistic comes handy when analyzing subjective measures. When comparison or interpretation have to be made, the kappa statistic gives a good view of the agreements and contradictions without overfitting them. They provide the kappa statistic in their work pertaining to computational linguistics and cognitive science for content analysis.

But the onset of predictive analytics has proved to be highly advantageous recently, since it has helped the data scientists to discover the hidden pattern among the available attributes in a patient's medical history. The stream has also helped to predict the onset and the severity of the disease from the available pattern persisting in the dataset.

The main objective of the proposed system is to find association between features and classifying patterns for prediction and monitoring of diabetes. And by applying efficient association and classification algorithms after feature relevance analysis, predict diabetes in better way. This system includes functionalities and interfaces for smart phone to continuously manage blood glucose level. It is capable of giving call automatically upon emergency to concerned doctor and ambulance. The proposed system provides an efficient classifier for the purpose of classification of diabetes and predicting its onset.

The Sect. 2 briefs the proposed system and its architecture, Sect. 3 relates the correlation analysis, classification and comparison and the correspondence analysis and Sect. 4 presents the results and the understanding summarized as conclusion.

2 Proposed Work

This proposed system concentrates upon predictive analysis of diabetes treatment by applying data mining technique on electronic medical records. After diagnosing the disease the patient has to be medicated and monitored throughout their lives. The research work also focus on diagnosing, monitoring and educating patients on their medication and pragmatic technological resources for maintaining blood glucose level.

The proposed system provides a cheap pervasive healthcare unit for continuously monitoring diabetic patients. The layout of the system is explained in Fig. 1. The proposed system provides a device equipped with different kinds of sensors for monitoring the pulse rate, blood glucose level, pressure of the patient. The data analyzing framework is explained as below. 96 when the readings are taken they are transmitted to the mobile application on the smart phone. The mobile application gives a history of the patients health conditions. If any deviation is detected or emergency sensed, the application sends outgoing calls to the hospital and the nearby police station. The system architecture for the diagnostic setup is explained in Fig. 1. The proposed system provides an efficient classifier for the purpose of classification of diabetes and predicting its onset. The architecture has been shown to be in sections like Data Mining Framework and Data Renderer framework. The Data Mining Framework, contains the following components.

- Data Preprocessor
- Data Integrator
- Data Mining Classifier Builder
- Predictive Analysis Engine
- Report Generator

The system comprises a Data Preprocessor which consumes the training data and performs normalization and cleanses the data. The Data Integrator performs the process of transforming the data using middleware to suit the data mining framework.

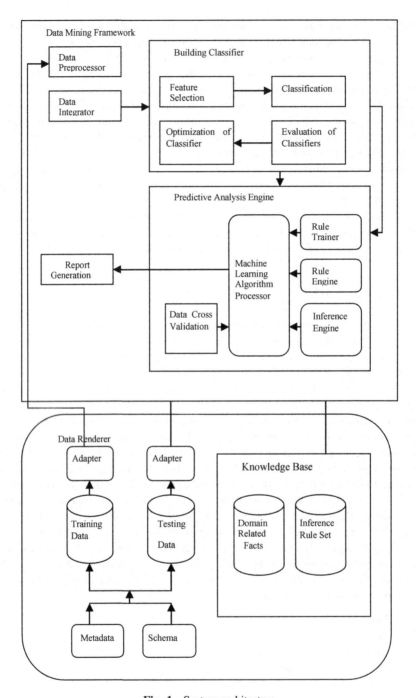

Fig. 1. System architecture

This is followed by building of an efficient classifier. The process performs feature selection and classification. It performs comparative analysis over several classifiers presents a summary of best results for analysis. The optimizer takes the input in order to build a classifier which provides best results, converging the qualities of the best suited algorithms. The results are provided to the prediction module which applies machine learning algorithms [9, 10]. The inference engine processes the rules and facts to provide the evaluations. The machine learning algorithms use the trained classifier in order to predict over the testing data for the disease patterns. A tenfold cross validation is applied in order to make the prediction better [6–8]. The major tasks involved in this proposed system are:

- Preprocessing
- Building Classifier

2.1 Preprocessing

Preprocessing involves cleansing the dataset to make it complete and consistent. Data needs preprocessing because the data tends to be noisy, inconsistent and incomplete. The data and its inherent quality directly correlate with the mining processes effectiveness and efficiency and its quality.

Preprocessing involves Data cleaning, integration, transformation, reduction and discretization. Resampling methods are basically divide the dataset to training and test set. They perform feature selection and model building with the training set and model assessment with test set. Resampling is implemented with range of techniques like cross validation (CV), bagging and bootstrap-based methods. In the context of the dataset considered herein, the resampling technique is used to improve the efficiency of the classifiers. The dataset used in the proposed system is described as below.

2.2 Datasets

The dataset is taken from UCI repository, known as PIMA Indians Diabetes Dataset of National Institute of Diabetes and Digestive and Kidney Diseases, contains 9 attributes and their descriptions are given in the Table 1 below. These records were collected from 768 persons. The persons were selected randomly with age above 20 years old.

Table 1. Dataset description

S. no	Attribute name	Attribute description
1	NPG	Occurrence of pregnancy
2	PGL	Concentration level noted in 2-h OGT test
3	DIA	Diastolic blood pressure(in mmHg)
4	TSF	Triceps skin folds thickness (in mm)
5	INS	Serum insulin noted at 2-h interval
6	BMI	Body mass index (in Kg/mm2)
7	DPF	Diabetes pedigree function (Family History)
8	AGE	Age of person (in years)
9	Class	Has diabetes or not

2.3   Feature Selection

Feature Selection is selection of the most relevant features to perform interpretation easier, model building simpler and training times faster. It is used to reduce the attribute set to the most influential set alone [26]. In the proposed system, several filtering algorithms are used and the attribute selection of these algorithms is summarized as below.

Linear Correlation measures how strongly the attributes are related with the outcome. It computes and tests the significance of the linear correlation of each pair of continuous input attributes (Table 2).

Table 2. Comparison of percentage of correctly classified samples

Algorithm	No. of attributes	List of attributes
Relief	4	PGL, BMI, DPF, AGE
Fisher	6	PGL, BMI, AGE, NPG, DPF, INS
Step	5	PGL, BMI, NPG, DPF, DIA
Run	2	PGL, AGE

*Total No of Attributes: 9

The result of Linear Correlation over the dataset in the proposed system ranks the correlation of the attributes in the following order: PGL, BMI, AGE, NPG, DPF, INS, TSF, DIA. The correlation r between two variables is provided by Eq. 1

$$r = \left[\frac{1}{n-1}\right] * \sum \{[(xi - x)/Sx] * [(yj - y)/Sy]\} \tag{1}$$

where n is the number of subjects who were analyzed and their total number of records. The formula is a simple division of summation of variance divided by standard deviation which is denoted by S_x and S_y.

2.4   Correspondence Analysis

Association analysis is a very viable technique which gives correlation between various features and how they are influenced by others. The goal is to provide effective comparative inference.

The Chi-square statistic is calculated as follows in Eq. 2:

$$x^2 = \sum_{i=1}^{r} \sum_{j=1}^{c} \frac{(fo_{ij} - fe_{ij})^2}{fe_{ij}} \tag{2}$$

where r is row and c is column. The foij and feij are frequencies of the values across the specified row and column on the contingency table formed from the training set that is being supplied. In the proposed work, Correspondence Analysis ranks the following attributes in their order of significance: PGL, INS, AGE, BMI, NPG, DPF.

The relief filter results are found to be more in line with the findings of linear correlation and correspondence analysis with minimal set of attributes compared to other feature selection algorithms. So filtering is performed using relief filter and classification is carried out. The classification process in briefed as below.

2.5   Building Classifier

Classification is the task of predicting the class labels for data records as guided by classifiers. Classification can be supervised or unsupervised. In supervised classification the class labels are known and in unsupervised classification, class labels are not known wherein prediction using clustering is performed [5, 12, 13]. Classification can be performed using various techniques as listed below.

- Decision Tree Based Classification
- KNN based clustering
- Random Forest

Amid all classification algorithms as analyzed from the survey and the comparison performed, [15, 18] the proposed system takes up the following algorithms to analyze the dataset. The algorithms are ID3, RND and J48. The afore mentioned classifiers are considered for accuracy and Random Tree, C4.5 Decision Tree and K-Nearest Neighbor prove to be reasonably good as inferred from earlier work. These are tested out with different pre-processing techniques and feature selection, then the algorithms are short listed.

3   Results and Discussion

The dataset is tested out with several classifiers after fisher filter as stated and justified in previous section. The classification is carried out with filtering and without filtering and also carried out with feature reduction and the results are compared. Based on the comparison the optimal classifiers are chosen and they are taken into hybrid ensemble classification with Voting and Stacking. The results are found to be much better for Voting with training. A supervised learning algorithm interprets the training data and produces a function which is studied from the data, from which new mappings can be achieved. The algorithm correctly determines the class labels for these unseen data particles. For the dataset under consideration Gini coefficient is calculated. Gini coefficient measures the inequality among values of a frequency distribution. A Gini coefficient of zero expresses perfect equality where all values are the same. The formula for Gini Index is as below

$$G = 1 - \sum_{1=1}^{k} \mathrm{pi}^2 \tag{3}$$

Table 3 summarizes the Gini Index calculated for the dataset. The smallest attribute splits the node. It helps us infer the purity and the influence of the attribute over the decision making process.

The Table 4 provides the comparison of the performance of various classification algorithms based on the accuracy, response time, precision and recall. The classification is performed without filtering and then with filtering for all algorithms. Later, from the results of Correspondence analysis, and Linear Correlation, Feature selection is performed and attributes of the dataset are reduced. Later again the classifiers are applied over the reduced set. The results are compared herein. Table 4 gives a comparative analysis on the accuracy of various classifiers using various methods: without filtering the dataset, by applying the filtering concept and with the choice of feature selection in order to find the best choice of classifier.

Table 3. Gini index

Attribute	Gini coefficient
NPG	0.301
PGL	0.133
INS	0.165
DIA	0.153
DPF	0.375
BMI	0.198
AGE	0.146
TSF	0.133

It is observed that always the result of accuracy is better to go with filtering and it is found that the algorithms like C4.5 and K-NN provide good results other than Random Tree which always gives a better percent accuracy.

Table 4. Comparison of the kappa statistic and other parameters

Algorithm	%correctly classified samples	Time taken to process (in sec)	Cost	Kappa statistic
Random Forest	94.66	0.27	41	0.88
IBK	93.48	0	50	0.86
J48	86.58	0.3	103	0.7

Kappa statistic is a more robust measure that will help us analyze the performance of the classifiers in an unambiguous manner. The following is Cohler's Kappa statistic, where Po is Probability of random agreement and Probability of observed proportionate agreement.

$$k = \frac{P_o - P_e}{1 - P_e} \tag{4}$$

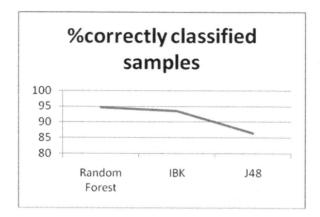

Note: Along X - Axis - Algorithm and Along Y - Axis - Performance on percentage of correctly classified samples

Fig. 2. Comparison of correctly classified samples

The above Fig. 2 shows a comparison of correctly classified samples among various algorithms like Random Forest, IBK and J48. The comparison shows that the random forest gives good result and the IBK and J48 are in decreasing order.

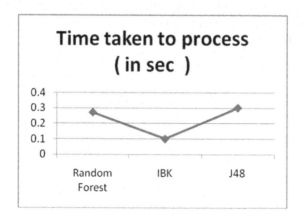

Note: Along X - Axis - Algorithm and Along Y - Axis - Performance on Time taken to process the samples

Fig. 3. Comparison of time taken to process

The above Fig. 3 shows a comparison of time for processing samples among various algorithms like Random Forest, IBK and J48. The comparison shows that the random forest and J48 give good result and J48 is comparatively long and the IBK is on the decreasing edge and takes least time.

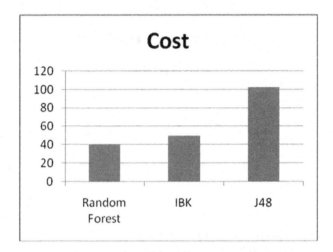

Note: Along X - Axis - Algorithm and Along Y - Axis - Performance on cost
estimation of processing the samples

Fig. 4. Comparison of cost of classifiers

The above Fig. 4 shows a comparison of cost of correctly classified samples among various algorithms like Random Forest, IBK and J48. The comparison shows that the random forest gives good result and the IBK comes next and J48 are in most costly. The cost analogy shows how the predictions have consequence by going against the ground reality which may be true or false.

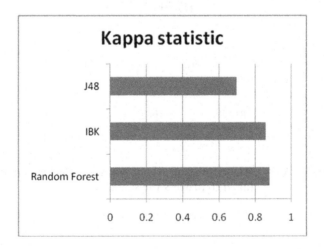

Note: Along X - Axis - Algorithm and Along Y - Axis - Performance on
Kappa evaluation of classified samples

Fig. 5. Comparison of kappa value

The Kappa Statistic as shown in Fig. 5 shows how well the actual and predicted values are correlated to each other. The statistic shows that IBK and Random Forest are better in showing the actual truth. It is another tool for evaluating the performance of the classifiers. The Figs. 2, 3, 4 and 5 show that the ranking of the performance of the classifiers is like Random Forest, IBK followed by J48. Though the processing time is less in IBK, the cost, kappa and percent correctly classified samples state confirm the order.

4 Conclusion

The proposed system provides a cheaper device in order to provide continuous monitoring of diabetic patients to avoid any emergency situations providing pervasive healthcare at much cheaper rate to common man. On the diagnosis part, the proposed system performs optimized classification using attribute selection, pre-processing with resampling and classification with the analyzed top most algorithms in order of performance. The algorithms are compared and feature reduction along with filtering over the classifiers equipped with training data discussed in the proposed system proves to be much better in its accuracy, cost, kappa review and time taken.

Acknowledgment. This research work is a part of the All India Council for Technical Education (AICTE), India funded Research Promotion Scheme project titled "Efficient Prediction and Monitoring Tool for Diabetes Patients Using Data Mining and Smart Phone System" with Reference No: 8- 169/RIFD/RPS/POLICY-1/2014-15.

References

1. Smita, P.S.: Use of data mining in various field: a survey paper. IOSR J. Comput. Eng. (IOSR-JCE) **16**(3), 18–22 (2014)
2. Tomar, D., Agarwal, S.: A survey on data mining approaches for healthcare. Int. J. Bio-Sci. Bio-Technol. **5**(5), 241–266 (2013)
3. Chaurasia, V., Pal, S.: Early prediction of heart diseases using data mining techniques. Carib. J. Sci. Tech. **1**, 208–217 (2013)
4. Fanga, L., et al.: Feature selection method based on mutual information and class separability for dimension reduction in multidimensional time series for clinical data. Biomed. Sig. Process. Control **21**, 82–89 (2015)
5. Halper, F.: Predictive Analytics for Business Advantage. TDWI Research, pp. 1–32 (2014)
6. Iyer, A., Jeyalatha, S., Sumbaly, R.: Diagnosis of diabetes using classification mining techniques. Int. J. Data Mining Knowl. Manag. Process **5**(1), 1–14 (2015)
7. Juliyet, L.C., Amanullah, M.K.: The surveillance on diabetes diagnosis using data mining techniques. Int. J. Sci. Res. Technol. **1**(4), 34–39 (2015)
8. Nagarajan, S., Chandrasekaran, R.M., Ramasubramanian, P.: Data mining techniques for performance evaluation of diagnosis in gestational diabetes. Int. J. Curr. Res. Acad. Rev. **2**(10), 91–98 (2014)
9. Butwall, M., Kumar, S.: A data mining approach for the diagnosis of diabetes mellitus using random forest classifier. Int. J. Comput. Appl. **120**(8), 36–39 (2015)

10. Thirumal, P.C., Nagarajan, N.: Utilization of data mining techniques for diagnosis of diabetes mellitus - a case study. Asian Res. Publ. Netw.-J. Eng. Appl. Sci. **10**(1), 8–13 (2015)
11. Sen, S.K., Dash, S.: Application of meta learning algorithms for the prediction of diabetes disease. Int. J. Adv. Res. Comput. Sci. Manag. Stud. **2**(12), 396–401 (2014)
12. Shivakumar, B.L., Alby, S.: A survey on data-mining technologies for prediction and diagnosis of diabetes. In: International Conference on Intelligent Computing Applications, pp. 167–173 (2014)
13. Visalatchi1, G., Gnanasoundhari, S.J., Balamurugan, M.: A survey on data mining methods and techniques for diabetes mellitus. Int. J. Comput. Sci. Mob. Appl. **2**(2), 100–105 (2014)
14. Venkatalakshmi, B., Shivsankar, M.V.: Heart disease diagnosis using predictive data mining. Int. J. Innov. Res. Sci. Eng. Technol. **3**(3), 1873–1877 (2014)
15. Agrawal, P., Dewangan, A.K.: A brief survey on the techniques used for the diagnosis of diabetes-mellitus. Int. Res. J. Eng. Technol. **2**(3), 1039–1043 (2015)
16. Deepika, N., Poonkuzhali, S.: Design of hybrid classifier for prediction of diabetes through feature relevance analysis. Int. J. Innov. Sci. Eng. Technol. **2**(10), 788–793 (2015)
17. Wang, S., Minku, L.L., Yao, X.: Resampling-based ensemble methods for online class imbalance learning. IEEE Trans. Knowl. Data Eng. **26**, 1–13 (2014)
18. Poonkuzhali, S., Sindhuja, M., Jeyalakshmi, J., Sreesubha, S.: Diabetes mellitus risk factor prediction through feature relevance analysis and hybrid classifier. In: Advances in Innovative Engineering and Technologies - Proceedings of the International Conference on Innovative Engineering and Technologies, pp. 317–332 (2016)
19. Yousefi, L., Saachi, L., Bellazzi, R., Chiovato, L., Tucker, A.: Predicting comorbidities using resampling and dynamic bayesian networks with latent variables. In: 2017 IEEE 30th International Symposium on Computer-Based Medical Systems (CBMS), Thessaloniki, pp. 205–206 (2017)
20. Hashi, E.K., Zaman, M.S.U., Hasan, M.R.: An expert clinical decision support system to predict disease using classification techniques. In: 2017 International Conference on Electrical, Computer and Communication Engineering (ECCE), Cox's Bazar, pp. 396–400 (2017)
21. Vaishali, R., Sasikala, R., Ramasubbareddy, S., Remya, S., Nalluri, S.: Genetic algorithm based feature selection and MOE Fuzzy classification algorithm on Pima Indians Diabetes dataset. In: 2017 International Conference on Computing Networking and Informatics (ICCNI), Lagos, pp. 1–5 (2017)
22. Negi, A., Jaiswal, V.: A first attempt to develop a diabetes prediction method based on different global datasets. In: 2016 Fourth International Conference on Parallel, Distributed and Grid Computing (PDGC), Waknaghat, pp. 237–241 (2016)
23. Jung, M.: Toward designing mobile software to predict hypoglycemia for patients with diabetes. In: 2016 IEEE/ACM International Conference on Mobile Software Engineering and Systems (MOBILESoft), Austin, TX, pp. 29–30 (2016)
24. Jankovic, M.V., Mosimann, S., Bally, L., Stettler, C., Mougiakakou, S.: Deep prediction model: the case of online adaptive prediction of subcutaneous glucose. In: 2016 13th Symposium on Neural Networks and Applications (NEUREL), Belgrade, pp. 1–5 (2016)
25. Botros, F.S., Taher, M.F., ElSayed, N.M., Fahmy, A.S.: Prediction of diabetic foot ulceration using spatial and temporal dynamic plantar pressure. In: 2016 8th Cairo International Biomedical Engineering Conference (CIBEC), Cairo, pp. 43–47 (2016)
26. LaPierre, N., Rahman, M.A., Rangwala, H.: CAMIL: clustering and assembly with multiple instance learning for phenotype prediction. In: 2016 IEEE International Conference on Bioinformatics and Biomedicine (BIBM), Shenzhen, pp. 33–40 (2016)

27. Salekin, A., Stankovic, J.: Detection of chronic kidney disease and selecting important predictive attributes. In: 2016 IEEE International Conference on Healthcare Informatics (ICHI), Chicago, IL, pp. 262–270 (2016)
28. Sheng, K., Liu, Z., Zhou, D.: An adaptive resampling algorithm based on CFSFDP. In: 2017 2nd IEEE International Conference on Computational Intelligence and Applications (ICCIA), Beijing, China, pp. 41–45 (2017)
29. Viera, A.J., Garrett, J.M.: Understanding interobserver agreement: the kappa statistic. Fam. Med. **37**(5), 360–363 (2005)

Parallel Fuzzy Cognitive Map Using Evolutionary Feature Reduction for Big Data Classification Problem

M. V. Judy[(✉)] and Gayathri Soman

Department of Computer Applications,
Cochin University of Science and Technology, Cochin, Kerala, India
judy.nair@gmail.com, gayathrisoman025@gmail.com

Abstract. Big data classification is a challenging task because of the enormous volume, variety velocity associated with it. As the amount of data increases it is more difficult for data scientist in collecting, cleaning and analyzing data. To find useful and meaningful data from unstructured data is an important task. Meaning full data can be found using different classification techniques. There are different techniques used so far to gain useful knowledge from big data such as K-Means clustering algorithm, Association rule mining algorithm, linear regression algorithms, logistic regression algorithms, Naïve Bayesian etc. Fuzzy Cognitive Maps (FCM) is another efficient approach which is being used for decision making. The difficulty of using FCMs for big data classification is with the number of large available parameters associated with the data set. Hence in this paper we propose a parallel fuzzy cognitive map using map Reduce framework which learns and classifies from a reduced feature set using parallel evolutionary genetic algorithm. The methodology is tested on Bench Mark Data sets and results show the efficiency of the method.

Keywords: Big data classification · Genetic algorithms · MapReduce
Fuzzy cognitive map · Evolutionary feature reduction

1 Introduction

Big Data has the following characteristics of volume, velocity, variety, veracity which exceed the typical data mining algorithms to process. Hence there is a need for new and enhanced method for analyzing and processing big data. The data mining techniques should have the capacity to address the large amount of unstructured data in motion. Mining algorithms should be able to process the distributed data with complex and dynamic characteristics.

Big Data classification is used for knowledge discovery and intelligent decision making. Various proven classification techniques are available that falls into two major categories of supervised and unsupervised learning strategies. The classification task has two major phases, learning phase which takes the huge and complex data sets as input and evaluation phase which tests the accuracy of classification patterns. These techniques use parallel and distributed frameworks for data reduction and classification. Section 2 briefly describes the related work.

© Springer Nature Singapore Pte Ltd. 2018
J. K. Mandal and D. Sinha (Eds.): CSI 2017, CCIS 836, pp. 226–239, 2018.
https://doi.org/10.1007/978-981-13-1343-1_22

In this paper an evolutionary approach using genetic algorithm is used to reduce feature set and fuzzy cognitive maps are used for decision making. Section 3 gives an overall background of the techniques involved. Section 4 explains the proposed method in detail. The results and conclusion is provided in Sects. 5 and 6 respectively.

2 Related Work

FCMs can be used for a wide range of research and industrial areas, such as political science, electrical engineering, military science, medicine, history, supervisory systems, etc. In [3] Giles used Fuzzy cognitive maps to deal with 'diabetes' in medical sciences. FCM were used in [4] to evaluate the credit risk of particular companies. In [5] Giabbanelli used FCM to diagnose obesity based on physiological behavior. Reichelt in [6] used FCM to evaluate execution risk of IT projects and the dependency between them. Rule based fuzzy cognitive maps were proposed by Carvalho and Tome in [7]. RBFCM are FCMS which included timing and other new methods with uncertainty propagation. Fuzzy grey cognitive maps are an extension of FCM which was used to deal with multiple meaning environments proposed by Salmeron in [8]. Lakovidis and Papageorgiou developed Intuitionistic fuzzy cognitive maps [9]. iFCM not only represent the relationship between two concepts but also the degree to which the expert hesitates to express that influence. To handle complex dynamic causal systems Dynamic cognitive network was proposed in [10]. To handle dynamic maps Aguilar also proposed a dynamic random fuzzy cognitive map in [11]. Kottas proposed Fuzzy cognitive networks [12] this systems always reach equilibrium points. They use an updating mechanism which receives feedback from the real system. To simulate real-time variable states Cai proposed an evolutionary fuzzy cognitive maps [13]. Park and Kim [14] proposed fuzzy time cognitive maps, which included time in node's relationships. Fuzzy rules were incorporated to FCM in [15]. In [16] belief-degree-distributed fuzzy cognitive maps were proposed in which causal relationship are expressed by belief structure. A FCM based on rough set theory was proposed by Chunying in [17] called rough cognitive maps. Time Automara Based Fuzzy cognitive Maps were developed in [18] which were used to distribute emotional services in an Aml environment.

As the amount of data increases the number of features also increases. Selecting valuable features from these available features is an import task since only very few features would be useful for us. Feature selection methods can be mainly classified in supervised and unsupervised. In supervised feature selection the class labels are known before hand while in unsupervised the class labels are known. The supervised feature selection methods can be mainly classified into filter, wrapper and wrapper methods according to [19]. Filter methods are usually used as a preprocessing step. Here features are selected depending on the rank they have obtained using different statistical tests. Conditional Mutual Information criteria for feature ranking are used by the author in [20]. For text classification in [21] twelve feature selection metrics are considered. The features are ranked using all the available metrics and using a threshold 100 words is selected. In [22, 23] a ranking criteria is developed based on class densities. While in [24, 25] a feature relevance criteria is used to rank the features. Selection of threshold is a disadvantage in this method. Gram-Schmidt orthogonalization method is used in [26] for feature ranking. Wrapper methods actually acts as a search problem where different subsets are prepared, evaluated and they are compared with other combinations. A tree structure is used in Branch and Bound method [19, 27] which is used to evaluate different subsets for a given feature selection number. Embedded Methods are another feature selection method. In this method the feature selection is done as a part of training. Network pruning is a method which is used to obtain optimum network architecture for neural networks, in this method nodes having small magnitude features and the nodes connecting to those nodes are excluded [28, 29]. A cost function is derived in [30] to eliminate random features. A regression model is used in [31–33] chemo metric applications to reduce the number of features. A multitask learning approach is used in [34] to improve the prediction performance. Sparseness in the feature space is selected as a feature selection method for text classification in [35]. Hidden structures are found from unlabeled data in unsupervised learning. Without knowledge of class labels clustering techniques [36] tries to discover natural groupings in a set of objects. Semi-supervised feature selection is other class of feature selection which uses both supervised and unsupervised data for learning. To score a set of features a clustering indicator construction is used in [37].

3 Technical Background

3.1 Fuzzy Cognitive Maps

Fuzzy Cognitive Maps have been developed from cognitive maps, which were initially proposed by Axelrod in 1976 [1]. The concepts and the causal relationships between these concepts were the two main components of cognitive maps. The concepts were represented using nodes and the causal relationships using links between the nodes. Depending upon the causal relationship between the concepts the links have a positive or negative value. But in many cases these causal relationships may be too complex to be represented using just positive and negative links. This lead to the development of FCMs.

Fuzzy Cognitive maps were proposed by Kosko [2] in 1986. A FCM and cognitive maps differences in the way in which they represent the causal relationships. The strength of fuzzy logic and cognitive maps are combined in FCMs. Using FCMs one can easily represent human knowledge in natural human language than other concept mapping techniques. With the help of Fuzzy cognitive map it is easy to represent causal relationships among concepts. Concepts represent an entity, a state, a variable, or a characteristic of the system. The concepts are connected using directed links. The value on the links also known as the weight specifies quantitatively the extent to which concept A has caused concept B. The directed links are represented using "+", "−" or 0 value. "+" indicates that increase or decrease in one concept causes an increase or decrease in other concept respectively. "−" indicates that an increase or decrease in one concept causes changes in reverse direction in other concept. And a value of zero indicates that there is no relationship between concept A and B. That is this directed link between concepts shows the strength of the conditions between two concepts. This

FCM's can be used for decision making also. In this case the first nodes represent the concepts while the last nodes represent the decision or the classes. In this FCM's each concept node may or may not be connected to the decision nodes. I.e., a link between a concept node and a decision node exist only if that particular decision depends on the concept give in the concept node. There would be no link between the concept nodes. An example of a diagram showing the FCM's used for decision making is shown in the Fig. 1 below. Here the nodes C1, C2, C3 are the concept nodes and D1 and D2 are the decision nodes. Decision nodes are also called output nodes. Figure 1 shows an example of a FCM used for decision making. In the figure. C1, C2, C3 and C4 are the concept nodes and D1 and D2 are decision nodes. The Decision node D1 depends on the concepts C1, C2 and C3, while D2 depends on C3, C2 and C4. The relation between concept nodes and decision nodes are shown by a weight value. In the figure the weight w11 shows the relation between concept C1 and decision D1. Similarly the weight values w21, w32, w31, w32 and w12 shows the relation between C2–D1, C3–D2, C3–D1, C3–D2 and C1–D2 respectively.

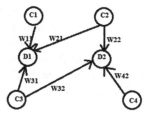

Fig. 1. Fuzzy cognitive maps for decision making

3.2   Map Reduce

Nowadays, the growing trend of application have led to large amount of data which is difficult to handle. Map-Reduce has been used as an effective method to analyze big data and to implement scalable parallel algorithms. The input to map-reduce model should be given as a <key, value> pair, so all structured and unstructured data must be first converted to this form. Map reduce function mainly consists of two types of function the Map and the Reduce function. It mainly consists of three main steps, the Map, Shuffle and the Reduce function. Distribution of data id done by Map and shuffle function and the computation is performed by the reduce function. The Map function converts the unstructured data into structured data. A map function takes a set of value as input and outputs a set of key-value pairs. This is given as input to reduce function. A reducer receives all the data for an individual "key" from all the mappers and outputs any number of <key, value> pair. All the Map functions must be completed before the reduce function is applied (Fig. 2).

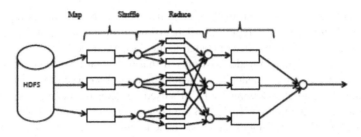

Fig. 2. Framework of Map-Reduce.

3.3   Genetic Algorithms for Feature Selection

In this paper we are using genetic algorithm for feature reduction, which is the most advanced algorithm for feature selection. It is based on biological evolution and natural genetics. GAs can be used to optimize the performance of a predictive model, by selecting the most relevant features. GAs produce a better approximation operating on a population of individuals. Each generation creates a new population by selecting individuals to their level of fitness in the problem domain and using operators to recombine them together. The generated offspring would sometimes undergo mutation. The new generated population better suits to the environment than the individuals they were created from. The total number of features in the data set represents the number of genes in GAs. Genes are represented using binary values and they represent if a feature is included or not.

The first step in GAs is to create and initialize the individuals of a population. Each positive gene means that the particular feature is included. The second step is to assign fitness to the individuals. The fitness is evaluated by calculating the selection error. For calculating the selection error the model is first trained using the training data and then tested using the testing data. If the selection error is high it means a low fitness. Those individuals with a higher fitness have high changes of being selected. The most commonly used fitness assignment is "Rank based" method. In this method, individuals are sorted according to their selection error, and then fitness is assigned to each individual depending on the position in the individual rank. The third step is selection. In this step the individuals for the next generation are selected. Those individuals who are more fitted into the environment are most likely to be selected, i.e. the selection operator selects the individuals according to their fitness level. Roulette wheel is one of the most commonly used selection method. In this method all individuals are placed in roulette with areas proportional to their fitness. Then the individuals are selected at random after rotating the roulette. The selection operation have selected half of the population, this is followed by a crossover operator which recombines the selected individuals to generate a new population. In this method two individuals are selected at random and they are combined to form four off springs for the new population, until the new population has the same size as the old one. Each of the offspring features can come from one parent or another is decided by the uniform crossover method. After the process of crossover the new generation generated may have chances of low diversity, because they generate off springs that have very similar to parents. These drawbacks can be eliminated by changing some of the features in the off springs at random. This is done by the fifth step called mutation. In mutation a random number between 0 and 1 is selected and if this number is lower than a value called the mutation rate then that particular feature is flipped.

4   Proposed Method

4.1   Overall Framework

The figure depicts the overall workflow of the proposed method. In this method, the feature set is reduced using MR – EEFS (Enhanced Evolutionary Feature Selection, this id described in Sect. 4.2. The reduced data set is given as input to FCM. The FCM is constructed by capturing the tendency of the input dataset as explained in Sect. 4.3.1. Then the FCM is implemented using the Map-Reduce paradigm., this is explained in Sect. 4.3.2 (Fig. 3).

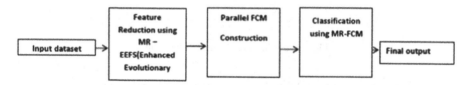

Fig. 3. Proposed method workflow

4.2   Enhanced Evolutionary Feature Reduction Using Map Reduce (EEFR - MR)

Evolutionary feature reduction process which combines the features of GA and map reduce is used. The Fig. 4 shows the proposed map reduce framework.

This section describes the parallelization of GA, in which parallelization is done using the map-reduce method to obtain a reduced feature set which is given as input to next state. Consider that T is the training set which is stored in HDFS. Let n denote the number of map task. The split task of map reduce divides T into n disjoint subsets. Subsets are formed by splitting the input dataset row wise. Each obtained subset Ti {i element of {1, 2, …, n}} is processed by individual map task Mi respectively. All the subsets contain same number of features as the dataset are portioned sequentially. The input to each map phase is a <key, value> pair, were the key is the chromosome id and the value is the subset of the dataset. Each map phase uses the GA for feature selection and the output of each map phase is a <key, value> pair, were key (ki) is the chromosome id and value is the fitness value (fi). This set fi indicates the features selected by the GA. In the next step the combiner takes the average of the fitness values of a particular key, i.e., finds the average of all the feature values obtained for a particular chromosome id. The reduce phase performs crossover, mutation and selection to obtain

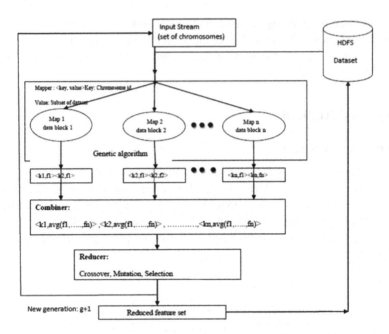

Fig. 4. Evolutionary feature reduction

the reduced feature set. The reduced feature set R is represented as R = {R1, ..., Rn} and this is stored in HDFS. The overall workflow of obtaining the reduced feature set from the dataset is shown in Fig. 4.

4.3   Construction of Parallel FCM for Decision Making

FCM networks can be represented using simple adjacent matrix or weight matrix. Here weight matrix is obtained by taking the correlation between different features of the feature set A obtained in the previous step. In this paper a parallel FCM is proposed. Parallelization is brought by using Map reduce with standard FCM's.

4.3.1   Create Weight Matrix from Data Set Using Map Reduce

The weight matrix is obtained by taking the correlation between all the features obtained in previous step. As the obtained useful feature set may also be of size above thousands, so it would be difficult to find the correlation between these features as a whole. In order to make the computation process more simple we are using a map reduce paradigm to find the weight matrix from the feature set. Figure 5 shows the flowchart of the weight matrix generation. The reduced feature set R that was stored in HDFS is taken as input in this step. Let n denote the number of map task. The split task of map reduce divides R into n disjoint subsets. Subsets are formed by splitting the input dataset column wise. Each obtained subset Ri {i element of {1, 2, ..., n}} is processed by individual map task Mi respectively. The input to each map phase is a <key, value> pair, were the key is the (i, j) th position and the value is the subset of R whose row is i and column number is j. Each map phase finds the correlation between the features values present in the subset (i, j) and the output of each map phase is a <key, value> pair, were key (ki) is the (i, j) position and value is the correlation value (ci). In the next step the combiner combines the correlation values of a (i, j) pair obtained from different maps. The reduce phase finds the average of the correlation value of a (i, j) pair. The output obtained from the reducer is the weight matrix which is the correlation between each feature values and this is stored in HDFS.

The overall workflow of obtaining the weight matrix from the reduced feature set is shown in Fig. 5.

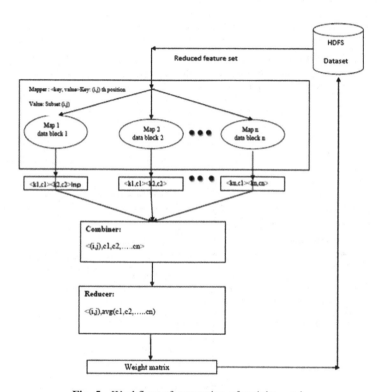

Fig. 5. Workflow of generation of weight matrix

4.3.2 Parallel FCM

The architecture of PFCM is shown in Fig. 6. The weight matrix Wij, obtained in the previous step is taken from HDFS and given as input to map reduce paradigm. The input to each map function is a <key, value> pair, were the key indicates the subset of concept values obtained from the reduced feature set R(r1, r2, ..., rn, label) and value represent the subset of weight matrix; i.e., the weight matrix of the subset of concept selected. Each Individual FCM gives the partial solution local to that FCM which is used to find the final global solution. i.e.; each map function calculates Ai using the below equation

$$A_i^{(k+1)} = f\left(A_i^{(k)} + \sum_{j\neq i}^{N} A_j^{(k)}.W_{ij}\right)$$

Where $A_i^{(k+1)}$ is the value of Concept Ci at simulation step k + 1, $A_i^{(k)}$ is the value of concept Ci at simulation step k, W_{ij} is the weight of the interconnection from concept Cj to concept Ci. And f is the threshold function given as follows.

$$f = \frac{1}{1+e^{-\lambda x}}$$

The reduce phase takes the union of the outputs of all the map functions. Reduce function is used to combine the results of all mappers which gives the final A vector. Then the result is stored in HDFS.

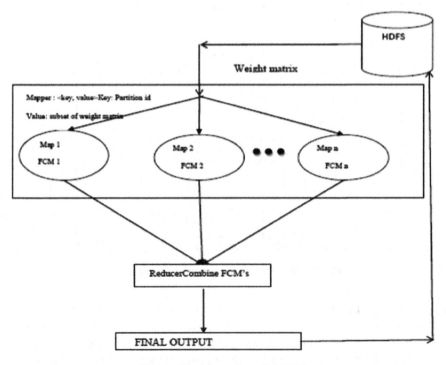

Fig. 6. Workflow of parallel FCM

5   Experimental Framework and Analysis

5.1   Datasets and Methods

The quality of proposed PFCM is tested using two datasets. First the epsilon dataset is used this dataset was actually created in 2008 for the Pascal large Scale learning challenge. The LIBSVM version is used here. Second dataset is Covtype-2 dataset. This dataset is collected from UCI machine learning repository. Details about the datasets are given in Table 1.

Table 1. Details about datasets

Data	No. of records	No. of attributes	Splits
Covtype - 2	581012	54	576
Epsilon	500000	2000	512

5.2   Hardware and Software Used

Processor used was "i3" 4rth Generation Systems [10 nodes: 1 Master node + 9 Slave nodes], 4 GB RAM memory was used and a Hard-Disk space of 500 GB. Operating system used was Ubuntu version 16.04 LTS. Map-Reduce were implemented using Hadoop 2.00-cdh 4.7.1 and Apache Spark 1.0.0. Map-Reduce 1 (Cloudera's open-source Apache Hadoop distribution).

5.3   Feature Selection Performance

To compare the performance of MR-EEFS with MR-EFS and sequential CHC [38], a set of experiments were done using the subsets of the epsilon dataset. MR-EEFS is applied on these subsets and the values obtained after applying sequential CFC and MR-EFS is taken from [38]. The execution times are presented in Table 2 and Fig. 7 shows the runtime of MR-EEFS over whole dataset. In case of sequential CHC it shows a quadratic shape which states that the time taken to tackle the whole dataset would be impractical. While the case of MR-EFS and MR-EEFS was nearly constant. In Table 1 the time taken by MR-EEFS for 20,000 instances is even less than the time taken by sequential CHC for 2000 instances.

Table 2. Execution times over the epsilon subsets.

Instances	Sequential CHC	MR-EFS	MR-EEFS
1000	391	419	499
2000	1352	409	488
5000	8667	413	491
10000	39576	431	509
15000	91272	445	517
20000	159315	455	535

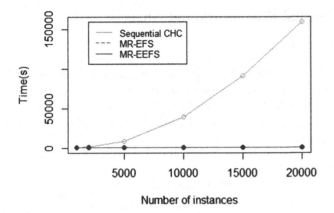

Fig. 7. Execution times of the sequential CHC, MR-EFS and MR-EEFS

5.4 Classification Results

This section presents the results obtained by applying several classifiers over the reduced epsilon dataset and covtype-2 with its features previously selected by using MR-EEFS. The measure used is area under the curve (AUC). This measure is defined as the area under the Receiver Operating Curve (ROC). The formula used for calculation is given in the following Eq. (2). TPR is true positive rate and TNR is True negative Rate which is obtained from the confusion matrix. AUC results are shown in Table 3. Figures 8 and 9 shows the graphical results.

$$AUC = [(TPR + TNR)/2]$$

Table 3. Accuracy with epsilon and covtype-2 data set

Data set	Logistic regression	Naive Bayesian	SVM	PFCM
Covtype - 2	75.23'	77.56	75.67	77.87
Epsilon	0.649	0.67	0.65	0.699

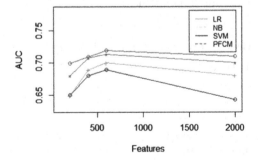

Fig. 8. Accuracy with epsilon dataset

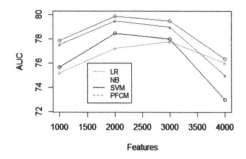

Fig. 9. Accuracy with covType-2 dataset

6 Conclusion

In this work a new modeling and simulation approach based on fuzzy cognitive maps is used for big data classification. FCM is considered as an efficient technique for decision making. But the inefficiency of FCM to handle large number of concepts makes it difficult to apply FCM for big data classification. Hence a new method is proposed to implement FCM for big data classification. First the feature set is reduced using evolutionary method that is implemented with Map Reduce and then the learning is parallelized with different map tasks. Hence the efficiency of FCM is increased. From the experiments it has been analyzed that a Map-Reduce based parallel FCM works efficiently on large data sets as compared to the sequential SVM.

References

1. Axelrod, R.: Structure of Decision: The Cognitive Maps of Political Elites. Prentice-Hall, Englewood Cliffs (1976)
2. Kosko, B.: Fuzzy cognitive maps. Int. J. Man-Mach. Stud. **24**, 65–75 (1986)
3. Giles, B.G., et al.: Integrating conventional science and aboriginal perspectives on diabetes using fuzzy cognitive maps. Soc. Sci. Med. **64**(3), 562–576 (2007)
4. Zhai, et al. (2009)
5. Giabbanelli, P.J., Torsney-Weir, T., Mago, V.K.: A fuzzy cognitive map of the psychosocial determinants of obesity. Appl. Soft Comput. **12**(12), 3711–3724 (2012)
6. Reichelt, K., Lyneis, J.: The dynamics of project performance: benchmarking the drivers of cost and schedule overrun. Eur. Manag. J. **17**(2), 135–150 (1999)
7. Carvalho, J.P., Tome, J.A.: Rule based fuzzy cognitive maps: Expressing time in qualitative system dynamics. In: Proceedings of the 10th IEEE International Conference on Fuzzy System, pp. 280–283 (2001)
8. Salmeron, J.L.: Modeling grey uncertainty with fuzzy grey cognitive maps. Expert Syst. Appl. **37**(12), 7581–7588 (2010)
9. Iakovidis, D.K., Papageorgiou, E.I.: Intuitionistic fuzzy cognitive maps for medical decision making. IEEE Trans. Inf. Technol. Biomed. **15**(1), 100–107 (2011)
10. Miao, Y., Liu, Z.Q., Siew, C.K., Miao, C.Y.: Dynamical cognitive network: an extension of fuzzy cognitive map. IEEE Trans. Fuzzy Syst. **9**(5), 760–770 (2001)

11. Aguilar, J.: A dynamic fuzzy cognitive map approach based on random neural networks. Int. J. Comput. Cognit. **1**(4), 91–107 (2003)

12. Kottas, T.L., Boutalis, Y.S., Christodoulou, M.A.: Fuzzy cognitive networks: a general framework. Intell. Decis. Technol. **1**, 183–196 (2007)

13. Cai, Y., Miao, C., Tan, A.-H., Shen, Z., Li, B.: Creating an immersive game world with evolutionary fuzzy cognitive maps. IEEE J. Comput. Graph. Appl. **30**(2), 58–70 (2010)

14. Wei, Z., Lu, L., Yanchun, Z.: Using fuzzy cognitive time maps for modeling and evaluating trust dynamics in the virtual enterprises. Expert Syst. Appl. **35**(4), 1583–1592 (2008)

15. Song, H.J., Miao, C.Y., Wuyts, R., Shen, Z.Q., D'Hondt, M., Catthoor, F.: An extension to fuzzy cognitive maps for classification and prediction. IEEE Trans. Fuzzy Syst. **19**(1), 116–135 (2011)

16. Ruan, D., Hardeman, F., Mkrtchyan, L.: Using belief degreedistributed fuzzy cognitive maps in nuclear safety culture assessment. In: Proceedings of Annual Meeting North American Fuzzy Information Processing Society, pp. 1–6 (2011)

17. Chunying, Z., Lu, L., Dong, O., Ruitao, L.: Research of rough cognitive map model. In: Shen, G., Huang, X. (eds.) ECWAC 2011, Part II. CCIS, vol. 144, pp. 224–229. Springer, Heidelberg (2011). https://doi.org/10.1007/978-3-642-20370-1_37

18. Acampora, G., Loia, V., Vitiello, A.: Distributing emotional services in ambient intelligence through cognitive agents. Serv. Oriented Comput. Appl. **5**(1), 17–35 (2011)

19. Kohavi, R., John, G.H.: Wrappers for feature subset selection. Artif. Intell. **97**, 273–324 (1997)

20. Fleuret, F.: Fast binary feature selection with conditional mutual information Mach. Learn. Res. **5**, 1531–1555 (2004)

21. Forman, G.: An extensive empirical study of feature selection metrics for text classification. J. Mach. Learn. Res. **3**, 1289–1306 (2003)

22. Javed, K., Babri, H.A., Saeed, M.: Feature selection based on class-dependent densities for high-dimensional binary data. IEEE Trans. Knowl. Data Eng. **24**, 465–477 (2010)

23. Peng, H., Long, F., Ding, C.: Feature selection based on mutual information: criteria of max-dependency, max-relevance, and min-redundancy. IEEE Trans. Pattern Anal. Mach. Intell. **27**, 1226–1238 (2005)

24. Kira, K., Rendell, L.A.: The feature selection problem: traditional methods and a new algorithm. In: Proceedings of Tenth National Conference on Artificial Intelligence, pp. 129–134 (1992)

25. Acuna, E., Coaquira, F., Gonzalez, M.: A comparison of feature selection procedures for classifier based on kernel density estimation. In: Proceedings of the International Conference on Computer, Communication and Control Technologies, vol. 1, pp. 468–472 (2003)

26. Stoppiglia, H., Dreyfus, G., Dubios, R., Oussar, Y.: Ranking a random feature for variable and feature selection. J. Mach. Learn. Res. **3**, 1399–1414 (2003)

27. Narendra, P., Fukunaga, K.: A branch and bound algorithm for feature subset selection. IEEE Trans. Comput. **6**, 917–922 (1977)

28. Setiono, R., Liu, H.: Neural-network feature selector. IEEE Trans. Neural Netw. **8**, 654–662 (1997)

29. Romero, E., Sopena, J.M.: Performing feature selection with multilayer perceptrons. IEEE Trans. Neural Netw. **19**, 431–441 (2008)

30. Stracuzzi, D.J., Utgoff, P.E.: Randomized variable elimination. J. Mach. Learn. Res. **5**, 1331–1364 (2004)

31. Wu, D., Zhou, Z., Feng, S., He, Y.: Uninformation variable elimination and successive projections algorithm in mid-infrared spectra wavenumber selection. Image Signal Process. (2009)

32. Centner, V., Massart, D.-L., de Noord, O.E., de Jong, S., Vandeginste, B.M., Sterna, C.: Elimination of uninformative variables for multivariate calibration. Anal. Chem. **68**, 3851–3858 (1996)
33. Alsberg, B.K., Woodward, A.M., Winson, M.K., Rowl, J.J., Kell, D.B.: Variable selection in wavelet regression models. Anal. Chim. Acta **368**, 29–44 (1998)
34. Caruana, R., de Sa, V.: Benefitting from the variables that variable selection discards. J. Mach. Learn. Res. **3**, 1245–1264 (2003)
35. Peng, Y., Xuefeng, Z., Jianyong, Z., Yunhong, X.: Lazy learner text categorization algorithm based on embedded feature selection. J. Syst. Eng. Electron. **20**, 651–659 (2009)
36. Law, M.H., Figueiredo, M.A.T., Jain, A.K.: Simultaneous feature selection and clustering using mixture models. IEEE Trans. Pattern Anal. Mach. Intell. **26**, 1154–1166 (2004)
37. Zhao, Z., Liu, H.: Semi-supervised feature selection via spectral analysis. In: Proceedings of the 7th SIAM Data Mining Conference (SDM), 641–646 (2007)
38. Peralta, D., del Río, S., Ramírez-Gallego, S., Triguero, I., Benitez, J.M., Herrera, F.: Evolutionary feature selection for big data classification: a mapreduce approach

Cluster Optimization in Wireless Sensor Networks Using Particle Swarm Optimization

S. R. Deepa[✉] and D. Rekha

VIT University, Chennai, India
{deepa.sr2013,rekha.d}@vit.ac.in

Abstract. Clustering approaches have been used to an extensive range of issues and also in Wireless Sensor Network (WSN) domain efficiently to address scalability problem. This paper proposes a Particle Swarm Optimization (PSO) technique to enhance the lifetime of wireless sensor networks. Better scalability is achieved through clustering process to make sure of even distribution of nodes into clusters and thus eliminating leftover nodes problem which will be a major cause for draining out the energy of sensor nodes and results in reduced lifetime of overall network. The Spanning tree based data routing process will ease the task of cluster heads while forwarding the data further towards base station. The proposed work is carried out in NS-2, the results show that PSO outperforms the existing techniques such as DRINA, BCDCP, OEERP, E-OEERP in terms of network lifetime, throughput, packet delivery ratio, residual nodes and packet drop count.

Keywords: Routing protocol · Wireless sensor networks
Particle Swarm Optimization

1 Introduction

The sensor nodes used in Wireless Sensor Network (WSN), sense the real world events and transmit data to base station for further processing. Sensors assist the society, since they can be integrated into vehicles, eco space and many devices. They can help to avoid terrible events such as collapsing of buildings, preserve natural resources, improves productivity and security. It also helps in developing new technologies such as smart home applications. As the technology advances in integrated circuit system, electro mechanical system wireless systems, the usage of wireless sensor networks are increased extensively. The size of the microprocessors has reduced in time and there is reduction also in its cost. This reduction in size, cost and increase in computation of microprocessors has led to the development and usage of more sensors. Wireless Sensor Networks are used extensively in sensing and reporting about floods, pollution, water usage, improving crop quality and fertilizers [1–4].

Many of the sensors get connected to controlling devices and devices which process (for through LAN), a rapidly increasing sensor nodes communicate the information through wireless channels to a base station. Most of the applications need dense

© Springer Nature Singapore Pte Ltd. 2018
J. K. Mandal and D. Sinha (Eds.): CSI 2017, CCIS 836, pp. 240–253, 2018.
https://doi.org/10.1007/978-981-13-1343-1_23

sensor deployment and hence wireless communication is needed. Hence, a wireless sensor node has to perform sensing, processing of sensed data, transmission and store information. The sensor nodes monitor in coordination with each other to form a Wireless Sensor Network. The Sensors communicate among themselves and also with the base station. This centralized base station does further processing, analysis and storage [5].

Evolutionary computation and bio inspired algorithms are used to enhance the energy efficiency of wireless networks. Evolutionary algorithms are based on principles of biological evolution [6–8]. The Swarm Intelligence (SI) is a novel distributed intelligent technique for solving optimization problems that indigenously motivated from the biological instances by flocking or swarming process in vertebrates. Particle Swarm Optimization (PSO) includes swarming nature which can be seen in bird flocks, fish school, or swarms of bees etc, from which the idea is emerged [17, 18]. The biggest advantages of PSO are its rapid convergence. In PSO, candidate solutions called particles move in an n-dimensional solution space searching for the best possible point. In WSNs, the PSO algorithm is generally run on autonomous sensor nodes or on the base station. Particle Swarm Optimization is bio-inspired algorithm. Clustering a Wireless Sensor Network increases the Network Lifetime. In this work Particle Swarm Optimization (PSO) is used for cluster optimization in Wireless Sensor Networks. The Wireless Sensor Network is considered as a weighted, connected graph and minimum spanning tree is used for routing data from cluster head to the base station.

The Paper is further organized as follows. Section 2 describes the problem challenges of Wireless Sensor Network. Section 3 gives the details of related work in clustering WSN. Section 4 gives problem statement and proposed methodology. Section 5 gives the performance evaluation and simulation parameters. Conclusion is given in Sect. 6.

2 Problems and Challenges of Wireless Sensor Networks

This section gives the information about energy constraint and residual nodes formation which is considered as the most vital design challenge and problem of a Wireless Sensor Network.

2.1 Energy Consumption

One of the challenges in the wireless sensor network design is energy limited batteries of sensor nodes. The sensor nodes get energy through batteries. Replacing or recharging of battery is required (e.g., using solar power) when the energy is drained after performing the data transmissions. The design of protocols at higher layers and energy efficiency of sensor node greatly depend on the working of physical layer [9]. The leakage current and energy involved in switching are important for energy consumption of a processor.

$$Energy = E_{power} + E_{lkg} = C_{total}V_{dd} + V_{dd}I_{leak}\Delta t \tag{1}$$

In Eq. (1) E_{lkg} is leakage energy, C_{total} is the capacitance, V_{dd} is the voltage supplied, I_{leak} is current leaked, and Δt is the time for computing.

2.2 Scalability and Residual Nodes Formation

The sensor nodes used in network may be very high ranging from few hundred nodes to thousands, depending on the application. Unless any event occurs, many nodes can be left in the sleep mode, with few sensors providing data [10]. WSN consists of densely deployed sensor nodes; hence there are chances that many nodes may detect the same event which leads to data redundancy. This suggests the idea of grouping nodes into clusters so as to reduce the redundant data. The cluster head collects data from the cluster nodes and transmit unique data to the base station. The cluster head performs data aggregation. Some of the cluster issues in WSN are:

(a) Sensor node count in a cluster, methodology of selecting cluster head.
(b) Problems of having nodes not falling into any of the clusters, they are known as residual node. Many protocols and mechanisms exists which handle these issues.

3 Related Work

A substantial work is done to find suitable clustering and routing protocol in Wireless Sensor Networks. The most important and very critical among all the other factors is the Energy efficiency. The lifetime of Network greatly depends on energy.

The energy efficiency of WSN is improved with clustering. It also improves the network lifetime and also the scalability. This improvement is since all nodes forward data to cluster head and only cluster head is involved in routing data to base station [11]. Only the cluster heads are to be managed with clustering rather than managing the whole network.

Base Station Controlled Dynamic Clustering protocol (BCDCP) is a protocol used for clustering and routing in WSN. The sensor nodes are simple and the base station has high computation ability. This protocol has two phases one for initializing network and transmitting information. Here the cluster heads are randomly chosen in rotations and clusters are formed. The clusters are balanced in order to avoid overload of cluster head. BCDCP improves lifetime of the network and energy is saved. Iteratively clusters are split. The network is first split into two, and then continues to split into smaller networks until expected number of clusters is obtained. After the centralized base station gets the power information of the nodes in the target area, cluster splitting algorithm creates clusters and cluster head selection is done. It divides the complete network into two sub-clusters; the procedure is repeated to obtain smaller clusters. The algorithm terminates when predefined number of clusters are obtained. The entire field is covered by placing the CHs at maximum distance [12]. There is possibility of residual node formation in such networks.

Data Routing for In-Network Aggregation (DRINA) algorithm enhances the points of aggregation and the routing tree is built using only fewer control packets. The DRINA algorithm builds a tree to route the data, by considering minimum shortest paths which connect every source nodes to the destination with increase in data fusion. The DRINA algorithm works with the nodes such as Collaborator node which gathers information by finding an event. The data is sent to the Coordinator node [13]. Coordinator node may become a collaborator after election. It performs the centralized fusion of information and sends the fused information to destination. A Tree is constructed to route information. Some of the nodes are elected as coordinator (cluster head). Base station receives sensed data [13]. The network lifetime is reduced because of residual nodes.

Optimized Energy Efficient Routing Protocol (OEERP) uses uniform battery draining of nodes [14]. It is one of the clustering protocols. Cluster Heads (CHs) are elected randomly. After the cluster head election, it broadcasts an advertisement message which is received by every node in transmission range, present within target area. The sensor nodes join particular Cluster Head by sending reply message with request message [14]. These nodes at some time may be included as a member of a cluster or they may be a cluster head also. The number of residual nodes keeps varying in time. High Energy is consumed in sending the data that is sensed from residual nodes to sink node, since many control messages are sent to identify the neighbor. A node remaining as residual node for a long time will exhaust soon. Therefore all nodes should have a chance to be members of clusters or to be a cluster head.

Enhanced Optimized Energy Efficient Routing protocol (E-OEERP) is also one of the cluster based routing protocol which reduces and eliminates individual node or the residual nodes and enhances the lifetime of the network than the existing protocols. It is achieved with the combination of Particle Swarm Optimization (PSO) in clustering process and the gravitational search algorithm (GSA) for route formation. The performance of the E-OEERP in terms of network lifetime, throughput, and packet delivery ratio are found and compared with the protocols like LEACH, DRINA, OEERP, BCDCP protocols [15]. The E-OEERP showed much high performance in terms of enhancing the sensor network lifetime [16]. The energy consumption can still be reduced.

The spanning tree based PSO algorithm is proposed to increase the lifetime of Wireless sensor network. The Problem statement and the proposed methodology is discussed in the next section and the results will show the enhanced performance in terms of the packet delivery ratio, throughput, network lifetime and reduced number of left-out-nodes or the residual nodes in the target area.

4 Methodology

In this paper the wireless sensor network lifetime is enhanced by using the Spanning tree based routing protocol with PSO. The PSO technique is used to bring out the efficient cluster optimization process in the network and the spanning tree mechanism is to find the optimal path for sending the information from the member nodes to the base station with reduced delay. Thus both the clustering and information transmission process in WSN can be made efficient using the combination of the PSO and the spanning tree technique.

4.1 Particle Swarm Optimization

One of the key factors for applying PSO is to find the way to map the problem solution obtained into the PSO particle. Bird flocking optimizes few objective function. Each particle will be aware of the best value (pbest) and its best position in the target area. Whatever has to be optimized in WSN clustering, has to be captured in terms of particles and the objective function. Then the sensors/base station to runs the PSO on their resident processor. Finally, the resulting gbest solution is taken as the final solution, and an action is initiated based on the solution [19]. Here the network energy efficiency has to be improved with the optimization of clustering process. Cluster head selection has to be done. Once cluster heads are selected then sensor nodes in their transmission range are included in the respective clusters. Therefore sensor node is considered as a particle. Each particle will know the best of the group (gbest), among pbests.

The fitness function for a particle is

$$F = \beta \frac{E_{CHa}}{E_{ma}} + (1 - \beta) \frac{D_{ma}}{D_{CHa}} \tag{2}$$

In Eq. (2) $\beta = 0.5$, E_{ma}, E_{CHa} are average residual energy values of member nodes and cluster heads respectively and D_{ma}, D_{CHa} are average distance of member nodes to base station and average distance of cluster heads to base station respectively. The fitness function is a maximization function.

Figure 1 shows the flowchart of PSO. Each sensor node i has initial velocity V_i and position X_i. $rand_1$ and $rand_2$ are numbers randomly generated. In the search space every iteration of PSO enhances the velocity and position of the particles. The updating of velocity is done by considering three acceleration components. The components are ω which is the coefficient of inertia, c_1 which is a constant denoting cognitive acceleration and c_2 which is a constant denoting social acceleration. In the gbest iteration, the particles having better fitness value become cluster heads. The nodes in the sensing region of cluster head become the cluster members. The algorithm terminates after fixed number of iterations are reached.

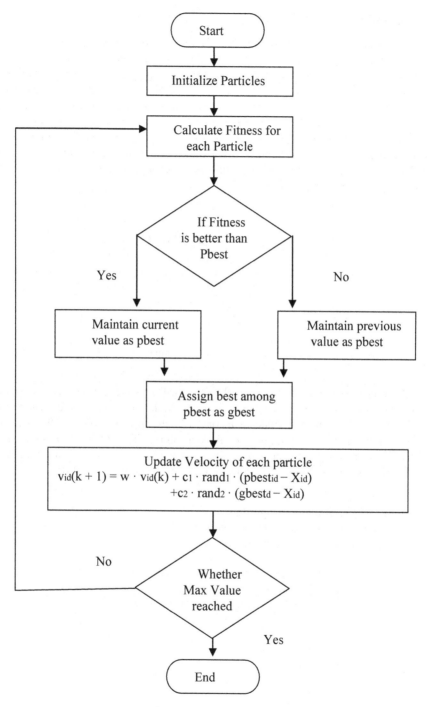

Fig. 1. Flowchart for PSO.

4.2   Spanning Tree Based Routing

After the cluster optimization is done, the data sensed by the nodes has to be transmitted to the base station whenever an event occurs. The cluster head performs aggregation and routes the data to the base station using spanning tree algorithm. For this algorithm to apply we need to consider the WSN as an undirected, connected graph. For a specific tree, the spanning tree connects all the vertices. There can be multiple spanning trees for a graph. With each edge assigned with some weight, the Minimum spanning tree is the spanning tree with less weight. The spanning tree is shown in Fig. 2. Each of the branches is assigned with random weights. As seen in Fig. 2 the spanning tree is highlighted. Different ways of connecting the vertices leads to many other spanning trees [20].

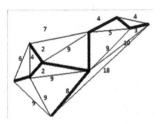

Fig. 2. Spanning tree graph

A Minimum spanning tree is a graph which will consider all the vertices in the network as nodes and does not contain any cycles. In the tree the root node will be the node having smaller ID. Other nodes will connect to the specific root node. The pseudo code for spanning tree algorithm is given in Algorithm 1. The WSN is considered as a weighted, connected graph and minimum spanning tree is found. This minimum spanning tree is a route to transmit data from cluster head to base station.

Algorithm 1 The spanning tree algorithm
Define: r_m is the root identifier, node m chooses
      d_m is the minimum shortest path distance from r_m to
     node m
     $g_m = (m, r_m, d_m)$ will be the message sent by node m
     $p_{m\,is}$ the parent ID of node m
     $h_{rev,m}$ to be the time when node m received the message
     from its parent node.
Initial values:
     g_m to (m, m, 0) for all m Є N
     p_m to m for all m Є N
     $h_{rev,\,m}$ to 0 for all m Є N

Span_set (node ID m, time t, timeframe S)
       1 if source of an event is not m,
       2 return

3 else {broadcast using one hop g_m and timer B is started,it expires every S sec

4 while true,

5 if timer B expires and ($r_m = m$ or $t > h_{rev, m}+S$),

6 set g_m to (m, m, 0)

7 set p_m to m

8 set $h_{rev, m}$ to t

9 broadcast using one-hop g_m

10 if from node j receiving a message g_j,

11 if $r_j < r_m$, or ($r_j = r_m$ and $d_j+1 < d_m$),

    or ($r_j= r_m$, $d_j +1 = d_m$, and j $\leq p_m$),

12 set g_m to (m, r_j, $d_j +1$)

13 set p_m to j

14   set $h_{rev, m}$ to t

15Broadcast using one hop g_m and restart timer B}

5 Simulation Parameters and Performance Evaluation

The proposed technique of Particle Swarm Optimization with Spanning tree algorithm to improvise the Network lifetime of Wireless Sensor Networks is carried out using Network Simulator – 2.34 (NS-2.34) with various packages. The following are the parameters considered to analyze the efficiency of proposed technique:

1. Packet Delivery Ratio
2. Throughput
3. Network Lifetime
4. Packet Drop
5. Number of Residual Nodes

To realize the betterment of the above parameters, the proposed technique is compared with existing protocols such as BCDCP, DRINA, OEERP and Enhanced-OEERP mentioned here as E-PSO.

Table 1 gives parameter's initial values of wireless sensor network and PSO parameters.

Table 1. Basic parameters of network with initial values

Parameter	Value
Population	100
Transmission/sensing region	200 * 200 m
Sensor node's energy initially	200 J
Acceleration constants	c1 = c2 = 2
Inertial weight range	0.9 to 0.4
Cluster radius	30 m
Range of sensor node	36 m
Rate of transmission	409 Kbps
Power required for transmission	0.02 W
Power required for receiving data	0.01 W
Packet size	512 bytes

5.1 Packet Delivery Ratio

The overall performance of the network is determined by the packet delivery ratio which is calculated as below

$$PDR = Rp / Tp \qquad (3)$$

Equation (3) R_p is total packets received and T_p is total transmitted packets. Higher the number of packets received by the nodes in network, better the performance. Table 2 shows the Packet Delivery Ratio (PDR) comparison with various existing protocol.

Table 2. Packet delivery ratio comparison

Protocol	PSO with spanning tree	E-PSO	OEERP	BCDCP	DRINA
No. of nodes	100	100	100	100	100
PDR	99.946	97.2	92.79	89.07	95.396

The Fig. 3 demonstrate the improvised PDR in the proposed PSO with Spanning tree technique compared to all the existing protocols and significant consistency in the packet delivery ratio. The graphs are generated using the xgraph package along with ns-2.34.

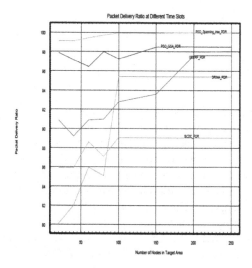

Fig. 3. Packet delivery ratio graph

5.2 Throughput

The Table 3 shown below gives the throughput analysis of the PSO technique with the spanning tree with existing protocols like E-OEERP mentioned as E-PSO, BCDC,

Table 3. Throughput

Protocol	PSO with spanning tree	E-PSO	OEERP	BCDCP	DRINA
No. of nodes	100	100	100	100	100
Throughput	870.10	780.1	633.2	500	601

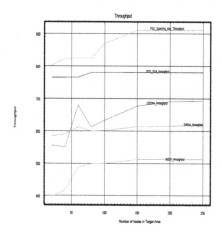

Fig. 4. Throughput

DRINA and OEERP. Effective way of transmitting data to the base station defines the throughput. The graph in Fig. 4 shows that, proposed methodology improves the throughput than other protocols.

5.3   Network Lifetime

The critical parameter in Wireless Sensor Network is Energy or the battery of the sensor nodes. Irrespective of the efficiency of the routing protocol, the sensor node will reach a state where energy reaches its minimum level. Hence there is a need for conserving the energy of a sensor node and intern enhancing the lifetime of whole network. In various time slots the total energy consumption is measured for proposed method and comparison is done with other existing algorithms by assigning the nodes with 200 joules of energy, in Table 4. Usage of Energy for protocols mentioned is gradually increasing. Figure 5 shows that the Total Energy Consumption of the proposed PSO with spanning tree protocol is less in comparison with rest of the algorithms mentioned. Network lifetime is improved by improving energy efficiency.

Table 4. Network lifetime

Protocol	PSO with spanning tree	E-PSO	OEERP	BCDCP	DRINA
Simulation time taken	300 s	300 s	70 s	10 s	100 s
Initial energy	200 J	200 J	200 J	200 J	200 J
Energy consumed	55 J	130 J	200 J	200 J	100 J

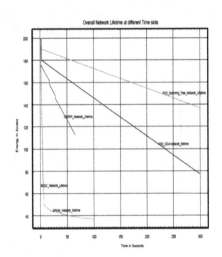

Fig. 5. Network lifetime

5.4   Packet Drop

There are various factors when a sensor node in the target area will drop certain number of packets during processing, aggregating or during the transmission of packets to the respective cluster heads or to the base station. With respect to all these issues, the proposed technique of PSO with Spanning tree is analyzed for packet drop count and there is a significant reduction in proposed technique compared to all other existing protocols as shown in Table 5 and Fig. 6.

Table 5. Packet drop count

Protocol	PSO with spanning tree	E-PSO	OEERP	BCDCP	DRINA
No of Nodes	100	100	100	100	100
No. of Packets Dropped	0		12	12	99	405

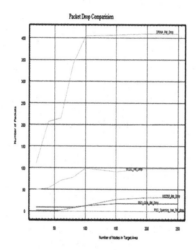

Fig. 6. Packet drop graph

5.5   Residual Node Count

When there are no residual nodes or less number of residual nodes, this iteration can be considered as global best. At this point cluster formation process can end. The individual nodes after cluster formation are shown in Table 6. The graph in Fig. 7 infers that, the proposed PSO with spanning tree reduces the number of residual nodes to almost nil thus more efficient than the algorithms existing. Since all the individual nodes become cluster members at some point in time, the lifetime of the network is increased significantly.

Table 6. Residual nodes

Protocol	PSO with spanning tree	E-PSO	OEERP	BCDCP	DRINA
No. of nodes	100	100	100	100	100
No. of residual nodes	0	0	4	21	10

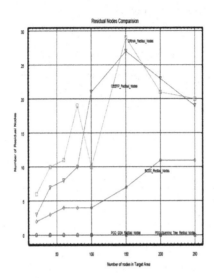

Fig. 7. Residual node count

6   Conclusion

The Spanning Tree based Routing Protocol with PSO for improvising lifetime of WSN is proposed in this paper. The Performance of the proposed work is compared with existing protocols. The combination of the particle swarm optimization technique for cluster optimization and spanning tree algorithm for routing outperforms the existing work in terms of various parameters like the packet delivery ratio, the network lifetime and throughput. The packet drop is reduced. The proposed work greatly enhanced the network life time of the wireless sensor network with complete elimination of residual nodes formation in the target area. As a part of the future work, the methodology can be extended to a network with mobile nodes and the wireless sensor network lifetime can be enhanced

References

1. Maraiya, K., Kant, K., Gupta, N.: Application based study on wireless sensor network. Int. J. Comput. Appl. **21**(8), 9–15 (2011)
2. Akyildiz, et al.: A survey on sensor network. IEEE Commun. Mag. **40**, 102–114 (2002)

3. Balakrishnan, H.: An application-specific protocol architecture for wireless micro sensor networks. IEEE Trans. Wirel. Commun. **1**(4), 660–670 (2002)
4. Akyildiz, I.F., Su, W., Sankarasubramaniam, Y., Cayirci, E.: A survey on sensor networks. IEEE Commun. Mag. **40**(8), 102–114 (2002)
5. Estrin, D., Girod, L., Pottie, G., Srivastava, M.: Instrumenting the world with wireless sensor networks. In: Proceedings of the International Conference, on Acoustics, Speech and Signal Processing (ICASSP 2001), Salt Lake City, vol. 4, pp. 2675–2678 (2001)
6. Arivudainambi, D., Rekha, D.: An evolutionary algorithm for broadcast scheduling in wireless multihop networks. Wirel. Netw. **18**(7), 787–798 (2012)
7. Arivudainambi, D., Rekha, D.: Broadcast scheduling problem in TDMA adhoc networks using immune genetic algorithm. Int. J. Comput. Commun. Control **8**, 18–29 (2013)
8. Arivudainambi, D., Rekha, D.: Memetic algorithm for minimum energy broadcast problem in wireless ad hoc networks. Swarm Evol. Comput. **12**, 57–64 (2013)
9. Yick, J., Mukherjee, B., Ghosal, D.: Wireless sensor network survey. Comput. Netw. **52**, 2292–2330 (2008)
10. Romer, K., Mattern, F.: The design space of wireless sensor networks. IEEE Trans. Wirel. Commun. **11**, 54–61 (2004)
11. Martirosyan, A., Boukerche, A., Pazzi, R.W.N.: A taxonomy of cluster-based routing protocols for wireless sensor networks. In: International Symposium on Parallel Architectures, Algorithms, and Networks (i-span 2008), Sydney, NSW, pp. 247–253 (2008)
12. Shah, R.C., Rabaey, J.M.: Energy aware routing low energy adhoc sensor networks. In: Proceedings of the IEEE Wireless Communications and Networking Conference, vol. 1, pp. 350–355 (2002)
13. Zhicheng, D., Li, Z., Wang, B., Tang, Q.: An energy aware cluster-based routing protocol for wireless sensor and actor network. J. Inf. Technol. **8**(7), 1044–1048 (2009). https://doi.org/10.3923/itj.2009.1044.1048
14. Chand, K.K. Bharati, P.V., Ramanjaneyulu, B.S.: Optimized energy efficient routing protocol for life-time improvement in wireless sensor networks. In: Proceedings of the International Conference on Advances in Engineering, Science and Management, pp. 345–349 (2012)
15. RejinaParvin, J., Vasanthanayaki, C.: Particle swarm optimization- based clustering by preventing residual nodes in wireless sensor networks. IEEE Sens. J. **15**, 4264–4274 (2015)
16. Mitton, N., Razafindralambo, T., Simplot-Ryl, D., Stojmenovic, I.: Towards a hybrid energy efficient multi-tree-based optimized routing protocol for wireless networks. Sensors **12**, 17295–17319 (2012)
17. Ji, C., Zhang, Y., Gao, S., Yuan, P., Li, Z.: Particle swarm optimization for mobile ad hoc networks clustering. IEEE International Conference on Networking, Sensing and Control **1**, 372–375 (2004)
18. Kennedy, J., Eberhart, R.: Particle swarm optimization. In: Proceedings of the IEEE International Conference on Neural Network, Piscataway, NJ, USA, pp. 1942–1948 (1995)
19. Kulkarni, R.V., Venayagamoorthy, G.K.: Particle swarm optimization in wireless-sensor networks: a brief survey. IEEE Trans. Syst. Man Cybern.—Part C Appl. Rev. **41**, 262–267 (2011)
20. Lee, M., Wong, V.W.S.: An energy-aware spanning tree algorithm for data aggregation in wireless sensor networks. In: PACRIM 2005 IEEE Pacific Rim Conference on Communications, Computers and Signal Processing, pp. 300–303 (2005)

Bio Computing

Identification of Benign and Malignant Cells from Cytological Images Using Superpixel Based Segmentation Approach

Shyamali Mitra[1], Soumyajyoti Dey[2], Nibaran Das[2(✉)],
Sukanta Chakrabarty[3], Mita Nasipuri[2], and Mrinal Kanti Naskar[1]

[1] Department of Electronics and Telecommunication Engineering,
Jadavpur University, Kolkata, India
shyamali.mitraa@gmail.com, mrinaletce@gmail.com
[2] Department of Computer Science and Engineering,
Jadavpur University, Kolkata, India
deysoumya03@gmail.com, nibaran@gmail.com,
mitanasipuri@gmail.com
[3] Theism Medical Diagnostics Centre, Dumdum, Kolkata, India
drsukantachakraborty@gmail.com

Abstract. Proper Segmentation of cytological images is a prerequisite for appropriate localization of nucleus of cancer cells to classify the specimen as benign or malignant. Most of the works till date pursue segmentation for a specific or single type of cancer cells. The present work considers cytological images from various types of cancer cells. As nuclei from the different types of cells carry different attributes, segmentation becomes a challenging task. Here a superpixel based segmentation techniques with different morphological and clustering algorithms such as anisotropic diffusion, DBscan, Fuzzy C-means etc. have been proposed to distinguish nucleus from different kinds of cells. Finally the segmented nuclei are used to extract features for classification using five different classifiers separately and observed an improved recognition accuracy.

Keywords: Fine Needle Aspiration Cytology · Anisotropic diffusion
SLIC · DB SCAN clustering · Fuzzy C-means clustering
Entropy based superpixel

1 Introduction

Cancer is one of the most dreadful diseases in today's life [1]. It is one of the biggest challenging areas in medical science because it's cure depends on the correct diagnosis at the right stage. Often the symptoms of this disease are noticeable or perceivable at the last stage when it is impossible for the patient to survive. Therefore, the correct diagnosis of malignancy at the right time is very crucial to enhance the chances of survival. From many years, researchers are trying the best way of diagnosis for its cure. A physical exam of the affected part of the patient is conducted and then medical history is studied (if applicable), especially symptoms and family history to diagnose cancer. Among all the diagnosis processes, a very common diagnosis is Fine Needle

© Springer Nature Singapore Pte Ltd. 2018
J. K. Mandal and D. Sinha (Eds.): CSI 2017, CCIS 836, pp. 257–269, 2018.
https://doi.org/10.1007/978-981-13-1343-1_24

Aspiration Cytology (FNAC) [2]. FNAC test is one type of biopsy process with shortest turnaround time and less harmful than a surgical biopsy. In this procedure, the cells are first collected from the infected area through needle and then the pathologist smears on the slide using Leishman Giemsa staining. After that, the smear is viewed by the pathologist under the microscope for observation. In the microscopic image, the light pink colored portions are viewed as the cytoplasm and the deep pink colored portions, the nuclei. The overcrowded portions of the nuclei are observed by the pathologist as a general feature of malignant cells. Our objective is to distinguish each of the nucleus from the cytological images because it is the shape or size or various aspects of nuclei that are taken into consideration for the classification of a specimen as benign or malignant.

From last few decades, the researchers are trying to develop an automated computer aided diagnosis system for cytological images [3–6]. In this paper, our first goal is to segment the nuclei from the cytological images by using some traditional segmentation processes like anisotropic diffusion [7], superpixel based segmentation [8], DB SCAN clustering [9], Fuzzy-C-means clustering [10] etc. After isolating the portion of nuclei from the rest of cytoplasm, some features like compactness, eccentricity, area, convex-area of nuclei etc. are extracted for classification of benign and malignant tumors using some well-known classifiers such as k-Nearest Neighbor (k-NN), Random Forest, Support Vector Machines (SVMs), Multilayer Perceptron (MLP), Naïve Bayes and finally develop a comparative analysis.

2   A Literature Survey

A lot of works are reported on cytological image segmentation and classification [1–14]. Lezoray et al. [11] have performed segmentation of cytological images using an extension of watershed as an optimal region-growing operator using color information in several color spaces. A pool of cells has been calculated by experts to tally the segmentation success rate. All cells are isolated irrespective of their spatial configuration. The average success rate as reported is 94.5% for the nuclei and 93% for the cytoplasm.

In [12] Kowal et al. present a system of computer-aided diagnosis of breast cancer using Gaussian mixture model to segment cytological images. They propose a segmentation procedure that integrates results of adaptive thresholding and Gaussian mixture clustering. Next, cells are classified using four different classifiers: k-nearest neighbors, naive Bayes, decision trees and classifiers ensemble. Diagnostic accuracy obtained for the experiments that are conducted varied according to different classification approaches and oscillated up to 98% for quasi optimal subset of features.

Filipczuk et al. [5] propose a circular Hough transform based segmentation of cell nuclei, where shapes of the nuclei are estimated by circles. The resultant circles are then filtered to keep only high-quality approximations for further investigation by a support vector machine which classifies detected circles as correct or incorrect on the basis of texture features and the percentage of nuclei pixels according to a nuclei mask obtained using Otsu's thresholding method. A set of 25 features of the nuclei is used in the classification of the cells by four different classifiers (fuzzy c-means, k-means, Gaussian mixture model, and competitive neural networks).

A smart diagnosis system for breast cancer classification [10] has been developed by George et al. where nuclei boundaries are segmented based on Hough transform in combination with watershed algorithm. For each segmented region features describing texture and shape of the nucleus are calculated. The extracted features are used to train several neural network architectures to investigate the most suitable network model for classifying the cells. Four classification models are used namely multilayer perceptron (MLP) using back-propagation algorithm, probabilistic neural networks (PNN), learning vector quantization (LVQ) and support vector machine (SVM). The classification results are obtained using 10-fold cross validation.

In the study [4], Jeleń et al. have presented a system that classifies a malignancy stage of cancer that is malignant due to the pre-screening process before taking an FNA. One of the most popular and widely used scheme for grading cytological tissue is the Bloom-Richardson grading scheme. In this system, three factors viz. degree of structural differentiation, pleomorphism, occurrence of hyperchromatic and mitotic figures are taken into account to categorize cancerous tissues. They have used automated segmentation procedure that involved the level set method. All level set methods start with an initial level set function, the closer the initial level set function to the final segmentation, the more likely the method converge quickly to the segmentation process. To automate the segmentation process and start with a good initial level set function, they use an iterative clustering approach for automatic image thresholding.

In Issac Niwas's paper [13], it is investigated whether complex wavelets can provide better performance than the more common real valued wavelet transform. The proposed methodology for the computation of nuclei textural features included the preprocessing stage for segmenting the nuclei region followed by the decomposition of the isolated nuclei regions by means of complex wavelet transform and the computation of the nuclei multiscale features using co-occurrence matrix based features. Based on the extracted features samples are then classified by a k-NN classifier. The correct classification results are obtained as 93.9% for the complex wavelets whereas 70.3% for the real wavelets.

Das et al. [14] have published a paper on texture-based approach for diagnosis of FNAC images where they have performed saturation using thresholding segmentation. First the saturation channel of HSI (Hue Saturation Intensity) image is extracted. After HSI saturation thresholding, the nuclei are segmented by channel subtraction. Here the features are extracted by using GLCM (grey level co-occurrence matrix) and LBP (local binary pattern) algorithms. For classification, Logistic classifier is used.

3 Materials and Method

3.1 Dataset Description

The cytological images of FNAC test are collected from a pathology centre named "Theism Medical Diagnostics Centre, Dumdum, Kolkata, West Bengal" under the supervision of the pathologist. The images are taken from Olympus microscope at 40x optical zoom with 5-megapixel resolution. Around 100 cytological images are collected among which 50 samples are malignant and 50 samples are benign.

4 Present Work

As mentioned earlier, in the present work image segmentation has been done to isolate nuclei from the cells and extract different features from the nuclei to classify each one of them into benign or malignant. Image segmentation is done using mathematical morphological operators like anisotropic diffusion, DB Scanning, open and close operators etc. The problem is difficult because there are large numbers of structural variations. In feature extraction part several features like area, convex area which can differentiate benign and malignant cells are taken into account. Finally, categorization is done using some standard classifiers like k-NN, Random Forest, SVM, Adaboost, MLP and compared their relative performances. The outline of the segmentation process is given in Fig. 2.

Fig. 1. Outline of the method

4.1 Segmentation Process

Image Segmentation is the most important area in image analysis to properly unveil the region of interest from the rest. The accuracy of subsequent steps like feature extraction and classification completely depend on a good segmentation algorithm. It is also a difficult problem because of complex nature of the nucleus and uncertainty in the microscopic image. For our images (in .jpg format) deep pink colored portions (i.e. nuclei) are extracted from the light pink colored portions (i.e. cytoplasm). To do that images are first transformed in RGB color model ($\mathbf{I_{RGB}}$). In RGB cytological images,

$$I_{RGB} = (F_R, F_G, F_B) \tag{1}$$

where, $F_R(x, y)$ = intensity of the pixel (x, y) in red channel, $F_G(x, y)$ = intensity of the pixel (x, y) in green channel $F_B(x, y)$ = intensity of pixel (x, y) in blue channel. The proposed method for the segmentation of nucleus is given below:

Image Segmentation Algorithm

```
Step-1: RGB input Image --> I(R, G,B)
Step-1.a: Split input Image into three channels I(R), I
    (G), I (B)
Step-2: Apply Anisotropic Diffusion algorithm on red,
    green and blue channelof  RGB input image conse-
    quently ---> Aniso_Diff(I(R)) ,Aniso_Diff(I(G)), An-
    iso_Diff(I(B))
Step 2(a): Merge these three channels after applying Ani-
    sotropic Diffusion.
    I(Aniso_Diff) = MERGE( Aniso_Diff(I(R)) An-
    iso_Diff(I(G))Aniso_Diff(I(B)))
Step 3: Apply Median Based SLIC segmentation algorithm on
    I(Aniso_Diff)
Step 3(a): RETURN lebel l(i) for every pixel i and adja-
    cency matrix.
Step 4: Apply Density Based SCAN clustering algorithm on
    the lebel l(i) and adjacency matrix.
Step 4(a): RETURN matrix I_DBScan
Step 5: Draw Region boundary on I_DBScan
Step 6: Binarize the matrix I_DBScan and inverse it.
Step 6(a): Erosion the image on Step-6
Step 7: Calculated Mean Intensity of the connected compo-
    nents with respect to the images on Step-2.
Step 7(a): Set values of the Mean Intensity on each pixel
    with respect to the images on Step-2.
Step 7(b): Contrasting the image on Step 7.a.
Step 8: Apply Fuzzy C means Clustering Algo on the image
    on Step 7.b.
Step 9: Calculate the Area of the connected components of
    the image (Step-8).
Step 9(a): If the area is less than or equal to 700 pix-
    els then SET pixels value = 0
Step-10:  Aply erosion the image and dilasion.
Step-10.a: Masking the image (Step-10) on the original
    image (Step-1).
Step-11: Apply entrophy based superpixel algorithm on the
    image (Step-10.a)
Step-12:  Segmented Image.
```

First the input image is split into three channels to process each resulted channel independently. Next Anisotropic diffusion algorithm [7] is applied on each channel of RGB image because this can be operated only on 2D grey scale image. The equation for anisotropic diffusion is given by,

$$F_t = div(c(x,y,t)\nabla F) = c(x,y,t)\Delta F + \nabla c.\nabla F \qquad (2)$$

Where c is the diffusion coefficient. Most of the noise reduction techniques perform blurring without preserving the edges. Hence edges also get blurred. On the contrary anisotropic diffusion technique smooths intra-regions in the image whereas the edges of inter-region are preserved by choosing different diffusion iterations. This algorithm works well for preservation of edges of the nuclei. Non-linear approach of anisotropic diffusion algorithm is used to preserve as well as enhance edge details. Nonlinear anisotropic diffusion filters sharpen edges over a wide range of slope scales and reduce noise conservatively with dissipation purely along object boundaries. The 4-nearest neighbors' discretization of the Laplacian operator can be used to calculate the next iterations given in Eq. 3

$$\left. \begin{array}{l} \nabla_N F_{R(x,y)} \equiv F_{R(x-1,y)} - F_{R(x,y)} \\ \nabla_W F_{R(x,y)} \equiv F_{R(x,y-1)} - F_{R(x,y)} \\ \nabla_S F_{R(x,y)} \equiv F_{R(x+1,y)} - F_{R(x,y)} \\ \nabla_E F_{R(x,y)} \equiv F_{R(x,y+1)} - F_{R(x,y)} \end{array} \right\} \qquad (3)$$

$$F_{R(i,j)}^{t+1} = F_{R(i,j)}^t + \lambda [c_N * \nabla_N F_R + c_S * \nabla_S F_R + c_E * \nabla_E F_R + c_W * \nabla_W F_R]_{(i,j)}^t \qquad (4)$$

$$F_{G(i,j)}^{t+1} = F_{G(i,j)}^t + \lambda [c_N * \nabla_N F_G + c_S * \nabla_S F_G + c_E * \nabla_E F_G + c_W * \nabla_W F_G]_{(i,j)}^t \qquad (5)$$

$$F_{B(i,j)}^{t+1} = F_{B(i,j)}^t + \lambda [c_N * \nabla_N F_B + c_S * \nabla_S F_B + c_E * \nabla_E F_B + c_W * \nabla_W F_B]_{(i,j)}^t \qquad (6)$$

where t is the no of iterations and $0 \leqslant \lambda \leqslant 1/4$ N, S, E, W are the mnemonic subscripts denote the neighboring pixels in the North, South, East and West directions respectively of the pixel centered at (x, y). The symbol '∇' denotes differences of nearest-Neighbor and

$$c_{N(x,y)}^t = g\left(\left| \nabla_N F_{R(x,y)}^t \right| \right) \qquad (7)$$

where $g(x)$ defined by $g(x) = e^{\left(-\left(\|x\|/k\right)^2\right)}$ and $g(x) = \dfrac{1}{1+\left(\frac{\|x\|}{k}\right)^2}$

Here $\lambda = 0.15$ and k = 20 are chosen. If the magnitude of the gradient is large, it can indicate the edges whereas low magnitude are as always point out noise. From Eqs. 4, 5 and 6 we get

$$I_{Anisotropic} = F_{R(i,j)}^{t+1} \cup F_{G(i,j)}^{t+1} \cup F_{B(i,j)}^{t+1} \qquad (8)$$

Now Median Based SLIC (Simple Linear Iterative Clustering) segmentation algorithm [8] is applied on $I_{Anisotropic}$. The image ($I_{Anisotropic}$) is divided into 2000 superpixels. The resulting superpixels whose area less than 10 pixels are eliminated and the super pixel attributes are computed from the median colored value.

Now Spatial DB (density based) SCAN [9] clustering algorithm is applied on this labeled image which is generated from previously applied superpixel algorithms. The high density regions of the labeled image are located and these regions are separated by lower density regions.

It is assumed that $I_{db-scan}$ be the new labeled image corresponding to new clustered regions after applying density based clustering algorithm. Then the boundaries of labeled regions are drawn in $I_{db-scan}$. The image with region boundary is denoted by $I_{boundary}$. A binary image (I_{Binary}) is generated from the image $I_{boundary}$ and black and white color on this binary image are interchanged to make black the boundary of nuclei and cytoplasm and other portions of the entire image make white. $I' = [1\ 1\ ...\ 1]_{m \times n} - [I_{Binary}]_{m \times n}$. Now morphological operation is applied here, erode the image I' with the presence of a structural element ş, $I' \ominus ş = \{z \mid ş_z \subseteq I'\}$ where $ş_z$ is the translation of ş. Assume, $I'' \equiv I' \ominus ş$. The mean intensity of the connected components of the image I'' is calculated with respect to the images $F_{R(i,j)}^{t+1}, F_{G(i,j)}^{t+1}, F_{B(i,j)}^{t+1}$.

Mean Intensity of each connected component is calculated as $(MI) =$

$1/n \left[\sum_{j=1}^{n} f\left(x_j,\ y_j\right) \right]$ where n is the no of pixels and $f(x_i, y_i)$ is the intensity value of the pixel (x_j, y_j). The values of Mean Intensity are stored in each pixels of the connected components. $F1(x, y) = MI_{red}^i$ for all x,y where (x, y) are the pixels of ith connected components with respect to red channel. Similarly $F2(x, y) = MI_{green}^i$ $F3(x, y) = MI_{blue}^i$.

$$I_{contour} = F1 \cup F2 \cup F3 \qquad (9)$$

$I_{contour}$ is split into three channels and convert each channel into gray scale image and finally they are merged. After that Fuzzy C-means clustering [10] algorithm is applied on that image. Here 15 clusters are chosen and a new clustered image (I_{fcm}) is generated. Now the image I_{fcm} has some irrelevant portions. It is observed that the areas of irrelevant portions consist of nearly 700 pixels (which is chosen arbitarily). To remove those irrelevant portions of connected component of the image are calculated. For i^{th} connected component $CC_i(x, y) = 0$ if area of CC_i is less than or equal to 700 pixels. After that some morphological operations like erosion and dilation are applied. Now the original pink colored nuclei are superimposed on the masked background.

To separate the overlapped portions in nuclei Entropy based superpixel algorithm is introduced. The entire image is divided into 750 superpixels, and the overlapping portions are separated by superpixels labels following the entropy rate on a graph

$$G = (V, A)$$
$$H(A) = - \sum \mu\_i \sum p\_(i,j)(A)\ log\ (p\_(i,j)(A)) \qquad (10)$$

The balancing term can be written as

$$B(A) \equiv H(Z\_A) - N\_A = -\sum pZ\_A(i) \; log \; (pZ\_A(i)) - N\_A \qquad (11)$$

The objective function which combines the balancing factor and entropy rate is

$$Max[H(A) + \lambda B(A)] \; where \; \lambda \geqslant 0 \qquad (12)$$

Here the overlapping portions are divided by the maximum value of this objective function. Finally the segmented image has produced, which will be helpful to distinguish between malignant and benign cells. In the segmented image, there are only the portions of deep pink colored nuclei separated from one another (Fig. 3).

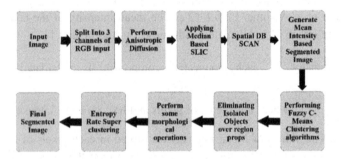

Fig. 2. Different steps of segmentation steps

5 Feature Extraction

Feature extraction redefines a large set of redundant data into a set of features or feature vector of reduced dimension. First the segmented images are taken and they are transformed to binary images by adjusting the threshold value. Next the features of the connected components of these binary images are calculated. Here largest 70 connected components are taken by comparing the areas of connected components. After that three types of features namely (a) Eccentricity [15] (b) Compactness [16] (c) Area/(convex area)^2 [17] are calculated. The features values are normalized by dividing their corresponding maximum values. Now histograms are evaluated from these normalized feature vectors. Here the histogram is computed because these features can be binned and to compare properly among those images.

6 Classification

Based on the features extracted in above step the classifiers classify the cells collected from different organs as either malignant or normal cells. To fully illustrate the difference between two classes the entire dataset is separated into two classes: Class #1 for benign and Class #2 for malignant. The dataset is divided into two parts: training set and test set using the ratio 2:1. For training purpose 67 images and for testing purpose

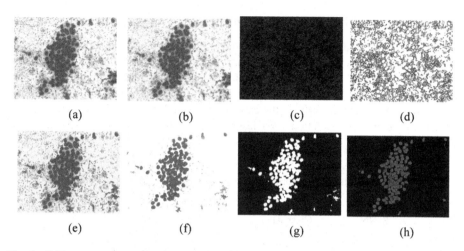

Fig. 3. Different steps of segmentation process (benign cell): (a) original image, (b) after anisotropic diffusion, (c) after SLIC and DB scan, (d) after morphology operations, (e) mean intensity based segmented image, (f) contrasting image (g) fuzzy C means, (h) final segmented image (Color figure online)

33 images are considered. To evaluate the performance five well known classifiers [18–20] namely k-NN, (k-Nearest Neighbor), Random Forest classifier, SVM, Adaboost and MLP are applied. The Segmentation techniques are developed under the environment of Matlab 2015a on a machine with the configuration of i3 processor with 4 GB RAM. For classification purpose WEKA 3.8 [21], a well-known open source machine learning software is used in the present work. To evaluate the performance, different performance metrics such as Precision $\left(\frac{TP}{TP+FP}\right)$, Recall $\left(\frac{TP}{TP+FN}\right)$, F-measure $\left(\frac{(2 \times Precision \times Recall)}{Precision + Recall}\right)$, Accuracy etc. are calculated. The empirically derived maximum output is shown in Fig. 4.

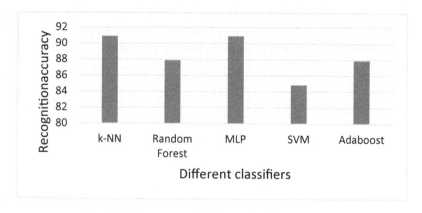

Fig. 4. Performance of different classifiers on test set

6.1   Experimental Result and Discussion

In the final segmented image presented in Fig. 3(h) only pink colored nuclei are kept by removing all noisy components by a minimum filter. From Table 1 it is concluded that classifiers k-NN and MLP scored almost equal and ranked higher in all sets whereas Adaboost and Random Forest rank lower and almost similar. SVM performs the worst among them. In most of the cases recall is high for Class# 2 which indicates the chances of misclassification for Class# 2 i.e. malignant cells are classified with higher accuracy.

Table 1. Statistical information on performance of different classifiers

Classifier		Precision	Recall	F-measure
K-NN	Class #1	1	0.813	0.897
	Class #2	0.85	1	0.919
	Weighted average	**0.923**	**0.909**	**0.908**
Random forest	Class #1	0.875	0.875	0.875
	Class #2	0.882	0.882	0.882
	Weighted average	0.879	0.879	0.879
MLP	Class #1	0.93	0.875	0.903
	Class #2	0.889	0.941	0.914
	Weighted average	0.91	**0.909**	**0.909**
SVM	Class #1	0.867	0.813	0.839
	Class #2	0.833	0.882	0.857
	Weighted average	0.849	0.848	0.848
ADABOOST	Class #1	0.833	0.938	0.882
	Class #2	0.933	0.824	0.875
	Weighted average	0.885	0.879	0.879

Table 2 shows the comparative chart on recognition accuracy. The maximum accuracy achieved in our method on test data set is $\sim 91\%$ which is quite convincing if we consider multiple types of cancer images. Figure 5 shows two misclassified segmented samples using MLP. The density of nucleus is seen to be very high for benign image whereas density is very low for malignant image leading to misclassification in both the cases.

Table 2. A comparative analysis among different existing techniques

Techniques	Data base information	Accuracy
Teramoto et al. [6]	Seventy-six (76) cases where 40 cases are of adenocarcinoma, 20 cases are of squamous cell carcinoma, and 16 cases are of small cell carcinoma collected at Fujita Health University, Toyoake City, Japan	71%
Żejmo et al. [22]	50 images from Szpital Zielona Gora, Poland	83%
Jelen et al. [4]	110 fine needle aspiration biopsy images are collected from Department of Pathology at the Medical University of Wrocław, Poland	94.24%
Gopinath et al. [23]	40 benign and 40 malignant of Thyroid images on-line image atlas of Papanicolaou Society of Cytopathology (http://www.papsociety.org/atlas.html)	96.6%
Das et al. [14]	100 samples of Benign and malignant cells from heterogeneous organs collected from slides of real patients from Theism Medical Diagnostics Centre, Kolkata, India	86%
Proposed method		91%

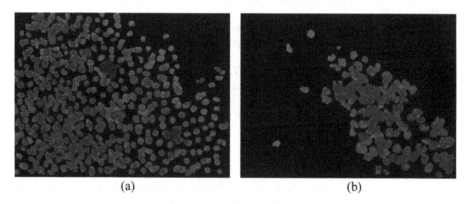

(a) (b)

Fig. 5. Examples of misclassified segmented image samples (a) benign samples misclassified as malignant (b) malignant samples misclassified as benign

7 Conclusion

In this paper, a new approach to automatic diagnosis of FNAC test for identification of benign and malignant cell is proposed. During the segmentation procedure we have used super pixel, density based clustering and Fuzzy- C- means clustering. After segmentation we have extracted different features such as eccentricity, compactness etc. from the images. The extracted features are used to classify test images based on the features of training sample images. We have found maximum recognition accuracy of 91% after using five different classifiers. In future work, some stronger features may be introduced for classification purpose and/or use Deep convolution neural network to improvise the recognition accuracy.

Acknowledgement. Authors are thankful to the "Center for Microprocessor Application for Training Education and Research" of Computer Science & Engineering Department, Jadavpur University, for providing infrastructure facilities during progress of the work. Authors are also thankful to Mr. Sandipan Choudhuri of Arizona State University, USA for his valuable suggestion and Dr. Debasree Mondal of Theism Medical Diagnostics Centre, Kolkata, West Bengal, India for providing us diagnosed samples.

References

1. World Health Organization (WHO): Cancer Factsheet of WHO. http://www.who.int/mediacentre/factsheets/fs370/en/. Accessed 28 Oct 2017
2. Ansari, N.A., Derias, N.W.: Fine needle aspiration cytology. J. Clin. Pathol. **50**(7), 541–543 (1997)
3. Wolberg, W.H., Street, W.N., Mangasarian, O.L.: Image analysis and machine learning applied to breast cancer diagnosis and prognosis. Anal. Quant. Cytol. Histol. **17**(2), 77–87 (1995)
4. Jeleń, L., Fevens, T., Krzyżak, A.: Classification of breast cancer malignancy using cytological images of fine needle aspiration biopsies. Int. J. Appl. Math. Comput. Sci. **18**(1), 75–83 (2008)
5. Filipczuk, P., Fevens, T., Krzy, A., Monczak, R.: Computer-aided breast cancer diagnosis based on the analysis of cytological images of fine needle biopsies. IEEE Trans. Med. Imaging **32**(12), 2169–2178 (2013)
6. Teramoto, A., Tsukamoto, T., Kiriyama, Y., Fujita, H.: Automated classification of lung cancer types from cytological images using deep convolutional neural networks. Biomed. Res. Int. **2017**, 1–6 (2017)
7. Weickert, J.: Anisotropic diffusion in image processing. Image Rochester NY, vol. 256, no. 3, p. 170 (1998)
8. Achanta, R., Shaji, A., Smith, K., Lucchi, A., Fua, P., Süsstrunk, S.: SLIC superpixels compared to state-of-the-art superpixel methods. IEEE Trans. Pattern Anal. Mach. Intell. **34** (11), 2274–2282 (2012)
9. Sander, J., Ester, M., Kriegel, H.-P., Xu, X.: Density-based clustering in spatial databases: the algorithm GDBSCAN and its applications. Data Min. Knowl. Discov. **2**(2), 169–194 (1998)
10. George, Y.M., Bagoury, B.M., Zayed, H.H., Roushdy, M.I.: Automated cell nuclei segmentation for breast fine needle aspiration cytology. Signal Process. **93**(10), 2804–2816 (2013)
11. Lezoray, O., Abderrahim, E., Hubert, C., Gilles, G., Michel, L., Hubert, R.M.: Segmentation of cytological images using color and mathematical morphology. Acta Stereol. **18**(1), 1–14 (1999)
12. Kowal, M., Filipczuk, P., Obuchowicz, A., Korbicz, J.: Computer-aided diagnosis of breast cancer using Gaussian mixture cytological image segmentation. J. Med. Inform. Technol. **17**, 257–262 (2011)
13. Issac Niwas, S., Palanisamy, P., Sujathan, K., Bengtsson, E.: Analysis of nuclei textures of fine needle aspirated cytology images for breast cancer diagnosis using Complex Daubechies wavelets. Signal Process. **93**(10), 2828–2837 (2013)

14. Das, P., Chatterjee, T., Chakraborty, S., Mondal, D., Das, N.: A texture based approach for automatic identification of benign and malignant tumor from FNAC images. In: BT - 2nd IEEE International Conference on Recent Trends in Information Systems, ReTIS 2015, Kolkata, 9–11 July 2015, pp. 249–254 (2015)

15. Iles, P.J.W.: Average cell orientation, eccentricity and size estimated from tissue images. University of Waterloo (2005)

16. Chen, X., Zhou, X., Wong, S.T.C.: Automated segmentation, classification, and tracking of cancer cell nuclei in time-lapse microscopy. IEEE Trans. Biomed. Eng. 53(4), 762–766 (2006)

17. Dey, P., Ghoshal, S., Pattari, S.K.: Nuclear image morphometry and cytologic grade of breast carcinoma. Anal. Quant. Cytol. Histol. 22(6), 483–485 (2000)

18. Sarkhel, R., Das, N., Das, A., Kundu, M., Nasipuri, M.: A multi-scale deep quad tree based feature extraction method for the recognition of isolated handwritten characters of popular indic scripts. Pattern Recognit. 71, 78–93 (2017)

19. An, T.K. Kim, M.H.: A new diverse AdaBoost classifier. In: 2010 International Conference on Artificial Intelligence and Computational Intelligence, vol. 1, pp. 359–363 (2010)

20. Liaw, A., Wiener, M.: Classification and regression by randomForest. R News 2(Dec), 18–22 (2002)

21. Hall, M., Frank, E., Holmes, G., Pfahringer, B., Reutemann, P., Witten, I.H.: The WEKA data mining software: an update. ACM SIGKDD Explor. Newsl. 11(1), 10–18 (2009)

22. Żejmo, M., Kowal, M., Korbicz, J., Monczak, R.: Classification of breast cancer cytological specimen using convolutional neural network. J. Phys: Conf. Ser. 783(12060), 1–11 (2017)

23. Gopinath, B., Shanthi, N.: Support vector machine based diagnostic system for thyroid cancer using statistical texture features. Asian Pac. J. Cancer Prev. 14(1), 97–102 (2013)

Identifying MicroRNA Markers From Expression Data: A Network Analysis Based Approach

Paramita Biswas[✉] and Anirban Mukhopadhyay

Department of Computer Science and Engineering, University of Kalyani,
Kalyani 741235, West Bengal, India
paramita.biswas1991@gmail.com, anirban@klyuniv.ac.in

Abstract. The identification of biomarkers is very important to know the presence or severity of a particular disease state in the patient body. According to the latest studies on miRNAs and their behaviors, it is known to us that miRNAs involve in the regulation mechanism of several biological processes. Sometimes the abnormal change in miRNA expressions in different conditions may lead to malignant growth in tissues. In this article, our proposed approach not only helps to detect differentially coexpressed modules but also helps to identify biomarker candidates from those modules. The proposed algorithm uses the WCGNA software package to explore coexpression profiles of the miRNAs. The algorithm has been applied to existing miRNA datasets to point out the miRNA markers. Then, biological validation analysis has been performed for the obtained miRNA markers.

Keywords: MicroRNA marker · Microarray analysis
Differentially coexpressed network · Topological overlap
Intramodular connectivity · MiRNA-target interaction · Carcinomas

1 Introduction

In order to determine the presence of malignant cell or tissue in human genome, candidate biomarker [18] identification is essential. Several kinds of research have shown that biomarker has the potential to estimate status and risk of the diseases in the patient body. It also helps to detect response to the therapy. With the advancement of molecular biology, now microRNAs are considered as new biomarkers [1,17].

The miRNA is a small RNA fragment, which has not taken a part in the translation process [3]. Each miRNA consists of almost 22 nucleotides [3]. MicroRNAs involve in RNA silencing and regulate gene expression in many living organisms, by targeting mRNA [2]. Some studies have already revealed that miRNAs not only regulate several cellular mechanisms, but also act as tumor suppressors in the tumorigenesis process [7]. Therefore, extraction of useful knowledge and

© Springer Nature Singapore Pte Ltd. 2018
J. K. Mandal and D. Sinha (Eds.): CSI 2017, CCIS 836, pp. 270–284, 2018.
https://doi.org/10.1007/978-981-13-1343-1_25

information through miRNA expression analysis gives a significant impact in cancer research. Due to the short size of miRNAs, the biomarker identification through expression analysis became challenging [13]. In this context, the advanced microarray technology has emerged as a boon to the computational biologists. It has made it possible to observe the thousands gene expression in a single chip. It also makes researchers be capable of monitoring these expression profiles across different tissue samples in different experimental conditions.

Recently, network-based approaches become very popular to study the gene expression profiles, since they are capable of exploring and analyzing significant properties such as bio-diversity, phenotypic variation, connectivity etc. [4]. A network is represented by a graph structure consisting of a node set V and a link set E. An adjacency matrix representation best suited for describing a network, denoted by $A = a_{ij}$, where each non-diagonal entry, a_{ij} represents either weighted connectivity or just adjacency between the node i and j. The value of $a_{ij} = 0$ denotes no such edge lies between the node i and j. The node degree in a network can be defined as the number of links incident to that node. The node with a maximum degree is considered as the hub of the network. Most of the biological processes or activities can be easily viewed as a network, where genes, proteins or other bio-molecules represented by nodes and interaction between them represented by links [4]. In this study, we examine coexpression network of miRNAs. Here each node corresponds to each miRNA, the edge between two such miRNAs indicates there is a association between those miRNAs and the weight of the edge implies degree of similarity between those miRNAs.

In this context, a number of network based approaches exist to analyze gene expression signature in different condition. Choi et al. [6] performed a differential coexpression analysis of microarray dataset by employing Fisher's z-test based link scoring technique, to show cancer-induced changes in two distinct networks. Topological overlap measure is very helpful to observe the neighborhood connectivity. Therefore, it is widely used in several literature to explore differential correlation across the networks [9–11]. Another approach named DifCoEx [19], aims at grouping differentially coexpressed gene pairs using statistical framework followed by a hierarchical clustering technique. A recently proposed method, DCoSpect, uses spectral clustering technique to identify differentially coexpressed modules from the dataset [15]. Most of these approaches use different coexpression scoring technique to measure the degree of the relationship between the gene pair across different conditions and perform statistical significance tests to detect biologically significant genes.

In this article, our approach not only aims to detect differentially coexpressed modules but also finds candidate biomarker using intramodular connectivity analysis. The algorithm is applied to a microRNA expression dataset. The expression dataset has m miRNAs and s samples which can be represented as a 2D matrix $X_{m*s} = [x_{ij}]$, where each entry x_{ij} denotes the ith miRNA's expression level for each jth sample [14]. Firstly, we are calculating correlation between the miRNA in different state of samples. Next, we try to find differentially coexpressed modules with the help of hierarchical clustering. Finally, we identify most significant hub nodes as candidate miRNA marker from those differentially coexpressed modules. For this purpose, we choose neighborhood sharing score based intramodular connectivity measurement technique. Those identified miRNAs are further studied for their biological significance analysis.

2   Proposed Method

In this section, we discuss our proposed algorithm for distinguishing miRNA markers from expression data. The overall process of our candidate biomarker identification and their biological validation analysis comprises three stages. The stages are discussed below.

2.1   Coexpression Similarity Measurement:

First, we measure the degree of similarity between the miRNAs depending on their expression profiles. The degree of similarity determines the level of agreement between miRNAs across different samples and conditions.

Preparing Correlation Matrices: For this purpose, we apply Pearson Correlation Coefficient formula [16], as correlation analysis measures the strengths of association between a pair of miRNAs and the direction of the relationship. In this correlation estimation technique, the coefficient values lie between -1 and $+1$. The coefficient value $+1$ indicates there exist a pure +ve linear relationship and -1 indicates there exist a pure -ve linear relationship. If the coefficient value lies between -1 and $+1$, expresses the degree of linear dependency within the miRNAs. If the coefficient value very close to -1 or $+1$, indicates the stronger correlation within the miRNAs and the value equals to zero, indicates the miRNAs are independent. If a dataset has s samples of two miRNAs (a, b), then the Eq. 1 is used to find the value of the correlation coefficient (p_{ab}) between them. In the equation, a_i and b_i represents the expressions of the corresponding miRNAs, in $i = 1, 2, ..., s$ samples. We prepare the correlation matrix using Pearson Correlation Coefficient formula for each pair of miRNAs (a, b), for each condition κ. Here, we have taken the absolute coefficient values. We denote the similarity matrix or correlation matrix by $P_{ab}^\kappa = |p_{ab}|$.

$$p_{ab} = \frac{s \sum a_i b_i - \sum a_i \sum b_i}{\sqrt{(s \sum a_i^2 - (\sum a_i)^2)(s \sum b_i^2 - (\sum b_i)^2)}} \tag{1}$$

Coexpressed Network Construction: Our next step is building coexpression network. If there exists correlation coefficient score for a pair of miRNAs in their respective correlation matrix then the miRNAs are considered as adjacent to each other in coexpression network. The correlation coefficient value is considered as the weight of the edge between the adjacent nodes. This way we build completely connected weighted coexpression networks from the correlation matrices for different condition. Here P^1 and P^2 denotes correlation matrices for condition 1 and condition 2 respectively. Now we perform pairwise difference [19]

$(\delta_{ab} = P^1 - P^2)$ between the correlation matrices using Eq. 2. We construct differentially coexpressed network depending on the pairwise difference matrix. All miRNAs are participating in this completely connected weighted network with their differential score as an edge weight.

$$D : \delta_{ab} = (\sqrt{\frac{1}{2}|sign(p_{ab}^1) * (p_{ab}^1)^2 - sign(p_{ab}^2) * (p_{ab}^2)^2|})^{\beta} \qquad (2)$$

In the differential score matrix D, the higher value of δ_{ab} indicates that the significant change of coexpression status between miRNA pairs (a, b) within two different conditions. β is considered as a tuning parameter or soft threshold parameter. The parameter β is introduced to emphasize the large differential score compared to less meaningful lower differences. Usually the positive integer is preferred as β value. The increment in β values gives less priority in smaller changes in the correlation. Accordingly, higher value of β helps to identify statistically significant data [19]. Theoretically, the value of β shows an inverse relationship with the sample size. Therefore, if the sample size increases, then smaller values of β is preferred. In this experiment, we always check the significance of the result after changing the β values and biological network criteria is studied accordingly.

2.2 Differentially Coexpressed Module Detection

The coexpression network analysis helps to distinguish a subset of strongly connected nodes (modules) [22]. Our approach for module detection uses the node dissimilarity measure followed by a clustering technique. To accomplish this, we first derive a Topological Overlap [8,20,21] based node dissimilarity matrix $\Im$ from these differential score matrix D using Eq. 3. The dissimilarity matrix $\Im$ score lies between 0 and 1.

$$\Im : \tau_{ab} = \begin{cases} 1 - \dfrac{\sum_{\kappa}(\delta_{a\kappa}\delta_{b\kappa}) + \delta_{ab}}{min(\sum_{\kappa}\delta_{a\kappa}\sum_{c}\delta_{b\kappa}) + 1 - \delta_{ab}}, & \text{if } a \neq b \\ 1, & \text{otherwise} \end{cases} \qquad (3)$$

Topological overlap measure helps us to identify neighbor sharing miRNAs from the differential coexpression network. A low value (high similarity) of τ_{ab} indicates that the miRNA pair (a, b) associated with a same large group of neighbor miRNAs in the network and they (a, b) share significant relationship with each other [19]. This miRNA group considered as "topological overlap" of the miRNA pair (a, b) in the differential coexpression network. To detect the set of miRNAs that have maximum topological overlap, we employ clustering techniques. Here, dissimilarity matrix $\Im$ is taken as input for clustering and module detection. We choose average linkage hierarchical clustering technique. In order to extract the modules from the obtained dendrogram after hierarchical clustering, dynamic-TreeCut [12] algorithm is used.

2.3   Identification of Module Hubs

Hub identification is very important for biological network analysis. The most centrally located node in the network is referred to as the hub of the network. Usually, the degree of the nodes is considered for hub detection. As our network graph is completely connected so all the nodes have same degree distribution. Therefore, we calculate intramodular connectivity to identify hub nodes in each module. Here topological overlap based matrix score [22] is used to measure the connectivity of each node in each module according to the Eq. 4.

$$\omega_a = \sum_{b=1}^{m} \tau_{ab} \tag{4}$$

where τ_{ab} denotes a topological overlap score within the nodes a and b. Here, m denotes the number of nodes connected with the node a. If a node has the largest group of neighbor overlap with other nodes in the network, then its topological overlap based connectivity score ω_a should be high.

Proposed Algorithm for Module Detection and Hub Identification is shown in Algorithm 1.

Algorithm 1: Proposed Algorithm for Module Detection and Hub Identification

---

Input   : *Two state (normal, tumor) miRNA expression data matrix $X_{m \times s}$, m=number of miRNAs, s=number of samples.*

Output: *Differentially Coexpressed modules and their Hubs.*

Step 1: *Normalization of $(X_{m \times s})$*
  $X_{norm} \leftarrow Norm(X_{m \times s})$.

Step 2: *Separate normal state data $(N_{m \times s_1})$ and tumor state data $(T_{m \times s_2})$ from X_{norm}, where $s_1, s_2 \in s$*

Step 3: *Compute correlation coefficient matrices P^N, P^T from both matrices $N_{m \times s_1}$ and $T_{m \times s_2}$.*
  $P^N(i,j) \leftarrow corr(n_i, n_j)$,   where $n_i, n_j \in N_{m \times s_1}$ and $i, j \in m$.
  $P^T(i,j) \leftarrow corr(t_i, t_j)$,   where $t_i, t_j \in T_{m \times s_2}$ and $i, j \in m$.

Step 4: *Building differential coexpression matrix as follows:*
  $\delta(i,j) \leftarrow |P^N(i,j) - P^T(i,j)|$,   for all $i, j \in m$

Step 5: *Compute the neighborhood sharing score $\tau(i,j)$ for each pair of node in δ.*

Step 6: *Preparing node dissimilarity matrix dist as follows:*
  $dist(i,j) \leftarrow 1 - \tau(i,j)$,   for all $i, j \in m$

Step 7: *Hierarchical clustering is applied over the dissimilarity matrix dist.*

Step 8: *module $\leftarrow$ Differentially coexpressed modules are detected after cutting the resulting dendrogram at proper level.*

Step 9: *Compute intramodular connectivity for each node i in each module:*
  $\omega_i \leftarrow \sum_{j=1}^{m} \tau(i,j)$,   for all $i, j \in m$

Step 10: *In a module, node i is selected as hub if ω_i gives maximum connectivity score.*

---

3   Results and Discussion

In this section, we present the results of the proposed algorithm. The algorithm performed on a existing microRNA dataset. Our experiments are accomplished by using R software with WGCNA library. In order to detect the modules, hierarchical clustering and dynamicTree-Cut [12] method has been applied. After performing the same experimental setup with different minimum cluster sizes, we found that minimum cluster size equals to 10 gives the most stable number of modules for our dataset, as shown in the Fig. 1. Therefore, we choose the minimum cluster size equal to 10 for dynamic Tree-Cut algorithm. We have identified miRNA modules that are differentially coexpressed and hub nodes are detected from those modules. Then genes, targeted by identified miRNAs has been explored. Gene Ontology and pathway analysis is performed to provide evidence for their biological relevance.

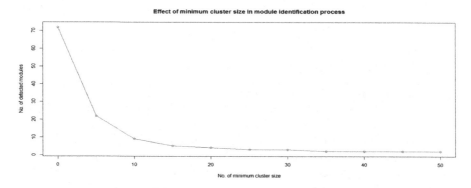

Fig. 1. The figure represents the effect of minimum cluster size on the number of modules identification. From the figure it is clear that we get most stable no. of modules with the minimum cluster size equals to 10.

3.1 Dataset Details

We have collected publicly available dataset from the website http://www.broad. mit.edu/cancer/pub/miGCM. The complete dataset contains 217 number of miRNAs and they are collected from the mammalian species. We have extracted six datasets with the normal and tumor samples from different tissues like breast, colon, kidney, lung, prostate and uterus. Each dataset consist of the 217 miRNAs [13]. The detail description of the number of tumors and normal samples from the each tissue types are provided in Table 1. Now we prepare our dataset in such a way that it contains 217 miRNA ids along the rows & their expression value corresponding to each type of sample stored in each cell along the columns. Then we normalize the entire dataset & separate the normal and tumor samples with the same set of miRNA lists. The sample vectors of each dataset are normalized to have mean 0 with variance 1. Finally the processed dataset consists of two classes, the first class contains all the normal samples (32 samples) and other class contains all the tumor samples (57 samples).

Table 1. Number of normal and tumor samples present in each tissue type.

Tissues	Normal sample	Tumor sample	Total sample
Breast	3	6	9
Colon	5	10	15
Kidney	3	5	8
Lung	4	6	10
Prostate	8	6	14
Uterus	9	10	19
Total	32	43	75

3.2   Experimental Analysis

The proposed algorithm has been applied to the normalized data [5]. We use Pearson's correlation coefficient to establish the degree of association within miRNAs and the direction of the relationship across different sample conditions. Depending on the correlation between the miRNA pairs, an undirected completely connected weighted coexpression network is defined. Furthermore, we have studied the topological properties of the network. In the next step, we examine the neighborhood connection of the individual nodes with topological overlap based dissimilarity measurement technique. Then module assignment has been performed by employing hierarchical clustering followed by dynamic-TreeCut [12]. Next, we consider intramodular connectivity measure to get the node having maximum neighborhood share. These highly connected nodes within modules identified as a hub of the modules.

3.3   Study on the Dataset

We have identified 9 differentially coexpressed modules. These modules consist of a total 217 miRNAs. Each module is represented by specific color, viz Grey (27 miRNAs), Turquoise (66 miRNAs), Blue (35 miRNAs), Brown (18 miRNAs), Yellow (18 miRNAs), Green (15 miRNAs), Red (14 miRNAs), Black (13 miRNAs), Pink (11 miRNAs). The dendrogram consisting miRNAs and their corresponding module colors are shown in Fig. 2. Here the miRNAs, belonging to Grey module, cannot establish any kind of relationship with other miRNAs in our experiment. Therefore, we are not considering grey module for further analysis. As these 8 modules are undirected, completely connected weighted network so we are unable to use adjacency connectivity measure. Thus we are using topological overlap based connectivity measure to obtain most centrally located nodes or hubs.

The 8 miRNAs are selected as a hub for each module with maximum connectivity score. Their probe ids are EAM109, EAM211, EAM345, EAM337, EAM177, EAM205, EAM361, EAM293. Hub miRNAs with their probe id and neighborhood connectivity score are summarized in Table 2. As our goal is to identify miRNA marker related to the human genome, therefore, only six miRNAs are considered for further study. The miRNAs with probe id EAM345 and EAM177 belongs to other mammalian species, that is why these miRNAs are not considered for further study. The biological significance analysis of the obtained miRNA markers, has been carried out by using a publicly available online database, miRTarBase. There are many other databases available

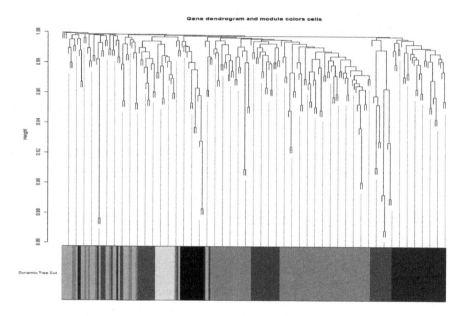

Fig. 2. The figure represents dendrogram consisting miRNAs and their corresponding module colors. (Color figure online)

Table 2. Modules and their respective miRNA markers.

Modules	Hub miRNAs	Node connectivity in percentage
Turquoise	hsa-miR-7	98.28
Blue	hsa-miR-144	96.06
Yellow	hsa-miR-93	94.12
Red	hsa-miR-138	92.33
Black	hsa-miR-326	91.74
Pink	hsa-miR-188	90.19

online for studying miRNA target interactions (MTIs). We choose miRTarBase because it has acquired almost three hundred and sixty thousand miRNA-target interactions (MTIs). The database also provides the several experimental (e.g. reporter assay, western blot, microarray, etc.) validity results for the collected MTIs. Not only that, the miRTarBase always checks the other similar databases to update their collection. According to their validation method, each of the MTIs is marked as strong and weak. The Figs. 3 and 4 show the miRNA-target interactions (MTIs) for each detected miRNAs. In these figures node color differs to represent the distinction between miRNAs and genes. The different edge colors present the strength of interaction depending on the validation method. In Table 3, the miRNA markers and few strongly connected target genes with their associated disease names are enlisted. Surprisingly, almost all miRNA target genes are associated with several types of carcinomas. Here we can see that miRNA hsa-miR-138 target genes associated with 13 type of carcinomas. This analysis indicates that there exist strong relationship between the detected miRNAs and carcinoma diseases.

The KEGG (Kyoto Encyclopedia of Genes and Genomes) database is very helpful to observe the cancer related pathways. To investigate relationship among the identified miRNA targets and cancer-related diseases, KEGG pathway enrichment analysis has been performed. The Database for Annotation, Visualization and Integrated Discovery (DAVID) is publicly available at http://david.abcc.ncifcrf.gov/. We crosschecked our KEGG pathway analysis result

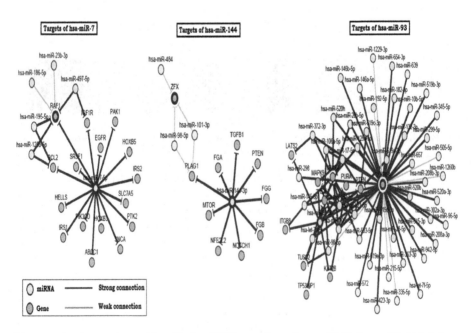

Fig. 3. The figure shows identified miRNA markers (hsa-miR-7, hsa-miR-144 & hsa-miR-93) and their target miRNAs and genes.

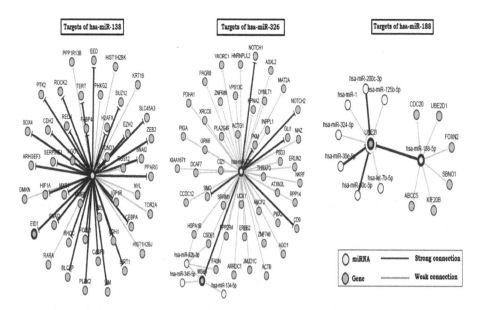

Fig. 4. The figure shows identified miRNA markers (hsa-miR-138, hsa-miR-326 & hsa-miR-188) and their target miRNAs and genes.

Table 3. For each selected miRNA marker, few target genes and their associated cancer type are retrieved by miRTarBase.

Sl No.	miRNAs	Target genes	Cancer type association
1	hsa-miR-7	IRS1, IRS2, BLC2, PIK3CD	Thyroid carcinoma (THCA)
		EGFR, HOXB3, SNCA, PAK1, IGF1R	Stomach adenocarcinoma (STAD)
		HOXB5	Breast invasive carcinoma (BRCA)
		PTK2, SRSF1	Liver hepatocellular carcinoma (LIHC)
		HELLS, SLC7A5	Head & Neck squamous cell carcinoma (HNSC)
		RAF1	Lung squamous cell carcinoma (LUSC)
		ABCC1	Kidney renal papillary cell carcinoma (KIRP)
2	hsa-miR-144	ZFX, FGA, FGB, NOTCH1	Stomach adenocarcinoma (STAD)
		PLAG1	Kidney renal clear cell carcinoma (KIRC)
		TGFB1	Uterine Corpus Endometrial Carcinoma (UCEC)

(*continued*)

Table 3. (*continued*)

Sl No.	miRNAs	Target genes	Cancer type association
		PTEN	Breast invasive carcinoma (BRCA)
		FGG	Prostate adenocarcinoma (PRAD)
		NFE2L2	Lung adenocarcinoma (LUAD)
		MTOR	Cholangiocarcinoma (CHOL)
3	hsa-miR-93	CDKN1A, PURA	Kidney renal clear cell carcinoma (KIRC)
		TUSC2	Pancreatic adenocarcinoma (PAAD)
		E2F1, ITGB8	Prostate adenocarcinoma (PRAD)
		MAPK9	Liver hepatocellular carcinoma (LIHC)
		KAT2B, LATS2, PTEN	Lung squamous cell carcinoma (LUSC)
		TP53INP1	Kidney Chromophobe (KICH)
		VEGFA	Stomach adenocarcinoma (STAD)
4	hsa-miR-138	RHOC, MMP3, PPARG	Esophageal carcinoma (ESCA)
		GNAI2, EZH2, H2AFX, FABP4, PLEK2, LPL, RELN, MXD1, SLC45A3, CDH1, TERT, ZEB2, SOX4, VIM, CDH2	Stomach adenocarcinoma (STAD)
		BLCAP	Liver hepatocellular carcinoma (LIHC)
		SERPINE1, PTK2, EED	Lung adenocarcinoma (LUAD)
		SIRT1	Bladder Urothelial Carcinoma (BLCA)
		IGF1R, CBL	Uterine Corpus Endometrial Carcinoma (UCEC)
		HIF1A, SNAI2	Kidney Chromophobe (KICH)
		CASP3,	Lung squamous cell carcinoma (LUSC)
		EID1	Breast invasive carcinoma (BRCA)
		CCND3, ROCK2	Thyroid carcinoma (THCA)
		ARHGEF3	Kidney renal papillary cell carcinoma (KIRP)
		FOSL1	Cholangiocarcinoma (CHOL)
		SUZ12, CEBPA	Pancreatic adenocarcinoma (PAAD)

(*continued*)

Table 3. (*continued*)

Sl No.	miRNAs	Target genes	Cancer type association
5	hsa-miR-326	NOTCH1	Breast invasive carcinoma (BRCA)
		NOTCH2	Lung squamous cell carcinoma (LUSC)
		GLI1, SMO	Head & Neck squamous cell carcinoma (HNSC)
		CD9, MSH3	Kidney renal clear cell carcinoma (KIRC)
6	hsa-miR-188	UBE2I	Kidney renal clear cell carcinoma (KIRC)
		CBL	Uterine Corpus Endometrial Carcinoma (UCEC)

using these DAVID tool. Our study of the target-gene involvement in several pathways with their p-values from different databases, are listed in Table 4. We found Prostate cancer, Lung cancer, Endometrial cancer, Proteoglycans in cancer, Central carbon metabolism in cancer, Choline metabolism in cancer, HTLV-1 infection and Hepatitis B related pathways were enriched with miRNA target-genes. These results indicate that the detected miRNA markers are showing a deep involvement with several cancer pathways. Hence, we are able to find biologically significant miRNA markers.

Table 4. Top five significant KEGG pathways analysis using DAVID Tool for the target genes of each of the selected miRNA marker.

Probe-id	miRNA	Pathway (p-value)
EAM109	hsa-miR-7	Prostate cancer (1.23E−08)
		Small cell lung cancer (5.42E−08)
		ErbB signaling pathway (7.49E−08)
		Glioma (9.20E−08)
		Endometrial cancer (5.08E−07)
EAM211	hsa-miR-144	Proteoglycans in cancer (0.002)
		PI3K-Akt signaling pathway (0.016)
		Pathways in cancer (0.032)
		MicroRNAs in cancer (0.053)
		mRNA surveillance pathway (0.055)

(*continued*)

Table 4. (*continued*)

Probe-id	miRNA	Pathway (p-value)
EAM337	hsa-miR-93	HTLV-I infection (2.71E−06)
		Pathways in cancer (5.20E−06)
		Hepatitis B (5.36E−06)
		Endocytosis (2.10E−05)
		Bladder cancer (4.01E−05)
EAM205	hsa-miR-138	Pathways in cancer (1.37E−04)
		Transcriptional misregulation in cancer (6.20E−04)
		p53 signaling pathway (8.19E−04)
		Proteoglycans in cancer (0.001)
		MicroRNAs in cancer (0.001)
EAM361	hsa-miR-326	Thyroid hormone signaling pathway (3.91E−04)
		Central carbon metabolism in cancer (0.002)
		Prostate cancer (0.006)
		Proteoglycans in cancer (0.006)
		Endometrial cancer (0.009)
EAM293	hsa-miR-188	HTLV-I infection (4.16E−04)
		Proteoglycans in cancer (0.004)
		Fc epsilon RI signaling pathway (0.006)
		ErbB signaling pathway (0.011)
		Choline metabolism in cancer (0.017)

4   Conclusion

In this article, an algorithm has been proposed to identify differentially coexpressed miRNA marker from miRNA expression dataset. We have collected real-life miRNA expression dataset across different sample conditions. These dataset consist of several tissue types, i.e. Breast, Colon, Kidney, Lung, Prostate and Uterus. The algorithm starts with the construction of completely connected differentially coexpressed network for the normalized dataset. Then we use topological overlap measure to get maximum neighborhood sharing score for each node which suggests the degree of concordance between the nodes.

We extract 8 differentially coexpressed modules by applying hierarchical clustering technique followed by dendrogram cutting procedure. Furthermore, we also study the topological properties of those networks and 8 hubs are identified. Each node represents each miRNAs. According to the various biological relevance study, we found that few detected miRNA markers have significant association with several types of cancers. In future, we will try to incorporate feature selection and optimization techniques to improve our algorithm performance.

References

1. Abeel, T., Helleputte, T., Van de Peer, Y., Dupont, P., Saeys, Y.: Robust biomarker identification for cancer diagnosis with ensemble feature selection methods. Bioinformatics **26**(3), 392–398 (2009)
2. Ambros, V.: The functions of animal micrornas. Nature **431**(7006), 350–355 (2004)
3. Bartel, D.P.: MicroRNAs: genomics, biogenesis, mechanism, and function. Cell **116**(2), 281–297 (2004)
4. Barter, R.L., Schramm, S.J., Mann, G.J., Yang, Y.H.: Network-based biomarkers enhance classical approaches to prognostic gene expression signatures. BMC Syst. Biol. **8**(4), S5 (2014)
5. Bolstad, B.M., Irizarry, R.A., Astrand, M., Speed, T.P.: A comparison of normalization methods for high density oligonucleotide array data based on variance and bias. Bioinformatics **19**(2), 185–193 (2003)
6. Choi, J.K., Yu, U., Yoo, O.J., Kim, S.: Differential coexpression analysis using microarray data and its application to human cancer. Bioinformatics **21**(24), 4348–4355 (2005)
7. Della Vittoria Scarpati, G.: Analysis of differential miRNA expression in primary tumor and stroma of colorectal cancer patients. BioMed Res. Int. **2014**, 840921 (2014)
8. Ravasz, E., Somera, A.L., Mongru, D.A., Oltvai, Z.N., Barabási, A.: Hierarchical organization of modularity in metabolic networks. Science **297**(5586), 1551–1555 (2002)
9. Fukushima, A.: DiffCorr: an R package to analyze and visualize differential correlations in biological networks. Gene **518**(1), 209–214 (2013)
10. Hsu, C.L., Juan, H.F., Huang, H.C.: Functional analysis and characterization of differential coexpression networks. Scientific Rep. **5**, 13295 (2015)
11. Langfelder, P., Horvath, S.: WGCNA: an R package for weighted correlation network analysis. BMC Bioinform. **9**(1), 559 (2008)
12. Langfelder, P., Zhang, B., Horvath, S.: Defining clusters from a hierarchical cluster tree: the dynamic tree cut package for R. Bioinformatics **24**(5), 719–720 (2008)
13. Lu, J., Getz, G., Miska, E.A., Alvarez-Saavedra, E., Lamb, J., Peck, D., Sweet-Cordero, A., Ebert, B.L., Mak, R.H., Ferrando, A.A.: Microrna expression profiles classify human cancers. Nature **435**(7043), 834–838 (2005)
14. Mukhopadhyay, A., Maulik, U.: An SVM-wrapped multiobjective evolutionary feature selection approach for identifying cancer-microrna markers. IEEE Trans. NanoBioscience **12**(4), 275–281 (2013)
15. Ray, S., Chakraborty, S., Mukhopadhyay, A.: DCoSpect: a novel differentially coexpressed gene module detection algorithm using spectral clustering. In: Das, S., Pal, T., Kar, S., Satapathy, S.C., Mandal, J.K. (eds.) Proceedings of the 4th International Conference on Frontiers in Intelligent Computing: Theory and Applications (FICTA) 2015. AISC, vol. 404, pp. 69–77. Springer, New Delhi (2016). https://doi.org/10.1007/978-81-322-2695-6_7
16. Raza, K., Jaiswal, R.: Reconstruction and analysis of cancer-specific gene regulatory networks from gene expression profiles. Int. J. Bioinform. Biosci. (IJBB) **3**(2), 25–34 (2013)
17. Sauter, E.R., Patel, N.: Body fluid micro(mi)RNAs as biomarkers for human cancer. J. Neuclic Acids Investig. **2**(1), 1 (2011)
18. Taguchi, Y., Murakami, Y.: Principal component analysis based feature extraction approach to identify circulating microrna biomarkers. PloS One **8**(6), e66714 (2013)

19. Tesson, B.M., Breitling, R., Jansen, R.C.: DiffCoEx: a simple and sensitive method to find differentially coexpressed gene modules. BMC Bioinform. **11**(1), 497 (2010)
20. Ye, Y., Godzik, A.: Comparative analysis of protein domain organization. Genome Res. **14**(3), 343–353 (2004)
21. Yip, A.M., Horvath, S.: Gene network interconnectedness and the generalized topological overlap measure. BMC Bioinform. **8**(1), 22 (2007)
22. Zhang, B., Horvath, S.: A general framework for weighted gene co-expression network analysis. Stat. Appl. Genetics Mol. Biol. **4**(1), 1–43 (2005)

Eye Tracking with Involuntary Head Movements for a Vision-Based Rehabilitation System

Arpita Ray Sarkar[1(✉)], Goutam Sanyal[1], and Somajyoti Majumder[2]

[1] Department of Computer Science and Engineering,
National Institute of Technology, Durgapur 713209, WB, India
sarkartrishna@gmail.com, nitgsanyal@gmail.com
[2] Faculty of Engineering and Technology, NSHM, Durgapur 713212, WB, India
somajyoti.majumder@nshm.com

Abstract. Rehabilitation plays a very important role to achieve highest possible level of self-dependence by people with disability or affected with stroke or injury/surgery to spine or brain. Several assistive technologies, including the popular computer vision-based technologies made this task simpler and easier and affordable. The main difficulty is to track eyes accurately of the person with involuntary head movements using computer vision based techniques, where eye-tracking is used as the basic and essential step towards rehabilitation. Majority of the works (reported in literature) do not intend for real-time application for rehabilitation as higher complexity, longer processing time, requirement of special or wearable hardware prevent them to be used for intended application of rehabilitation. The present research uses Haar-classifier for detection of face and eye from the cluttered background and then Improved Hough transform is applied for accurate eye centre tracking. Experiment has been carried out with a person having involuntary head movements in different difficult/critical environments. The average efficiency of detection for the most critical situation (during night for user with spectacles at a distance of 213 cm or 7 ft) has reached 99%, which establishes the acceptance of the method for day-and-night rehabilitation of people.

Keywords: Computer vision · Involuntary head movements · Eye tracking
Rehabilitation · Improve hough transform

1 Introduction

Eye tracking is an approach to detect the movement of the eyes relative to the head or to identify the point of interest (gaze) where the viewer is looking at. Eye tracking has been found to be very useful for assessment of fatigue of drivers, attention detection of customers for different products in a super market, surveillance by the security personals through monitoring of unexpected behaviour (prolonged and mysterious looking to objects) of people, controlling robots and prosthetics [1, 2] etc. But, probably the most important application of eye tracking is for rehabilitation of patients suffering from cerebrovascular (i.e. stroke) and other neurological disorders (e.g. cerebral palsy,

© Springer Nature Singapore Pte Ltd. 2018
J. K. Mandal and D. Sinha (Eds.): CSI 2017, CCIS 836, pp. 285–299, 2018.
https://doi.org/10.1007/978-981-13-1343-1_26

Rett Syndrome, Parkinson's and Alzheimer's disease, schizophrenia etc.) or injury or surgery to head or spine.

Rehabilitation is essential for such patients to gain highest possible level of self-dependency. Eye tracking is being used successfully and widely either to detect the movements of the eyes while performing some activities on a computer to assess the day-to-day performance of the patients and thereby improvement of the patients or to assist daily activities and support communications in daily life [3]. This rehabilitation approach, often termed as vision based rehabilitation, has become more popular due to its low-cost, easy-to-use, simple and non-invasive nature.

But often these cerebrovascular or neurological disorders are associated with involuntary head movements which create hindrances and difficulties towards accurate and satisfactory eye tracking. These head movements, also called tremor are rhythmic, involuntary and oscillatory in nature and ranging from 3 Hz to 12 Hz depending upon the type of disorder [4, 5]. Though a number of eye tracking systems have been developed by different researchers as well as some are available commercially, but accurate eye tracking with involuntary head movements is still a challenging domain of research. This works as the background for the present work.

The objective of the current work is to develop an eye tracking system for tracking the eyes of a person with involuntary head movements of low-amplitude using a single camera and without any special attachment. Real-time experiments with the person lying on a bed in inclined position at a distance of 7 ft from the camera under different lighting conditions during daytime and nights have been carried out to establish the robustness and flexibility of the system. Simultaneously the head movements have also been characterized through an accelerometer-cum-gyroscopic sensor (MPU 6050) and Atmel micro-controller (Arduino).

2   Related Works

Reliable eye tracking is very much essential for utilizing it towards successful human-computer interaction for various applications. Detection of proper head movements and thereafter either elimination or accepting it as the alternative modes of communication are the two next associated steps for this purpose. Different methods using computer vision techniques with the help of single camera, multiple cameras, IR lights and different sensors, such as ultrasonic sensor, accelerometer, gyro sensor have been employed for proper and accurate detection of head movement. Descriptions of such available works are presented in the following paragraphs.

Zhu and Ji [6, 7] have used Pupil Centre Corneal Reflection (PCCR) for eye gaze tracking along with natural head movements with two new schemes. Backgrounds in medical and physical domains along with knowledge in image processing techniques are required in those schemes. However, such complex schemes are difficult to implement in real-time applications. Optimizations of the algorithms, equations and phases would have been beneficial. Use of flexible hardware could provide better acceptance and opportunity for real-time applications. Nevertheless, schemes are not validated on a database containing various test subjects with different environmental conditions. Similarly PCCR method has been used for gaze tracking along with an ultrasonic sensor for measuring the z-distance between the user and the screen [8]. However, this method is complex and requires sufficient processing time to respond in real time and may not be useful for real-time applications. Also, the method has not been tested under varied conditions, such as different background, different illuminations, different users etc. for establishing its robustness.

A hybrid head and eye tracking approach for reconstructing realistic human head and eye movement in virtual avatars has been presented in [9]. This approach is divided in three modules, macro module (uses Microsoft Kinect depth sensor), micro module (uses modified version of the open source ITU Gaze Tracker using low-cost USB web camera) and the fusion module. This approach may not be useful for real-time applications due to use of three tier methods and numbers of hardware leading to longer processing and response time.

Lai et al. [10] have described a three dimensional gaze tracking method fusing head pose tracking and appearance-based gaze estimation. But this approach still provides moderate estimation accuracy. Besides, the method has not been evaluated against different and difficult/critical environmental conditions, such as far-away distance (e.g. 5 ft/152 cm or more), lower illuminations (especially during night), users with glasses etc.

Real-time gaze Tracking Algorithm with head movement Compensation (RTAC) has been developed by Huang, Wang and Ping [11] to use with a simple hardware. RTAC differs with the conventional methods in terms of modeling the eye. The allowable range for this approach is low and operational range (i.e. 30 cm) is also not appreciable for real-time applications. Only three readings have been evaluated which are not sufficient to establish the capability of the approach.

Application of Artificial Neural Network (ANN) is another approach which has been used successfully to detect the gaze direction based on the after concatenation of the head and eye movements [12]. However, no performance-evaluation has been carried out here. Also comparison with different existing methodologies is also absent. So, it is difficult to conclude whether such system can be utilized for real-time applications or not.

A three tier static head-pose estimation algorithm and a visual 3-D tracking algorithm using image processing and pattern recognition has been described in [13] for implementation as a driver awareness monitoring application. But it needs more software solution optimization before implementing in real-time situations.

Kim et al. [14] has presented a head and eye tracking method which uses the epipolar method along with feature point matching to find out the position of the head and its rotational angle. But this work lacks sufficient theoretical proof and needs proper optimization. The processing time is also not reported. Besides, it requires numbers of dedicated hardware which makes it relatively expensive for real-time implementation.

A new method for estimating gaze direction considering the head posture has been presented in [15], where the head posture is established through triangle attribute constituted by eyes and mouth. The experiment has been carried out for a short distance of 40 cm only and on single subject with normal illumination only. More experimental proofs are required for different subjects, far-away distances, lower illuminations and cluttered backgrounds for establishing the robustness and acceptance of the method in real-time applications.

Most of the above methods are either complex or uses expensive hardware for implementation. Often the processing time for response is higher making them unacceptable for real-time applications. Nevertheless, none of the methods are evaluated against difficult/critical environmental conditions, especially far-away distances (may be 5 Ft/153 cm or more), lower illuminations (which is common during the night), different cluttered backgrounds and users with spectacles/glasses. Performance in low illumination is most challenging, but essential requirement for application in real fields which has been missed totally by the researchers/developers. These restrict the above methods/approaches for application to real-time rehabilitation.

The present research work has the potential for real-time application for rehabilitation as established through the experiments carried out under difficult and critical situations. The methodology has been evaluated under normal situations often found in case of home-based rehabilitation, where the person/patient may lie on the bed at a far-way distance in low illumination during the night wearing spectacles. The unique capability of the present approach for eye-tracking is detection of face and eyes through Haar-cascade classifiers followed by eye-centre estimation by Improved Hough Transform.

3   Methodology

Eye tracking can be achieved accurately through execution of essential steps. Accurate eye tracking has to be achieved through few essential steps. This has led to use to wearable eye trackers to capture the image of the eyes. This causes discomfort to the users as well as it cannot be worn throughout the day. This problem can be resolved by placing the camera away from the person and it becomes useful for day-and-night rehabilitation. Several image processing techniques are performed on the initial images captured by the camera to obtain the best quality images for final tracking.

In the first step, detection of face region is done removing the cluttered background from the captured image. Subsequently, the detected face region undergoes another round of operation for detection of eye region. Advantage of this approach over the direct detection of eye regions is that the computational load and the processing time are reduced substantially. This is because, here instead of the whole image, only portion of the image containing the object of interest is processed. This approach helps to overcome the poor quality of the image due to use of available cheaper webcams. The associated steps for eye tracking are described in detail below.

3.1   Face and Eye Detection

Detection of face region from the captured image comes as the first step of the overall process. It is very much essential to detect correctly the face region from cluttered background. Thereafter, region containing only eye is extracted from the face region detected previously.

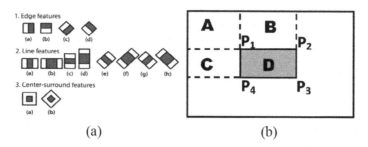

(a)   (b)

Fig. 1. (a) Haar-like features [16] (b) Integral-image based computation of sum of the pixels within rectangle D

Haar-like feature-based cascade classifiers is considered as one of the best tools for detection of faces and eye regions from any image, proposed by Paul Viola and Michael Jones [16] in 2001. Figure 1(a) represents some Haar-like features, often used for various detections. Here, the size of the window is decided based up on the requirement and moved over the input image to calculate the Haar-like features using integral image for each sub-section of the image. Integral image at any location (x, y) is defined as the sum of all pixels within the rectangle ranging from the top left corner at location (0, 0) to bottom right corner at location (x, y):

$$I(x, y) = \sum_{x' \leq x, y' \leq y} i(x, y) \tag{1}$$

where i(x, y) denotes the grey level of input image. Calculation of the rectangle features depends up on the calculation of all integral images. For instance, the sum of the pixels within region D as shown in Fig. 1(b), can be calculated using the integral images at P_1, P_2, P_3, P_4 and it can be written as:

$$D = A + B + C + D - (A + B) - (A + C) + A \tag{2}$$

$$\text{or } D = I(P_4) - I(P_2) - I(P_3) + I(P_1) \tag{3}$$

AdaBoost (Adaptive Boosting) proposed by Yoav Freund and Robert Schapire, is a machine learning technique for using in conjunction with other learning algorithms [17]. To develop a real-time and efficient face detection system, Viola and Jones has fused the fast features calculation with the AdaBoost algorithm and the cascade technique. All possible windows at different positions and scales are checked for detection of objects (faces or eyes) in an image. Cascade of classifiers are employed for face or eye detection in real-time. Every stage of cascade when trained by the Ada-Boost algorithm, will accept around 100% of the positive images (includes the desired objects) and 20–50% of the negative (includes non-objects) images are rejected. Rejection of any sub-window at k-stage leads to the conclusion that it doesn't contain a face or eye and subsequently ignored in the next stages. If all the n stages are linked, the detection rate of object in an image becomes higher.

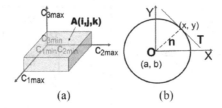

Fig. 2. (a) Three dimensional representation of accumulator (b) Relationship between (x, y, θ) and (a, b).

3.2   Eye Centre Detection

Detection of eye centres is the next step to be performed on the extracted eye regions and this can be performed using a number of techniques, such as application of colour based filter, shape based filter or detection using Hough circles [18, 19] etc. For detection of eye centres, cascade classifiers, similar to that of faces and eye regions, can also be used. However, here detection of eye centres is performed through Improved Hough circle based approach [19].

Hough transform is a preferred method to detect circle in an image owing to its applicability to any function in the form $g(v, c) = 0$. Here v and c are denoted as the co-ordinate and co-efficient vector respectively. The co-ordinates of point on the circle satisfy (4)

$$(x - c_1)^2 + (y - c_2)^2 = c_3^2 \tag{4}$$

where (c_1, c_2) and c_3 denote the co-ordinate of centre and the radius of the circle respectively. The three parameters (c_1, c_2, c_3), if mapped to a three dimensional rectangular co-ordinate system, cubic accumulator $A(i, j, k)$ is generator as depicted in Fig. 2(a). So, the process of detection of points on the circle simply turns into refinement and gradually increment of the values of c_1 and c_2 in $c_1 c_2 c_3$ plane. The value of c_3 can be obtained using Eq. (4). The value stored in the accumulator $A(i, j, k)$ will thus denote the number of many conical intersections in the three dimensional parametric space.

Hough transform is very useful for detection of circles in images easily, but the main difficulties to use it in digital image processing are its associated large numbers of parameter of round function, poor efficiency of detection, higher computational complexity. This leads to compulsory improvement of the Hough transform for application to two dimensional parametric space. The necessary steps for Improved-Hough transform based circle-detection have been described below.

- Step - I: The centre of the circle is to be determined in two dimensional Hough transform space
- Step - II: Next the radius of the circle is calculated by statistical histogram

It is clear from the Fig. 2(b) that the tangent T to the circle touches the circle at the point (x, y) and the normal n to the tangent passes through this tangent point and the centre of the circle. So, the centre of the circle can be found out using this. The normal component can be calculated using grey-scale edge detection operator. Then the three dimensional parameters (x, y, θ) can be mapped to two dimensional space (a, b), where (x, y) and θ are the co-ordinate and the angle with the x-axis of the normal vector respectively. It is obvious from Fig. 2(b) that

$$\tan \theta = \frac{(y - b)}{(x - a)} \tag{5}$$

$$\text{or } b = a \tan \theta + (y - x \tan \theta) \tag{6}$$

Equation (7) as mentioned below can be used to calculate the radius of the circle.

$$r^2 = (x - a_0)^2 + (y - b_0)^2 \tag{7}$$

where (a_0, b_0) denotes the co-ordinate of the centre of the circle and can be obtained from Step - I. A statistical histogram of the related radius can be plotted for all the points (x_k, y_k) and the maximum peak will denote as the radius. The associated steps of the algorithm for Improved-Hough transform can be written as:

- First edges are to be found and then for each edge point the following steps are to be performed.
- Using the edge point as the centre and radius r, a circle is to be drawn and all co-ordinates that the circle passes through in the accumulator are to be increased
- Then one or several maxima in the accumulator are identified
- Thus calculated parameters (r, a_0, b_0) corresponding to the maxima are mapped back to the original image

Finally the detected eye centres are mapped to a global co-ordinate so as to create a relation between the eye centres and co-ordinates on a display monitor or screen placed at a distance from the user for activation of the desired icons.

3.3   Effect of Head Rotation

Accuracy of detection of eye centres demands that the face needs to be parallel to the image capture plane (i.e. the camera) as shown in Fig. 3(a) which corresponds to circular shape of the pupil when projected on the image capture plane. But this is often hampered due to involuntary head movement which is very common for stroke patients or patients with other neurological disorders. The frequency of such involuntary head movement ranges from 3 Hz to 12 Hz with the range of amplitude from 0.001 cm to 1 cm [20]. For such cases the head of the patients oscillates horizontally with mostly eye fixed as shown in Fig. 3(b). The pupil can be visualized till there is any occlusion. The chance of occlusion reduces with increase in the distance between the patient and the image capture plane (i.e. camera). But the overall projected size of the pupil changes which may lead to erroneous reading.

Pure rotation of the head horizontally around the vertical axis results in elliptical shape of the pupil when projected on the image capture plane as presented in Fig. 3(c). If the radius of the pupil is considered as r calculated from the circular projection, then the change in this radius can be measured from the geometry presented in Fig. 3(c). For pure rotation of head horizontally through an angle of θ, the projected length of the radius on the image capture plane as shown in Fig. 3(c) becomes r_1, given by:

$$r_1 = r \cos \theta \tag{8}$$

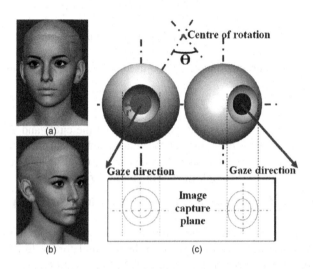

Fig. 3. (a) Human head with eyes looking towards the front (b) Head rotated horizontally with eyes fixed (c) 3D model of the eyeballs along with its projection on the image capture plane for the above two head positions.

Up to 25° of rotation, the cosine value lies within 90% of the initial value. As the peak value from the statistical histogram is identified as the radius of the circle leading to detection of the centre thereafter, there is very less chance to identify the smaller value (r_1) as the radius of the circle. Even if r_1 is identified as the radius of the circle, the centre will be concentric with that of the circle with radius r. So, effect of involuntary head movements for accurate eye-centre detection is compensated automatically inside the methodology itself. But this is true for the cases where persons/patients located at a distance (here 7 Ft or 2.13 m) from the camera, as the curvature of the pupil/iris may not affect in case of longer in-between distance. Besides, the angle of head-rotation beyond 25° is hardly possible for such patients and hence not considered for further research. It is also to note that with the increase in frequency (close to 12 Hz), the angle of head-rotation decreases substantially.

4   Experiments

The main aim of the present research work is to evaluate the performance of an eye tracking system to be used for rehabilitation of patients suffering from (or suffered) stroke, cerebral palsy, Parkinson's or Alzheimer's disease or other locked-in patients who lost the communication abilities and having involuntary head movement in horizontal plane. Daily activities of the patients with involuntary head oscillations can be supported by such a rehabilitation system and necessary assistance/help can be provided based up on the gaze tracking on some pre-defined basic need icons.

As the system is supposed to provide assistance to the patients with involuntary head movements day and night, it is essential to evaluate the performance of the system at day and night in different illuminations inside a room with persons wearing spectacles and without spectacles. Besides, it is also essential to characterize the involuntary head movement of the person/patient for understanding the nature of the head movement and its co-relation with the eye tracking in terms of scope and limitations.

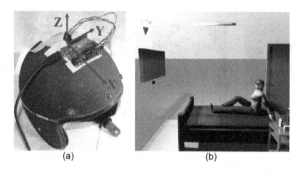

(a)   (b)

Fig. 4. (a) Human head with eyes looking towards the front (b) Head rotated horizontally with eyes fixed (c) 3D model of the eyeballs along with its projection on the image capture plane for the above two head positions.

For the purpose of characterisation of head movements a MEMS based accelerometer-cum-gyro (MPU 6050) sensor is used with Arduino Uno microcontroller. Both the sensor and the microcontroller are attached to a helmet to be worn by the patient for this purpose as shown in Fig. 4(a). The rotation and acceleration data measured by the sensor are transferred to the computer from the microcontroller. This data is further analysed for characterisation of the head movement.

The hardware for the eye tracking system consists of an Intel NUC Kit (with 2.4 GHz Intel Celeron Processor N2820, DDR3 RAM and Intel HD Graphics), a USB camera (Logitech HD Webcam C525 with capability for auto-focus and auto-light correction) and a monitor. Standard available monitors are used for the display purpose. To make the system portable and cheaper, low cost and portable projector and a screen can be used to replace the monitor. The experimental set-up is presented in Fig. 4(b).

Visual Studio has been selected as the programming platform with support from Open CV libraries. The in-built trainer as well as detector of OpenCV provides advantage while development. A large numbers of pre-trained classifiers for faces, eyes, smiles etc. developed by different researchers over the time are easily available for direct use. It is also possible to develop own classifiers using positive and negative images. Pre-built libraries and classifiers have been used in the present work.

As the first step, camera captures the video and frames are loaded one-by-one. These individual frames are then processed with the required xml files (i.e. classifier files). Three consecutive detections are merged as one. Pruning operation is necessary to apply on these frames to exclude regions of less interest (i.e. less chance to contain a face). Based upon the requirement, the smallest size of the face to be detected is identified. Eyes are also detected in similar manner and a rectangular box marks the detected regions. Subsequently, the eye centres are detected from the eye regions (region of interest) and marked with '+' signs. The geometric midpoint of those two eye centres are calculated and marked in the picture with black diamond '◊' sign. Figure 5 depicts the different associated steps for the detection.

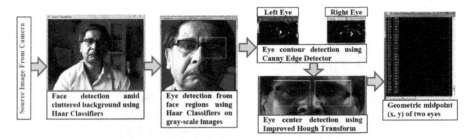

Fig. 5. Different associated steps of image processing for eye centre detection from a video using improved hough transform

The experiments have been performed in a normal room with dimension 12×12 ft as because the proposed system will be used by the people staying in normal rooms of homes or hospitals or physiotherapy clinics. Figure 4(b) presents a schematic view of the experimentation room. The user sits on the bed in an inclined position. The camera is placed at a distance of 7 ft (2.13 m) from the patient. The light source is placed in front of the user as often found in homes. The monitor is used to display the need icons to the user and so mounted on the wall to face the user directly. Initially, video data are stored on the computer and later processed for further analysis. A 68 year old patient with involuntary head movements has been engaged to gather the data for different illuminations (during day and night) and parameters/conditions (with and without spectacles). Third-party software has been used to store the online video data with the detection signs on the computer.

5   Results and Discussion

The MPU 6050 accelerometer-cum-gyro sensor was fixed with the axes as shown in Fig. 4(a). The user (patient) had head movements in the horizontal plane (X-Y) plane only around the vertical Z-axis. The gyroscopic data about the Z-axis and acceleration data along Y-axis only have been acquired through serial port and saved. Data around other axes (if any) is not considered. The gyroscopic and acceleration data for limited number of head rotations are plotted in Fig. 6(a) and (b) respectively.

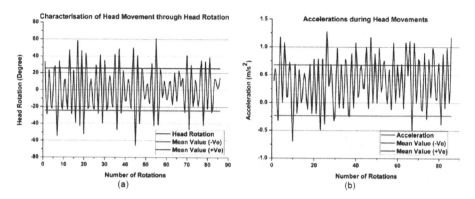

Fig. 6. (a) Gyroscope data (b) Acceleration data for the rhythmic head movements

The gyroscopic data reveals the oscillatory nature of the head movement and it ranges on the average from 26° on the positive side to −25° on negative side. Similarly the mean value of acceleration on the positive side is 0.68 m/s^2 and that on the negative side is −0.23 m/s^2 respectively. This has resulted in generation of a frequency of 4 Hz for head movements.

The video data of eye tracking stored on the computer with detection marks and estimation of geometric midpoint (x, y) of two eyes were later analysed to evaluate the performance of the eye tracking system with head movements. The average number of frames for the video data set is 308 for different lighting conditions (day and night) with user wearing spectacles and without spectacles.

The in-between distance of user and the light source, location and intensity of the light source are some of the major factors which affect the average illuminations. The illumination during daytime is higher due to presence of natural light and in night, it is lower. However, attempt has been made to keep the illumination of the room normal as maintained in daily life. The average values of illuminations during the experiments with the light source at the front for daytime and night were measured to be 230 lx and 28 lx respectively.

The detection of eye centres is considered as correct when both the eye centres have been detected in a single frame. Percentage of correct detection for any video data set is the total number of such correctly detected frames against the total number of frames captured. Figure 7(a) shows the percentage of correct detection at daytime and night for users with and without spectacles. The mean values and standard deviations of the data for this case are presented in Fig. 7(b).

The average percentage of correct detection for user with spectacles during daytime for the in-between distance of 7 Ft is found to be 94. However, the range of data lies between 78 to 100% with a standard deviation of 6.86. But, the percentage of correct detection during daytime without spectacles is found to be higher than that of with spectacles due to absence of glaring on the glasses. A typical image with glaring of the spectacles has been presented in Fig. 8(a). The mean value of correct detection (percentage) in this case is 96 with a lower standard deviation of 2.71. Here the range of data is found to be ranging between 91% and 98%.

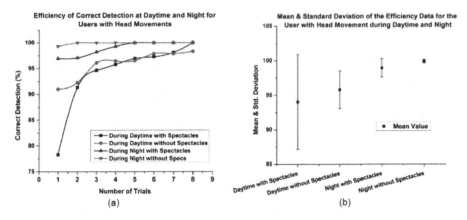

Fig. 7. (a) Efficiency of correct detection of eye-centres during day and night for user with and without spectacles (b) Mean and standard deviation of the efficiency data.

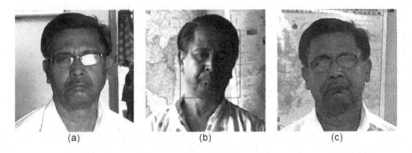

Fig. 8. Factors affecting the correct detection of eyes and eye centres (a) glaring of glasses (b) non-uniform illumination (c) uniform illumination.

The performance of the system/methodology is found to be better in night than that during daytime. The average percentages of detections in the night under very low illumination (28 lx) for user with and without spectacles are 98.94 and 99.91 respectively due to uniform illumination on the face owing to single source of light placed in front of the user. During daytime, natural light enters the room through door(s) and numbers of windows leading to non-uniform illumination on the face. This has been shown in Fig. 8(b) and (c) which depict the presence of non-uniform and uniform illuminations on the face of the user during daytime and night respectively. The range of data is also very narrow. The standard deviation of the data for user with spectacles is 1.35 and for users without spectacles 0.25 respectively. This reveals the repeatability nature of the data.

Vision-based rehabilitation system should have very high detection accuracy and repeatability to be accepted as a 24 × 7 support system. The most critical situation for correct detection may occur in the night when the illumination is low and user wears spectacles. Glaring, reflection and availability of sufficient lights are the major hindrances for such situation. The present approach has obtained the average overall value of detection (for users with and without spectacles) as 95% for cases during the daytime, whereas the same for night is found to be 99.4%.

A detailed comparison of the present work with other existing similar works has been presented in the table below. The above discussion reveals that the present method can provide 100% efficiency of detection, when proper and uniform illumination is used. It is evident from the table that such performance has not been achieved by any other work. Also, the following works may not be suitable for real-time applications as these have not gone through proper evaluation in reality, especially in case of lower illumination in night for users with spectacles (Table 1).

Table 1. Comparison of the presented work with other related works

Paper references	Objectives/experiments	Dist.	Performance	Low-light experiments
Jung et al. [8]	Gaze tracking with compensation of natural head movements	70–80 cm [Z-dist.]	Gaze detection error: 0.69° (standard deviation 0.14)	Not performed
Li et al. [9]	Realistic eye movements in virtual avatars	40–60 cm	Euclidean dist. between pupil centres (mean) = 2.46 pixels (with glasses) [86%] and 2.87 pixels (without glasses) [100%] w.r.t. to 2.87 pixels (ground truth)	Not performed
Lai et al. [10]	Estimation of binoculars 3-D lines of sight	70–80 cm	Mean error: 2–5°	Not performed
Huang et al. [11]	Improvement of usability and practicality of non-contact gaze tracking	30 cm	Mean error: 1°	Not performed
Zhang et al. [15]	Gaze estimation	40 cm	6 out of 8 images are detected correctly	Not performed
Present method	Eye tracking for selection of icons	213 cm	Daytime: 94% (with specs.), 95.8% (no specs.); Night: 98.94% (with specs.), 99.91% (no specs.)	Yes (28 lx)

6   Conclusion

Computer vision is one of the assistive technologies, which has huge potential for application towards rehabilitation due to its affordable cost, simplicity, easy-to-use and non-invasive nature. Often the eyes or the gaze of the patients are tracked continuously using different cameras either to monitor the performance of the patient while executing a task/exercise or to provide day-and-night support for patients who lost communication abilities. But involuntary head movement, which is very common for these patients, poses hindrances for effective and proper eye or gaze tracking. A number of works reported in the literature, though may be theoretically excellent, failed to establish their acceptance and reliability for real-time applications. The present approach uses simple, low-cost, easy-to-use, readily available components for tracking the eyes of the patient for providing 24 × 7 support as well as rehabilitation. Haar-classifiers have been used to detect the face and the eye from the captured image amidst the cluttered background. Eye centres are detected through Improved Hough Transform. The proposed methodology has been evaluated against difficult/critical situations often common to normal day-to-day lives of the patients. It is very important to note that the present approach attained approximately 99% efficiency of detection even in low illumination during night for the user at a distance of 2.13 m away and wearing spectacles and having involuntary head movements. Such higher efficiency has not been achieved by any of the previous works reported in the literature. Presently work is going on to establish the mapping function between the detected eye centres and the PoG (Point of Gaze) on the screen (or monitor) to activate the icons displayed on the screen for support and rehabilitation.

References

1. Castellini, C., Sandini, G.: Gaze tracking for robotic control in intelligent teleoperation and prosthetics. In: 2nd Conference on Communication by Gaze Interaction (COGAIN 2006), Gazing into the Future, Italy, pp. 73–77 (2006)
2. Orman, Z., Battal, A., Kemer, E.: A study on face, eye detection and gaze estimation. Int. J. Comput. Sci. Eng. Surv. 2(3), 29–46 (2011)
3. Zhou, H., Hu, H.: A survey - human movement tracking and stroke rehabilitation. Technical report, University of Essex, UK (2004)
4. Smaga, S.: Tremor. Am. Fam. Phys. 68(8), 1545–1552 (2003)
5. Bhidayasiri, R.: Differential diagnosis of common tremor syndromes. Postgrad. Med. J. 81(962), 756–762 (2005)
6. Zhu, Z., Ji, Q.: Eye gaze tracking under natural head movement. In: IEEE Computer Society Conference on Computer Vision and Pattern Recognition, pp. 918–923 (2005)
7. Zhu, Z., Ji, Q.: Novel eye gaze tracking techniques under natural head movement. IEEE Trans. Biomed. Eng. 54(12), 2246–2260 (2007)
8. Jung, D., et al.: Compensation method of natural head movement for gaze tracking system using an ultrasonic sensor for distance measurement. Sensors 6(1), 1–20 (2016)
9. Li, Y., Wei, H., Monaghan, D.S., O'Connor, Noel E.: A low-cost head and eye tracking system for realistic eye movements in virtual avatars. In: Gurrin, C., Hopfgartner, F., Hurst, W., Johansen, H., Lee, H., O'Connor, N. (eds.) MMM 2014. LNCS, vol. 8325, pp. 461–472. Springer, Cham (2014). https://doi.org/10.1007/978-3-319-04114-8_39
10. Lai, C., Chen, Y., Chen, K., Chen, S., Shih, S., Hung, Y.: Appearance-based gaze tracking with free head movement. In: 22nd International Conference on Pattern Recognition, pp. 1869–1873 (2014)
11. Huang, Y., Wang, Z., Ping, A.: Non-contact gaze tracking with head movement adaptation based on single camera. Int. J. Comput. Electr. Autom. Control Inf. Eng. 3(11), 2568–2571 (2009)
12. Nimi, M.R., Renji, S.: ANN based head movement detection with eye tracking. Int. J. Comput. Sci. Inf. Technol. 6(2), 1513–1517 (2015)

13. Murphy-Chutorian, E., Trivedi, M.M.: Head pose estimation and augmented reality tracking: an integrated system and evaluation for monitoring driver awareness. IEEE Trans. Intell. Transp. Syst. **11**(2), 300–311 (2010)
14. Kim, J., et al.: Construction of integrated simulator for developing head/eye tracking system. In: International Conference on Control, Automation and Systems, pp. 2485–2488 (2008)
15. Zhang, W., Wang, Z., Xu, J., Cong, X.: A method of gaze direction estimation considering head posture. Int. J. Sig. Process. Image Process. Pattern Recogn. **6**(2), 103–112 (2013)
16. Viola, P., Jones, M.: Rapid object detection using a boosted cascade of simple features, In: IEEE Conference on Computer Vision and Pattern Recognition, vol. 1, pp. 511–518 (2001)
17. Freund, Y., Schapire, R.E.: A decision-theoretic generalization of on-line learning and an application to boosting. J. Comput. Syst. Sci. **55**(1), 119–139 (1997)
18. Soltany, M., Zadeh, S.T., Pourreza, H.: Fast and accurate pupil positioning algorithm using circular hough transform and gray projection. In: Proceedings of of International Conference on Computer Communication and Management, vol. 5, pp. 556–561 (2011)
19. Chen, D., Bai, J., Qu, Z.: Research on pupil center location based on improved hough transform and edge gradient algorithm. In: National Conference on Information Technology and Computer Science, China, pp. 47–51 (2012)
20. Calzetti, S., Baratti, M., Gresty, M., Findley, L.: Frequency/amplitude characteristics of postural tremor of the hands in a population of patients with bilateral essential tremor: implications for the classification and mechanism of essential tremor. J. Neurol. Neurosurg. Psychiatry **50**, 561–567 (1987)

Importance of Thermal Features in the Evaluation of Bacterial Blight in Rice Plant

Ishita Bhakta[✉], Santanu Phadikar, and Koushik Majumder

Maulana Abul Kalam Azad University of Technology,
BF-142, Sector-I, Salt Lake, Kolkata 700064, West Bengal, India
ishita.official@gmail.com,
sphadikar@yahoo.com, koushikzone@yahoo.com

Abstract. The aim of the study is to investigate the potential of texture and thermal features extracted from the thermograph of the rice leaves in bacterial leaf blight forecasting. Thermal images have some advantages over visual images. Visual images are capable of capturing only symptoms visible in bare eyes whereas thermal images can capture invasive temperature changes of an object when any chemical changes occur within it, which may not create any visual changes. In this paper, thermal images are used to identify the internal changes of the rice leaves before any visual changes occur due to the bacterial leaf blight disease. Thermal images of the leaves at normal, primary stage of infection and highly infected stage are collected from field. For this experiment, 158 samples of each stage (normal leaves, leaves at primary stage of infection and highly infected leaves) are considered. Images are preprocessed to standardize the environment of image acquisition. Then images are segmented to extract the region of interest using Otsu's algorithm. Temperature variation and texture features are extracted from the segmented images using the Flir Tools and Gray-level co-occurrence matrix method respectively. The temperature differences of normal leaves, leaves at primary stage of infection and highly infected leaves are evaluated using summary statistics. Paired t-test values are computed to find the significance of the result. The result shows that there is significant difference among these three stages of leaves with respect to thermal feature. But, with respect to the texture features there is no significant difference. Hence, the result verifies the importance of thermal features in bacterial leaf blight forecasting.

Keywords: Rice disease forecasting · Bacterial leaf blight
Temperature variation

1 Introduction

India is the second most populated country in the world [1]. As per estimates by the Central Statistics Office (CSO), Government of India, the share of agriculture was approximately 17% of the Gross Domestic Product (GDP) during 2015–16 which was 43% in 1970s [2]. Over 70% of the rural households depend on agriculture [3]. Rice is one of the major crops cultivated here [4]. The productivity of rice is affected by

© Springer Nature Singapore Pte Ltd. 2018
J. K. Mandal and D. Sinha (Eds.): CSI 2017, CCIS 836, pp. 300–313, 2018.
https://doi.org/10.1007/978-981-13-1343-1_27

various factors like diseases, weed, natural calamities etc. Xan-thomonas Oryzae pv. Oryzae is one type of bacteria that causes blight in rice leaves in tropical environment with favorable temperature between 25°C–34°C and 70% humidity in lowland areas [5]. Bacterial blight is one of the most severe diseases of rice [4]. The severity of the disease increases in susceptible rice varieties under high nitrogen fertilization. It may cause yield loss of about 70% [4]. At the booting stage, it causes broken kernels with low quality grains. The symptoms of the disease vary with time. At first stage, it causes yellowing of the leaves. As the disease progresses, it turns yellow to greyish-green to straw-colored and ultimately rolls up and dies [4]. The time taken to grow all these visual symptoms in favorable environment is 3 to 4 months [4]. Before all these visual symptoms grow in the rice leaves, some internal chemical changes occur that cause temperature variation. If these variations can be captured and analyzed, then it may help us to forecast the disease occurrence at preliminary stage. This timely prediction can help the farmers to prevent the disease and reduce the yield loss in large amount. This will also increase the quality of grains. With this goal, thermal images of the rice leaves are captured at regular time intervals to monitor temperature variations at different stages of the disease.

Thermal imaging is a technique that can capture the invisible pattern in an object through infrared radiation [6]. It provides a contact-less imaging procedure based on temperature variations [6] to observe physiological changes in an object. A good amount of application of this technology is found in medical field to diagnose and monitor internal clinical changes in diseases [7]. Thermography helps to quantify the internal inflammation within the object, which is not visible in bare eyes [7]. In last decade, numerous studies have been accomplished to detect and classify rice diseases like brown spot, leaf blast, sheath blight etc. In following section, some of these studies [8–14] are briefed out to establish the importance of thermal image based analysis in rice disease forecasting.

In [8] Phadikar and Sil have proposed a prototype of rice disease detection system based on image processing and soft computing techniques. They have considered leaf blast and brown spot diseases for experimentation and applied entropy based thresholding approach to segment the acquired digital images of the diseased plants. Diseased areas are detected with boundary detection algorithm. Diseased and normal images are classified with unsupervised learning approach. Further authors have improved the result of their work in another study carried out in the year of 2011 [9]. In this work, the authors have selected fourteen features out of thirty-six features with information gain theory. This feature selection algorithm has increased the accuracy of the model. After that in 2012 the authors have classified the rice leaf diseases based on morphological changes [10]. The accuracy of their system in Bayes and SVM classifier was 79.5% and 68.1%. Kim et al. have used a rice disease epidemiology model EPIRICE to predict epidemics of rice diseases in South Korea [11]. They have considered leaf blast and sheath blight for their experimentation. In [12] authors have classified the rice panicle blast level from hyperspectral images with the help of "bag of spectra words" (BoSW) model. For classification they have used support vector machine. Their system has gained accuracy of 81.41% for six level classification and 96.40% for two level classification. In [13] authors have extracted different types of vegetation indices from digital images of the rice leaves for both brown spot and blight diseases. The extracted texture features were used for classification of these two diseases in fifteen different classifiers to find the best classification model for this study. In [14] authors have developed an incremental rule based classification system for rice disease prediction. This dynamic classifier is based on the concept of particle swarm optimization and association rule mining.

After studying all these literatures, it is observed that visual images of rice plant and leaf are mostly used for disease prediction and detection. Some literatures [15–18] have used the thermal images for disease detection and canopy measurement. But, there is no evidence of using thermal images for disease prediction of plant images. At the initial stage of any pathogen causes some chemical changes in the plant cell, which are not visible in the bare eyes. Visual changes are observed after a significant time when some of the cells are damaged. Thus, prediction of diseases can not be done using the visual images. Based on the assumption that "chemical and cellular changes in rice plant over the diseased regions may replicate similar changes in temperature over the diseased areas of rice leaves", thermal images may be used for diseases prediction. With this assumption, thermal images of rice leaves at normal, primary stage of infection and highly infected stage are analyzed to observe the change in temperature and texture features. This observation further helps to design an automated rice disease-forecasting model for bacterial leaf blight.

Rest of the paper is organized as follows – Sect. 2 describes the materials and methods used in this study. Section 3 discusses the result of the experiment and finally Sect. 4 concludes the paper with proper research directions.

2   Materials and Methods

In this paper, the pattern changes due to bacterial leaf blight are captured and analyzed in four phases. First step is data collection. In this phase, thermal images are collected from a specific field. Then data are processed to standardize the environment of data collection. The uniform images are then segmented to detect region of interest. Correct segmentation helps to remove additional background and focus only on the affected leaf area. At last, features are extracted from this region to characterize the pattern of disease evolution with time.

2.1   Data Collection

Thermal images were collected from a rice field during the month of September and October, 2017. Annual average rainfall of this region was about 141 mm, temperature was about 28 °C and humidity was about 74%. To capture images, Flir C5 thermal camera was used. Initially we collected images from 368 rice plants after 45 days of plantation and marked properly for prospective evaluation. These plants were labelled as normal. Then the rice plants were inoculated with the bacterial suspension. After one week of inoculation, Images were collected from the same plants to capture any internal changes. These plants were labelled as primary stage of infection. The visual symptoms of the disease appeared in 158 plants after two weeks of inoculation. Images were collected from the affected leaves of these plants. These images are labelled as highly infected leaves. From all these collected images, a dataset is prepared which contains 158 highly infected leaves and their respective images at normal and primary infection stage. So, this dataset contained total 474 images, of which 158 were normal leaves, 158 were leaves at primary stage of the disease and 158 were highly infected leaves.

In Fig. 1 sample images are shown at these three stages. Figure 1(a) represents a normal leaf image whereas Fig. 1(b) represents the same leaf after disease inoculation and Fig. 1(c) represents the leaf after the growth of visual symptoms.

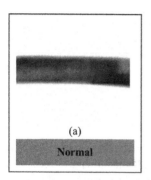
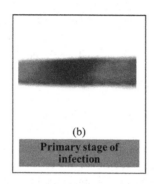
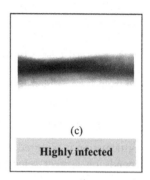

(a)   (b)   (c)

Normal   Primary stage of infection   Highly infected

Fig. 1. Sample thermal images of rice leaves infected with bacterial leaf blight at different stages. (a) Leaf before the disease, (b) leaf at the initial stage of disease and (c) leaf fully infected with the disease. (Color figure online)

2.2   Data Processing

Pre-processing of the data is required as the images are acquired in diverse environmental conditions with different temperature and humidity. Flir Tools software [19] was used to provide uniformity to the environment with 0.95 emissivity, 20°C reflectance temperature and IR resolution of 80 × 60. Further, color palette of these images were changed with Flir tools to assign region specific color. The regions with same level of apparent temperature are assigned same color. Here Rainbow color palette in Flir tools is used for better understanding of temperature variation over the leaves.

Figure 2 represents the same set of leaf images as in Fig. 1, after changing the color palette to Rainbow. This color palette can distinctly classify the regions based on temperature variations. This helps us to capture and store this variation with disease progression for further computation using the Flir tools. Further, rainbow color images are converted into grayscale to ease the computation procedure.

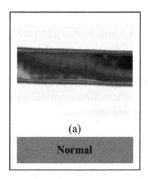 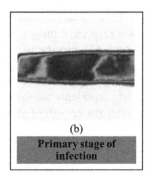 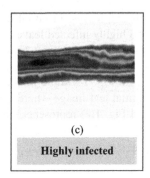

Fig. 2. Thermal images of rice leaves infected with bacterial leaf blight after changing color model. (a) Leaf before the disease, (b) leaf at the initial stage of disease and (c) leaf fully infected with the disease. (Color figure online)

2.3 Segmentation

Segmentation is required to detect the region of interest. Accuracy of feature extraction depends on correct selection of region of interest. The collected images were segmented to figure out the leaf area and eliminate the background. The standard threshold based segmentation method Otsu [20] is used for segmentation, as it is the most popular and easy method in this category.

Figure 3 represents the segmented images of the same set of leaves in Fig. 1 at different stage of disease.

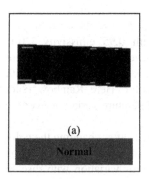 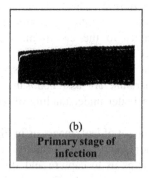 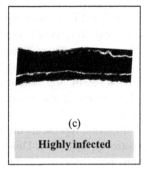

Fig. 3. Segmented leaf images. (a) Leaf before the disease, (b) leaf at the initial stage of disease and (c) leaf fully infected with the disease.

2.4 Feature Extraction

We have extracted mainly two types of feature from thermal images of the rice leaves - temperature and texture feature. Temperature feature was extracted with Flir Tools software whereas texture features were extracted from gray level co-occurrence matrix. Each of these features are explained in following sections.

Temperature

Temperature variation in experimented images has been extracted with the help of Flir Tools. Three statistical measurements were taken to evaluate temperature variation in normal, primary stage of disease and fully infected leaves. These are – Mean, Standard deviation and Median.

Texture Feature

Texture features were extracted from gray level co-occurrence matrix. The grey level co-occurrence matrix [21] counts the co-occurrence of image pixels with grey values i and j at a distance d, defined in polar coordinates (d, Θ). Θ can take the values 0°, 45°, 90°, 135°, 180°, 225°, 270° and 315°. The grey level co-occurrence matrix (GLCM) defines spatial relationship of pixels in an image. It is calculated with the Eq. (1).

$$G(i,j) = \sum_{x=1}^{m} \sum_{y=1}^{n} \begin{cases} 1, & if\ I(x,y) = i\ and \\ & I\begin{pmatrix} x+d_x, \\ y+d_y \end{pmatrix} = j \\ 0, & Otherwise \end{cases} \tag{1}$$

Where m * n = size of image I, d = (dx, dy) displacement vector. From this matrix, mean (μ_i, μ_j) and standard deviation (σ_i, σ_j) were computed for further calculations. In this research work, four features were extracted using equations mentioned in Table 1 to evaluate the change in rice leaves due to bacterial blight. These are listed below.

Table 1. Formula to calculate texture features

Feature	Formula
Contrast	$\sum_i \sum_j (i,j)^2 G(i,j)$
Correlation	$\sum_i \sum_j \frac{(i,j)G(i,j) - \mu_i \mu_j}{\sigma_i \sigma_j}$
Energy	$\sum_i \sum_j G(i,j)^2$
Homogeneity	$\sum_i \sum_j \frac{1}{1+(i-j)^2} G(i,j)$

1. Contrast [22, 23] – It measures the sharpness of images. High contrast means better visual sharpness. Low contrast means blurred images.
2. Correlation [22, 23] – It measures the probability of co-occurrence of a specified pixel pairs.
3. Energy [22, 23] – It measures textural uniformity of an image and also known as Angular Second Moment and Uniformity.
4. Homogeneity [22] – It measures the consistency in image qualities. High values of homogeneity means more regularity and lack of local changes in image surfaces.

3   Results and Discussion

For this study, 158 samples from each stage (normal leaves, leaves at primary stage of infection and highly infected leaves) were taken. Features were extracted at each stage. The variation in temperature and texture features at each stage are plotted in Figs. 4, 5, 6, 7, 8, 9, 10, 11, 12 and 13. A set of Boxplots for the feature set are drawn to represent the shape, central tendency and variability of the distribution. Figures 4, 5, 6, 7 and 8 represents these Box plots for temperature, contrast, correlation, energy and homogeneity respectively.

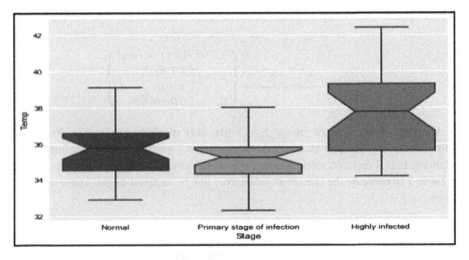

Fig. 4. Temperature variation boxplot

From Fig. 4 it is evident that when normal rice leaf is affected by bacterial blight then temperature of leaf is reduced gradually up to the final stage of the disease. At the final stage, the leaf cells die. As a result, fully infected leaf losses its natural temperature and reaches the environmental temperature. The effect of this temperature variation is reflected in the box plot of temperature variation. This effect can be explained with the position of median in each box.

Figure 5 represents the variation of contrast feature for normal leaves, leaves at primary stage of infection and highly infected leaves. The normal leaf has low contrast as intensity value of each pixel is closer to each other. When disease manifestation starts in the leaf, then some portion of the leaf become yellowish whereas other portion remains green. This color variation results in high contrast. For this reason, the contrast of the diseased leaves increases in the box plot. In case of highly infected leaves, contrast reduces than primary stage of the disease but increases than normal state.

In Fig. 6, correlation in normal images is higher than diseased images. As, in normal leaves pixel intensity value are highly correlated. But, when disease appears in the leaves then intensity values are changed which affect the correlation among the pixels. This effect is evident in this box plot. The intensity variation reduces in fully

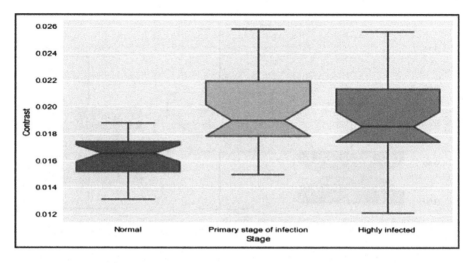

Fig. 5. Contrast variation boxplot (Color figure online)

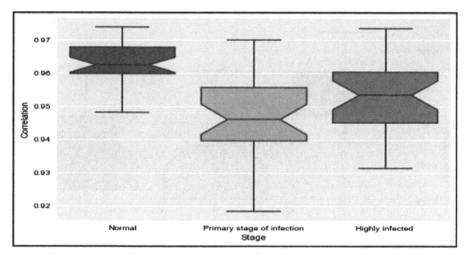

Fig. 6. Correlation variation boxplot

infected leaves as major part of the leaf contain dead cells. Thus, correlation in fully infected leaves is higher than primary diseased leaves but lower than normal leaves.

Figure 7 represents the variation in energy feature for normal leaves, leaves at primary stage of infection and highly infected leaves. Energy represents the squared sum of GLCM values. Low energy means same values in GLCM and high energy means unequal values in GLCM [24]. From the box plot of energy variation in rice leaves, it is clear that in normal leaves GLCM values are similar which means energy is low. When disease occurs, the values in GLCM are changed and energy increases.

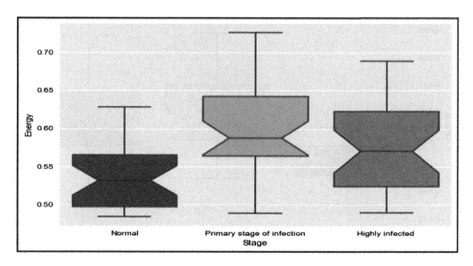

Fig. 7. Energy variation boxplot

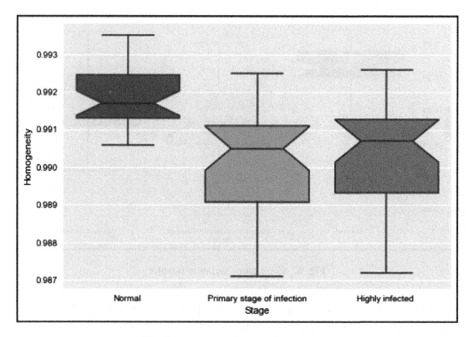

Fig. 8. Homogeneity variation boxplot

Finally, in case of fully infected leaves, again the GLCM values become similar and energy is reduced.

Figure 8 represents the homogeneity of image textures. High values of this feature signify the lack of intra-regional changes. That means images are locally homogenous in nature. The homogeneity of normal leaf images is high as they are homogeneous in

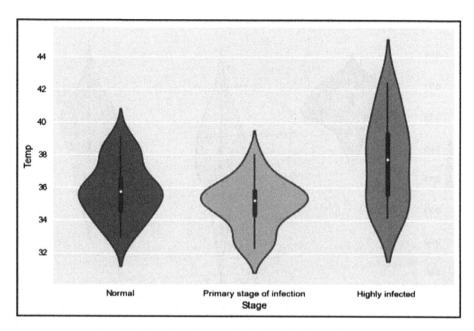

Fig. 9. Probability density function of temperature variation

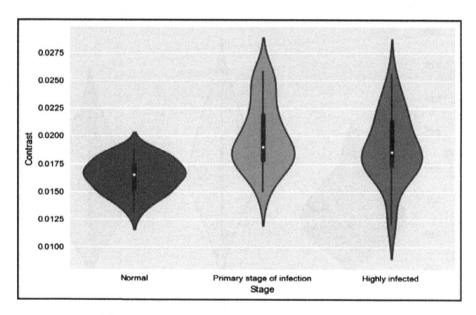

Fig. 10. Probability density function of contrast variation

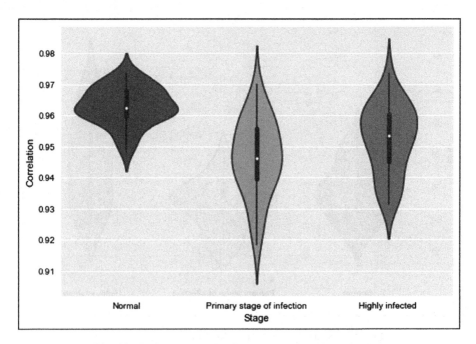

Fig. 11. Probability density function of correlation variation

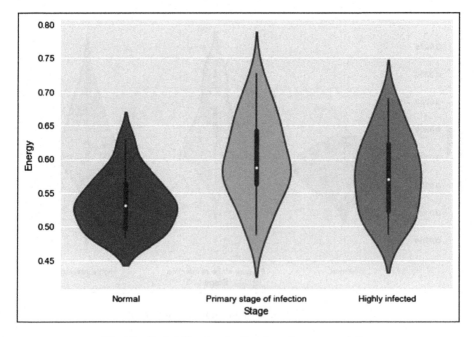

Fig. 12. Probability density function of energy variation

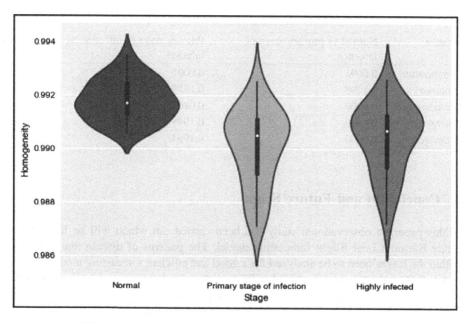

Fig. 13. Probability density function of homogeneity variation

nature. When disease symptoms grow within the leaf then homogeneity reduces. At last when leaf cells are going to be dead then again homogeneity increases as local changes in images decrease.

Figures 9, 10, 11, 12 and 13 represents the probability density function of the thermal and texture features. The previous box plots only shows the summary statistics of the feature set. But these plots show the full distribution of the feature set.

With box plot and probability density function, we can not specify the statistical significance of the observation. To find this statistical significance of the result obtained, paired t-test is done between every two stages. At first, paired t-test is carried out between "normal" and "primary stage of infection" and after that between "primary stage of infection" and "highly infected" leaves. The result of the paired t-test for each features are tabulated in Table 2. The values in the table represents the p-values of the feature set. If the p-value is less than 0.05 then there is a significant difference between observed dataset with respect to the selected feature. From Table 2 it is clear that there is significant difference in temperature for "normal to primary stage of infection" leaves and "primary stage of infection to highly infected" leaves. But in case of contrast, there is no significant difference among these three stages. For correlation, energy and homogeneity features significant difference is found when normal leaves are getting infected gradually. But when the cells of highly infected leaves died there is no significant difference.

The paired t-test result shows that temperature is the only feature that can significantly differentiate the normal, primary stage of infection and highly infected leaves affected by the Bacterial Leaf Blight for an automated system. Hence, with this analysis the importance of thermal feature in Bacterial Leaf Blight forecasting has been verified.

Table 2. Paired t-test result (p-value)

Feature	Normal vs primary stage of infection	Primary stage of infection vs highly infected
Temperature	0.0091	0.0001
Contrast	0.1798	0.1979
Correlation	0.0000	0.0803
Energy	0.0000	0.1949
Homogeneity	0.0000	0.1964

4   Conclusion and Future Scope

In this paper an observational study has been carried out which will be helpful for future Bacterial Leaf Blight forecasting model. The patterns of disease manifestation within the leaves need to be analyzed for a good and efficient forecasting model. In this paper, these patterns are recognized with respect to temperature and texture features. The variation in these features are analyzed with summary statistics and probability density functions. Paired t-test is carried out to find out the statistical significance of these variations. The result of the analysis shows that the variation in temperature statistics is only significant for three stages of the disease – normal, primary stage of infection and highly infected. Thus it proves the statistical significance of thermal feature with p-value less than 0.05 in Leaf Blight forecasting.

In future, these observations will help to analyze the pattern of disease evolution and design a forecasting model to control the epidemic of blight diseases with reduced yield loss.

References

1. Coale, A.J., Hoover, E.M.: Population Growth and Economic Development. Princeton University Press, Princeton (2015)
2. Central Statistics Office (CSO)—Ministry of statistics and program implementation, gross domestic product, 17 April 2017. http://www.mospi.gov.in/central-statistics-office-cso-0
3. Arjun, K.M.: Indian agriculture-status, importance and role in Indian Economy. Int. J. Agric. Food Sci. Technol. **4**(4), 343–346 (2013)
4. Chose, L.M., Ghatge, B., Subramanyan, V.: Rice in India. Indian Council of Agricultural Reserarch, New Delhi (1956)
5. Datta, D.: Principles and Practices of Rice Production. International Rice Research Institute, Los Baños (1981)
6. Lloyd, J.M.: Thermal Imaging Systems. Springer, New York (2013). https://doi.org/10.1007/978-1-4899-1182-7
7. Vollmer, M., Möllmann, K.P.: Infrared Thermal Imaging: Fundamentals, Research and Applications. Wiley, Hoboken (2017)
8. Phadikar, S., Sil, J.: Rice disease identification using pattern recognition techniques. In: 11th International Conference on Computer and Information Technology, pp. 420–423. IEEE (2008)

9. Phadikar, S., Sil, J., Das, A.K.: Feature selection by attribute clustering of infected rice plant images. Int. J. Mach. Intell. **3**(2), 74–88 (2011)

10. Phadikar, S., Sil, J., Das, A.K.: Classification of rice leaf diseases based on morphological changes. Int. J. Inf. Electron. Eng. **2**(3), 460–463 (2012)

11. Kim, K.H., Cho, J., Lee, Y.H., Lee, W.S.: Predicting potential epidemics of rice leaf blast and sheath blight in South Korea under the RCP 4.5 and RCP 8.5 climate change scenarios using a rice disease epidemiology model. EPIRICE Agric. Forest Meteorol. **203**, 191–207 (2013)

12. Huang, S., Qi, L., Ma, X., Xue, K., Wang, W., Zhu, X.: Hyperspectral image analysis based on BoSW model for rice panicle blast grading. Comput. Electron. Agric. **118**, 167–178 (2015)

13. Phadikar, S., Goswami, J.: Vegetation indices based segmentation for automatic classification of brown spot and blast diseases of rice. In: 3rd International Conference Recent Advances in Information Technology (RAIT), pp. 284–289. IEEE (2016)

14. Sengupta, S., Das, A.K.: Particle Swarm Optimization based incremental classifier design for rice disease prediction. Comput. Electron. Agric. **140**, 443–451 (2017)

15. Prince, G., Clarkson, J.P., Rajpoot, N.M.: Automatic detection of diseased tomato plants using thermal and stereo visible light images. PLoS ONE **10**(4), e0123262 (2015)

16. Mohanty, S.P., Hughes, D.P., Salathé, M.: Using deep learning for image-based plant disease detection. Front. Plant Sci. **7**, 1419–1425 (2016)

17. Hackl, H., Baresel, J.P., Mistele, B., Hu, Y., Schmidhalter, U.: A comparison of plant temperatures as measured by thermal imaging and infrared thermometry. J. Agron. Crop Sci. **198**(6), 415–429 (2012)

18. Banerjee, K., Krishnan, P., Mridha, N.: Application of thermal imaging of wheat crop canopy to estimate leaf area index under different moisture stress conditions. Biosys. Eng. **166**, 13–27 (2018)

19. User's manual FLIR Tools, 27 October 2017. http://dronexpert.nl/wp-content/uploads/2017/06/flir-tools-manual.pdf

20. Gonzalez, R.C., Woods, R.E.: Digital Image Processing. Prentice Hall, Upper Saddle River (2002)

21. Pathak, B., Barooah, D.: Texture analysis based on the gray-level co-occurrence matrix considering possible orientations. Int. J. Adv. Res. Electr. Electron. Instrum. Eng. **2**(9), 4206–4212 (2013)

22. Soh, L.-K., Tsatsoulis, C.: Texture analysis of SAR sea ice imagery using gray level co-occurrence matrices. IEEE Trans. Geosci. Remote Sens. **37**(2), 780–795 (1999)

23. Haralick, R.M., Shanmugam, K.: Textural features for image classification. IEEE Trans. Syst. Man Cybern. **6**, 610–621 (1973)

24. Zhao, Q., Shi, C.Z., Luo, L.P.: Role of the texture features of images in the diagnosis of solitary pulmonary nodules in different sizes. Chin. J. Cancer Res. **26**(4), 451 (2014)

An Automated Approach Towards Digital Photo-Trichogram for Hair Fall Diagnosis

Naren Debnath[1], Nibaran Das[2($\boxtimes$)], Somenath Sarkar[3],
and Mita Nasipuri[2]

[1] Department of Computer Science and Engineering, Adamas University,
Kolkata, India
narendebnath2@gmail.com
[2] Department of Computer Science and Engineering, Jadavpur University,
Kolkata, India
nibaran@gmail.com, mitanasipuri@gmail.com
[3] Department of Dermatology, Bankura Sammilani Medical College,
Bankura, West Bengal, India
dr.somenathsarkar@gmail.com

Abstract. Identification of a specific type of alopecia or hair loss is essential to get rid of hair loss issues. But identification of it is a challenging task to the medial experts. Among different techniques, Digital Photo-Trichogram is one of the popular non-invasive medical procedures for diagnosis of alopecia. In the present work we propose a novel system which is able to measure automatically the growth of hair without manual interaction and experts' opinion. The developed system can estimate hair fall related issues with the help of parameters such as unit area density, approximate average height and width of hair, determination of vellus or terminal hair automatically from the picture of shaved region of alopecia effected area. The system is tested with the samples collected from Calcutta School of Tropical Medicine, Kolkata and achieve satisfactory results.

Keywords: Index Terms—Digital Photo-Trichogram · Binarization
Inter-pixel gap · Horizontal and vertical scan

1 Introduction

Digital Photo-Trichogram is one of the non-invasive medical procedures for diagnosis of hair fall disease or alopecia. In this method a portion of the scalp (1 mm^2 to 2 mm^2 area) is shaved and then the shaved portion is washed with dye for better contrast of the captured image. After using the dye, a few numbers of suitable images of the shaved portion are captured using either a very high resolution digital camera or a Digital USB Microscope. There are other methods to diagnose alopecia, but Digital Photo-Trichogram is nearly the most suitable and convenient method for current medical cases. In India, dermatologists use their own cognition to detect and provide remedy for hair loss. Since the number of patients increases every day, and their busy schedule, a system is necessary for faster detection of the stages of alopecia. For recognizing and

© Springer Nature Singapore Pte Ltd. 2018
J. K. Mandal and D. Sinha (Eds.): CSI 2017, CCIS 836, pp. 314–329, 2018.
https://doi.org/10.1007/978-981-13-1343-1_28

providing remedies for hair loss, very few computerized systems are available, among which, TrichoScan® [1] is a popular one. But this software using Digital Photo-Trichogram needs a good proportion of manual interaction for detecting features of hair such as height, width, to determine whether the stage of hair is vellus or terminal. Saraogi et al. [2] have identified the limitation of this software. Though existing works do not provide any significant contribution, we have found only one research work by Esfandiari et al. [3] which shows the use of Artificial Neural Network, for diagnosis of hair loss using some numerical data allied to alopecia. In this research Two-Layer Neural Network algorithms is used to detect the type of alopecia. They have tried to diagnose the amount of hair loss using the factors like age, gender, genetic factors, pregnancy, surgery record, zinc deficiency, iron deficiency and effect of the use of cosmetics. This diagnosis was only based on some numerical test data obtained by consultation with doctors and medical tests. The algorithms used in the paper are Levenberg-Marquardt, Resilient Back Propagation, Powell-Beale Conjugate Gradient, Fletcher Reeves Conjugate Gradient, Polak-Rebier Conjugate Gradient, and Scaled Conjugate Gradient. The aforementioned factors for alopecia are the input parameters for neural network. They obtained the Mean Square Error (MSE) and Mean Absolute Error (MAE) to evaluate the performance of the neural network. Other works are related to the evaluation of the TrichoScan® about its suitability and capability. In Saraogi et al. [2] it is showed that optimality of detection of anagen/telogen hair provides incorrect result and it is an overestimation of total hair density and the density of vellus hair doesn't correlate the clinical severity of alopecia. It also showed that single hair strands falsely divided into double hair strands at the point of exit from the scalp surface and identified as telogen hair. Gassmueller et al. [4] validated that there is excellent co-relation between TrichoScan® software and manual marking of hair for about 10 patients. Holfmanet et al. [5] reported that TrichoScan® method is more reproducible with smaller margin of operator error than with manual marking. To address the issue in the present work we have estimated the density of the hair loss to find out the features of hair strands such as height, width, percentage of vellus hair etc. Sauvola's [6] Binarization method is used followed by a novel method of horizontal and vertical scanning. The database is created from The School of Topical Medicine, Medical College, Kolkata, WB, India under the supervision of medical practitioners. This paper is organized as: the immediate next sub-section states the motivation towards this work followed by another subsection describing about the nature of hair and hair loss. After that some of the related tasks are discussed followed by the present work. In the present work we have discussed the data collection procedure along with the proposed methodology. At the closure there is detailed discussion of experimental results with the conclusion.

1.1 Motivation

In India only 25% of people with a general hair loss problem consult with dermatologists. Rest randomly search for the non-prescribed remedies and due to ignorance many of them reach up to the verge of extinction of hair. Many patients, often, after consulting with a dermatologist, stop following the prescribed medicines in intermediary period and also break the communication with the respective doctors. Keeping all these factors in mind and to save precious time of patients, a system that can diagnose the hair loss pattern and provide remedy for the respective hair loss problem is much needed in our country. Some semi-automatic systems such as TrichoScan Smart, TrichoScan Pro exist in other country only for the diagnosing purpose. So it is our endeavor to develop a system that can automatically diagnose and provide a suggestion for remedy of hair loss disease and also to help dermatologists to provide better suggestion to their patients in a much more convenient manner in Indian sub-continental conditions.

1.2 Hair and Hairloss

Hair is a composition of a special type of protein called Keratin. Cuticle, Cortex and Medulla is the three concentric layers of each hair strand. Hair grows in four different phases – Anagen, Catagen, Telogen, and Exogen. Different People have different textures of hair, and hair-colors based on different environmental conditions. Very few people take a good care of hair, as a result of which most of the people suffer from hair fall. It is noticed by medical practitioners that 50 to 150 hair strands shed daily, which is normal in nature, greater amount of it is considered as hair loss.

Hair loss patterns in male and female are called Male Pattern Hair Loss (MHPL) and Female Pattern hair Loss (FHPL) respectively. We have considered only MPHL in this work. There are different categories of hair loss, such as Androgenetic Alopecia, Alopecia Areata, Telogen Effluvium, Traction Alopecia, Trichotillomania, Cicatricial Alopecia and Hair Fall due to Hair-Shaft Abnormalities [7]. Androgenetic Alopecia and Alopecia Areata is mostly observed alopecia in Indian people. The main agent responsible for Androgenetic Alopecia is Dehydrotestosterone, a very powerful Androgen hormone. It reduces the scalp hair and increases body and genital hair. Apart from this, various other diseases like hormonal changes, consumption of drugs, environmental factors, and genetic factors accelerate the hair loss problem and result in cause complete hair loss [3].

2 Related Work

Segmentation of images is the process of dividing the image pixels into two groups, background pixels and foreground pixels. Bi-level information of an image can be obtained through segmentation which reduces the computational load and enables the utilization of simplified analysis method compared to 256 grey level information [4]. There are a number of segmentation algorithms existing and they are categorized as thresholding, region based, cluster based, graph based etc. [8]. Thresholding and region based are mostly used segmentation methods among the all others. Thresholding based segmentation is again categorized as Global threshold based and Local threshold based [9]. Due to non-uniform illumination over the captured image, local pixel value difference, error in capturing images, the global thresholding method is insufficient. We have used Local threshold based segmentation method in our work. Sauvola, Bersen, Niblack [10] are three of many other local thresholding methods which we have used.

Local Variance Method: Local variance method to calculate threshold is used by both Niblack and Sauvola. Local mean m(x,y) and standard deviation of a window sized r × r of a pixel are used in these techniques.

Niblack's Method: Niblack's method used the following equation to calculate the threshold TP(x,y) at (x,y) position using window size r × r:

$$TP_{(x,y)} = m_{(x,y)} + k\delta_{(x,y)} \tag{1}$$

In this equation m(x,y) and δ(x,y) are the local mean and the standard deviation of the pixel at (x,y) inside the window and k the bias. The value of k = −0.2 and r = 15 produce satisfactory results. The change of threshold according to the change of contrast in the local neighbourhood of the pixel at (x,y) is adapted by the local mean m (x,y) and standard deviation δ(x,y). The level of adaptation which varies the threshold value is controlled by the value of k.

Sauvola's Method: Mean m(x,y) and standard deviation δ(x,y) are used to calculate the threshold value in Sauvola's method using a window size r × r given as:

$$T_{(x,y)} = m_{(x,y)} \left[1 + k \left(\frac{\delta_{(x,y)}}{R} - 1 \right) \right] \tag{2}$$

Local Grey Range using Bernsen's Method: In Bernsen's method local grey range technique is used where the values between the maximum and minimum gray range within the local neighborhood window are used to determine the threshold value.

The local threshold value $T_{(x,y)}$ within a window size r × r is obtained as:

$$T_{(x,y)} = 0.5 \left(I_{\max(i,j)} + I_{\min(i,j)} \right) \tag{3}$$

$I_{\max(i,j)}$ and $I_{\min(i,j)}$ are the maximum and minimum values within the local neighbourhood window and results the contrast.

$$C_{(i,j)} = \left(I_{\max(i,j)} - I_{\min(i,j)} \right) \geq 15 \tag{4}$$

The mean value of $I_{max}(i,j)$ and $I_{min}(i,j)$ is used to calculate the midrange value as the threshold within the local neighbourhood window. In this method no bias controls the threshold value. The value r = 31 provides satisfactory results.

Figure 1(ii) displays the comparison of the above mentioned three binarization method using Digital Photo-Trichogram image.

3 Present Work

3.1 Database Preparation

Database design is the most challenging task of any pattern recognition problem for the validation of different algorithms. The design of the databases of scalps is the most important and crucial task of the present work. The methodology of Digital Photo-Trichogram process is followed under the present work for creation of the database. The overall process consists of: (1) shaving off a small portion of the scalp of patients, (2) dying the shaved area of the scalp for better contrast, (3) capturing the image of that area using a digital camera. The other records of patients are also kept appropriately for the proper treatment and future references. As this kind of image database is being designed for the first time for research in Image Processing in India, due to lack of appropriate standard some data are rejected. The other difficulties we have faced during collection of images are, non-availability of proper resources such as (USB digital microscope), environmental burden, lack of the patient's time, and proper shaving and cleansing material for the imaging of affected scalp area. A set of images from image database is given in Fig. 1(i).

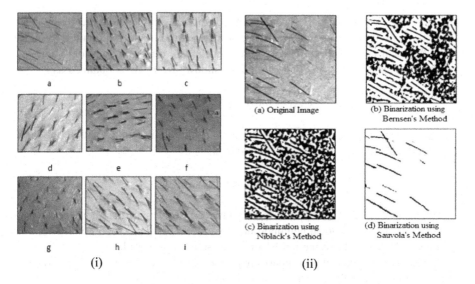

(a) Original Image

(b) Binarization using Bernsen's Method

(c) Binarization using Niblack's Method

(d) Binarization using Sauvola's Method

(i)   (ii)

Fig. 1. (i) Examples of sample images form the collected database (ii) Comparison of three binarization method on sample image a.

3.2 Proposed Method

Hair strand(s) which is (are) considered as foreground object, filled with distinct random colour using 8-neighborhood pixel after binarization. If any of the neighbors of the current black pixel of a particular object is also black then the current pixel is assigned to the distinct random color and this process is continued recursively until any other black neighbor pixel exists for that object.

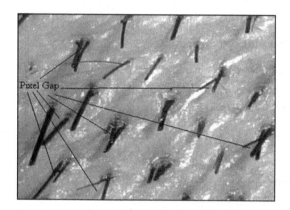

Fig. 2. Inter-pixel gap between hair strands

Separation and Counting of Hair Strands

After segmentation by using Sauvola's method, and filling with distinct random colour, we found a considerable amount of inter-pixel (background colour) gaps in between the same overlapped object. Considering this background inter-pixel gaps in the overlapping hair strands shown in Fig. 2, have been separated by using the following method. Separating a particular object (overlapped or single hair strand) is done by scanning horizontally as well as vertically. For each horizontal and vertical scan the below mention in Algorithm 1 is used.

Algorithm 1
Input − a preprocessed image of Digital Photo- Trichogram
 Output − approximate total no. of hair strand
  <u>Data Structures:</u>
cp(i,j) − current pixel of the current object
bgc − background pixel colour
 obp − object pixel colour
  Steps
Initialize **tcount**=0
Row Scan:.
Initialize **hcount**=0, **phcount**=0
For each row pixels
if (**cp(i-1,j)** == **bgc** and **cp(i,j)** == **obp)** then
        hcount= **hcount** + 1
if (**hcount**>**phcount)** then
phcount= **hcount**
(Repeat steps 3 to 4 for no. of rows for the particular object)
Column Scan:.
Initialize **vcount**=0,**pvcount**=0
For each column pixels
if (**cp(i,j-1)** == **bgc** and **cp(i,j)** == **obp)** then
            vcount= **vcount** + 1
if (**vcount**>**pvcount)**
pvcount= **vcount**
Repeat steps 6 to 7 for no. of columns for a particular object
if (**phcount**>**pvcount)**
tcount= **tcount** + **phcount**
  else
        tcount= **pvcount** + **pvcount**
Repeat steps 2 through 8 until all the object pixels are scanned
The variable **tcount** is used in both of the following algorithms.

Calculation of Approximate Average Width

As the width of hair strands is not equal along the length of each hair strand, so a minimal average of vertical and horizontal pixel width is calculated. In this method each horizontal and vertical scanning is done for each row pixels and column pixels side by side till the current hair strand pixels are encountered. The following algorithm is used for horizontal and vertical scan.

Algorithm 2:
Input – *a processed Digital Photo-Trichogram image*
Output – *approximate average width of each hair strand*
<u>*Data Structures:*</u>
cp(i,j) – *current pixel of current object*
bgc – *background pixel colour*
obp – *object pixel colour*
Steps:
   1. *Initialize* ***avwc***=*0*
   2. *Initialize* ***twc***= *0*, ***ob***= *0*
Row scan:.
   3. *Initialize* ***hpc*** = *0*
   4. *If* ((***cp(i-1,j)*** == ***bgc*** *and* ***cp(i,j)*** == ***obp***) *or*
     (***cp(i-1,j)*** == ***obp*** *and* ***cp(i,j)*** == ***obp***) *or* (***cp(i-***
     1,j) == ***obp*** *and* ***cp(i,j)*** == ***bgc***)) *then*
hpc=***hpc*** + *1*
(Repeat step 4 until end row pixel is reached)
  Column Scan:.
   5. *Initialize* ***vpc*** = *0*
   6. *If* ((***cp(i,j-1)*** == ***bgc*** *and* ***cp(i,j)*** == ***obp***) *or*
     (***cp(i,j-1)*** ==
obp *and* ***cp(i,j)*** == ***obp***) *or* (***cp(i-1,j)*** == ***obp*** *and*
cp(i,j) == ***bgc***)) *then*
vpc= ***vpc***+ *1*
(Repeat step 6 until end column pixel is reached)
   7. *If* (***hpc***== *0* *and* ***vpc***!= *0*) *then*
   8. ***twc*** = ***twc***+ ***vpc***
ob=***ob***+ *1*
- *else if* (***vpc***== *0* *and* ***hpc***!= *0*) *then*
     twc = ***twc***+ ***hpc***
   ob=***ob***+ *1*
- *else if* ***hpc***>***vpc*** *then*
- ***twc*** = ***twc***+ ***vpc***
    ob=***ob***+ *1*
else if ***vpc***>***hpc*** *then*
- ***twc*** = ***twc***+ ***hpc***
    ob=***ob***+ *1*
*(Repeat steps 3 through 7 until all the object pixels
are scanned)*
   9. ***avwc***= ***avwc***+ (***twc/ob***)
*(Repeat 1 through 8 until all the objects pixels are
scanned)*
   10.***avwc*** = ***avwc/tcount***
   11.*Stop.*

Calculation of Approximate Average Height

As the orientation of objects couldn't be corrected, the method applied here is by counting the horizontal and vertical edge wise pixels of each object including overlapped object and multiplying the number of edge wise pixels by the number of objects (for single and overlapping objects). To count the horizontal and vertical edge wise pixels the following algorithm is used.

```
Algorithm 3:
Input - a processed Digital Photo-Trichogram image
Output - The approximate height of each hair strand
Data Structures:
cp(i,j) - current random coloured pixel
Steps:
    1. Initilization of avhc = 0
    2. Initialize hc=0, hr = 0
    3. Scan the pixels from left to right
If (s == cp(i,j))
    hc++
break
(Repeat until all the horizontal initial edge pixels are
compared)
    4. Scan the pixels from top to bottom
If (s == cp(i,j))
    hr++
    break
(Repeat until all the vertical initial edge pixels are
compared)
    5. If (hc>hr) then
avhc = avhc + hc × tot. no. of adjacent hair strands
    else
        avhc = avhc + hr × tot. no. of adjacent hair
strands
  (Repeat steps 1 to 5 until all the objects are covered)
    6. avhc = avhc/tcount
    7. Stop.
avhc is the approximate average height of each object.
```

4 Experimental Results and Discussion

After applying the proposed methodology, the result obtained is shown in Fig. 3. Sauvola's method is used in proposed methodology varying the value of parameter k from 0 to 40 and the optimal result is obtained at k = 15 and 32. These two values of k have been chosen for better binarization and clear primary separation of hair strands.

Tables 1, 2 and 3 display the results of data samples obtained only in the first phase of diagnosis, due to unavailability of the patient of the first phase in the second phase.

Table 4 specifically displays the percentage of telogen hair for six patients. Table 5 shows the comparison of the results of data samples obtained in two phases of the diagnosis.

Table 1. Number of hair strand count

Sl. #	Name of images	Object count by (in pixels)	
		Manual count	Proposed method
1	Image 1	17	19
2	Image 2	67	77
3	Image 3	34	34
4	Image 4	31	33
5	Image 5	41	39
6	Image 6	36	37
7	Image 7	28	27
8	Image 8	45	37
9	Image 9	33	31
10	Image 10	32	29
11	Image 11	27	24
12	Image 12	27	25
13	Image 13	33	26
14	Image 14	34	45
15	Image 15	34	39
16	Image 16	31	38
17	Image 17	18	19
18	Image 18	48	48
19	Image 19	35	49
20	Image 20	42	47
21	Image 21	41	58

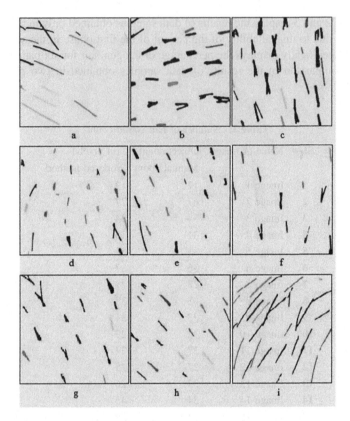

Fig. 3. Sample images after applying proposed methodology

Table 2. Number of hair strand count

Sl. #	Name of images	Height measure (in pixels)	
		Manual count	Proposed method
1	Image 1	106	98
2	Image 2	75	68
3	Image 3	48	50
4	Image 4	46	44
5	Image 5	57	52
6	Image 6	55	47
7	Image 7	60	45
8	Image 8	61	82
9	Image 9	45	41
10	Image 10	62	61
11	Image 11	65	59

(continued)

Table 2. (*continued*)

Sl. #	Name of images	Height measure (in pixels)	
		Manual count	Proposed method
12	Image 12	67	52
13	Image 13	48	41
14	Image 14	111	129
15	Image 15	99	132
16	Image 16	90	105
17	Image 17	94	95
18	Image 18	60	80
19	Image 19	54	48
20	Image 20	58	55
21	Image 21	65	69

Table 3. Width measure of hair strands

Sl. #	Name of images	Width measure (in pixels)	
		Manual count	Proposed method
1	Image 1	6	4
2	Image 2	6	6
3	Image 3	6	7
4	Image 4	5	5
5	Image 5	6	6
6	Image 6	5	6
7	Image 7	6	6
8	Image 8	7	6
9	Image 9	6	8
10	Image 10	5	6
11	Image 11	5	6
12	Image 12	6	5
13	Image 13	5	6
14	Image 14	6	5
15	Image 15	7	5
16	Image 16	7	6
17	Image 17	7	7
18	Image 18	5	6
19	Image 19	5	6
20	Image 20	5	6
21	Image 21	6	6

Table 4. Percentage of telogen hair in 6 patients in both the test phases

Sl #	Name of images	Numbers of hair strands		Percentage of telogen hair
		First phase of diagnosis	Second phase of diagnosis	
1	Image 1	14	19	10.52
2	Image 2	70	77	8.75
3	Image 3	19	64	0.0
4	Image 4	18	69	0.0
5	Image 5	34	58	3.57
6	Image 6	25	31	0.0

Table 5. Width measure in 6 patients in both the test phases

Sl #	Name of images	Width measure (in pixels)	
		First phase of diagnosis	Second phase of diagnosis
1	Image 1	6	8
2	Image 2	6	8
3	Image 3	6	7
4	Image 4	5	7
5	Image 5	6	7
6	Image 6	8	11

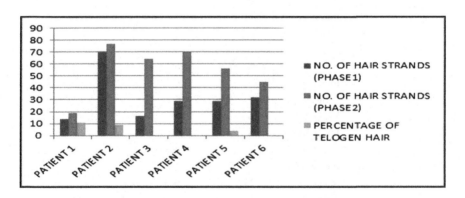

Fig. 4. Height of each hair strand of 6 patients

In this work the results are obtained automatically in terms of number of objects (individual and overlapped hair strands), approximate average height and width of each hair strand. So our proposed system is able to measure automatically the growth of hair and no manual interaction is needed except uploading the image. From Table 1 to Table 3 we can so far conclude that this system is able to identify the growth of hair in the shaved region (the diagnosed area) by which it is possible to identify the improvement in hair growth. The diagnosis is done in two phases. The data obtained in

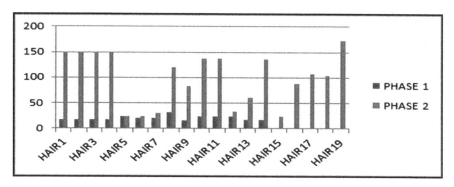

Fig. 5. Height of each hair strand of PATIENT 1

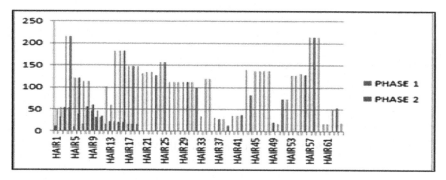

Fig. 6. Height of each hair strand of PATIENT 2

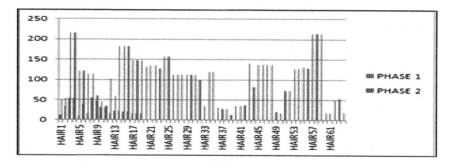

Fig. 7. Height of each hair strand of PATIENT 3

these two test phases are used for comparison in terms of the growth of the number of hairs on the shaved region, height and width of hair strands, are shown in Table 5.

In Fig. 4 we have shown that the comparison of the total number of hair in two phases of the diagnosis and number of telogen hairs in six patients. From Figs. 5, 6, 7,

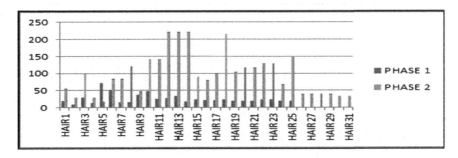

Fig. 8. Height of each hair strand of PATIENT 4

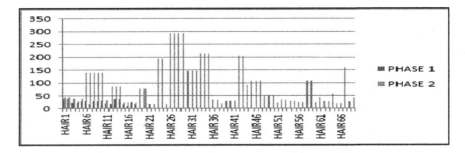

Fig. 9. Height of each hair strand of PATIENT 5

8 and 9 show the comparison of height of hair strands in both the phases of the diagnosis for each five patients.

5 Conclusion

The diagnostic method used here is non-invasive Digital Photo-Trichogram. People with busy schedule with a severe hair loss problem can be helped using this system using a computer and dermatologists may also be helped for better treatment once the overall system is developed. The most challenging part of this project was to collect sufficient and a good amount of data samples of the scalp images using Digital Photo-Trichogram method, as this kind of data samples are not readily available. To the best of our knowledge, there is no previous research except one TrichoScan®, a proprietary computer aided semi-automatic hair loss diagnostic system. The other challenging task was to segment the overlapped hair strands and to measure the approximate average height and width of total number of hair strands.

Acknowledgement. Authors are thankful to the "Center for Microprocessor Application for Training Education and Research" of Computer Science & Engineering Department, Jadavpur

University, for providing infrastructure facilities during progress of the work. Authors are also thankful to Dermatology department, Calcutta School of Tropical Medicine for providing useful data.

References

1. TrichoScan ......makes hair growth measurable - Home (n.d.). http://trichoscan.com/pages/english/home.php. Accessed 15 May 2014
2. Saraogi, P.P., Dhurat, R.S.: Automated digital image analysis (TrichoScan®) for human hair growth analysis: ease versus errors. Int. J. Trichology 2(1), 5–13 (2010). https://doi.org/10.4103/0974-7753.66905
3. Esfandiari, A., Kalantari, K.R., Babaei, A.: Hair loss diagnosis using artificial neural networks. Int. J. Comput. Sci. Issues 9(5(2)), 174–180 (2012)
4. Gassmueller, J., Rowold, E., Frase, T., Hughes-Formella, B.: Validation of TrichoScan® technology as a fully-automated tool for evaluation of hair growth parameters. Eur. J. Dermatol. 19(3), 224–231 (2009). https://doi.org/10.1684/ejd.2009.0640
5. Basic Structure of Hair (n.d.). http://www.fbi.gov/
6. Sauvola, J., Pietikäinen, M.: Adaptive document image binarization. Pattern Recogn. 33(2), 225–236 (2000). https://doi.org/10.1016/S0031-3203(99)00055-2
7. Mulinari-Brenner, F., Bergfeld, W.F.: Hair loss: diagnosis and management. Clevel. Clin. J. Med. (2003). https://doi.org/10.3949/ccjm.70.8.705
8. Maru, D., Shah, B.: Image segmentation techniques and genetic algorithm. Int. J. Adv. Res. Comput. Eng. Technol. (IJARCET) 2(4), 1483–1487 (2013)
9. Dass, R., Devi, S.: Image segmentation techniques. Int. J. Electron. Commun. Technol. (IJECT) 3(1), 66–70 (2012)
10. Singh, T.R., Roy, S., Singh, O.I., Sinam, T., Singh, K.M.: A new local adaptive thresholding technique in binarization. Int. J. Comput. Sci. Issues 8(6), 271–277 (2012)

Advanced Diagnosis of Deadly Diseases Using Regression and Neural Network

Sumit Das[1]($\boxtimes$), Manas Kumar Sanyal[2], and Debamoy Datta[3]

[1] Information Technology, JIS College of Engineering, Kalyani 741235, India
sumit.it8l@gmail.com
[2] Department of Business Administration, University of Kalyani,
Kalyani 741235, India
manassanyall23@gmail.com
[3] Electrical Engineering, JIS College of Engineering, Kalyani 741235, India
datta.debamoy@gmail.com

Abstract. We see that the diagnosis of disease is very difficult these days and for ordinary doctors even it becomes perplexing to handle the situation we use the combined power of artificial neural network and Regression analysis. In this paper we use certain new techniques by combining the capabilities of statistical analysis and Artificial Neural Network. We also give a relation of BMI with age by using data mining and use that for our analysis. Here in our paper we also identify placebo i.e. a patient actually does not have the symptoms but because he/she thinks that they have the disease and hence tells to a doctor that he/she has the disease. We identify a parameter called α and theoretically justify that using it we can identify which one is placebo. It is distinguished that probability and fuzzy logic are independent but considering one thing that occurrence of disease is based on probability i.e. two outcomes the disease may happen or may not happen but evaluation of symptoms is essentially fuzzy i.e. "Feeling VERY cold"or "Feeling EXTREMELY cold". So we intimately connect these two different concepts. Hence we use a membership function in our paper to calculate probabilities.

Keywords: Gini coefficient · Reliability · Neurons · BMI

1 Introduction

In this paper we consider two things first of all we notice that a person becomes more prone to disease as his age increases. So we define a Reliability parameter for a person's organ after we get his age and BMI i.e. Body Mass Index as input and we use a neural network for that purpose. Now after the network has been trained we define the reliability as:

$$R = e^{-\gamma t}$$

Where, R is the output response of the neurons. R is actually the activation function for a neuron in other words our neuron becomes a radial basisnetwork. As this gives the probability of failing of a patient's organ as an exponential distribution. Let us see its

J. K. Mandal and D. Sinha (Eds.): CSI 2017, CCIS 836, pp. 330–351, 2018.
https://doi.org/10.1007/978-981-13-1343-1_29

authenticity consider t → ∞ this gives Reliability 0. This is justified on the grounds that as the age of a person increases the person is more likely to suffer from the disease, similarly we can observe that as t → 0 Reliability becomes 1. This can be explained on the similar grounds. But because of the artificial Neural Networks our above formula becomes flexible. Let's see how: Now, consider

$$\gamma_1 < \gamma_2 < \gamma_3$$
$$t_1 < t_2 < t_3$$

So,

$$\gamma_1 * t_1 < \gamma_2 * t_2 < \gamma_3 * t_3$$

So,

$$-\gamma_1 * t_1 > -\gamma_2 * t_2 > -\gamma_3 * t_3$$

Therefore

$$R_1 > R_2 > R_3$$

Therefore, gamma takes a fraction of the product of BMI and age of the input. We did this because suppose a person has a disease has age 67 and another person has a disease at 70 so the probability of happening of disease also varies from person to person. Therefore, our R takes care of that as it depends on neural network so it learns intelligently and discovers the pattern and makes accurate classification. Now in our case this thing is more accurately described by Radial bias network. Now BMI is determined by the regression analysis from a standard data that is collected [3]. We use R programming for this purpose. Also, consider that BMI is determined for many people, for healthy persons the BMI value and for ill person the BMI value are different as the loss of appetite is one of the major effects of most of the diseases. Not all patients that come to the doctor are ill and hence we actually treat a fraction of the originally sampled population. It would be very great if we can filter this population such that we are sure that most of the patients are either ill or healthy, that is where we use the BMI values of the population and determine the Gini coefficient.

2 Background Study

Each and every person in his life is at some point of time has fallen prey to disease. Life threatening condition only occurs if it is not diagnosed properly we need a solution that is where artificial intelligence comes into play [1]. The application of Neural networks, regression analysis and expert systems have been subject to considerable research in these few years researcher considered an expert system to evaluate various symptoms of a patient [2]. If potentially serious condition is found then the patient is advised to have tests. In studies the paper focused on specific disease pulmonary tuberculosis and trained neural networks and developed one artificial neural network model for classi-fication (multilayer perceptron—MLP) and another risk group assignment (self-organizing map—SOM) for PTB in hospitalized patients in a high complexity hospital in Rio de Janeiro City [3]. They used 7 variables—radiologic classification, age, gender, cough, night sweats, weight loss and anorexia. Thus we see age is also important apart from the symptoms and test data. In this inspiring paper used a new meta-heuristic algorithm, centripetal accelerated particle swarm optimization (CAPSO), is applied to evolve the ANN learning and accuracy [4]. The algorithm is based on an improved scheme of particle swarm algorithm and Newton's laws of motion. In our studies, it has been observe that the paper uses a special process that combines the power of data mining [5]. They use Logical Analysis of Data (LAD). LAD is a supervised learning, artificial intelligence, data mining technique that possesses dis-tinctive advantages which proved to be of use in PAHM. They showed that in the testing process LAD can detect and diagnose the asset's state based on the generated knowledge during the learning process. This process of learning and pattern generation serve to reinforce the theoretical knowledge and uncover new knowledge about a certain diagnostic problem in PAHM. This gives us the idea that data mining, regression and other statistical methods if could be combined with the power of expert systems and artificial neural network then the diagnosis will become very accurate. Our research study focuses on utilizing maximum out of these techniques and combining them to achieve the desired results.

3 Methodology

The Fig. 1 shows the proposed architecture for our system. Now the evaluation of symptoms of a disease is essentially fuzzy. Considering that a statement made by patient contains linguistic terms for example the statement "I am feeling EXTREMELY COLD". Thus a symptom is inherently associated with words like extremely, very etc. Also we note that occurrence of disease is inherently associated with probability that a disease may happen or may not happen. Thus intuition tells that these two different concepts are interlinked. We consider the following things

$$P \propto \mu$$

This is our assumption based on the arguments that the range of both of them coincide and also by above arguments.

$$P = k\mu$$

Where k is the constant of proportionality. Now according to our arguments when the person absolutely has the symptoms then we are definitely sure the person has the disease so when $\mu = 1$ then $P = 1$ which gives $k = 1$. Now we would like to describe what this function f is in the figure. We train our network such that first result gives 0 when the age is large, BMI has large deviation from the normal and $(1 - G)$ is 0.

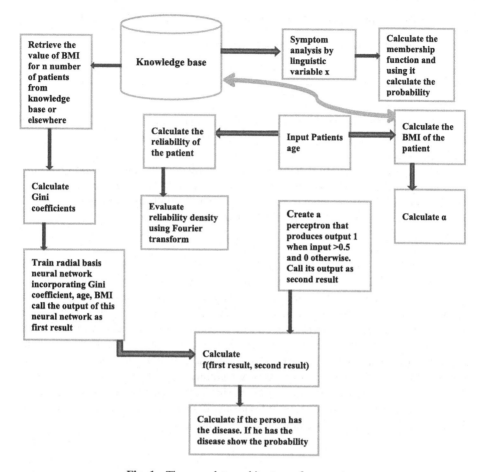

Fig. 1. The complete architecture of our system

Where G is the Gini coefficient, so a radial basis network is used for the first input. That is actually first result is reliability. Second result can be described mathematically as:

$$u(z) = \left.\begin{array}{l} 1, z > 0.5 \\ 0, z \leq 0.5 \end{array}\right\}$$

That is why perceptron is used now. The input z to the perceptron is:

$$z = R * \mu$$

If the perceptron produces 1, We say that the person has the disease with probability μ else we say the person is healthy. Thus we get a relationship between the first result and second result.

3.1 Fourier Transforms and It's Interesting Relationship with Reliability

Consider that any function can be represented as:

$$R(t) = \int_{-\infty}^{\infty} r(w)e^{(-iwt)}dw$$

i.e. we assume that our reliability is composed of many sinusoidal and co-sinusoidal signals. As $e^{(-iwt)}$ is actually $\cos(wt) + i * \sin(wt)$. So let us see the physical interpretation of this:

See the plot of reliability –Vs-time in the plot given in the Fig. 1, suppose at time $t = 0$ the system has certain amount of reliability then at $t = 0$ it is offered maintenance so the reliability increases upto a certain point. Then it falls again in an interval T/2 where T is the time period of sinusoidal signal Now we know that

w = (2 * π)/T

or, T = (2 * π)/w

so for T/2, w = (4 * π)/T. So in this interval it first increases then decreases and the whole cycle is repeated like this by periodic maintenance. Now consider the person as a system when the person takes Medicine His reliability increases and he recovers from the disease but it does not means that he remains healthy forever so after a peak point his reliability decreases so it is in a way of sinusoidal behavior but in reality as the person ages his reliability decreases exponentially, So we can consider this exponential response to be made up of superposition of numerous sinusoidal and cosinusoidal response. So in ordinary life things are very complicated functions but we can assume them to be made up of interference or superposition of many such sinusoidal curves. So we wish to analyze the whole thing in frequency domain. i.e. we can interpreter(w) as the amplitude in the frequency domain (Figs. 2 and 3).

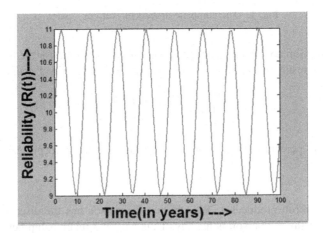

Fig. 2. Representation of a sinusoidal component of reliability, the equation is actually of the form y = A + Bsin(wt + φ) so we wish to analyze the spectrum. (this figure is in time domain)

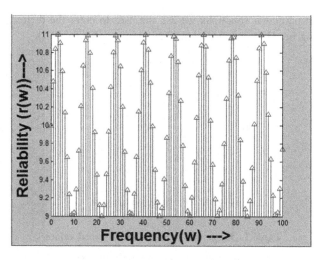

Fig. 3. This is in frequency domain where each arrow represents the amplitude r(w) in particular frequencies. (just an example)

So let us define another term reliability density. We define it as:

$$I = \int_0^{w_c} (r(w))^2 dw$$

Where w_c represents the critical frequency it is defined as the frequency when half time period is the maintainence time i.e.

$$w_c = (4 * \pi)/(\text{maintainence time})$$

So let us interpret this. In analogy with vibration where the energy of vibration is proportional to the square of the amplitude in a window of [w, w + Δw] we can interpret this interms of our reliability as more the value of I more are we sure we need less Maintainence in that energy is defined as the ability to be in working state in analogy to energy in physics where energy is defined as the ability to do work. Now:

$$I = f(\text{Maintainence time})$$

3.2 Fuzzy Logic Combined with Bayesian Network and Reliability with the Aid of Neural Networks

We use a Bayesian network to combine these things together (Fig. 4):

Where s1, s2,..., Sn represents the symptoms. D is the event of occurrence of disease and A is the event of being in the age group that is very prone to disease. Now consider certain things that we use fuzzy function to determine the probabilities associated with particular functions we ask the user to enter the degree of symptoms he/she is feeling i.e. How much do you feel: symptomX (Table 1).

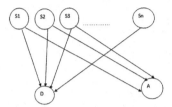

Fig. 4. The Bayesian network

Table 1. Linguistic variables and assigned values.

Linguistic variable	Assign values(x)
Extreme	5
Very much	4
Moderate	3
Somewhat	2
A little bit	1
Not at all	0

User enters digits between 0 and 5. Let us call our variable as D. Then in zadeh's notation [5]:

$$D = \{\frac{\int_0^5 \mu(x)dx}{x}\}$$

Where the integral is actually not integration but a symbol adapted by zadeh.

$$\mu(x) = \left(\exp\left(-\frac{x^2}{(x-5)^2}\right) - 1\right)^2, 0 \leq x \leq 5$$

now we want to do analysis on this matter a bit more. Let us define another so, let us calculate the probability that

$$P(D|S1) = \mu_1(x)$$
$$P(D|S2) = \mu_2(x)$$
$$\ldots P(D|Sn) = \mu_n(x)$$

Now let us calculate P(A)

$$P(A) = 1 - (R(1/(100 - t)))$$

Let us give an explanation for this R(t) gives the probability that the patient does not have the disease so $1 - R(t)$ gives the probability having the disease. Now consider that a person can live maximum 100 years following which death is eminent. So when $t \to 100$, $R(t) \to 0$. Before this we had considered Ideal case for determining the Reliability by assuming that a person can have any age. So Now our concern is to find the final probability. Now we define another parameter $\beta = $ BMI/age. Where BMI is the Body Mass Index. The BMI can be a good measure of person's appetite and health. So we see that as age increases beta value decrease and as BMI increases beta value increases. So the physical interpretation of BMI is actually Body to mass Index per unit age. So we can assume that our probability is a function of beta. Now Disease occurs when the body has malnutrition or it is weak as a result the Immunity system is not able to provide protection. In both cases BMI can be an effective measure.

So It is natural to assume that as beta increases we can expect that symptoms decreases or mathematically:

When $\mu = 1$, $\beta = $ undefined and $\mu = 0$ then beta is 1. So $1/(\beta - 1) = f(\log \mu)$. Let us see that when $\mu = 0$, $\log 0$ is undefined hence beta is 1. So reciprocal of (beta $- 1$) is a function of $\log \mu$

Let

$$\alpha = \frac{1}{\beta - 1}$$

$$d\alpha = \left(\frac{\delta \alpha}{\delta \log(\mu)}\right) * d(\log \mu)$$

Now let d μ be negligible then its logarithm cannot be Neglected so

$$d\alpha = \left(\frac{\delta \alpha}{\delta \log(\mu)}\right) * 1/\mu$$

Or,

$$d\alpha = \left(\frac{\delta \alpha}{\delta(\mu)}\right) * \left(\frac{d\mu}{dx}\right) * \left(\frac{1}{\mu}\right)^2$$

Now for determining $\left(\frac{\delta \alpha}{\delta(\mu)}\right)$. First input is BMI and following which symptoms are fed then a graph is plotted between beta and μ and the slope is determined from the graph itself. So we make an approximation when $\mu = 1$ we have α_{crit} so actually $\left(\frac{\delta \alpha}{\delta(\mu)}\right)$ is $\alpha_{crit}/1$ as it is the slope of α vs μ, but we plotted the graph between β and μ so we do the following calculations

$$\alpha = \frac{1}{\beta - 1}$$

Or,

$$\beta = \frac{1 + \alpha}{\alpha}$$

Or, $\left(\frac{\delta\alpha}{\delta(\mu)}\right) = \left(\frac{\delta\alpha}{\delta(\beta)}\right)\left(\frac{\delta\beta}{\delta(\mu)}\right)$ by chain rule.

$$\left(\frac{\delta\alpha}{\delta(\beta)}\right) = -\frac{1}{(\beta - 1)^2}$$

For the persons considered (μ) parameters are not available only their age group and their BMI are known from the statistical data we obtained [3]. Assuming they are healthy persons β can be calculated as $\beta_{calculated} = BMI/(\text{mean of age group considered})$ and consider that our $\beta_{calculated}$ is valid for $\mu = 0$ that is for healthy population showing no symptom of the disease but putting the value of $\mu = 0$ in the equations gives us undefined. So we use the following trick

$$\left(\frac{dy}{dx}\right)_{(x_1, y_1)} = \frac{y_1}{x_1}$$

Or, $\frac{dy}{d(x+1)} = \frac{y_1 + c}{x_1 + 1}$. (Replacing x by x + 1) [Since y also changes as x changes we assume y changes by c].

So the above was algebraic manipulations using valid rules of calculus so

$$\frac{\delta\beta}{\delta(1 + \mu)} = \left(\frac{\beta_{calculated} + c}{1 + 0}\right)$$

Or, $\frac{\delta(\mu + 1)}{\delta(\beta)} = \frac{1}{\beta_{calculated} + c}$

Or, $\frac{\delta(\mu)}{\delta(\beta)} = \frac{1}{\beta_{calculated} + c}$

Or, $\frac{\delta(\beta)}{\delta(\mu)} = \beta_{calculated} + c$

which is the slope at the required point and we use this slope only. Since we did not have the statistical data relating beta and μ so we neglect c in the light of our argument that since μ is a logistic function its value lies between zero and one and β is usually large so a small change in β will cause a very small change in μ.

We notice that $1/d\alpha$ is actually a fraction hence we can well assume that our probability is a function of these values. Now consider the tailors expansion of our fuzzy membership function:

$$\mu = \left(1 + \frac{x^2}{(x-5)^2} - 1\right)^2$$

as $e^{-x} \simeq (1-x)$

or, $\mu \simeq \frac{x^4}{(x-5)^4}$

Therefore, $\frac{d\mu}{dx} = \frac{d}{dx}\left(\frac{x^4}{(x-5)^4}\right)$

which can be easily determined. So our $d\alpha$ is easily calculated. The physical interpretation of $d\alpha$ is that as its value increases the patient is more likely to suffer from the disease and this concept helps in eliminating any placebo. Suppose the person is healthy but is saying that he has a symptom called x say, but his BMI would remain normal hence if there is any placebo then it can be easily estimated. It is a natural observation that a patient sometimes tells a doctor those symptoms which he/she does not have because the patient "thinks" that he/she has the symptom which is only a placebo that only experienced doctors are able to identify. This approach works best for most of the diseases.

3.3 Gini Coefficient and Determining the Primitive Health of a Sampled Population

Gini coefficient [6] is a valid measure of concentration that is determined from Lorenz curve and gives 0 when all observations are evenly distributed (i.e., we have zero concentration) and 1 when we have extreme concentration. It is defined mathematically as:

$$G = 1 - \frac{1}{n}\sum_{i=1}^{n}(v_{i-1} + v_i)$$

Where $v_i = (\sum_{j=1}^{i} x_j)/(\sum_{j=1}^{n} x_j)$

$$u_i = \frac{i}{n}$$

Where $i = 0, \ldots\ldots, n$

But for doing this the data is ordered $0 < x_1 < x_2 < \cdots < x_n$.

Where x is the observation. Taking v along y axis and u along x axis and plotting in the third quadrant we get Lorentz curve.

Now G can be a good measure of the degree of randomness. Now consider that we sampled a group of population for BMI and BMI is evenly distributed then we can say that the population as a whole is healthy. Now consider another population where the BMI is a bit different for a group that is there is some concentration or in simple words BMI is large for a particular group of the sampled population then we can definitely say that some part of the population is suffering from disease. Which part we will determine from further calculations but this primitive approach helps to filter out those groups that have disease and those that do not. This greatly removes the burden of calculation.

When G = 1 then at least some persons in the population does have the disease. Now let us consider our population, we used the package in R. The BMI values were stored in the vector called BMI (Fig. 5).

Fig. 5. Calculation of GINI coefficient for our sampled population, with the input Body mass index values for males aged 20 and over.

Since the value of Gini coefficient is very small hence we are justified that our sampled population [7] is a healthy one. This is also shown by the Lorentz curve [8] (Fig. 6).

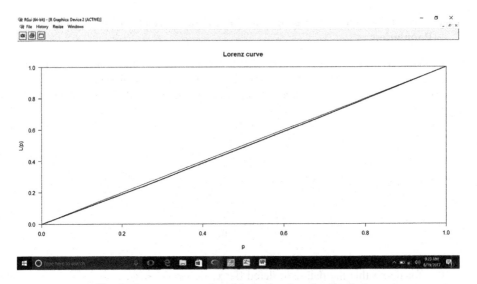

Fig. 6. Lorentz curve plotted in R showing the distribution

We first took our data and considered the mean age group i.e., suppose the age group considered was 20 to 29 years we took the mean i.e. 24.5 to be the age for that BMI hence we tried a linear regression model here is the result (Fig. 7):

Here we get the relationship of the form:

$$\text{mean BMI} = (20.3 \pm 3.2) + (0.06 \pm 0.03) * \text{age} + (0.006 \pm 0.002) \\ * (\text{no of persons examined})$$

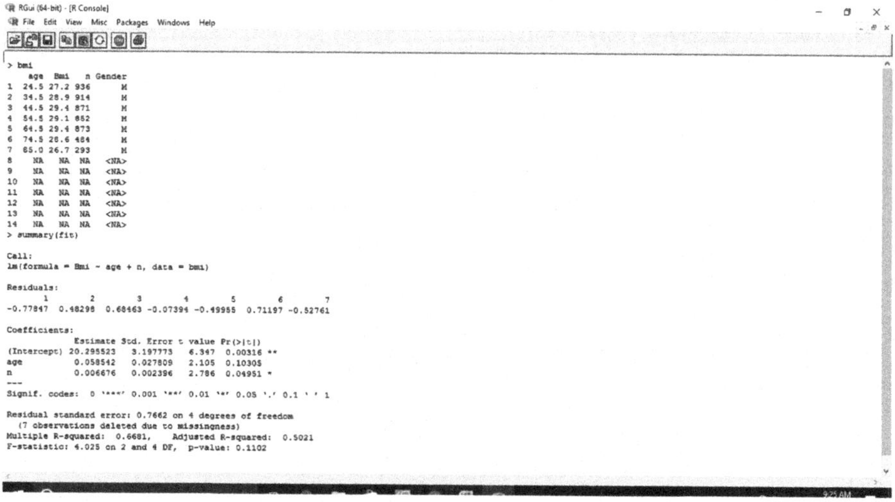

Fig. 7. Consider our data that we collected

But consider the value of multiple R-squaredvalue it is 66.81% indicating that the model accounts for 66.81% of the variance in mean BMI value (Fig. 8).

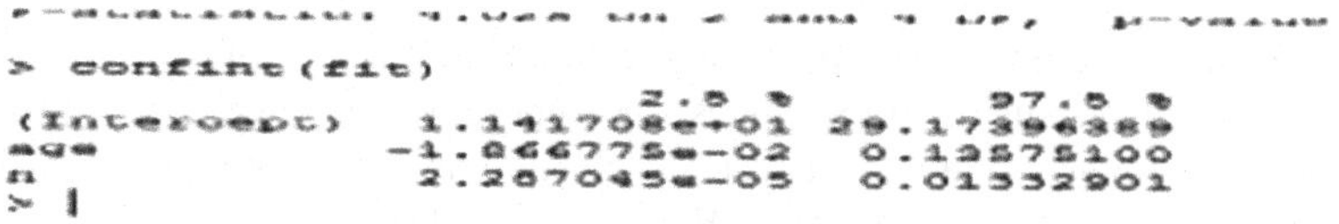

Fig. 8. The confidence of our Model

It gives us whether we can trust this model or not as we can see from the above figure that when n lies in the interval $[2.3 * 10^{-5}, 0.01]$ we can be 95% confident on our results. Hence we can say outside this interval we can be 60 to 70% sure of our model. Hence we modify our model (Fig. 9).

As we can see what we did is we used square of the age to approximate our data here the value of multiple R-squared [9] is 93.9% indicating that this model accounts for 93.9% of the variance in Mean BMI value.

Hence our Modified formula is:

$$\text{mean BMI} = (21.9 \pm 1.63) + (0.29 \pm 0.06) * \text{age} - (0.0028 \pm 0.0008) * (\text{age}^2)$$
$$- (0.00012 \pm 0.002) * (\text{no of persons examined})$$

Fig. 9. Showing our modified regression model

Hence we got our modified model of BMI and other parameters. The p value [10] for the variable n is >0.5 and hence this value is rejected and our final formula is:

$$\text{mean BMI} = (21.9 \pm 1.63) + (0.29 \pm 0.06) * \text{age} - (0.0028 \pm 0.0008) * (\text{age}^2)$$

The spread LevelPlot ()function in R creates a scatter plot of the absolute standardized Residuals versus the fitted values, and superimposes a line of best fit. For this we imported the library called car. This package is not available in the base package of R so we needed to install it separately (Figs. 10 and 11).

The ncvTest ()function produces a score test of the hypothesis of constant error variance against the alternative that the error variance changes with the level of the fitted values. A significant result suggests heteroscedasticity non-constant errorvariance.

So ultimately we see that upto certain extent our regression model is OK. As we have less amount of data. This is the maximum we can reach but thinking intuitively we see that mean BMI is nearly constant and changes a little with age. Now this is a fact that we can observe even from the common sense that for people aged more than 20 their BMI varies little with age (in our model nearly 0.3%). Hence we can say that our model is consistent with observation. So we are justified using this formula (Fig. 12).

$$\beta = \frac{\text{BMI}}{\text{age}} = \frac{21.9 \pm 1.63}{\text{age}} + (0.29 \pm 0.06) - (0.0028 \pm 0.0008) * \text{age}$$

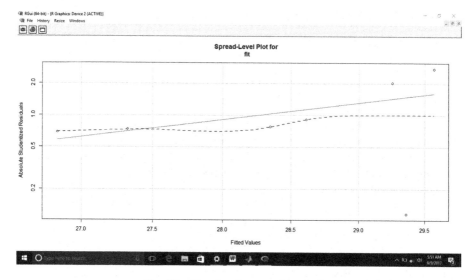

Fig. 10. Showing the spread level plot.

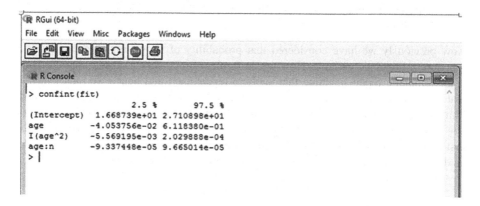

Fig. 11. Results of ncvTest(fit)

Fig. 12. Showing the confidence of our improved model.

3.4   Final Probability of the Disease from Our Bayesian-Network

Finally by the theorem of total probability we calculate the probability of disease as:

$$P(D) = \sum_{i=1}^{n} P(D|s_i, A) * P(s_i, A)$$

Now we know from the basic rules of calculus that $P(A|B)$ is defined as the probability of happening of the event A provided B has already happened.

Now we can consider that when si and A have already happened then we are absolutely sure that the Disease had actually happened. So $P(D|s_i, A) = 1$ always. So, our equation finally becomes:

$$P(D) = \sum_{i=1}^{n} P(s_i, A)$$

Or, $P(D) = \sum_{i=1}^{n} P(s_i) * P(A)$
As $P(si, A) = P(si \text{ and } A)$
Which we have already determined.

$$P(D) = \sum_{i=1}^{n} \mu_i(x) * P(A)$$

Where P(A) is the absolute value of the reliability which is calculated.

But before implementing this in MATLAB we would want to filter the data using R.

3.5   Change of Fuzzy Function with Time Our New Modified Fuzzy Function

Now previously we have considered that probability of happening of a disease as a function of linguistic variable. Now we do further refinements. Consider that our body is an automatic repair machine that tends to repair itself and hence we may consider that body recovers from the disease. Thus our membership also changes with time. Thus our membership function is a function of x and t. Now a patient may visit a doctor any number of times so our counting is t = 0 when the patient visits the doctor for the first time and then it we take the measure of time the next time he visits a doctor. So, let us do analysis in 3D plane containing three variables x, t & μ (Fig. 13).

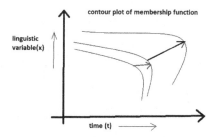

Fig. 13. A typical example of a contour plot of membership function μ (just a hypothetical example)

Consider an example of contour plot of the membership function we want to derive an equation for our new membership function. We notice that our membership function should be such that it decreases with time or equivalently speaking: $M = \int \nabla\mu * dx * dt$

We call M as irrecovery function the symbol of integration in this case is actual integration.

Should have some finite value. Let us see what this integral means. See that if μ remains constant or changes very slightly with change in x and t. Then the gradient of μ should be very large as can be visualized from the contour plot, Gradient is represented by the arrows which is normal to the curve. Consider the first curve as $\mu = \mu_1$, second curve as $\mu = \mu_2$, and third curve as $\mu = \mu_3$, such that $\mu_1 < \mu_2 < \mu_3$.

Case1:

As can be seen from the black arrow its length is maximum as we can see that for the third curve for large value of x and t we get our μ.

Let us suppose $\mu_1 = 0.1, \mu_2 = 0.2, \mu_3 = 0.3$ so it is clear that for large change in (x, t) we get a small change from μ_2 to μ_3 so μ remains approximately constant with time, therefore, we have large gradient.

Case2:

Consider the red arrow its magnitude is small as for small change in (x, t) we get a large change from μ_1 to μ_2 so μ changes rapidly with our independent variables. And we see for this case the gradient is small.

The derivation of our equation:

Now see that as M increases within a finite boundary the volume under the μ also increases. Now φ is a scalar constant that is different for different persons. Now we can clearly see that M is directly proportional to the weighted volume under the surface. We say weighted as the dependence on volume depends on a particular person. Suppose a person A has less amount of μ value as compared to the person B. So we can say that their M values will be different so as their dependence on the volume. But φ is constant for that particular person.

K is the proportionality constant.

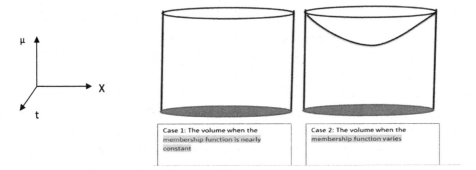

Fig. 14. Showing the dependence of volume on the variation of membership function by imagining a cylindrical volume whose top surface is the function surface and the bottomplane is the (x, t) plane we expect the value of membership function to decrease with time or upon increase it increase showing direct proportionality relationship.

As per the Fig. 14 as the value of the M increases or decreases accordingly as the weighted volume increases or decreases.

$$\left(\iint \nabla\mu * ds\right) \propto \left(\iiint \Phi \, dv\right)$$

$$\iint \nabla\mu * ds = k * \iiint \Phi \, dv$$

Or, $\int \nabla . (\nabla\mu) \, dv = k * \int \Phi \, dv$ by Gauss's divergence theorem
Or, $\nabla^2\mu = k * \Phi$
with the initial conditions:

$$\mu(5,0) = 1$$
$$\mu(0,0) = 0$$
$$\lim_{t\to\infty} \mu(x,t) = \infty$$

Hence we derived our partial differential equation of the membership function.

3.6   Solution of Our Partial Differential Equation

Now this is a non-homogeneous equation we convert it to homogeneous Form by assuming a substitution of the form $\mu(x,t) = f(x,t) + \frac{1}{2} * k * \Phi * x^2$
So, the equation becomes: $\nabla^2 f = 0$
Firstly we found f then we found our μ. Now this was easy as the above equation is just Laplace equation which can be solved by the separation of variables

Our derived equation is: $\mu(x,t) = \frac{1 - \frac{25k\Phi}{2}}{\sin(5p)} * \sin(px) * e^{pt} + \frac{1}{2}k\Phi x^2$

which satisfies all our equations and the boundary condition. We see the physical interpretation of this consider in the paper [12]. Here they link probability with membership function. Consider each time the patient visits the doctor means that the patient has not recovered from the disease. Hence this formula accurately describes this situation. Output:

Now the value of radial basis function lies between 0 and 1 and the value of the membership function also lies between 0 and 1. So ultimately, the product of these two functions should lie between 0 and 1. On the basis of this training and input data can be designed. Here is the simplified version of the algorithm without incorporating the Bayesian framework as discussed. Based on this algorithm we develop proper MATLAB codes.

Algorithm without Bayesian network:

1. for($i = 1$ to n)
    a. Display "enter your age";
    b. age $\leftarrow$ (age in years);
    c. A(i, 0) $\leftarrow$ age
    d. % calculate BMI for a single patient %
    e. $BMI(i, 0) \leftarrow (21.9 + 1.63) + (0.29 + 0.06) * age - (0.0028 + 0.0008) * (age^2)$;
    f. end
2. % now calculate the Gini coefficient by developing an entire algorithm or in our case we used R to calculate.
3. G $\leftarrow$ (enter the Gini coefficient)
4. For($i = 1$ to n)
    a. Input1(i, 0) $\leftarrow$ {BMI(i, 0) * (1 − G) * A(i, 0)};
    b. Train1(i, 0) $\leftarrow$ {1};
    c. end
5. % now we declare our network
6. Net1 $\leftarrow$ newrb(Input1, Train1, 0.5)
7. % where 0.5 is spread after this we take samples.
8. For($i = 1$ to n)
    a. P1 $\leftarrow$ (enter the age);
    b. $P2 \leftarrow (21.9 + 1.63) + (0.29 + 0.06) * P1 - (0.0028 + 0.0008) * (P1^2)$;
    c. P3 $\leftarrow$ G;
    d. P = {P1 * P2 * P3};
    e. R = sim(Net1, P);
    f. end
9. %Next we calculate the μ
10. Symptom = {'symptom1', 'symptom2', 'symptom3'};
11. % we consider in this case we have 3 symptoms
12. For($i = 1$ to n)
    a. Display "how much do you feel, symptom(i, 0)"
    b. Display "enter 5 if **extreme**"

c. Display "enter 4 if **very much**"
d. Display "enter 3 if **moderate**"
e. Display "enter 2 if **somewhat**"
f. Display "enter 1 if **a little bit**"
g. Display "enter 0 if **Not at all**"
h. x ← (enter the value);
i. p ← 0.5
j. k ← 1
k. Φ ← 1

l. $\text{meu}(i, 0) \leftarrow \dfrac{1 - \frac{25k\Phi}{2}}{\sin(5p)} * \sin(px) * e^{pt} + \frac{1}{2} k\Phi x^2$

m. end
13. % now we generate a perceptron
14. Input2 = {1, 1, 1, 1, 0.4, 0.3, 0.2, 0.1, 0, 0.6, 0.7, 0.8, 0.9};
15. Train2 = {1, 1, 1, 1, 0, 0, 0, 0, 0, 1, 1, 1, 1}
16. U ← newp(Input2, Train2)
17. % finally we feed our samples
18. For(i = 1 to n)
  a. L ← meu * R;
  b. Result ← sim(U, L)
  c. If(Result == 1)
    i. Display "The person has the disease with the probability"
    ii. Display "meu"
    iii. End
  d. Else
    i. Display "The person is healthy"
    ii. End
19. % now we calculate our alpha
20. For(i = 1 to n)
  a. $\text{Alpha}(i, 0) \leftarrow \dfrac{1}{\frac{BMI}{age} - 1}$
  b. T(i, 0) = {1}
  c. end
21. % we note that these alpha are for healthy persons so these acts as input for our perceptron and should produce 1
22. % we generate perceptron network to determine the presence of placebo
23. NPlacebo ← newp(Alpha, T)
24. % so if for any unknown alpha it produces 1 then there is no placebo else we say there is a placebo.

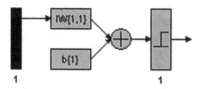

Fig. 15. Showing our perceptron generatedin MATLAB.

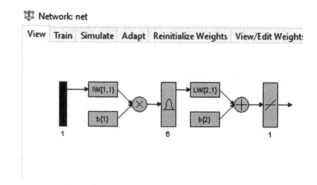

Fig. 16. Showing our perceptron generatedin MATLAB.

4 Results

Disease has become a great problem for the mankind and diagnosing it for poor has become even more difficult (Fig. 15). We know that because of these very reason lots of diseases that can be cured very easily is becoming a nightmare for a certain fraction of civilians. Doctors charge a hefty amount of fees from poor unable to afford the fees they rush towards the jaws of death. Hence our paper is an attempt to take a step forward in the way the diagnosis of disease is done (Fig. 16). In an interesting paper compared logistic regression model with the prediction of artificial Neural Network [11]. They used SPSS for the regression analysis. Whereas we consider linear regression and Gini coefficient to filter the population or sample that is to be fed to the neural network and then finally we get our results we use R and MATLAB for this purpose. In this way we combine the capacity of both. Now from the paper by [12], we can already see the connection of fuzzy logic with probability. From the paper [13], we get a method to measure the overall performance of our software as:

$$\text{classification accuracy} = \frac{1}{|N|} \sum_{i=1}^{|N|} \text{assess}(n_i)$$

$$\text{assess}(n) = \begin{cases} 1, & \text{if classify}(n) \\ 0, & \text{otherwise} \end{cases}$$

Classify (n) returns the classification of n calculated with neural network. i.e., in Layman's term if our system is able to classify we denote it as 1 but now to adjust to our need as we use probability for our classification and call it as modified classification accuracy.

$$\text{assess}(n) = \mu$$

Where μ is our time dependent fuzzy logic function as it is our measure of the probability of occurrence of the disease and our assess(n) becomes 1 when we are absolutely able to categorize that the patient has the disease and is 0 when according to our software does not classify the disease. Now N was the set of data to be classified and our N would be much smaller as we had filtered the population based on the Gini coefficient. As we consider only that fraction of population whose statistical concentration is more? Hence finally the things become:

$$\text{modified classification accuracy} = \frac{1}{|N|} \sum_{i=1}^{N} \text{total assess}(n_i)$$

$$\text{total assess}(n_i) = \frac{1}{\iint_{x=0,t=0}^{x=m,t=n} dxdt} \int_{x=0,t=0}^{x=m,t=n} \mu_i dxdt$$

We note that it is ordinary integration not zadeh's notation of fuzzy sets.

Where m = the value of the linguistic variable for the patient, n = time gap for second visit, so if it is the first visit we take t = 0. So we have $\mu 1$ that is our actual probability of observation and $\mu = 0$ is the case when our software tells the person does not have the disease. Thinking from a different perspective it is possible that our patient may not have provided the actual input. Considering the placebo effect, a patient may think that he is suffering from a symptom that is actually not there so the linguistic variable may not be 100% true representation of his condition. Hence we consider the average of the membership function for assessment. But in the software we just use the original μ to make things simple.

5   Conclusion

This study concludes on the fact that this, methodology could be successfully applied in any medical diagnosis field. Our intelligent system can adapt itself and is flexible in the sense that changing conditions such as age of the person, the population type etc. We can detect any symptoms not only that it is more reliable than an ordinary doctor as sometimes even eminent doctors are at difficulty in solving the problems the probabilistic reasoning is highly useful in the sense that it gives us the confidence to our results this is a big difference that we make in this field. "A doctor increases their income but does not think about the poor, whereas an engineer on the other hand gains benefits by increasing the prosperity of a country". Therefore, our works intelligently support the quote to serve the nation for humankind in the area of medical diagnosis to some extent. In addition, the world is becoming data oriented where the entire population matters rather than individual. Thus, in future work various methods of data analytics could encapsulate with this work for father enhancement.

References

1. Das, S., Biswas, S., Paul, A., Dey, A.: AI doctor: an intelligent approach for medical diagnosis. In: Bhattacharyya, S., Sen, S., Dutta, M., Biswas, P., Chattopadhyay, H. (eds.) Industry Interactive Innovations in Science, Engineering and Technology. LNNS, vol. 11, pp. 173–183. Springer, Singapore (2018). https://doi.org/10.1007/978-981-10-3953-9_17

2. Adebayo, A.O., Fatunke, M., Nwankwo, U., Odiete, O.G.: The design and creation of a malaria diagnosing expert system. School of Computing and Engineering Sciences, Babcock University, P.M.B.21244 Ikeja, Lagos, Nigeria. https://ijact.in/index.php/ijact/article/download/338/288

3. https://www.springerprofessional.de/development-of-two-artificial-neural-network-m

4. Beheshti, Z., Shamsuddin, S.M.H., Beheshti, E., Yuhaniz, S.S.: Enhancement of artificial neural network learning using centripetal accelerated particle swarm optimization for medical diseases diagnosis. Soft. Comput. 18(11), 2253–2270 (2014). https://doi.org/10.1007/s00500-013-1198-0

5. Yacout, S.: Logical Analysis of Maintenance and Performance Data of Physical Assets, ID34. 978-1-4577-1851-9/12/$26.00 ©2012 IEEE (2012)

6. Gini coefficient: Wikipedia, The Free Encyclopedia, 1 September 2017. https://en.wikipedia.org/w/index.php?title=Gini_coefficient&oldid=798388811. Accessed 9 Sept 2017

7. Fryar, C.D., Gu, Q., Ogden, C.L., Flegal, K.M.: Anthropometric reference data for children and adults: United States, 2011–2014. National Center for HealthStatistics. Vital Health Stat. 3(39) (2016). https://www.cdc.gov/nchs/data/series/sr_03/sr03_039.pdf

8. Lorenz Curve: Wikipedia, The Free Encyclopedia, 17 July 2017. https://en.wikipedia.org/w/index.php?title=Lorenz_curve&oldid=790975050. Accessed 9 Sept 2017

9. Coefficient of Determination: Wikipedia, The Free Encyclopedia, 6 September 2017. https://en.wikipedia.org/w/index.php?title=Coefficient_of_determination&oldid=799285669. Accessed 9 Sept 2017

10. P-value: Wikipedia, The Free Encyclopedia. https://en.wikipedia.org/w/index.php?title=P-value&oldid=799574149. Accessed 9 Sept 2017

11. Sakai, S., Kobayashi, K., Toyabe, S.I., Mandai, N., Kanda, T., Akazawa, K.: Comparison of the levels of accuracy of an artificial neural network model and a logistic regression model for the diagnosis of acute appendicitis (n.d.). https://doi.org/10.1007/s10916-007-9077-9

12. Das, S., Sanyal, M., Datta, D., Biswas, A.: AISLDr: artificial intelligent self-learning doctor. In: Bhateja, V., Coello Coello, C.A., Satapathy, S.C., Pattnaik, P.K. (eds.) Intelligent Engineering Informatics. AISC, vol. 695, pp. 79–90. Springer, Singapore (2018). https://doi.org/10.1007/978-981-10-7566-7_9

13. Delen, D., Walker, G., Kadam, A.: Predicting breast cancer survivability: a comparison of three data mining methods. Artif. intell. Med. June 2005. https://www.ncbi.nlm.nih.gov/pubmed/15894176

Social Computing

A Scheme of PV Cell Operated BLDC Motor to Drive Fans and Pumps in Rural Areas

Santanu Mondal[1(✉)] and Madhurima Chattopadhyay[2]

[1] Electronics and Instrumentation Engineering,
Techno India, Salt Lake, Kolkata 700091, India
santanu_aecl1984@yahoo.co.in
[2] Applied Electronics and Instrumentation Engineering,
Heritage Institute of Technology, Kolkata 700107, India
madhurima.chattopadhyay@heritageit.edu

Abstract. This paper describes the development of a schematic model for a photovoltaic (PV) panel fed sensorless drive of permanent magnet brushless DC motor for improvement in power utilization as substitute of conventional motors. In general, photovoltaic based systems require a few converters (AC-DC/DC-AC) for rural appliances which produce a power loss of around 20–30% for each. In order to drive BLDC motors, one can easily avoid this conversion loss by directly connecting the BLDC motor to the DC bus form the PV panel. Before real time implementation, we studied the schematic system through mathematical expressions in MATLAB/Simulink based platform in which, a simulation model of photovoltaic array has been designed with rated I-V characteristics. Hence, the power obtained from the PV panel is supplied to BLDC motor drive through proper circuitry which incorporating three phase inverter. The sensorless drive for the BLDC motor uses d-q model for rotor position estimation and the simulation work assumes a normal irradiance of 1000 W/m^2. In the implemented hardware, a battery is placed in between solar panel and the motor drive in order to maintain constant supply. The main objective of the proposed work is to drive a BLDC motor operated fan/pump in rural areas through solar power by eliminating unwanted conversion loss as well as shock hazards.

Keywords: Sensorless BLDC motor · Capacity factor · SPWM
Photovoltaic

1 Introduction

Photovoltaic energy is a clean energy, with a long service life and high reliability. Thus, it can be considered as one of the most sustainable renewable energies [1]. It is significant that direct current (DC) is generated from PV cell and this is always advantageous to circulate the energy as it is. Most of the modern high end house hold appliances require AC-DC converter for functioning. Therefore, if we try to drive these equipment's with solar power, two sets of such converters are essential which introduces power loss at each conversion stage, shown in Fig. 1. In order to sustain our ac supply with a solar power back up, a huge loss will be generated from the converter end

© Springer Nature Singapore Pte Ltd. 2018
J. K. Mandal and D. Sinha (Eds.): CSI 2017, CCIS 836, pp. 355–368, 2018.
https://doi.org/10.1007/978-981-13-1343-1_30

which sometimes is even higher than the energy produced from PV panel [2–4]. The overall system efficiency can only improve if we minimize these losses by incorporating DC devices with DC micro-grid. Moreover, in most of the solar powered rural areas, people have to be satisfied with solar lantern/LED lights as normal PV panel cannot operate market available 60–100 W ceiling fan. But most of the appliances used in day to day life like mobile charger, LED TV, Laptops etc. can make use of DC source directly generated from solar power. Through this present study, we are trying to provide comfort to these people by using power efficient BLDC [3] motor based fans. This solution not only brings well-being to the poor villagers but also introduces safety with comparatively low maintenance.

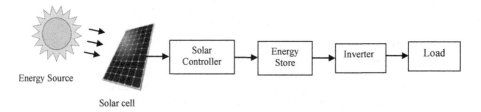

Fig. 1. Schematic diagram of grid system

Moreover, the sensorless commutation of BLDC motor commences with less heating along with less maintenance compared to sensored one [4, 5]. Thus makes the drive temperature independent energy efficient system as in sensored, hall sensors deteriorates [9, 10] the performance beyond certain temperature. In general, pulse width modulation (PWM) technique is common for drives that operate at moderate rotational speed applications. Here to imply this in variable speed application for low power consumption SPWM is more competent to cater the purpose.

This work presents a photovoltaic cell energized sensorless BLDC motor drive. The sensorless drive along with the commutation technique is discussed in Sect. 1 and followed by the mathematical modelling of the solar panel drive system in Sect. 2. The real time implementation of PV cell based BLDC drive is presented in Sect. 3. Section 4 presents the output results of the hardware and simulation model. Finally conclusion is given by Sect. 5 with the essence of the outcomes from the real time implementation of the proposed scheme.

2   PV Panel Fed BLDC Motor Drive

This development considers a 3-phase, star connected BLDC motor and PV panel. Figure 2 shows the block diagram of BLDC motor with sensorless drive using PV panel. This model uses the SPWM (Sinusoidal Pulse Width Modulation Method) commutation technique by assuming d-q model of the BLDC motor. We have also considered Probability Density Function (PDF) of PV Panel, capacity factor and model of Energy Storage.

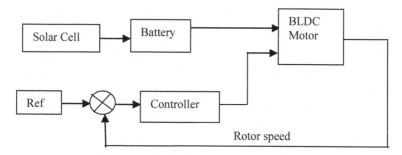

Fig. 2. Block diagram of sensorless BLDC Motor with PV panel

2.1 Modeling of BLDC Drive Using Sinusoidal Pulse Width Modulation Method

In SPWM, a sinusoidal reference waveform is compared with a triangular carrier waveform to generate gate pulses for switching of inverter shown in Fig. 3 [11]. The SPWM is the most extensively used PWM control method due to ease of performance, lower harmonic output and less switching losses. In this method, a high frequency triangular carrier signal is compared with a low frequency sinusoidal modulating signal in an analog or logic comparator device. The frequency of line voltage at the inverter output depends on frequency of modulating sinusoidal signal [12].

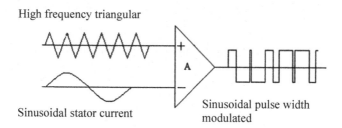

Fig. 3. Principle of SPWM generation

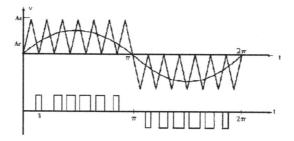

Fig. 4. Sinusoidal PWM generation technique

Basically, each switch is controlled by comparing a sinusoidal reference wave with a triangular carrier wave. The switching state is changed when the sine waveform intersects the triangular waveform [13]. The fundamental frequency of the output is the same as the reference wave, and the amplitude of the output is determined by relative amplitudes of the reference (sinusoidal) and carrier waves (triangular). A high switching frequency leads to a better filtered sinusoidal output waveform.

The sinusoidal commutation is more precise than trapezoidal because it controls the position of rotor continuously. Therefore, it is necessary to apply a sinusoidal current, 120° out of phase with each other, to each of the motor winding [13]. Hence the resulting current vector will be in phase with the rotor position and a more precise torque will be obtained, free from the typical ripple of sinusoidal switching which is described by Fig. 4. Clark transformation is used to convert parameters from a-b-c axis to alpha beta axis.

$$\begin{bmatrix} V_\alpha \\ V_\beta \end{bmatrix} = 2/3 \begin{bmatrix} 1 & -1/2 & -1/2 \\ 0 & \sqrt{3/2} & -\sqrt{3/2} \end{bmatrix} \begin{bmatrix} V_a \\ V_b \\ V_c \end{bmatrix} \tag{1}$$

It converts fixed reference frame to rotating reference frame.

$$\begin{bmatrix} V_d \\ V_q \end{bmatrix} = \begin{bmatrix} \cos\Phi & \sin\Phi \\ -\sin\Phi & \cos\Phi \end{bmatrix} \begin{bmatrix} V_\alpha \\ V_\beta \end{bmatrix} \tag{2}$$

$$\begin{bmatrix} V_d \\ V_q \end{bmatrix} = 2/3 \begin{bmatrix} \cos\Phi & \cos(\Phi-\gamma) & \cos(\Phi+\gamma) \\ -\sin\Phi & -\sin(\Phi-\gamma) & -\sin(\Phi+\gamma) \end{bmatrix} \begin{bmatrix} V_a \\ V_b \\ V_c \end{bmatrix} \tag{3}$$

Where, γ is $2 * \pi/3$ and Φ is rotor angle or angle between alpha-beta axis and d-q axis. The BLDC control block is given by q-axis control, d-axis control and torque speed control. The q-axis and d-axis control block is given by Eqs. 4 and 5 respectively.

$$\frac{1}{sL_d} = V_q - (i_{d.}\omega_e L_d) - \omega_e Y_{af} - 1.4i_q \tag{4}$$

$$\frac{1}{sL_d} = V_q - (i_{q.}\omega_e)L_q) - i_d R \tag{5}$$

Torque speed control block is given by Eqs. 6 and 7

$$T_e = i_q Y_{af} + (L_d - L_q)(I_d - I_q) \tag{6}$$

$$T_e - T_m - \left(\frac{2B}{P}\right)\omega_e = P\theta/J_s \tag{7}$$

Where, L_q and L_d is inductance, R is stator resistance, Y_{af} is rotor flux constant, J is moment of inertia, B is friction vicious gain, P is number of poles. Inverse Clark and Park transformation is implemented from equation to get three phase stator current from d-q axis.

$$\begin{bmatrix} I_\alpha \\ I_\beta \end{bmatrix} = 2/3 \begin{bmatrix} \cos\Phi & -\sin\Phi \\ \sin\Phi & \cos\Phi \end{bmatrix} \begin{bmatrix} I_d \\ I_q \end{bmatrix} \tag{8}$$

$$\begin{bmatrix} I_a \\ I_b \\ I_c \end{bmatrix} = \begin{bmatrix} 1 & 0 \\ -1/2 & \sqrt{3}/2 \\ -1/2 & -\sqrt{3}/2 \end{bmatrix} \begin{bmatrix} I_\alpha \\ I_\beta \end{bmatrix} \tag{9}$$

$$\begin{bmatrix} I_a \\ I_b \\ I_c \end{bmatrix} = \begin{bmatrix} \cos\Phi & -\sin\Phi \\ \cos(\Phi-\gamma) & -\sin(\Phi-\gamma) \\ \cos(\Phi+\gamma) & -\sin(\Phi+\gamma) \end{bmatrix} \begin{bmatrix} I_d \\ I_q \end{bmatrix} \tag{10}$$

2.2 Modeling of the PV Panel

A PV panel converts sunlight to direct current electricity and usually consisting of two layers of silicon (semi-conductor material) and a separation layer, are wired together and assembled into panels or modules. When the cells are bare to sunlight, photons from the sun interact with electrons in the upper silicon layer. The equivalent circuit of a solar cell is shown in Fig. 5. Typically a solar cell can be modelled by a current source and an inverted diode connected in parallel to it.

Applying Kirchhoff's current law and current will obtain

$$I = I_{ph} - I_d - I_p \tag{11}$$

$$I_{ph} = \frac{G}{G_{ref}}(I_{ph,ref} + \mu_{sc}.\Delta T) \tag{12}$$

$$I_d = I_0\left[\exp\left(\frac{V+I.R_s}{a}\right) - 1\right] \tag{13}$$

$$I_0 = DT_c^3 exp\left(\frac{-q\epsilon_g}{A.K}\right) \tag{14}$$

$$I_p = \frac{V+R_s I}{R_p} \tag{15}$$

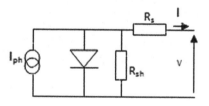

Fig. 5. Equivalent circuit of a solar cell

Where $\mathbf{I_{ph}}$ is the photocurrent, $\mathbf{I_d}$ is the diode current, $\mathbf{I_p}$ is the leak current. G is the irradiance, $\mathbf{G_{ref}}$ is the irradiance at standard test condition, **a** is the modified ideality factor, $\Delta T = T_c - T_{c,ref}$, T_c is the actual cell temperature(K), $T_{c,ref}$ is the standard test condition. μ_{sc} is the coefficient temperature of short circuit current and $I_{ph,ref}$ is the photo current at STC.

The present simulation work is done using MATLAB/Simulink. In Table 1 shows the Capacity Factor for the month of April & July, 2016 and Table 2 shows the specifications of BLDC motor and PV panel. The complete simulation model of the photovoltaic based sensorless BLDC motor is shown in Figs. 6, 7 and 8. Each subsystem is created according to the modelling equations.

2.3 PV Panel Probability Density Function

The irradiance of the sunlight varies with weather. Therefore, consideration of the average radiation is inadequate to predict the influence of clouds on power generation. So, it is very necessary to explain the solar radiation in statistical way. To describe the random occurrence of solar irradiance, the irradiance-probability density function is necessary. Three most common probability density functions are used. These are Lognormal, Beta and Weibull.

The average power output of photovoltaic panel can be calculated by the following equations

$$P_a = \int P(S)f(s)ds \tag{16}$$

$$P(S) = V(S)I(S) \tag{17}$$

where $f(S)$ is the function of probability density and $P(S)$ is the power of the PV panel.

2.4 Determination of Capacity Factor

The probability approach is used to determine the performance and the power generation of the photovoltaic panel. There are many different types of PV panels commercially available in the market. It is necessary to choose panel that is suitable for a particular location [6]. Apart from of the panel size, while designing a photovoltaic system, the choice of the PV panel is based on the comparison of the capacity factor in different months for the considered panel. The capacity factor is the ratio of average power output to rated power of the PV panel. The capacity factor of the said panel is determined and the expression is given by Eq. 18.

$$CF = 1/P_r \int P(S)f(s)ds \tag{18}$$

Table 1. Capacity factor for the month of April & July, 2016

Month	Time			
	10 a.m.	12 p.m.	2 p.m.	4 p.m.
April	0.34	0.54	0.49	0.13
July	0.26	0.56	0.48	0.22

2.5 Energy Storage Model

In this current research, we have used three cell Li-Poly battery as an energy storage device in between the solar cell and motor. It will be essential to run the motor at night in absence of sun light. The storage capacity of the battery as well as energy consumed by a specified motor will decide how long (hours) the motor will be operating in rated speed. Again during summer, the generated energy is excess of the load demand provided the state of charge does not exceed the battery capacity and also shown higher energy outputs. This is a superior matching between the generation and demand [8].

In a system with a large size battery and small size panel will result in slower charge and discharge rates in the batteries. Most of the converted energy will be stored in battery when the instantaneous generation is in excess of the load, therefore, the energy loss will be low and the frequent loss of load due to the instantaneous variation can be reduced. The computation of the optimum number of photovoltaic panels and batteries was based on Loss of Power Supply Probability (LPSP) concept [7] and the economy of the system. Power Supply Probability Loss can be distinct as the average long-term fraction of the load and also defined as:

$$LPSP = Prob.\{E_b(t) \leq E_{bmin}(t)\}$$

Where, $E_b(t)$ is the stored energy in batteries & $E_{b\,min}(t)$ is the minimum allowable energy level.

The generated energy by the PV panel can be expressed with time t as:

$$E(t) = N_p E_p(t)$$

Where N_p is the PV module number and $E_p(t)$ is the generated energy by PV module.

3 Real Time Implementation

The following section postulates and compares the real time simulation results with that of the MATLAB simulations. The real time implemented hardware is shown in Fig. 9.

4 Results

The real time implemented hardware setup shown in Fig. 9. The simulation results shows that by using the proposed sensorless method the desired rpm reach within 0.005 s shown in Fig. 10. The I-V characteristic of PV panel is shown in Fig. 11. Figure 12 shows capacity factor vs. time. Output current waveform of SPWM realized in simulation and hardware shown in Figs. 13 and 14 respectively.

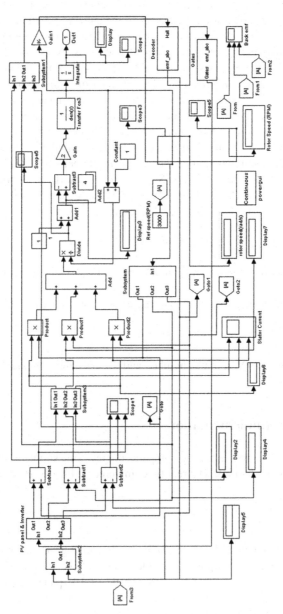

Fig. 6. The BLDC model developed in MATLAB

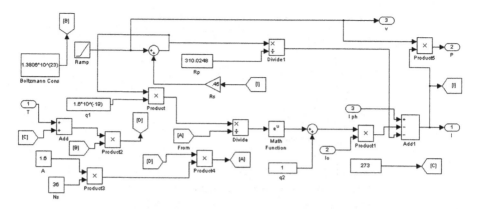

Fig. 7. Simulink model of PV panel

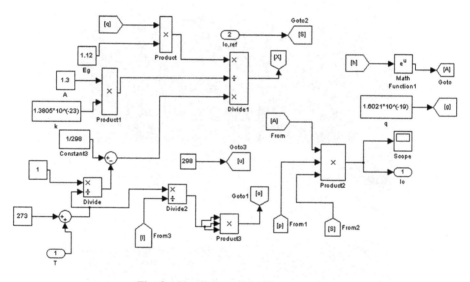

Fig. 8. Simulink model of Io generation

Table 2. Specifications of BLDC motor and PV panel

Parameters of motor & PV panel values	
No. of poles	4
DC source voltage	54
Irradiance	1000 w/m^2
Rated speed	3000 rpm
Self-inductance	0.0272 H
Damping constant	0.2
Load torque	4 N-m
Parallel resistance of PV panel	310.0248 Ω
Coefficient temp. of short circuit current	1.3×10^{-3}
Cell temperature at STC	298 k

Fig. 9. The real time implemented hardware setup

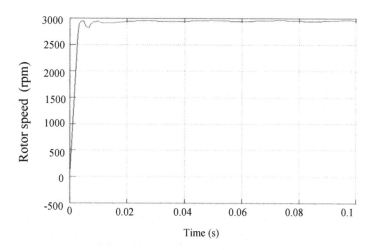

Fig. 10. Speed waveform of BLDC motor

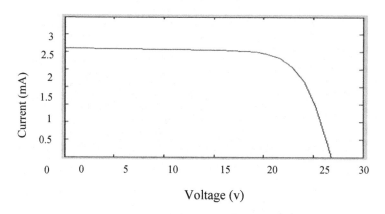

Fig. 11. The I-V characteristics of PV panel

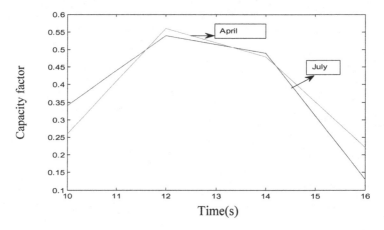

Fig. 12. Capacity factor vs. time plot

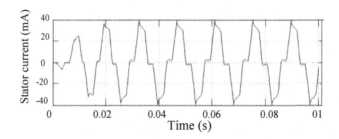

Fig. 13. Output current waveform of SPWM realized in simulation

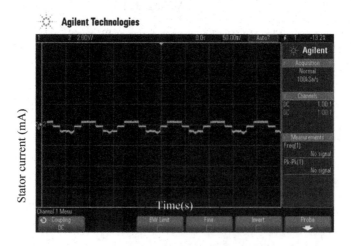

Fig. 14. Output stator current waveform of SPWM realized in hardware

5 Conclusion

Present paper has proposed a novel instrumentation scheme for cooling and water pumping especially in rural areas though solar powered BLDC sensorless motor drive. This work has been performed both in simulation and in real time hardware. This work implements SPWM commutation algorithm to provide a wide range of speed variation. The real time implemented outputs are satisfactorily replicating the simulated results. This work successfully implements a PV panel fed BLDC motor drive and validates it through real time and software simulation results. In accordance with it is seen that conventional AC induction motor based cooling systems require higher number of solar panels than that of BLDC fed drives, thus BLDC based cooling systems are not only power efficient but also are less costly as they require far less amount of solar cells per panel. This motor is appropriate for various applications due to very low maintenance, lower acoustic noise, high power density and higher speed ranges compare to other motor drives.

References

1. Kim, T.-H., Ehsani, M.: Sensorless control of the BLDC motors from near-zero to high speeds. IEEE Trans. Power Electron. **19**(6), 1635–1645 (2004)
2. Samin, J., et al.: Optimal sizing of photovoltaic systems in varied climates. Sol. Energy **6**(2), 97–107 (1997)
3. Chen, C.-H., Cheng, M.-Y.: A new cost effective sensorless commutation method for brushless DC motors without phase shift circuit and neutral voltage. IEEE Trans. Power Electron. **22**(2), 644–653 (2007)
4. Mondal, S., Nandi, A., Mallick, I., Ghosh, C., Giri, A.: Performance evaluation of brushless DC motor drive for three different types of MOSFET based DC-DC converters. In: IEEE International Conference, DevIC 2017, 23–24 March 2017. ISBN 978-1-5090-4724-6
5. Mondal, S., Mitra, A., Chattopadhyay, M.: Mathematical modeling and Simulation of Brushless DC motor with ideal back EMF for a precision speed control. In: IEEE International Conference on Electrical, Computer and Communication Technologies, ICECCT-2015. ISBN 978-1-4799-6084-2
6. Zhang, C., Bian, D.: APWM control algorithm for eliminating torque ripple caused by stator magnetic field jump of brushless DC motors. In: Proceedings of the 7th World Congress on Intelligent Control and Automation, Chongqing, 25–27 June 2008
7. Rahman, S., Kroposki, B.D.: Photovoltaics and demand side management performance analysis at a university building. IEEE Trans. Energy Convers. **8**(3), 491–498 (1993)
8. Zhou, J.H., Zhong, Z.W., Luo, M., Shao, C.: Wavelet-based correlation modelling for health assessment of fluid dynamic bearings in brushless DC motors. Int. J. Adv. Manuf. Technol. **41**, 421–429 (2009)
9. Shrestha, G.B., Goela, L.: Study on optimal sizing of stand-alone photovoltaic stations. IEEE Trans. Energy Convers. **13**(4), 373–378 (1998)
10. Gupta, R.A., Kumar, R., Bansal, A.K.: Artificial intelligence applications in permanent magnet brushless DC motor drives. Artif. Intell. Rev. **33**, 175–186 (2009)

11. Mondal, S., Mitra, A., Chowdhury, D., Chattopadhyay, M.: A new approach of sensorless control methodology for achieving ideal characteristics of brushless DC motor using MATLAB/Simulink. In: Third International Conference on Computer, Communication, Control and Information Technology (C3IT), 7–8 February. IEEE (2015). ISBN 978-1-4799-4446-0

12. Jinghua, Z., Zhengxi, L.: Research on hybrid modulation strategies based on general hybrid topology of multilevel inverter. In: Proceedings of International Symposium on Power Electronics, Electrical Drives, Motion, Ischia (2008)

13. Chowdhury, D., Mitra, A., Mondal, S., Chattopadhyay, M.: A new implementation scheme in robotic vehicle propulsion using brushless DC motor. In: Mandal, J., Satapathy, S., Sanyal, M., Bhateja, V. (eds.) Proceedings of the First International Conference on Intelligent Computing and Communication, vol. 458, pp. 387–394. Springer, Singapore (2017). https://doi.org/10.1007/978-981-10-2035-3_39

Development of a Power Efficient Hearing Aid Using MEMS Microphone

Souvik Mallik, Debjyoti Chowdhury,
and Madhurima Chattopadhyay[(✉)]

Applied Electronics and Instrumentation, Heritage Institute of Technology,
Kolkata 700107, India
souvik.211190@gmail.com, {debjyoti.chowdhury,
madhurima.chattopadhyay}@heritageit.edu

Abstract. In this paper, MEMS based capacitive microphone is designed for low cost power efficient hearing aid application. The developed microphone along with the associated circuitry is mounted at the back of the human ear in form of a wearable device. The designed microphone consists of a flexible circular silicon nitrite (Si_3N_4) diaphragm and a polysilicon perforated back plate with air as dielectric between them. The incident acoustic waves on the sensor cause deflection of the diaphragm to alter the air gap between the perforated back plate (fixed electrode) and the diaphragm (moving plate) which causes a change in capacitance. The acoustic pressure applied to the microphone is from 0 Pa to 100 Pa for an operating range of 100 Hz–10 kHz which corresponds to the audible frequency range in case of human beings. The main purpose of this work is to increase the longevity of battery used in conventional hearing aids. The designed MEMS microphone with Si_3N_4 diaphragm is capable of identifying acoustic frequencies (100 Hz to 10 kHz) which corresponds to a specific change in absolute pressure from 0 Pa to 100 Pa for 2 micron thick diaphragm with a sensitivity of about 0.08676 mV/Pa. The design of the sensor and the characteristics analysis are performed in FEM based simulation software which are later validated in real time.

Keywords: MEMS · Microphone · Circular diaphragm · FEM
Hearing aid · Low power

1 Introduction

Partial hearing loss is the most common form of human impairment. Among the world population about 3.7 million people are of the age group 16–64 and the rest 6.3 million are above 65 years of age who suffer from such problem. The various types of hearing losses suffered by human beings are conductive (ear canal, ear drum and ear bones), sensorineural (inner ear) and mixed hearing loss (ear canal, ear drum, inner ear) such diseases can be helped by hearing aid devices depending on the severity of the hearing loss [1]. There are many types of hearing aids depending upon how they are worn by the patient i.e. behind the ear (BTE), in the ear (ITE), in the canal (ITC) and completely in the canal (CIC). The hearing aids commercially available have the problem of directionality, sensitivity and audio range. Based on the sensing element a microphone can be capacitive

© Springer Nature Singapore Pte Ltd. 2018
J. K. Mandal and D. Sinha (Eds.): CSI 2017, CCIS 836, pp. 369–375, 2018.
https://doi.org/10.1007/978-981-13-1343-1_31

(condenser), piezoelectric and piezo-resistive. A capacitive microphone computes the change in acoustic pressure by the change in capacitance [2] (Fig. 1).

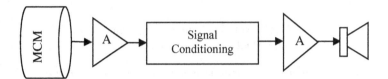

Fig. 1. Basic block diagram of the proposed hearing aid

The most common capacitive microphones are Electret capacitive microphone (ECM) and MEMS capacitive microphone (MCM) [3–5]. In this work, MCM is selected because of its ultra-small fabrication geometries, excellent stability to temperature and low power consumption along with the ability to fabricate the underlying amplifier circuitry on the same substrate. This paper is organized as follows Sect. 1 introduces the work. Section 2 describes the design of MEMS capacitive microphone and the principle of its operation of the respectively. Section 3 introduces the set of steps a unique capacitance to voltage read out for the developed MEMS microphone. Finally, Sect. 5 explains the results and discussions in the simulation of microphone for hearing aid applications along with concluding remarks.

2   Design of MEMS Microphone

The designed microphone consists of a flexible circular silicon nitrite (Si_3N_4) diaphragm and a polysilicon perforated back plate with air as dielectric between them. In this work, the designed microphone consists of a Si3N4 diaphragm over a polysilicon perforated back plate [6–8]. Figure 2 shows the basic structure of the designed condenser microphone with Si3N4 diaphragm of thickness 2 micro-meters and Si back plate of thickness 5 micro-meters with diaphragm area of 7850 sq. micro-meter. The diaphragm when stretched by an acoustic wave a change in air gap distance occurs for an applied DC bias voltage.

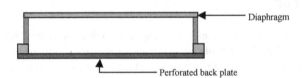

Fig. 2. Basic structure of the designed MEMS microphone

An incident acoustic wave strikes the diaphragm of the designed sensor to cause change in average distance from the perforated back plate. This change in distance produces a change in overall capacitance and charge, giving rise to a time varying output voltage, V on the electrodes. The capacitance of the parallel plate microphone is expressed by Eq. 1 [9].

$$C = \varepsilon_0 \varepsilon_r \frac{A}{d} \tag{1}$$

Where, A is the area of back plate, d is the distance between diaphragm and back plate, ε_0 and ε_r is the absolute and relative permittivity of the medium (Fig. 3).

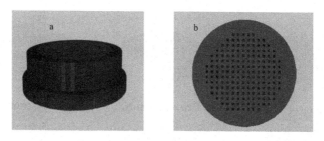

Fig. 3. The designed MEMS microphone (a) side view (b) bottom view

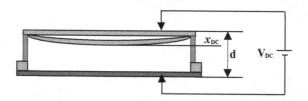

Fig. 4. Basic block diagram of the designed MEMS microphone

When a DC voltage V_{DC} is applied between the two electrodes shown by Fig. 4, an electric charge $Q_{DC} = C_0 V_{DC}$ appears on the surface of the membrane, where C_0 is given by Eq. 2 [10].

$$C_o = \frac{A.\varepsilon_0}{(d - x_{DC})} \tag{2}$$

Where, x_{DC} is the static average displacement due to the DC electrostatic force and d the actual distance between the movable and fixed plate. Incident acoustic waves changes the average distance from the back plate which is given by Eq. 3.

$$x = d - x_{DC} + x_{AC} = d_0 + x_{AC} \tag{3}$$

Where, x_{AC} is the average displacement of the vibrating membrane. The sensitivity of capacitive microphone is given by Eq. 4 [11].

$$\text{Sensitivity} = V_0 \times \left[\frac{C_f}{C_0} - 1 \right] \times \frac{1}{\Delta P} \text{V/Pa} \tag{4}$$

3   MEMS Microphone Fabrication Steps

The fabrication steps start by developing the perforated back plate form the Si wafer, outer body of the MEMS microphone is formed by depositing Si_3N_4 atop the Si wafer through LPCVD [12]. The diaphragm is formed by filling up the cavity with phosphosilicate glass (PSG) and deposition of Poly Silicon over it to form the diaphragm. The PSG is later etched out while forming the perforated back plate, shown in Fig. 5.

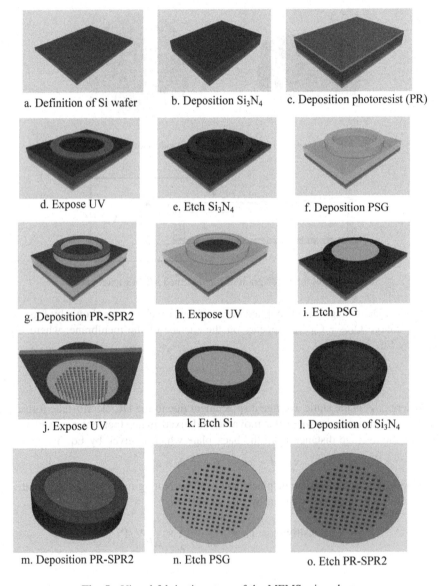

a. Definition of Si wafer   b. Deposition Si_3N_4 c. Deposition photoresist (PR)

d. Expose UV   e. Etch Si_3N_4 f. Deposition PSG

g. Deposition PR-SPR2   h. Expose UV   i. Etch PSG

j. Expose UV   k. Etch Si   l. Deposition of Si_3N_4

m. Deposition PR-SPR2   n. Etch PSG   o. Etch PR-SPR2

Fig. 5.   Virtual fabrication steps of the MEMS microphone

4 Real Time Implemented MEMS Microphone and Amplification Circuit

The amplifier for the developed MEMS microphone, shown in Fig. 6(b) was built around a low cost dual-channel audio amplifier TDA2822 M by STMicroelectronics having a gain a 3 dB [13]. A bias voltage of 5 V was given to the amplifier using a portable 5 V button lithium battery, shown by Fig. 6(a).

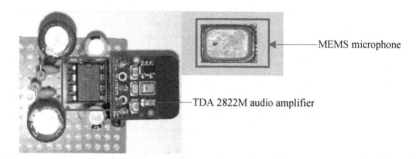

Fig. 6. (a) The developed TDA2822 M based audio amplifier (b) the developed MEMS microphone

5 Results

This section postulates the sensor outputs. In order to achieve linear characteristics, the applied pressure range to these sensors is restricted between 0–100 Pa [14] shown in Fig. 7 [15].

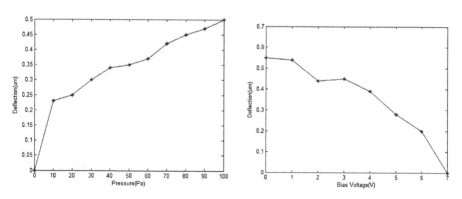

Fig. 7. For a special range of applied pressure 0–100 Pa

Fig. 8. Deflection of diaphragm for change in bias voltage

The above Fig. 8 shows the deflection of the microphone diaphragm for change in applied voltage, the pull-in voltage for the designed microphone is around 7 V [16–18] from the above figure.

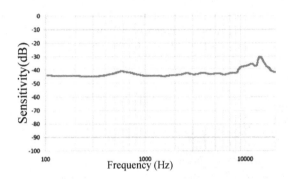

Fig. 9. The frequency response of the developed MEMS microphone

The sensitivity of the MEMS microphone is shown in Fig. 9, which after amplification by TDA 2822 M is around −48.9 dB in the frequency bandwidth from 100 Hz to 10 kHz.

6 Conclusion

This paper presents a low cost power efficient hearing aid, which consists of an MEMS microphone and an analog-amplifying chip. The MEMS microphone has a movable membrane and a perforated back-plate part manufactured using micromachining techniques. The MEMS microphone was first virtually fabricated in a FEM based simulation platform to obtain the right design parameters. The sensitivity of the MEMS microphone was about −48.9 dB in a bandwidth from 100 Hz to 10 kHz. The used of a MEMS microphone coupled with a low cost amplifier (i.e. TDA 2822 M) proves an suitable substitute for conventional hearing aids.

References

1. Bergqvist, J., Gobet, J.: Capacitive microphone with a surface micromachined backplate using electroplating technology. J. Microelectromech. Syst. 3(2), 69–75 (1994)
2. Chowdhury, S., Jullien, G.A., Ahmadi, M.A., Miller, W.C.: MEMS acousto-magnetic components for use in a hearing instrument. Presented at SPIE's Symposium on Design, Test Integration, and Packaging of MEMS/MOEMS, Paris (2000)
3. Ganji, B.A., Majlis, B.Y.: Design and fabrication of a new MEMS capacitive microphone using a perforated aluminum diaphragm. Sens. Actuators, A **149**, 29–37 (2009)
4. Ganji, B.A., Majlis, B.Y.: High sensitivity and small size MEMS capacitive microphone using a novel slotted diaphragm. Microsyst. Technol. **15**(9), 1401–1406 (2009)

5. Ganji, B.A., Majlis, B.Y.: Slotted capacitive microphone with sputtered aluminum diaphragm and photoresist sacrificial layer. Microsyst. Technol. **16**, 1803–1809 (2010)
6. Hsu, P.C., Mastrangelo, C.H., Wise, K.D.: A high density polysilicon diaphragm condenser microphone. In: Conference Record IEEE 11th International Workshop on MicroElectro Mechanical Systems (MEMS), pp. 580–585 (1988)
7. Jing, C., Liu, L., Li, Z., Tan, Z., Xu, Y., Ma, J.: On the single-chip condenser miniature microphone using DRIE and back side etching techniques. Sens. Actuators, A **103**, 42–47 (2003)
8. Kabir, A.E., et al.: Very high sensitivity acoustic transducers membrane and gold back plate. Sensors Actuators-A **78**, 138–142 (1999)
9. Kronast, W., Muller, B., Siedel, W., Stoffel, A.: Single-chip condenser microphone using porous silicon as sacrificial layer for the air gap. Sens. Actuators, A **87**, 188–193 (2001)
10. Li, X., Lin, R., Kek, H., Miao, J., Zou, Q.: Sensitivity- improved silicon condenser microphone with a novel single deeply corrugated diaphragm. Sens. Actuators, A **92**, 257–262 (2001)
11. Ma, T., Man, T.Y., Chan, Y. C., Zohar, Y., Wong, M.: Design and fabrication of an integrated programmable floating-gate microphone. In: Proceedings of the Fifteenth IEEE International Conference on Micro Electro Mechanical Systems, pp. 288–291 (2002)
12. Miao, J., Lin, R., Chen, L., Zou, Q., Lim, S.Y., Seah, S.H.: Design considerations in micromachined silicon microphones. Microelectron. J. **33**, 21–28 (2002)
13. Ning, J., Liu, Z., Liu, H., Ge, Y.:. A silicon capacitive microphone based on oxidized porous silicon sacrificial technology. In: Proceedings of the 7th International Conference on Solid-State and Integrated Circuits Technology, vol. 3, pp. 1872–1875 (2004)
14. Ning, Y.B., Mitchell, A.W., Tait, R.N.: Fabrication of a silicon micromachined capacitive microphone using a dry-etch process. Sens. Actuators **A3**, 237–242 (1996)
15. Pappalardo, M, Caliano, G, Foglietti, V, Caronti, A, Cianci, E.: A new approach to ultrasound generation: the capacitive micromachined transducers. University Roma, Rome, Italy (2002)
16. Pappalardo, M., Caronti, A.: A new alternative to piezoelectric transducer for NDE and medical applications: the capacitive ultrasonic micromachined transducer (cMUT). University Roma, Rome, Italy (2002)
17. Yang, C.: The sensitivity analysis of a MEMS microphone with different membrane diameters. J. Mar. Sci. Technol. **18**, 790–796 (2010)
18. Chao, C.-P., Tsa, C.-Y., Chiu, C.-W., Tsai, C.-H., Tu, T.-Y.: A new hybrid fabrication process for a high sensitivity MEMS microphone. Microsyst. Technol. **19**, 1425–1431 (2013)

Leveraging ICT for Food Security:
An Analysis in the Context of PDS in India

Arun Kumar Biswal[(⊠)] and Mamata Jenamani

Indian Institute of Technology Kharagpur, Kharagpur 721302,
West Bengal, India
{akb,mj}@iem.iitkgp.ernet.in

Abstract. The Indian food security system, commonly known as the Public Distribution System (PDS) is plagued with inefficiency. While implementing the recommendations of various national committees; Government of India has initiated many ICT intervention projects to improve the efficiency and effectiveness of the system. This paper analyses the various ICT initiatives and its impact on Food Security in India. We collect secondary data both on *the progress of various ICT projects* and *the performance of PDS system in the subsequent period* through defined Key Performance Indicators (KPIs).We use multiple regression model to investigate the relation between these dependent and independent variables. Our analysis shows that there exists a positive correlation between reforms like ICT intervention and effectiveness of food security system. As food security in India is a global issue, the implications of ICT intervention projects on performance of the system can be a topic of interest in India and other developing countries.

Keywords: Food security · ICT · Public distribution system · E governance
NFSA · India

1 Introduction

It is the British Government in 1939 which is credited with the introduction of first public distribution of food grains in India in a structured manner. They started the operation at Bombay and gradually extended to other areas. Since its inception, the system has gone through much evolution (Refer Table 1) to reach its present form of Targeted Public Distribution System (TPDS). With the aim of focusing on the poor, Government of India (GoI) launched the TPDS scheme in June 1997. It is considered as a principal instrument in the hands of Governments for ensuring food security to the most vulnerable sections against rise in prices of essential commodities. It is a poverty alleviation programme and contributes towards the social well being of people. Commonly known as the food security system, TPDS constitutes the central government's *procurement and interstate transportation* of the food grains and the state governments' subsequent *distribution* to the identified poor at subsidized rate. The two prime objectives of the system are to guarantee a market for the farmers and to ensure food security for the poor. With a network of more than five lakh Fair Price Shops (FPSs), PDS in India is one of the largest distribution mechanisms of its type in the

© Springer Nature Singapore Pte Ltd. 2018
J. K. Mandal and D. Sinha (Eds.): CSI 2017, CCIS 836, pp. 376–390, 2018.
https://doi.org/10.1007/978-981-13-1343-1_32

world. Essential commodities for the poor like Rice, Wheat, Sugar, Kerosene and the like are supplied to approximately 18 crore families at subsidized prices. With the implementation of NFSA 2013, the system guarantees food for two thirds of the population with an estimated annual cost in the range of Rs. 95,000 crore to 1,12,000 crore [1].

Table 1. Evolution of PDS. Source: Own summarization based on data from http://www.fao.org/docrep/x0172e/x0172e06.htm#P1406_137724

Year	Sequence of events
1939	• Introduction of the Rationing system in Bombay
1942	• Creation of Department of Food under Government of India
1943	• Decision by Indian Govt to end the rationing system
1950	• Reintroduction of rationing system post independence due to inflationary pressure in the economy
1956	• Government abandoned procurement and relaxed all control norms due to ample availability of food grains in the open market
1958	• Government again put control on trading and reintroduced PDS due to drop in production • Diversification of commodity basket by adding Sugar, cooking coal and kerosene oil
1965	• Creation of Food Corporation of India(FCI) and Commission for Agricultural Cost and Prices (CACP)
1992	• Launch of Revamped Public distribution System
1997	• Introduction of Targeted Public Distribution System (TPDS) with specific focus on the poor • Introduction of Decentralized procurement scheme
2000	• Antyodaya Anna Yojana(AAY) scheme was launched to target poorest of the poor
2001	• Government notified PDS Control Order (2001) to administer TPDS
2013	• National Food Security Act 2013 came into force
2015	• Government notified PDS Control Order(2015) under National Food Security Act (NFSA)

Though, the rationing system and its successor, the Public Distribution System (PDS) is the backbone for delivering food security, it suffers from problems like resource wastage, corruption, leakage, ghost beneficiary, non-accountability, non-transparency, inefficiency, ineffectiveness and delay in resources and services distribution [2]. Rotting of food grains at warehouses, stealing and over charging by FPS owners, distribution of low quality grains to beneficiaries, inclusion and exclusion errors, heavy bureaucratic procedures are some of the many malaise of the system. Therefore, even if the food subsidy, as a percentage of GDP, has increased from 0.5% in 2007–08 to 0.8% in 2012–13 [1], the benefits are not reaching the intended recipients. Over the years, experts and researchers have pointed out the issues related to the Indian PDS. The Programme Evaluation Organization of the Planning Commission undertook a survey in 2005 to evaluate the performance of TPDS. Based on the survey results, the report concludes that, to transfer one rupee to a beneficiary, government spends Rs. 3.65 [3]. It estimates, 58 percent of the central pool issued subsidized food grain gets diverted and not reaching to the intended beneficiaries. Even the latest study estimates leakages at more than 40% at all India level [4, 5].

Due to its social and political sensitiveness, successive governments have set up committees to suggest ways and means to improve the effectiveness and efficiency of the Targeted Public Distribution System. For example, Wadhwa committee recommends end to end computerization of the entire PDS supply chain to minimize human intervention as one of the measures [6]. Considering the severity of the inefficiency in the system the committee preferred to submit a separate report suggesting computerization of all processes in the entire PDS supply chain starting from procurement from farmers to end distribution by the FPS dealers [7]. Modernization of Targeted Public Distribution System (TPDS) with end-to-end computerization of the supply chain is a priority area for improving the efficiency of the system. With the enactment of NFSA 2013, it has acquired greater importance as 'Right to Food' is guaranteed to the people under this Act.

The objective of this paper is to discuss the various ICT projects initiated by Government of India, its progress and the impact. The authors believe that food security in India is of global interest, and implications of ICT intervention projects on performance of TPDS can be a topic of interest in India and other developing countries. The rest of the paper is organized as follows. In Sect. 2 we review the existing literature on application of ICT tools in the field of long term developmental issues like Education, Food Security, Health Care and Public Service Management. Section 3 highlights the opportunities for ICT intervention in TPDS and the relevant projects. In Sect. 4, we discuss the progress on various components of the projects and in Sect. 5 we highlight the possible benefits with a subsection on the regression model. Finally, Sect. 6 concludes the study.

2 Literature Review

In this section, we review the existing literature on ICT adoption in supply chain, benefits, barriers and technologies. Although this review is not exhaustive, it covers a significant number of papers that have been published in the recent years. We classify the literature based on the application of ICT in the key sectors like Education, Food Security, Health Care, and Public Service management and Supply Chain Management. Table 2 summarizes the studies relevant to these sectors. ICT revolution is a major contributor towards cheaper and easier transfer of income supplements to the targeted poor for social safety nets like food security [8]. Banerjee, Darbas, Brown and Roth [9] study how reforms like technological innovation in food grain supply management have been effective in reducing food insecurity in India and Bangladesh. Masiero [10] through the case study on PDS shows how the link between e-governance and development could be leveraged for policy formulation in the context of food security. Lashgarara, Mirdamadi, Hosseini and Chizari [11] identify ICT as one of the most important solution to the food security problem. The authors suggest ways to increase food security through use of ICT including (i) Accessing real time information, (ii) Reducing transaction cost, (iii) Encouraging agricultural diversification and

(iv) Gaining access to global knowledge base. In another study they identify that, old technologies like Radio, Television, Audio cassettes and Phones are more cost effective and relevant to address food insecurity in rural areas of IRAN [12]. McLaren, Metz, van den Berg, Bruskiewich, Magor and Shires [13] state that ICT could be the answer to last mile problem of disseminating information to farmers and this would empower them to make better production and marketing decisions. McEntee and Agyeman [14] apply geographic information systems (GIS) technology to provide spatial mapping of food access as well as more sophisticated analyses of food price and availability. Hwang and Smith [15] find that ICT and GIS can positively influence food security when utilized within a web mapping framework. Traceability of food items along the supply chain provides added capability to be agile, ensure quality and safety, and affect policies related to food security [16]. By using GIS and global navigation satellite systems (GNSS) and integrating with communication technologies, computers and tractors, the authors develop protocols that can trace food items from source to final destination.

Table 2. ICT application in developmental issues

Application area	Citations
Education	[17–25]
Food security	[8–16, 26–30]
Health care	[31–35]
Public service management	[36–41]
Supply chain management	[42–50]
ICT adoption issues, barriers	[51–60]

Many authors highlight the positive correlation between ICT implementation and the performance indicators in the field of education, research and innovation [17, 19, 25]. Mama and Hennessy [22] find that for successful implementation of ICT initiative in school, it is very essential to understand in depth the teachers' rationales and behaviors. Similarly Peeraer and Van Petegem [23] identify the factors which determine the integration of ICT in the field of education.

Ray [37] propose a framework to improve accountability in public services through the use of ICT tools by emphasizing on the traditional accountability relationships among various stake holders like citizens, political authority and service provider. Luyombya [40] through empirical analysis establish the contribution of Information and Communication Technology (ICT) such as computers, for creating and managing digital records in the Ugandan Public Service (UPS). Singh and Karn [38] address the issue of the implementation of right to information act through the use of ICT and suggest methodology for its further improvement.

3   ICT Intervention Opportunities in the TPDS

As shown in Fig. 1, the TPDS in its existing form operates through a multi-level process in which the centre and states share responsibility. It is the central government's responsibility to procure food grains, from farmers at Minimum Support Price (MSP) as fixed by the CACP. In case of decentralized procurement introduced in 1997, the state governments buy and maintain stocks under the central pool. The centre also allocates grains to each state proportionately on the basis of number of eligible beneficiaries with their entitlement quantity. Out of the total number of poor in each state; it is the responsibility of the state governments to identify the eligible households based on mutually agreed criteria. The central government transports the food grains up to the main depots (FCI controlled) in each state and then the concerned state governments deliver the allocated grains to the beneficiaries through distributors and Fair Price Shops (FPS).

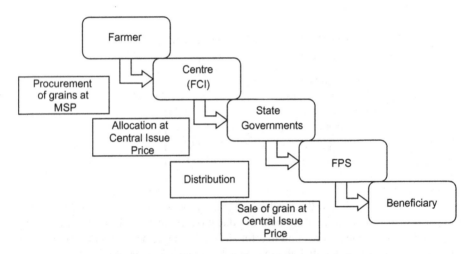

Fig. 1. PDS supply chain Source: http://www.prsindia.org

In this legacy system of TPDS, the beneficiary families get paper ration cards which indicate their eligibility to avail food grains at subsidized prices. The record of eligibility and monthly transactions is maintained manually which is prone to human errors and tampering. Also, during allocation and stock movement from Central depots to States and then to regional levels warehouses, the entire process is carried out manually. Some notable deficiencies of this system includes (i) Multiple ration cards issued to one person, (ii) Lack of authentic identification for users, (iii) Faulty system of record keeping, (iv) Diversion of PDS food grains to market (iv) Lack of monitoring system to track the trucks in transit and (v) Lack of real time monitoring of inventory and centralized record keeping. Each of the above identified problems provides opportunity for application of ICT tools for its solution. To address the issue of multiple card holders, inclusion and exclusion error, digital database should be maintained for all the beneficiaries with final grain distribution through biometric identification. Further, if the total food grains allocated to a particular state can be compared with the actual disbursement to beneficiaries then diversion can be prevented.

For achieving this objective, primary focus should be on automating the allocation process at all stages of the PDS supply chain. A fool proof monitoring system is required that can cover the transactions and transport at all levels starting from FCI controlled central store to fair price shops. In Table 3, we summarize and map the PDS processes with the sources of pilferage and the proposed ICT modules that govt has initiated to address it.

Table 3. Mapping of planning module to sources of error

Sources of error	PDS Process	Proposed ICT solution	Planning module
Inclusion and exclusion Error, Ghost card	Identification of Beneficiary	Digitization of beneficiary database , Biometric Identification	Digitization of database
Lack of information to Farmers	Procurement	Use of portal, Mobile application,	Computerization of supply chain
No real time information of Inventory	Storage	RFID enabled application, Integrated information system	
Diversion during transit	Transportation	GPS solution	
Lack of prior Information to Beneficiary	Distribution	Information through SMS, Toll free number, Transparency Portal, Online allocation	Transparency portal
Manual recording of transactions at FPS	Distribution	FPS automation to minimize human intervention	FPS automation
Lack of attention to Beneficiary complain	Grievance Redressal	Grievance redressal mechanism	Grievance redressal Mechanism

4   ICT Projects Implementation

4.1   The Strategy

In the eleventh five year plan (2007–2012), the Department of Food and Public Distribution (DFPD) launched two pilot schemes for computerization of TPDS operations. Under the non-plan scheme, the government approved Smart Card based delivery of Essential Commodities for implementation on pilot basis in two States (Chandigarh and Haryana). The two main objectives of this pilot project were (i) to make the delivery mechanism more efficient and (ii) to assess if the smart card based distribution system is scalable. Under the plan scheme, computerization of the TPDS system was approved on a pilot basis for three states with an estimated budget of Rs. 53.47 crore [61]. Capturing information, tracking the food grains used in the PDS supply chain through the application of ICT tools and involving citizens and other stake holders were the prime motives behind implementation of this pilot project. The scale and complexity involved in the project constrained the government to limit the implementation of this ICT solution only up to the block level. The above schemes initiated by various governments lacked in end to end coverage and integration in a comprehensive manner. To overcome this, the government in the twelfth five year plan (2012–2017) prepared a planned scheme to provide financial and technical support for the computerization scheme with a cost sharing mechanism between centre and state. The implementation scheme comprised two components where component-I comprised of digitization of database, automation of supply chain, transparency portal and grievance redressal mechanism and component-II proposed automation of FPS. National Informatics Centre (NIC) was entrusted with the role of technical consultant on behalf of the centre. Established in 1976, NIC under Ministry of Communication and Information Technology, Government of India (GoI) is one of India's major organizations promoting informatics led development and prime builder of e-Governance applications. The lesson learned from previous state initiatives and NIC's pilot projects made the basis for implementation of the Planned Scheme. The total budget for the planned schemes under various components with central and state share is given in Table 4.

Table 4. Details of ICT Budget Source: http://www.pdsportal.nic.in/Files/Final-Status_Paper.pdf

Name of plan scheme		Planned budget (Rs. Crore)			Approval date	Fund released till May 2015	
		Central	State	Total		Amount	No of states
12th five year plan (2012–2017)	Comp-I	489.37	394.70	884.07	Oct, 2012	269.17	29
	Comp-II	1798.44	1590.95	3389.4	-	-	-

Although the baseline target date for digitization of beneficiary database and computerization of supply-chain was fixed as October, 2012 and March, 2013 respectively, most of the states failed to finalize their action plan and submit financial proposals facing practical problems during implementation and lack of clarity on various aspect of the scheme. So the government recognized the need of a detailed guideline for implementation of the scheme which could also provide a comprehensive way forward for its implementation. As per the need, the department with the help of NI prepared the implementation guidelines to be used by Food and Civil Supplies (F&CS) departments of States/UTs and finally issued it in the month of September 2013.

4.2   The Progress

Since the year 2011, computerization of TPDS operation is treated as a Mission Mode Project (MMP) under the National e Governance Plan (Ne GP). As per the guidelines, the central government diligently follows up with States and Union territories (UTs) to review their progress. The progress on various aspects of ICT implementation is summarized in this section. Figure 2 depicts the planned versus actual expenditure on the central fund released for ICT projects. Although the actual expenditure is almost in line with the plan, there is a substantial difference between the initial estimate and the revised estimate in the year 2014–15. In Table 5, we summarize the progress of implementation under Component-I and Component-II of the planned schemes for all the 36 States/UTs. We can observe that the progress is non uniform among the states and there is a substantial gap.

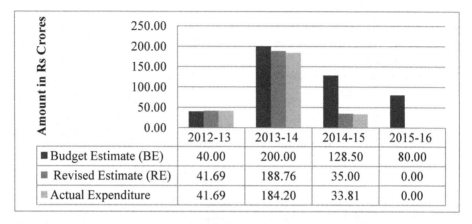

	2012-13	2013-14	2014-15	2015-16
■ Budget Estimate (BE)	40.00	200.00	128.50	80.00
■ Revised Estimate (RE)	41.69	188.76	35.00	0.00
■ Actual Expenditure	41.69	184.20	33.81	0.00

Fig. 2. Plan Vs Actual expenditure on ICT projects Source: Author's own computation based on data available on http://dfpd.nic.in/writereaddata/images/tpds-Annex-1.pdf

5 Benefits Obtained from PDS Reform and Role of ICT

The benefits from ICT projects can be evaluated by quantifying the intended benefits to the organization solely attributable to ICT intervention. This is quite problematic and there is no single method that can be applied to all situations. Also without successful implementation of the project, the performance cannot be judged. In this section, we observe the trend of TPDS performance parameters during the reform process.

5.1 Trend from National Sample Survey Data

The monthly per capita consumption from PDS, share of PDS quantity from total consumption and the percentage of households reporting consumptions are the quantifiable parameters to gauge the success of reform in TPDS. The trend over a period of time (2004–05 to 2011–12) is shown in Figs. 3, 4 and 5.

Although the improvement cannot be solely attributed to ICT intervention, the trend is encouraging and establishing a positive correlation.

Table 5. Status of ICT adoption in PDS (as on 09.08.2016) Source: Own summarization based on data available on http://dfpd.nic.in/writereaddata/images/Annex-ii.pdf

Sl. no	Name of ICT initiative	Status (no. of States & UTs)		
		Completed	In progress	No progress
1	Digitization of Ration cards/Beneficiary database	36	0	0
2	Aadhar seeding in ration cards	5	29	2
3	Digitization of Godown database	29	6	1
4	Online allocation of food grain	23	3	10
5	Supply Chain Computerization	15	1	20
6	Transparency Portal	36	0	0
7	Call centres/Toll free helpline	35	1	0
8	Online grievances	32	0	4

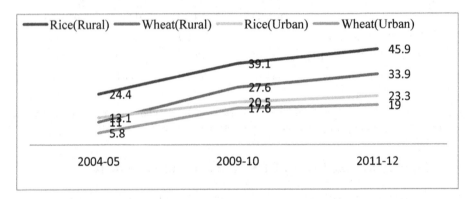

Fig. 3. % of households reporting consumption from PDS during 30 days

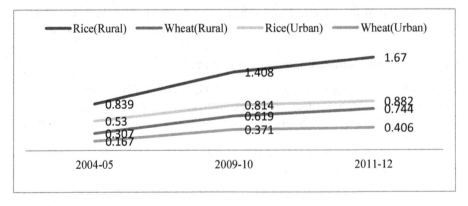

Fig. 4. Monthly per capita consumption from PDS (in Kg)

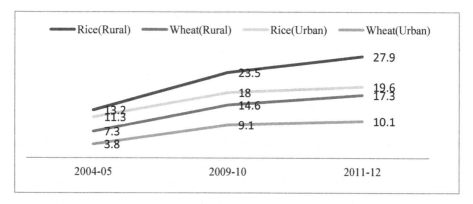

Fig. 5. % share of PDS consumed

5.2 The Regression Model

In this subsection we investigate if there exists any relationship between the level of ICT implementation in a specific state and the corresponding PDS performance of that state. We consider the PDS food grain leakage percentage as a performance indicator and collect state wise data from available sources [5]. As shown in Fig. 6, we develop a regression model considering the State wise progress of various ICT initiatives as independent variables and the corresponding state wise loss (leakage percentage from PDS) as dependent variable. We collect data for the States/UTs of India and analyse the model using MS Excel 2007 and present the out put through Table 6.

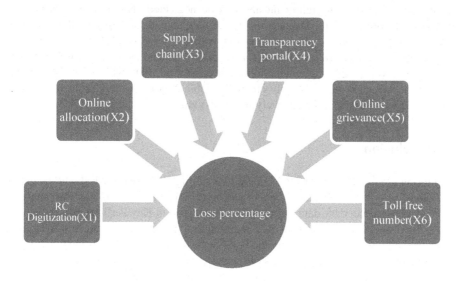

Fig. 6. The regression model

Table 6. Summary output

Regression Statistics					
Multiple R	0.251148961				
R Square	0.063075801				
Adjusted R Square	-0.267603329				
Standard Error	28.76054848				
Observations	24				
ANOVA					
	_df_	_SS_	_MS_	_F_	_Significance F_
Regression	6	946.6764306	157.7794	0.190746	0.975243442
Residual	17	14061.87553	827.1691		
Total	23	15008.55196			
	Coefficients	_Standard Error_	_t Stat_	_P-value_	
Intercept	48.46936593	19.78743083	2.449503	0.025439	
X Variable 1	-0.017801211	0.204782986	-0.08693	0.931745	
X Variable 2	0.044751083	0.256360244	0.174563	0.863485	
X Variable 3	-0.190262183	0.306724034	-0.6203	0.543284	
X Variable 4	-0.006125881	0.200590791	-0.03054	0.975993	
X Variable 5	0.07189794	0.185856178	0.386847	0.703669	
X Variable 6	-0.006519597	0.159937316	-0.04076	0.967959	

The corresponding higher P-values against the predictor coefficients imply that, statistically these are not significant and can be neglected. This may be because of limited data points and inconsistencies in the available data. Also for the response variable, we take projected value due to non availability of actual data for the reform period. However, negative coefficients for majority independent variables indicate that, with higher level of ICT implementation the leakage from PDS will be less. As can be observed, automation of the supply chain (Variable X3) is more significant for minimising losses owing to comparatively lower P-Value.

6 Conclusion

Monitoring the functioning of TPDS operations through the use of ICT should be given the highest priority as substantial benefit can be achieved through its use. Our analysis of the available secondary data shows the positive trend in Key Performance Indicators of the Food Security System post ICT intervention. Transparency and improved efficiency is the only solution to sustain the Food Security System. ICT has the potential of reshaping the activities and processes of the system and building relationships between citizens and the government. To expedite the implementation of the ICT projects, timelines should be fixed with the aid and assistance of the Central and State governments. Project monitoring should be entrusted to an independent agency both at the central and state level to ensure transparency. The core members of the Central and State Committees should preferably not be shifted till specified targets are achieved. The success of ICT projects depends largely on human skills and capabilities. So, education and training initiatives must be considered as priority actions and staffs need to be trained to handle new processes and activities. Collaboration and coordination among the concerned stake holders should be encouraged to increase efficiency and effectiveness of the system.

References

1. Balani, S.: Functioning of public distribution system: an analytical report (2013)
2. Kumar, S., Pal, S.K.: Empirically developed integrated ICT framework for PDS in developing countries. In: 2013 Third World Congress on Information and Communication Technologies (WICT), pp. 234–239 (2013)
3. Planning Commission: Performance evaluation of targeted public distribution system (TPDS) (2005)
4. Drèze, J., Khera, R.: Understanding leakages in the public distribution system. Econ. Polit. Wkly. **50**, 39 (2015)
5. Gulati, A., Saini, S.: Leakages from public distribution system (PDS) and the way forward. Under Review as an ICRIER Working Paper under ICRIER-ZEF Project (2015)
6. Wadhwa, J.D.: Report on the State of Delhi. Central Vigilance Committee on Public Distribution System (2007)
7. Justice Wadhwa Committee: Report on computerization of PDS Operations (2009)
8. Anderson, K., Strutt, A.: Food security policy options for China: lessons from other countries. Food Policy **49**, 50–58 (2014). Part 1
9. Banerjee, O., Darbas, T., Brown, P.R., Roth, C.H.: Historical divergence in public management of foodgrain systems in India and Bangladesh: opportunities to enhance food security. Glob. Food Secur. **3**, 159–166 (2014)
10. Masiero, S.: Redesigning the Indian food security system through e-governance: the case of Kerala. World Dev. **67**, 126–137 (2015)
11. Lashgarara, F., Mirdamadi, S.M., Hosseini, S.J.F., Chizari, M.: The Role of food-security solutions in the protection of natural resources and environment of developing countries. Ann. N. Y. Acad. Sci. **1140**, 68–72 (2008)
12. Lashgarara, F., Mirdamadi, S.M., Hosseini, S.J.F.: Identification of appropriate tools of information and communication technologies (ICT) in the improvement of food security of Iran's rural households. Afr. J. Biotechnol. **10**, 9082–9088 (2013)
13. McLaren, C.G., Metz, T., van den Berg, M., Bruskiewich, R.M., Magor, N.P., Shires, D.: Chapter 4 informatics in agricultural research for development. Adv. Agron. **102**, 135–157 (2009)
14. McEntee, J., Agyeman, J.: Towards the development of a GIS method for identifying rural food deserts: geographic access in Vermont USA. Appl. Geogr. **30**, 165–176 (2010)
15. Hwang, M., Smith, M.: Integrating publicly available web mapping tools for cartographic visualization of community food insecurity: a prototype. GeoJournal **77**, 47–62 (2012)
16. Gebbers, R., Adamchuk, V.I.: Precision agriculture and food security. Science **327**, 828–831 (2010)
17. Andreea-Diana, S.: The importance of involving pupils from the rural area in using ICT skills and tools – a milestone. Procedia – Soc. Behav. Sci. **128**, 36–43 (2014)

18. Benstead, K., Spacey, R., Goulding, A.: Changing public library service delivery to rural communities in England. New Libr. World **105**, 400–409 (2004)
19. Blignaut, A.S., Hinostroza, J.E., Els, C.J., Brun, M.: ICT in education policy and practice in developing countries: South Africa and Chile compared through SITES 2006. Comput. Educ. **55**, 1552–1563 (2010)
20. Çapuk, S., Kara, A.: A discussion of ICT integration within developed and developing world context from critical perspectives. Procedia – Soc. Behav. Sci. **191**, 56–62 (2015)
21. Fitzgerald, B., Savage, F.: Public libraries in Victoria, Australia: an overview of current ICT developments, challenges, and issues. OCLC Syst. Serv.: Int. Digital Libr. Perspect. **20**, 24–30 (2004)
22. Mama, M., Hennessy, S.: Developing a typology of teacher beliefs and practices concerning classroom use of ICT. Comput. Educ. **68**, 380–387 (2013)
23. Peeraer, J., Van Petegem, P.: ICT in teacher education in an emerging developing country: Vietnam's baseline situation at the start of 'The Year of ICT'. Comput. Educ. **56**, 974–982 (2011)
24. Tongkaw, A.: Multi perspective integrations information and communication technologies (ICTs) in higher education in developing countries: case study Thailand. Procedia – Soc. Behav. Sci. **93**, 1467–1472 (2013)
25. Wiseman, A.W., Anderson, E.: ICT-integrated education and national innovation systems in the Gulf Cooperation Council (GCC) countries. Comput. Educ. **59**, 607–618 (2012)
26. Biswal, A.K., Jenamani, M., Kumar, S.K.: Warehouse efficiency improvement using RFID in a humanitarian supply chain: Implications for Indian food security system. Transp. Res. Part E: Logist. Transp. Rev. **109**, 205–224 (2018)
27. Masiero, S.: Reconstructing the state through ICTs?: a case of state-level computerization in the Indian public distribution system. In: Proceedings of the Sixth International Conference on Information and Communication Technologies and Development: Full Papers, vol. 1, pp. 113–122. ACM (2013)
28. Masiero, S.: Transforming state-citizen relations in food security schemes: the computerized ration card management system in Kerala (2012)
29. Sreenivas, T.: Whether the way state delivers services is redefined concomitantly with changes in the society that are mediated by ICT?: a case of supply chain management of public distribution system operations in the Chhattisgarh state of India, September 6, 2012. pp. 5–7. CPRafrica (2012)
30. Ostry, A., Morrison, K.: Developing and utilizing a database for mapping the temporal and spatial variation in the availability of "local foods" in British Columbia. Environments **36**, 19 (2008)
31. Villarroel, V., Seoane, J., Pozo, F.D.: Analysis of information and communication needs in rural primary health care in developing countries. IEEE Trans. Inf Technol. Biomed. **9**, 66–72 (2005)
32. Chandrasekhar, C., Ghosh, J.: Information and communication technologies and health in low income countries: the potential and the constraints. Bull. World Health Organ. **79**, 850–855 (2001)
33. Haszlinna Mustaffa, N., Potter, A.: Healthcare supply chain management in Malaysia: a case study. Supply Chain Manag.: Int. J. **14**, 234–243 (2009)
34. Nkrumah Gordon, A., Ebo Hinson, R.: Towards a sustainable framework for computer based health information systems (CHIS) for least developed countries (LDCs). Int. J. Health Care Qual. Assur. **20**, 532–544 (2007)
35. Novo-Corti, I., Varela-Candamio, L., García-Álvarez, M.T.: Breaking the walls of social exclusion of women rural by means of ICTs: the case of 'digital divides' in Galician. Comput. Hum. Behav. **30**, 497–507 (2014)

36. Seri, P., Zanfei, A.: The co-evolution of ICT, skills and organization in public administrations: evidence from new European country-level data. Struct. Change Econ. Dyn. **27**, 160–176 (2013)
37. Ray, S.: Reinforcing accountability in public services: an ICT enabled framework. Transform. Gov.: People, Process Policy **6**, 135–148 (2012)
38. Singh, S., Karn, B.: "Right to Information Act" – a tool for good governance through ICT. J. Inf. Commun. Ethics Soc. **10**, 273–287 (2012)
39. Weber, K.M., Heller-Schuh, B., Godoe, H., Roeste, R.: ICT-enabled system innovations in public services: experiences from intelligent transport systems. Telecommun. Policy **38**, 539–557 (2014)
40. Luyombya, D.: ICT and digital records management in the Ugandan public service. Rec. Manag. J. **21**, 135–144 (2011)
41. Shirazi, F., Gholami, R., Añón Higón, D.: The impact of information and communication technology (ICT), education and regulation on economic freedom in Islamic Middle Eastern countries. Inf. Manag. **46**, 426–433 (2009)
42. Harris, I., Wang, Y., Wang, H.: ICT in multimodal transport and technological trends: unleashing potential for the future. Int. J. Prod. Econ. **159**, 88–103 (2015)
43. Mensah, P., Merkuryev, Y., Longo, F.: Using ICT in developing a resilient supply chain strategy. Procedia Comput. Sci. **43**, 101–108 (2015)
44. Prajogo, D., Olhager, J.: Supply chain integration and performance: the effects of long-term relationships, information technology and sharing, and logistics integration. Int. J. Prod. Econ. **135**, 514–522 (2012)
45. Singh, A., Mishra, N., Ali, S.I., Shukla, N., Shankar, R.: Cloud computing technology: reducing carbon footprint in beef supply chain. Int. J. Prod. Econ. **164**, 462–471 (2015)
46. Fan, T., Tao, F., Deng, S., Li, S.: Impact of RFID technology on supply chain decisions with inventory inaccuracies. Int. J. Prod. Econ. **159**, 117–125 (2015)
47. Ali, J., Kumar, S.: Information and communication technologies (ICTs) and farmers' decision-making across the agricultural supply chain. Int. J. Inf. Manag. **31**, 149–159 (2011)
48. Kushwaha, G.S.: Competitive advantage through information and communication technology (ICT) enabled supply chain management practices. Int. J. Enterp. Comput. Bus. Syst. **1**, 3 (2011)
49. Kabra, G., Ramesh, A.: Analyzing ICT issues in humanitarian supply chain management: a SAP-LAP linkages framework. Glob. J. Flex. Syst. Manag. **16**, 157–171 (2015)
50. Dey, A., Jenamani, M., Thakkar, Jitesh J.: Lexical TF-IDF: an n-gram feature space for cross-domain classification of sentiment reviews. In: Shankar, B.U., Ghosh, K., Mandal, D.P., Ray, S.S., Zhang, D., Pal, S.K. (eds.) PReMI 2017. LNCS, vol. 10597, pp. 380–386. Springer, Cham (2017). https://doi.org/10.1007/978-3-319-69900-4_48
51. Bakhshizadeh, H., Hosseinpour, M., Pahlevanzadeh, F.: Rural ICT interactive planning in Ardabil province: Sardabeh case study. Procedia Comput. Sci. **3**, 254–259 (2011)
52. Bhuasiri, W., Xaymoungkhoun, O., Zo, H., Rho, J.J., Ciganek, A.P.: Critical success factors for e-learning in developing countries: a comparative analysis between ICT experts and faculty. Comput. Educ. **58**, 843–855 (2012)
53. Grazzi, M., Vergara, S.: ICT in developing countries: are language barriers relevant? evidence from Paraguay. Inf. Econ. Policy **24**, 161–171 (2012)
54. Gupta, B., Dasgupta, S., Gupta, A.: Adoption of ICT in a government organization in a developing country: an empirical study. J. Strateg. Inf. Syst. **17**, 140–154 (2008)
55. Kelvin, O.O., Oghenetega, I., Jackson, A.: A review of issues in information and communication technology (ICT) planning and implementation in academic libraries in Nigeria. Libr. Hi Tech News **29**, 11–17 (2012)

56. Kyobe, M.: Investigating the key factors influencing ICT adoption in South Africa. J. Syst. Inf. Technol. **13**, 255–267 (2011)
57. Rahayu, R., Day, J.: Determinant factors of e-commerce adoption by SMEs in developing country: evidence from Indonesia. Procedia – Soc. Behav. Sci. **195**, 142–150 (2015)
58. Sandeep, M.S., Ravishankar, M.N.: The continuity of underperforming ICT projects in the public sector. Inf. Manag. **51**, 700–711 (2014)
59. Sobanke, V., Adegbite, S., Ilori, M., Egbetokun, A.: Determinants of technological capability of firms in a developing country. Procedia Eng. **69**, 991–1000 (2014)
60. Gichoya, D.: Factors affecting the successful implementation of ICT projects in government. Electron. J. e-government **3**, 175–184 (2005)
61. Department of Food and Public Distribution, Government of India: Status Paper on Computerisation of TPDS Operations (2014)

Mobile, Nano, Quantum Computing

Calculating Transmittance and Field Enhancement of n-Layer MIM Surface Plasmon Structure for Detection of Biological Nano-Objects

Arpan Deyasi[1(✉)], Pratibha Verma[2], and Angsuman Sarkar[3]

[1] Department of Electronics and Communication Engineering,
RCC Institute of Information Technology, Kolkata, India
deyasi_arpan@yahoo.co.in

[2] Department of Electronics and Communication Engineering, NIT Agartala,
Jirania, India
vermapratibha1007@gmail.com

[3] Department of Electronics and Communication Engineering,
Kalyani Government Engineering College, Kalyani, India
angsumansarkar@ieee.org

Abstract. In this paper, transmittance property of n-layer metal-insulator-metal surface plasmon structure is analytically investigated in the visible range of electromagnetic spectrum. Here n-layer signifies the critical number of layers after which increase in layer number insignificantly modifies the photonic behavior of the structure. Corresponding field enhancement is also computed to study the critical dimensions and external incident angles for maximum energy reflection. Peak in transmittance spectra is calculated when propagation constant of plasmon surface and that of incident wave becomes nearly equal. Results will help to detect biological nano-objects whose signature viruses have the same wavelength when transmittance peak occurs.

Keywords: Transmittance · Field enhancement · MIM structure
Surface plasmon · Resonance · Angle of incidence

1 Introduction

In a metal-dielectric interface, if free electrons are going to oscillate rapidly in longitudinal direction [1] when they are coherent and delocalized, and that phenomenon is termed as surface plasmon. At this condition, dielectric constant of the metal becomes a function of frequency, and also becomes a complex number. This phenomenon is described by J. C. Maxwell as the propagation of electron density in a progressive manner [2] along the interface, and henceforth, the occurrence is considered as dynamic [3]. This structure is used in spectroscopic application [4], designing of molecular sensors [5], Nano-photonic device [6], detection of optical power [7], nanometric measurement [8] etc.

© Springer Nature Singapore Pte Ltd. 2018
J. K. Mandal and D. Sinha (Eds.): CSI 2017, CCIS 836, pp. 393–401, 2018.
https://doi.org/10.1007/978-981-13-1343-1_33

Slavik *et al.* [9] proposed novel sensor with better resolution and sensitivity using SPR with lower cost and power consumption. Gold is used for sensing applications much earlier to the work of Slavik where the effect of environment monitoring is considered [10]. Peng proposed temperature sensor [11] based on SPR inside PCF by using different liquids in the air holes to reduce the loss. Maximum resonance for SP based sensors is found at normal incidence condition [12]. Recently grating-based SPR biosensor is proposed [13] in the vicinity of infrared wavelength, and improvement of figure of merit is calculated by varying the structural parameters. Thermometer is designed using liquid crystal based hollow fibre [14] with very high sensitivity. Now-a-days, optical waveguide based SPR sensor based smartphone is proposed [15].

In the present work, transmittivity and filed enhancement of SPR structure is proposed with particular investigation of peak position. Corresponding wavelength will produce resonance when it matches with the signature wavelength of any biological nano-objects e.g., virus. Thus identification of detection of the object can be made by varying angle of incidence along with appropriate structural parameters. Here number of layers is increased and properties are calculated for that multilayer arrangement where further introduction of additional layers will not produce any significant change in the photonic properties.

2 Mathematical Formulation

Reflectance of perpendicular and parallel polarized waves for complex index of refraction

$$r_\perp = \frac{n_1 \cos(\theta_{incident}) - n_2 \cos(\theta_{refracted})}{n_1 \cos(\theta_{incident}) + n_2 \cos(\theta_{refracted})} \tag{1}$$

$$r_{||} = \frac{n_2 \cos(\theta_{incident}) - n_1 \cos(\theta_{refracted})}{n_2 \cos(\theta_{incident}) + n_1 \cos(\theta_{refracted})} \tag{2}$$

Perpendicular polarized or transverse electric, light cannot excite surface Plasmon resonance because of the oscillations of the electric field do not couple with the longitudinal modes of vibration of the sample media.

Fresnel co-efficient for a parallel polarized incident waves is-

$$r_{||} = \frac{\left(\frac{n_2}{n_1}\right)^2 \cos(\theta) - i\sqrt{\sin^2 \theta - \left(\frac{n_2}{n_1}\right)^2}}{\left(\frac{n_2}{n_1}\right)^2 \cos(\theta) + i\sqrt{\sin^2 \theta - \left(\frac{n_2}{n_1}\right)^2}} \tag{3}$$

For physical systems-

$$R_{\parallel} = \left[\frac{n_1 \sqrt{1 - \left[\frac{n_1}{n_2} \sin(\theta_{incidence})\right]^2} - n_2 \cos(\theta_{incidence})}{n_1 \sqrt{1 - \left[\frac{n_1}{n_2} \sin(\theta_{incidence})\right]^2} + n_2 \cos(\theta_{incidence})} \right]^2 \tag{4}$$

When $n_1 < n_2$, external reflection results and when $n_1 > n_2$, internal reflection occurs. If $n_1 = n_2$, then no reflection occurs because there is no optical boundary to interact with.

For multilayer, reflectance co-efficient between layer 'i' and 'j' is:

$$r_{ij} = \frac{n_j^2 \sqrt{n_i^2 - n_{ambient}^2 \sin^2 \theta} - n_i^2 \sqrt{n_j^2 - n_{ambient}^2 \sin^2 \theta}}{n_j^2 \sqrt{n_i^2 - n_{ambient}^2 \sin^2 \theta} + n_i^2 \sqrt{n_j^2 - n_{ambient}^2 \sin^2 \theta}} \tag{5}$$

The absorptive term also contributes to a phase shift at each layer by a phase factor φ_i of i.

$$\phi_i = \frac{2\pi d}{\lambda} \sqrt{n_i^2 - n_{ambient}^2 \sin^2 \theta} \tag{6}$$

where d_i is the thickness of layer i.

For parallel polarized systems, the characteristic matrix describing each layer is:

$$M_i = \begin{bmatrix} \cos\left(\frac{2\pi}{\lambda} n_i h_i \cos \theta_i\right) & -i \sin\left(\frac{2\pi}{\lambda} n_i h_i \cos \theta_i\right) \\ -i\sqrt{\frac{\mu_i}{n_i^2}} \cos(\theta_i) \sin\left(\frac{2\pi}{\lambda} n_i h_i \cos \theta_i\right) & \cos\left(\frac{2\pi}{\lambda} n_i h_i \cos \theta_i\right) \end{bmatrix} \tag{7}$$

The field strength in an n-layer system and their Fresnel behavior is:

$$Q_i = M_i^{-1} \prod_{i=1}^{n-1} M_i Q_{n-1} \tag{8}$$

where Q_i is defined as the matrix of the field strength at each layer is:

$$Q_1 = M_1^{-1} \prod_{i=1}^{n-1} M_i Q_{n-1} \tag{9}$$

3 Results and Discussion

For n-layer, effect of variation of incidence angle on transmittance, field enhancement and reflectance for different structural and external parameters are discussed which depicts that transmittance is heightened up as incidence angle is raised but fall down after critical angle. Field enhancement is only maximum at critical angle and then follows the symmetry nature at both sides of peak point. Incidence angles with reflectance for 4-layer follows the same nature as of 3-layer IMI structure [11] except the enhancement in magnitude of reflectance.

Figure 1 shows the transmittance of n layer profile for different values of incidence angle. With increase of incidence angle the transmittance increases and reaches to the maximum, but beyond certain limit it decreases sharply. At critical angle most of the energy gets passed along the surface. But beyond critical angle the ratio of the transmitted signal to the total incident signal i.e. the transmittance decreases very rapidly because of the total internal reflection.

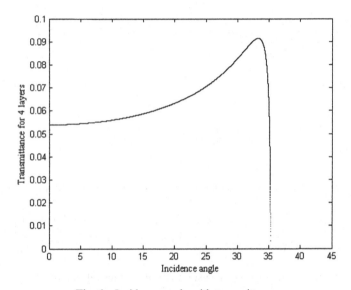

Fig. 1. Incidence angle with transmittance

Figure 2 shows the transmittance for different values of thickness of gold layer profile with incidence angle. This shows that for a given thickness of the gold layer incidence angle the transmittance of gold layer increases with increase in thickness. Refractive index of a material is fixed and critical angle depends on the refractive index of the material, thus it is also fixed for a material. So transmittance falls for different thickness of gold layer at the same critical angle of incidence.

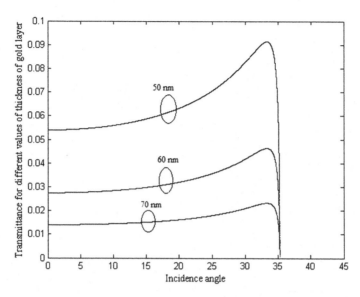

Fig. 2. Incidence angle vs. transmittance for different values of thickness of gold layer

Figure 3 shows the transmittance for different values of wavelength of He-Ne laser light profile for different values of incidence angle. Here as the wavelength of He-Ne laser light increases the transmittance also increases with increase in incidence angle. As with the increase in wavelength light travels more distance inside the material so transmittance increases. But beyond critical angle the transmittance decreases rapidly as total internal reflection increases.

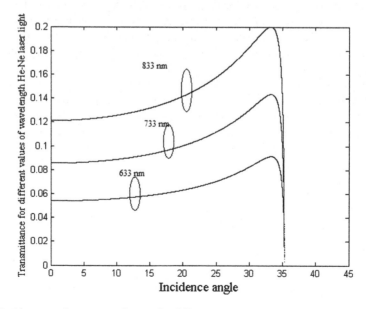

Fig. 3. Incidence angle vs. transmittance for different values of wavelength of He-Ne laser light

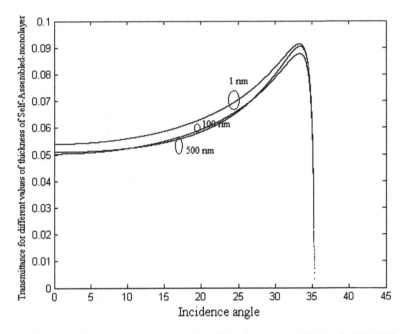

Fig. 4. Incidence angle vs. transmittance for different values of thickness of SAM layer

Figure 4 shows the transmittance for different values of thickness of self assembled monolayer profile for different values of incidence angle. This shows that for a given thickness of SAM layer the transmittance increases with increase in incidence angle. Refractive index of a material is fixed and critical angle depends on the refractive index of the material, thus it is also fixed for a material. So transmittance falls for different thickness of SAM layer at the same critical angle of incidence. But for different values of thickness of the SAM layer the variation is small as compared to the gold layer.

Figure 5 shows the field enhancement for different values of thickness of gold layer profile for different values of incidence angle. It shows that with the increase in thickness the peak value of electric field decreases. Keeping all other parameters constant the field density is higher in thin layer than thick layer as field accumulation is higher in case of thin layer. So peak value of electric field intensity is higher in thin layer as compared to the thick layer.

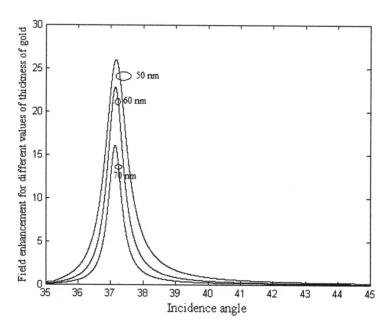

Fig. 5. Incidence angle vs. field enhancement for different values of thickness of gold layer

Figure 6 shows the field enhancement for different values of thickness of self assembled monolayer profile for different values of incidence angle. As when the incidence angle increases the field intensity at the layer surface goes on increasing. At critical incidence angle, the field intensity is at maximum at the surface as most of the energy passes along the surface. If again the incidence angle increases then energy starts going inside the layer, thus reducing the field intensity at the surface. So there is the peak electric field at the surface at critical angle in the graph. But unlike the gold layer here the field intensity profile is same for all the thickness of self assembled monolayer. For different thickness field distribution is superimposed one on another.

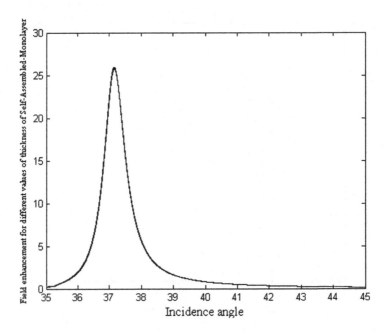

Fig. 6. Incidence angle vs. field enhancement for different values of SAM layer

4 Conclusion

Transmittance of n-layer surface plasmon structure and corresponding field enhancement is analytically calculated at visible range of electromagnetic spectrum with detailed mathematical formulation. Here n-layer signifies the fact that after increasing number of layers, the optical properties will change insignificantly, and thus form application perspective, this result can be considered as generalized for a multi-layer structure. Peak of transmittance spectra is calculated for is dependence on different structure parameters and operating wavelength and field enhancement is obtained for maximum reflection of energy. Result will play critical role in detecting virus or other biological smaller objects when the peak occurs at that signature wavelength of the virus.

References

1. Ishimaru, A., Jaruwatanadilok, S., Kuga, Y.: Generalized surface plasmon resonance sensors using metamaterials and negative index materials. Prog. Electromagn. Res. **51**, 139–152 (2005)
2. Sharma, A.K., Jha, R., Gupta, B.D.: Fiber-optic sensors based on surface plasmon resonance: a comprehensive review. IEEE Sens. J. **7**, 1118–1129 (2007)
3. Homola, J., Yee, S.S., Gauglitz, G.: Surface plasmon resonance sensors: review. Sens. Actuators, B **54**, 3–15 (1999)

4. Ding, S.Y., et al.: Nanostructure-based plasmon-enhanced raman spectroscopy for surface analysis of materials. Nat. Rev. Mater. **1**, 16021 (2016)
5. Boozer, C., Kim, G., Cong, S., Guan, H., Londergan, T.: Looking towards label-free biomolecular interaction analysis in a high-throughput format: a review of new surface plasmon resonance technologies. Curr. Opin. Biotechnol. **17**, 400–405 (2006)
6. Hong, B., Sun, A., Pang, L., Venkatesh, A.G., Hall, D., Fainman, Y.: Integration of faradaic electrochemical impedance spectroscopy into a scalable surface plasmon biosensor for in tandem detection. Opt. Express **23**(23), 30237–30249 (2015)
7. Feng, D., Zhou, W., Qiao, X., Albert, J.: High resolution fiber optic surface plasmon resonance sensors with single-sided gold coatings. Opt. Express **24**(15), 16456–16464 (2016)
8. Li, H., Peng, W., Wang, Y., Hu, L.: Theoretical analyses of localized surface plasmon resonance spectrum with nanoparticles imprinted polymers. In: IEEE Communications and Photonics Conference and Exhibition, pp. 1–8 (2011)
9. Slavík, R., Homola, J.: Optical multilayers for LED-based surface plasmon resonance sensors. Appl. Opt. **45**, 3752–3759 (2006)
10. Meriaudeau, F., Downey, T.R., Passian, A., Wig, A., Ferrell, T.L.: Environment effects on surface-plasmon spectra in gold-island films potential for sensing applications. Appl. Opt. **37**, 8030–8037 (1998)
11. Peng, Y., Hou, J., Huang, Z., Lu, Q.: Temperature sensor based on surface plasmon resonance within selectively coated photonic crystal fiber. Appl. Opt. **51**, 6361–6367 (2012)
12. Melo, E.F., Fontana, E.: Design of surface plasmon resonance sensors having maximum response at normal incidence. In: Frontiers in Optics 2012/Laser Science XXVIII, OSA Technical Digest (online) (2012). FTu3A.18
13. Tahmasebpour, M., Bahrami, M., Asgari, A.: Design study of nanograting-based surface plasmon resonance biosensor in the near-infrared wavelength. Appl. Opt. **53**, 1449–1458 (2014)
14. Lu, M., Zhang, X., Liang, Y., Li, L., Masson, J.F., Peng, W.: Liquid crystal filled surface plasmon resonance thermometer. Opt. Express **24**, 10904–10911 (2016)
15. Bremer, K., Walter, J., Roth, B.: Optical waveguide based surface plasmon resonance sensor system for smartphones, imaging and applied optics: OSA technical digest (online) (2016). AIW2B.1

A Comparative Analysis of CNF and XOR-AND Representations for QCA Majority Gate Estimation

Ayan Chaudhuri[1], Mahamuda Sultana[2], Diganta Sengupta[3(✉)],
Chitrita Chaudhuri[4], and Atal Chaudhuri[4]

[1] Techno India, Kolkata, India
ayanchaudhuri27@gmail.com
[2] Techno India College of Technology, Kolkata, India
sg.mahamuda@gmail.com
[3] Techno India – Batanagar, Kolkata, India
sg.diganta@gmail.com
[4] Jadavpur University, Kolkata, India
{cchitrita,atalc23}@gmail.com

Abstract. Complimenting the rising research of reversible computation, Quantum Dot Cellular Automata (QCA) has emerged as a potential alternative for CMOS. Although in its nascent stage, QCA promises logical reversibility; thereby adhering to the near zero power dissipation attribute of reversibility. Architectures built using quantum dot cells are majorly cascades of Majority Voters - the fundamental gate in QCA. This study investigates two predictive procedures to pre-determine the number of Majority Voters required for realizing a given Boolean function on QCA platform. One procedure utilizes the concept of optimized XOR-AND formulation of a Boolean function represented in CNF whereas the other procedure determines the Majority Voter count based on Karnaugh map approach. Pre-determination of Majority Voter count can result in analysis of efficiency deciding parameters (area etc.) beforehand, hence the motivation of the study.

Keywords: QCA · Majority voter · XOR-AND · Reversible logic
Reversible computation

1 Introduction

Addressing issues faced by CMOS due to dimensional scaling such as short channel, power dissipation and quantum effects, alternative information processing devices have gained the attention of researchers. Results reflect proposals for Quantum Dot Cellular Automata (QCA) [1], Carbon Nanotubes [2], Single Electron Transistors (SETs) [3], Nanomagnet-based Logic (NML) [4] and Tunneling Phase Logic (TPL) [5] devices. QCA forms the recent implementation of the original "Cellular Automata Principle" [6] and is the subject for this study. The paradigm for QCA states the presence of two or four quantum dots in a single cell with mobile charges occupying half of the dots. Hence a cell comprising of four dots can be addressed as a paired two dot cell.

© Springer Nature Singapore Pte Ltd. 2018
J. K. Mandal and D. Sinha (Eds.): CSI 2017, CCIS 836, pp. 402–415, 2018.
https://doi.org/10.1007/978-981-13-1343-1_34

Cascades of these cells create Nano-architectures. A unique combination of five such cells forms the fundamental gate of Quantum Dot Cellular Automata and is known as the Majority Voter gate (henceforth written as MV), Fig. 1.

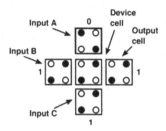

Fig. 1. Majority Voter – the fundamental gate of QCA

The inputs of the MV can be manipulated for realizing the fundamental Boolean logic gates [7] and thereby design any arbitrary Boolean specification. Hence majority voter gate count and QCA cell cascades form the primitive measures for determining the efficiency of a Nano-architecture built using QCA cells. We propose two methods for estimation of MV count for a given Boolean specification prior to its realization using QCA cells. One of the approaches formulate a CNF Boolean specification into a XOR-AND Boolean equivalent and generate MV count thereafter. The other approach follows the traditional Karnaugh Map approach to determine the MV count.

The rest of the paper is organized as follows: The next section concentrates on the related work. Section 3 illustrates the proposed approaches for MV count. Section 4 presents the analysis results followed by conclusion and future scope in Sect. 5.

2   Related Work

Quantum Dot Cellular Automata has been a topic of research for the last decade and has witnessed a plethora of architecture design proposals over the years. One of the notable being the Programmable Logic Array (PLA) implemented using QCA [8]. In this proposal, the authors have designed a fixed geometrical layout of cells for realizing any Boolean specification on a given set of inputs. The QCA PLA proposal is basically an advanced proposal of reconfigurable QCA logic devices (QCA FPGAs). In either case, FPGA or PLA, a CNF Boolean specification serves as the input.

Arbitrary Boolean specifications when realized using Majority Voters require interconnection within the subsequent MVS. This is done using series of QCA cells termed as QCA wires but the length and width of the wire generate various rotational, displacement and missing cell defects as shown by Dysart [9]. Dysart has utilized *"Probabilistic Transfer Matrix (PTM)"* to determine the reliability of a QCA circuit depending upon the cell structure.

Kong et al. [10] has harvested *Majority Logic* concept to provide an optimal QCA layout for three variable Boolean functions. They also provide a generalized decomposition theorem for decomposing any Boolean function claiming their study to remove all the redundancies in QCA designs. Pudi and Sridharan [11] have proposed fresh decomposition theorems for designing low delay adders in QCA. They use three bit majority functions in deciding the nth carry from the initial carry in an n-bit adder recursively. Other recent adder design proposals using QCA platform are presented in [12] (binary) and [13] (decimal).

Wang et al. [14] have proposed a new concept termed as the *"Majority Expression Look-up Table (MLUT)"* generated by optimized majority expressions for four variable Boolean specifications. They further optimize the majority network using a unique redundancy removal process proposed by them. Calculation of the cost function for QCA designs have been provided by Liu et al. in [15].

3   Proposed Method

This section presents the two proposed procedures for MV count estimation. The first one illustrates the XOR-AND decomposition process (both non-optimized and optimized) and the second one illustrates the Karnaugh map approach.

3.1   XOR-AND Decomposition Approach

The XOR algebra effectively yields a gate-minimum result otherwise not achievable using conventional mapping methods. The non-optimized approach for XOR-AND decomposition of a Boolean specification is provided in Sect. 6.3 of [16]. The process of XOR-AND decomposition using the algorithm in [16] has been illustrated in Appendix – A in this study. We present a novel process for post-decomposition optimization.

Given a Boolean XOR-AND specification, we have generated a set of minimization rules for certain combinations of minterms as stated in Table 1. These substitutions provide optimized XOR-AND expressions. Thereafter the MV count is generated from the optimized (minimized) expressions. The rules have been generated by truth table analysis of the XOR specifications.

Close observation of Table 1 reveals that the optimized expression converts a XOR-AND specification into an AND equivalent with inverted literals. AND expressions have been used in this study to calculate the MV count as per a set of rules as described in Table 2. The rules have been specifically generated in this study for four variable AND function but can be extended to n-variable AND operation.

Where

$M_i(x, y, z) = xy + xz + yz$; + resembles OR operation for the ith Majority Voter Gate

Output of M_i serves as the input of M_{i+1}.

Table 2 illustrates the process of realization of an n-variable minterm into cascades of Majority Voters, 'n' restricted to 4 in the present case. Table 2 also provides the MV count for the minterms. Hence, three Majority Voter gates are required for four variable minterm whereas two Majority Voter gates are required to realize a three variable minterm. Table 3 provides the MV count for all the minterms in Table 1.

Table 1. Minimization rules for XOR-AND expressions

Expression	Optimized expression	Expression	Optimized expression	Expression	Optimized expression
abcd ⊕ abc	abcd'	bcd ⊕ b	(cd)'b	abc ⊕ bc	a'bc
abcd ⊕ abd	abc'd	bcd ⊕ c	(bd)'c	abc ⊕ a	(bc)'a
abcd ⊕ acd	ab'cd	bcd ⊕ d	(bc)'d	abc ⊕ b	(ac)'b
abcd ⊕ bcd	a'bcd	acd ⊕ ac	acd'	abc ⊕ c	(ab)'c
abcd ⊕ ab	(cd)'ab	acd ⊕ ad	ac'd	cd ⊕ c	cd'
abcd ⊕ ac	(bd)'ac	acd ⊕ cd	a'cd	cd ⊕ d	c'd
abcd ⊕ ad	(bc)'ad	acd ⊕ a	(cd)'a	bd ⊕ b	bd'
abcd ⊕ bc	(ad)'bc	acd ⊕ c	(ad)'c	bd ⊕ d	b'd
abcd ⊕ bd	(ac)'bd	acd ⊕ d	(ac)'d	bc ⊕ b	bc'
abcd ⊕ cd	(ab)'cd	abd ⊕ ab	abd'	bc ⊕ c	b'c
abcd ⊕ a	(bcd)'a	abd ⊕ ad	ab'd	ad ⊕ a	ad'
abcd ⊕ b	(acd)'b	abd ⊕ bd	a'bd	ad ⊕ d	a'd
abcd ⊕ c	(abd)'c	abd ⊕ a	(bd)'a	ac ⊕ a	ac'
abcd ⊕ d	(abc)'d	abd ⊕ b	(ad)'b	ac ⊕ c	a'c
bcd ⊕ bc	bcd'	abd ⊕ d	(ab)'d	ab ⊕ a	ab'
bcd ⊕ bd	bc'd	abc ⊕ ab	abc'	ab ⊕ b	a'b
bcd ⊕ cd	b'cd	abc ⊕ ac	ab'c		

Table 2. Rules for MV realization of AND operation for four variable minterms

AND expression	Majority voter realization	MV count
abcd	M_1 (a,b,0) → M_2 (ab,c,0) → M_3 (abc,d,0)	3
abc	M_1 (a,b,0) → M_2 (ab,c,0)	2
abd	M_1 (a,b,0) → M_2 (ab,d,0)	2
acd	M_1 (a,c,0) → M_2 (ac,d,0)	2
bcd	M_1 (b,c,0) → M_2 (bc,d,0)	2
ab	M_1 (a,b,0)	1
ac	M_1 (a,c,0)	1
ad	M_1 (a,d,0)	1
bc	M_1 (b,c,0)	1
bd	M_1 (b,d,0)	1
cd	M_1 (c,d,0)	1

Till now we have discussed the MV count for a single optimized minterm. The MV count also depends upon the number of minterms in the simplified XOR-AND expression from the Boolean specification and is given by Eq. (1).

Table 3. MV count for n-variable minterms, n∈[1, 4]

Expression	MV count	Expression	MV count	Expression	MV count
abcd'	3	(cd)'b	2	a'bc	2
abc'd	3	(bd)'c	2	(bc)'a	2
ab'cd	3	(bc)'d	2	(ac)'b	2
a'bcd	3	acd'	2	(ab)'c	2
(cd)'ab	3	ac'd	2	cd'	1
(bd)'ac	3	a'cd	2	c'd	1
(bc)'ad	3	(cd)'a	2	bd'	1
(ad)'bc	3	(ad)'c	2	b'd	1
(ac)'bd	3	(ac)'d	2	bc'	1
(ab)'cd	3	abd'	2	b'c	1
(bcd)'a	3	ab'd	2	ad'	1
(acd)'b	3	a'bd	2	a'd	1
(abd)'c	3	(bd)'a	2	ac'	1
(abc)'d	3	(ad)'b	2	a'c	1
bcd'	2	(ab)'d	2	ab'	1
bc'd	2	abc'	2	a'b	1
b'cd	2	ab'c	2		

$$MV\ Count = \lfloor n/2 \rfloor * 3 \tag{1}$$

$$n = \#\ of\ terms\ in\ the\ simplified\ XOR - AND\ Expression$$

Let us define MV count presented in Table 3 to be $MV_{Count-1}$ and that given by Eq. (1) as $MV_{Count-2}$. The cumulative MV count is given by Eq. (2).

$$MV_{Count} = MV_{Count-1} + MV_{Count-2} \tag{2}$$

Illustrative Example 1

Number of Majority Voter Gates required realizing the given Boolean specification.

$$f = \sum(2, 3, 5, 7, 8, 12, 13, 14) \tag{3}$$

The XOR-AND equivalent for the Eq. (3) is given by Eq. (4).

$$f = a \oplus c \oplus ad \oplus bc \oplus bd \oplus acd \tag{4}$$

The process for generation of Eq. (4) is provided in Appendix – A.
$MV_{Count-1}$ for Eq. (4) = (0 + 0 + 1 + 1 + 1 + 2) = 5 (from Table 3)
$MV_{Count-2}$ for Eq. (4) = 9 (using Eq. (1))

$$\therefore MV_{Count} = MV_{Count-1} + MV_{Count-2} = 5 + 9 = 14.$$

Hence, 14 Majority Voter gates are required to realize the Boolean specification given by Eq. (3) using QCA.

Illustrative Example 2

In the worst case scenario, a simplified four variable XOR-AND expression will have at most fifteen terms. The XOR-AND expression for such a specification is presented in Eq. (5).

$$f = a \oplus b \oplus c \oplus d \oplus ab \oplus ac \oplus ad \oplus bc \oplus bd \oplus cd \oplus abc \oplus abd \oplus acd \oplus bcd \oplus abcd \tag{5}$$

Using our optimizing technique presented in Table 1, the optimized XOR-AND expression is presented in Eq. (6).

$$f = a \oplus a'b \oplus a'c \oplus a'd \oplus a'bc \oplus a'bd \oplus a'cd \oplus a'bcd \tag{6}$$

$MV_{Count-1}$ for Eq. (6) = (0 + 1+1 + 1+2 + 2+2 + 3) = 12 (from Table 3)
$MV_{Count-2}$ for Eq. (6) = 12 (using Eq. (1))

$$\therefore MV_{Count} = MV_{Count-1} + MV_{Count-2} = 12 + 12 = 24.$$

Hence, 24 Majority Voter gates are required to realize the Boolean specification given by Eq. (5) using QCA.

3.2   Karnaugh Map Approach

The Karnaugh map (K-Map) approach simplifies the Boolean Specification in CNF using a K-Map and then calculates the MV count from the simplified CNF Boolean Expression. The MV count for minterms are presented in Table 4.

$MV_{Count-1}$ for K-Map approach is given by Table 4.
$MV_{Count-2}$ for K-Map approach is given by Eq. (7).

$$MV_{Count-2} = n - 1 \tag{7}$$

$$n = \# \, of \, minterms \, in \, the \, Boolean \, Expression$$

∴ The cumulative MV count is given by Eq. (2).

Illustrative Example 1

Number of Majority Voter Gates required realizing the given Boolean specification.

$$f = \sum(2, 3, 5, 7, 8, 12, 13, 14) \tag{8}$$

The simplified expression for Eq. (8) using K-Map is given by Eq. (9)

Table 4. Majority Voter gates required for respective minterms

Expression	MV count	Expression	MV count	Expression	MV count
a'c'	1	a'b'c'	2	b'c'd'	2
a'd	1	a'b'd	2	b'c'd	2
a'c	1	a'b'c	2	b'cd	2
bc'	1	a'bc'	2	b'cd'	2
bd	1	a'bd	2	ab'd'	2
bc	1	a'bc	2	a'bd'	2
ac'	1	abc'	2	abd'	2
ad	1	abd	2	ab'd'	2
ac	1	abc	2	a'b'c'd'	3
b'c'	1	ab'c'	2	a'b'c'd	3
b'd	1	ab'd	2	a'b'cd	3
b'c	1	ab'c	2	a'b'cd'	3
a'd'	1	a'c'd'	2	a'bc'd'	3
bd'	1	a'c'd	2	a'bc'd	3
ad'	1	a'cd	2	a'bcd	3
a'b'	1	a'cd'	2	a'bcd'	3
a'b	1	bc'd'	2	abc'd'	3
ab	1	bc'd	2	abc'd	3
ab'	1	bcd	2	abcd	3
c'd'	1	bcd'	2	abcd'	3
c'd	1	ac'd'	2	ab'c'd'	3
cd	1	ac'd	2	ab'c'd	3
cd'	1	acd	2	ab'cd	3
b'd'	1	acd'	2	ab'cd'	3

$$f = ac' + ab' + bcd' \tag{9}$$

$MV_{Count-1}$ for Eq. (9) = (1 + 1 + 2 = 4) (using Table 4)
$MV_{Count-2}$ for Eq. (9) = 2 (using Eq. (7))

$$\therefore MV_{Count} = MV_{Count-1} + MV_{Count-2} = 4 + 2 = 6.$$

Discussion.
It can be well inferred that the worst case scenario arises for the two given expressions in Eqs. (10) and (11). Close observation of these two terms reveal that simplified expression contains eight terms each, given by Eqs. (12) and (13) respectively for Eqs. (10) and (11).

$$f = \sum(0, 3, 5, 6, 9, 10, 12, 15) \tag{10}$$

$$f = \sum(1, 2, 4, 7, 8, 11, 12, 14) \tag{11}$$

$$f = a'b'c'd' + a'b'cd + a'bc'd + a'bcd' + abc'd' + abc'd + ab'cd' + abcd \tag{12}$$

$$f = a'b'c'd + a'b'cd' + a'bc'd' + a'bcd + abc'd + abcd' + ab'c'd' + ab'cd \tag{13}$$

Table 5. Comparative analysis for ten standard function using the two proposals

Standard functions	MV count using optimized XOR-AND	MV Count using Karnaugh Map
$f = abc$	2	2
$f = abc + a'b'c'$	12	5
$f = abc + ab'c'$	5	5
$f = ab + bc$	7	3
$f = ab + a'b'c$	11	4
$f = a'bc + a'b'c' + abc'$	9	8
$f = ab + bc + ac$	6	5
$f = ab + b'c$	5	3
$f = ab + bc + a'b'c'$	7	6
$f = abc + a'b'c + ab'b' + a'bc'$	3	11

4 Comparative Analysis

In this section we provide the MV count for ten standard functions using both the proposed procedures (Table 5).

Figure 2 presents the graphical representation of Table 5.

From Table 5 and Fig. 2, it can be observed that the two approaches provide different MV counts for different functions. Hence, the choice of procedure for the best result is unpredictable. Therefore, we executed the two procedures independently on an arbitrary large set (100 functions) of data as presented in Appendix – B. Figure 3 presents the graphical representation of the analysis on the large set of data.

Figure 3 reflects that the choice of a certain procedure to pre-determine the MV count in advance is not possible within the scope of the present study. Hence, we conclude that for pre-determining the MV count for a certain Boolean specification, both the procedures should be executed and the best result to be considered.

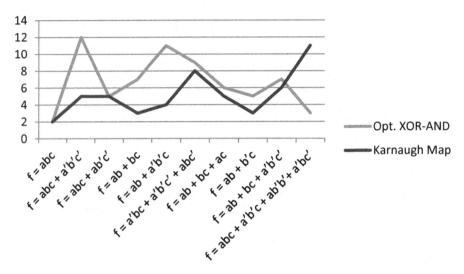

Fig. 2. Graphical representation of Table 5

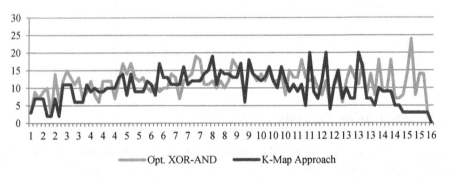

Fig. 3. Comparative analysis of the two procedures on an arbitrary set of data (Appendix – B)

5 Conclusion

We have proposed two approaches for pre-determining the Majority Voter gate count for realization of an arbitrary Boolean specification on QCA platform. One procedure decomposes the Boolean function into optimized XOR-AND expression and calculates the Majority Voter count and the other procedure uses the tradition CNF Boolean simplification approach to determine the Majority Voter count. We have done a comparative analysis of both the approaches and have witnessed that the choice of procedure is specification dependent. Hence, we propose addressing a given Boolean expression using both the approaches and then finalize on the minimum count for the Majority Voter gates.

The proposed optimization procedure for the XOR-AND decomposition can be further explored to design a better optimization technique fetching gate-minimum results irrespective of Boolean specifications.

Appendix – A

This Appendix illustrates the process of XOR-AND extraction from a given arbitrary Boolean specification using Sect. 6.3 of [16]. For sake of simplicity, we take the same example given in Illustrative Example 1, Eq. (3). Let the given Boolean specification be

$$f = \sum(2,3,5,7,8,12,13,14)$$

The following algorithm presents the process of XOR-AND extraction.

Algorithm.

Step1: To draw the minimization chart and list all minterms in the Boolean specification on the first column denoted by f_1 in Table 6.

Step2: To list all minterm possibilities in the first row. Start with one, all possible pairs of variables, then all triples of variables and so on up to columns for all the variables possibility.

Step3: Placing 1's in all possible variable columns that have unprimed variables in minterms as shown in Table 6.

Step4: To obtain the function in final XOR-AND, crossing ($\times$) all columns containing even number of 1's.

Therefore using Table 6, the final XOR-AND expression (Eq. (4)) taking into account only tick marks ($\sqrt{}$) in Table 6 is

$$f = a \oplus c \oplus ad \oplus bc \oplus bd \oplus acd$$

Table 6. Minimization chart (Courtesy: Dajani, O.: emerging design methodology and its implementation through RNS And QCA. Dissertations 646, Wayne State University (2013))

f_1	1	a	b	c	d	ab	ac	ad	bc	bd	cd	abc	abd	acd	bcd	abcd
0010				1			1		1		1	1		1	1	1
0011											1			1	1	1
0101										1			1		1	1
0111															1	1
1000		1				1	1	1				1	1	1		1
1100						1						1	1			1
1101													1			1
1110												1				1
	$\times$	$\sqrt{}$	$\times$	$\sqrt{}$	$\times$	$\times$	$\times$	$\sqrt{}$	$\sqrt{}$	$\sqrt{}$	$\times$	$\times$	$\times$	$\sqrt{}$	$\times$	$\times$

Appendix – B

MV count on a larger set of data (Fig. 3 has been generated using this data)

# Minterms	Boolean Specifications (CNF) f=	MV count using Optimized XOR-AND	MV Count using Karnaugh Map
1	$\sum(13)$	3	3
2	$\sum(3,14)$	9	7
2	$\sum(12,15)$	7	7
2	$\sum(7,9)$	9	7
2	$\sum(0,4)$	10	2
2	$\sum(5,13)$	2	2
2	$\sum(1,14)$	14	7
2	$\sum(2,3)$	6	2
3	$\sum(1,7,11)$	12	11
3	$\sum(4,11,14)$	15	11
3	$\sum(5,6,9)$	13	11
3	$\sum(0,6,8)$	11	6
3	$\sum(1,3,4)$	13	6
3	$\sum(2,7,10)$	7	6
3	$\sum(3,5,15)$	9	11
4	$\sum(0,1,2,13)$	12	9
4	$\sum(1,3,6,13)$	8	10
4	$\sum(3,7,10,15)$	6	9
4	$\sum(1,4,9,11)$	12	9
4	$\sum(2,11,12,15)$	12	10
4	$\sum(1,2,12,13)$	12	10
4	$\sum(0,4,9,15)$	7	10
5	$\sum(0,3,6,7,9)$	12	13
5	$\sum(3,5,8,11,14)$	17	14
5	$\sum(6,7,8,10,11)$	14	8
5	$\sum(0,6,11,12,13)$	17	14
5	$\sum(2,9,13,14,15)$	13	9
5	$\sum(4,7,10,11,12)$	12	9
5	$\sum(1,2,6,8,12)$	13	9
6	$\sum(1,2,4,5,13,15)$	10	12
6	$\sum(2,3,7,10,12,14)$	9	11
6	$\sum(2,4,6,7,12,15)$	11	8
6	$\sum(0,3,4,6,10,15)$	9	17
6	$\sum(1,2,8,11,12,15)$	10	13
6	$\sum(1,3,4,9,10,13)$	10	13

(continued)

(*continued*)

# Minterms	Boolean Specifications (CNF) f=	MV count using Optimized XOR-AND	MV Count using Karnaugh Map
6	$\sum(2,4,6,10,11,15)$	14	11
7	S(0,1,3,6,9,13,14)	13	11
7	S(2,6,8,9,11,14,15)	7	11
7	$\sum(1,2,5,6,9,12,15)$	12	16
7	$\sum(1,4,8,10,12,14,15)$	13	11
7	$\sum(1,4,6,9,10,12,13)$	14	12
7	$\sum(1,3,6,10,11,12,13)$	19	12
7	$\sum(2,3,4,8,9,10,14)$	18	12
8	$\sum(0,3,4,5,6,7,9,15)$	11	14
8	$\sum(0,3,4,6,7,8,10,13)$	11	15
8	$\sum(2,5,6,7,8,11,13,14)$	12	19
8	$\sum(3,4,6,7,10,13,14,15)$	10	11
8	$\sum(1,2,6,8,10,11,12,13)$	12	15
8	$\sum(1,3,4,7,8,12,14,15)$	10	14
8	$\sum(1,3,4,6,11,13,14,15)$	12	14
9	$\sum(1,2,4,6,7,9,10,11,14)$	18	13
9	$\sum(1,2,4,5,7,8,10,12,14)$	16	13
9	$\sum(0,1,2,4,7,9,11,14,15)$	14	17
9	$\sum(2,4,5,6,10,11,12,13,14)$	8	6
9	$\sum(1,2,4,6,7,8,10,11,12)$	16	18
9	$\sum(2,3,4,8,9,11,12,14,15)$	14	14
9	$\sum(0,3,5,8,9,12,13,14,15)$	12	13
10	$\sum(1,2,3,4,8,9,12,13,14,15)$	14	12
10	$\sum(0,2,3,5,6,7,10,11,12,14)$	12	13
10	$\sum(1,2,4,5,7,8,10,11,13,15)$	15	16
10	$\sum(2,3,4,5,6,7,8,9,11,12)$	12	12
10	$\sum(0,1,4,6,7,8,9,12,13,15)$	12	10
10	$\sum(0,1,2,4,5,8,11,13,14,15)$	14	16
10	$\sum(0,2,3,4,6,7,9,12,13,15)$	8	12
11	$\sum(0,1,2,3,4,5,7,10,13,14,15)$	15	9
11	$\sum(2,3,4,5,6,8,9,11,12,13,14)$	13	11
11	$\sum(0,2,4,6,7,8,9,10,11,13,14)$	13	9
11	$\sum(0,1,2,3,5,6,7,9,10,14,15)$	18	11
11	$\sum(2,3,4,5,6,7,8,10,11,14,15)$	13	5
11	$\sum(1,2,4,5,6,8,11,12,13,14,15)$	12	20
11	$\sum(0,1,4,5,10,11,12,13,14,15)$	13	9
12	$\sum(0,1,2,4,6,7,8,9,11,13,14,15)$	10	7
12	$\sum(0,2,4,5,6,7,8,9,10,11,12,13)$	8	12

(*continued*)

(continued)

# Minterms	Boolean Specifications (CNF) $f=$	MV count using Optimized XOR-AND	MV Count using Karnaugh Map
12	$\sum(0,1,2,4,6,7,9,10,11,12,13,14)$	12	20
12	$\sum(0,1,2,4,5,6,8,10,11,12,14,15)$	5	4
12	$\sum(0,2,3,4,5,7,8,10,11,13,14,15)$	11	11
12	$\sum(0,1,2,3,4,6,7,9,10,12,14,15)$	13	15
12	$\sum(0,1,2,3,4,5,6,7,8,10,12,15)$	6	7
13	$\sum(1,2,3,4,5,7,8,10,11,12,13,14,15)$	12	10
13	$\sum(0,1,2,3,5,6,7,8,9,11,12,13,15)$	16	7
13	$\sum(0,1,2,3,5,6,7,10,11,12,13,14,15)$	13	7
13	$\sum(1,3,4,5,6,7,8,9,10,11,12,14,15)$	11	20
13	$\sum(1,2,3,4,5,6,8,10,11,12,13,14,15)$	17	16
13	$\sum(0,1,2,3,4,5,6,7,8,9,10,14,15)$	8	7
13	$\sum(0,2,4,5,7,8,9,10,11,12,13,14,15)$	14	7
14	$\sum(0,1,2,3,4,5,6,7,9,10,11,12,13,15)$	8	5
14	$\sum(1,2,3,4,5,6,7,8,9,10,12,13,14,15)$	18	10
14	$\sum(0,1,2,3,4,6,7,8,9,10,11,12,13,15)$	9	9
14	$\sum(0,1,2,3,4,5,6,8,10,11,12,13,14,15)$	9	9
14	$\sum(1,2,3,4,5,6,7,8,9,10,11,12,13,15)$	18	9
14	$\sum(0,1,2,4,5,7,8,9,10,11,12,13,14,15)$	7	5
14	$\sum(0,1,2,3,4,5,6,7,8,11,12,13,14,15)$	7	5
15	$\sum(0,1,2,3,4,5,6,7,8,9,10,11,13,14,15)$	8	3
15	$\sum(0,2,3,4,5,6,7,8,9,10,11,12,13,14,15)$	14	3
15	$\sum(1,2,3,4,5,6,7,8,9,10,11,12,13,14,15)$	24	3
15	$\sum(0,1,2,3,4,5,7,8,9,10,11,12,13,14,15)$	8	3
15	$\sum(0,1,3,4,5,6,7,8,9,10,11,12,13,14,15)$	14	3
15	$\sum(0,1,2,3,5,6,7,8,9,10,11,12,13,14,15)$	14	3
15	$\sum(0,1,2,3,4,5,6,8,9,10,11,12,13,14,15)$	3	3
16	$\sum(0,1,2,3,4,5,6,7,8,9,10,11,12,13,14,15)$	0	0

References

1. Lent, C., Tougaw, P., Porod, W., Bernstein, G.: Quantum cellular automata. Nanotechnology **4**(1), 49–57 (1993)
2. Bachtold, A., Hadley, P., Nakanishi, T., Dekker, C.: Logic circuits with carbon nanotube transistors. Science **294**(5545), 1317–1320 (2001)
3. Kastner, M.: The single-electron transistor. Rev. Mod. Phys. **64**, 849–858 (1992)
4. Vacca, M., Graziano, M., Zamboni, M.: Majority voter full characterization for nanomagnet logic circuits. IEEE Trans. Nanotechnol. **11**(5), 940–947 (2012)

5. Fahmy, H., Kiehl, R.: Complete logic family using tunneling-phase-logic devices. In: The Eleventh International Conference on Microelectronics, ICM 1999, Kuwait, pp. 22–24 (1999)
6. Schiff, J.: Cellular Automata: A Discrete View of the World. Wiley, New York (2007)
7. Porod, W., et al.: Quantum-dot cellular automata: computing with coupled quantum dots. Int. J. Electron. **86**(5), 549–590 (1999)
8. Tougaw, D., Johnson, E., Egley, D.: Programmable logic implemented using quantum-dot cellular automata. IEEE Trans. Nanotechnol. **4**(11), 739–745 (2012)
9. Dysart, T.: Modeling of electrostatic QCA wires. IEEE Trans. Nanotechnol. **12**(4), 553–560 (2013)
10. Kong, K., Shang, Y., Lu, R.: An optimized majority logic synthesis methodology for quantum-dot cellular automata. IEEE Trans. Nanotechnol. **9**(2), 170–183 (2010)
11. Pudi, V., Sridharan, K.: New decomposition theorems on majority logic for low-delay adder designs in quantum dot cellular automata. IEEE Trans. Circuits Syst.-II: Express Briefs **59** (10), 678–682 (2012)
12. Perri, S., Corsonello, P., Cocorullo, G.: Area-delay efficient binary adders in QCA. IEEE Trans. Very Large Scale Integr. (VLSI) Syst. **22**(5), 1174–1179 (2014)
13. Gladshtein, M.: Quantum-dot cellular automata serial decimal adder. IEEE Trans. Nanotechnol. **10**(6), 1377–1382 (2011)
14. Wang, P., Niamat, M., Vemuru, S., Alam, M., Killian, T.: Synthesis of majority/minority logic networks. IEEE Trans. Nanotechnol. **14**(3), 473–483 (2015)
15. Liu, W., Lu, L., O'Neill, M., Swartzlander Jr., E.: A first step toward cost functions for quantum-dot cellular automata designs. IEEE Trans. Nanotechnol. **13**(3), 476–487 (2014)
16. Dajani, O.: Emerging Design Methodology and Its Implementation Through RNS And QCA. Dissertations 646, Wayne State University (2013)

Logic Design and Quantum Mapping of a Novel Four Variable Reversible s2c2 Gate

Mahamuda Sultana[1], Ayan Chaudhuri[2], Diganta Sengupta[3(✉)], and Atal Chaudhuri[4]

[1] Techno India College of Technology, Kolkata, India
sg.mahamuda@gmail.com
[2] Techno India, Kolkata, India
ayanchaudhuri27@gmail.com
[3] Techno India – Batanagar, Kolkata, India
sg.diganta@gmail.com
[4] Jadavpur University, Kolkata, India
atalc23@gmail.com

Abstract. Reversible Logic has emerged as a topic of massive research owing to its promising heat arresting attribute and being an inherent part of quantum computing. CMOS has already started witnessing physical threshold limits with architectures based on classical irreversible logic functions. Several application specific reversible gates have been proposed in the previous decade. This communication proposes a novel four variable reversible gate capable of implementing a standalone full adder/subtractor. The gate has exhibited better statistics in peer comparisons. The work in this paper illustrates the complete design and construction of the proposed gate along with the quantum realization.

Keywords: Reversible logic · Reversible gate · Quantum computing
Reversible full adder · Reversible full subtractor

1 Introduction

With increasing chip densities, scaling and large scale miniaturization [1], CMOS has already reached the physical threshold limits upholding Moore's law. Bennett [2] has shown that the heat dissipated [3] by conventional digital architectures can be arrested if the computations are made reversible [4] (Definition 1). The claims made in [3] have been recently proven in [5] forming the main source of motivation for research on reversible computing. The fundamental reversible gate library comprises of the Toffoli [6] (Definition 2), Fredkin [7], Feynman [8] and the Peres gates [9]; we have implemented the Toffoli Netlist for the proposed gate using the basic Unidirectional Algorithm of [10, 11] and further optimized using negative control lines [12]. An n-variable reversible gate comprises of 'n' inputs and 'n' outputs. Hence, a four variable reversible gate comprises of 4 input bits. Four bits generate $2^4 = 16$ combinations. These 16 combinations can interchange positions in 16! ways. Therefore there are 16! four variable reversible gates. Each of these 16! Gates may realize specific Boolean functions. The proposed gate realizes a full adder and also the basic Boolean gates, thereby

© Springer Nature Singapore Pte Ltd. 2018
J. K. Mandal and D. Sinha (Eds.): CSI 2017, CCIS 836, pp. 416–427, 2018.
https://doi.org/10.1007/978-981-13-1343-1_35

providing provisions for designing any complex Boolean specification. Adders form the most fundamental unit of arithmetic architectures; hence this study concentrates on the design of a four variable reversible adder. The proposed adder has been compared with several existing peers in literature and found to fare better. The comparisons have been made in terms of the quantum metrics (Definition 3). The proposal also serves as a standalone parity generator/checker unit.

Definition 1: *A function 'f' is reversible if it reflects a One-to-One mapping of the Input-Output Vector $I_v = \{I_1, I_2 \ldots I_n\}$ and $O_v = \{O_1, O_2 \ldots O_n\}$ of 'f' respectively and is ONTO. Cumulatively a reversible function 'f' should be bijective in nature. A reversible gate can be termed as a composite Boolean logic implementing a reversible function and should possess the following properties:*

- I_v can be uniquely determined from O_v.
- I_v-O_v Mapping is one-to-one and onto; Bijective.
- Fan out is restricted to FO1 (Fan-Out of 1).
- Feedbacks are prohibited in reversible gates.

Definition 2: A Multiple Control Toffoli (MCT) gate can be denoted by TOFx(C; T); $C \cap T = \emptyset$; where C is a set of Control Lines controlling the single Target line T; for a given variable set $\{a_1, a_2, a_3 \ldots a_n\}$.

∴ A No-Control-Single-Target gate always inverts the signal passing through it and is denoted as TOF1 $\{x_1\}$. Similarly in a Single-Control-Single-Target gate, TOF2 $\{x_1, x_2\}$, the target line x_2 gets inverted if x_1 is high. This gate is typically called the Feynman gate. TOF3 $\{x_1, x_2, x_3\}$ is generally referred to as the Toffoli Gate where x_1 and x_2 are the control lines and x_3 is the target line which gets inverted when both x_1 and x_2 are high.

Definition 3: *The parameters required to measure the quality of a network is known as Quantum Metrics. They are defined as the Quantum Cost, fundamental gate count required to realize the network, Complexity (Definition 4) and the Two Qubit Gate count of the network.*

Definition 4: *The Complexity of a reversible function $f(X) = \{X_1, X_2, \ldots X_{m-1}\}$ is denoted by $C_f = \sum_{i=0}^{m-1} \delta(A_i, B_i)$; where A_i and B_i are the corresponding 2^m input-output patterns of f(X) and δ equals the Hamming Distance (Definition 5) between A_i and B_i.*

Definition 5: *The numbers of variations at corresponding bit positions of two bit streams A and B is known as the Hamming Distance and is denoted by $(\delta(A, B))$.*

The rest of the paper is organized as follows. The next section provides the related survey of relevant existing work followed by elaboration of our proposed work in Sect. 3. Section 4 provides the complete analysis of our proposed gate with peer comparisons with existing counterparts and concludes in the next section.

2   Related Work

An adiabatic or physically reversible network neither supports energy-heat conversion nor change in entropy. Reversible circuits can be termed as deterministic state machines since the pre-operation state can be uniquely determined by the post-operation state vectors. This attribute of reversible functions generated massive research in search for viable reversible networks and synthesis algorithms. Proposals for application specific reversible gates became one of the research dimensions. A number of four variable reversible gates have been proposed to implement arbitrary logic functions till date. A brief survey of all the existing four variable reversible gates can be found in [13]. Some literary proposals also exhibit conservative logic and parity preserving gates. A conservative logic gate has equal high logic count at the input as well as the output vectors. A parity preserving gate maintains equal parity in its input-output vector sets.

Binary full adder realizations have been proposed using TSG [14], HNG [15], SCG [16] and IG [17] gates. RPS [18] gate has been used to realize a decimal full adder. Haghprasad and Navi have designed a reversible BCD Adder using the HNFG [19, 20] gates whereas Biswas et al. have proposed designs for reversible BCD adders and carry skip BCD adders using the MTSG [21] gate. Rashmi, Umarani and Shreedhar have designed 4:2 carry save adders using the FAG [22] gate and reversible sequential circuits using the DFG [22] gate. Chaudhuri et al. have proposed a reversible four variable TCG [23] gate which realizes the 2's complement operation using a single gate. This gate can form the basis for subtraction in terms of 2's complement addition.

Vasudevan et al. have proposed two reversible gates, R1 [24] and R2 [24], for online testability of reversible logic circuits. The authors claim that R1 can be used to realize any Boolean function either independently or in cascade and R2 is used to introduce online testability in the reversible circuit. For example, the XNOR and the NAND function can be realized using a single R1 gate but NOR and AND logic require two R1 gates. Our proposed gate can implement AND, OR, NOT, XOR and XNOR functions using a single s2c2 gate as will be discussed later. Shukla et al. have proposed the CSMT [25] gate capable of realizing binary to gray code conversions.

The other proposals have implemented Parity Generators/Checkers, Code Converters, De-Multiplexers, Decoders and Cryptographic Applications using the MKG [19], ALG [26], DKG [27], MRG [27] and BVMF [28] gates.

3   Proposed Reversible s2c2 Gate

The primary motivation for the design of the four variable reversible gate is to realize a standalone full adder/subtractor. The proposed gate also seconds as a parity generator/checker. Table 1 provides the truth table for the proposed s2c2 gate along with the Hamming Distance between I_v-O_v and the complexity. Table 2 provides permutation matrix for Table 1. Figure 1 provides the high level diagram for the s2c2 gate

Table 1. Truth table of proposed s2c2 gate

Inputs				Outputs				δ_i
A	B	C	D	P	Q	R	S	
0	0	0	0	0	0	0	0	0
0	0	0	1	0	0	1	0	2
0	0	1	0	0	0	0	1	2
0	0	1	1	0	1	1	1	1
0	1	0	0	0	0	1	1	3
0	1	0	1	0	1	0	1	0
0	1	1	0	0	1	1	0	0
0	1	1	1	0	1	0	0	2
1	0	0	0	1	0	1	1	2
1	0	0	1	1	1	0	1	1
1	0	1	0	1	0	1	0	0
1	0	1	1	1	0	0	0	2
1	1	0	0	1	1	0	0	0
1	1	0	1	1	1	1	0	2
1	1	1	0	1	0	0	1	3
1	1	1	1	1	1	1	1	0
Complexity								20

Table 2. Permutation matrix for s2c2 gate

$$
\begin{pmatrix}
1 & 0 & 0 & 0 & 0 & 0 & 0 & 0 & 0 & 0 & 0 & 0 & 0 & 0 & 0 & 0 \\
0 & 0 & 1 & 0 & 0 & 0 & 0 & 0 & 0 & 0 & 0 & 0 & 0 & 0 & 0 & 0 \\
0 & 1 & 0 & 0 & 0 & 0 & 0 & 0 & 0 & 0 & 0 & 0 & 0 & 0 & 0 & 0 \\
0 & 0 & 0 & 0 & 0 & 0 & 0 & 1 & 0 & 0 & 0 & 0 & 0 & 0 & 0 & 0 \\
0 & 0 & 0 & 1 & 0 & 0 & 0 & 0 & 0 & 0 & 0 & 0 & 0 & 0 & 0 & 0 \\
0 & 0 & 0 & 0 & 0 & 1 & 0 & 0 & 0 & 0 & 0 & 0 & 0 & 0 & 0 & 0 \\
0 & 0 & 0 & 0 & 0 & 0 & 1 & 0 & 0 & 0 & 0 & 0 & 0 & 0 & 0 & 0 \\
0 & 0 & 0 & 0 & 1 & 0 & 0 & 0 & 0 & 0 & 0 & 0 & 0 & 0 & 0 & 0 \\
0 & 0 & 0 & 0 & 0 & 0 & 0 & 0 & 0 & 0 & 0 & 1 & 0 & 0 & 0 & 0 \\
0 & 0 & 0 & 0 & 0 & 0 & 0 & 0 & 0 & 0 & 0 & 0 & 0 & 1 & 0 & 0 \\
0 & 0 & 0 & 0 & 0 & 0 & 0 & 0 & 0 & 0 & 1 & 0 & 0 & 0 & 0 & 0 \\
0 & 0 & 0 & 0 & 0 & 0 & 0 & 0 & 1 & 0 & 0 & 0 & 0 & 0 & 0 & 0 \\
0 & 0 & 0 & 0 & 0 & 0 & 0 & 0 & 0 & 0 & 0 & 0 & 1 & 0 & 0 & 0 \\
0 & 0 & 0 & 0 & 0 & 0 & 0 & 0 & 0 & 0 & 0 & 0 & 0 & 1 & 0 & 0 \\
0 & 0 & 0 & 0 & 0 & 0 & 0 & 0 & 0 & 1 & 0 & 0 & 0 & 0 & 0 & 0 \\
0 & 0 & 0 & 0 & 0 & 0 & 0 & 0 & 0 & 0 & 0 & 0 & 0 & 0 & 0 & 1
\end{pmatrix}
$$

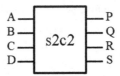

Fig. 1. High level diagram of the proposed s2c2 gate

The output expressions are as follows:

$$P = A$$
$$Q = (A \oplus C)(B \oplus D) \oplus BD \equiv (A \oplus C)(B + D) + BD$$
$$R = A \oplus B \oplus D$$
$$S = A \oplus B \oplus C$$

The output variable R and S double as the parity 3 bit parity checkers and 2 bit parity generators.

We have generated Toffoli Netlist for our proposed gate using the Unidirectional Algorithm and the Bi-Directional Algorithm of [10, 11] and further optimized it using the proposal in [12]. The synthesis has been done using the tool RCViewer+ [29]. The program codes for the Unidirectional and the Bi-Directional algorithms are as follows:

Program Code for Unidirectional Algorithm:

```
TOF3 (A, B, D)
TOF3 (A, B, C)
TOF3 (A, C, B)
TOF3 (A, B, D)
TOF3 (A, B, D)
TOF2 (A, B)
TOF2 (B, D)
TOF2 (B, C)
TOF3 (C, D, B)
TOF2 (C, D)
TOF2 (D, C)
TOF2 (C, D)
```

Program Code for Bi-Directional Algorithm:

```
TOF3 (A, C, B)
TOF2 (A, B)
TOF2 (A, C)
TOF2 (A, D)
TOF3 (B, C, D)
TOF2 (B, D)
TOF3 (C, D, B)
TOF3 (B, C, D)
```

```
TOF2 (B, C)
TOF2 (C, D)
TOF2 (D, C)
TOF2 (C, D)
```

Figures 2 and 3 provide the relevant Toffoli Netlists for the respective algorithms. The left and the right hand sides of the figures represent the input and the output sides respectively.

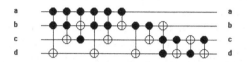

Fig. 2. Toffoli Netlist for s2c2 gate using unidirectional algorithm

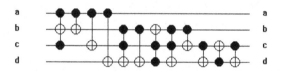

Fig. 3. Toffoli Netlist for s2c2 gate using bi-directional algorithm

The Toffoli Netlist generated using the Bi-Directional Algorithm only could be optimized as the Netlist designed using the Unidirectional Algorithm proved to be optimized using RCViewer+ [29]. The optimization was done incorporating negative control lines as presented in Fig. 4.

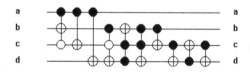

Fig. 4. Toffoli Netlist for s2c2 gate post optimization

Table 3 provides the Gate Count, Quantum Cost (Definition 6) and the Number of Two Qubit Gates required for the three Netlists provided in Fig. 1 through Fig. 3.

Table 3. Relevant metrics for Toffoli Netlists

Toffoli Netlist using	Gate count	Quantum cost	# Two Qubit gates
Unidirectional algorithm	12	32	36
Bi-Directional algorithm	12	26	28
Optimized bi-directional	10	24	26

Definition 6: *The Quantum Cost (QC) of a reversible function f(X) is defined as $\sum_{i=1}^{n} TOFx_i$; where $TOFx_i$ is the cost of the ith Toffoli Gate.*

The Quantum Costs of TOF1, TOF2, TOF3 and TOF4 are 1, 1, 5 and 13 respectively.

It can be observed from Table 3 that the optimized Netlist definitely fares better in terms of the three metrics used.

Table 4 exhibits the Boolean logic representations using the proposed gate for certain constant inputs. It can be noted that the three fundamental classical electronics gates, viz. AND, OR and NOT, can be realized using the s2c2 gate. Hence, we can settle that any digital architecture can be realized using the proposed s2c2 gate. The last two rows in Table 4 provide the input combinations for which s2c2 behave as a full adder/subtractor. Close observation reveals that the C_{in} pin is transmitted directly to the output thereby laying provisions for the gate to be used for Ripple Carry Adder designs and well as Carry Look Ahead Adder designs. Also the gate supports signal duplication (generating higher fan outs as Definition 1 rules out provisions for greater than one fan outs). Hence, in cases where signal branching is dominant, the proposed gate with specific input combinations can increase the fan out. Another important function realized is the XNOR gate which finds acceptance in cryptographic environments.

Table 4. Boolean logic realization using the proposed gate

Inputs				Outputs				Logic realizations
A	B	C	D	P	Q	R	S	
A	1	1	1	A	1	A	A	Signal duplication (FO3)
1	B	1	1	1	B	B	B	Signal duplication (FO3)
1	1	C	1	1	1	1	C	Through signal
1	1	1	D	1	D	D	1	Signal duplication (FO2)
0	B	1	1	0	1	B'	B'	Negation (NOT)
0	B	1	0	0	B	B	B'	Duplication (FO2) + Negation (NOT)
1	B	0	0	1	B	B'	B'	NOT duplication
A	B	0	0	A	A'B	A $\oplus$ B	A $\oplus$ B	XOR duplication
1	B	0	D	1	B + D	(B $\oplus$ D)'	B'	OR, XNOR
0	B	0	D	0	BD	(B $\oplus$ D)	B	AND, XOR
1	B	1	D	1	BD	(B $\oplus$ D)'	B	AND, XNOR
A	B	1	1	A	A' + B	(A $\oplus$ B)'	(A $\oplus$ B)'	XNOR
Cin	B	0	A	Cin	AB $\oplus$ Cin(A $\oplus$ B)	A $\oplus$ B $\oplus$ Cin	B $\oplus$ Cin	Full Adder + Control Through + XOR
Cin	B	1	A	Cin	AB $\oplus$ Cin'(A $\oplus$ B)	A $\oplus$ B $\oplus$ Cin	(B $\oplus$ Cin)'	Full Subtractor + Control Through + XNOR

4   Comparative Analysis

The proposed gate has been compared to existing counterparts in literature. Table 5 sums up the analysis based on the Quantum Metrics (Definition 3). Figure 5 provides the graphical representation for Table 5.

Table 5. Comparative analysis based on quantum metrics

Name of the gate	GC	QC	TQG	C_f
FAG	11	19	19	24
SCG	15	43	51	32
DFG	16	46	48	28
MRG	4	6	8	24
TSG	10	28	30	28
HNG	4	8	12	16
R1	10	18	18	36
R2	7	7	7	32
HNFG	5	5	5	24
MKG	9	21	21	24
IG	3	9	11	16
RPS	17	99	61	24
ALG	10	42	34	32
MTSG	5	21	17	22
DKG	15	29	31	28
BVMF	7	15	15	28
TCG	10	34	26	33
Proposed s2c2 Gate using				
Basic/Unidirectional Algorithm	12	32	36	20
Bi-Directional Algorithm	12	26	28	
Optimized Bi-Directional Algorithm	10	24	26	

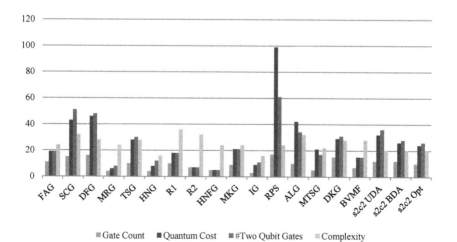

Fig. 5. Graphical representation of Table 5

It can be observed that the proposed gate excels over most of the existing counterparts and possesses the lowest complexity barring R1 and IG gates. Table 6 and Fig. 6 present the number of classical electronics gate required to implement the proposed s2c2 gate.

Table 6. Comparative analysis with respect to classical electronics gate

Name of the gate	AND	OR	NOT	XOR
FAG	1	0	0	4
SCG	3	2	2	3
DFG	4	2	1	2
MRG	1	0	0	4
TSG	3	1	3	3
HNG	1	0	0	4
R1	2	0	0	6
R2	0	0	0	3
HNFG	0	0	0	2
TCG	0	2	0	3
MKG	2	0	3	4
IG	2	0	1	4
RPS	9	0	3	8
ALG	4	0	1	7
MTSG	2	0	0	4
DKG	3	1	2	5
BVMF	3	1	2	4
Proposed s2c2	2	2	0	4

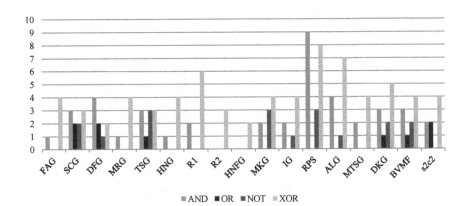

■ AND ■ OR ■ NOT ■ XOR

Fig. 6. Graphical representation of Table 6

As mentioned earlier, a certain number of four variable reversible gates have been proposed in literature realizing full adders. Our proposal not only realizes a full adder but also a full subtractor. Table 7 provides the comparison with existing realizations of full adders in terms of gate count.

Table 7. Comparative analysis of full adder realizations

Name of gate	# Gates	# Garbagr outputs	Full subtractor
TSG	1	2	False
IG	2	3	False
HNG	1	2	False
SCG	1	2	True
Proposed s2c2	1	2	True

Table 7 reflects that the proposed gate is at same length or better in peer comparisons in terms number of gates and garbage outputs but barring SCG, no other gate is capable of realizing standalone full subtractor. For example inverting the input pin 'C' in Table 5 converts the gate from a full adder to a full subtractor. Also in terms of other quantum metrics, the proposed gate fares better with respect to the existing peers mentioned in Table 7. For example, HNG gate exhibits better results in all the Quantum metrics in Table 4 but falls short in realization of a full subtractor. Hence, taking into account the Quantum Metrics, basic Boolean gate realization, XOR, XNOR function, Parity checker-generator function realizations; which have been the fundamental benchmarks in new four variable reversible gate proposals in literature; we claim that our gate fares betters than the existing counterparts in literature.

5   Conclusion

This study presents a novel four variable reversible gate. The gate reflects better results in peer comparison in terms of the Quantum Metrics and other relevant parameters. Since the proposed gate realizes all the basic Boolean gates and also the XOR and XNOR functions, hence we claim that any complex Boolean specification can be realized using the gate. The proposed gate can be further extended to design the complete architecture for 16 bit binary and BCD adders. Since, a single gate can realize both the full adder and the full subtractor; hence dedicated subtractor units can also be designed.

References

1. Zhirnov, V., Cavin, R., Hutchby, J., Bourianoff, G.: Limits to binary logic switch scaling - a Gedaken Model. Proc. IEEE **91**(11), 1934–1939 (2003)
2. Bennett, C.: Logical reversibility of computation. IBM J. Res. Dev. **17**(6), 525–532 (1973)

3. Landauer, R.: Irreversibility and heat generation in the computing process. IBM J. Res. Dev. **5**(3), 183–191 (1961)
4. Frank, M.: Introduction to reversible computing: motivation, progress and challenges. In: 2nd Conference on Computing Frontiers, pp. 385–390 (2005)
5. Bérut, A., Arakelyan, A., Petrosyan, A., Ciliberto, S., Dillenschneider, R., Lutz, E.: Experimental verification of Landauer's principle linking information and thermodynamics. Nature **483**(7388), 187–189 (2012)
6. Toffoli, T.: Reversible Computing. Tech Memo MIT/LCS/TM-151, MIT Lab for Computer Science (1980)
7. Fredkin, E., Toffoli, T.: Conservative logic. Int. J. Theor. Phys. **21**, 219–253 (1982)
8. Feynman, R.: Simulating physics with computers. Int. J. Theor. Phys. **21**(6), 467–488 (1982)
9. Peres, A.: Reversible logic and quantum computers. Phys. Rev. A **32**(6), 3266 (1985)
10. Miller, D., Maslov, D., Dueck, G.: A transformation based algorithm for reversible logic synthesis. In: Design Automation Conference, pp. 318–323 (2003)
11. Maslov, D., Dueck, G., Miller, D.: Synthesis of Fredkin-Toffoli reversible networks. IEEE Trans. Very Large Scale Integr. (VLSI) Syst. **13**(6), 765–769 (2005)
12. Datta, K., Sengupta, I., Rahaman, H.: A post-synthesis optimization technique for reversible circuits exploiting negative control lines. IEEE Trans. Comput. **64**(4), 1208–1214 (2015)
13. Vasudevan, D., Lala, P., Di, J., Parkerson, J.: Reversible-logic design with online testability. IEEE Trans. Instrum. Meas. **55**(2), 406–414 (2006)
14. Thapliyal, H., Srinivas, M.: Novel reversible 'TSG' gate and its application for designing components of primitive reversible/quantum ALU. In: Fifth International Conference on Information, Communications and Signal Processing (2005)
15. Maity, G., Maity, S.: Implementation of HNG using MZI. In: Third International Conference on Computing Communication & Networking Technologies (ICCCNT), pp. 1–6 (2012)
16. Sengupta, D., Sultana, M., Chaudhuri, A.: Realization of a novel reversible SCG gate and its application for designing parallel adder/subtractor and match logic. Int. J. Comput. Appl. **31**(9), 30–35 (2011)
17. James, R., Jacob, K., Sasi, S.: Design of compact reversible decimal adder using RPS gates. In: World Congress on Information and Communication Technologies (WICT), pp. 344–349 (2012)
18. Haghparast, M., Navi, K.: A novel reversible full adder circuit for nanotechnology based systems. J. App. Sci. **7**(24), 3995–4000 (2007)
19. Haghparast, M., Navi, K.: A novel reversible BCD adder for nanotechnology based systems. Am. J. App. Sci. **5**(3), 282–288 (2008)
20. Islam, M., Rahman, M., Begum, Z.: Fault tolerant reversible logic synthesis: carry look-ahead and carry-skip adders. In: International Conference on Advances in Computational Tools for Engineering Applications, ACTEA 2009, pp. 396–401 (2009)
21. Rashmi, S., Umarani, T., Shreedhar, H.: Optimized reversible montgomery multiplier. Int. J. Comput. Sci. Inf. Technol. **2**(2), 701–706 (2011)
22. Arun, M., Saravanan, S.: Reversible arithmetic logic gate (ALG) for quantum computation. Int. J. Intell. Eng. Syst. **6**(3), 1–9 (2013)
23. Biswas, A., Hasan, M., Chowdhury, A., Babu, H.: Efficient approaches for designing reversible binary coded decimal adders. Microelectron. J. **39**(12), 1693–1703 (2008)
24. Biswas, P., Gupta, N., Patidar, N.: Basic reversible logic gates and it's QCA Implementation. Int. J. Eng. Res. Appl. **4**(6), 12–16 (2014)
25. Shukla, V., Singh, O., Mishra, G., Tiwari, R.: Application of CSMT gate for efficient reversible realization of binary to gray code converter circuit. In: 2015 IEEE UP Section Conference on Electrical Computer and Electronics (UPCON), pp. 1–6 (2015)

26. Bhagyalakshmi, H., Venkatesha, M.: Design of a multifunction BVMF reversible logic gate and its applications. Int. J. Comput. Appl. **32**(3), 0975–8887 (2011)

27. Chaudhuri, A., Sultana, M., Sengupta, D., Chaudhuri, A.: A novel reversible two's complement gate (TCG) and its quantum mapping. In: 2017 Devices for Integrated Circuit (DevIC), pp. 252–256. IEEE, Kolkata (2017)

28. Sultana, M., Prasad, M., Roy, P., Sarkar, S., Das, S., Chaudhuri, A.: Comprehensive quantum analysis of existing four variable reversible gates. In: 2017 Devices for Integrated Circuit (DevIC). IEEE, Kolkata, pp. 116–120 (2017)

29. Arabzadeh, M., Saeedi, M. In: RCViewer+: a viewer/analyzer for reversible and quantum circuits. (Accessed version 2.5 2008-2013). http://ceit.aut.ac.ir/QDA/RCV.htm

A Design and Application Case Study of Binary Semaphore Using 2 Dimensional 2 Dot 1 Electron Quantum Dot Cellular Automata

Sunanda Mondal[1]([⊠]), Mili Ghosh[1], Kakali Datta[1], Debarka Mukhopadhyay[2], and Paramartha Dutta[1]

[1] Department of Computer and System Sciences, Visva Bharati University, Santiniketan, India
sund.mondal@gmail.com, ghosh.mili90@gmail.com, kakali.datta@gmail.com, paramartha.dutta@gmail.com
[2] Department of Computer Science, Amity School of Engineering and Technology, Amity University, Kolkata, India
debarka.mukhopadhyay@gmail.com

Abstract. Quantum-dot Cellular Automata (QCA) appeared as a comprehensive solution to the shortfalls CMOS technology is facing in case of nanoscale implementations. This emerging nanotechnological paradigm promises high speed, energy efficient computing. In this present scope, the concept of binary semaphore has been implemented using J-K Flipflop with the 4-dot 2-electron variant of Quantum-dot Cellular Automata. Later we analyze the proposed layout with respect to suitable well established metrics. In addition we provide a case study of the proposed semaphore layout on traffic control system which comes out to offer a way more optimized in respect of power utilization.

Keywords: 4-dot 2-electron QCA · Coulomb's law · Majority voter
Semaphore · Binary semaphore · J-K flipflop

1 Introduction

Efficient solution to technological limitations of existing technologies (Sem (2012)) in nanoscale encourages researchers to find out efficient alternatives. Quantum-dot Cellular Automata (QCA) was first proposed by Lent and Tougaw in Lent and Tougaw (1997). QCA ensures edge-driven flow of data and energy, information processing near the ground state, high density, high energy efficiency and ultra fast computation speed (Lent and Tougaw (1997)).

The most researched counterpart of QCA is the 4 Dot 2 Electron version (Farazkish et al. (2008); Oya et al. (2003)). The designs of some well known logic constructs such as MUX, adders, flipflops have been reported in Mukhopadhyay et al. (2011); Mukhopadhyay and Dutta (2012b); Navi et al. (2010); Dutta and

© Springer Nature Singapore Pte Ltd. 2018
J. K. Mandal and D. Sinha (Eds.): CSI 2017, CCIS 836, pp. 428–448, 2018.
https://doi.org/10.1007/978-981-13-1343-1_36

Mukhopadhyay (2013). Several reversible circuits are also available in Debarka Mukhopadhyay (2012); Thapliyal and Ranganathan (2013); Mondal et al. (2015).

Semaphore is a well known concept in the purview of operating system. Semaphore is basically a variable which serves the purpose of I/O controlling. It is widely used to control the access of shared resources in mutual exclusion basis. There are two kinds of semaphore:

- Binary Semaphore which can take only two values, either 0 or 1 to symbolize availability or unavailability of resources.
- Counting Semaphore which may assume more than two values and generally used for the purpose of resource count.

In the present article the binary semaphore is implemented using 2 Dot 1 Electron version of QCA. In Huang et al. (2007) an interesting application of flipflops has been offered to regulate traffic signal. Subsequently in the present scope we have made a case study of our implementation over traffic signaling system using the proposed 2 Dot 1 Electron QCA based binary semaphore. We have considered traffic signals at a T-junction with four sets of traffic signal for each road and at a X-crossing with five sets of traffic signal for each road.

The arrangement of the rest of the article is done in the following manner. A brief discussion is made on the preliminaries of the 2 Dot 1 Electron version of QCA along with requisite clocking in Sect. 3. Later on the concept of binary semaphore as well as the design of J-K Flipflop are presented in Sect. 4. In addition Sect. 4.2, the binary semaphore has been implemented using the said version of QCA. The output states are then justified in Sect. 5. An analysis of the proposed design has been carried out in Sect. 6. Section 7, contains a case study of the proposed binary semaphore in the traffic signaling system. In Sect. 8, the energy and power requirement of the proposed layout is evaluated. Section 9 presents a comparison of our proposed traffic control system with the existing one. Finally a conclusion has been presented in Sect. 10.

2   Historical Background

In the domain of 4 Dot 2 Electron counterpart of QCA there are quite a few reportings regarding logical circuit designs in QCA such as Walus et al. (2003), energy and power related issues of QCA circuits such as Srivastava et al. (2011); Srivastava et al. (2016).

In Walus et al. (2003), basic arithmetic structures based on QCA are analyzed. This paper justified arithmatic circuits using a newly developed simulator called QCADesigner. This article, by the help of an exclusive cost function application in that the circuit delay behaves proportionally to the number of clock zones present between input and output in addition to the number of gates because of latching.

The article Srivastava et al. (2011) contributes QCAPro, an error estimation technique for evaluating i. polarization error as well as ii. loss due to switching power. The tool can also provide power loss estimation in QCA architectures with sharp clock transitions. This tool can figure out maximum and minimum power loss, average power loss in a QCA circuit during switching of inputs.

In Roy (2016), presented is a new methodology to estimate the power consumption and the tunneling rate of the QCA circuits with the help of some mathematical expressions regarding the wave nature of electrons. Based on this methodology the device power can be estimated with more precision inside the tunneling junction. This paper provided QCA device power computation methodology with the help of Schrödinger wave equations.

3   QCA Review

As shown in the Fig. 1 the 2 Dot 1 Electron QCA cells are rectangular in shape. Thus these cells can be aligned either vertically or horizontally. For different alignments convention of binary data representation is also different as shown in the figure. As the name suggests the cells contain 2 quantum-dots and one electron which can tunnel between the two quantum dots. Similar to the other QCA variants, the cell to cell interaction in case of 2 Dot 1 electron QCA is done by the electrostatic principle due to Coulomb.

(a)   (b)

Fig. 1. The 2-dot 1-electron QCA cell polarity

3.1   Wire

As cell to cell information takes place as per Coulomb's principle, this feature could be exploited to construct a wire like construct to transmit information from one end to other. In case of 2 Dot 1 Electron QCA, the binary wire is basically a linear arrangement of likely oriented cells as shown in Fig. 2. In such type of construct, if the input is held at one end the same information can be retrieved from the other end of the binary wire.

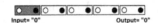

Fig. 2. Binary wire

3.2   Inverter

Due to the unique structural property of 2 Dot 1 Electron QCA cells, inversion can be done in two ways. Firstly by placing an oppositely oriented cell between two likely oriented cells. Secondly by placing the cells in inverting corner positions. Both of the aforesaid inverters are shown in the Figs. 3 and 4.

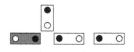

Fig. 3. Inverter

(i) Inverting   (ii) Non-inverting   (iii) Non-inverting   (iv) Inverting

Fig. 4. Cell placement in corner positions

3.3 Fan-Out Gate

Fan-out is a logic construct needed to drive a particular information to more than one logic circuits. The fan-out component of QCA consists of two sets of perpendicular branches. After the first branch off from the original input, one of the sides get inverted due to the inverted corner property. Thus to get back the actual input in the desired direction we need another perpendicular branching. Such a construct is shown in the Fig. 5.

Fig. 5. The 2-dot 1-electron fan-out gate

3.4 Planar Wire Crossing

Unique structural benefit of 2 Dot 1 Electron QCA ensures planar crossing of binary wires without hampering the information being carried by the wires. This can be achieved with only one restriction being imposed on the wires that the wires must have a clock zone difference of two as shown in the Fig. 6.

Fig. 6. Planar wire crossing

3.5   Majority Voter Gate

The majority voter gate (MV) in 2 Dot 1 Electron QCA consists of four such cells as shown in the Fig. 7. Any three of them can be treated as the inputs and the rest one will be treated as the output cell. For the particular alignment as shown in the Fig. 7 the third input will be inverted automatically. This automatic inversion is done due to the fact that the bottom input and the output cell alignment is an inverting corner position. The logic function of the MV gate is shown in Eq. 1.

$$M(A, B, C') = AB + BC' + AC' \tag{1}$$

(a)

(b)

Fig. 7. Majority voter gate (a) Digital representation and (b) QCA implementation

If the C input to the majority gate is opted as the programming input and fixed its value to either logic "1" or logic "0", OR and AND gate will be obtained respectively. This is because

$$M(A, B, 1) = A \cdot B \tag{2}$$

$$M(A, B, 0) = A + B \tag{3}$$

Similarly, if B input is chosen to be the programming input to the majority, we obtain

$$M(A, 1, C) = A + C' \tag{4}$$

and

$$M(A, 0, C) = A \cdot C' \tag{5}$$

Also for A input to the majority gate we obtain

$$M(1, B, C) = B + C' \tag{6}$$

and

$$M(0, B, C) = B \cdot C' \tag{7}$$

Hence, the output of the MV gate together can be written as

$$\text{Output} = \begin{cases} B \cdot C' & \text{in case A=0} \\ B + C' & \text{in case A=1} \\ A \cdot C' & \text{in case B=0} \\ A + C' & \text{in case B=1} \\ A + B & \text{in case C=0} \\ A \cdot B & \text{in case C=1} \end{cases} \tag{8}$$

3.6   Clocking

As pointed out (Mukhopadhyay et al. (2011)), the CMOS clock and the Quantum-dot Cellular Automata clock are completely different from functional aspects. When CMOS clock is used to synchronize between logic constructs, the other one used to supply energy so that the input signal can propagate through the entire circuit. In case of QCA the clocking of circuits is achieved by regulating the applied voltage to the capacitor to achieve different clock zones. The QCA clock also regulates the data flow direction. Many earlier reportings in the domain of QCA such as Mukhopadhyay and Dutta (2012c); Mukhopadhyay et al. (2011) have reported that the quantum-dot cellular automata clocking is quasi adiabatic in nature. The clocking consists of four clock zones each of which is made up of four clock phases each namely switch, hold, release and relax.

- At the very begining of the switch phase, the electron's energy is low enough. During this phase of clock, the clock amplitude is increased and as a result the energy of the electrons is raised. With this enhanced energy level electrons get de-localized. So, switch phase is basically a low energy to high energy transition phase. Till the very end of this phase the clock signal amplitude attains its maximum strength and so does the electron energy.
- The hold phase as the name implies, maintains the maximum strength of the clock signal amplitude. The electrons are de-localized from their quantum-dot position. The cells do not possess any polarity information. Thus at this phase cells attain the null state.
- Release phase is basically a high energy to low energy transition phase. Till the very end of the release phase, the clock signal amplitude attains its minimum strength. With the clock signal amplitude the electron's energy starts to reduce and by the end of this phase electron's energy comes down at its minimum level. hence the electrons are latched at the quantum-dots and the cells attain a definite polarity. The computations are done at this phase.
- Relax phase maintains the polarity of the cells which are obtained by the end of the release phase.

As reflected in Fig. 8 each clock zone is $\frac{\pi}{2}$ out of phase with its succeeding zone.

3.7   Advantages of 2-Dot 1-Electron QCA

2 Dot 1 Electron version of QCA possesses several advantages over the 4 Dot 2 Electron version of QCA due to some of its unique structural characteristic. The major advantages can be listed as below:

- As the name suggests, in case of the 2 Dot 1 Electron version each cell is composed of an electron and 2 holes which is exactly half of the 4 Dot 2 Electron version of QCA. So for similar architecture with equal number of cells the energy requirement will be much less in case of 2 Dot 1 Electron QCA due to less number of electrons. If the number of cells is very few then the

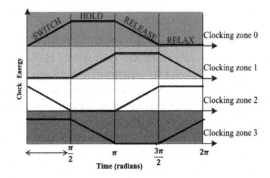

Fig. 8. QCA clocking with differently colored clock zones: Pink for clock zone 0, Sky blue for clock zone 1, White for clock zone 2, Green for clock zone 3 (Color figure online)

difference in energy requirement does not make any sense. But if the number of cells are large enough then the difference in energy requirement plays a significant role.

- In case of the 2 Dot 1 Electron variant there is no ambiguous cell configuration as compared with case of 4 Dot 2 Electron QCA. The 4 Dot 2 Electron version contains 4 quantum-dots and 2 electrons. So, the number of cell configurations will be $\binom{4}{2} = 6$ as apparent in Fig. 9. However, only two out of them are valid. On the contrary in 2 Dot 1 electron QCA there are exactly two $\binom{2}{1} = 2$ types of cell configurations and both of them are valid.
- The majority voter (MV) gate in the 2 Dot 1 electron version is a universal gate itself as one of the inputs get inverted. In case of 4 Dot 2 electron version we need to incorporate an inverter gate in addition to make it a universal gate.

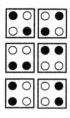

Fig. 9. The 4-dot 2-electron QCA possible configurations

4   Binary Semaphore

An integer variable, S is declared as the semaphore data type. Only one process can use it at a time and hence it is used for controlling access by multiple processes to a common resource in parallel programming or multiuser environment.

Binary semaphore can take the values 1 and 0 signifying 'unlocked' and 'locked' or 'available' and 'unavailable' respectively.

Apart from initialization, a semaphore, S can be accessed only through two atomic operations *wait* or P operation and *signal* or V operation. P and V stand for the Dutch words 'proberen' and 'verhogen' meaning 'to test' and 'to increment', respectively. Operation V increments the semaphore S, while operation P decrements it. The classical definitions of *wait* and *signal* are.

In 1965 E.W. Dijkstra proposed a new concept called semaphore to control mutual exclusion to shared resources between concurrent processes. As mentioned earlier binary semaphore can have only two values either a "1" or a "0" which indicates the availability or the unavailability of the resources respectively.

Semaphore is a protected variable which can be accessed by two well known atomic operations namely (1) "P" or "*wait*" operation and (2) "V" or "*signal*" operation. The "*wait*" operation is used to check the availability and reduces the value of semaphore "S". The "*signal*" operation signals the availability and increments the value of semaphore "S". These functions can be better understood from the following equations

$$wait(S) : \text{while } S \leq 0 \text{ do } \textit{no-op};$$
$$S = S - 1;$$
$$signal(S) : S = S + 1;$$

S is a variable which takes into account the number of available resources. The value of this variable S can be modified using the two operations $P(S)$ and $V(S)$ i.e. wait and signal operations respectively. The wait operation is invoked when resource allocation is desired. The signal operation is invoked when a process is on with a resource. Both the operations $P(S)$ and $V(S)$ are atomic operations through which mutual exclusion is imposed on semaphore S. If multiple processes try to attempt to get access a non-sharable resource at the same time only one process could get the access. Others will be kept on waiting. The operations ensure that no process is going to wait for an infinite time.

Figure 10 shows the state transition diagram of a binary semaphore where Q_0 represents the state when the resource is available and Q_1 represents the state when the resource is being accessed and hence unavailable. i is an input variable, $i = 0$ means a resource access is requested, $i = 1$ means no resource access is requested. Initially, no resource is requested and the system is at state Q_0. If there is no request for the resource, i.e. $i = 1$ then the system remains at state Q_0. When there is a request for the resource, then the value of i is decremented by 1, i.e. $i = 0$ then the system transits from state Q_0 to state Q_1, representing that the resource is occupied and hence unavailable. When the system is in state Q_1 and there is a request for the resource, $i = 0$, then the system remains at state Q_1. Again when the system is in state Q_0 and the resource is released the the value of i is incremented by 1 i.e. $i = 1$ and the system goes back to the state Q_0.

S-R flipflop is unable to process four state transitions shown in Fig. 10 as $Q(t+1) = Q(t)$ when $S = R$ as reflected in the article Dutta and Mukhopadhyay

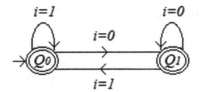

Fig. 10. State diagram for a binary semaphore

(2013). So, S-R flipflop is not capable of implementing the binary semaphore. Thus we implemented the binary semaphore using J-K flipflop in 2 Dot 1 Electron QCA.

4.1   J-K Flipflop

J-K flipflop is the most widely used and is considered to be a versatile universal flipflop (Dutta and Mukhopadhyay (2013)). The logic diagram is shown in Fig. 11 and the characteristic table is given in Table 1.

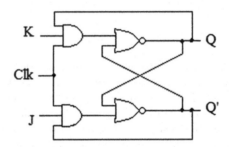

Fig. 11. Logic diagram of J-K flipflop

The Karnaugh map for J-K flipflop is

Q \ JK	00	01	11	10
0	0	0	1	1
1	1	0	0	1

From the Karnaugh map, we get the characteristic equation:

$$Q(t+1) = J\overline{Q(t)} + \overline{K}Q(t) \tag{9}$$

The schematic diagram for implementation of J-K flip is shown in Fig. 12 where M symbolizes the majority voter gate structure as shown in Fig. 7(a).

Table 1. Characteristic table for J-K flipflop

$Q(t)$	J	K	$Q(t+1)$
0	0	0	0
0	0	1	0
0	1	0	1
0	1	1	1
1	0	0	1
1	0	1	0
1	1	0	1
1	1	1	0

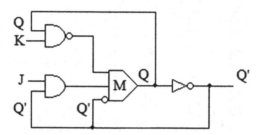

Fig. 12. Schematic diagram for 2-dot 1-electron QCA J-K flipflop

4.2   Design of Binary Semaphore

The schematic diagram of binary semaphore using 2-dot 1-electron QCA J-K flipflop is shown in Fig. 13 and the architecture of the same is available in Fig. 14. To introduce delay after any state is achieved we require to add a counter. A gray code counter (Datta (2017)) may be incorporated here with the proposed circuit to suppliment delay (Table 2).

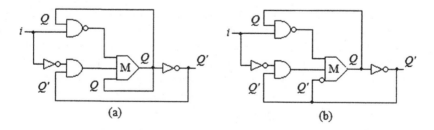

Fig. 13. Schematic diagram for 2-dot 1-electron QCA Binary semaphore

Table 2. Transition table for binary semaphore

$Q(t)$	i	$Q(t+1)$
0	1	0
0	0	1
1	0	0
1	1	1

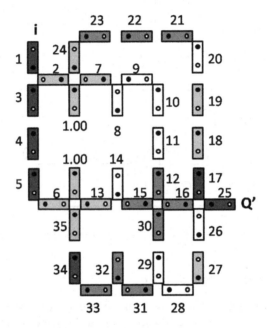

Fig. 14. Implementation of binary semaphore using 2-dot 1-electron QCA

5   Output of Binary Semaphore

No open source simulator is available to simulate 2 Dot 1 Electron QCA architectures. So, we have to justify the correctness of our proposed circuits using
some well established principle. In the present scope, we are going to justify our
proposed work using Coulomb's principle. The mathematical formulations based
on coulomb's principle are shown in Eqs. 10 and 12. The potential energy calculations between two point charges are evaluated using the equations suggested
in Mukhopadhyay and Dutta (2012a); Ghosh et al. (2015a).

$$U = Kq_1q_2/r \tag{10}$$

$$Kq_1q_2 = 9 \times 10^9 \times (1.6)^2 \times 10^{-38} \tag{11}$$

$$U_T = \sum_{t=1}^{n} U_t \tag{12}$$

where U is the potential energy between two point charges, K is the **Coulomb's constant**, q_1, q_2 are the point charges and while two point charges maintain a distance r between them. U_T reflecting the cumulative potential energy that an electron experiences because of the presence of its neighbors which is calculated using Eq. 12. In case of 2 Dot 1 Electron QCA, electrons have negative charge whereas quantum dots have induced positive charge. Electron tends to align at the farthest position from another electron and as close as possible to a quantum dot. Electrons try to attain a position with minimum potential energy. Thus we have to find out the potential energy of an electron at each possible position (for 2 Dot 1 Electron QCA cell only two possible positions) and the position which gives the minimum potential energy, electron will attain that position. For our enumeration we have considered the breadth and the length of a QCA cell as 13 nm and 5 nm respectively all along. And the distance between two likely oriented adjacent cells is 5 nm (Hook et al. (2011)). During the potential energy calculations for horizontal cells the left quantum dot is marked as x and the right quantum dot is marked as y. Similarly for vertical cells the upper quantum dots are marked as x and the lower quantum dot is marked as y. In these potential energy calculations quantum dots are considered to have induced positive charge as they can contain electron. So, the potential energy calculation between one electron and one quantum dot has a negative outcome due to different polarization of charge.

The respective output calculations are presented in Table 3.

To the best of our knowledge, QCA semaphore is unique. It is very difficult to claim to refer it as optimum in fact there is no specific guideline following which it is possible to downsize a circuit preserving its characteristics. What is presented in Fig. 14 is an instance of well thought out design with as minimum number of QCA cells as possible to the best of our ability. However it is not to claim that this is the optimum one that can not further be downsized.

6   Design Analysis

In Ghosh et al. (2015b), for the analysis of a typical QCA architecture viz. stability and area utilization.

Let a be the length of the edge of 4-dot 2-electron QCA cells. Let p nm and q nm be the length and the breadth of a 2-dot 1-electron QCA cell respectively. For the binary semaphore using 2-dot 1-electron QCA, we require 37 cells. The area covered effectively is $37pq$ nm^2. The area covered by the design is $5(p+q) \times (6p + 7q)$ nm^2. Thus, the area utilization ratio is $37 : 5(p + q) \times (6p + 7q)$. Thus, area utilization is high. Five clock phases are required for the architecture.

7   Case Study

In this context we are considering the crossing of two roads, one along horizontal direction and the other along vertical direction as reflected in Fig. 15. Both the roads allow two way traffic and hence, at the crossing a car can move in any of

Table 3. Output states of binary semaphore using 2-dot 1-electron QCA

Cell index	Position of electron	Total potential energy (in the scale of 10^{-20} J)	Comments
1	-	-	Input i
2	-	-	Same as polarity of cell 1
3–6	-	-	Same as reverse polarity of cell 1
7	a	14.102	Electron latches at b due to
	b	1.368	less energy
8	-	-	Same as polarity of cell 7
9–12	-	-	Same as reverse polarity of cell 7
13	a	−3.329	Electron latches at a due to
	b	−0.537	Less energy
14–15	-	-	Same reverse polarity of cell 13
16	a	5.891	Electron latches at b due to
	b	0.537	Less energy
17–23	-	-	Same as reverse polarity of cell 18
24	-	-	Same as reverse polarity of cell 23
25	-	-	Same as reverse polarity of cell 16
26–27	-	-	Same as polarity of cell 16
28–30	-	-	Same as reverse polarity of cell 27
31–32	-	-	Same as reverse polarity of cell 28
33–35	-	-	Same as reverse polarity of cell 31

the four possible directions. Pedestrians would like to cross the road in horizontal and vertical directions. Therefore, we require sixteen traffic lights in all.

In Fig. 15, we can see four cars A, B, C and D moving from all the four directions. At the crossing each car can move to its left or can move straight or can move to its right either to go right or take a U-turn. Car A may move left if the signal 1 is green, it may move straight if the signal 2 is green, it may move right or take a U-turn if the signal 3 is green. Similarly, car B can move left, straight and right if the signals 4, 5 and 6 are respectively green; car C can move left, straight or right if the signals 7, 8 and 9 are respectively green whereas car D can move left, straight or right if the signals 10, 11 and 12 are respectively green. Thus, the movement of car A is controlled by the traffic lights 1, 2 and 3, that of car B is controlled by the traffic lights 4, 5 and 6, that of car C is controlled by the traffic lights 7, 8, and 9 and that of car D is controlled by the traffic lights 10, 11 and 12.

The pedestrians may cross the roads from left to right and vice-versa along the horizontal direction, when the signal 13 is green when no car is allowed to move to and along the vertical direction. Similarly, the pedestrians may cross the roads from north to south and vice-versa along the western crossing, when

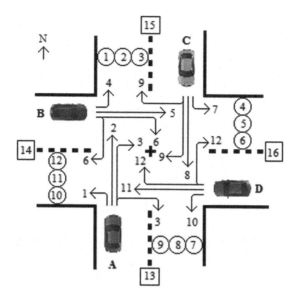

Fig. 15. Traffic signal control at a four-road junction (Color figure online)

the signal 14 is green and then no car is allowed to move to and from the west; the pedestrians may cross the roads from east to west and vice-versa along the northern crossing, when the signal 15 is green and then no car is allowed to move to and from the north; the pedestrians may cross the roads from north to south and vice-versa along the eastern crossing, when the signal 16 is green and then no car is allowed to move to and from the east. Thus, we have four cases as follows:

- The signal 13 is green: The signals 1, 2, 3, 6, 8, 10, 14, 15 and 16 must be red and any one of the signals 5, 9 or 12 may be green. However, the signals 4, 7 and 11 may be green.
- The signal 14 is green: The signals 1, 4, 5, 6, 9, 11, 13, 15 and 16 must be red and any one of the signals 3, 8 or 12 may be green. However, the signals 2, 7 and 10 may be green.
- The signal 15 is green: The signals 2, 4, 7, 8, 9, 12, 13, 14 and 16 must be red and any one of the signals 3, 6 or 11 may be green. However, the signals 1, 5 and 10 may be green.
- The signal 16 is green: The signals 3,5, 7, 10, 11, 12, 13, 14 and 15 must be red and any one of the signals 2, 6 or 9 may be green. However, the signals 1, 4 and 8 may be green.

From the above study, we conclude that there are two sets of phases with four phases in each set. The signals are either red or green according to the first set as shown in Table 4 and according to the second set as shown in Table 5.

Algorithm 1 shows how the traffic light signals may be operated. The parameter $delay_i$ indicates the duration for this a light at phase $i, i = I, II, III, IV,$

Table 4. Phases of traffic signals (modified) according to the first set

Phase	Red signals	Green signals
I	$R_I = \{1, 2, 3, 5, 6, 8, 9, 10, 14, 15, 16\}$	$G_I = \{4, 7, 11, 12, 13\}$
II	$R_{II} = \{1, 4, 5, 6, 8, 9, 11, 12, 13, 15, 16\}$	$G_{II} = \{2, 3, 7, 10, 14\}$
III	$R_{III} = \{2, 3, 4, 7, 8, 9, 11, 12, 13, 14, 16\}$	$G_{III} = \{1, 5, 6, 10, 15\}$
IV	$R_{IV} = \{2, 3, 5, 6, 7, 10, 11, 12, 13, 14, 15\}$	$G_{IV} = \{1, 4, 8, 9, 16\}$

Table 5. Phases of traffic signals (modified) according to the second set

Phase	Red signals	Green signals
I	$R_I = \{1, 2, 3, 5, 6, 8, 10, 12, 14, 15, 16\}$	$G_I = \{4, 7, 9, 11, 13\}$
II	$R_{II} = \{1, 3, 4, 5, 6, 8, 9, 11, 13, 15, 16\}$	$G_{II} = \{2, 7, 10, 12, 14\}$
III	$R_{III} = \{2, 4, 6, 7, 8, 9, 11, 12, 13, 14, 16\}$	$G_{III} = \{1, 3, 5, 10, 15\}$
IV	$R_{IV} = \{2, 3, 5, 7, 9, 10, 11, 12, 13, 14, 15\}$	$G_{IV} = \{1, 4, 6, 8, 16\}$

may be red or green. The parameter $blinkdelay_i$ indicates the duration for this a light at phase $i, i = I, II, III$, may be blinking so that cars moving may prepare themselves to stop or cars standing may prepare to move. This parameter, $delay_i$, will depend on the incoming traffic conditions, i.e. if fewer cars are coming in then $delay_i$ is set to a low value. However, $blinkdelay_i$ may have a constant value and $blinkdelay_i \ll delay_i$.

8   Energy and Power Requirements

The energy related parameters to be used to analyze the proposed designs are available in Dutta and Mukhopadhyay (2015); Ghosh et al. (2016). These parameters are developed to analyze 4 Dot 2 Electron QCA but are applicable to any structural variant of QCA. The parameters we are going to use are namely E_{clock}, the minimum clock signal energy to be supplied to the QCA architecture for its execution; E_{diss} the dissipated energy from the architecture; v_1, the frequency of incident energy; v_2, the frequency of energy dissipation; τ_1, required time to move from quantum level n to quantum level n_1; τ_2, required time to dissipate energy into the environment; τ, the switching time; t_p, propagation time through the architecture and $v_2 - v_1$ is the differential frequency. These parameters for the proposed design are calculated in Table 6. Let the Quantum number, reduced Plank's constant, electron mass, number of cells in the architecture, number of clock phases used be denoted by n, $\hbar$, m, N, k respectively. We have considered $n = 10$ and $n_1 = 2$ for no speific reason. Table 6 includes values of different energy parameters of the proposed semaphore devoiding consideration of any delay counter.

Algorithm 1. Traffic signal control at a four road junction

initialize $S = 0$;

repeat

    for $i = I$ to IV **do**

        Set $delay_i$; // according to traffic condition

        Set $blinkdelay_i$ // time for which the green light will blink before becoming red

        $S = S - 1$; // enter critical section

        while $delay_i \neq 0$ **do**

            Set light signals in R_i as red

            Set light signals in G_i as green

            Decrement $delay_i$

        end

        while $blinkdelay_i \neq 0$ **do**

            Set light signals in R_i as blinking red

            Set light signals in G_i as blinking green

            Decrement $blinkdelay_i$

        end

        $S = S + 1$ // exit critical section

    end

until *forever*;

9 Comparative Study with Existing Technology

The existing trafiic control system is developed using a counter IC which is used for sequential circutry. The IC 555, a timer generates pulse for the main IC 4017 counter. The glow of different lights is completely determined and controlled by the IC 555 NE5 (2017). So, To compare our proposed layout of traffic control mechanism using binary semaphore, we have considered the IC 555. We have done a power rating comparison of the proposed design with a real chip purely on the basis of theoretical properties. In the absence of any practical implementation as yet, the comparison has to be performed on the basis of theoretical design only.

Chip NE 555 Specifications NE5 (2017)

- Supply Voltage = 4.5 V to 15 V
- Supply Current (Vcc = +5 V) = 3 mA to 6 mA
- Supply Current (Vcc = +15 V) = 10 mA to 15 mA
- Output Current (maximum) = 200 mA
- Maximum Power Dissipation = 600 mW
- Power Consumption (Minimum operating) = 30 mW@5 V, 225 mW@15 V
- Operating Temperature = 0 °C to 75 °C

As we can see in Table 6 the energy required to run the proposed layout is 1.320 aJ and the switching time is 8.629 fs. So the power required by the proposed

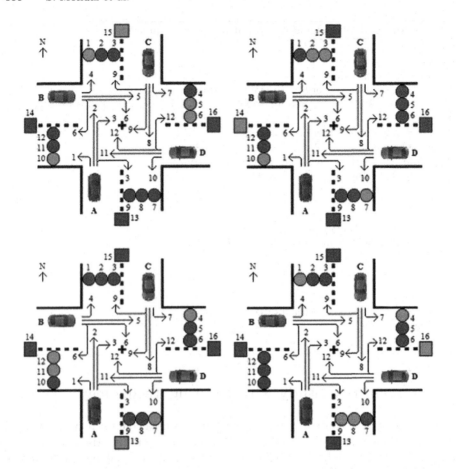

Fig. 16. Traffic signal control (modified) according to the first set of phases (a) Phase 1 (b) Phase 2 (c) Phase 3 (d) Phase 4

architecture is

$$P = \frac{1.320\,\text{aJ}}{8.629\,\text{fs}}$$
$$= 0.153\,\text{mW} \tag{13}$$

The minimum power requirement of IC 555 is 30 mW which is considerably higher than what our proposed layout (Figs. 16 and 17).

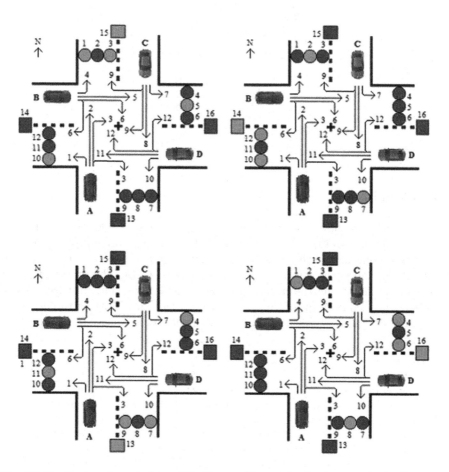

Fig. 17. Traffic signal control (modified) according to the first set of phases (a) Phase 1 (b) Phase 2 (c) Phase 3 (d) Phase 4

Table 6. Energy parameter evaluations

Parameter	Value
$E_m = E_{clock} = \dfrac{n^2\pi^2\hbar^2 N}{2ma^2}$	1.320 aJ
$E_{diss} = \dfrac{\pi^2\hbar^2}{2ma^2}(n^2-1)N$	1.307 aJ
$\nu_1 = \dfrac{\pi\hbar}{2ma^2}(n^2-n_2^2)N$	3.824 PHz
$\nu_2 = \dfrac{\pi\hbar}{2ma^2}(n^2-1)N$	0.1195 PHz
$\nu_2 - \nu_1 = \dfrac{\pi\hbar}{2ma^2}(n_2^2-1)N$	5.056 PHz
$\tau_1 = \dfrac{1}{\nu_1}$	0.021 fs
$\tau_2 = \dfrac{1}{\nu_2}$	8.368 fs
$\tau = \tau_1 + \tau_2$	8.629 fs
$t_p = \tau + (k-1)\tau_2 N$	1.247 ps

10   Conclusion

In this article, we have effectively designed semaphore 2-dot 1-electron QCA based J-K flipflop and the design is extended to develop traffic signal control.

In the present article the concept of binary semaphore has been implemented using J-K flipflop in the purview of 2 Dot 1 Electron QCA. The proposed layout was then justified using the potential energy calculations. The proposed design has been analyzed in terms of the energy and power issues. Further the proposed semaphore design has been utilized to implement traffic controlling system.

References

International technology roadmap for semiconductor (ITRS). http://www.itrs.net

NE555 Chip Specification. http://www.datasheetcatalog.com/datasheets_pdf/N/E/5/5/NE555.shtml. Accessed 17 Apr 2017

Datta, K., Mukhopadhyay, D., Dutta, P.: Design of two-bit gray code counter using two-dimensional two-dot one-electron QCA. In: Mandal, J.K., Dutta, P., Mukhopadhyay, S. (eds.) CICBA 2017. CCIS, vol. 776, pp. 75–84. Springer, Singapore (2017). https://doi.org/10.1007/978-981-10-6430-2_7

Debarka Mukhopadhyay, P.D.: QCA based novel unit reversible multiplexer. Adv. Sci. Lett. **16**(1), 163–168 (2012)

Dutta, P., Mukhopadhyay, D.: New architecture for flip flops using quantum-dot cellular automata. In: Satapathy S., Avadhani, P., Udgata, S., Lakshminarayana, S. (eds.) Proceedings of the 48th Annual Convention of Computer Society of India Vol II Advances in Intelligent Systems and Computing. Springer, Cham, vol. 249, pp. 707–714 (2013). https://doi.org/10.1007/978-3-319-03095-1_77

Dutta, P., Mukhopadhyay, D.: A study on energy optimized 4 dot 2 electron two dimensional quantum dot cellular automata logical reversible flip-flops. Microelectron. J. **46**, 519–530 (2015)

Farazkish, R., Azghadi, M., Navi, K., Haghparast, M.: New method for decreasing the number of quantum-dot cells in QCA circuits. World Appl. Sci. J. **6**, 793–802 (2008)

Ghosh, M., Mukhopadhyay, D., Dutta, P.: A 2 dot 1 electron quantum cellular automata based parallel memory. In: Mandal, J.K., Satapathy, S.C., Sanyal, M.K., Sarkar, P.P., Mukhopadhyay, A. (eds.) Information Systems Design and Intelligent Applications. AISC, vol. 339, pp. 627–636. Springer, New Delhi (2015a). https://doi.org/10.1007/978-81-322-2250-7_63

Ghosh, M., Mukhopadhyay, D., Dutta, P.: A 2 dot 1 electron quantum cellular automata based parallel memory. In: Mandal, J.K., Satapathy, S.C., Sanyal, M.K., Sarkar, P.P., Mukhopadhyay, A. (eds.) Information Systems Design and Intelligent Applications. AISC, vol. 339, pp. 627–636. Springer, New Delhi (2015b). https://doi.org/10.1007/978-81-322-2250-7_63

Ghosh, M., Mukhopadhyay, D., Dutta, P.: A study on 2 dimensional 2 dot 1 electron quantum dot cellular automata based reversible 2:1 MUX design: an energy analytical approach. Int. J. Comput. Appl. **38**(2–3), 82–95 (2016). https://doi.org/10.1080/1206212X.2016.1218239

Hook IV, L.R., Lee, S.C.: Design and simulation of 2-D 2-dot quantum-dot cellular automata logic. IEEE Trans. Nanotechnol. **10**(5), 996–1003 (2011)

Huang, J., Momenzadeh, M., Lombardi, F.: Design of sequential circuits by quantum dot cellular automata. Microelectron. J. **38**, 525–537 (2007)

Lent, C., Tougaw, P.: A device architecture for computing with quantum dots. Proc. IEEE **85**, 541–557 (1997)

Mondal, S., Mukhopadhyay, D., Dutta, P.: A novel design of a logically reversible half adder using 4-dot 2-electron QCA. In: National Conference on Computing, Communication and Information Processing, pp. 123–130 (2015)

Mukhopadhyay, D., Dutta, P.: QCA based novel unit reversible multiplexer. Adv. Sci. Lett. **16**(1), 163–168 (2012a)

Mukhopadhyay, D., Dutta, P.: Quantum cellular automata based novel unit 2:1 multiplexer. Int. J. Comput. Appl. **3**, 22–25 (2012b)

Mukhopadhyay, D., Dutta, P.: Quantum cellular automata based novel unit reversible multiplexer. Adv. Sci. Lett. **5**, 163–168 (2012c)

Mukhopadhyay, D., Dinda, S., Dutta, P.: Designing and implementation of quantum cellular automata 2:1 multiplexer circuit. Int. J. Comput. Appl. **25**(1), 21–24 (2011)

Navi, K., Farazkish, R., Sayedsalehi, S., Azghadi, M.R.: A new quantum-dot cellular automata full-adder. Microelectron. J. **41**, 820–826 (2010)

Oya, T., Asai, T., Fukui, T., Amemiya, Y.: A majority-logic device using an irreversible single-electron box. IEEE Trans. Nanotechnol. **2**(1), 15–22 (2003). https://doi.org/10.1109/TNANO.2003.808507

Roy, S.S.: Simplification of master power expression and effective power detection of QCA device (wave nature tunneling of electron in QCA device). In: 2016 IEEE Students 8217, Technology Symposium (TechSym), pp. 272–277 (2016). https://doi.org/10.1109/TechSym.2016.7872695

Srivastava, S., Asthana, A., Bhanja, S., Sarkar, S.: QCAPro - an error-power estimation tool for QCA circuit design. In: 2011 IEEE International Symposium of Circuits and Systems (ISCAS), pp. 2377–2380 (2011). https://doi.org/10.1109/ISCAS.2011.5938081

Thapliyal, H., Ranganathan, N.: Design of efficient reversible logic-based binary and BCD adder circuits. J. Emerg. Technol. Comput. Syst. **9**(3), 17:1–17:31 (2013). https://doi.org/10.1145/2491682

Walus, K., Jullien, G.A., Dimitrov, V.S.: Computer arithmetic structures for quantum cellular automata. In: 2003 The Thrity-Seventh Asilomar Conference on Signals, Systems Computers, vol. 2, pp. 1435–1439 (2003). https://doi.org/10.1109/ACSSC. 2003.1292223

A Novel Approach Towards Optimized Synthesis of Four Variable Reversible Function Using Toffoli-Fredkin Based Mixed Templates

Kushal Shaw, Subham Pal, Sinjini Banerjee, Priyabrata Sahoo[✉],
and Atal Chaudhuri

Department of Computer Science and Engineering, Jadavpur University,
Kolkata 700032, India
shawkushal@ymail.com, subham2011pal@gmail.com,
sinjini2236@gmail.com, pbsahoo.3@gmail.com,
atalc23@gmail.com

Abstract. In the arena of reversible computation, several algorithms for synthesizing reversible circuit have contributed a major part. Good number of algorithms for optimized reversible circuit design is available in literature. In our previous work we proposed a synthesis algorithm for four variable reversible circuits using Toffoli Gates only, which outperforms already proposed synthesis algorithm in terms of both gate count and as well as quantum cost. The current work proposes another synthesis algorithm for four bit reversible functions using pre-designed templates combining both Toffoli and Fredkin gates. Template design considers optimal Control Sets for combined Toffoli and Fredkin gates in terms of gate count. These combined Toffoli-Fredkin templates further improve upon the gate count. Comparative study of previously proposed synthesized algorithms having Toffoli gates alone with mixed Toffoli-Fredkin version clearly exhibits the gate count improvements.

Keywords: Four variable reversible gate · Reversible logic
Reversible logic synthesis algorithm · Toffoli Netlist · Fredkin Netlist

1 Introduction

Concept of reversibility has shown silver line to handle the problems associated with current CMOS [2, 6] based digital circuits for power consumption and heat generation. Though the concept of reversible computing has gained remarkable attention in last couple of decades, yet the paradigm is going through an incipient stage attending an immense global research. As the fundamental operation of quantum computation has to be reversible, reversibility is the key attribute of our discussion. The reversible gate library consists of Toffoli Gate [1], Fredkin Gate [19], Feynman Gate [3] and Peres Gate [5]. In our previous work [22], we proposed an algorithm for synthesizing four variable reversible functions using positive controlled Toffoli gates, where we received better result compared to earlier available unidirectional synthesis algorithm [12].

In our earlier proposed algorithm attention are given to gate minimization leading to reduction in gate cost as well, but in the initial phase we designed only Toffoli based

© Springer Nature Singapore Pte Ltd. 2018
J. K. Mandal and D. Sinha (Eds.): CSI 2017, CCIS 836, pp. 449–462, 2018.
https://doi.org/10.1007/978-981-13-1343-1_37

templates. Now we have export the possibility of using Fredkin Gate, another popular reversible gate, in the same motivation of gate reduction. Basically Fredkin gate is a swap gate, thus it needs Toffoli gates to be included for template design.

For example: Suppose we need to convert 0001 from 0110, according to our previous proposed algorithm, TOF2 (c, d) → TOF2 (d, c) → TOF2 (d, b) is sufficient enough for this conversion, but by using only Fredkin gate this conversion is never possible. Thus we proposed an algorithm consisting both Toffoli and Fredkin gates to convert 0001 from 0110 and gates required for this conversion are FRED2 (c, d) → TOF2 (d, b). This example shows reduction in gate count compared to the previous synthesizing algorithm using only Toffoli gates.

In Sect. 2 the proposed method is detailed. Initially control line sets are listed individually for Toffoli and Fredkin which are then combined to Toffoli-Fredkin templates design.

In Sect. 3 the pseudo code of the corresponding algorithm using the templates is presented.

In Sect. 4 the proposed algorithm is compared with other existing algorithms using Toffoli gates alone. The proposed algorithm shows positive improvement over the previous algorithms.

Section 5 concludes the work followed by references.

Definition 1:
A function consisting of n-variables $f(x_1, x_2, \ldots\ldots, x_n)$ can be defined as **reversible** if and only if:

The number of inputs and outputs must be equal.

The function holds one-to-one mapping between input vectors and output vectors, i.e. the input states can be determined from the output states.

Definition 2:
A generalized **Toffoli** gate of n * n is defined as input vectors $I_v = (x_1, x_2, \ldots\ldots, x_{n-1}, x_n)$ and output vectors $O_v = (x_1', x_2', \ldots\ldots, x_n')$ where, $x_1' = x_1, x_2' = x_2, \ldots\ldots, x_{n-1}' = x_{n-1}$ and $x_n' = (x_1 \text{ AND } x_2 \text{ AND } \ldots\ldots \text{ AND } x_{n-1}) \oplus x_n$.

Toffoli gates can be combined to construct any reversible circuit. Hence it is also called as universal reversible logic gate.

Definition 3:
A generalized **Fredkin** gate of n * n passes it first n − 2 inputs unchanged to corresponding outputs, and swaps its last two outputs if first n − 2 inputs are all 1. Fredkin gate is also called as a controlled swap gate which maps three inputs (C, I_1, I_2) onto three outputs (C, O_1, O_2). If C = 0 then I_1 maps to O_1 and I_2 maps to O_2. If C = 1 then I_1 maps to O_2 and I_2 maps to O_1 i.e. two outputs are swapped.

2 Proposed Method

The novel work in this paper describes how to synthesis a 4-variable reversible function [20] (*Definition 1*), i.e. a reversible gate which has four inputs and as well as four outputs. As several synthesis algorithms are already proposed regarding this manner, now the key factor is to reduce the number of gates which will automatically cut down the ultimate space complexity of the circuit.

The proposed algorithm in this article consists of two different categories – I. *Control Line Set Generation* and II. *Toffoli-Fredkin Template Generation*. A truth table consists of n-variables, has 2^n combinations, from 0 to $2^n - 1$. Since proposed algorithm can only contribute in the area of 4-variable reversible functions, hence f (0) = {0000} and $f(2^4 - 1) = f(15) = \{1111\}$. Any f(i + 1) can be expressed as f (i + 1) = f(i) + 1; 1 <= i <= 14. Here f(i) reflects the corresponding output for the given input $(i)_{decimal}$.

I. Control Line Set Generation

In order to synthesis a given 4-variable reversible truth table, it should be checked whether the first row of the table contains {0000} or not. Let f(i) = wxyz, where z is LSB and w is MSB. If f(0) = {0101}, then uncontrolled Toffoli gates TOF(z) and TOF (x) are applied to all the entries corresponding to column z and x respectively in the truth table. Next checking should be done for f(1), whether f(1) = {0001} or not. If f(1) is not {0001}, then any number between {0010} to {1111} is present in that particular place. Since we have already synthesized f(0) to {0000}, hence there remains only 14 possibilities. Toffoli gates (*Definition* 2) and Fredkin gates (*Definition* 3) are available for synthesis purpose. Both these gates have different Control Line Set to be applied. Set of all control lines are given in Tables 2 and 3. The same process has to be followed for f(2) to f(14). Once we are done with f(14), we can see that f(15) is generated automatically because no other combination is available for that place.

Figure 1 presents the Control Line Set applicable for Toffoli gates. Let us consider f(i) = wxyz. The control lines have to be generated in a way such that none of the previously synthesized row hampers. Any of the variables among w, x, y and z can be used as control line for f(1). For f(2), the value of f(1) has been checked. Since it is {0001} i.e. (w = 0, x = 0, y = 0 and z = 1), z is removed from the list and no lower significant bit than z is available to be combined with it. So the control line set remains {w, x, y}. Control lines for f(3) has been generated by checking the value of f(2). Since f(2) = {0010}, hence y is removed from the Control Line Set for f(3). And since z is lower significant bit than y, it is combined with y to create a new control yz. This process goes on till f(14) and every f(i) depends on the Control Line Set of f(i − 1). No Toffoli or Fredkin gate is required for f(15) as it will be automatically shifted to its proper position.

From Fig. 1, the total number of Control Line Set for Toffoli gates can be defined as $\sum_{i=1}^{14} f(i) = 31$.

As per Definition 3, Fredkin gate is nothing but a swap gate. If contols and targets for two consecutive Toffoli gates are (m, n) and (n, m) respectively, then total number of gates can be reduced to implement the circuit by using Fredkin gate. Figure 2 presents all the possible controls along with their targets for Fredkin gates as a replacement of Toffoli gates.

w	x	y	z	Control Line Set
0	0	0	0	NIL
0	0	0	1	{w, x, y, z}
0	0	1	0	{w, x, y}
0	0	1	1	{w, x, yz}
0	1	0	0	{w, x}
0	1	0	1	{w, xy, xz}
0	1	1	0	{w, xy}
0	1	1	1	{w, xyz}
1	0	0	0	{w}
1	0	0	1	{wx, wy, wz}
1	0	1	0	{wx, wy}
1	0	1	1	{wx, wyz}
1	1	0	0	{wx}
1	1	0	1	{wxy, wxz}
1	1	1	0	{wxy}
1	1	1	1	{NULL}

Fig. 1. Control line set generation for Toffoli gates

w	x	y	z	Control Line Set	Target
0	0	0	0	NIL	NIL
0	0	0	1	{NULL}	{wz, xz, yz}
0	0	1	0	{NULL}	{wy ,xy}
0	0	1	1	{w, y, z}	{wy, wz, xy, xz}
0	1	0	0	{NULL}	{wx}
0	1	0	1	{w, x, z}	{wx, wz, xy, yz}
0	1	1	0	{x, y}	{wx, wy}
0	1	1	1	{xy, xz, yz}	{wx, wy, wz}
1	0	0	0	{NULL}	{NULL}
1	0	0	1	{w}	{xz, yz}
1	0	1	0	{w}	{xy}
1	0	1	1	{wy, wz}	{xy, xz}
1	1	0	0	{NULL}	{NULL}
1	1	0	1	{wx}	{yz}
1	1	1	0	{NULL}	{NULL}
1	1	1	1	{NULL}	{NULL}

Fig. 2. Control line set generation for Fredkin gates

II. Toffoli-Fredkin Template Generation

This section illustrates the process of Toffoli-Fredkin Template Generation for synthesis of a given reversible truth table of four variables. This process will map a 4-bit pattern into f(i), where f(i) = wxyz. First row of the given truth table will map into f(0) by using uncontrolled Toffoli gate(s) as necessary. The process starts form f(1), assuming f (1) is not equal to {0001}. Now there are 14 possible combinations are available from which {0001} can be reached. The Toffoli-Fredkin Template is given in Fig. 3.

w	x	y	z	Toffoli Template	Toffoli-Fredkin Template
0	0	1	0	t2 y z → t2 z y	f2 y z
0	0	1	1	t2 z y	t2 z y
0	1	0	0	t2 x z → t2 z x	f2 x z
0	1	0	1	t2 z x	t2 z x
0	1	1	0	t2 y z → t2 z y → t2 z x	f2 y z → t2 z x
0	1	1	1	t2 z y → t2 z x	t2 z y → t2 z x
1	0	0	0	t2 w z → t2 z w	f2 w z
1	0	0	1	t2 z w	t2 z w
1	0	1	0	t2 y z → t2 z y → t2 z w	f2 y z → t2 z w
1	0	1	1	t2 z y → t2 z w	t2 z y → t2 z w
1	1	0	0	t2 x z → t2 z x → t2 z w	f2 x z → t2 z w
1	1	0	1	t2 z x → t2 z w	t2 z x → t2 z w
1	1	1	0	t2 y z → t2 z y → t2 z x → t2 z w	f2 y z → t2 z x → t2 z w
1	1	1	1	t2 z y → t2 z x → t2 z w	t2 z y → t2 z x → t2 z w

Total 14 Combinations

Fig. 3. Toffoli-Fredkin template to generate {0001} from

The Toffoli-Fredkin Templates for conversion of the remaining 13 possibilities i.e. {0010} to {1110} are shown in Fig. 4 through Fig. 16. After {1110} gets its proper

w	x	y	z	Toffoli Template	Toffoli-Fredkin Template
0	0	1	1	t2 y z	t2 y z
0	1	0	0	t2 x y → t2 y x	f2 x y
0	1	0	1	t2 x z → t2 x y → t2 y x	t2 x z → f2 x y
0	1	1	0	t2 y x	t2 y x
0	1	1	1	t2 y z → t2 y x	t2 y z → t2 y x
1	0	0	0	t2 w y → t2 y w	f2 w y
1	0	0	1	t2 w z → t2 w y → t2 y w	t2 w z → f2 w y
1	0	1	0	t2 y w	t2 y w
1	0	1	1	t2 y z → t2 y w	t2 y z → t2 y w
1	1	0	0	t2 x y → t2 y x → t2 y w	f2 x y → t2 y w
1	1	0	1	t2 x z → t2 x y → t2 y x → t2 y w	t2 x z → f2 x y → t2 y w
1	1	1	0	t2 y x → t2 y w	t2 y x → t2 y w
1	1	1	1	t2 y z → t2 y x → t2 y w	t2 y z → t2 y x → t2 y w

Total 13 Combinations

Fig. 4. Toffoli-Fredkin template to generate {0010} from

position in the table one can observe that {1111} also gets its position automatically. Templates are designed in a way such that conversion of f(i) does not impact f(0) to f (i − 1) Figs. 5, 6, 7, 8, 9, 10, 11, 12, 13, 14, 15, and 18.

w	x	y	z	Toffoli Template	Toffoli-Fredkin Template
0	1	0	0	t2 x z → t2 x y → t3 y z x	t2 x z → f3 z x y
0	1	0	1	t2 x y → t3 y z x	f3 z x y
0	1	1	0	t2 x z → t3 y z x	f3 y x z
0	1	1	1	t3 y z x	t3 y z x
1	0	0	0	t2 w z → t2 w y → t3 y z w	t2 w z → f3 z w y
1	0	0	1	t2 w y → t3 y z w	f3 z w y
1	0	1	0	t2 w z → t3 y z w	f3 y w z
1	0	1	1	t3 y z w	t3 y z w
1	1	0	0	t2 x z → t2 x y → t3y z x →t3 y z w	f3 w x z → f3 z w y
1	1	0	1	t2 x y → t3 y z x → t3y z w	f3 z x y → t3 y z w
1	1	1	0	t2 x z → t3 y z x →t3 y z w	f3 y x z → t3 y z w
1	1	1	1	t3 y z x → t3 y z w	t3 w x z → t3 y z w

Total 12 Combinations

Fig. 5. Toffoli-Fredkin template to generate {0011} from

w	x	y	z	Toffoli Template	Toffoli-Fredkin Template
0	1	0	1	t2 x z	t2 x z
0	1	1	0	t2 x y	t2 x y
0	1	1	1	t2 x z → t2 x y	t2 x z → t2 x y
1	0	0	0	t2 w x → t2 x w	f2 w x
1	0	0	1	t2 w z → t2 w x → t2 x w	t2 w z → f2 w x
1	0	1	0	t2 w y → t2 w x → t2 x w	t2 w y → f2 w x
1	0	1	1	t2 w z → t2 w y → t2 w x → t2 x w	t2 w z → t2 w y → f2 w x
1	1	0	0	t2 x w	t2 x w
1	1	0	1	t2 x z → t2 x w	t2 x z → t2 x w
1	1	1	0	t2 x y → t2 x w	t2 x y → t2 x w
1	1	1	1	t2 x z → t2 x y →t2 x w	t2 x z → t2 x y → t2 x w

Total 11 Combinations

Fig. 6. Toffoli-Fredkin template to generate {0100} from

w	x	y	z	Toffoli Template	Toffoli-Fredkin Template
0	1	1	0	t3 x y z → t3 x z y	f3 x y z
0	1	1	1	t3 x z y	t3 x z y
1	0	0	0	t2 w z → t2 w x → t3 x z w	t2 w x → f3 x w z
1	0	0	1	t2 w x → t3 x z w	f3 z w x
1	0	1	0	t2 w z → t2 w y → t2 w x → t3 x z w	f3 w x y → f3 x w z
1	0	1	1	t2 w y → t2 w x → t3 x z w	f3 w x y → t3 x z w
1	1	0	0	t2 w z → t3 x z w	f3 x w z
1	1	0	1	t3 x z w	t3 x z w
1	1	1	0	t2 w z → t2 w y →t3 x z w	f3 w y z → t3 x z w
1	1	1	1	t2 w y → t3 x z w	t2 w y → t3 x z w

Total 10 Combinations

Fig. 7. Toffoli-Fredkin template to generate {0101} from

w	x	y	z	Toffoli Template	Toffoli-Fredkin Template
0	1	1	1	t3 x y z	t3 x y z
1	0	0	0	t2 w y → t2 w x → t3 x y w	t2 w y → f3 y w x
1	0	0	1	t2 w z → t2 w y→ t2 w x → t3 x y w	t2 w z → t2 w y → f3 y w x
1	0	1	0	t2 w x → t3 x y w	f3 y w x
1	0	1	1	t2 w z → t2 w x → t3 x y w	t2 w z → f3 y w x
1	1	0	0	t2 w y → t3 x y w	f3 x w y
1	1	0	1	t2wz → t2 w y → t3 x y w	t2 w z → f3 x w y
1	1	1	0	t3 x y w	t3 x y w
1	1	1	1	t2 w z → t3 x y w	t2 w z → t3 x y w

Total 9 Combinations

Fig. 8. Toffoli-Fredkin template to generate {0110} from

w	x	y	z	Toffoli Template	Toffoli-Fredkin Template
1	0	0	0	t2 w z → t2 w y → t2 w x → t4 x y z w	t2 w z → t2 w y → f4 y z w x
1	0	0	1	t2 w y → t2 w x → t4 x y z w	t2 w y → f4 y z w x
1	0	1	0	t2 w z → t2 w x → t4 x y z w	t2 w z → f4 y z w x
1	0	1	1	t2 w x → t4 x y z w	f4 y z w x
1	1	0	0	t2 w z → t2 w y → t4 x y z w	t2 w z → f4 x z w y
1	1	0	1	t2 w y → t4 x y z w	f4 x z w y
1	1	1	0	t2 w z → t4 x y z w	f4 x y w z
1	1	1	1	t4 x y z w	t4 x y z w

Total 8 Combinations

Fig. 9. Toffoli-Fredkin template to generate {0111} from

w	x	y	z	Toffoli Template	Toffoli-Fredkin Template
1	0	0	1	t2 w z	t2 w z
1	0	1	0	t2 w y	t2 w y
1	0	1	1	t2 w z →t2 w y	t2 w z → t2 w y
1	1	0	0	t2 w x	t2 w x
1	1	0	1	t2 w z →t2 w x	t2 w z → t2 w x
1	1	1	0	t2 w y →t2 w x	t2 w y → t2 w x
1	1	1	1	t2 w z → t2 w y → t2 w x	t2 w z → t2 w y → t2 w x

Total 7 Combinations

Fig. 10. Toffoli-Fredkin template to generate {1000} from

w	x	y	z	Toffoli Template	Toffoli-Fredkin Template
1	0	1	0	t3 w y z → t3 w z y	f3 w y z
1	0	1	1	t3 w z y	t3 w z y
1	1	0	0	t3 w x z → t3w z x	f3 w x z
1	1	0	1	t3 w z x	t3 w z x
1	1	1	0	t3 w x z → t3 w z y → t3 w z x	f3 w y z → t3 w z x
1	1	1	1	t3 w z y → t3 w z x	t3 w z y → t3 w z x

Total 6 Combinations

Fig. 11. Toffoli-Fredkin template to generate {1001} from

w	x	y	z	Toffoli Template	Toffoli-Fredkin Template
1	0	1	1	t3 w y z	t3 w y z
1	1	0	0	t3 w x y → t3 w y x	f3 w x y
1	1	0	1	t3 w x z → t3 w x y → t3 w y x	t3 w x z → f3 w x y
1	1	1	0	t3 w y x	t3 w y x
1	1	1	1	t3 w x z → t3 w y x	t3 w x z → t3 w y x

Total 5 Combinations

Fig. 12. Toffoli-Fredkin template to generate {1010} from

w	x	y	z	Toffoli Template	Toffoli-Fredkin Template
1	1	0	0	t3 w x z → t3w x y → t4 w y z x	t3 w x z → f4 w z x y
1	1	0	1	t3 w x y → t4 w y z x	f4 w z x y
1	1	1	0	t3 w x z → t4 w y z x	f4 w y x z
1	1	1	1	t4 w y z x	t4 w y z x

Total 4 Combinations

Fig. 13. Toffoli-Fredkin template to generate {1011} from

w	x	y	z	Toffoli Template	Toffoli-Fredkin Template
1	1	0	1	t3 w x z	t3 w x z
1	1	1	0	t3 w x y	t3 w x y
1	1	1	1	t3 w x z → t3 w x y	t3 w x z → t3 w x y

Total 3 Combinations

Fig. 14. Toffoli-Fredkin template to generate {1100} from

w	x	y	z	Toffoli Template	Toffoli-Fredkin Template
1	1	1	0	t4 w x y z → t4 w x z y	f4 w x y z
1	1	1	1	t4 w x z y	t4 w x z y

Total 2 Combinations

Fig. 15. Toffoli-fredkin template to generate {1101} from

w	x	y	z	Toffoli Template	Toffoli-Fredkin Template
1	1	1	1	t4 w x y z	t4 w x y z

Finally 1 combination

Fig. 16. Toffoli-Fredkin template to generate {1110} from

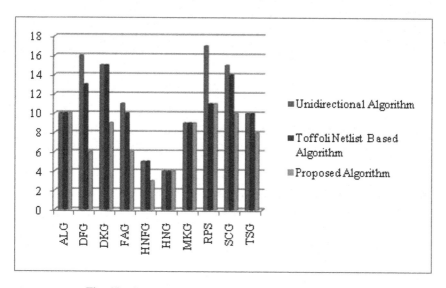

Fig. 17. Comparative analysis with respect to gate count

3 Algorithm

Input: Given a 4-variable unique reversible truth table

Output: To generate a synthesized truth table (0000 to 1111 in ascending order) using predefined Toffoli-Fredkin based mixed templates.

Begin

Read the truth table and store it into a 16x4 matrix, say arr[i][j], where i=number of rows and j=number of columns.

For j = 0 to 3
Do
    If (arr[0][j] equals 1)
    Then
        For i= 0 to 15
        Do
            arr[i][j] = 1 XOR arr[i][j];
      */*Complements the element at arr[i][j]*/*
        End For

    Write the corresponding uncontrolled Toffoli gate into a temporary file.
    End If
End For

For i=1 to 14
Do
    Synthesize the ith row using Toffoli-Fredkin based mixed templates to achieve sequential combination 0000-1111.

  Choose a template in a way such that previous i-1 rows are not affected during synthesis of ith row.
*/*Algorithm follows Table 3 – Table 16*/*
End For

Retrieve the temporary file in reverse order to generate the final set of Toffoli and Fredkin gates in order to achieve synthesized truth table.

End

4   Comparative Analysis

We have synthesized 10 already proposed 4-variable reversible gates using our own Toffoli-Fredkin mixed templates based algorithm. Also the number of gates has been calculated along with the synthesis. The gate count of our mixed algorithm is compared with the gate count from Unidirectional Algorithm proposed in [12, 16] and Toffoli Netlist Based Synthesis Algorithm proposed in the previous work [22]. Table 1 below provides the result obtained from comparative study.

Table 1. Comparative analysis

Reversible gate	Gate count		
	Unidirectional algorithm	Toffoli Netlist based synthesis algorithm	Proposed algorithm
ALG	10	10	10
DFG	16	13	6
DKG	15	15	9
FAG	11	10	6
HNFG	5	5	3
HNG	4	4	4
MKG	9	9	9
RPS	17	11	11
SCG	15	14	10
TSG	10	10	8

Figure 17 reveals the graphical comparison between the Unidirectional Algorithm, Toffoli Netlist Based Synthesis Algorithm and algorithm proposed in this literature. The figure exhibits the comparative analysis with respect to the gate count. From this characteristic graph, it can be observed that Toffoli-Fredkin mixed templates based algorithm fares much better result than earlier proposed algorithms in terms of number of gates.

5   Conclusion

We have proposed a novel synthesis algorithm for any 4-variable reversible function in this literature. In the present form, the described algorithm can be extended to include Toffoli gates with negative logic. Since this algorithm can synthesis only four variable reversible functions, it can be generalized for n-variables too. The library can be extended further to store Control Line Set for mixed Toffoli-Fredkin architecture.

Appendix

The Appending section describes the process of generating Toffoli-Fredkin templates to synthesis a four variable reversible function. The algorithm has been described in Sect. 3. We are taking an already proposed 4-variable reversible gate DKG and will synthesis it following the previously mentioned algorithm.

Table 2. Truth table of DKG gate

Input	Output
abcd	**wxyz**
0000	0000
0001	0001
0010	0101
0011	0110
0100	1001
0101	1010
0110	1110
0111	1111
1000	0100
1001	0011
1010	0111
1011	0010
1100	1101
1101	1000
1110	1100
1111	1011

Table 3A. Synthesis procedure using templates

Output	S1	S2	S3	S4
wxyz	**wxyz**	**wxyz**	**wxyz**	**wxyz**
0000	0000	0000	0000	0000
0001	0001	0001	0001	0001
0101	0100	**0010**	0010	0010
0110	0111	0111	**0011**	0011
1001	1001	1001	1001	1000
1010	1010	1100	110	1101
1110	1111	1111	1011	1010
1111	1110	1110	1110	1111
0100	0101	0011	0111	0111
0011	0011	0101	0101	0101
0111	0110	0110	0110	0110
0010	0010	0100	0100	0100
1101	1100	1010	1010	1011
1000	1000	1000	1000	1001
1100	1101	1011	1111	1110
1011	1011	1101	1101	1100
t2 x z	**f2 x y**	**t3 y z x**	**t2 w z**	**f2 w x**

Table 3B. Synthesis procedure using templates

S5	S6	S7	S8	S9
wxyz	**wxyz**	**wxyz**	**wxyz**	**wxyz**
0000	0000	0000	0000	0000
0001	0001	0001	0001	0001
0010	0010	0010	0010	0010
0011	0011	0011	0011	0011
0100	0100	0100	0100	0100
1101	**0101**	0101	0101	0101
0110	**0110**	0110	0110	0110
1111	**0111**	0111	0111	0111
1011	1011	1010	**1000**	1000
1001	1001	1000	1010	**1001**
1010	1010	1011	1001	**1010**
1000	1000	1001	1011	**1011**
0111	1111	1110	1100	**1100**
0101	1101	1100	1110	**1101**
1110	1110	1111	1101	**1110**
1100	1100	1101	1111	**1111**
t3 x z w	**f2 w z**	**t2 w y**	**f3 w y z**	**INPUT**

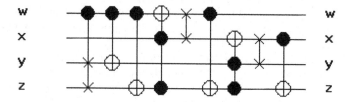

Fig. 18. Toffoli-Fredkin realization of synthesized DKG gate (gate count: 9)

The output part of Table 2 will be the input for our algorithm proposed in this literature. Since f(0) = {0000} and f(1) = {0001} are already synthesized, the algorithm will be followed to map f(2) to {0010}. Table 3A and B represent required templates for the synthesis purpose.

References

1. Toffoli, T.: Reversible computing. MIT Lab for Computer Science, Tech Memo MIT/LCS/TM-151 (1980)
2. Landauer, R.: Irreversibility and heat generation in the computing process. IBM J. Res. Dev. **5**(3), 183–191 (1961)

3. Feynman, R.P.: Simulating physics with computers. Int. J. Theor. Phys. **21**(6), 467–488 (1982)
4. Agrawal, A., Jha, N.K.: Synthesis of reversible logic. In: Proceedings of DATE, pp. 21 384–21 385, February 2004
5. Peres, A.: Reversible logic and quantum computers. Phys. Rev. A **32**(6), 3266 (1985)
6. Bennett, C.: Logical reversibility of computation. IBM J. Res. Dev. **17**(6), 525–532 (1973)
7. Soeken, M., Dueck, G.W., Miller, D.M.: A fast symbolic transformation based algorithm for reversible logic synthesis. In: Devitt, S., Lanese, I. (eds.) RC 2016. LNCS, vol. 9720, pp. 307–321. Springer, Cham (2016). https://doi.org/10.1007/978-3-319-40578-0_22
8. Wille, R., Große, D., Dueck, G.W., Drechsler, R.: Reversible logic synthesis with output permutation. In: 22nd International Conference on VLSI Design, New Delhi, pp. 189–194 (2009)
9. Arabzadeh, M., Saeedi, M: RCViewer+ : a viewer/analyzer for reversible and quantum circuits (2008–2013, version 2.5). http://ceit.aut.ac.ir/QDA/RCV.htm
10. Rashmi, S.B., Umarani, T.G., Shreedhar, H.K.: Optimized reversible montgomery multiplier. Int. J. Comput. Sci. Inf. Technol. **2**(2), 701–706 (2011)
11. Datta, K., Sengupta, I., Rahaman, H.: A post-synthesis optimization technique for reversible circuits exploiting negative control lines. IEEE Trans. Comput. **64**(4), 1208–1214 (2015)
12. Datta, K., Ghuku, B., Sandeep, D., Sengupta, I., Rahaman, H.: A cycle based reversible logic synthesis approach. In: Third International Conference on Advances in Computing and Communications, pp. 316–319 (2013)
13. Frank, M.P.: Introduction to reversible computing: motivation, progress and challenges. In: 2nd Conference on Computing Frontiers, pp. 385–390 (2005)
14. Dueck, G.W., Maslov, D.: Reversible function synthesis with minimum garbage outputs. In: Proceedings of 6th International Symposium on Representations and Methodology of Future Computing Technologies, pp. 154–161, March 2003
15. Dueck, G.W., Maslov, D., Miller, D.M.: Transformation-based synthesis of networks of Toffoli/Fredkin gates. In: Proceedings of IEEE Canadian Conference on Electrical and Computer Engineering, pp. 211–214, May 2003
16. Miller, D.M., Maslov, D., Dueck, G.W.: A transformation based algorithm for reversible logic synthesis. In: Proceedings of DAC, pp. 318–323, June 2003
17. Maslov, D., Dueck, G.W., Miller, D.M.: Toffoli network synthesis with templates. IEEE Trans. Comput.-Aided Des. Integr. Circuits Syst. **24**(6), 807–817 (2005)
18. Barenco, A., et al.: Elementary gates for quantum computation. Phys. Rev. A Gen. Phys. **52**(5), 3457–3467 (1995)
19. Fredkin, E., Toffoli, T.: Conservative logic. Int. J. Theor. Phys. **21**, 219–253 (1982)
20. Sultana, M., Prasad, M., Roy, P., Sarkar, S., Das, S., Chaudhuri, A.: Comprehensive quantum analysis of existing four variable reversible gates. In: Devices for Integrated Circuit (DevIC), Kalyani, 23–24 March 2017 (2017)
21. Chaudhuri, A., Sultana, M., Sengupta, D., Chaudhuri, A.: A novel reversible two's complement gate (TCG) and its quantum mapping. In: Devices for Integrated Circuit (DevIC), Kalyani, 23–24 March 2017 (2017)
22. Banerjee, S., Sahoo, P., Sultana, M., Chaudhuri, A., Sengupta, D., Chaudhuri, A.: Toffoli Netlist based synthesis of four variable reversible functions. In: 3rd IEEE International Conference on Research in Computational Intelligence and Communication Network, Kolkata (ICRCICN-2017), pp. 315–320 (2017)

Data Mining

An Improved and Intelligent Boolean Model for Scientific Text Information Retrieval

Amarnath Pathak$^{(\boxtimes)}$ and Partha Pakray

Department of Computer Science and Engineering,
National Institute of Technology Mizoram, Aizawl, India
amar4gate@gmail.com, parthapakray@gmail.com

Abstract. Diverse nature of text contents present in scientific documents and evolving complexity of user queries intended for their retrieval, demand revision in conventional indexing and query search mechanisms to effectively address issues and challenges of Information Retrieval (IR) and Intelligent Data Mining. Conventional boolean model of IR, in particular, shows restrictive behavior in matching query terms against the indexed terms which leads to retrieval of only few relevant documents. Moreover, the boolean model seeks for co-occurrence of the constituents of query term and discards searching the constituents individually. Motivated by all such shortcomings, we have proposed an IR system, equipped with features of OR search and OR+Stemming search, whose better exploring abilities facilitate search for constituent and stemmed constituent terms. Experimental results depicting remarkable improvement in evaluation measures serve as testament to distinguished abilities of proposed enhancements.

Keywords: Information Retrieval (IR) · Stemming · Precision
Natural Language Processing · Data mining · IR models

1 Introduction

Retrieval of text information from scientific documents constitutes one of the prominent application areas of Natural Language Processing and Data Mining. Information Retrieval (IR) concerns mining meaningful and relevant information, in form of ranked set of documents, from large pool of documents. However, quite often the indexed documents contain inexact and imprecise form of the queried term. For example, query term may be part of a larger indexed term, indexed term may be one of the constituents of query term, indexed term may be stemmed form of the query term or even worse, the indexed term may be semantically similar to the query term. An IR system should intelligently handle such situations of inexact query match. Intelligence of IR system is manifested in its ability to rank retrieved documents and ability to retrieve documents, containing constituent terms, stemmed constituent terms and semantically similar

© Springer Nature Singapore Pte Ltd. 2018
J. K. Mandal and D. Sinha (Eds.): CSI 2017, CCIS 836, pp. 465–476, 2018.
https://doi.org/10.1007/978-981-13-1343-1_38

terms of a given user query, in situations of inexact query match. Boolean model, Vector Space model and Probabilistic model are the popular classical IR models which have served the purpose for years. Although Boolean IR model is characterized by clean formalism and easy implementation, its underlying working idea of exact matching may result in retrieval of too few or too many documents [8].

Conventional IR models and the techniques of text information retrieval have undergone several remarkable modifications in recent past which have helped conventional IR systems in adapting to the domain of scientific document retrieval. In particular, refinement in query search mechanisms and indexing techniques have been exceptionally efficient in escalating performance and effectiveness of retrieval. An IR system is evaluated in terms of its preciseness to retrieve relevant documents and its potential to retrieve relevant documents ahead of irrelevant ones. Experimental observations and past studies reveal that conventional indexing techniques fail to account for composite expressions and expressions containing scientific terms, foreign words and terms having special characters/symbol. Such expressions are either exclusively discarded or misinterpreted as completely different expression by the indexer thus resulting in lowered precision measures. Moreover, conventional query search mechanism of IR systems, such as AND search, looks for co-occurrence of the constituent query terms and refrains from exhaustive exploration of indexed documents.

Motivated from above mentioned shortcomings of conventional IR systems, we have proposed an improved and intelligent boolean model based scientific text information retrieval system which embodies two modifications with regard to query search mechanism. OR search mechanism offers improved exploration of constituent terms and OR+Stemming search furthers the effectiveness of retrieval by searching stemmed terms alongside original terms. Significant improvement of OR search over AND search and marginal improvement of OR+Stemming search over OR search are reflected in the experimental results furnished by the proposed IR system.

Rest of the paper is organized as follows: Sect. 2 reviews related works on existing IR models and scientific text retrieval mechanisms. Section 3 details system architecture and working description of proposed IR system. Section 4 thoroughly details experimental designs, results obtained from the proposed system and analysis of obtained results. Section 5 concludes the paper and points direction for future research.

2   Related Works

In this paper we have essentially tried to investigate possible modifications in conventional boolean IR model and experimentally verified that augmenting conventional boolean model with OR search and OR+Stemming search mechanisms results in significant performance improvement.

Performance comparison of classical IR models, namely Boolean Model, Vector Space Model and Probabilistic model, have been detailed and discussed in

[16]. Boolean model relies on exact matching and works on all or none principle i.e. either all or none of the documents are retrieved. Vector space model, one of the earliest historical models [21], relies on partial matching, term weighting and Term Frequency - Inverse Document Frequency (tf - idf) measures for IR and offers better recall rates than the boolean model. Probabilistic model works on principle of nearly exact match rather than exact match, offers better recall rate than the previous two models, but suffers from reduced speed [19]. A combination of probabilistic and boolean IR models has been examined in context of World Wide Web document retrieval and the same has been found to improve retrieval performance [20].

In [5], authors have used light stemmers for 3 Indian languages, namely Hindi, Bengali and Marathi, while evaluating probabilistic IR models on the three languages. An IR system, using Yet Another Suffix Stripper (YASS) stemmer, for Bengali monolingual information retrieval finds mention in [17]. However, it is worth noticing that simple suffix stripping based stemmers often underperform in case of highly inflected Indian languages, which necessitates the need to design robust stemmers for handling such languages [1].

Use of evolutionary algorithms, particularly Adaptive Genetic Algorithm with variable crossover and mutation probability, in context of extended boolean models, promises faster attainment of better results [12]. Fuzzy IR model constitutes another popular enhancement of classical IR models [4,10]. Apparent nature of Fuzzy search does not let the searching stick to all or no searching (as in the case of boolean IR model) but instead lets the searching oscillate between degree of match verses strict match [6].

Besides, classical IR models have undergone modifications with respect to their indexing and query search mechanisms to facilitate speedy and effective retrieval. Substitution tree based indexing mechanisms, in particular, promise economical usage of system memory and swift indexing of index terms [15,18]. Moreover, textual entailment and measuring semantic similarity between query terms and index terms often aid to effectiveness of IR [11,13]. An elaborate architecture comprising of text and math entailment modules for scientific document retrieval has been discussed and detailed in [14].

Furthermore, integration of IR techniques with emerging deep learning techniques has been found to successfully accomplish numerous desired objectives such as locating potential buggy files for a given bug report [7]. It has been experimentally observed that Deep Neural Networks and IR collectively achieve higher bug localization accuracy than the individual models.

Apache Nutch[1], Lucene[2], Indri[3] and Wumpus[4] are among popular Open-Source IR Systems which cater to the users' demand of speedy and effective retrieval [2]. Many such IR systems are equipped with features of handling mul-

---

[1] http://nutch.apache.org/.
[2] https://lucene.apache.org/core/.
[3] https://www.lemurproject.org/indri/.
[4] http://www.wumpus-search.org/.

tiple fields per document and automatic query expansion [3,9] which prove their worthiness as and when required.

3   System Architecture and Working Description

Apache Nutch (see footnote 1) using Apache Lucene (see footnote 2) as its indexing core, Nutch crawler and Nutch query search module equipped with distinguished features of OR and OR+Stemming search, constitute indispensable components of proposed system's architecture. Other essential components and their outputs have been highlighted in italics in following description and have been red marked in Fig. 1. In this section, we describe system's architecture and step-wise algorithmic working principle. Step-wise working of system is as follow:

1. URLs of documents in the corpus are recursively read into a text file, *urls.txt*. Each of these URLs corresponds to a scientific document of the corpus.
2. *Injector* collects seed URLs contained in *urls.txt*. *Injector* converts injected URLs to *CrawlDb* entries and merges injected URLs into *CrawlDb*. However, before crawling, *Injector* strictly verifies pattern of URLs and permits them to proceed for crawling provided that they confirm to valid regex patterns, contained inside Nutch configuration file, *regex-urlfilter.txt*. *regex-urlfilter.txt* can be modified to allow or disallow URLs designating a particular file type.
3. *Generator* generates a list of URLs, called *Fetchlist*, from *CrawlDb* and places the *Fetchlist* into *Segment Directory*.
4. *Fetcher* fetches the contents of URLs in *Fetchlist* and *Fetched Contents* are stored back into *Segment Directory*.
5. *Fetched Contents* are parsed by the *Parser* and *Parsed Contents* are stored back into *Segment Directory*. Thus, a *Segment Directory* comprises of *Fetchlist*, *Fetched Contents* and *Parsed Contents*, and there can be several such segments depending on number of URLs in the URL list.
6. Updater updates *CrawlDb* with the contents in the *Segment Directory*.
7. *Link inverter* inverts links of the XHTML documents to give preference to inlinks (number of pages pointing to current document) over outlinks (number of pages to which the document is pointing). *LinkDb* stores inlink information which later helps in ranking.
8. Steps 3–7 above are repeated for each segment in the *Segment Directory*.
9. Apache Lucene Indexer uses inverted indexing mechanism and information from *CrawlDb*, *LinkDb* and *Segment Directory* to create an *Index*.
10. Given a user query, the basis *AND search module* and the proposed *OR search* and *OR+Stemming search* modules operate over *Index* to retrieve set of relevant documents corresponding to the query term.

Query search modules of proposed system extend the architecture of basic *AND search module* of Apache Nutch. Given a query term, the searcher modules now search the term in two distinct fashions, namely OR search and OR+Stemming search. *OR search module* splits the query term into its constituents and searches them individually in the *Index*. *OR+Stemming search module* improves effectiveness of retrieval by searching constituent terms as well as stemmed terms. Moreover, at any stage, system refrains from reporting redundant results which may stem from apparent nature of the two search mechanisms. Redundant results, if any, hamper the system evaluation process. Section 4.5 further elaborates the three search mechanisms used in the proposed system.

Figure 1 describes system architecture and working of the system.

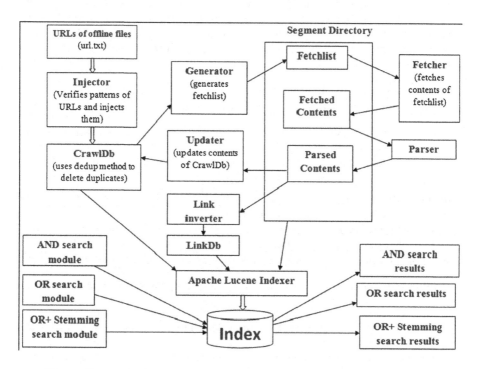

Fig. 1. System architecture and working description (Color figure online)

4 Experimental Design and Results

4.1 Corpus Description

Proposed IR system has been experimented with a total of 102 scientific documents derived from NTCIR-12 MathIR task[5]. Each document has an average size of 150 Kb and the size of complete corpus is 16.9 MB. NTCIR-12 MathIR task used two distinct corpora - arXiv corpus and Wikipedia corpus.

1. **arXiv corpus:** arXiv corpus is characterized by 105120 scientific articles selected from several arXiv categories[6] such as math, cs, physics:math-ph,

---

[5] http://ntcir-math.nii.ac.jp/.
[6] https://arxiv.org/list/math-ph/1101.

stat and physics:hep-th and adapted to suitable HTML+MathML format. Each technical document contained in arXiv corpus is divided into paragraphs which comprise of 8,301,578 distinguished search units which equal 60 million math formulae. As the arXiv corpus has been written by technical experts, it is intended for users having some level of mathematical understanding.

2. **Wikipedia corpus:** Wikipedia corpus is characterized by a total of 319,689 articles selected from English Wikipedia and converted to simpler XHTML format having no images. Articles in the corpus contain around 590,000 formulae which have been encoded using LaTeX, presentation and content MathML. In contrast to arXiv corpus, Wikipedia corpus contains articles intended for non-experts.

Scientific documents in our experiment have been uniformly chosen from both the corpus. Adequate care has been taken to ensure that:

1. Each document possesses considerable size and contains more than one query from the query set.
2. Few documents contain inflected forms of query terms such as plural form, progressive forms, stemmed query term and so on. For example, given the query term to be *Cauchy's inequality*, some of the documents contain terms such as Cauchy, equality, equal and equaling.
3. Few documents contain expanded query terms, meaning query term present as part of some larger term. For example, given the query term to be *abelian*, some of the documents contain terms such as non-abelian, abelian group etc.

Table 1 gives concise description about the corpus used for experimentation.

Table 1. Dataset description

Size of corpus	No. of documents	Source of documents
16.9 MB	102	arXiv corpus and Wikipedia corpus of NTCIR-12 MathIR task

4.2   Queryset Description

Performance of proposed system has been evaluated using a qyeryset[7] comprising of 37 scientific queries with substantial number of queries having multiple terms. A query tuple in queryset is characterized by query term and, a query ID which identifies the term. Presence of multiple terms in a query helps evaluate OR search mechanism (discussed in detail in Subsect. 4.5) of proposed IR system. Besides, some query terms, such as *Hölder's inequality* and *Schrödinger equation*, contain special characters and foreign words which remarkably test system's performance under special circumstances.

---

[7] https://github.com/pathakamarnath/IR-Query-Set/blob/master/queryset6.0.txt.

4.3 Gold Dataset and Result Set

Format of Gold dataset and Result set, used in our system evaluation, strictly adhere to TREC EVALATION[8] formats. Gold dataset is the standard dataset with which the retrieval results embodied in result set are compared. Gold dataset has four distinct fields, namely Query ID (qid), Iteration (iter), Document number (docno) and Relevance (rel). The dataset lists out standard results, in form of set of documents, for each of the query terms. The trivial Iteration field (iter) is set to some dummy value and remains unnoticed during evaluation process. Relevance (rel) is an integer in the range −1 to 127 where positive integer values symbolize relevant documents and negative values symbolize irrelevant documents corresponding to a given query term. Gold dataset used in our system evaluation contains 373 entries with 6 of the entries explicitly marked as irrelevant.

Result set has 6 distinct fields, namely Query ID (qid), Iteration (iter), Document number (docno), Rank (rank), Similarity (sim) and RunID (run_id), to uniquely identify each of the retrieved documents for each query term. However, only 3 out of 6 fields, namely Query ID (qid), Document number (docno) and Similarity (sim), are examined by evaluation tool and others are discarded. Similarity (sim) measure is float in nature and ranges from 0.0 to 1.0. *sim* measure attains eminent values for documents which contain exact query term (and/or) repetition of query term. Besides, *sim* measure rules out the essence of rank as the notion of rank is implicit in it. However, we have deprived our system of similarity and ranking features by assigning dummy value to both these fields. Lastly, the trivial RunID field has been set to some dummy value, *demo*, as it barely contributes to evaluation process.

Snapshots depicting some of the entries of Gold dataset and Result set are shown in Figs. 2 and 3 respectively.

4.4 Evaluation Result Set

System's performance has been evaluated using *trec_eval* evaluation tool which compares entries of Result set with those of Gold dataset. For a given query term, the order of entries in Result set and Gold dataset need not agree. An evaluation result set, generated by the *trec_eval* tool, summarizes effectiveness of IR system in terms of certain parameters, salient ones being mean average precision (*map*), Precision at 5 (*P_5*), Precision at 10 (*P_10*) and binary preference-based measure (*bpref*). Precision is computed by dividing number of retrieved relevant documents by total number of retrieved documents. For a given query, Precision at k (*P_k*) signifies number of retrieved relevant documents out of first k retrieved documents. For example, as seen from Figs. 2 and 3, the *P_5* measure for first query (qid=1) will be 1 since all the 5 retrieved documents are relevant. However, the final *P_5* measure is average of *P_5* measures of all the queries. *bpref* is a measure of number of judged relevant documents which are retrieved ahead of

---

[8] http://trec.nist.gov/trec_eval/.

qid	iter	docno	rel
1	0	0812.1117_1_23	1
1	0	0902.1972_1_126	1
1	0	0909.0323_1_12	1
1	0	0901.3829_1_6	1
1	0	0910.5122_1_21	1
1	0	0904.0205_1_10	1
2	0	0812.1117_1_31	1
2	0	0812.1117_1_33	1
2	0	0901.3829_1_6	1
2	0	0901.3829_1_17	1
2	0	0901.3829_1_14	1
3	0	0812.2005_1_11	1
3	0	0812.2005_1_13	1
3	0	1003.3863_1_10	1
3	0	1003.3863_1_12	1
3	0	1003.3863_1_11	1
3	0	1001.4180_1_8	1
3	0	1001.4180_1_16	1
3	0	0812.1117_1_23	1

Fig. 2. Snapshot of gold dataset

qid	iter	docno	rank	sim	run_id
1	Q0	0901.3829_1_6	1	0.9	demo
1	Q0	0910.5122_1_21	1	0.9	demo
1	Q0	0812.1117_1_23	1	0.9	demo
1	Q0	0909.0323_1_12	1	0.9	demo
1	Q0	0904.0205_1_10	1	0.9	demo
2	Q0	0812.1117_1_33	1	0.9	demo
2	Q0	0812.1117_1_31	1	0.9	demo
2	Q0	0901.3829_1_17	1	0.9	demo
2	Q0	0901.3829_1_14	1	0.9	demo
2	Q0	0901.3829_1_6	1	0.9	demo
3	Q0	0812.2005_1_13	1	0.9	demo
3	Q0	1001.4180_1_8	1	0.9	demo
3	Q0	0812.2005_1_11	1	0.9	demo
3	Q0	1001.4180_1_16	1	0.9	demo
3	Q0	1003.3863_1_10	1	0.9	demo
3	Q0	0812.1117_1_23	1	0.9	demo
3	Q0	0904.0205_1_11	1	0.9	demo
3	Q0	1003.5732_1_12	1	0.9	demo
3	Q0	0812.3534_1_10	1	0.9	demo
3	Q0	0901.3829_1_14	1	0.9	demo
3	Q0	0906.4646_1_157	1	0.9	demo
3	Q0	0909.0323_1_12	1	0.9	demo

Fig. 3. Snapshot of result set

judged irrelevant documents. In order to compute *map*, precision score for each query is computed whenever a relevant document is retrieved. For a given query, average precision score is computed by dividing sum of all the precision scores by total number of relevant documents retrieved for the query. Finally, the mean of all the average precision scores, computed over total number of queries in the queryset, equates to *map*.

All the four evaluation parameters acquire considerably high values, close to 1, for an effective IR system.

4.5   Query Search Mechanisms

Query search mechanisms refer to distinct fashions in which a query term is searched in the underlying index. We have employed three distinct search mechanisms, namely AND, OR and OR+Stemming, to search the query term and compared their effectiveness in terms of parameters mentioned in previous subsection. An IR system employing AND search mechanism looks for exact match of the query term with indexed terms. OR search mechanism splits the query term into its constituents and searches them individually in the underlying index. OR+Stemming search furthers the effectiveness of retrieval by employing stemming of constituent terms and searching constituent terms as well as stemmed terms. The well known Porter Stemming Algorithm[9] has been employed in performing stemming of constituent terms.

4.6   System Evaluation Results

System evaluation is characterized by Corpus, Queryset, Gold dataset, Query search mechanism employed and Result set furnished by the IR system. *trec_eval* evaluation tool compares Gold dataset and Result set and outputs evaluation result set embodying values of different evaluation parameters. Corpus, Queryset and Gold dataset have been kept common for the three Query search mechanisms. Effectiveness of the search mechanisms have been compared on grounds of four salient evaluation parameters, namely *P_5*, *P_10*, *map* and *bpref*, and the obtained results have been tabulated in Table 2. Figure 4 shows a bar chart depicting performance comparison of the three search mechanisms.

Table 2. Values of evaluation parameters for three different search mechanisms

Parameters	AND	OR	OR+Stemming
P_5	0.6424	0.7676	0.7730
P_10	0.3909	0.5622	0.5703
map	0.5668	0.7757	0.7945
bpref	0.5668	0.7941	0.8147

4.7   Result Analysis

A significant increase in values of evaluation parameters, in case of OR search mechanism, is credited to its enhanced exploring ability. AND search discards

---

[9] https://tartarus.org/martin/PorterStemmer/.

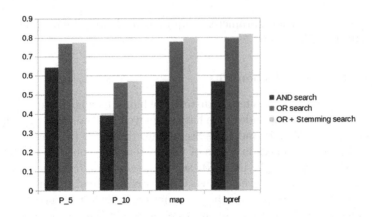

Fig. 4. Performance comparison of AND, OR and OR+Stemming search

the documents in which constituent terms do not co-occur whereas OR search examines and retrieves all such documents and even those documents which embody few of the constituent terms. For instance, given the user query to be *Green's functions*, AND search only retrieves the documents containing exact term, i.e. *Green's functions*, whereas OR search retrieves the documents containing exact term plus the additional documents containing individual constituent terms, namely *Green's* and *functions*. OR+Stemming search induces marginal performance improvement by searching stemmed constituents terms alongside original terms. Marginal improvement presumably owes to the fact that considerable number of constituent terms are already in their stemmed form. For the above user query, OR+Stemming search additionally retrieves the documents containing terms *Green, function, Green* and/or *function*.

Also, bpref and map attain nearly equal values which owes to the fact that both evaluation measures have been found to attain equivalent values for test set with complete judgments. However, bpref is more robust in situations of incomplete judgment.

Furthermore, bpref and map measures procure fairly high values, particularly for systems employing OR search and OR+Stemming search mechanisms. This is driven by the system's behavior to retrieve relevant documents ahead of irrelevant ones and such a behavior is also reflected in P_10 evaluation measure being lower than P_5 measure. Comparatively lower values of P_10 measures are indicative of the fact that after retrieving 5 documents for a query and as the number of retrieved documents approaches 10 for a query, system has a tendency to retrieve irrelevant documents.

Moreover, all the three search mechanisms fail to attain precision values (*P_5, P_10*) close to 1 which pertains to system's inability to handle query terms containing special characters, foreign terms, highly inflected terms and terms separated using dashes or apostrophe. For instance, IR system fails to retrieve the documents having query term *Schrödinger* since it contains the special character ö (o with umlaut).

5   Conclusion and Future Scope

Scientific documents are characterized by scientific terms and expressions which significantly differ from normal text in terms of complexity and representation. Improvement in basic query search mechanism of conventional boolean IR model constitutes one of the primary requirements for scientific text information retrieval as it eventually imparts considerable improvement to effectiveness of IR system. We have experimented with basic query search mechanism (AND search) of Apache Nutch based IR system and proposed two possible modifications, namely OR search and OR+Stemming search. Improved exploring abilities and apparent nature of the two search techniques bestow remarkable improvements to precision measures and the same has been observed experimentally.

Some of the notable future modifications are mentioned as under:

1. Stemming of indexed terms besides query terms.
2. Integrating WordNet and Word2Vec with the underlying IR system for searching semantically similar terms.
3. Equipping index and search modules with potential to handle special characters and foreign terms.

Above modifications are likely to supplement values of evaluation measures and escalate performance of retrieval significantly.

Acknowledgement. The work presented here falls under the Research Project Grant No. YSS/2015/000988 and supported by the Department of Science & Technology (DST) and Science and Engineering Research Board (SERB), Govt. of India. The authors would like to acknowledge the Department of Computer Science & Engineering, National Institute of Technology Mizoram, India for providing infrastructural facilities and support.

References

1. Bhaskar, P., Das, A., Pakray, P., Bandyopadhyay, S.: Theme based English and Bengali ad-hoc monolingual information retrieval in fire 2010. Corpus **1**, 25–32 (2010)
2. Büttcher, S., Clarke, C.L., Cormack, G.V.: Information Retrieval: Implementing and Evaluating Search Engines. MIT Press, Cambridge (2016)
3. Chauhan, R., Goudar, R., Sharma, R., Chauhan, A.: Domain ontology based semantic search for efficient information retrieval through automatic query expansion. In: 2013 International Conference on Intelligent Systems and Signal Processing (ISSP), pp. 397–402. IEEE (2013)
4. Cross, V.: Fuzzy information retrieval. J. Intell. Inf. Syst. **3**(1), 29–56 (1994)
5. Dolamic, L., Savoy, J.: UniNE at FIRE 2008: Hindi, Bengali, and Marathi IR. In: Working Notes of the Forum for Information Retrieval Evaluation, pp. 12–14 (2008)
6. Kraft, D.H., Colvin, E., Marchionini, G.: Fuzzy Information Retrieval. Morgan & Claypool (2017). http://ieeexplore.ieee.org/xpl/articleDetails.jsp?arnumber=7833477

7. Lam, A.N., Nguyen, A.T., Nguyen, H.A., Nguyen, T.N.: Bug localization with combination of deep learning and information retrieval. In: 2017 IEEE/ACM 25th International Conference on Program Comprehension (ICPC), pp. 218–229, May 2017

8. Lashkari, A.H., Mahdavi, F., Ghomi, V.: A Boolean model in information retrieval for search engines. In: 2009 International Conference on Information Management and Engineering, pp. 385–389. IEEE (2009)

9. Lemos, O.A., de Paula, A.C., Zanichelli, F.C., Lopes, C.V.: Thesaurus-based automatic query expansion for interface-driven code search. In: Proceedings of the 11th Working Conference on Mining Software Repositories, pp. 212–221. ACM (2014)

10. Lucarella, D., Morara, R.: First: fuzzy information retrieval system. J. Inf. Sci. **17**(2), 81–91 (1991)

11. Lynum, A., Pakray, P., Gambäck, B., Jimenez, S.: NTNU: measuring semantic similarity with sublexical feature representations and soft cardinality. In: SemEval@ COLING, pp. 448–453 (2014)

12. Maitah, W., Al-Rababaa, M., Kannan, G.: Improving the effectiveness of information retrieval system using adaptive genetic algorithm. Int. J. Comput. Sci. Inf. Technol. **5**(5), 91–105 (2013)

13. Pakray, P., Bandyopadhyay, S., Gelbukh, A.: Textual entailment using lexical and syntactic similarity. Int. J. Artif. Intell. Appl. **2**(1), 43–58 (2011)

14. Pakray, P., Sojka, P.: An architecture for scientific document retrieval using textual and math entailment modules. Karlova Studnka, Czech Republic, Recent Advances in Slavonic Natural Language Processing (2014)

15. Pathak, A., Pakray, P., Sarkar, S., Das, D., Gelbukh, A.: MathIRS: retrieval system for scientific documents. Comput. Sist. **21**(2), 253–265 (2017)

16. Raman, S., Chaurasiya, V.K., Venkatesan, S.: Performance comparison of various information retrieval models used in search engines. In: 2012 International Conference on Communication, Information Computing Technology (ICCICT), pp. 1–4, October 2012

17. Sarkar, K., Gupta, A.: An empirical study of some selected ir models for Bengali monolingual information retrieval. arXiv preprint arXiv:1706.03266 (2017)

18. Schellenberg, M.T.: Layout-based substitution tree indexing and retrieval for mathematical expressions. Rochester Institute of Technology (2011)

19. Steyvers, M., Griffiths, T.L.: Rational analysis as a link between human memory and information retrieval. In: The Probabilistic Mind: Prospects for Bayesian Cognitive Science, pp. 329–349 (2008)

20. Yoshioka, M., Haraguchi, M.: On a combination of probabilistic and Boolean IR models for WWW document retrieval. ACM Trans. Asian Lang. Inf. Process. (TALIP) **4**(3), 340–356 (2005)

21. Zhai, C.: Statistical language models for information retrieval. Synth. Lect. Human Lang. Technol. **1**(1), 1–141 (2008)

Categorization of Bangla Web Text Documents Based on TF-IDF-ICF Text Analysis Scheme

Ankita Dhar[1]([⊠]), Niladri Sekhar Dash[2]([⊠]), and Kaushik Roy[1]([⊠])

[1] Department of Computer Science, West Bengal State University,
Kolkata, India
ankita.ankie@gmail.com, kaushik.mrg@gmail.com
[2] Linguistic Research Unit, Indian Statistical Institute, Baranagar, India
ns_dash@yahoo.com

Abstract. With the rapid growth and huge availability of digital text data, automatic text categorization or classification is a comparatively more effective solution in organizing and managing textual information. It is a process of automatically assigning a text document into one of the predefined sets of text categories. Although plenty of methods have been implemented on English text documents for categorization, limited studies are carried out on the Indian language texts including Bangla. Against this background, this paper analyzes the efficiency of some of the existing text classification methods available to us and proposes to supplement these with a new analysis method for classifying the Bangla text documents obtained from online web sources. The paper argues that addition of Inverse Class Frequency (ICF) measure to the Term Frequency (TF) and Inverse Document Frequency (IDF) methods can yield better responses in the act of feature extraction from a language like Bangla. The combination of all three processes generates a set of features which is further fed to train the MultiLayer Perceptron (MLP) classifier to produce promising results in identifying and classifying text documents to their respective domains and categories. Comparison of this classifier with others confirms that this has higher accuracy level in case of Bangla text documents. It is expected that MLP can produce satisfactory performance in terms of high dimensionality and relatively noisy feature vectors also.

Keywords: Bangla text classification · Term Frequency
Inverse Document Frequency · Inverse Class Frequency
MLP · Corpus

1 Introduction

In this era of digitalization, numbers of digital text documents are growing rapidly and are available in great amount. The possibility is due to the high capacity of software, hardware, powerful computing, and storage device with ease of availability at affordable prices. Huge availability of various text documents requires an efficient organization and retrieval. To have easy access to these text documents, classification of these text documents need to be done using some standard automatic text classification techniques. Classifying a large set of unlabelled text documents manually into their

J. K. Mandal and D. Sinha (Eds.): CSI 2017, CCIS 836, pp. 477–484, 2018.
https://doi.org/10.1007/978-981-13-1343-1_39

predefined categories is extremely time-consuming, difficult, error-prone, expensive and hence not feasible at all.

Automatic text classification or categorization system is the best possible solution to the problem. Text classification refers to the supervised learning task of using a labeled training set of text documents which assign a category to a new text document based on a model generated by a classifier. There are two important characteristics that differ text categorization or classification task from other classification problems. The first major characteristic is the high dimensional dataset and to ensure the sparse and noisy data. The high dimensionality of a dataset is the direct fallout of using the vector space model that represents the text document as a vector of words. The second characteristic is the number of categories or domains. Classifying text documents into more than two categories is a challenging task where the content of text documents from various domains is sometimes closely related to each other.

The rest of the paper is arranged as follows: related work is discussed in Sect. 2; the proposed work which includes generation of the dataset, tokenization, pre-processing, extraction of the feature values and its dimensionality reduction are discussed in Sect. 3; Sect. 4 describes result analysis including the description of the classifier being used and finally, concluded in Sect. 5.

2   Existing Work

From the literature review of text classification, it can be observed that languages like English and Arabic have gained great attention by the researchers followed by Chinese, Persian but very few types of research have been done on Indian languages. For English language, DeySarkar et al. [1] proposed a clustering-based approach using 13 datasets based on Naive Bayes classification algorithm. Guru and Suhil [2] introduced Term_Class relevance as the feature selection method on the 20Newsgroup dataset using SVM and KNN classifiers for their experiment. Jin et al. [3] proposed a bag-of-embeddings model on two datasets: Reuters21578 and 20Newsgroups, using Stochastic Gradient Descent (SGD) classifier for classification problem. Wang et al. [4] carried out their experiment on Reuters21578 and 20Newsgroups datasets based on term frequency and t-test feature selection methods and classification are done using various commonly used classifiers.

In case of Arabic text classification, Al-Radaideh and Al-Khateeb [15] used associative rule-based classifiers in their experiment for classifying Arabic medical text documents. Light stemming and rootification approaches along with TFIDF and dependency grammar properties have been employed on Kalimat corpus by Haralambous et al. [16].

Gupta and Gupta [5] implemented hybrid approach by taking two classification algorithms namely, Naive Bayes and Ontological Based classifiers for classifying Punjabi text documents. ArunaDevi and Saveetha [11] classified Tamil text documents by extracting compound features from CIIL and Mozhi corpus. Swamy and Thappa [12] used Vector Space Model and TF-IDF weighting scheme based on Zipf's law for classifying 100 text documents each for Kannada, Tamil, and Telugu and applied Decision Tree (J48), Naive Bayes (NB) and KNN as classifiers for their experiment.

Patil and Bogiri [13] implemented LINGO clustering algorithm for classifying 200 Marathi news text documents. Bolaj and Govilkar [14] proposed dictionary based classification approach by computing the feature vector using Marathi dictionary and classifying the text documents using classification algorithm like Multinomial Naive Bayes, SVM, Modified KNN, and ontology-based classification.

For Bangla text classification, to the best of our knowledge, N-Gram based technique has been used by Mansur et al. [6] to categorize Bangla newspaper text corpus assembled from a single newspaper (i.e., Pratham Alo) including just one-year data. Another study by Mandal and Sen [7] shows the comparison of four supervised learning techniques for categorizing labeled news web documents into five categories. The classification has been carried out on 1000 text documents and the total number of tokens is 22,218. Accuracy achieved for four classifiers namely; SVM, NB, DT (C4.5) and KNN are 89.14%, 85.22%, 80.65% and 74.24% respectively. Kabir et al. [8] applied Stochastic Gradient Descent (SGD) Classifier for classifying Bangla text documents from 9 different categories. Other commonly used classifiers have been used for comparison purpose. The accuracies achieved: SGD Classifier is 93.85%, Ridge Classifier is 93.44%, Perceptron is 91.42%, Passive-Aggressive is 93.19%, SVM is 93.78%, NB is 91.89%, and Logistic-Regression is 93.05%. A comparative study of different types of methods of classifying Bangla text document is provided in the work of Islam et al. [9]. In another work of Islam et al. [10], it can be seen that by applying TFIDF as feature selection method and SVM as classifier they achieve accuracy of 92.57% for classifying Bangla text documents covering twelve text categories.

3   Proposed Model

Prior to the extraction of feature values and accomplishing classification task, it is essential to perform tokenization which is basically the segmentation of sentences into tokens and pre-processing where the tokens that carry no relevant domain-specific information are removed. At the pre-processing stage, elimination of stop words-punctuations, postpositions, conjunctions, English equivalent words, and English and Bangla numerals which are frequently used in a Bangla text documents is performed. Now, extractions of proper feature sets are required to train the model for achieving an encouraging result for text document classification. The following block diagram (Fig. 1) demonstrates the overall process of automatic Bangla text categorization system implemented in this experiment. A detailed description of the model is provided below.

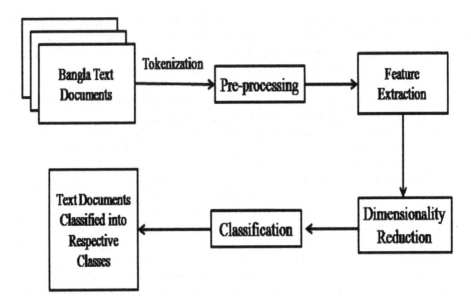

Fig. 1. Bird's eye view of the proposed model

3.1   Data Collection

The Bangla text documents used for the experiment have been obtained from various online Bangla news text corpus produced by some Bangla daily newspapers, online webpages and online magazines:

(a)   AnandabazarPatrika: http://www.anandabazar.com
(b)   Bartaman: http://allbanglanewspapers.com/bartaman
(c)   Ebelatabloid: http://www.ebela.in
(d)   https://deshirecipe.wordpress.com
(e)   http://www.ebanglarecipe.com
(f)   http://www.banglaadda.com
(g)   http://amaderchhuti.com
(h)   https://www.ebanglatravel.com
(i)   http://recipebangla.com.

From this corpus, total 4000 Bangla text documents are obtained covering eight categories. There are 500 text documents from each of the eight domains, namely, Business (B), Entertainment (E), Food (F), Medical (M), Science & Technology (ST), Sports (SP), State (S) and Travel (T). After tokenization, the number of tokens extracted is 12,43,860 and after removal of punctuation marks, postpositions, conjunctions, pronouns, English and Bangla numerals, and English equivalent words, the number of tokens finally collected is 9,57,623.

3.2   Feature Extraction and Selection

For this experiment, the standard method like TF-IDF are improvised into TF-IDF-ICF by incorporating Inverse Class Frequency (ICF) in TF-IDF to develop the feature values from the text documents.

The TF here represents the frequency of a term t in a particular text document d. The IDF generally measures the relevance of a term t in d. The IDF of a term t is determined using equation (Eq. 1) where N represents the total text documents and DF (Document Frequency) is the number of text documents where term t occurs.

$$IDF_t = \log \frac{N}{DF_t} \tag{1}$$

The TF-IDF [7] for a term t in a text document d is measured using the following equation (Eq. 2) given below.

$$TF - IDF = TF * IDF_t \tag{2}$$

The ICF basically measures the occurrences of a term t in a number of text categories using the following equation (Eq. 3) provided below with C categories.

$$ICF_t = \log \frac{C}{CF_t} \tag{3}$$

The TF-IDF-ICF scheme for a term t in a text document d is measured using the following equation (Eq. 4) given below.

$$TF - IDF - ICF = TF * IDF_t * ICF_t \tag{4}$$

Before providing the feature set to the classifier, it is subjected to the reduction technique to reduce its dimensionality of the feature vectors by removing that multi-collinearity (those features that are redundant or in other words, have the same value for all the instances are discarded from the feature set) for improving the learning model. Here, PCC (Pearson's Correlation Coefficient) is used as reduction technique to estimate the value of an attribute by calculating the correlation between it using the following equation (Eq. 5) given below [17].

$$PCC = \frac{\sum (I - \bar{I})(J - \bar{J})}{\sqrt{\sum (I - \bar{I})^2 (J - \bar{J})^2}} \tag{5}$$

4   Experimental Setup

For this experiment, the MultiLayer Perceptron (MLP) is used as a model classifier and trained by backpropagation technique to classify the instances with learning rate of 0.29, momentum of 0.25 and iterated over 1600 times with 50 (hidden layer) neurons.

All such values to the MLP have been assigned based on a trial run. MLP is chosen as it is popularly used classifier in text classification field [18]. The domain-wise accuracies are illustrated through a graph in the following figure (Fig. 2). The recognition accuracy has been achieved using the following formula (Eq. 6):

$$\text{Accuracy} = \frac{Correctly\_classified\_text\_documents}{Total\_number\_of\_text\_documents} * 100\% \tag{6}$$

The detail of the result obtained by applying various commonly used classifiers like Naive Bayes Multinomial (NBM), Naive Bayes (NB), Decision Tree (J48), PART and KNN along with MLP on this dataset before applying reduction technique and with reduced feature set is given in Table 1.

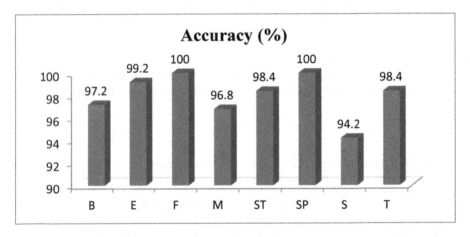

Fig. 2. Obtained accuracies for eight domains

Table 1. Accuracy with or without reduction

Classifiers	Before reduction	After reduction
MLP	97.65%	98.03%
NBM	94.62%	95.82%
NB	53.42%	59.75%
J48	92.62%	92.42%
PART	92.30%	92.47%
KNN	96.12%	97.09%

The statistical analysis using Friedman nonparametric test [1] is presented in the following table (Table 2) below. It has been selected due to its nature of not depending on the specific model being used in the experiment. The Friedman test $\left(\chi_F^2\right)$ is computed with the help of equations (Eqs. 7 and 8). The statistical analysis shows the value of $\left(\chi_F^2\right)$ for 5 (k−1) degrees of freedom along with a significance (α) of 0.05 is 24.314, with k classifiers and N datasets.

$$\chi_F^2 = \frac{12N}{k(k+1)}\left[\sum_j R_j^2 - \frac{k(k+1)^2}{4}\right] \tag{7}$$

$$R_j = \frac{1}{N}\sum_i R_j^i \tag{8}$$

Table 2. Statistical analysis using Friedman test

Classifier	Dataset					Mean rank
	#1	#2	#3	#4	#5	
MLP	98.28 (1)	98.45 (1)	98.73 (1)	98.89 (1)	98.76 (1)	$R_1 = 1.0$
NBM	95.98 (3)	95.44 (3)	96.34 (3)	96.08 (3)	96.19 (3)	$R_2 = 3.0$
NB	58.52 (6)	59.26 (6)	59.15 (6)	61.74 (6)	61.37 (6)	$R_3 = 6.0$
J48	93.09 (4)	92.58 (4)	92.71 (5)	92.44 (4)	92.77 (5)	$R_4 = 4.4$
PART	92.27 (5)	92.13 (5)	92.79 (4)	93.05 (5)	92.89 (4)	$R_5 = 4.6$
KNN	97.08 (2)	97.14 (2)	97.42 (2)	97.26 (2)	97.18 (2)	$R_5 = 2.0$

5 Conclusion

This paper shows that the application of TF-IDF-ICF feature with dimensionality reduction technique can bring in precision in classifying the text documents to their respective categories. From the present experiment, it is evident that based on this reduction technique adopted for Bangla text documents classification, it is possible to achieve high accuracy. In future, the system can be tested on a larger dataset with a large number of text categories. Also, other commonly used standard reduction techniques can be applied along with different feature extraction and selection techniques as well. Various classifiers can also be applied for comparison with the proposed system. It is hoped that the cross-interpolation of different techniques may excited encouraging performance in case of text domain identification and classification provided the input text documents are sufficiently processed for extracting required data and information to train the system.

Acknowledgement. One of the authors thank DST for support in the form of INSPIRE fellowship.

References

1. Sarkar, S.D., Goswami, S., Agarwal, A., Akhtar, J.: A novel feature selection technique for text classification using Naive Bayes. Int. Sch. Res. Not. **2014**, 10 (2014)
2. Guru, D.S., Suhil, M.: A novel Term_Class relevance measure for text categorization. In: Proceedings of International Conference on Advanced Computing Technologies and Applications, pp. 13–22 (2015)
3. Jin, P., Zhang, Y., Chen, X., Xia, Y.: Bag-of-Embeddings for text classification. In: Proceedings of the 25tth International Joint Conference on Artificial Intelligence, pp. 2824–2830 (2016)
4. Wang, D., Zhang, H., Liu, R., Lv, W.: Feature selection based on term frequency and T-Test for text categorization. In: Proceedings of the 21st ACM International Conference on Information and Knowledge Management, pp. 1482–1486 (2012)
5. Gupta, N., Gupta, V.: Punjabi text classification using Naive Bayes, centroid and hybrid approach. In: Proceedings of the 3rd Workshop on South and South East Asian Natural Language Processing, pp. 109–122 (2012)
6. Mansur, M., UzZaman, N., Khan, M.: Analysis of N-Gram based text categorization for bangla in a newspaper corpus. In: Proceedings of International Conference on Computer and Information Technology, p. 08 (2006)
7. Mandal, A.K., Sen, R.: Supervised learning methods for bangla web document categorization. Int. J. Artif. Intell. Appl. **05**, 93–105 (2014)
8. Kabir, F., Siddique, S., Kotwal, M.R.A., Huda, M.N.: Bangla text document categorization using stochastic gradient descent (SGD) classifier. In: Proceedings of International Conference on Cognitive Computing and Information Processing, pp. 1–4 (2015)
9. Islam, S., Jubayer, F.E., Ahmed, S.I.: A comparative study on different types of approaches to Bengali document categorization. In: Proceedings of International Conference on Engineering Research, Innovation and Education, p. 06 (2017)
10. Islam, S., Jubayer, F.E., Ahmed, S.I.: A support vector machine mixed with TF-IDF algorithm to categorize Bengali document. In: Proceedings of International Conference on Electrical, Computer and Communication Engineering, pp. 191–196 (2017)
11. ArunaDevi, K., Saveetha, R.: A novel approach on Tamil text classification using C-Feature. Int. J. Sci. Res. Dev. **2**, 343–345 (2014)
12. Swamy, M.N., Thappa, M.H.: Indian language text representation and categorization using supervised learning algorithm. Int. J. Data Min. Tech. Appl. **02**, 251–257 (2013)
13. Patil, J.J., Bogiri, N.: Automatic text categorization marathi documents. Int. J. Adv. Res. Comput. Sci. Manag. Stud. **03**, 280–287 (2015)
14. Bolaj, P., Govilkar, S.: Text classification for marathi documents using supervised learning methods. Int. J. Comput. Appl. **155**, 6–10 (2016)
15. Al-Radaideh, Q.A., Al-Khateeb, S.S.: An associative rule-based classifier for Arabic medical text. Int. J. Knowl. Eng. Data Min. **03**, 255–273 (2015)
16. Haralambous, Y., Elidrissi, Y., Lenca, P.: Arabic language text classification using dependency syntax-based feature selection. In: Proceedings of International Conference on Arabic Language Processing, p. 10 (2014)
17. Ahlgren, P., Jarneving, B., Rousseau, R.: Requirements for a cocitation similarity measure, with special reference to pearson's correlation coefficient. J. Am. Soc. Inform. Sci. Technol. **54**, 550–560 (2003)
18. Prusa, J.D., Khoshgoftaar, T.M.: Improving deep neural network design with new text data representations. J. Big Data **04**, 16 (2017)

Load Balancing of Unbalanced Matrix Problem with More Machines

Ranjan Kumar Mondal[1(✉)], Payel Ray[1], Enakshmi Nandi[1], Biswajit Biswas[2], Manas Kumar Sanyal[2], and Debabrata Sarddar[1]

[1] Department of Computer Science and Engineering, University of Kalyani, Kalyani, India
ranjan@klyuniv.ac.in, payelray009@gmail.com, pamelaroychowdhurikalyani@gmail.com, dsarddar1@gmail.com
[2] Department of Business Administration, University of Kalyani, Kalyani, India
biswajit.biswas0012@gmail.com, manassanyal123@gmail.com

Abstract. In nowadays cloud computing as a developing web accommodation model has been propagating to offer different Internet resources to users. Cloud computing occupies a range of computing Internet applications for facilitating the finishing of sizable voluminous-scale tasks. Cloud computing is a web predicated distributed computing. There is more than a million number of servers connected to the Internet to provide several types of accommodations to provide cloud users. Constrained numbers of servers execute fewer numbers tasks at a time. So it is not too easy to execute all tasks at a time. Some systems execute all tasks, so there are needed to balance all loads. Load balance minimizes the completion time as well as executes all tasks a particular way.

There are not possible to remain equal number servers to execute equal tasks. Tasks to be executed in cloud computing would be less than the connected servers sometime. Excess servers have to execute a fewer number of tasks. Here we are going to present an algorithm for load balancing and performance with minimization completion time and throughput. We apply here a very famous Hungarian method to balance all loads in distributing computing. Hungarian Technique helps us to minimize the cost matrix problem.

Keywords: Load balancing · Load balancing algorithms · Cloud computing
Hungarian method

1 Introduction

We know cloud computing [1] is a web-based service. It has moved the computing applications and data from the device into data centers. Cloud computing has modified IT companies employed to intend software. Since cloud computing has been running in its developing phase. As a result, there are a lot of complications stay on in cloud computing [1]. For example:

- To ensure capable access control (authentication and authorization).

© Springer Nature Singapore Pte Ltd. 2018
J. K. Mandal and D. Sinha (Eds.): CSI 2017, CCIS 836, pp. 485–494, 2018.
https://doi.org/10.1007/978-981-13-1343-1_40

- Network level immigration for the constraint of a minor amount cost and time to shift work.
- For data transition phase and resting phase give correct protection to the data.
- Data defense, the disclosure of perceptive data is achievable, and the significant complexity of cloud computing is load balancing. During the process of load balancing, dissimilar kinds of information, for instance, some works waiting in the queue, work arrival time, also CPU processing time at each processor and neighboring systems also may be replaced amongst the systems to get the proficient and developed total performance. So, many algorithms have proposed for Load Balancing purpose. In this article, we have proposed an innovative algorithm for proper load balancing to obtain better CPU processing time for subjects of improved excellence presentation.

2 Load Balancing Definition

We know load balancing [2] is a basic word utilize for giving out extensive processing loads to slighter processing systems for improving the large performance of the system. In a distributed system surroundings, it is the process of sharing out loads amongst a variety of other systems of a distributed system to get better both resource use along with work response time. An ideal balancing algorithm ought to keep away from overloading or underloading of any exact system.

In cloud environment background, the choice of load balancing algorithm is strenuous; this is because it occupies complementary constraints like security, reliability, throughput, etc. So, the important majority objective of a balancing algorithm in a cloud computing system is to develop the response time of work by distributing entire loads of the system. The algorithms have to additionally make sure that it is not overloading any particular system.

Load balancers are able to attempt in two different methods: one is cooperative, and another is non-cooperative. In a cooperative way, the system's effort at the same time to attain the ordinary objectives of optimizing the total response time. In the non-cooperative mode, the jobs are running separately to develop the response time of local jobs.

2.1 The Types of Algorithms

Load Balancing [2] primarily decides the task that how to choose the next system and to transfer a new request to transfer the load from the overloaded process to under loaded process. It spreads the incoming requesting load among the available systems to improve the performance drastically by the Cloud manager. There are two types of an algorithm based on their operation method; they are a static load balancing algorithm (SLA) and dynamic load balancing algorithm (DLA).

A. **SLA:** It does not rely on the current position. It decides on the host; the demand will be performed before setting up the demand.

B. **DLA:** The load balancer analyzes the present condition of load strategies at every existing host performs to ask for a suitable host. First-Come-First-Served, Throttled, Honey Foraging Algorithm, etc. are the model of dynamic scheduling algorithm are better than a static algorithm and appropriate for a lot of requests, which can carry the various workloads, which would be unable to predict.

3   Related Works

Cloud computing provides a compilation of services to the consumer, for example, multi-media sharing, online software, game and online storage. Each system performs a task or a sub-task in a cloud environment, [3]. The OLB algorithm is set to remain every system busy despite the present workloads of every system [3, 4, 6]. OLB algorithm allocates tasks to presented systems in arbitrary order [5]. The MCT algorithm assigns jobs to the systems having the expected minimum completion time of this job over other systems [6]. The MM scheduling algorithm assumes the same scheduling approach as the MCT [6] algorithm to assign a job, the system to complete this job with minimum completion time over other systems [7]. The LBMM scheduling algorithm [8] implements MM scheduling approach and load balancing strategy. It can evade the unnecessarily copied assignment. Load Balancing with Job Switching [9] minimize loads of heavy loaded machine to under loaded machine by switching a particular work. Load Balancing of Unbalanced Matrix with Hungarian Method [10] uses Hungarian algorithm where works are greater than all machines. Load balancing of the unbalanced cost matrix [11] is same as the previous algorithm.

4   Criteria for Performance

Our planning load balancing algorithm is considered to obtain together all scheduling criterion such as most significant CPU consumption, lowest **TAT**, highest throughput, smallest waiting time and context switches. We discuss the AT, BT, WT, TAT, RT, and Throughput [3].

Arrival Time (AT):	The time when something will enter the process in the main memory.
Waiting Time (WT):	The time when how long, the process waiting in the ready queue.
Burst Time (BT):	The time when how long, the process holds the CPU.
Turnaround Time (TAT):	In general, turnaround time (TAT) means the amount of **time** taken to fulfill a request.
Response Time (RT):	Response time is the total amount of time it takes to respond to a request for service.
Throughput:	Throughput is the highest rate of production or the highest speed at which something can be developed.

5 Problem Definition

There are several systems in a cloud organization. That is to say; each system has the dissimilar potential to perform the duty; hence, only consider the CPU of the system is not as much as necessary while a system is preferred to perform a task or subtask. So, to pick an efficient system to perform a job is extremely significant in cloud computing surroundings. Due to the task having unusual attributes for the consumer to give completion. Hence it needs a few of the resources definite, for occurrence, when implementing organism series assembly, it probably has big constraint toward memory. And to reach the top result in the completion of every job, so we plan tasks property to acknowledge a dissimilar state decision variable in which it is according to a resource of task constraint to set decision variable. An agent collects associated information of all system linked to this cloud system, for instance, CPU capability, available memory, and bandwidth rate.

The cloud computing surrounding is compiled from various systems, wherever the possessions of all system might differ. Also, the computing capability offered by the available CPU, the convenient memory size, and bandwidth rate are dissimilar. Cloud computing presents the resources of all system, so the existing resource of each system possibly will differ in a full of activity condition. From task completion available CPU, existing memory, and bandwidth rate are the essential things for the completion.

Accordingly, in the study, the existing CPU ability, the existing memory size, and bandwidth rate obtained as the threshold for estimating manager system values. An illustration instance of precise as goes after:

(I) The available CPU capability $\geq$ 753 MB/s
(II) The available memory $\geq$ 251298 KB/s
(III) Bandwidth Rate $\geq$ 8.18 MB/s.

To allocate a variety of works to dissimilar computing systems, in such a way that the entirety assignment cost is to be the smallest amount, known as the assignment problem.

If the numeral works are not equal to a numeral of the computing systems, then it is known to be unequal assignment problem.

Assume a problem which consists of a group of 'i' systems $N = \{N_1, N_2, ..., N_i\}$. A group of 'j' works $\{W = W_1, W_2, ..., W_j\}$ is considered which are to be allocated for finishing on 'm' available computing systems. The finishing cost of each work on all the computing systems is known and mentioned in the matrix of the order of n. The objective is to decide the minimum cost. This problem is solved by well-known a prevalent method called Hungarian method [12].

5.1 Hungarian Method

Step 1: The input of this algorithm is an *n*n square*.
Step 2: To find the least element from each row and subtract it from every element in the corresponding row.
Step 3: In the same way, for each column, get the least element and deduct it from every element in the corresponding column.
Step 4: Face all zeros in the subtracted matrix with least numeral of horizontal and vertical lines. If numerals of lines are n, then an optimal assignment exists. The algorithm stops. Otherwise, if numerals of lines are less than n then, go to after that step.
Step 5: Get the least element that is uncovered by a line in Step 4. Deduct with a smallest uncovered element from all uncovered elements, and add a smallest uncovered element to all elements that are covered twice.

6 Proposed Work

Whenever the matrix of an assignment problem is a non-square matrix, that is, when the quantity of sources system is unequal to the quantity of destinations system, the assignment problem is called an unbalanced assignment problem. This kind of problems, replica rows (or columns) are added to the matrix to complete it to shape a square matrix. The replica rows or columns will contain all elements as zeroes. The Hungarian method could be used to solve this type of crisis.

6.1 Algorithm

To present an algorithmic representation of the method, let us consider a problem which consists of a set of 'i' systems $N = \{N_1, N_2, ..., N_i\}$. A set of 'j' works $W = \{W_1, W_2, ..., W_j\}$ is considered which is to be allocated for finishing on 'm' available computing systems and the finishing value C_{mn}, where m = 1, 2, ..., i and n = 1, 2, ..., i, where j > i, i.e., the numeral of works is more than a numeral of computing systems.

Step-1: Say: *m*n* matrix where m<n.
Step-2: Apply Hungarian Algorithm
Step-3: Assign each work to their corresponding machine.
Step-4: Stop.

Example: Presume a company has six systems that are used for four works. Each work is able to be allocated to one and only one system at the same time.

The cost of every work on every machine is specified in the following Table.

Assignment Problem

Works/Machines	N_{11}	N_{12}	N_{13}	N_{14}	N_{15}	N_{16}
W_{11}	10	19	8	15	21	18
W_{12}	10	18	17	17	42	23
W_{13}	13	26	19	14	19	22
W_{14}	22	19	18	18	38	22
W_{15}	14	17	10	19	24	11

The following is the original cost matrix:

10	19	8	15	21	18
10	18	17	17	42	23
13	26	19	14	19	22
22	19	18	18	38	22
14	17	10	19	24	11

Make the Matrix Square

The cost matrix holds more rows than columns; we attach replica columns with zeros to compose the matrix square:

10	19	8	15	21	18
10	18	17	17	42	23
13	26	19	14	19	22
22	19	18	18	38	22
14	17	10	19	24	11
0	0	0	0	0	0

Deduct Row Minimum

Because every row has a zero, deducting row minimum it does not affect.

2	11	0	7	13	10	(-8)
0	8	7	7	32	13	(-10)
0	13	6	1	6	9	(-13)
4	1	0	0	20	4	(-18)
4	7	0	9	14	1	(-10)
0	0	0	0	0	0	

Subtract Column Minimum

Every column contains a zero, subtracting column minima has no effect.

Face up all Zeros with the Least Number of Lines

There are four lines needed to face all zeros:

2	11	0	7	13	10	
0	8	7	7	32	13	
0	13	6	1	6	9	
4	1	0	0	20	4	Y
4	7	0	9	14	1	
0	0	0	0	0	0	Y
Y		Y				

Create Additional Zeros

The number of lines is lesser than 5. The smallest uncovered number is 1. We deduct this number from all uncovered elements and add it to all elements covered twice:

2	10	0	6	12	9
0	7	7	6	31	12
0	12	6	0	5	8
5	1	1	0	20	4
4	6	0	8	13	0
1	0	1	0	0	0

Cover up all Zeros with the Least Number of Lines

There are five lines required to face all zeros:

2	10	0	6	12	9	Y
0	7	7	6	31	12	
0	12	6	0	5	8	
5	1	1	0	20	4	
4	6	0	8	13	0	Y
1	0	1	0	0	0	Y
Y		Y				

Construct Supplementary Zeros

The figure of lines is lesser than six. The least uncovered digit is one. We deduct this number from all uncovered elements and add it to all elements covered twice:

3	10	0	7	12	9
0	6	6	6	30	11
0	11	5	0	4	7
5	0	0	0	19	3
5	6	0	9	13	0
2	0	1	1	0	0

Face all Zeros with the Least Number of Lines

There are 6 lines needed to face all zeros:

3	10	0	7	12	9	Y
0	6	6	6	30	11	Y
0	11	5	0	4	7	Y
5	0	0	0	19	3	Y
5	6	0	9	13	0	Y
2	0	1	1	0	0	Y

The Most Favorable Project

Since there are 6 lines required, the zeros face an best possible result:

3	10	0	7	12	9
0	6	6	6	30	11
0	11	5	0	4	7
5	0	0	0	19	3
5	6	0	9	13	0
2	0	1	1	0	0

This matrix keeps up a correspondence to the following most favorable result in the new matrix:

10	19	**8**	15	21	18
10	18	17	17	42	23
13	26	19	**14**	19	22
22	**19**	18	18	38	22
14	17	10	19	24	**11**

7 Experiment

Figure 1 illustrates the finishing time for all tasks at dissimilar computing systems. The threshold is the average finishing time of task t_i in all executing systems. For calculating the performance of our proposed algorithm, our approach is compared with MM and LBMM by the case shown in Fig. 1. Figure 1 expresses the evaluation finishing time of all executing system among our approach, LBMM, and MM. The finishing times for completing all tasks by using our approach, MM and LBMM are 17, 42 and 27 s, in that order. Our approach complete the minimum finishing time and better load balancing than other algorithms, such as LBMM and MM in this case.

8   Comparison

Our proposed load balancing of unbalanced cost matrix can get improved load balancing and performance than other algorithms, such as LBMM and MM from the following the figure.

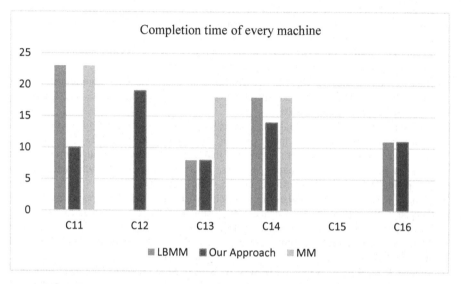

Fig. 1. The evaluation of finishing time (sec) of each task at diverse systems.

9   Conclusion

The present paper, we have planned an well-organized algorithm LBH for the cloud computing network to allocate tasks to computer systems along with their resource ability in the same way, LBH be able to attain superior load balancing and performance than other algorithms, for instance LBMM and MM from the experiment.

The objective of this work is to achieve load balancing by LBH algorithm, that composes all system in executing condition. At the side ofs, in our proposed work, the LBH algorithm is too developed to build the least completion time on the system of all tasks. Additionally, in a comprehensive case, the cloud technology is not only static system but dynamic system as well. In Addition, our proposed technique will be extending to preserve and run when the system is fundamental cloud computing system in future work.

References

1. Mell, P., Grance, T.: The NIST definition of cloud computing, pp. 20–23 (2011)
2. Mondal, R.K., Ray, P., Sarddar, D.: Load balancing. Int. J. Res. Comput. Appl. Inf. Technol. **4**(1), 01–21 (2016). ISSN Online: 2347-5099, Print: 2348-0009, DOA: 03012016
3. Ritchie, G., Levine, J.: A fast, effective local search for scheduling independent works in heterogeneous computing environments. J. Comput. Appl. **25**, 1190–1192 (2005)
4. Braun, T.D., et al.: A comparison of eleven static heuristics for mapping a class of independent tasks onto heterogeneous distributed computing systems. J. Parallel Distrib. Comput. **61**, 810–837 (2001)
5. Wang, S.C., Yan, K.Q., Liao, W.P., Wang, S.S.: Towards a load balancing in a three-level cloud computing network. In: CSIT, pp. 108—113 (2010)
6. Hung, C.-L., Wang, H.-H., Hu, Y.-C.: Efficient load balancing algorithm for cloud computing network. In: International Conference on Information Science and Technology (IST 2012), pp. 28–30, April 2012
7. Kokilavani, T., Amalarethinam, D.G.: Load balanced min-min algorithm for static meta-task scheduling in grid computing. Int. J. Comput. Appl. **20**(2), 43–49 (2011)
8. Wu, M.-Y., Shu, W., Zhang, H.: Segmented min-min: a static mapping algorithm for meta-tasks on heterogeneous computing systems. In: Proceedings of the 9th Heterogeneous Computing Workshop (HCW 2000), pp. 375–385. IEEE (2000)
9. Mondal, R.K., et al.: Load balancing with job switching in cloud computing network. In: Satapathy, S.C., Bhateja, V., Udgata, S.K., Pattnaik, P.K. (eds.) Proceedings of the 5th International Conference on Frontiers in Intelligent Computing: Theory and Applications. AISC, vol. 516, pp. 305–312. Springer, Singapore (2017). https://doi.org/10.1007/978-981-10-3156-4_31
10. Mondal, R.K., Ray, P., Nandi, E., Biswas, B., Sanyal, M.K., Sarddar, D.: Load balancing of unbalanced matrix with hungarian method. In: Mandal, J.K., Dutta, P., Mukhopadhyay, S. (eds.) CICBA 2017. CCIS, vol. 776, pp. 256–270. Springer, Singapore (2017). https://doi.org/10.1007/978-981-10-6430-2_20
11. Mondal, R.K., Ray, P., Nandi, E., Sen, P., Sarddar, D.: Load balancing of the unbalanced cost matrix in a cloud computing network. In: Computer, Communication and Electrical Technology: Proceedings of the International Conference on Advancement of Computer Communication and Electrical Technology (ACCET 2016), West Bengal, India, 21–22 October 2016, p. 81. CRC Press (2017)
12. Kuhn, H.W.: The Hungarian method for the assignment problem. Nav. Res. Logist. (NRL) **2**(1–2), 83–97 (1955)

An HMM Based POS Tagger for POS Tagging of Code-Mixed Indian Social Media Text

Partha Pakray$^{(\boxtimes)}$, Goutam Majumder, and Amarnath Pathak

Department of Computer Science and Engineering,
National Institute of Technology Mizoram, Aizawl, India
parthapakray@gmail.com, goutam.nita@gmail.com, amar4gate@gmail.com

Abstract. Text emanated from users' posts and comments on social media constitutes important piece of information for wide ranging Natural Language Processing (NLP) applications, such as Sentiment Analysis, Sarcasm Detection, Named Entity Identification, Question Answering and Information Retrieval (IR). Part–of–Speech (POS) tagging, a prerequisite for all such applications, augments tag information to the raw text. However, an inherent tendency of social media users to include multilingual contents in their posts, called code-mixing, poses challenge to POS tagging. Besides, intricate and free style writing add to the complexity of problem. To cope with the issue, a Hidden Markov Model (HMM) based supervised algorithm has been introduced for POS tagging of code–mixed Indian social media text. Publicly available social media text of Indian Languages (ILs), particularly English, Hindi, Bengali and Telugu, have been used to train and test the proposed system. Correctness of system annotated tags has been evaluated on ground of F-measure.

Keywords: POS Tagging · HMM · NLP · Code-Mixed Data
Social media

1 Introduction

Wide scale use of social media has accelerated social and digital transformation. Social media platforms are often used by different class of people for their respective concerns, ranging from personal to professional. Personal posts are chiefly characterized by individual's view and outlook whereas promotional posts embed product promotion and end users' reviews. Comprehensive analysis of end users' reviews and comments help product manufacturers in decision making and adapting their products accordingly. Besides, analysis of sentiment, embedded in posts, help demarcate positive and negative reviews. In a nutshell, contents of social media posts serve as crucial input to wide ranging NLP applications, such as Sentiment Analysis, Sarcasm Detection, Named Entity Recognition, Question Answering and Information Retrieval. However, apparent nature of algorithms,

© Springer Nature Singapore Pte Ltd. 2018
J. K. Mandal and D. Sinha (Eds.): CSI 2017, CCIS 836, pp. 495–504, 2018.
https://doi.org/10.1007/978-981-13-1343-1_41

used in such application domains, necessitates POS tagging of text contents a priori. POS tagging augments tag information to constituent words of sentences, thus enriching their information content.

Social media platforms offer ample flexibility to their users in writing posts, comments and reviews. For example, contents of the post needn't adhere to grammatical constructs, contents may be noisy and even worse, contents may be multilingual i.e. comprising of words from different languages. Code mixing refers to inherent tendency of multilingual social media users to embed multilingual contents in their posts. Embedding often occurs at phrase, word and morpheme level. For example, a native Bengali user is likely to adulterate his English post with Bengali words. Whereas code mixing occurs at intra-sentence level, an interchangeably used perplexing term code-switching refers to mixing of different linguistic units at inter-sentence level [1,5]. Solecistic and free style writing, noisy contents and code mixed contents pose challenge to POS tagging and distinguish contents of social media from those of conventional sources. Different linguistic backgrounds of words in code-mixed sentences necessitate revamping existing POS Tagging techniques.

An exhaustively trained HMM based supervised system, described in this paper, helps cope with the issue. System exploits publicly available training and test data of NLP tools contests at ICON 2016[1]. Dataset comprises of intermixed words from English, Hindi, Bengali and Telugu languages. HMM based tagger uses class conditional probability and makes simplifying assumptions for annotating fine-grained and coarse-grained tags to the words in test dataset. Details on task and fine-grained to coarse-grained tag mapping can be found in [8,9], respectively.

Rest of the paper is organized as follows: Sect. 2 describes related works on POS Tagging; Sect. 3 describes HMM based POS Tagger system and its underlying working idea; Sect. 4 describes experimental designs, system results and result analysis; Sect. 5 concludes the paper and points directions for future research.

2   Related Works

POS tagging is a well studied problem of NLP and Computational Linguistic domains. For languages, such as English, German, Spanish, and Chinese, several POS taggers have already acquired considerably high accuracies.

A Maximum Entropy Classifier and Bidirectional Dependency Network based POS tagger acquires per–word accuracy of 97.24% [7,14]. A Support Vector Machine (SVM) based POS tagger, discussed in [11], attains accuracy of 97.16% for English on WSJ corpus.

Problems related to POS tagging of English to Spanish code–switched discourse has been reported in [13]. For this task, different heuristics based POS tag information have been combined from existing monolingual taggers. It also explores the use of different language identification methods to select POS tags

---

[1] http://ltrc.iiit.ac.in/icon2016/.

from the appropriate monolingual taggers. The Machine Learning approach, using features from monolingual POS tagger, attains accuracy of 93.48%. As the data has been manually transcribed from recordings, POS tagger does not incur difficulties due to code–mixing.

POS tagging for English–Hindi code mixed social media content has been reported in [15]. Efforts have been made to address issues of code–mixing, transliteration, non–standard spelling and lack of annotated data. Moreover, it is for the first time that problem of transliteration in POS tagging of code–mixed social media text has been addressed. In particular, the contributions include formalization of the problem and related challenges in processing Hindi–English code–mixed social media text, creation of annotation dataset and some initial experiments for language identification, transliteration, normalization and POS tagging of code–mixed social media text.

A language identification method for POS tagging has been developed and reported in [3]. Proposed method helps identifying language of words. Proposed method employs heuristics to form the chunks of same language. The method attains an accuracy of 79%. However, in absence of Gold language tags accuracy falls to 65%. The work reported in paper also highlights importance of language identification and transliteration in POS tagging of code–mixed social media data.

Use of distributed representation of words and log linear models for POS tagging of code–mixed Indian social media text has been reported in [12]. Furthermore, integrating pre-processing and post-processing modules with Conditional Random Field (CRF) has been found to procure reasonable accuracy of 75.22% in POS tagging of Bengali–English mixed data [4]. A supervised CRF using rich linguistic features for POS tagging of code–mixed Indian social media text finds mention in [6].

3   System Description

In this work, a supervised *bigram* Hidden Markov Model (HMM) has been implemented to identify the POS of code–mixed Indian Social Media Text. HMM based POS tagger uses two key simplifying assumptions for reducing computational complexity. Working principle of supervised algorithms, HMM based POS tagging and simplifying assumptions have been discussed and detailed in following subsections.

3.1   Working Principle of Supervised Algorithms

A supervised POS Tagging algorithm uses labeled training data of the form $(x^{(1)}, y^{(1)}) \cdots (x^{(m)}, y^{(m)})$, where $x^{(i)}$ refers to an input word and $y^{(i)}$ refers to corresponding POS label. Ultimate objective of training is to learn the optimal hypotheses, $f : \mathcal{X} \to \mathcal{Y}$, which will correctly map a previously unseen word, x, to its corresponding tag, f(x). Shorthand notations, $\mathcal{X}$ and $\mathcal{Y}$, refer to set of input words and set of corresponding POS labels, respectively.

Equation 1 signifies that given x to be a word of code-mixed sentence, objective of our learning algorithm is to find the tag, $y \in Y$, for which $P(y|x)$ is maximum.

$$f(x) = arg \max_{y \in Y} P(y|x) \tag{1}$$

Thus, the trained model outputs most probable tag y for the given word x.

3.2 HMM Based POS Tagging and Simplifying Assumptions

Joint probability distribution, $P(x, y)$, is referred to as Generative model. Equations 2 and 3 express $P(x, y)$ in term of class conditional probabilities $P(x|y)$ and $P(y|x)$, respectively.

$$P(x, y) = P(y)P(x|y) \tag{2}$$

$$P(x, y) = P(x)P(y|x) \tag{3}$$

Using Eqs. 2 and 3, $P(y|x)$ can be re-written as Eq. 4.

$$P(y|x) = [P(y)P(x|y)]/[P(x)] \tag{4}$$

However, if we are interested in finding optimal y, expressed as $\hat{y}$, static denominator of Eq. 4 can be ignored (see Eq. 5).

$$\hat{y} = arg \max_{y} P(y|x) = arg \max_{y} P(y)P(x|y) \tag{5}$$

Thus Eq. 5 expresses our objective function, given in Eq. 1, in terms of class conditional probability $P(x|y)$ and apriori probability $P(y)$.
Consider following notations:

1. w^n: Word sequence of length n.
2. t^n: Tag sequence of length n.
3. $\hat{t^n}$: Optimal tag sequence of length n.

Given w^n, our objective is to find the optimal tag sequence $\hat{t^n}$. Using Eq. 5, $\hat{t^n}$ can be written as:

$$\hat{t^n} = arg \max_{t^n} P(t^n|w^n) = arg \max_{t^n} P(t^n)P(w^n|t^n) \tag{6}$$

Probability values $P(t^n)$ and $P(t^n|w^n)$ are referred to as prior probability and likelihood probability, respectively (See Eq. 7).

$$\hat{t^n} = arg \max_{t^n} \underbrace{P(t^n)}_{prior} \underbrace{P(w^n|t^n)}_{likelihood} \tag{7}$$

Let tags $t_1, t_2, ..., t_n$ (denoted by shorthand notation t_{1-n}) constitute tag sequence t^n and words $w_1, w_2, ..., w_n$ (denoted by shorthand notation w_{1-n})

constitute word sequence w^n. Using these notations, $P(t^n)$ and $P(w^n|t^n)$ can be re-written as Eqs. 8 and 9 respectively.

$$P(t^n) = P(t_1)P(t_2|t_1)P(t_3|t_{1-2})P(t_4|t_{1-3})...P(t_n|t_{1-\{n-1\}}) \qquad (8)$$

$$P(w^n|t^n) = P(w_1|t_1)P(w_2|w_1,t_{1-2})P(w_3|w_{1-2},t_{1-3})..P(w_n|w_{1-\{n-1\}},t_{1-n}) \qquad (9)$$

HMM based POS taggers make following two assumptions to simplify Eqs. 8 and 9:

1. The probability of a tag appearing is dependent only on the previous tag and independent of other tags in tag sequence also known as bi–gram assumption.
2. The probability of word appearing depends only on its own POS tag and independent of other POS tags and words.

Using first assumption, Eq. 8 can be simplified and re-written as Eq. 10.

$$P(t^n) = P(t_1)P(t_2|t_1)P(t_3|t_2)P(t_4|t_3)...P(t_n|t_{n-1}) \approx \prod_{i=1}^{n} P(t_i|t_{i-1}) \qquad (10)$$

Using second assumption, Eq. 9 can be simplified and re-written as Eq. 11.

$$P(w^n|t^n) = P(w_1|t_1)P(w_2|t_2)P(w_3|t_3)...P(w_n|t_n) = \prod_{i=1}^{n} P(w_i|t_i) \qquad (11)$$

Equation 12, which is used by HMM based POS Tagger to estimate the most probable tag sequence, is obtained by plugging simplified Eqs. 10 and 11 into Eq. 6.

$$\hat{t^n} = arg\max_{t^n} P(t^n|w^n) \approx arg\max_{t^n} \prod_{i=1}^{n} P(t_i|t_{i-1})P(w_i|t_i) \qquad (12)$$

Probability values $P(t_i|t_{i-1})$ and $P(w_i|t_i)$ in Eq. 12, referred to as tag transition probability and word emission probability, are computed from the labeled training corpus.

For example, tag transition probability $P(t_i|t_{i-1})$, for the two tags t_i and t_{i-1}, can be computed by dividing count of occurrences of t_i after t_{i-1} by count of t_{i-1} (see Eq. 13).

$$P(t_i|t_{i-1}) = \frac{Count(t_{i-1}, t_i)}{Count(t_{i-1})} \qquad (13)$$

Furthermore, word emission probability $P(w_i|t_i)$, for word w_i and tag t_i, is computed by dividing count of number of times word w_i has been assigned tag t_i by count of number of times tag t_i appears in the dataset (see Eq. 14).

$$P(w_i|t_i) = \frac{Count(t_i, w_i)}{Count(t_i)} \qquad (14)$$

4 Experiment Design and Results

4.1 Dataset Description

To train and test HMM based POS Tagger implementation, publicly available train and test data of NLP tools contest at ICON 2016 have been used. Broadly, the dataset comprises of three sets/language pairs (Bengali–Hindi (BN–EN), Hindi–English (HI–EN) and Telugu–English (TE–EN)) of code–mixed social media text of Indian Languages, collected from Facebook, Twitter and WhatsApp. For each language pair and for each source, the dataset has been further bifurcated into fine–grained and coarse–grained code–mixed data.

Figure 1 shows samples of Coarse–Grained and Fine–Grained training dataset. Details of tag sets used in training data is available in [10].

@bionicsix1	univ	@		@bionicsix1	univ	@
@phanerozoic11	univ	@		@phanerozoic11	univ	@
@pari_cious	univ	@		@pari_cious	univ	@
bohut	hi	G_SYM		bohut	hi	QT_QTF
achay	hi	G_J		achay	hi	JJ
ayay	hi	G_V		ayay	hi	V_VM
.	univ	G_X		.	univ	RD_SYM
Mixed	en	G_J		Mixed	en	JJ
dabay	hi	G_N		dabay	hi	N_NN
Wala	hi	G_PRT		Wala	hi	RP_RPD
mix	en	G_N		mix	en	N_NN
n	en	CC		n	en	CC
maida	hi	G_N		maida	hi	N_NN
.	univ	G_X		.	univ	RD_SYM
Apna	hi	G_PRP		Apna	hi	PR_PRL
hee	hi	G_PRT		hee	hi	RP_RPD
koi	hi	G_PRP		koi	hi	DM_DMI
taste	en	G_J		taste	en	JJ
bana	hi	G_V		bana	hi	V_VM
liya	hi	G_V		liya	hi	V_VAUX
:)	univ	E		:)	univ	E
(a)				(b)		

Fig. 1. Sample of training dataset: (a) Coarse_Grained and (b) Fine_Grained

4.2 Code–Mixed Index (CMI) of the Dataset

For inter-corpus comparisons, level of code-mixing needs to be measured for each dataset comprising of words from different languages. Code–Mixed Index (CMI) compares non-frequent words in the dataset against total number of language dependent words [2]. CMI is computed by subtracting count of words belonging to most frequent language in the dataset (n) from total number of language dependent words (N) and dividing the result by total number of language dependent words (see Eq. 15).

$$CMI = \frac{N - n}{N} \qquad (15)$$

CMI statistics of training dataset is shown in Table 1.

Table 1. CMI statistics of training dataset (BN–Bengali, HI–Hindi, TE–Telugu, EN–English, FB–Facebook, TWT–Twitter and WA–WhatsApp)

Code–Mixed language	Dataset type	FB	TWT	WA
BN–EN	Fine-Grained	0.486	0.486	0.197
	Coarse-Grained	0.230	0.267	0.002
HI–EN	Fine-Grained	0.139	0.565	0.789
	Coarse-Grained	0.641	0.216	0.113
TE–EN	Fine-Grained	0.265	0.338	0.285
	Coarse-Grained	0.372	0.265	0.255

4.3   Results

F-measure of HMM based POS Tagger for coarse-grained and fine-grained tag sets are listed in Tables 2 and 3, respectively. As seen from the two tables, for each language pair, *F-measure* of predicted coarse-grained tags are better as compared to *F-measure* of predicted fine-grained tags.

Table 2. F-measure of coarse–grained tag sets

Code–Mixed language	FB	TWT	WA
BE–EN	82.25	75.90	84.35
HI–EN	76.02	85.64	76.04
TE–EN	79.89	75.08	78.26

Table 3. F-measure of fine–grained tag sets

Code–Mixed language	FB	TWT	WA
BE–EN	76.55	72.37	81.74
HI–EN	68.81	81.05	66.11
TE–EN	72.96	72.88	72.46

4.4 Performance Comparison with Other Systems

In ICON 2016 Tool Contest on POS Tagging for Code-Mixed Indian Social Media (Facebook, Twitter and, WhatsApp) Text, a total of 13 system results were submitted for evaluation. Performances of systems were evaluated on grounds of F-measure. Ranks of our NLP-NITMZ team for each language pair and for each of the datasets have been tabulated in Table 4. Our team, using HMM based POS Tagger, ranked first in coarse–grained POS Tagging of Facebook code–mixed data of Bengali–English language pair. Team ranked second in coarse–grained POS Tagging of Twitter and WhatsApp code–mixed data of Bengali–English language pair. Team also ranked second in fine–grained POS Tagging of Facebook and Twitter code–mixed data of Bengali–English language pair.

Table 4. Rank list of NLP–NITMZ team for fine–grained (FG) and coarse–grained (CG) tag sets

Dataset	Code–Mixed language	Rank (FG)	Rank (CG)
FB	BN–EN	2	1
TWT		2	2
WA		4	2
FB	HI–EN	13	5
TWT		9	4
WA		11	5
FB	TE–EN	8	7
TWT		12	8
WA		12	7

4.5 Result Analysis

Decrease in F-measure for fine-grained dataset owes to ambiguity in tag annotation to the words in training dataset. In fine-grained training datasets, same word has been annotated differently for its different occurrences and this holds true for majority of words. For example, Hindi word "kya" has been 18 times annotated as G_PRP and 1 time annotated as PSP, out of its 19 occurrences in Hindi–English Facebook course-grained training data. In contrast, the same word has been 5 times annotated as PR_PRQ, 13 times annotated as DM_DMQ and 1 time annotated as PSP, out of its 19 occurrences in Hindi–English Facebook fine-grained training data. Ambiguity in tag annotation often reduces word–emission probability which eventually degrades F-measure.

5   Conclusion

Multilingual social media users have flooded social media platforms with code–mixed and noisy contents. Code–mixed data needs to be POS tagged for its productive utilization in NLP application domains. To cope with the challenge of POS tagging heterogeneous and noisy code–mixed data, an HMM based POS Tagger has been implemented and evaluated using code–mixed social media text of Indian Languages. Obtained system results and values of F-measure, for different language pairs and social media categories, prove worthiness of HMM based POS Tagger, particularly for coarse–grained POS tagging.

Using heuristics for reducing search space of probable tag sets, using Neural Network approach for training and testing and increasing number of instances in the training dataset are some of the notable future modifications which are likely to improve current evaluation scores.

Acknowledgement. Authors would like to acknowledge Third phase of Technical Education Quality Improvement Programme (TEQIP-III) for providing financial support. Authors are also thankful to Department of Computer Science & Engineering, National Institute of Technology Mizoram for providing infrastructural facilities and support.

References

1. Bokamba, E.G.: Code-mixing, language variation, and linguistic theory: evidence from Bantu languages. Lingua **76**(1), 21–62 (1988)
2. Gambäck, B., Das, A.: On measuring the complexity of code-mixing. In: Proceedings of the 11th International Conference on Natural Language Processing, Goa, India, pp. 1–7 (2014)
3. Gella, S., Sharma, J., Bali, K.: Query word labeling and back transliteration for Indian languages: shared task system description. FIRE Working Notes 3 (2013)
4. Ghosh, S., Ghosh, S., Das, D.: Part-of-speech tagging of code-mixed social media text. In: EMNLP 2016, p. 90 (2016)
5. Gumperz, J.J.: Discourse Strategies, vol. 1. Cambridge University Press, Cambridge (1982)
6. Gupta, D., Tripathi, S., Ekbal, A., Bhattacharyya, P.: SMPOST: parts of speech tagger for code-mixed indic social media text. arXiv preprint arXiv:1702.00167 (2017)
7. Heckerman, D., Chickering, D.M., Meek, C., Rounthwaite, R., Kadie, C.: Dependency networks for inference, collaborative filtering, and data visualization. J. Mach. Learn. Res. **1**(Oct), 49–75 (2000)
8. Jamatia, A., Das, A.: Part-of-speech tagging system for Indian social media text on twitter. In: Social-India 2014, First Workshop on Language Technologies for Indian Social Media Text, at the Eleventh International Conference on Natural Language Processing (ICON-2014), pp. 21–28 (2014)
9. Jamatia, A., Das, A.: Task report: tool contest on POS tagging for codemixed Indian social media (Facebook, Twitter, and Whatsapp) Text@ icon 2016. In: The Proceeding of ICON 2016 (2016)

10. Jamatia, A., Gambäck, B., Das, A.: Part-of-speech tagging for code-mixed English-Hindi Twitter and Facebook chat messages. In: Association for Computational Linguistics (2015)
11. Màrquez, L., Giménez, J.: A general POS tagger generator based on support vector machines. J. Mach. Learn. Res. (2004)
12. Pimpale, P.B., Patel, R.N.: Experiments with POS tagging code-mixed Indian social media text. arXiv preprint arXiv:1610.09799 (2016)
13. Solorio, T., Liu, Y.: Part-of-speech tagging for English-Spanish code-switched text. In: Proceedings of the Conference on Empirical Methods in Natural Language Processing, pp. 1051–1060. Association for Computational Linguistics (2008)
14. Toutanova, K., Klein, D., Manning, C.D., Singer, Y.: Feature-rich part-of-speech tagging with a cyclic dependency network. In: Proceedings of the 2003 Conference of the North American Chapter of the Association for Computational Linguistics on Human Language Technology-Volume 1, pp. 173–180. Association for Computational Linguistics (2003)
15. Vyas, Y., Gella, S., Sharma, J., Bali, K., Choudhury, M.: POS tagging of English-Hindi code-mixed social media content. In: EMNLP, vol. 14, pp. 974–979 (2014)

Multistage Preprocessing Approach for Software Defect Data Prediction

Meetesh Nevendra[1](✉) and Pradeep Singh[2]

[1] Department of Information Technology, National Institute of Technology,
Raipur, India
m.nevendra456@gmail.com
[2] Department of Computer Science and Engineering,
National Institute of Technology, Raipur, India
psingh.cs@nitrr.ac.in

Abstract. Naïve Bayes is one of the most simplest and efficient classification algorithms and is therefore being widely used. It has been utilized in several situations, like web mining, image process, fraud detection, and text mining. This approach has an assumption that features are independent of each other and their weights are equally important. However, a feature might or might not be interrelated. In cases where features are interrelated, the performance of the algorithm might decrease. In order to see the dependency between one feature and another, "mRMR" (Minimum redundancy maximum relevance) feature selection method was introduced. In this study, by applying the preprocessing steps with a Naïve Bayes classification methodology, we have shown the difference with and without applying preprocessing steps. The method has been applied to the defect datasets and experiments were carried out on NASA PROMISE repository. The obtained result shows that the feature selection, discretization with a classifier (Naïve Bayes) is more successful than the others.

Keywords: SDLC · mRMR · SMOTE · NB

1 Introduction

In a software development life cycle (SDLC) there have been numerous stages. These stages have been introduced stepwise like planning, analysis, and design, development, and test phases. All the phases are important stages in SDLC but the test phase is the most important. It consists of two parts namely verification and validation. It gives the assurance when the product is defect-free. The cost of rectifying a defect detected by a developer is much less than when found by a customer at their own side [1]. In recent years, lots of researcher's are taking attention in test-oriented approach in machine learning, and are producing lots of new testing approaches. With these approaches, the software modules are automatically being classified as defective or non-defective. The relation between the software quality and defect prediction has been already studied [2]. Software quality has been proposed by various researchers, such as Zhao et al. [3], Hassan et al. [4] and Suresh et al. [5].

© Springer Nature Singapore Pte Ltd. 2018
J. K. Mandal and D. Sinha (Eds.): CSI 2017, CCIS 836, pp. 505–515, 2018.
https://doi.org/10.1007/978-981-13-1343-1_42

For simplicity and effectiveness of the algorithm, the Naïve Bayes classification approach is widely used. It is used in many scenarios, such as web mining, image processing, fraud detection, and text mining. Naïve Bayes approach has an assumption that each and every feature is independent of each other and their weights are equally important. However, there can be a possibility that the features may or may not be interrelated. In cases where the features are interrelated, the performance may decrease. The Naïve Bayes algorithm can be grouped into two types [6] i.e. semi-naïve Bayes and feature-weighting methods. The semi-naïve Bayes method achieves better classification performance, and while applying feature-weighting techniques, highly predictive features are increased and less predictive features are decreased.

In this experiment, following preprocessing step with Naïve Bayes classification method is proposed. In order to get the best feature among all the features and to check the dependency between one another, the MRMR feature selection method is introduced. The method has been applied to the defect data sets and experiments were carried out using NASA PROMISE data sets. The problem arises in software defect prediction because of lack of framework [7]. In order to avoid the misleading results the general framework was proposed by Song et al. [8]. The application of preprocessing steps before the classification methods generate better results than the simply application of the classification method over datasets. The preprocessing steps consist of several stages like feature selection, normalization, discretization, and imbalancing.

The rest of the paper is organized as follows. We describe the related work in Sect. 2. In Sect. 3 we elaborate metrics and datasets. Then we elaborate our experiments in Sect. 4. The experiment results are shown in Sect. 5. Finally, we conclude our work in Sect. 6.

2   Related Work

2.1   Software Defect Prediction Studies

Before releasing the product the developer has to check the product is defect prone or non-defect-prone software modules. For achieving the high prediction performance, the testing activities have been increased. There is a lot of machine learning techniques have been applied to solve the software defect prediction problem. And they are: Artificial Neural Network [9], Random Forest [10], Logistic Regression [11], Support Vector Machines [12], and Naïve Bayes [13].

2.2   Naïve Bayes Studies

Naïve Bayes is one of the very simplest, efficient, and robustness classification algorithm that's why is it widely used. It is one of the top ten algorithms in data mining [14]. Settouti et al. [15] show the performance of several classification algorithms by using UCI Machine Learning Repository as bench market data sets. After comparison to several classification algorithms, Naïve Bayes algorithm given the ninth-ranked. It is used in many scenarios, such as web mining [16], image processing [17], fraud detection, and text mining. Because of the performance of the Naïve Bayes is solid, the researchers are taking attention to this fields and try to improve the performance [18], Arar et al. [19] have been improved the performance of the Naïve Bayes with some changes on them.

2.3   Software Defect Prediction Used by Naïve Bayes

Naïve Bayes is one of the most widely used algorithms in the field of software defect prediction. Menzies et al. [20] told that Naïve Bayes is given best result with the use of filtering and feature selection technique. The result of filtering and feature with Naïve Bayes is more successful than the simple Naïve Bayes. A lot of question and answer given in the [21].

3   Metrics and Datasets

In this study, we use seven defect data sets which are from NASA datasets and it is taken from tera-PROMIS repositories. Each data set is used for the software module. In a dataset each instance consists of two parts features and class which corresponds the defective information, if there is one or more defect, it is labeled as the defective module, and if not labeled as a non-defective module.

Table 1 show the seven datasets used in our experiments. The second column shows the Lines of code (KLOC), and in the third column shows the total no of the feature present in the data sets, the fourth column shows the percentages of defective in the data set.

Table 1. General characteristics of the datasets.

Name	Size of KLOC	Feature	Defective
CM1	20	37	12.2%
PC1	40	37	8.03%
PC2	26	36	1.0%
PC3	40	37	12.45%
PC4	36	37	12.72%
KC3	18	39	18.0%
MW1	8	37	10.23%

4   Methodology

The learning model is built on training data, no testing data is involved. For preprocessing the steps were applied in both pieces of training as well as testing data. Training data and testing data is made from the complete dataset, the dataset is divided into two parts randomly ten times, for partitioning the training and testing data we use ten-fold cross-validation. One subset is used for training data and one is used for testing data.

The learning model framework is implemented in PYTHON, MATLAB and R. The MATLAB is used for the feature selection process, R is used for discretization, and the rest of preprocessing (normalization and balancing) and classification technique is implemented in PYTHON. The learning model we have created in this study is shown in Fig. 1. On the further of this section, we will discuss the preprocessing steps:

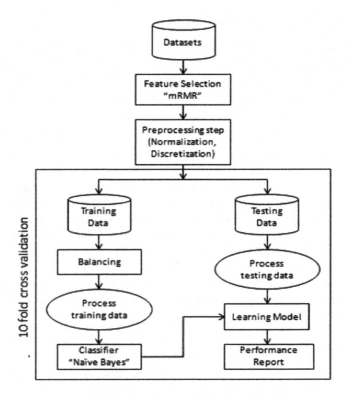

Fig. 1. Learning model framework

4.1 Feature Selection

The each and every feature in the datasets is different to each other and each feature has different tasks. However, it cannot be given the defect estimation model. The feature selection process performs on complete dataset. For the feature selection process we will apply the "mRMR" [22] feature selection, and we will take the five features among the all the features in the dataset. The "mRMR" feature selection is defined as follows:

$$mRMR = \max_s \left[\frac{1}{|s|} \sum_{f_i \in S} I(f_i; c) - \frac{1}{|S|^2} \sum_{f_i; f_j \in S} I(f_i; f_j) \right] \qquad (1)$$

Where,

- S is the set of feature for the class c. f_i and f_j is individual feature depending upon class c.

- The equation shows the mutual information values between the feature f_i with respect to class and average value of all mutual information between the feature f_i and the feature f_j.

4.2 Normalization

After the apply feature selection process on datasets, we split the data into two parts for training and testing. In training and testing data we apply the normalization. For the normalization, we use min-max normalization [23]. The min-max normalization shifted the data to a certain range. So that the standard derivation and negative impact has been reduced. The feature u is converted to u' and the formula is:

$$u' = \frac{u - min_f}{max_f - min_f} \left(new\_max_f - new\_min_f\right) + new\_min_f \tag{2}$$

Where,

- min_f is the minimum value of the feature f.
- max_f is the maximum value of the feature f.
- new_min_f is the new converted minimum value.
- new_max_f is the new converted maximum value.

4.3 Discretization

Discretization method applies over software metrics shown by Fayyad and Irani [24]. The various study has shown over software defect prediction by discretization method [25] and many discretization methods have been applied to Naïve Bayes classifier [26, 27]. The description of this method is in [26, 28]. There are several steps in regular discretization and they are:

- The discretized continuous feature values are ranked.
- To separate the data a cutoff point is selected.
- The continuous values are divided or combined according to the ranges.
- To apply the discretization process stopping criterion is selected.

In this paper discretization is applied after the feature selection process in training and testing data. For discretization, we use MDLP (minimum description length principle) [29] method in order to treat non-discrete datasets from a distributed perspective.

4.4 Balancing Class Distributor

The balancing process applies over only in training datasets. Balancing is often in software defect, when the number of defective modules (majority class) more than that of non-defective (minority class). There are several ways for the balancing, such as oversampling, under sampling etc. but we chose the SMOTE method [30], and applied to the training data. The mathematical formula for generating SMOTE sample is:

$$x_{\{new\}} = x_i + \lambda \times \left(x_{\{zi\}} - x_i\right) \tag{3}$$

Where:

$x_{\{new\}}$ is a new sample, x_i is existing sample, λ is random number in the range [0, 1].
The interpolation will create a sample on the line between $x_{\{zi\}}$ and x_i.

4.5   Naïve Bayes Classifier

After completion of preprocessing steps the Naïve Bayes classifier is applied and a learning model is created, the testing data is applied to the learning model for predicting the results. The Naïve Bayes classifier is one of the most effective classifier methods. The Naïve Bayes formula is:

$$P(C_k|X) = \frac{P(C_k)P(X|C_k)}{P(X)} \tag{4}$$

Where,

- Ck denotes to class, K - 0, 1 (defective or non-defective)
- $X = (x_1, x_2, \ldots, x_n)$ represent features.

4.6   Performance Measures

In order to compare the obtained result in this study with another, the same criteria is used. To evaluation of prediction the following measures is generated are: (I) Precision, (II) Recall, (III) F1-major and (IV) Accuracy.

$$\text{Precision} = tp/(tp + fp) \tag{5}$$

The precision is in Eq. (1) where tp = true positive, fp = false positive. The result generated between the best values is 1 and the worst value is 0.

$$\text{Recall} = tp/(tp + fn) \tag{6}$$

Where tp = true positive and fn = false negatives. Recall has ability to find all the positive samples.

$$F1 - \text{major} = 2 * (\text{precision*recall})/(\text{precision} + \text{recall}) \tag{7}$$

F1 score can be interpreted as a weighted average of the precision and recall. The result generated between the best values is 1 and the worst value is 0.

$$\text{Accuracy} = (tp + tn)/(tp + tn + fp + fn) \tag{8}$$

Where tp = true positive, tn = true negative, fn = false positive and fp = false positive. It is also known as description of systematic errors.

5   Experimental Result and Discussion

The results of our experiments from seven data sets are given in Table 2. The result is in the form of precision, recall, F1-major, and accuracy. Results are generated by averaging of 10 times run the program for each data set. For that, we are using the ten-fold cross-validation. The last row shows the average results of all datasets. Obtained results are compared with different approaches in Table 2. In Table 3 we compare all the recall value with FDNB approach [23] in which feature selection and log filtering preprocessing were applied to the data.

Table 2. Comparison of our all approaches.

Data set	FS+DIC+NB				FS+NO+BL+NB				FS+NO+NB			
	Rec.	*Acc.*	*Pre.*	*F1*	*Rec.*	*Acc.*	*Pre.*	*F1*	*Rec.*	*Acc.*	*Pre.*	*F1*
CM1	**0.85**	**0.92**	**0.85**	**0.84**	0.73	0.85	0.73	0.77	0.74	0.83	0.74	0.77
PC1	**0.92**	**0.92**	**0.92**	**0.92**	0.78	0.9	0.78	0.82	0.82	0.91	0.82	0.85
PC2	0.87	**0.99**	0.87	0.92	0.61	**0.99**	0.61	0.74	0.82	**0.99**	0.82	0.89
PC3	0.78	**0.88**	0.78	0.8	0.73	0.8	0.73	0.75	0.8	0.8	0.8	0.8
PC4	**0.87**	**0.93**	0.86	**0.89**	0.81	0.92	0.81	0.81	0.82	0.92	0.82	0.81
KC3	**0.84**	**0.9**	**0.84**	**0.85**	0.75	0.87	0.75	0.79	0.75	0.88	0.75	0.78
MW1	**0.86**	**0.9**	**0.86**	**0.88**	0.33	0.78	0.33	0.39	0.55	0.85	0.55	0.61
AVG.	**0.86**	**0.92**	**0.85**	**0.87**	0.68	0.87	0.68	0.72	0.76	0.88	0.76	0.79
Dataset			FS+ NB				NB					
	Rec.		*Acc.*		*Pre.*		*F1*		*Rec.*	*Acc.*	*Pre.*	*F1*
CM1	**0.85**		0.84		**0.85**		**0.84**		0.83	0.89	0.83	**0.84**
PC1	0.91		0.91		0.91		0.9		0.89	0.89	0.89	0.89
PC2	0.95		0.98		0.95		**0.97**		**0.96**	0.98	**0.96**	**0.97**
PC3	**0.85**		0.85		**0.85**		**0.84**		0.21	0.79	0.21	0.17
PC4	**0.87**		**0.93**		0.87		**0.89**		0.85	0.91	0.85	0.86
KC3	0.81		0.89		0.81		0.81		0.79	0.89	0.79	0.8
MW1	0.65		0.84		0.65		0.7		0.82	0.89	0.82	0.84
AVG.	**0.84**		**0.89**		**0.84**		**0.85**		0.76	0.89	0.76	0.77

As we can see that in Fig. 2(a) for Recall, most of the datasets are performing well with preprocessing data (feature selection, discretization) set with Naïve Bayes classifier. In Fig. 2(b) for Accuracy, the data sets are performing well with preprocessing data (feature selection, discretization) set with Naïve Bayes classifier. In Fig. 2(c) for precision, most of the datasets are performing well with preprocessing data (feature selection, discretization) set with Naïve Bayes classifier. In Fig. 2(d) for F1-major, most of the datasets are performing well with preprocessing datasets (feature selection, discretization) with Naïve Bayes classifier.

Table 3. Compression of recall value with all given models.

Datasets	FS+DIC+NB	FS+NO+BL+NB	FS+NO+NB	FS+NB	NB	FDNB
CM1	**0.85**	0.73	0.74	**0.85**	0.83	0.82
PC1	**0.92**	0.78	0.82	0.91	0.89	0.78
PC2	0.87	0.61	0.82	0.95	**0.96**	0.69
PC3	0.78	0.73	0.8	**0.85**	0.21	0.82
PC4	0.87	0.81	0.82	0.87	0.85	**0.97**
KC3	**0.84**	0.75	0.75	0.81	0.79	0.67
MW1	**0.86**	0.33	0.55	0.65	0.82	0.54
AVG.	**0.86**	**0.68**	**0.76**	**0.84**	**0.76**	**0.76**

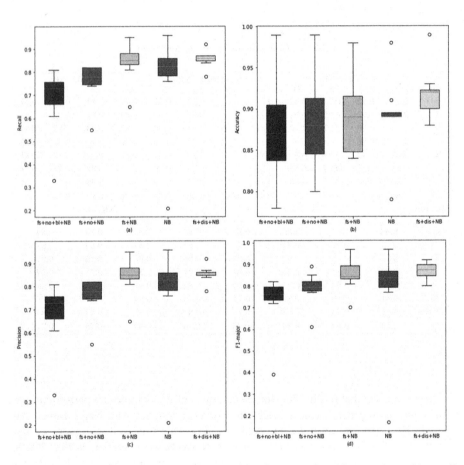

Fig. 2. Box plot representation on the complete data set. On this we show (a) recall, (b) accuracy, (c) precision, and (d) F1-major.

The result in Table 3 (FS+DIC+NB) was obtained by performing feature selection, discretization, and Naïve Bayes classifier with all data sets. For dividing training and testing dataset, we use ten-fold cross-validation. The average value of recall, accuracy, precision, and F1-major are 0.86, 0.92, 0.85, and 0.87. In third column (FS+NO+BL +NB) were obtained by performing feature selection, normalization, and balancing and Naïve Bayes classifier with all datasets. Accuracy, precision, and F1-major are 0.68, 0.87, 0.68, and 0.72. In fourth column (FS+NO +NB) were obtained by performing feature selection, normalization, and Naïve Bayes classifier with all data sets.

For dividing training and testing dataset, we use ten-fold cross-validation. The average value of recall, accuracy, precision, and F1-major are 0.76, 0.88, 0.76, and 0.79. In fifth column (FS+NB) were obtained by performing feature selection and Naïve Bayes classifier with all data sets. For dividing training and testing dataset, we use ten-fold cross-validation. The average value of recall, accuracy, precision, and F1-major are 0.84, 0.89, 0.84, and 0.85. In the sixth column, only Naïve Bayes classification will apply to generate the result on whole data sets. For dividing training and testing dataset, we use ten-fold cross-validation. The average value of recall, accuracy, precision, and F1-major are 0.76, 0.89, 0.76, and 0.77. The best results are in bold according to the precision, recall, f1-major, and accuracy with respect to the learning model (Table 2).

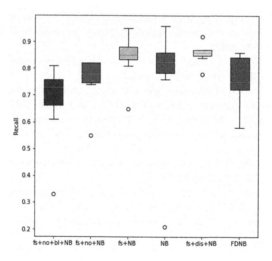

Fig. 3. Compare recall value with all the methods.

6 Conclusion and Future Work

In this study we take the seven publicly available and widely used NASA data sets, firstly we perform the feature selection process in the datasets and get the required features from it, then apply the preprocessing steps which are normalization, discretization, and balancing, in the required feature data.

After we apply Naïve Bayes classifier and build a learning model. Ones a learning model is created we predict the result. We compare this result with several preprocessing, without preprocessing data and with FDNB method in Table 3. In comparison with all the method, we found that the discretization over selected features is performed well with Naïve Bayes classifier. In this study, it was clear that defect data sets need to be preprocessed before build the learning model, and if not then learning model can give misleading results. Also using all datasets in preprocessing steps could result in overestimated performance. The complete model was made through training data and was validated over testing data.

In future we would like to introduced transfer learning in this field so that one-one cross-project were performed, and also the process could be applied to different datasets.

References

1. Pelayo, L., Dick, S.: Applying novel resampling strategies to software defect prediction. In: Annual Conference of the North American Fuzzy Information Processing Society – NAFIPS, pp. 69–72 (2007)
2. Basili, V.R., Melo, W.L., Briand, L.C.: A validation of object-oriented design metrics as qualityindicators. IEEE Trans. Softw. Eng. 22, 751–761 (1996)
3. Zhao, F., et al.: A hybrid eBusiness software metrics framework for decision making in cloud computing environment. IEEE Syst. J. 11(2), 1049–1059 (2017)
4. Zhang, F., Hassan, A.E., McIntosh, S., Zou, Y.: The use of summation to aggregate software metrics hinders the performance of defect prediction models. IEEE Trans. Softw. Eng. 45, 476–491 (2016)
5. Suresh, Y., Pati, J., Rath, S.K.: Effectiveness of software metrics for object-oriented system. Procedia Technol. 6, 420–427 (2012)
6. Zaidi, N., Cerquides, J.: Alleviating Naive Bayes attribute independence assumption by attribute weighting. J. Mach. Learn. Res. 14, 1947–1988 (2013)
7. Arora, I., Tetarwal, V., Saha, A.: Open issues in software defect prediction. Procedia Comput. Sci. 46, 906–912 (2015)
8. Song, Q., Jia, Z., Shepperd, M., Ying, S., Liu, J.: A general software defect-proneness prediction framework. IEEE Trans. Softw. Eng. 37, 356–370 (2011)
9. Arar, Ö.F., Ayan, K.: Software defect prediction using cost-sensitive neural network. Appl. Soft Comput. 33, 263–277 (2015)
10. Zakariah, M.: Classification of large datasets using random forest algorithm in various applications: survey. Int. J. Eng. Innov. Technol. 4, 189–198 (2014)
11. Hall, T., Beecham, S., Bowes, D., Gray, D., Counsell, S.: A systematic review of fault prediction performance in software engineering. IEEE Trans. Softw. Eng. 38, 1276–1304 (2011)

12. Pradhan, A.: Support vector machine-a survey. Int. J. Emerg. Technol. Adv. Eng. **2**, 82–85 (2012)
13. Ryu, D., Baik, J.: Effective multi-objective Naïve Bayes learning for cross-project defect prediction. Appl. Soft Comput. J. **49**, 1062–1077 (2016)
14. Wu, X., et al.: Top 10 algorithms in data mining. Knowl. Inf. Syst. **14**(1), 1–37 (2008)
15. Settouti, N., Bechar, M.E.A., Chikh, M.A.: Statistical comparisons of the Top 10 algorithms in data mining for classification task. Int. J. Interact. Multimed. Artif. Intell. **4**, 46 (2016)
16. Shirakawa, M., Nakayama, K., Hara, T., Nishio, S.: Wikipedia-based semantic similarity measurements for noisy short texts using extended Naive Bayes. IEEE Trans. Emerg. Top. Comput. **3**, 205–219 (2015)
17. Vitello, G., Sorbello, F., Migliore, G.I.M., Conti, V., Vitabile, S.: A novel technique for fingerprint classification based on fuzzy C-Means and Naive Bayes classifier. In: 2014 Eighth International Conference on Complex, Intelligent and Software Intensive Systems (CISIS), pp. 155–161 (2014)
18. Zhang, J., Chen, C., Xiang, Y., Zhou, W., Xiang, Y.: Internet traffic classification by aggregating correlated naive bayes predictions. IEEE Trans. Inf. Forensics Secur. **8**, 5–15 (2013)
19. Arar, Ö.F., Ayan, K.: A feature dependent Naive Bayes approach and its application to the software defect prediction problem. Appl. Soft Comput. **59**, 197–209 (2017)
20. Menzies, T., Greenwald, J., Frank, A.: Data mining static code attributes to learn defect predictors. IEEE Trans. Softw. Eng. (1), 2–13 (2007)
21. Feng, G., Guo, J., Jing, B.-Y., Sun, T.: Feature subset selection using Naive Bayes for text classification. Pattern Recognit. Lett. **65**, 109–115 (2015)
22. Ding, C., Peng, H.: Minimum redundancy feature selection from microarray gene expression data. In: Proceedings of the 2003 IEEE of the Bioinformatics Conference, CSB 2003, vol. 3, pp. 523–528. IEEE (2003)
23. Jain, Y., Bhandare, S.: Min max normalization based data perturbation method for privacy protection. Int. J. Comput. Commun. Technol. **2**, 45–50 (2011)
24. Fayyad, U.M., Irani, K.B.: On the handling of continuous-valued attributes in decision tree generation. Mach. Learn. **8**, 87–102 (1992)
25. Hewett, R.: Mining software defect data to support software testing management. Appl. Intell. **34**, 245–257 (2011)
26. Kaya, F.: Discretizing Continuous Features for Naive Bayes and C4.5 Classifiers. University of Maryland Publications (2008)
27. Lu, J., Yang, Y., Webb, G.I.: Incremental discretization for naïve-bayes classifier. In: Li, X., Zaïane, O.R., Li, Z. (eds.) ADMA 2006. LNCS (LNAI), vol. 4093, pp. 223–238. Springer, Heidelberg (2006). https://doi.org/10.1007/11811305_25
28. Dougherty, J., Kohavi, R., Sahami, M.: Supervised and unsupervised discretization of continuous features. In: Machine Learning Proceedings 1995, pp. 194–202 (1995)
29. Irani, K., Fayyad, U.: Multi-Interval discretization of continuous-valued attributes for classification learning. In: Proceedings of the National Academy of Sciences USA, pp. 1022–1027 (1993)
30. Chawla, N.V., Bowyer, K.W., Hall, L.O., Kegelmeyer, W.P.: SMOTE: synthetic minority over-sampling technique. J. Artif. Intell. Res. **16**, 321–357 (2002)

Load Balancing with Inadequate Machines in Cloud Computing Networks

Payel Ray$^{(\boxtimes)}$ and Debabrata Sarddar

Department of Computer Science and Engineering,
University of Kalyani, Kalyani, India
payelray009@gmail.com, dsarddar1@gmail.com

Abstract. Cloud computing is a web-based distributed computing. There is more than million number of servers connected to cloud computing to provide different types of accommodations to provide cloud users. Limited numbers of servers execute more than a thousand jobs at a time. So it is not too easy to execute all jobs at a time. Some machines to execute all jobs, there is needed to balance all loads. Load balance minimizes the completion time as well as executes all jobs a particular way.

There are not possible to remain equal number servers to execute equal jobs. In sometimes jobs to be performed in the cloud will be less than the machines. Inhibited servers have to perform few jobs.

We propose an algorithm that some machines execute the tasks here a number of tasks less than the machines and balance all machine to make the most of the quality of services in cloud computing.

Keywords: Load balancing · Hungarian method · Cloud computing

1 Introduction

Human resources are the most significant parts of the Societies and associations so that the achievement of each association depends on its HRs. The associations attain their targets by means of information, familiarity, potency and skillfulness of human beings. As the HRs are physically share out, it is essential to set up an infrastructure for sharing the information, proficiency and experience of human beings. This new platform is named Expert Cloud [1].

In accordance with the description of NIST "Cloud computing is an Internet based computing and in which several groups of servers have been networked to allocate the distribution of data-processing jobs, centralized data storage and online access to the computer services or resources". We can say in different way, Cloud computing depends on resource distribution to attain coherence and wealth of scale, related to a utility over a network. It focuses on the maximization of the resource sharing effect [2].

A usual distributed system for example Expert Cloud contains the number of allocated HRs. These HRs can be added to each other to get the high performance and perform the job that one HR is not capable to make it by itself. To decrease the job completing time by the HR, the workload should be share out based on the HRs capability. This creates the load balancing necessary. The major principle of the load

© Springer Nature Singapore Pte Ltd. 2018
J. K. Mandal and D. Sinha (Eds.): CSI 2017, CCIS 836, pp. 516–522, 2018.
https://doi.org/10.1007/978-981-13-1343-1_43

balancing is that it makes possible networks and resources by providing as long as a maximum throughput with least response time. Dividing traffic between users, and therefore data can be sent and received without major delay [3, 4].

2 Related Works

Cloud computing provides a range of facilities to the user such as multi-media sharing, online office software, game and online storage. There are many type of Load balancing and resource management algorithms like static, dynamic or hybrid [5]. Static algorithms which frequently apply FCFS policy assign tasks to the resource based on simple information system for example the functionality of processor, capacity of memory etc. It shares out the jobs within the resources by representing formula. In this technique, the system doesn't require to gather the information from the surroundings constantly. The dynamic policies for example genetic algorithm utilize the present situation of the system for job allotment and at the final point the hybrid algorithms utilize the combination of static and dynamic ones. The hybrid algorithm switches to each of them at the right time. Although these algorithms provide the load balancing, they do not pay attention to the resource potential. They do not consider the requirements declared by the user for job execution as well. This signifies the lack of maximum resource utilization. We can divide load balancing algorithms into two categories. Those will be centralized and distributed. In the centralized process a single node is accountable for the management and load circulation throughout the entire system. This process is trouble-free but its problem is bottleneck. In the distributed process, every node gathers the load information about other nodes separately. The load balancing decision is local in this method. The method is suitable for the distributed environment such as Cloud. The method has overhead problem [6].

In cloud surroundings, every machine performs a job or a sub-job [7]. The OLB intends to keep each machine busy despite the current workloads of each machine [7, 8, 10]. Opportunistic Load Balancing algorithm allocates jobs to presented machines in arbitrary order [9]. The MCT algorithm allocates jobs to the machines having the expected minimum completion time of this job over other machines [10]. The MM scheduling algorithm presumes the similar scheduling approach as MCT [10] algorithm to assign a job, the machine to complete this job with MCT over other machines [11]. The Load Balance Min-Min (LBMM) scheduling algorithm [12] accepts MM scheduling approach and load balancing scheme. It can keep away from the unnecessarily copied assignment.

3 Proposed Method

To determine the matrix cost as well as a combination of tasks(s) vs. machine(s) of an unbalanced matrix problem, we would focus on a problem consisting of a set of 'm' machines $M = \{M1, M2,..., Mm\}$. A set of 'n' jobs $J = \{J1, J2,..., Jn\}$ is considered to be assigned for execution on the 'm' obtainable machines as well as the execution value Cij, where i = 1, 2,...,m as well as j = 1, 2, ..., n are mentioned in the cost matrix where m is greater than n.

4 Proposed Work

Every time, the matrix is not a square matrix, that is, the number of source nodes are not equivalent to the number of destination nodes. In such problems, dummy columns are added to the matrix to complete it to form a square matrix. The dummy columns will contain all costs elements as zeroes. The Hungarian method [13] may be used to solve the problem. We have discussed it with the following the example.

Algorithm:

1: *Say m*n matrix*
2: *Make the matrix square.*
   The cost matrix contains less columns than rows; we may insert dummy columns with zeros to create the matrix square:
3: *Subtract row with minimum value.*
4: *Subtract column with minimum value.*
5: *Face all zeros with a minimum number of lines.*
6: *Create additional zeros. If the number of lines is smaller than line then we subtract this number from all uncovered elements and add it to all elements that are covered twice:*
7: *Cover all zeros with a least number of lines.*
8: *Next, no one machine assigned with any subtask. Then we choose that machine having smallest completion time.*
9: *End.*

5 Example

Suppose a corporation has four machines being used for five jobs. Each job are capable to be assigned to one and only a machine at same time. The cost of each job on each machine is given in the following Table.

Assignment Problem

Jobs/machines	M_{11}	M_{12}	M_{13}	M_{14}
J_{11}	10	19	8	15
J_{12}	10	18	7	17
J_{13}	13	16	9	14
J_{14}	12	19	8	18
J_{15}	14	17	10	19

The following is the original cost matrix:

10	19	8	15
10	18	7	17
13	16	9	14
12	19	8	18
14	17	10	19

Make the Matrix Square

The cost matrix contains less columns than rows; we may insert dummy columns with zeros to create the matrix square:

10	19	8	15	0
10	18	7	17	0
13	16	9	14	0
12	19	8	18	0
14	17	10	19	0

Subtract Row with Minimum Value

This is cause each row contains a zero, subtracting row minima does not affect.

Subtract Column with Minimum Value

We subtract the column minimum from each column:

0	3	1	1	0
0	2	0	3	0
3	0	2	0	0
2	3	1	4	0
4	1	3	5	0
(-10)	(-16)	(-7)	(-14)	

Face all Zeros with a Minimum Number of Lines

There are four lines required to face all zeros:

0	3	1	1	0	x
0	2	0	3	0	x
3	0	2	0	0	x
2	3	1	4	0	
4	1	3	5	0	
				x	

Create Additional Zeros

The number of lines is smaller than 5. The smallest uncovered number is 1. We subtract this number from all uncovered elements and add it to all elements that are covered twice:

0	3	1	1	1
0	2	0	3	1
3	0	2	0	1
1	2	0	3	0
3	0	2	4	0

Cover all Zeros with a Least Number of Lines

There are five lines required to cover all zeros:

0	3	1	1	1	x
0	2	0	3	1	x
3	0	2	0	1	x
1	2	0	3	0	x
3	0	2	4	0	x

The Most Favorable Assignment

There are five lines required, all zeros face an best possible problem:

0	3	1	1	1
0	2	0	3	1
3	0	2	0	1
1	2	0	3	0
3	0	2	4	0

The following corresponds in the actual problem:

_10_	19	8	15
10	18	_7_	17
13	16	9	_14_
12	19	8	18
14	_17_	10	19

Next, no one machine assigned subtask T_4. Then we choose that machine having smallest completion time, i.e., minimum completion time of M_3 for task T_3 is 8.

$$
\begin{array}{cccc}
\textbf{\textit{10}} & 19 & 8 & 15 \\
10 & 18 & \textbf{\textit{7}} & 17 \\
13 & 16 & 9 & \textbf{\textit{14}} \\
12 & 19 & \underline{\textbf{8}} & 18 \\
14 & \textbf{\textit{17}} & 10 & 19 \\
\end{array}
$$

So, all subtasks are assigned to all machines.

6   Comparison

Our proposed algorithm with Hungarian method could get improved load balancing as well as performance than different algorithms, for example LBMM [4] and MM [5] from the following the figure (Fig. 1).

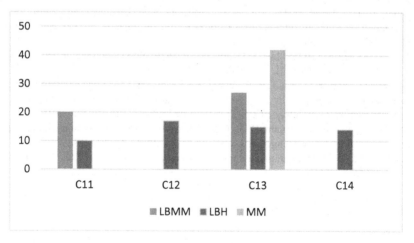

Fig. 1. The comparison of completion time of each task at a different node.

7   Conclusion

Nowadays, the range-queriable cloud storage is becoming increasingly important. However, most of the existing load balancing methods gain so much overhead which bounds the practice of range-queriable knowledge.

In this work, we proposed a new scheduling and load balancing algorithm Load Balancing with Inadequate Machines (LBIM) for the cloud computing network to assign jobs to computing nodes in accordance with their resource capacity. In the same way, LBIM can attain enhanced load balancing as well as function than other algorithms, such as LBMM and MM.

References

1. Navimipour, N.J., et al.: Expert cloud: a cloud-based framework to share the knowledge and skills of human resources. Comput. Hum. Behav. **46**, 57–74 (2015)
2. Mell, P., et al.: The NIST definition of cloud computing. National Institute of Standards and Technology, pp. 1–7 (2011). SP 800-145
3. Chaczko, Z., et al.: Availability and load balancing in cloud computing. In: International Conference on Computer and Software Modeling, vol. 14 (2011)
4. Babu, D., et al.: Honey bee behavior inspired load balancing of tasks in cloud computing environments. Appl. Soft Comput. **13**(5), 2292–2303 (2013)
5. Yan, K.Q., et al.: A hybrid load balancing policy underlying grid computing environment. Comput. Stand. Interfaces **29**(2), 161–173 (2007)
6. Sidhu, A.K., et al.: Analysis of load balancing techniques in cloud computing. Int. J. Comput. Technol. **4**(2), 2277–3061 (2013)
7. Silberschatz, A., Galvin, P.B., Gagne, G., Silberschatz, A.: Operating System Concepts, vol. 4. Addison-Wesley, Reading (1998)
8. Bruff, D.: The assignment problem and the Hungarian method. Notes Math **20**, 5 (2005)
9. Hung, C.-L., Wang, H.-H., Hu, Y.-C.: Efficient load balancing algorithm for cloud computing network. In: International Conference on Information Science and Technology (IST 2012), pp. 28–30, April 2012
10. Jain, A., Kumar, R.: Hybrid load balancing approach for cloud environment. Int. J. Commun. Netw. Distrib. Syst. **18**(3–4), 264–286 (2017)
11. Wang, S.C., Yan, K.Q., Liao, W.P., Wang, S.S.: Towards a load balancing in a three-level cloud computing network. In: 2010 3rd IEEE International Conference on Computer Science and Information Technology (ICCSIT), vol. 1, pp. 108–113. IEEE, July 2010
12. Kokilavani, T., Amalarethinam, D.G.: Load balanced min-min algorithm for static meta-task scheduling in grid computing. Int. J. Comput. Appl. **20**(2), 43–49 (2011)
13. Kuhn, H.W.: The Hungarian method for the assignment problem. Nav. Res. Logist. (NRL) **2** (1–2), 83–97 (1955)

Improvement of Electronic Governance and Mobile Governance in Multilingual Countries with Digital Etymology Using Sanskrit Grammar

Arijit Das[(✉)] and Diganta Saha

Department of Computer Science and Engineering, Jadavpur University,
Kolkata, India
arijitdas3@acm.org, neruda0101@yahoo.com

Abstract. With huge improvement of digital connectivity (Wifi, 3G, 4G) and digital devices access to internet has reached in the remotest corners now a days. Rural people can easily access web or apps from PDAs, laptops, smart phones etc. This is an opportunity of the Government to reach to the citizen in large number, get their feedback, associate them in policy decision with e governance without deploying huge man, material or resources. But the Government of multilingual countries face a lot of problem in successful implementation of Government to Citizen (G2C) and Citizen to Government (C2G) governance as the rural people tend and prefer to interact in their native languages. Presenting equal experience over web or app to different language group of speakers is a real challenge. In this research we have sorted out the problems faced by Indo Aryan speaking netizens which is in general also applicable to any language family groups or subgroups. Then we have tried to give probable solutions using Etymology. Etymology is used to correlate the words using their ROOT forms. In 5th century BC Panini wrote Astadhyayi where he depicted sutras or rules-how a word is changed according to person, tense, gender, number etc. Later this book was followed in Western countries also to derive their grammar of comparatively new languages. We have trained our system for automatic root extraction from the surface level or morphed form of words using Panian Grammatical rules. We have tested our system over 10000 bengali Verbs and extracted the root form with 98% accuracy. We are now working to extend the program to successfully lemmatize any words of any language and correlate them by applying those rule sets in Artificial Neural Network.

Keywords: Digital Etymology · Multilingual e Governance
Root form extraction · Panini · Neural network · Semantic search

1 Introduction

90% of the developing and transit countries are multi lingual that is there are officially more than one languages used for communication between citizens in the same country. India an example of such countries has 22 scheduled languages which has official recognition and gets encouragement to promote. Excluding this India has 122

© Springer Nature Singapore Pte Ltd. 2018
J. K. Mandal and D. Sinha (Eds.): CSI 2017, CCIS 836, pp. 523–530, 2018.
https://doi.org/10.1007/978-981-13-1343-1_44

major languages (spoken by more than 10 K people) and 1599 other languages. 70% population live in rural area and 90% of them can communicate only in their mother tongue. They feel comfortable to communicate over net in their native language or alternatively it may be said they interact more over net if they get chance to communicate in their native language.

Naturally it becomes the responsibility and intention of Govt. of multi lingual country to attract those people to e Governance initiative. The constraint of multi linguity can be used as an opportunity here. Govt. has already tried to deploy various websites and applications in front end only in the local languages. But here we have concentrated on a different problem and probable solution.

For C2G governance the most important issue is citizens' feedback. Now a days citizen can give input in their native language (if it is scheduled then normally soft key board is available). But if someone asks any question in Marathi and answer is available in Bengali the system fails to retrieve the answer. In general Search is general keyword matching based. For example if some farmer of Karnataka asking about some problem of coffee farming in Kannada language and the answer or related discussion is already there in Portuguese language as a conversation between two Brazilian farmers. Search engine fails to retrieve the answer as there are no common words and keyword matching algorithm fails.

So technically the problem is as there is a large no. of natural languages to communicate and the system fails to correlate them for search, sort or retrieve. Obviously one of the solution is Machine Translation of all text in other language to English as Internet has the highest data in English language but the problem is there is no dependable automatic machine translator which can convert any language to English with complete accuracy and this is technically an abnormally tedious job to translate each and everything in English and store them online which is nearly impossible.

Fortunately if we look into the anthropology we get Human being first knew how to speak and at the earliest phase those were merely sound signals. Then colloquial languages came. Then formally written alphabets came. Grammar was formed and literature was written but ancient Pandits did not allow the languages to grow haphazardly. That's why there is a huge similarity of Grammar in any language of the world. And historically we get at the early stage of formation of kingdom there was hardly two to three languages officially accepted all over the world. So every language has a root like Sanskrit is the root of all Indo Aryan language. This predicate is supported by the facts all the languages are classified in some group or subgroup and there is also a large inflection between sibling groups.

The first successful solution approach was UNL (Universal Networking Language) which conceptualized and universal language for communication over net but even after 20 years it can't give a universal framework which successfully works. We have taken a different approach Digital Etymology! Etymology is the study of the history of words, their origins, and how their form and meaning have changed over time. Which is commonly known as root form extraction in Sanskrit. We have proposed a probable solution to use the knowledge of Paninian Grammar in artificial neural network and measure the central tendency between any two words.

2   Problem Statement

In all ancient books like the Old Testament or Hindu legends it is mentioned that there was only one language in the world in the beginning era of human civilization. As they spread over the world build different civilization and adopt different languages.

As per the linguists and scientists there are 23 no. of language groups in the world. They are Indo-European, Uralic, Basque, Afro-Asiatic, Niger-Kordofanian, Nilo-Saharan, Khoisan, Altaic, Korean, Japanese, Chukotko- Kamchatkan, Sino-Tibetan, Daic, Austro-Asiatic, Austronesian, Andamanese, Australian, Eskimo-Aleut, Na-Dene, Amerindian, Caucasian, Dravidian and Burushaki. All the languages of a group have originated from one language. Relation between sibling sub grouped languages of same group result huge similarity of surface level words. Now in case of early days of internet communication the medium was mostly English. Later Spanish, Portuguese, French, German, Hindi, Mandarin expanded as medium. But now when internet is reaching in the rural area of developing and transit nation of multilingual countries use of local or native languages is increasing considerably. More it will spread more it will attract untouched native speakers. This is an opportunity for Govt. if language barrier can be overcome and embarrassing if the native speakers get distracted without getting support for their mother tongue over internet. In India for all scheduled languages support for keyboard, codification i.e. support for all insertion and retrieval in front end in native languages have been done. Now the problems are

- How to correlate same statement expressed in different languages?
- If they semantically express same thought how to determine and retrieve? (when question and answer are in different languages)
- How to consider opinions expressed in other languages during decision making? e.g. How to consider Tamil feedbacks when majority are in Hindi only?

These questions are extremely relevant in background processing for proper benefit of eGov.

3   Proposed Approach

We are proposing a universal language to represent semantic data extracted from natural language texts as a declarative formal language specifically designed. It can be used as a pivot language in interlingua machine translation systems or as a knowledge representation language in information retrieval applications.

UNL was first such approach to build a global language. We have presented here a probable approach which may be easily adopted and can overcome the difficulties of UNL.

We first reviewed all the probable language which can be backbone of our proposed universal language. We found German and Sanskrit for using skeletal framework for our proposed language. The reason is

1. Strong grammatical foundation.
2. Rich vocabulary and most importantly
3. The relocation of words in a sentence don't affect the meaning.

And for the last point Sanskrit gives the robust architecture. Word form (shabd rup) table a 8 × 3 matrix associates how a word changes according to number, gender, bivakti (to incorporate the meaning of prepositions in the sentence) and root form of the verb (dhaturup) a 3 × 3 matrix depicts how a verb changes according to tense, person and number.

Any sentence in any language (excluding some rare exception) is either SVO (subject-verb-object) or SOV (subject- object-verb). We propose to encode root form of inflected noun, verb in universal language and special comment field and store them. Therefore a sentence (e.g. I will go) expressed in language A will have same code as of the semantically same sentence (e.g. আমি যাব[[I will go in bengali]) expressed in language B though there is no common term between them so syntactical search fails to correlate them. Therefore theoretically by this method we can enlarge the domain of reach for an intelligent system to the whole world without any natural language barrier. This gives system an enormous power to search, sort, retrieve, decision making semantically like a human being as oppose to syntactically keyword matching like machines. As the root form are unique and linguists already have done a huge work on etymology, this system will generate a perfect backend process for semantic analysis which can even be extended to paragraphs or text corpus. Taking a simple example "I will go" and "আমিযাব" will have code গিঁমৃয়ািঁম or root গম--1st person simple future in coded form. Thus both the sentence have same code and though they don't have any common term or syntactically not related but following this method our system can determine that both the system bears same meaning or semantically same. Similarly with the help of "shabdorup" we can encode subject and object of the sentence also and making a composite code for each language.

So it is proved once the sentences are encoded following the above stated ruled it is easy to semantically relate. But now the challenges are

- How to generate the code in universal language from all natural languages?
- What will be the mathematical framework for this code generation?

We have started the work and formulated a probable route map to achieve these two goals which have been described in the next section.

4   Methodology

We propose a step by step process to generate the code (Fig. 1).

- 1. First determine the Parts of Speech (POS) of each word in a sentence using POS tagger.
- 2. Mark noun, pronoun and verb and anaphora reference from pronoun to noun.
- 3. Use supervised learning method specific to each native language to lemmatize them (e.g. running to run)
- 4. Pass them to complex neural network to determine the Sanskrit root
- 5. Generate the code
- 6. Add comment field for handling phrasal verb, idioms etc. to disambiguate the meaning.

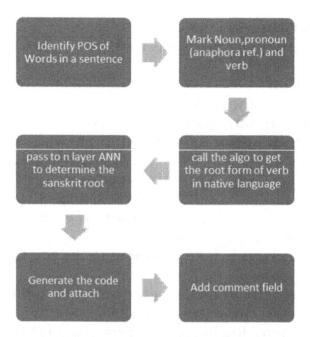

Fig. 1. Flowchart of the process

5 Work Done

We have already completed the process up to level three taking Bengali as a case study. Our system is giving more than 98% accurate result tested on 10000 verbs. The algorithm of the said process is given as Fig. 2.

Our next goal is to fit the set on n level complex neural network to get the Sanskrit root from Bengali root form. The approach is using radix topological sorting of dictionary words as perceptrons and synonyms or matching words (with least levenshtein distance) as sigmoid neurons. Still considerable work pending to announce the success of this experiment and we will publish the same in our next paper.

We have approached to use Parse Thicket to detect anaphora and other relation between words to be incorporated in comment section.

The study of how to improve the system, how to generalize it for all languages and use of semi supervised methods to reduce load on programmer, getting ideas from ongoing research globally are being done.

Algorithm 1: DAS & HALDER

Input: Bengali corpus to Shallow parser
(LTRC)

Output: Inflected verbs are collected in a file
Input.doc

Input to our system: Input.doc

Output of our system: Multiple files
classified according
to tense and person
consisting of root
form of verbs

1 begin

2   Corpus is taken as input to the Shallow
    parser

3   All the inflected verbs are collected in a
    file named as Input.doc

4   Input.doc is taken as input to our system

5   **if** বিভক্তি(in the Table 1) matches **then**

6   **if** *person matches* **then**

7   Verbs are passed to the respective
            method with the verbs and বিভক্তি
            for processing

8   Verbs are processed one by one

9   Panini's rules are applied on those
            verbs to extract root verbs

10   Root verb is stored in Output.doc
            file as well as separate file
            according to tense.

11   **else**

12   The verb collected from Shallow
            parser in Input.doc is not a verb

13   **else**

14   The verb collected from Shallow
        parser in Input.doc is not a verb

Fig. 2. Algorithm of step 3 of the process

6 Application

If successful the universal language will make a revolution in digital communication addressing the need of computing in natural languages.

All the byproduct developed and being developed in each steps are extremely essential in natural language processing research. We have already registered the automatic root verb extractor in ACL.

As there is a large no. of population in multi lingual countries research on this topic will serve the greater no. of people directly and immediately as opposed to incremental research problems of which outcome comes after a long delay and can benefit very small portion of the society.

It can save the endangered languages by attracting their native speakers to digital media.

Using uniform language in the backend will push us one step ahead for making uniform global village with single language and single nation without the barrier of state, country, race, color thus this will improve the global unity and values of feeling towards united mankind.

This kind of research also enhances cultural exchange heritage values and reduces the narrowness and insularity.

7 Scope for Improvement

As this is a highly interdisciplinary filed of research and specifically we need help from linguists, Sanskrit grammar experts and anthropologists so making a collaborative framework will ease the work.

Government can be directly involved for requirement specification for this universal language at least we need a single language for communication in the backend in this country with population of 120 crores of which dialect changes in every 8 km.

Now a days Govt. is trying to approach to citizens to involve them in governance, this will only be successful if rural people joins and they will join only if they get scope to express their view in mother tongue and that view also should be accountable for decision making thus investing in this research will have a recursive positive effect on e governance, Digital India, social structure, accountability and public administration.

References

1. Panini: Astadhyayi, 6th to 5th centuri BCE
2. Das, A., Halder, T., Saha, D.: Automatic extraction of Bengali root verbs using Paninian grammar. In: 2nd IEEE International Conference On Recent Trends in Electronics, Information & Communication Technology, Bangaluru, pp. 944–947 (2017)
3. Mridha, M.F., Saha, A.K., Das, J.K.: New approach of solving semantic ambiguity problem of bangla root words using universal networking language (UNL). In: 3rd International Conference on Informatics, Electronics and Vision, Dhaka, Bangladesh

4. Choudhury, M., Jalan, V., Sarkar, S., Basu, A.: Evolution, optimization and language change: the case of Bengali verb inflections. In: Proceedings of Ninth Meeting of the ACL Special Interest Group in Computational Morphology and Phonology, Prague, pp. 65–74

5. Islam, M.S.: Research on Bangla language processing in Bangladesh: progress and challenges. In: 8th International Language & Development Conference, Bangladesh, pp. 23–25

6. Pal, A.R., Saha, D., Naskar, S., Das, N.S.: Word sense disambiguation in Bengali: a lemmatized system increases the accuracy of the result. In: 2nd International Conference on Recent Trends in Information System, Kolkata, India

7. Ekbal, A., Haque, R., Bandyopadhyay, S.: Maximum entropy based Bengali part of speech tagging. In: Advances in Natural Language Processing and Applications Research in Computing Science, pp. 67–78

Security and Forensics

A Robust Video Steganographic Scheme Using Sudoku Puzzle for Secured Data Hiding

Sunanda Jana[1(✉)], Arnab Kumar Maji[2(✉)], and Rajat Kumar Pal[3]

[1] Department of Computer Science & Engineering,
Haldia Institute of Technology, Haldia, India
sunanda.onlyl@gmail.com
[2] Department of Information Technology,
North Eastern Hill Univerisity, Shillong 793022, India
arnab.maji@gmail.com
[3] Department of Computer Science & Engineering,
University of Calcutta, Kolkata, India
pal.rajatk@gmail.com

Abstract. Video Steganography is a method for securing data in a video file and hence it prevents the chance of theft. The proposed scheme uses the Video Steganography technique on the encrypted data (using RSA and AES) for providing maximum security and stability. In this work, a secured Video Steganographic scheme is proposed using Sudoku puzzle. The novelties of the work imply that nobody could be able to see as well as modify data during transmission as the secret message is first encrypted into cipher text twice using RSA and AES cryptographic technique then that cipher text is embedded in video using a Sudoku reference matrix. So, our proposed work combines both Cryptographic and Steganographic technique to enhance the security in maximum level with maintained computational complexity.

Keywords: Data communication · LSB · RSA · AES · PSNR
Sudoku puzzle · Steganography · Stego file · Cover/hidden file

1 Introduction

Data security basically aims at preserving the confidentiality and integrity of data and protecting the data from unauthorized users or hackers. Numerous methods such as Cryptography, Digital Watermarking and Steganography are established in order to increase the data security. The statement Steganography joins the Antique Greek words 'Steganos' signifying secured, hid, or ensured, and 'Graphene' signifying written work [1]. Steganography is the method of hiding the file, message, and image or video inside a new file such as message, video or image. In digital Steganography, electronic infrastructures may include the steganographic coding inside the transport layer such as program, image file, document file or protocol.

Steganography has various applications in military, personal, diplomatic and Intellectual Property Applications. Nowadays, in the digital world, ink and papers are replaced by many more handy and practical protections such as digital documents,

© Springer Nature Singapore Pte Ltd. 2018
J. K. Mandal and D. Sinha (Eds.): CSI 2017, CCIS 836, pp. 533–545, 2018.
https://doi.org/10.1007/978-981-13-1343-1_45

images, video, and audio files. With these, messages were hidden. Steganographic technique must be a significant share of the upcoming internet safety and privacy policies. In cryptography, encrypted data may expose some kind of secret data to the hackers but in Steganography, clandestine data is concealed in the cover file which does not make any suspicion [2].

The quantity of data hiding into the file is called as the embedding payload. The capacity of the Steganography scheme is to hide abundant data with minimum distortion in the data termed as the embedded efficiency. The best Steganography system must have a huge embedding efficiency with itself. The huge embedding efficiency means low distortion that leads to the high security in the network [2].

Merging Steganography with the cryptography technique provide an excellent security to the secret messages. This technique uses the RSA and Advanced Encryption Standard (AES) algorithms for obtaining more security for secret data compared to the existing method. The previous approach uses the Data Encryption Standard (DES) algorithm for encrypting the clandestine data with the Steganography technique. DES did not deliver much security when compared with the RSA and AES because the DES can be affected by Brute-Force attack. Also in some situation, S-box provides the same output for different input that can cause the problem of weak key.

To reduce these kinds of problems, this proposed approach uses the technique of RSA and AES algorithm. RSA is an asymmetric cryptographic algorithm, which uses two keys (public, private), one key for encryption and other key for decryption. AES is a block cipher that operates on block size of 128 or 192 or 256 bits for both encryption as well as decryption. 128 bits are considered in the proposed system for both encryption and decryption process. These two algorithm increases the security for message transmission. To increase the system stability, it could use the Sudoku puzzle technique for data hiding system. So it prevents the easy data hacking by unknown persons. Sudoku is a logic-based [14] combinational number located puzzle. It has 9×9 matrixes that could be further classified into the 3×3 block. Each 3×3 block placed with the digits from 0 to 9 each digit must be inserted only once in the matrix. These similar methods could be used in this system for Steganography process.

2 Different Existing Video Steganographic Scheme

Swetha et al. [2] defines that security of the complex data in the internet has become an important concern which leads to the data hiding methods.

Ginni et al. [1] states the video Steganography could be used to transmit more data from each frame. Videos can be divided into frames and each frame is used to hide the data. It also defines the video Steganography based on the LSB and MSB techniques.

Dasgupta et al. [3] describes the hash based LSB technique for improving the video Steganography system. It also measured the PSNR (Peak Signal Noise Ratio) value by comparing original and output video, which is used to find the quality of the Steganography video. This system provided highest PSNR value which increases the stego video's quality. It also describes the Mean Square Error (MSE) rate which is used to find the amount of data distortion available in the video Steganography. Finally, it proved that this approach has low MSE rate equated with the previous methods.

Antony et al. [4] describes the Steganography method which depends upon the Sudoku-puzzle. It also delivers the digital signature methods for providing high authentication and integrity as well as non-repudiation. It used the 24-bit colored image to hide the data, the 18×18 reference matrix used as a key and the digital signature which is embedded inside the cover image. It used the RSA algorithm to encrypt the secret messages. Then the encrypted message and public key of sender are packed in a unit which is further encrypted by RSA. Multiple encryptions make this technique to become highly secured.

Sameerunnisa et al. [5] states that data encrypted through RSA algorithm can be done before inserting the data into the video to prepare steganographic video. It proposed the method where the video could be parted into frames and audio. The encrypted data has been inserted with the audio then the entire Stego audio is encrypted though RSA algorithm. Also finally it added the frames with the encrypted audio. It intensifies the security of an approach.

Shakeela et al. [6] proposed the approach based on the double coding mechanism which increases the robustness of the approach. It performed in the wavelet domain using the pseudorandom codes and Morse code. The performance of this technique also evaluated through PSNR and MSE rate which provides good results.

Hu et al. [7] described that the way of hiding the video inside the video files. It defines that every frame of the secret video will be Non-uniform rectangular subdivided. The divided codes originated can be an encoded form of the original frame. These codes are hided in the least 4 bits of the host video. According to the experiments, it is clear that the data could be hiding in secure way and it has less data distortion when compared with the previous approach.

Kour et al. [8] described the various security methods and data hiding techniques used to create the LSB, ISB and MLSB based Steganography. It also clearly explained about the factors which are affecting the steganography and other advantages of steganography.

Vidya et al. [9] states that the data hiding techniques inside the images can be done by ken-ken puzzle. Solving of ken-ken puzzle is really a complex task. It will increase the security over the internet. It also analyzed its result against the quality metrics which provide higher quality of results. It is mostly used to enhance the graphic quality of the Stego image.

Chakraborty et al. [10] defined the steganography based on Sudoku embedding. Embedding is done through Sudoku solution matrix. It hides the data inside image, using RGB value for storing the data and Sudoku key matrix. The RG section contains the secret data and B section has the key value. It uses the same Sudoku matrix for both embedding as well as extraction phase. It increased the capacity of information by squeezing the data through DNA compression technique.

Pavithra et al. [11] studied about various cryptographic algorithm techniques and compared their performance evaluation. For different videos, the time taken by various cryptographic techniques are evaluated. From the results, it was found that the time taken for processing is less in AES algorithm when compared with DES and BLOW FISH.

Pancholi et al. [12] studied the performance of AES algorithm on a cloud network. Cloud services growth is increasing year by year. AES encryption is found to be the fastest method with high flexibility and scalability. The implementation of AES algorithm is simple. The memory requirement for AES algorithm is minimum when compared to Blowfish algorithm. AES encryption algorithm is highly performable with minimum memory requirement.

3   A Robust Video Steganographic Scheme Using Sudoku Puzzle

Steganography is a method for hiding the information behind the image or video or any other file for transmitting the data in a secured way [1]. Figure 1 depicts the way of how the Steganography system will work. The cover file defines the host video where the secret message will be stored. The data to hide represents the secret message. The secret message could be included into the host video through the use of Steganography application.

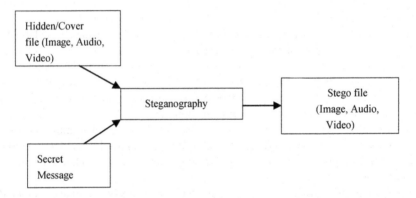

Fig. 1. Data hiding using Steganography

To hide information this approach uses cryptography techniques (RSA and AES algorithms) followed by Steganography technique using Sudoku puzzle. The data which is to be sent as a secret message is encrypted by using the RSA and AES algorithms. The RSA algorithm is based on the asymmetric encryption technique which is highly secured than the existing DES algorithm. The AES is a symmetric encryption algorithm, which is proficient in hardware as well as software and it can uphold a block length of 128 bits. AES encryption is more secure and faster when compared to other techniques. The encrypted data are hidden into the video frame by using the Sudoku puzzle as a key.

3.1   Encryption

During encryption, the video file is selected for hiding the data. Then video is converted into many frames using MATLAB function. Each frame is in.bmp (bitmap) extension. The data (secret message) is encrypted through RSA and AES algorithm. After these steps, the encrypted data and the single frame from the video are embedded together through the Sudoku puzzle technique. Then it shows the Stego output frames (Fig. 2).

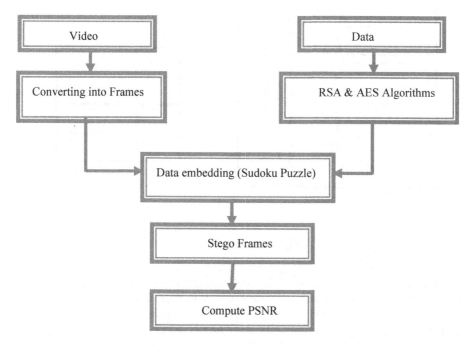

Fig. 2. Proposed methodology for the Video Steganography

During decryption, the encrypted video is selected and further split into many frames and each frame are in .bmp (bitmap) extension. From the frames, the data could be extracted which was embedded into Sudoku puzzle. Finally, the encrypted data is decrypted by using the RSA and AES algorithm.

3.1.1 RSA Algorithm
In our proposed technique RSA algorithm is used for encryption purpose. It operates on the trouble of factorizing huge numbers that have 2 and only 2 factors (Prime numbers) and it uses the public and private key mechanism. During the encryption the user needs to encrypt the data with receiver's public key. So at the acceptance end, the data is decrypted by the receiver private key.

3.1.2 AES (Advanced Encryption Standard)
Advanced Encryption Standard i.e. AES is a most popular symmetric encryption algorithm. AES was designed in a way such that it is proficient in both hardware and software. Block length of 128 bits is supported by AES.

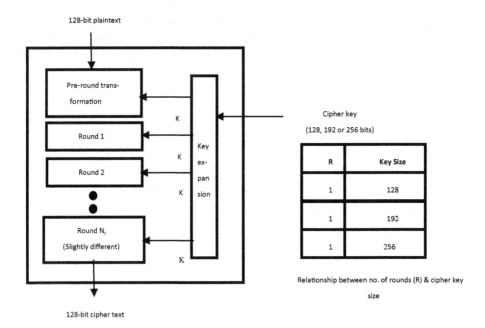

Fig. 3. Structure of AES.

Also it upholds a key length of 128, 192, and 256 bits. AES is adopted extensively and upholds for both hardware and software. A built-in flexibility of key length is available in AES, which allows a degree of 'future-proofing' in contradiction to progress in the capability to perform exhaustive key searches.

3.1.3   Operation of AES

AES is constructed based on 'substitution-permutation network'. A series of connected operations like replacing some input with specific output (substitution) and some are modified by shuffling the bits (permutation).

Byte computations are performed rather than bit computation. So 128 bits are considered as a 16-byte plaintext block. It is arranged like a matrix containing four columns and four rows. Depending on the length of the key, the number of rounds in AES will vary. Some relation to the number of rounds and key length are shown in Fig. 3. Each round uses dissimilar 128-bit round key, which was computed with the unique AES key (Fig. 4).

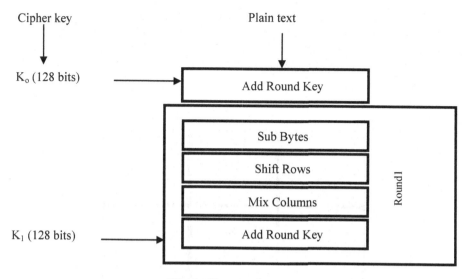

Fig. 4. First round process

5	3	4	6	7	8	9	1	2
6	7	2	1	8	5	3	4	8
1	9	8	3	4	2	5	6	7
8	5	9	7	6	1	4	2	3
4	2	6	8	5	3	7	9	1
7	1	3	9	2	4	8	5	6
9	6	1	5	3	7	2	8	4
2	8	7	4	1	9	6	3	5
3	4	5	2	8	6	1	7	9

Fig. 5. Sudoku solution

4	2	3	5	6	7	8	0	1
5	6	1	0	7	4	2	3	7
0	8	7	2	3	1	4	5	6
7	4	8	6	5	0	3	1	2
3	1	5	7	4	2	6	8	0
6	0	2	8	1	3	7	4	5
8	5	0	4	2	6	1	7	3
1	7	6	3	0	8	5	2	4
2	3	4	1	7	5	0	6	8

Fig. 6. Reference matrix

3.2   Generation of Sudoku and Reference Matrix

An image is represented as matrix of square pixels which are arranged in the form of rows and columns. An image with grey scale has pixels having intensity range 0 to 255. Usual grey scale image will have 8-bit color deepness equal to indicating 256 grey scales. A "true color" image has 24-bit color depth = $8 \times 8 \times 8$ bits = 256×256 256 colors = ~ 16 million colors. The Sudoku matrix is generated by the frame (9×9) from the single frame of a video which is chosen for the data embedding. The actual representation of Sudoku and reference matrix is as follows (Fig. 5).

The reference matrix is generated by subtracting a one value from the Sudoku solution. The representation of reference matrix is shown in Fig. 6. From the reference matrix 27 × 27matrix is generated. This could be obtained by arranging the reference matrix in 3 × 3 manner. The exact representation of 27 × 27 matrix is depicted in the below Fig. 7.

4	2	3	5	6	7	8	0	1	4	2	3	5	6	7	8	0	1	4	2	3	5	6	7	8	0	1
5	6	1	0	8	4	2	3	7	5	6	1	0	8	4	2	3	7	5	6	1	0	8	4	2	3	7
0	8	7	2	3	1	4	5	6	0	8	7	2	3	1	4	5	6	0	8	7	2	3	1	4	5	6
7	4	8	6	5	0	3	1	2	7	4	8	6	5	0	3	1	2	7	4	8	6	5	0	3	1	2
3	1	5	7	4	2	6	8	0	3	1	5	7	4	2	6	8	0	3	1	5	7	4	2	6	8	0
6	0	2	8	1	3	7	4	5	6	0	2	8	1	3	7	4	5	6	0	2	8	1	3	7	4	5
8	5	0	4	2	6	1	7	3	8	5	0	4	2	6	1	7	3	8	5	0	4	2	6	1	7	3
1	7	6	3	0	8	5	2	4	1	7	6	3	0	8	5	2	4	1	7	6	3	0	8	5	2	4
2	3	4	1	7	5	0	6	8	2	3	4	1	7	5	0	6	8	2	3	4	1	7	5	0	6	8
4	2	3	5	6	7	8	0	1	4	2	3	5	6	7	8	0	1	4	2	3	5	6	7	8	0	1
5	6	1	0	8	4	2	3	7	5	6	1	0	8	4	2	3	7	5	6	1	0	8	4	2	3	7
0	8	7	2	3	1	4	5	6	0	8	7	2	3	1	4	5	6	0	8	7	2	3	1	4	5	6
7	4	8	6	5	0	3	1	2	7	4	8	6	5	0	3	1	2	7	4	8	6	5	0	3	1	2
3	1	5	7	4	2	6	8	0	3	1	5	7	4	2	6	8	0	3	1	5	7	4	2	6	8	0
6	0	2	8	1	3	7	4	5	6	0	2	8	1	3	7	4	5	6	0	2	8	1	3	7	4	5
8	5	0	4	2	6	1	7	3	8	5	0	4	2	6	1	7	3	8	5	0	4	2	6	1	7	3
1	7	6	3	0	8	5	2	4	1	7	6	3	0	8	5	2	4	1	7	6	3	0	8	5	2	4
2	3	4	1	7	5	0	6	8	2	3	4	1	7	5	0	6	8	2	3	4	1	7	5	0	6	8
4	2	3	5	6	7	8	0	1	4	2	3	5	6	7	8	0	1	4	2	3	5	6	7	8	0	1
5	6	1	0	8	4	2	3	7	5	6	1	0	8	4	2	3	7	5	6	1	0	8	4	2	3	7
0	8	7	2	3	1	4	5	6	0	8	7	2	3	1	4	5	6	0	8	7	2	3	1	4	5	6
7	4	8	6	5	0	3	1	2	7	4	8	6	5	0	3	1	2	7	4	8	6	5	0	3	1	2
3	1	5	7	4	2	6	8	0	3	1	5	7	4	2	6	8	0	3	1	5	7	4	2	6	8	0
6	0	2	8	1	3	7	4	5	6	0	2	8	1	3	7	4	5	6	0	2	8	1	3	7	4	5
8	5	0	4	2	6	1	7	3	8	5	0	4	2	6	1	7	3	8	5	0	4	2	6	1	7	3
1	7	6	3	0	8	5	2	4	1	7	6	3	0	8	5	2	4	1	7	6	3	0	8	5	2	4
2	3	4	1	7	5	0	6	8	2	3	4	1	7	5	0	6	8	2	3	4	1	7	5	0	6	8

Fig. 7. Reference matrix of order 27 × 27.

3.3 Data Embedding

It first converts the secret data to secret digits through base-9 number system. If the changed secret digits are $S = s1, s2, \ldots, sn$, where n denotes the total quantity of covert digits. Two pixels of the frame images are selected and RGB values of each pair are chosen by the form of *Kt (x,y)*, and the pair are: *K1(R1,G1), K2(B1, R2), K3(G2, B2).* The RGB values are 8 bits having the number ranging from 0 to 255 so it could be converted for forming matrix. For every pair,

$$Pt.x = Kt.x \% 9,\ Pt.y = Kt.y \% 9$$

Here the *Pt.x* and *Pt.y* are chosen as the x and y axis elements of reference matrix M. The three candidate values are selected from the matrix which is Horizontal (CEH), Vertical (CEV) and Boxed (CEB). Then the minimum distance among the candidates are calculated. The following equation is used to find the minimum distance among the CEH, CEB, CEV.

$$M(x\text{min}, y\text{min}) = \min j = H, V, B\{|gi - xj| + |gi + 1 - yj|\}$$

where, g_i and g_{i+1} is used to represent the image frame pixel pair;

On the minimum distance candidate values the secret messages are placed inbase–9 encoded formats, which are represented below:

$$M[x_h, y_h] = M[x_v, y_v] = M[x_b, y_b] = s_i$$

where, S_i is used to indicate the secret message. With the left and right elements from position of M (Pt.x, Pt.y) of reference matrix the remaining positions are located (Fig. 8).

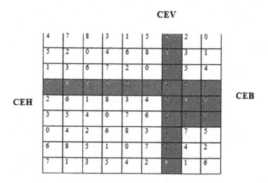

Fig. 8. CEH, CEV and CEB representation

From the above result it is shown that in the two pixels the 9 bits are included. Similarly, the same method to find the above CEH, CEV and CEB values is done for the other K2 and K3 pairs and finally the entire secret messages are embedded into the frame image.

3.4   Data Extraction

During the data extraction process the two pixels of same image (used for encrypt) is chosen from the video frame, which is paired in the manner of *K1 (R1, G1), K2 (B1, R2), K3 (G2, B2)*, that could be generalized by,

$$Pt.x = Kt.x \% 9, \ Pt.y = Kt.y \% 9$$

The *Pt.x* and *Pt.y* are placed at the x and y axis position, from that place the secret data are extracted. The process is repeated until the encrypted data is obtained. And the reverse process is used to decrypt the secret message.

4 Results and Discussion

4.1 Performance Evaluation

The perceptual imperceptibility of the data is designated by comparing the encrypted video frame with the original one through finding the MSE (Mean Square Error) and PSNR (Peak Signal to Noise Ratio) value. The MSE is used to find the amount of distortion occurred in the image. The PSNR is a parameter which is used to measure quality of image or video frame.

The equation for finding MSE value is: $MSE = \frac{1}{H*W} \sum_{i=1}^{H} (P(i,j) - S(i,j))$ where, the $P(i,j)$ is used to represent the original frame, the $s(i,j)$ is used to represent the secret frame, H and W represent the height and width of the both the frames.

From the MSE value the PSNR values could be calculated by the following equation:

$$PSNR = 10 log_{10} \frac{L^2}{MSE}$$

where, L is used to indicate the peak signal level of the grey scale image, which is taken as 255 as default. By this calculation the obtained PSNR value is high when compared to the previous approach. As the existing system uses the statistical key frame extraction technique, it also calculates the LSB value for hiding data in video but the PSNR value of the existing system is very low, which leads to the low quality of stegno image creation. But this proposed system has high PSNR value when equated with the previous method. The PSNR value comparison between the existing [3, 11] and proposed approach is depicted Table 1.

Table 1. The PSNR values of different methods

Methods	PSNR value
Chang et al. [15]	46.1012
Hong et al. [16]	48.2965
Khan et al. [17]	57.0777
Proposed method	68.0542

The PSNR comparison between the different image frames are depicted in the below graph (Fig 9).

■ Chang et al
■ Hong et al
■ khan et al
■ proposed

Fig. 9. The PSNR value comparison between different methods [15–17]

In this approach, the videos are split into image frames and the sample base video contains the frames of 182 with itself. The converted frames are then, used to embed the data within it. The encryption could be happened by using the RSA algorithm then the message embedding into the image frame, which could be done by using the technique called, Sudoku. Then finally, the embedded image is obtained, in the same way the data could be extracted from the Sudoku puzzle of cover frame then it is decrypted using the RSA.

The image frame before applying the encryption process and after encryption process are depicted in the below diagram (Fig. 10).

Fig. 10. Before Steganography

Fig. 11. After Steganography

It provides less variation compared with the previous approach as this method has high PSNR value and low MSE value (Fig. 11).

4.2 Computational Complexity

This part focuses on complexity issues of proposed work. In our proposed work, to embed a single character of secret message we need 3 pixels. So number of computations required to embed a secret message is $(3*m*x + l*w)$, where m is number of characters to b embedded, x is number of frames, l is length of frames, w is width of frames. So, the computational complexity of video Steganography method is $O(m)$ in the worst case. As we have used here RSA and AES algorithm before embedding so to know overall complexity of our algorithm we have to first calculate complexity of RSA as well as AES. Complexity of RSA is $O(\log n)$ where n is the key module and the complexity of AES algorithm is $O(m)$ where m is the block size. So, the computational complexity of our proposed method is $(m*\log n*3*m*x + l*w)$ i.e. $O(m \log n)$.

5 Conclusion

Steganography is the method of hiding the information and to prevent the unauthorized access from the illegal users. The proposed system uses the RSA due to its ability to provide better security for large file size henceforth computational complexity is reduced and AES algorithm is faster so it also reduces computational complexity. For providing maximum level of security proposed system uses RSA and AES cryptographic technique including video steganographic technique where image embedding is done by using the approach called Sudoku which uses the RGB pair value calculation for hiding the data, from that the data could be hided inside the image frame - which is obtained from the selected video. In the same way, while decrypting the message the image frames are extracted from the video, where the encrypted data is stored. Then the data is extracted by calculating the RGB pair values and finally decrypted the data by using the RSA and AES algorithm. The obtained results will produce the higher PSNR value when compared with the previous method. Also it has lower MSE rate.

References

1. Ginni, E.S., Pushpinder, E.: A review on secure video steganography technique using LSB & MSB. Int. J. Adv. Res. Comput. Commun. Eng. 5(3), 635–639 (2015)
2. Swetha, V., Prajith, V., Kshema, V.: Data hiding using video steganography-a survey. Int. J. Sci. Eng. Comput. Technol. 5(6), 206–213 (2015)
3. Dasgupta, K., Mandal, J.K., Dutta, P.: Hash based least significant bit technique for video steganography (HLSB). Int. J. Secur. Priv. Trust Manag. (IJSPTM) 1(2), 1–11 (2012)
4. Antony, L., Mathew, H.M., Jayakumar, P.: A new steganographic approach using Sudoku with digital signature. Int. J. Comput. Eng. Technol. (IJCET) 5(12), 177–185 (2014)
5. Sameerunnisa, S.K., Suhasini, K.S., Kommu, S.: Information security of video steganography utilizing RSA algorithm. Int. J. Adv. Res. Comput. Sci. Softw. Eng. 5(4), 284–289 (2015)
6. Shakeela, S., Arulmozhivarman, P., Chudiwal, R., Pal, S.: Double coding mechanism for robust audio data hiding in videos. In: Proceedings of IEEE International Conference on Recent Trends in Electronics, Information & Communication Technology (RTEICT), 20–21st May 2016, Bangalore, India, pp. 997–1001 (2016)
7. Hu, S.D.: A novel video steganography based on non-uniform rectangular partition. In: Proceedings of 14th International Conference on Computational Science and Engineering (CSE), 24–26th August 2011, Dalian, China, pp. 57–61, August 2011
8. Kour, J., Verma, D.: Steganography techniques–a review paper. Int. J. Emerg. Res. Manag. Technol. (IJERMT) 3(5), 132–135 (2014)
9. Vidya, G., Preetha, R.H., Shilpa, G.S., Kalpana, V.: Image steganography using ken ken puzzle for secure data hiding. Indian J. Sci. Technol. (IJST) 7(9), 1403–1413 (2014)
10. Chakraborty, S., Bandyopadhyay, S.K.: Steganography method based on data embedding by Sudoku solution matrix. Int. J. Eng. Sci. Invent. (IJESI) 2(7), 36–42 (2013)
11. Pavithra, S.: Performance evaluation of symmetric algorithms. J. Glob. Res. Comput. Sci. (JGRCS) 3(8), 43–45 (2012)
12. Pancholi, V.R., Patel, B.P.: Enhancement of cloud computing security with secure data storage using AES. Int. J. Innov. Res. Sci. Technol. (IJIRST) 2(09), 67–89 (2016)
13. Maji, A.K., Pal, K.P., Roy, S.: A novel steganographic scheme using Sudoku. In: 2013 International Conference on Electrical Information and Communication Technology (EICT), pp. 1–6 (2014)
14. Dey, D., Bandyopadhyay, A., Jana, S., Maji, A.K., Pal, R.K.: A novel image steganographic scheme using 8 × 8 Sudoku puzzle. In: Chaki, R., Saeed, K., Cortesi, A., Chaki, N. (eds.) Advanced Computing and Systems for Security. AISC, vol. 567, pp. 85–100. Springer, Singapore (2017). https://doi.org/10.1007/978-981-10-3409-1_6

15. Chang, C.C., Chou, Y.C., Kieu, T.D.: An information hiding scheme using Sdoku. In: 2008 Proceedings of Third International Conference on Innovative Computing, Information and Control (ICICIC), vol. 83, no. 12, pp. 2528–2535 (2008)
16. Hong, W., Chen, T.S.: A novel data embedding method using adaptive pixel pair matching. IEEE Trans. Inf. Forensics Secur. (IJETTCS) 7(1), 176–184 (2012)
17. Khan, M., Ahmad, J., Sajjad, M., Zubair, M.: Secure Image Steganography using Cryptography and Image Transposition. CoRR abs/1510.04413 (2015)

Identifying Soft Biometric Traits Through Typing Pattern on Touchscreen Phone

Soumen Roy[1(✉)], Utpal Roy[2], and Devadatta Sinha[1]

[1] Department of Computer Science and Engineering, University of Calcutta, 92 APC Road, Calcutta 700 009, India
soumen.roy_2007@yahoo.co.in,
devadatta.sinha@gmail.com
[2] Department of Computer and System Sciences, Visva-Bharati, Santiniketan 731235, India
roy.utpal@gmail.com

Abstract. In this paper, we are interested in identifying soft biometric traits such as gender (male/female), age group (below 18/18+), handedness (left/right) and hand(s) (both/single) used from the typing pattern on touchscreen phone in order to auto profiling the users online and to improve the performance of keystroke dynamics biometric system by incorporating such soft biometric scores as extra features. Four leading machine learning methods have been applied to map the typing patterns collected from 92 users through a web-based application developed by us. Obtained results in identifying such kind of traits for a typing pattern (time interval between sequences of key press and key release of entered characters) of a pre-defined text "Kolkata" are impressive. We also show the improvement of keystroke dynamics system 10% to 17% of gain accuracy using incorporation of such kind of traits with primary biometric data. This is the modest as well as an efficient approach in keystroke dynamics user authentication system in Android platform.

Keywords: Biometrics · Keystroke dynamics · Machine learning
Soft biometric

1 Introduction

Smartphone with Internet connectivity is the most common electronics gadget involves storage and access of sensitive data need to be secured. Typically, knowledge-based user identification\authentication methods such as PIN, password, and graph pattern based authentications are common and popular for its simple working principle. But people are very lazy while choosing a healthy PIN, password or graph pattern. As a result, this technique suffers from a various type of guessing attacks such as shoulder surfing attack, dictionary attack, and brute force attack. Now a day, integration of motor behavior parameter such as keystroke dynamics while typing rhythm is recommended to make the authentication process stricter and has the capability of decreasing the common guessing attacks. The way we speak (voice print), the way we walk (gait), the way we write (signature) are the behavioral biometric characteristics what we have

© Springer Nature Singapore Pte Ltd. 2018
J. K. Mandal and D. Sinha (Eds.): CSI 2017, CCIS 836, pp. 546–561, 2018.
https://doi.org/10.1007/978-981-13-1343-1_46

learned in our life, relate the issues in user identification\authentication. Apart from the behavioral biometrics, keystroke dynamic is the increasing field of research in information security concerns due to an unobtrusive and low-cost security solution. Keystroke dynamics is the process refers to measure how we type instead of what we type on a computer keyboard or touchscreen, which holds huge potential to identify the human due to neurophysiological factor. But the global performance of behavioral biometrics, more specifically keystroke dynamics system is lower than the morphological biometric characteristics such as the face print, iris print, fingerprint etc. due to the fact that this technique suffers from various troubles in data acquisition method to intra-class variation. As a result, typing pattern used as a factor in knowledge-based user authentication systems. In order to realize the fact and importance of using keystroke dynamics, this technique needs to be taken care.

With easy access to advanced technologies, we are witnessing a rapid growth in the number of smartphone users with also indirect effect on the growth of social networking users. This triggers the idea among us of introducing a method based on a keystroke dynamics technique to deduce the proper gender, age group, handedness and hand(s) used by the users. This could help to verify the proper gender and age group of the users automatically instead of taking the personal information based on trust. This may facilitate social network sites a fake free, genuine and more loyal user base.

According to a survey report [1], more than 62% of children shared their personal information and 39% of their parents were unaware of it and 71% of teens hide their online behavior from parents and 56% of parents are unaware of it. Another survey in India [2] reveals that 67% of the children under age 10 had a Facebook account and 82% of them received inappropriate messages. Social networking service is now very popular to keep in touch with friends. But there are many negative aspects. Spending more time on social networking sites reduces the actual productive time of the students; they are engaged in excessive use of this service which becomes an unconscious habit. Denti [3] in 2012 reported that user felt ill at ease when they were not allowed to regularly check up on their Facebook account. This service enables us to share a lot of personal information which leads to identity theft. Cohen [4] in 2011 reported that up to 15% of teens on social networks have been the target of cyber-bullying, while 88% have witnessed others being mean. Many Government authorities are actively trying to protect the children from these types of unknown threats coming from the massive use of the Internet. But no such potential technology has been developed so far that can distinguish a child from the adult. It is needless to say that rampant use of Internet has an adverse effect on the growing age children having diverse curiosity. The present study aims at restricting automatically the children from Internet threats and abuse of their talent. It has been observed that a user from child group could be discriminated among the adults by analyzing the typing style on the keyboard as well as on touch screen while typing a predefined text primarily.

To address the issues, keystroke dynamics is one of the easy behavioral biometrics characteristics can be used in practice. But keystroke dynamics user recognition itself suffers from various problems. Several studies have been conducted and proposed multiple methods such as multiple tries during data acquisition [5], biometric template updating [6], score fusion [7], the inclusion of soft biometrics [8] and much more. The performance of these biometric systems can be enhanced by integrating the soft biometric scores which can be used to search the genuine user more efficiently and accurately. As per the study [9],

> "Soft biometric traits are those characteristics that provide some information about the individual, but lack the distinctiveness and permanence to sufficiently differentiate any two individuals"

But as per the new definition from the study [10],

> "Soft biometric traits are physical, behavioral or adhered human characteristics, classifiable in predefined human complaint categories. These categories are, unlike in the classical biometric case, established and time-proven by humans with the aim of differentiating individuals"

In this paper, we have considered four soft biometric traits: gender, age group ($\leq$ 8/18 +), handedness and hand(s) used from typing pattern on the touchscreen. This information has low discriminating power but can be used to enhance the performance of the keystroke dynamics user recognition method.

Extraction and Selection of features is an important issue. We have worked on the following subset of timing features which were extracted from the available raw data (press and release time of each entered character): key hold/dwell time (time interval between pressed and released of same key), flight/latency time (time interval between two subsequent pressed, released, and pressed of current key and released of the previous key), and 2-gram/di-graph time (time interval between first key pressed and second key released). The other features such as key pressure, fingertips size, finger movements, choice of control keys, type of frequent errors and choice of errors correction mechanisms, gyroscope information, acceleration information, acceleration including gravity information, proximity information, the sound level, GPS data, browser name, browser code name, browser platform, browser version, browser engine name, browser agent name, browser language, cookie information, system clock resolution, operating system name and version, date and time of software installation are also can be measured for better performance in identification/authentication.

As per the experimental results, only timing features were used to discriminate the gender, age group, handedness, and hands used of the user which can be useful to reduce the error rate in the keystroke dynamics user authentication system. The typing patterns of one class are similar and sufficient dissimilar to other class. The science behind this is a physical structure, mentality, knowledge level, experience level, neurophysiological, neuropsychological factors of the user, which reflect on the keyboard and discriminates the patterns.

The study [8] proposed a novel framework to recognize the gender from keystroke dynamics dataset collected through a computer keyboard. They have also concluded that the inclusion of the gender information can enhance the performance of user recognition. All the works they have done based on the dataset collected through a conventional keyboard. Similar works have been done by [11], they have extracted the gender information along with some others soft biometric characteristics such as age group ($\leq$ 30/30+ or $\leq$ 32/32+), hand(s) used and handedness (left/right) of the individual. They have also used a conventional keyboard. Another study conducted by [12] also used a conventional keyboard to identify the age group below 18. But nowadays, keystroke dynamics with the conventional keyboard is going to be obsolete. It is due to the fact that smart android touch screen cell phone with all amenities is available with low cost in comparison to a Personal Computer. Therefore, it is more appropriate and demanded to identify the gender and age group from the data collected through Android touchscreen along with a conventional keyboard.

The main objective of this study is to develop a model that can identify the soft biometrics traits of users through the typing pattern on the touchscreen for a predefined text automatically to increase the accuracy by recognizing this soft biometrics information as additional features in keystroke dynamics user authentication system.

The major goal and contributions of the paper are as follows:

- Develop a soft biometric keystroke dynamics dataset of 92 subjects collected through a smartphone.
- Propose a novel model in identifying soft biometric traits such as gender, age group, handedness and hand(s) used to the typing pattern on the touchscreen phone which is more consistent in keystroke dynamics domain.
- Compare our proposed model with leading and proposed machine learning approach Support Vector Machine with Radial Basis Function (SVM-RBF) and statistically prove our approach is more suitable.
- We also developed keystroke dynamics data acquisition tools to collect the typing pattern on a computer keyboard and mobile phone in JavaScript for further research in identifying the age group, gender, handedness, hand(s) user on larger dataset develop on desktop and touchscreen with some extra features such as gyroscope and acceleration information.

The performance of the classification method to extract soft biometric trait is an important issue in keystroke dynamics domain. From the literature survey, we have seen that the performance of one classification method is varied if we change the dataset. In the paper [12], they have used 13 classification methods to extract the age group but they are confused to say the suitable classification method. In this paper, we have used Support Vector Machine with Radial Basis Function (SVM-RBF), Random Forest (RF), Naïve Bayes (NB) and Multi-nominal Log-Linear (MNLL). The performance of four leading machine learning methods is described, analyzed and compared.

The paper is assembled as follows. We started by reviewing previous works on soft biometric and shared datasets on keystroke dynamics in Sect. 2. We present the proposed method to recognize the gender and age group in Sect. 3. Section 4 presents the experimental results we obtained in our research and last section presents the limitation, scope of works, future works, and its conclusion.

2 Related Works and Analysis

The journey of keystroke dynamics has been started in 1980 by the study [13]. Throughout these three decades a huge number of papers have been published in the form of a journal, conference proceeding, and thesis, still, the accuracy of this technique is not reached its goal. In this section, we discuss publicly available keystroke dynamic datasets, extraction of soft biometric traits from typing pattern and the impact on keystroke dynamics user recognition system with the inclusion of soft biometric traits.

Ancillary information can significantly improve the recognition performance of biometric systems. Some ancillary information like gender can be extracted from the typing pattern as per Giot et al. [14], they obtained the accuracy of 91% to discriminate the gender on GREYC keystroke dynamics dataset created by [15] using libSVM [16], they also reported that 20% of gain accuracy can be achieved using only gender information as additional feature. Idrus et al. [11] show that it is possible to identify the gender, age group ($<30 \le$), handedness and hand(s) used while typing on a conventional keyboard and they reported the accuracy rate very close to 90%. Uzun et al. [12] showed that it is possible to distinguish the child group and adults through typing pattern on a conventional keyboard and they obtained the accuracy more than 90% for the simple familiar Turkish text. They have used 13 classification algorithms where SVM (Linear) is achieved minimum Equal Error Rate (EER) for familiar text but the performance is not consistent with the other text. Epp et al. [17] showed that it is possible to get the emotional state of an individual through keystroke dynamics through the typing pattern on a conventional keyboard. All the soft biometric traits have been extracted from the typing pattern on a conventional keyboard. No such work has been conducted in identifying the soft biometric traits such as gender and age group from the typing style on touch screen phone as per our knowledge. The objective of extracting soft biometric traits improves the performance of the biometric system. Jain et al. [18] obtained an improvement of 5% for fingerprint recognition using ethnicity (Asian/non-Asian), gender (Male/Female) and height in addition. Ailisto et al. [19] decreased the error rate from 3.9% to 1.5% for fingerprint recognition system using body weight measurement and boy fat percentage for additional information. Jain and Park [20] enabled fast search technique in the facial image using freckles, moles, and scars as additional information. Li et al. [21] achieved the performance improvement of 40% to 50% for face recognition using gender in addition.

We present some studies on soft biometric traits recognition based on typing pattern. As per our knowledge, only two studies focused on age group recognition from typing pattern collected through only a conventional computer keyboard in a controlled environment. Extraction of soft biometric or secondary biometric information (ethnicity, gender, age group, body weight, body fat...) from primary biometric characteristics (face print, fingerprint, typing style...) is not new. The main objective of these studies is to develop a model for auto profiling the individual or to enhance the performance of biometric systems in accuracy and time efficiency by incorporation of soft biometric traits extracted from the primary biometric dataset.

From the literature review, it has been found that most of the works on keystroke dynamics are based on the dataset developed from the conventional keyboard. But due to the advancement of the technological breakthrough more efficient android phone have come into the day to day life and most usage electronics gadgets. The keystroke dynamics data from the touchscreen keyboard are easily available due to the ample use of smartphone having all facilities. Now, it is more logical to concentrate on the keystroke dynamics study with the help of touchscreen data. From the survey of the literature, it has been found that no such work based on the keystroke dynamic dataset originates from the touch screen of the smartphone has been reported. In this study, we have used touch screen dataset instead of keystroke dynamics da available from the conventional keyboard.

To summarize the literature, SVM is more popular which has been used to train the system and as a classifier. All the researchers in the previous studies used lab-made datasets or experiments have been done in control environment. Now the question may arise, is this possible to predict the age group below 18 of the smartphone users from touch type? No work has been done to recognize the child user based on typing pattern on touch screen since the number of touchscreen users is rapidly increasing. Our approach is to develop an efficient model to distinguish the child users from adult and female user from male on typing pattern on a touchscreen device and develop a framework to address the real-life problems. To get the answer we have started our experiment. We have taken one dataset collected by us and we have taken four leading machine learning methods: Support Vector Machine (SVM), Random Forest (RF), Naïve Bayes (NB) and Multi-nominal Log-Linear (MLL).

3 Proposed Method

The first objective is to develop a dataset collected through touchscreen device from a large number of users belong to a different gender, age group, handedness, and qualification and then identify the soft biometric traits such as gender, age group below 18, handedness, and hands used from the way of touch type on touchscreen phone in order to address the issues in user recognition and widespread applications in E-commerce, Banking, and social networking sites, we have followed the following series of steps. Experimental setup and process during experiments are described below.

3.1 Data Acquisition

For the present purpose, we developed a keystroke dynamics dataset collected through a touchscreen phone using a web-based application developed by us. The frontend of the application is represented in Fig. 1. During the data acquisition, gender, age group, handedness, and hand(s) used information was collected for each subject. The dataset consists of typing pattern on touchscreen phone from the users belong to various categories in gender, age group, handedness, and educational qualification which is best suited for the purpose of identifying traits. The details of the data and sample distribution are described in Table 1. For the literature is concerned, there is no such dataset available so far to identify the soft biometrics traits as per our knowledge. Although, multiple datasets are publicly available on the Internet or we can get on request. But among them, most of the datasets have been developed through a conventional keyboard. But in this study, we are interested in working with the dataset collected through a touchscreen phone. Not only that, dataset also provides the traits information of each user. As per the study demands, the dataset collected by us is suitable. We have selected this dataset because it contains the instances by the users belong to various age group (7–18 and 19–65) and gender through the touchscreen environment. In our experiment, we have collected the typing pattern samples from 15 children (age below 18) and 77 adults of 92 subjects in one session with 7 repetitions for one text pattern ("Kolkata") through touchscreen mobile device (Moto G Plus 4th Gen., 5.5 in). Only one smartphone was used to collect the data. All the subjects were provided some instruction while start the typing process and they were informed about the experimental process in short. All subjects were requested to type a simple common word "Kolkata". Because they all are comfortable with that pre-defined text. The predefined text is consist of three simple syllables which is very easy to memorize and easy while typing. To get the consistent typing pattern we have chosen the predefined text "Kolkata" Details of the sample distribution of subjects are described in Fig. 2. Keypress (P) and release (R) timing of all entered keys in the predefined text were recorded raw data of typing pattern.

Fig. 1. Data acquisition tools.

The distribution of subjects clearly tells us the class distribution and the diversity of the subjects. Here, all the subjects are daily used touchscreen phone users.

3.2   Feature Extraction and Selection

Feature extraction process is carried out for selections the universal features which are distinctive in nature and easily available to all the users typing pattern. Basically, in keystroke dynamics, motor behavior, motion behavior, and pressure behavior feature subsets are captured. But motor behavior features are common to all type of keyboard and can be applied on a touchscreen device as well. Although, motion behavior only can be used in touch environment, where pressure can be measured with pressure sensitive keyboard. In our experiment, we have extracted the features from the raw data (key press and release time) used by [22]. The time interval between the combination of

Table 1. Data sample distribution

Categories	Classes	Number of instances	Percentage of class (%)
Gender	Male	497	77.17
	Female	147	22.83
Age group	Below 18	105	16.30
	18–25	294	45.65
	26–45	210	32.61
	46–60	35	5.43
Handedness	Right-handed	602	93.48
	Left-handed	42	6.52
Hand(s) used	Both hands	245	38.04
	One hand	399	61.96
Qualification	Secondary	133	20.65
	Higher secondary	175	27.17
	Graduation	133	20.65
	Master	175	27.17
	PhD	28	4.35

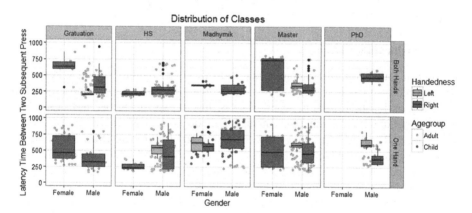

Fig. 2. Sample distribution of different classes for a particular feature (time interval of key press time of 'K' and 'o')

key press and release of each entered character were measured. The following are the features we have used: (1) Key Duration (KD): The time interval between one key press and same key release. (2) Press Press Latency Time (PP): The time interval between two subsequent presses. (3) Release Release Latency Time (RR): The time interval between two subsequent releases. (4) Release Press Latency Time (RP): The time interval between one key release and next key press. (5) Di-graph Latency Time (D): the time interval between one key press and next key release.

Feature selection is also an important issue in machine learning research. It enables the method to train faster and reduces the complexity of the model and makes it easy to interpret. It improves the evaluation performance of the model if the proper feature subset is chosen and it also reduces the overfitting. This part is necessary when the number of features is very large. In our experiment, we have used key hold time and the timing interval of combinations of keypress and release.

3.3 Pre-processing

Pre-processing step is divided into two subparts. First is to detect the outliers and clean the data and second is normalize the data. In order to improve the classification performance, preprocessing step is necessary since user typing style (raw data) contain noise and outliers. Typing pattern is not consistency due to emotional state, energy level, tiredness etc. Therefore typing style to be used in practice needs preprocessing to detect and remove outliers. Without data preprocessing or data cleaning classification performance may decline. We have replaced the outliers (value not in between 1st quartile and 2nd quartile) by the mean value of a specific feature. Then, we normalized the data within the range $[-1, 1]$ with the Eq. 1 for faster computing process. Here, x_i is the value which is to be normalized and μ is the mean value of x.

$$x_i = \frac{x_i - \mu}{\max(|x_i - \mu|)} \tag{1}$$

3.4 Classification Method

It has been found from the literature that most of the recognition work in keystroke dynamics domain has been used SVM with its many variants. It is the most used and common classification machine learning tools. In our experiment, we have used four leading machine learning methods named Support Vector Machine (SVM), Naïve Bayes (NB), Random Forest (RF) and Multi-nominal Log-Linear (MLL) to train the model and classification method. For SVM with RBF, we set the cost function (C, γ) or optimizing parameter value cost (C) = 128, gamma (γ) = 0.125.

Before developing the machine learning model, we selected the instances by an undersampling method where the instances of the different classes are equally distributed. We have first taken equal samples from the different classes and then divided it selecting samples randomly into two sizes (10% to 90% training and testing ratio) to create training and testing samples. The processes were executed (trained and evaluated) 100 times by taking a random selection of instances. Each time, the classification performances were recorded. The average results are described in this paper with 95% Confidence Interval (CI).

3.5 Performance Metrics

Statistical evaluation of the model can be measured by different metrics. Here, we have used five metrics to evaluate and compare the model performance: Accuracy, Sensitivity, Specificity, Area Under Curve (AUC) and Receiver Operating Curve (ROC). The ROC area represents the AUC. The ROC plot is a visual representation of the trade-off between True Positive Rate (TPR) and False Positive Rate (FPR). Each point in the above ROC curve is some threshold values. It varies to the degree of tolerance given to each individual threshold. Here, less FPR indicates more resistance and higher TPR indicates less usability of the model.

We have compared the previous machine learning method by t-test which is the statistic that checks if two means of accuracy and ROC are reliably different from each other. t value is the ratio between the variance between methods and the variance within methods. Where p-value is the probability that the pattern of obtained results by a method produced by random data. The value of p indicates the statistical significance of the model than other. We used the Confidence Interval (CI) to describe the amount of uncertainty associated with the results. CI at 95% is measured by the following equation:

$$CI = Mean\ value \pm 1.96\frac{\sigma}{\sqrt{N}} \tag{2}$$

Here σ and N = 100 represent the variation and the number of tries.

4 Experimental Results

The performance in accuracy in various training and testing ratio test options are presented in Fig. 3. The evaluation performance of the used four leading machine learning models is compared and analyzed in identifying soft biometric traits. In all cases, Random Forest approach is proved to be the suitable approach compared to previously used SVM and other two Naïve Bayes and Multi-nominal Log-Linear. In this paper, model evaluation performances are also compared with the help of ROC. The performance charts are presented in Fig. 4 where the evaluation performance of the used machine learning methods are compared and analyzed. Here we have used .5 training/testing (equal distribution of training and testing instances) ratio. The CI at 95% in an accuracy, sensitivity, specificity, and AUC are presented in Tables 2, 3, 4 and 5 in identifying age group, gender, handedness and hand(s) used respectively. We also compared the results with SVM by t-test. at .5 significant level results are compared. The sign 'v' indicates the better results and * indicates worth results than SVM, and no sign indicates similar results as SVM.

Accuracy comparison chart in identifying all four traits in different training ratios is presented in Fig. 3. It is clear from the figure that in all cases, RF is proved to be the suitable model than other used 3 methods in this domain.

Performance comparison chart by ROC represented in Fig. 4. The performance in identifying age group, handedness, and hand (s) used are impressive. But identifying the gender is not so good. The preliminary results were recorded; some more research work has to be done which has been described in future work section.

Training/testing ratio test option, 5 fold or 10 fold cross validation is the standard approaches to evaluate the model performance. In this domain, these methods may not be statistically meaningful in some applications. Therefore, record-wise and subject-

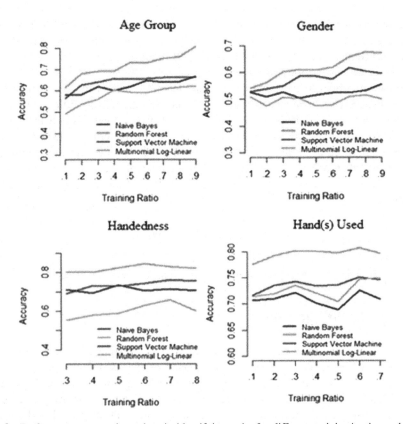

Fig. 3. Performance comparison chart in identifying traits for different training/testing ratio test options

wise cross-validation test option we have also used to evaluate our models. The details are described in Fig. 5.

Accuracy, Sensitivity, Specificity, and AUC were recorded with CI in identifying an age group for 50% training ratio test option in Table 2. The classifier, RF is proved to be the suitable than SVM at .5 significant level.

Accuracy, Sensitivity, Specificity, and AUC were recorded with CI in identifying gender for 50% training ratio test option in Table 3. The classifier, RF is proved to be the suitable than SVM at .5 significant level.

Accuracy, Sensitivity, Specificity, and AUC were recorded with CI in identifying handedness for 50% training ratio test option in Table 4. The classifier, RF is proved to be the suitable than SVM at .5 significant level.

Accuracy, Sensitivity, Specificity, and AUC were recorded with CI in identifying hand(s) used for 50% training ratio test option in Table 5. The classifier, RF is proved to be the suitable than SVM at .5 significant level.

In all cases, the classifier, RF is proved to be the suitable than SVM at .5 significant level in this domain. The different combination of feature subsets was used and

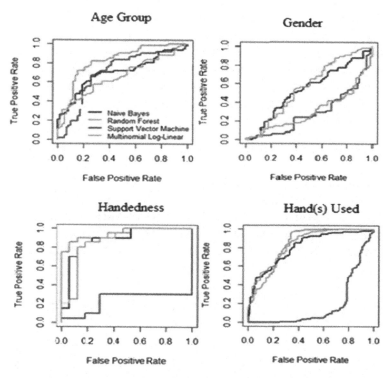

Fig. 4. Performance evaluation of four machine learning methods by ROC in 50% training ratio

Table 2. CI in identifying age group for .5 training/testing ratio test option

Classifiers	Accuracy (%)	Sensitivity (%)	Specificity (%)	AUC (%)
SVM	66.01 ± 1.43	68.24 ± 1.92	65.17 ± 2.02	71.06 ± 1.26
RF	**73.67 ± 1.23v**	**71.52 ± 1.77v**	**77.19 ± 2.19v**	**82.71 ± 1.18v**
NB	62.73 ± 1.79*	61.91 ± 2.03*	64.79 ± 2.71	68.25 ± 1.34*
MNLL	59.50 ± 1.33*	58.48 ± 1.65*	61.96 ± 2.27*	62.41 ± 1.46*

Table 3. CI in identifying gender for .5 training/testing ratio test option

Classifiers	Accuracy (%)	Sensitivity (%)	Specificity (%)	AUC (%)
SVM	59.33 ± 0.99	59.32 ± 1.80	60.35 ± 1.51	36.62 ± 1.17
RF	**62.63 ± 1.20v**	**63.70 ± 2.14v**	**62.79 ± 1.76v**	**31.51 ± 1.20***
NB	52.48 ± 0.93*	51.57 ± 1.10*	56.49 ± 2.33*	47.16 ± 1.42v
MNLL	50.12 ± 1.12*	50.59 ± 1.49*	50.73 ± 1.66*	51.05 ± 1.18v

compared there performance in Fig. 6. It is clear from the figure that a specific combination of the feature may not suit in identifying all traits.

Table 4. CI in identifying handedness for .5 training/testing ratio test option

Classifiers	Accuracy (%)	Sensitivity (%)	Specificity (%)	AUC (%)
SVM	74.28 ± 2.41	73.67 ± 3.19	80.49 ± 4.44	15.81 ± 1.41
RF	**81.56 ± 1.91v**	**81.81 ± 2.31v**	**82.59 ± 3.48v**	**90.96 ± 1.40v**
NB	71.65 ± 1.92*	78.34 ± 3.10*	68.33 ± 2.60*	77.41.33 ± 2.07v
MNLL	60.83 ± 2.31*	62.37 ± 3.45*	61.20 ± 2.96*	65.79 ± 3.12v

Table 5. Confidence interval at 95% in identifying hand(s) used for .5 training/testing ratio test option

Classifiers	Accuracy (%)	Sensitivity (%)	Specificity (%)	AUC (%)
SVM	73.06 ± 0.83	73.37 ± 1.32	73.01 ± 1.15	19.80 ± 0.78
RF	**79.91 ± 0.67v**	**86.04 ± 1.46v**	**75.85 ± 1.01v**	**86.83 ± 0.66v**
NB	70.81 ± 0.74*	68.21 ± 1.11*	74.59 ± 1.17*	80.26 ± 0.65v
MNLL	71.98 ± 0.75*	71.01 ± 1.43*	73.38 ± 0.97	82.97 ± 0.68v

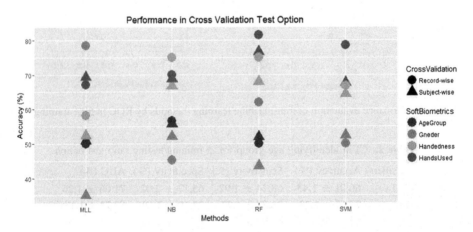

Fig. 5. Performance evaluation using record-wise and subject-wise cross-validation

The performance of keystroke dynamics biometrics can be improved by incorporation of soft biometric features. Table 6 indicates that the gain accuracy by fusion of soft biometric information. As per our experiment, age gender handedness, and hands used information can improve 10% to 17% of gain accuracy in android platform.

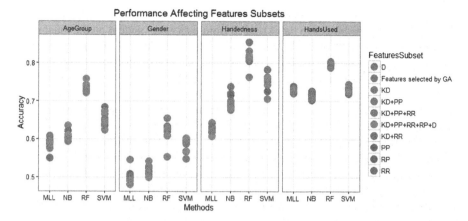

Fig. 6. Performance comparison in changing timing feature subsets

Table 6. Gain accuracy of keystroke dynamics biometrics incorporating soft biometric traits

Cross-validation	Gain accuracy (%)						
	Age	Gender	Handedness	Hands used	Age + gender	Age + gender + handedness	Age + gender + handedness + hands used
2 Fold	3.1	2.33	0.53	1.55	9.47	3.57	10.24
3 Fold	4.66	5.59	3.11	4.5	8.39	9.16	11.8
5 Fold	5.44	8.07	3.57	6.52	9.32	11.18	15.84
7 Fold	3.42	5.44	0.16	7.3	6.83	11.8	15.22
10 Fold	4.34	5.13	0.31	8.54	9.32	12.74	17.55

5   Conclusions and Future Work

In this paper, data acquisition protocols, tools, method, data preprocessing step, classification methods, and obtained results have been clearly described to extract soft biometric traits such as age group, gender, handedness, and hand(s) used from typing pattern on a touchscreen phone. Incorporation of such kind of traits with primary biometric characteristics is an effective way to enhance the state-of-the-art of keystroke dynamics also has been described.

Some of the keystroke dynamics datasets collected through the conventional keyboard are available but keystroke dynamics dataset collected through a smartphone with the subjects' age, gender, handedness, and hand(s) used information is not available as per our knowledge. We have developed a keystroke dynamics benchmark on Android platform in order to guide the future researchers in this area. Data acquisition is the most vital and essential part of keystroke dynamics. We have also developed keystroke capture tools which can be executed on the desktop and Android platforms for further study in this domain.

In this paper, we have proposed four machine learning models to identify the age group, gender, handedness and hand(s) used from the typing pattern on the touchscreen for a predefined text "Kolkata". The obtained results indicate Random Forest is the suitable machine learning method compared to previously proposed and common SVM-RBF in this domain.

We have considered the key hold time and the time interval between sequences of key press and release time. We have not considered key pressure, fingertips size, gyroscope data, acceleration speed in our experiment. These features may create a potentially efficient way to enhance the performance in this domain. There are many factors which may affect the process and increases the failure to enroll rate. More research work has to be done and many factors have to be included. In the Android platform, key pressure, acceleration, and fingertips size may be included where advanced sensing device, accelerometer are embedded in each smartphone, so this technique may get acceptable accuracy and can be used in practice.

This paper explained a solution for supporting gender, age group ($<18 \leq$), handedness, and hand (s) used identification through keystroke dynamics biometrics on the touchscreen on the Android platform which has good applications in real life. Results demonstrate that proposed approach represents an interesting step forward in the field where minor or female could be safe from looming threats from the Internet.

References

1. McAfee: The digital divide : how the online behavior of teens is getting past parents parent disconnect, June 2012
2. Variyar, M.: 82% children on Facebook receive vulgar messages. Hindustantimes (2013). http://www.hindustantimes.com/
3. Denti, L., Barbopoulos, I.: Sweden's largest Facebook study: a survey of 1000 Swedish Facebook users (2012)
4. Cohen, D.: Teen's behavior on Facebook is antisocial: report (2011). http://www.adweek.com/digital/facebook-teenagers-behavior/
5. Bartmann, D., Bakdi, I., Achatz, M.: On the design of an authentication system based on keystroke dynamics using a predefined input text. Int. J. Inf. Secur. Priv. 1(2), 1–12 (2007)
6. Pisani, P.H., Giot, R., Carlos, A., De Leon, P., De Carvalho, F., Lorena, A.C.: Enhanced template update: application to keystroke dynamics. Comput. Secur. 60, 134–153 (2016)
7. Teh, P.S., Yue, S., Teoh, A.B.: Feature fusion approach on keystroke dynamics efficiency enhancement. Int. J. Cyber-Secur. Digit. Forensics 1(1), 20–31 (2012)
8. Giot, R., Rosenberger, C.: A new soft biometric approach for keystroke dynamics based on gender recognition. Int. J. Inf. Technol. Manag. 11(August), 1–16 (2012). Spec. Issue Adv. Trends Biometrics
9. Jain, A.K., Dass, S.C., Nandakumar, K.: Can soft biometric traits assist user recognition? SPIE 5404, 561–572 (2004)
10. Dantcheva, A., Velardo, C., D'Angelo, A., Dugelay, J.L.: Bag of soft biometrics for person identification: new trends and challenges. Multimed. Tools Appl. 51(2), 739–777 (2011)
11. Idrus, S.Z.S., Cherrier, E., Rosenberger, C., Bours, P.: Soft biometrics for keystroke dynamics. In: Kamel, M., Campilho, A. (eds.) ICIAR 2013. LNCS, vol. 7950, pp. 11–18. Springer, Heidelberg (2013). https://doi.org/10.1007/978-3-642-39094-4_2

12. Uzun, Y., Bicakci, K., Uzunay, Y.: Could we distinguish child. users from adults using keystroke dynamics? (2014)
13. Gaines, R.S., Lisowski, W., Press, S.J., Shapiro, N.: Authentication by keystroke timing: some preliminary results. Technical report R-2526-NSF. Rand Corporation, May 1980
14. Giot, R., El-Abed, M., Rosenberger, C.: GREYC keystroke: a benchmark for keystroke dynamics biometric systems. In: IEEE 3rd International Conference on Biometrics Theory, Applications, and Systems, BTAS 2009 (2009)
15. Giot, R., et al.: GREYC keystroke : a benchmark for keystroke dynamics biometric systems (2009)
16. Chang, C., Lin, C.: LIBSVM: a library for support vector machines. ACM Trans. Intell. Syst. Technol. 2, 1–39 (2001)
17. Epp, C., Lippold, M., Mandryk, R.L.: Identifying emotional states using keystroke dynamics. In: Proceedings of 2011 Annual Conference on Human Factors in Computing Systems - CHI 2011, pp. 715–724 (2011)
18. Jain, A.K., Dass, S.C., Nandakumar, K.: Soft biometric traits for personal recognition systems. In: Zhang, D., Jain, A.K. (eds.) ICBA 2004. LNCS, vol. 3072, pp. 731–738. Springer, Heidelberg (2004). https://doi.org/10.1007/978-3-540-25948-0_99
19. Ailisto, H., Vildjiounaite, E., Lindholm, M., Mäkelä, S.M., Peltola, J.: Soft biometrics-combining body weight and fat measurements with fingerprint biometrics. Pattern Recognit. Lett. 27(5), 325–334 (2006)
20. Park, U., Jain, A.: Face matching and retrival using soft biometrics. IEEE Trans. Inf. Forensics Secur. 5(3), 406–415 (2010)
21. Li, Z., Zhou, X., Huang, T.S.: Spatial Gaussian mixture model for gender recognition. In: IEEE 16th International Conference on Image Processing (ICIP 2009) (2009)
22. Roy, S., Roy, U., Sinha, D.D.: ACO-random forest approach to protect the kids from internet threats through keystroke. Int. J. Eng. Technol. 2–9 (2017, accepted)

A Homomorphism Based Zero Knowledge Proof of Authentication for Chinese Remainder Theorem Based Secret Sharing

Parthajit Roy[✉]

Department of Computer Science, The University of Burdwan,
Burdwan 713104, West Bengal, India
roy.parthajit@gmail.com

Abstract. This paper proposes a secure computation model for zero knowledge proof of authentication for Chinese remainder theorem based secret sharing method. The model considers frauds in the system for more realism. The proposed model uses cryptographic hash function and discrete logarithm based ElGamal cryptosystems for its computations. The model computes the authentication in a homomorphic domain so that the information is not revealed, no matter whether all the persons are true shareholders or some of them are fraud. The proposed model definitely concludes that the system has a fraud.

Keywords: Homomorphic computation · Secure Hash Function
Discrete logarithm · Chinese remainder theorem
Secret sharing · Secure computation · Zero-Knowledge proof

1 Introduction

After the path breaking proposal of Public Key Cryptography by Diffie and Hellman [4] in the year 1976, four decades have gone and during this period, the subject has undergone many changes and has reached to its adolescence. The world has observed classical cryptosystems like RSA system [16], ElGamal system [5] to modern systems like elliptic curve based cryptography [10,12]. Several cryptographic protocols like digital signature, secure hash, secret sharing and many more have also been developed in the last four decades. There are a variety of such tools and protocols that made the field of cryptography rich enough.

All the techniques discussed above relies on the fact that the Eavesdropper is an outside entity. i.e. not the parties involved in the protocol. So, almost all of the techniques are computations on plain text to generate cipher texts. The Modern cryptographic protocols are even more realistic. They assume that the intruder may be present inside the system. So, trusting the insiders and revealing information to them may lead to information leakage. So, modern cryptographic

© Springer Nature Singapore Pte Ltd. 2018
J. K. Mandal and D. Sinha (Eds.): CSI 2017, CCIS 836, pp. 562–572, 2018.
https://doi.org/10.1007/978-981-13-1343-1_47

research directing towards secure computation or computation over cipher texts. Such types of computations are called homomorphic computations [22].

Homomorphism is a branch of mathematics where mapping between two of finite groups and their properties are studies. Homomorphic computation is a fascinating model where the computation in the homomorphic domain retains the computations of the plain text. Some early such proposal was given by Goldwasser et al. [7] where a square root over the product of two large primes was computed in the homomorphic cipher domain. Homomorphic computation on nth residue classes has been proposed by Paillier [15]. Okamoto et al. [14] has proposed factoring based secure computing. A pairing bases secure homomorphic computation has been proposed by Boneh et al. [3]. In their method, they have used Elliptic curve based bilinear Weil pairing for homomorphic encryption. An elaborated foundation on homomorphic encryption is done by Yi et al. [22].

Homomorphic encryption has a number of good applications in the field of modern cryptography. Its main objective is to keep data or identity, or location of the user secret in the whole process of computation. In secure face detection, homomorphic computation has successfully been applied by Ma et al. [11] and Nassar et al. [13] whereas in the field of Internet-of-Things (IoT) homomorphic computation has been applied by Zouari et al. [23].

Homomorphism is an important tool that can be used for privacy. Privacy is an unconditional issue in the field of Bioinformatics where the gene codes become exposed for research and computations. A secret genome search based on homomorphism in a decentralized architecture has been developed by Yamamoto et al. [20]. A privacy preservation model for location based service using K nearest neighborhood has been proposed by Yi et al. [21].

In this paper, a secure secret sharing model has been proposed. Secret sharing, on the other hand, is a branch of cryptography where a secret is being distributed among n shareholders in such a way that any combination of k persons can fully retrieve the secret and any combination of less than k persons does not get slightest idea of the secret. The first such proposal was given by Shamir [19]. His proposal was based on interpolation of polynomials. Independently, secret sharing based on linear equations was proposed by Blakley [2].

Chinese Remainder Theorem (CRT) based Secret sharing is another stunning branch of secret sharing where the secret is shared among n persons using CRT. An early such model has been proposed by Asmuth et al. [1]. A generalized model of secret sharing on Chinese Remainder Theorem has been proposed Iftene [8]. He also showed how to use it in secure e-voting system.

Zero Knowledge proof of identity is another interesting branch of cryptography where the proof of ownership of an information is established without revealing the information itself and thus avoid leakage of information. The first such model was proposed by Goldwasser et al. [6]. Some recent application in the field of wireless sensor network has been proposed by Khernane et al. [9] whereas an application of the same in Mobile to Mobile communication has been proposed my Schukat et al. [18]. A state of the art discussions on Zero-Knowledge proof up to year 2006 has been done by Rosen [17].

In this paper the problem has been identified as follows. Let a secret has been shared using CRT among n users by a designated authority. For the purpose of further security, the authority did not disclose the identity of the shareholders. This means, no shareholder knows who the other secret shareholders are. Let in the absence of the authority, the organization needs to know the secret. So, the organization announces the news in their website and asks the secret sharehold- ers to be present in a meeting. In the meeting, no body knows whether the other persons are true share holders or a fraud. As there may be frauds in the system revealing of information is a bad idea. The problem is, as the shareholders are unknown to each other, they don't want to revile their secrets without being sure about the identity of the other share holders. This paper proposes a solution that uses Secure Hash Functions and ElGamal encryption based models for authen- tication of the share holders in case of Chinese remainder theorem based secret sharing without revealing the information. Proposed model is a non-threshold secret sharing model, i.e. all the shareholders have to be present to recover the secret. The model gives a clear indication whether all the shareholders are true shareholders or not. The proposed model is also computationally efficient in the sense that it uses a single round for its computations.

The rest of the paper is organized as follows. Section 2 discusses the mathe- matical prerequisites that are needed to describe the model. Section 3 proposes the model of zero knowledge authentication. Strengths ans Weaknesses of the proposed model have been discussed in Sect. 4. Conclusion and future scopes are presented in Sect. 5 and references come thereafter.

2   Mathematical Preliminaries

This section deals with the mathematics related to group homomorphism, ElGa- mal cryptosystem and Chinese remainder theorem. The section also gives a brief idea of cryptographic hash functions and zero knowledge proof of identity.

A Homomorphism is a mapping $\psi : G \to H$, for two groups $(G, *)$ and $(H, \circ)$ s.t. $\forall a, b \in G, \psi(a), \psi(b) \in H$ and that $\psi(a * b) = \psi(a) \circ \psi(b)$. This also implies that if e_G, e_H are the identity elements of the group G and H respectively, then $\psi(e_G) = e_H$, which further implies that $\forall a \in G, \psi(a^{-1}) = \psi(a)^{-1}$ and therefore G forms a normal subgroup of H. Further, if the mapping $\psi(.)$ is a bijection and the set H is same as set G, then the homomorphism is called endomorphism.

The striking feature of homomorphism is that the computation can be per- formed in the homomorphic domain instead of the original group domain. Let us try to realize this by an example, Let us suppose that $a * b$ needs to be computed for some $a, b \in G$. What can be done is, instead of computing $a * b$ directly, they can be transfered to their corresponding homomorphic images as $\psi(a)$ and $\psi(b)$ and thereafter compute $h = \psi(a) \circ \psi(b) \in H$. Thereafter, compute the pre-image of h as $\psi^{-1}(h) = a * b$. Homomorphism ensures that $a * b$ will be recovered in the original domain.

The main advantage such type of indirect computation is secrecy of the original values a and b. Suppose Alice has a secret a and Bob has another secret b and they want to compute $a * b$ without revealing their actual information.

They will transform their plain text information a and b to $\psi(a)$ and $\psi(b)$ via homomorphic mapping and will reveal $\psi(a)$ and $\psi(b)$. The computation on $\psi(a)$ and $\psi(b)$ will be done and from $\psi(a) \circ \psi(b)$, which is actually $\psi(a * b)$ the pre-image will be computed. (For the time being, assume that from the product, they cannot recover the opponent's secret). The whole security of such model is based on the assumption that from $\psi(a), \forall a \in G$, is cryptographically hard. Obviously, computing a from $\psi(a) \forall a \in G$ must be easy if some extra information is known. This is called one way trap door functions. To summarize, an homomorphism is suitable for secure homomorphic computation, if and only if it has one way property.

ElGamal [5] system is the direct outcome of the discrete logarithm problem proposed by Diffie and Hellman [4]. The mathematical description of the system is as follows. Let p be a large prime and G is a multiplicative group realized over p. Let g be a be a generator of the group G. Let Alice owns these information. She then choses a secret number K_s and keeps it secret. She then computes P_k^A as public key and publishes $P_k^A = (G, g, K_p)$ where public key K_p is generated using Eq. 1.

$$K_p = g^{K_s} \bmod p \tag{1}$$

Let Bob wants to send a plain text to Alice. To send a plain text m Bob choses a random number $K_e, (K_e < p)$. This is known as *ephemeral key*. Bob then computes the following using Eqs. 2 and 3.

$$c_1 = g^{K_e} \bmod p \tag{2}$$

$$c_2 = m \times K_p^{K_e} \bmod p \tag{3}$$

He then sends the pair (c_1, c_2) over the insecure channel to Alice.

Alice in due course, performs her computations using Eq. 4 and subsequently she computes t^{-1}. She then multiplies t^{-1} with c_2 and retrieves the plain text m. This can be realized from Eq. 6.

$$t = c_1^{K_s} \tag{4}$$

$$t^{-1} = (c_1^{K_s})^{-1} \bmod p \tag{5}$$

$$
\begin{aligned}
t^{-1} \times c_2 \bmod p &= \left(c_1^{K_s}\right)^{-1} \times c_2 \bmod p \\
&= \left(\left(g^{K_e}\right)^{K_s}\right)^{-1} \times \left(m \times (K_p)^{K_e}\right) \bmod p \\
&= \left(g^{K_e \times K_s}\right)^{-1} \times \left(m \times \left(g^{K_s}\right)^{K_e}\right) \bmod p \\
&= \left(g^{K_e \times K_s}\right)^{-1} \times \left(m \times g^{K_s \times K_e}\right) \bmod p \\
&= m \times \left(g^{K_e \times K_s}\right)^{-1} \times \left(g^{K_s \times K_e}\right) \\
&= m \times 1 \\
&= m
\end{aligned}
\tag{6}
$$

The striking fact is that the ElGamal structure has endomorphism. To understand this, let us first define the homomorphic mapping using Eq. 7.

$$\psi(a) = g^a \ mod \ p \tag{7}$$

Now, consider two integers m_1 and m_2 are in possession of two different persons B and C and they want to compute $m_1 * m_2$ secretly. Let Alice has an ElGamal system (G, g, K_p). B and C can compute $m_1 * m_2$ secretly using Alice's ElGamal system. To do this, let B and C choses ephemeral keys K_{eb} and K_{ec} respectively. Thereafter B and C encrypts their plain texts m_1 and m_2 using Alice's public key. Let B generates (c_{1b}, c_{1c}) and C generates (c_{1c}, c_{2c}) respectively. They multiplies them using the following equation and sends the result to Alice for decryption.

$$(c_{1b}, c_{2b}) \times (c_{1c}, c_{2c}) = (c_{1b} \times c_{1c}, c_{2b} \times c_{2c}) \tag{8}$$

Clearly, multiplication is done in the homomorphic domain so none of B, C will be able to learn about other's plain text. What Alice decrypts is as follows.

$$t = (c_{1b} \times c_{1c})^{K_s} \tag{9}$$

and computes t^{-1} the inverse using Eq. 5. She then multiplies t^{-1} with $(c_{2b} \times c_{2c})$. The result she gets is,

$$
\begin{aligned}
&t^{-1}(c_{2b}.c_{2c}) \ mod \ p \\
&= \left((c_{1b} \times c_{1c})^{K_s}\right)^{-1} \times (c_{2b} \times c_{2c}) \ mod \ p \\
&= \left((g^{K_{eb}} g^{K_{ec}})^{K_s}\right)^{-1} \left(m_1 (K_p)^{K_{eb}} \times m_2 (K_p)^{K_{ec}}\right) \ mod \ p \\
&= \left((g^{K_{eb}} g^{K_{ec}})^{K_s}\right)^{-1} \left(m_1 (g^{K_s})^{K_{eb}} \times m_2 (g^{K_s})^{K_{ec}}\right) \ mod \ p \\
&= \left((g^{K_{eb}} g^{K_{ec}})^{K_s}\right)^{-1} \left(m_1 m_2 (g^{K_{eb}})^{K_s} (g^{K_{ec}})^{K_s}\right) \ mod \ p \\
&= m_1 m_2 \left((g^{K_{eb}} g^{K_{ec}})^{K_s}\right)^{-1} (g^{K_{eb}} g^{K_{ec}})^{K_s} \ mod \ p \\
&= m_1 m_2 \tag{10}
\end{aligned}
$$

Thus, Alice gets the multiplication of m_1 and m_2. The important observation is that if $\psi(m_1) * \psi(m_2)$ is performed in the homomorphic domain, then the resultant is multiplication in the original domain. This is what this paper is going to exploit.

The third thing that a cryptographic hash function has been used. A cryptographic hash function is a mapping from input of arbitrary length to an output of fixed length in such a way that is impossible to revert back. Hash functions has a number interesting properties. Given the output of the secure hash, it is impossible to reverse engineered to get back the plain text. Secondly, hash functions are preimage resistant. i.e. finding a collision is computationally impossible.

Hash functions are typically used for secret agreements. In this paper, standard SHA-512 (Designed by NSA) has been used for authentication protocol design.

Chinese remainder theorem says that given n linear congruent equations $x = r_i \bmod m_i, \forall i = 1, 2, \cdots, n$ with $gcd(m_i, m_j) = 1, \forall i, j$ with $i \neq j$, x has a unique solution in modulo $m_1 \times m_2 \times \cdots \times m_n$ domain.

In CRT based secret sharing method, a secret x is considered, and the remainder r_i is computed when it is divided by some prime p_i (Relatively co-primes are also works well) for $i = 1, \cdots, n$. The secrets (r_i, p_i) are transfered to person P_is. In this way the shares are shared. Whenever the secret needs to be reconstructed, the shareholders solve the linear congruent equations as follows.

$$x = r_1 \bmod p_1 \tag{11}$$

$$x = r_2 \bmod p_2 \tag{12}$$

$$\vdots$$

$$x = r_n \bmod p_n \tag{13}$$

The Chinese remainder theorem ensures that it has a unique solution. Further, if one of the information is missing, x cannot be guessed. There are thresholding models also for Chinese remainder theorem based secret sharing, but the present proposed model considers non thresholding model only.

All the necessary mathematics have been discussed in this section. Now we are ready to present the proposed model. Next section proposes this.

3 Proposed Zero Knowledge Authentication Model

The proposed model is a zero knowledge proof based authentication model for Chinese remainder theorem (CRT) based secret sharing. In the proposed model, it is assumed that a designated authority (DA) will share a secret x among n persons using CRT mased secret sharing model. In the proposed model, instead of co-prime divisors, the DA choses primes for modulus of CRT based secret sharing model. Typically, large primes. The DA then computes the shares. Let the shares are $(r_1, p_1), (r_2, p_2), \cdots, (r_n, p_n)$ and have been distributed to shareholders $S_1, S_2, \cdots, S_n$ respectively. He then multiplies all the primes and produces the hash of the result and makes it public. The computation of DA is summarized in Table 1.

It is clear that making the *aggrement* public is absolutely safe. No one can guess a bit of idea about the values *mult* of the original values of $p_1, p_2, \cdots, p_n$.

For authentication of the shareholders, some protocols are followed. The protocol is simple and deterministic. The shareholders have to compute the value *mult*. This means, they have to know the values $p_1, p_2, \cdots, p_n$. This is the only way to get the value of *aggrement*.

This paragraph focuses on the secret generation process. As, the DA didn't disclose the identities of the shareholders, it is hard for any shareholder to authenticate other share holders. Suppose, in the absence of DA, the company

Table 1. The computations of the designated authority.

Designated authority's computation
1. DA identifies the information x that he wants to share secretly. 2. DA selects suitable large primes $p_1, \cdots, p_n$ 3. DA breaks the information x using CRT based secrets $(r_1, p_1), (r_2, p_2), \cdots, (r_n, p_n))$ and shares them to holders $S_1, S_2, \cdots, S_n$ respectively. 4. DA computes $mult = p_1 \times p_2 \times \cdots \times p_n$. 5. DA computes $aggrement = SHA(mult)$ 6. DA makes the number of holders n and $agreement$ public in his web site.

needs to recover the secret. The company places the news in their website. In response, n persons turn out and claim that they are the actual shareholders. The next task of the company is to ask them to disclose their secrets. But, if one or some of them are frauds, then the information cannot be retrieved and the secrets of the valid shareholders will be disclosed to the frauds.

In the proposed model, no one, not even the company secretary, who is conducting the recovery process, will be able to learn about the secrets until all the n shareholders are authenticated. So, before revealing the actual secrets, the shareholders will be asked to prove their identity. This means, that they will have to prove that they posses the secrets. Shareholders then starts their protocol according to Table 2.

Table 2. The computations of the shareholder for proving their identity.

Shareholder's computation
1. Some person P (Secretary can be a good choice for this) makes her ElGaml system public. i.e. She makes (g, p, P_k) public. 2. Each S_i then does the following sequentially. S_1 encrypts his prime p_1 with the ElGamal system as $Secret_1 = (c_{11}, c_{21})$ and passes the result to S_2. S_2 then encrypts his prime p_2 with the ElGamal system as $Secret_2 = (c_{12}, c_{22})$. 3. S_2 then multiplies them as $secret_1 \times secret_2$ and passes to S_3. 4. S_3 then computes his $secret_3$ and multiplies $secret_1 \times secret_2 \times secret_3$. 5. The process continues up to nth shareholder computes $encrypt = secret_1 \times secret_2 \times \cdots \times secret_n$. 6. Person P then asked to recover the secret from $encrypt$. 7. Due to homomorphism of ElGamal as shown in equation 10 , P computes $result = p_1 \times p_2 \times \cdots \times p_n$ 8. all the hash of the $result$ is then computed. 9. If $SHA(result) = aggrement$, computed by DA as shown in Table 1, then the persons are all true shareholders. Otherwise there is fraud in the system.

Let us explain the working principle of the model. From Eq. 10 it is clear that ElGaml system has homomorphism property for multiplication. Now, whenever $Secret_1 = (c_{11}, c_{21})$ has been created by shareholder S_1 if it is passed to S_2, S_2 will not be able to recover the value of p_1 because it is encrypted using Secretary's public key. So, other than secretary, nobody can recover p_1. Shareholder S_2 then encrypts his prime p_2 using Secretary's public key and multiplies it with $secret_1$ and passes the result to shareholder S_3. S_3 also cannot recover the message for same reason. In this way all the messages are multiplied. The final outcome is $encrypt = secret_1 \times secret_2 \times \cdots \times secret_n$. The value encrypt is then submitted to the secretary for decryption. If it is assumed that shareholder S_1 choses ephemeral key e_1, S_2 chooses $e_2 \cdots S_n$ choses e_n, then the secretary computes the following using his private key (G, g, K_s) (K_s is the corresponding secret exponent of his public exponent K_p).

$$t = (c_{11} \times c_{12} \times \cdots \times c_{1n})^{K_s} \tag{14}$$

and computes t^{-1} the inverse using Eq. 5. She then multiplies t^{-1} with $(c_{21} \times c_{22} \times \cdots \times c_{2n})$. The result she gets is,

$$
\begin{aligned}
&t^{-1}.c_2 \bmod p \\
&= \left((c_{11} \times \cdots \times c_{1n})^{K_s}\right)^{-1} \times (c_{21} \times \cdots \times c_{2n}) \bmod p \\
&= \left((g^{K_{e1}} \times \cdots \times g^{K_{en}})^{K_s}\right)^{-1} \left(p_1 (K_p)^{K_{e1}} \times \cdots \times p_n (K_p)^{K_{en}}\right) \bmod p \\
&= \left((g^{K_{e1}} \times \cdots \times g^{K_{en}})^{K_s}\right)^{-1} \left(p_1 (g^{K_s})^{K_{e1}} \times \cdots \times p_n (g^{K_s})^{K_{en}}\right) \bmod p \\
&= \left((g^{K_{e1}} \times \cdots g^{K_{en}})^{K_s}\right)^{-1} \left(p_1 \times \cdots \times p_n (g^{K_{e1}})^{K_s} \cdots (g^{K_{en}})^{K_s}\right) \bmod p \\
&= p_1 \times \cdots \times p_n \left((g^{K_{e1}} \times \cdots \times g^{K_{en}})^{K_s}\right)^{-1} (g^{K_{e1}} \times \cdots \times g^{K_{ec}})^{K_s} \bmod p \\
&= p_1 \times \cdots \times p_n \tag{15}
\end{aligned}
$$

As a concrete example, let the secretary's ElGamal prime is $p = 83$ and the generator $g = 2$. Let the secretary's private key is $k_s = 11$. So, secretary's public key is $K_p = g^{K_s} \bmod p = 2^{11} \bmod 83 = 56$. Let B and C are the two shareholders. Let B has a prime for CRT and C has a prime for CRT. Let B's prime is $m_b = 5$ and C's prime is $m_c = 11$. Let B chooses the ephemeral key as $K_{eb} = 13$. B computes $c_{1b} = g^{K_{eb}} = 2^{13} \bmod 83 = 58$. He then encrypts the message and gets cipher text $c_{2b} = m_b \times K_p^{K_{eb}} \bmod p = 5 \times 56^{13} \bmod 83 = 64$. He then sends this pair $(c_{1b}, c_{2b}) = (58, 64)$ to C.

Let C's ephemeral key is $c_{ec} = 18$. So, he computes $c_{1c} = g^{K_{ec}} = 2^{18} \bmod 83 = 30$. He then encrypts the message and gets the cipher text $c_{2c} = m_c \times K_p^{K_{ec}} \bmod p = 11 \times 56^{18} \bmod 83 = 68$. So, his pair is $(c_{1c}, c_{2c}) = (30, 68)$. He then multiplies $((c_{1b}, c_{2b}) \times (c_{1c}, c_{2c})) \bmod p = ((58, 64) \times (30, 68)) \bmod 83$ and gets $(80, 36)$ and send this number to the secretary.

Secretary computes $80^{K_s} \; mod \; p = 80^{11} \; mod \; 83 = 58$. Then computes its inverse as $inv(58) \; mod \; 83 = 73$ and multiplies it with the second component i.e. she computes $73 \times 36 \; mod \; 83$ and gets the result 55, which is the product of the two primes 5 and 11 of B and C respectively.

In this way, from Eq. 15, the secretary computes the product $result = p_1 \times \cdots \times p_n$. But $result$ is a product of large primes and the factorization of the product of large primes is a computationally impossible task. Also, from this product (which is now made public by secretary), shareholders cannot reveal any information. This is because, they can divide the $result$ by their number but the resultant is a product of $n - 1$ primes. So, if n is greater than or equal to 3, then this resultant is at least a product of two large primes, which is also computationally impossible to factorize. Thereafter the hash of the $result$ has been computed. If the hash matches with the $agreement$ value proposed by the DA, then the shareholders are all authentic and they go for CRT based retrieval of secret x, otherwise the system has frauds and the process stops.

4   Security and Weaknesses

Last section proposed and explained homomorphic model for authentication model. This section discusses the strengths and weaknesses of the model.

The proposed model finally reveals the product of some large primes. This is absolutely safe. In the field of public key cryptography, it is widely known that product of large prime is very hard to factor. So, from the product of the large primes no information about the individual prime numbers will be revealed. If one or more of the persons are fraud, even then also, the product will not give any idea about individual primes. Finally, as the hash of the product is made public, no outside eavesdropper can learn anything about the product. So, the system is secure from both internal cheaters as well as from external intruders.

Though the model is secure, the whole computation is computationally intensive. This is because the message in the present case is a product of a number of large primes. Therefore for successful computation on n shares, the ElGamal modulo prime p should be like $p > p_1 \times \cdots \times p_n$. But small primes cannot be chosen. In that case factorization will be easier. So, the present paper restricts the number of shares. For this reason, in a practical sense, the number of shareholders should not be too large.

5   Conclusion

This paper proposes zero knowledge proof of authentication for Chinese remainder theorem based secret sharing method. The proposed model uses homomorphic computation for authentication purpose. For this, the model uses ElGamal based encryption system. The model is a realistic model that assumes the presence of frauds both withing the system as well as in outside. Further, the proposed model doesn't reveal any information about the secret until all the true shareholders are true shareholders. The Model also considers secure hash functions for hiding the plain text information and makes the digest of the information public for proving the authentication of the shareholders.

Though the model is promising, there are some weaknesses also. First of all, the model is computationally intensive. This is because the model computes huge number of exponentiation on modulo large prime domain. Secondly, the model works only for is a non-threshold CRT based secret sharing schemes. i.e. all the shareholders have to come together.

For the first weakness, the model can be further improvised to achieve better computational efficiency. For this Elliptic curves cryptosystems may be used which works well with relatively smaller primes. For the second problem, hash of all possible combinations of ^nc_k multiplications of primes can be made public by the designated authority DA. Further some more sophisticated mathematical models can be used as a remedy of both the weaknesses.

References

1. Asmuth, C., Bloom, J.: A modular approach to key safeguarding. IEEE Trans. Inf. Theory **29**(2), 208–210 (1983)
2. Blakley, G.R.: Safeguarding cryptographic keys. In: International Workshop on Managing Requirements Knowledge, p. 313 (1979)
3. Boneh, D., Goh, E.-J., Nissim, K.: Evaluating 2-DNF formulas on ciphertexts. In: Kilian, J. (ed.) TCC 2005. LNCS, vol. 3378, pp. 325–341. Springer, Heidelberg (2005). https://doi.org/10.1007/978-3-540-30576-7_18
4. Diffie, W., Hellman, M.: New directions in cryptography. IEEE Trans. Inf. Theory **22**(6), 644–654 (1976). https://doi.org/10.1109/TIT.1976.1055638
5. ELGamal, T.: A public key cryptosystem and a signature scheme based on discrete logarithms. IEEE Trans. Inf. Theory **31**(4), 469–472 (1985)
6. Goldwasser, S., Micali, S., Rackoff, C.: The knowledge complexity of interactive proof-systems. In: Proceedings of the Seventeenth Annual ACM Symposium on Theory of Computing. STOC 1985, pp. 291–304, ACM, New York (1985). https://doi.org/10.1145/22145.22178
7. Goldwasser, S., Micali, S.: Probabilistic encryption and how to play mental poker keeping secret all partial information. In: Proceedings of the Fourteenth Annual ACM Symposium on Theory of Computing. STOC 1982, pp. 365–377, ACM, New York (1982). https://doi.org/10.1145/800070.802212
8. Iftene, S.: General secret sharing based on the chinese remainder theorem with applications in e-voting. Electron. Notes Theor. Comput. Sci. **186**(Supplement C), 67–84 (2007). Proceedings of the First Workshop in Information and Computer Security (ICS 2006). http://www.sciencedirect.com/science/article/pii/S1571066107004604
9. Khernane, N., Potop-Butucaru, M., Chaudet, C.: BANZKP: a secure authentication scheme using zero knowledge proof for WBANs. In: 2016 IEEE 13th International Conference on Mobile Ad Hoc and Sensor Systems (MASS), pp. 307–315, October 2016
10. Koblitz, N.: Elliptic curve cryptosystems. Math. Comput. **48**(177), 203–209 (1987)
11. Ma, Y., Wu, L., Gu, X., He, J., Yang, Z.: A secure face-verification scheme based on homomorphic encryption and deep neural networks. IEEE Access **5**, 16532–16538 (2017)

12. Miller, V.S.: Use of elliptic curves in cryptography. In: Williams, H.C. (ed.) CRYPTO 1985. LNCS, vol. 218, pp. 417–426. Springer, Heidelberg (1986). https://doi.org/10.1007/3-540-39799-X_31. http://dl.acm.org/citation.cfm?id=18262.25413

13. Nassar, M., Wehbe, N., Bouna, B.A.: K-NN classification under homomorphic encryption: application on a labeled eigen faces dataset. In: 2016 IEEE International Conference on Computational Science and Engineering (CSE) and IEEE International Conference on Embedded and Ubiquitous Computing (EUC) and 15th International Symposium on Distributed Computing and Applications for Business Engineering (DCABES), pp. 546–552, August 2016

14. Okamoto, T., Uchiyama, S.: A new public-key cryptosystem as secure as factoring. In: Nyberg, K. (ed.) EUROCRYPT 1998. LNCS, vol. 1403, pp. 308–318. Springer, Heidelberg (1998). https://doi.org/10.1007/BFb0054135

15. Paillier, P.: Public-key cryptosystems based on composite degree residuosity classes. In: Stern, J. (ed.) EUROCRYPT 1999. LNCS, vol. 1592, pp. 223–238. Springer, Heidelberg (1999). https://doi.org/10.1007/3-540-48910-X_16. http://dl.acm.org/citation.cfm?id=1756123.1756146

16. Rivest, R.L., Shamir, A., Adleman, L.: A method for obtaining digital signatures and public-key cryptosystems. Commun. ACM **21**(2), 120–126 (1978). https://doi.org/10.1145/359340.359342

17. Rosen, A.: Concurrent Zero-Knowledge, 1st edn. Springer, Heidelberg (2006). https://doi.org/10.1007/3-540-32939-0

18. Schukat, M., Flood, P.: Zero-knowledge proofs in M2M communication. In: 25th IET Irish Signals Systems Conference 2014 and 2014 China-Ireland International Conference on Information and Communications Technologies (ISSC 2014/CIICT 2014), pp. 269–273, June 2014

19. Shamir, A.: How to share a secret. Commun. ACM **22**(11), 612–613 (1979). https://doi.org/10.1145/359168.359176

20. Yamamoto, Y., Oguchi, M.: A decentralized system of genome secret search implemented with fully homomorphic encryption. In: 2017 IEEE International Conference on Smart Computing (SMARTCOMP), pp. 1–6, May 2017

21. Yi, X., Paulet, R., Bertino, E., Varadharajan, V.: Practical k nearest neighbor queries with location privacy. In: 2014 IEEE 30th International Conference on Data Engineering, pp. 640–651, March 2014

22. Yi, X., Paulet, R., Bertino, E.: Homomorphic Encryption and Applications. Springer, Cham (2014). https://doi.org/10.1007/978-3-319-12229-8

23. Zouari, J., Hamdi, M., Kim, T.H.: A privacy-preserving homomorphic encryption scheme for the internet of things. In: 2017 13th International Wireless Communications and Mobile Computing Conference (IWCMC), pp. 1939–1944, June 2017

An Approach Towards Design and Analysis of a New Block Cipher Based Cryptographic System Using Modular Encryption and Decryption Technique (MEDT)

Debajyoti Guha[1(✉)], Rajdeep Chakraborty[1],
and Jyotsna Kumar Mandal[2]

[1] Techno India Group, Kolkata, West Bengal, India
debajyoti.aec@gmail.com, rajdeep_chak@rediffmail.com
[2] Department of CSE, University of Kalyani, Kalyani, India
jkm.cse@gmail.com

Abstract. In this article a new Cryptographic System based on Block Cipher has been planned where the Encryption and Decryption are done based on Modular Arithmetic. Hence the title of the article is suggested as Modular Encryption and Decryption Technique (MEDT). The plain text message which is a stream of bits, is assumed to be separated into a number of blocks & each block contains m bits, where m is anyone of (3, 9, 27, 81, 243). Number of zeros will be appended at the MSB of bit stream to make total number of bits odd in each block. The binary addition has been made on contiguous blocks taking modulus of addition as 2^m. The sum replaces the second block, first block remains unaltered. Similar operation will be continued for second and third blocks and so on till all the blocks are exhausted to get the cipher text. During summation the carry generated (if any) out of the MSB is discarded. The technique is applied on blocks with varying sizes from 3 to 3^n. The modulo subtraction technique is adopted for decryption to get back the plain text.

Keywords: Cryptographic System · Encryption · Decryption · Plain text
Cipher text · Block Cipher · Modulo arithmetic technique

1 Introduction

Computer security is all about studying cyber attacks with a view to defending against them. Understanding what makes systems vulnerable to these attacks is an important first step in avoiding or preventing them [6]. Scientists examined different classes of vulnerabilities including those caused by poorly written or configured software. Access control, authentication and data protection techniques have been introduced to keep one's message secret from others. The sound security practice may protect online transactions from frauds and forgery by ensuring integrity, reliability, security and non repudiation. Even one can say, today no system is secured unless practice and application of sound security protocols.

© Springer Nature Singapore Pte Ltd. 2018
J. K. Mandal and D. Sinha (Eds.): CSI 2017, CCIS 836, pp. 573–583, 2018.
https://doi.org/10.1007/978-981-13-1343-1_48

In Sect. 2 of this article we deal with the proposed scheme. A flow diagram of implementation and validation is given in Sect. 3. Comparative study of results is described in Sect. 4. Section 5 deals with conclusions, references and acknowledgment is given last.

2   The Modular Encryption and Decryption Technique (MEDT)

To implement the proposed work, the stream size of 729 bits has been taken. The scheme may be implemented for bigger stream sizes too. The input stream, Y, is initially segregated into a number of blocks (F1, F2..., F_x). Starting from LSB each block containing m bits (m = 3^i, i = 1, 2, 3...) and OR operation is performed on the first block in each round with odd number of 0 s as per the size of blocks in that corresponding round. So that S = F_1, F_2, F_3, .., F_x where x = 729/m. Starting from the MSB, the adjacent blocks are paired as (F_1, F_2), (F_2, F_3), (F_3, F_4), ..., (F_{x-1}, F_x). The Modulo Arithmetic Addition operation is applied to each pair of blocks for obtaining the cipher text. The process is repetitive with increasing block size till m = 243. To get back the original plain text message, Modular subtraction technique have been adopted.

2.1   The Algorithm for the Proposed Work

The input stream has been broken into blocks. Each block contains 3 bits and block pairing is done as explained in Sect. 2. The below steps are involved starting from the most significant side:

Round 1: For every adjacent block pair, the 1st block is added with the 2nd block with modulus of addition as 3 m for block size m. For 3-bit blocks, the addition modulus will be 9.

This round is repetitive for finite number of times and the number of iterations will form a part of the session key.

Round 2: Similar operation as described in Round 1 is performed with block size 9. The rounds will be continued between adjacent blocks till no blocks are left. The process is repeated, each time increasing the block size till m = 243.

Thus several rounds are completed till we reach **Round 5** where the block size is 243 and we get the encrypted bit-stream. Here a new content of F_X is obtained from addition of content from F_{X-1} and previous content from F_X. Therefore F_X now will be added to F_{X+1} and changes will be made in $F_{\backslash X+1}$ which increases the complexity of the algorithm resulting in the enhancement of security

During decryption, the opposite method i.e. modulo subtraction is performed, between the adjacent block pairs starting from LSB decreasing the block size from 243 to 3.

2.2   The Modulo Addition

The proposed technique is to throw away the carry from Most Significant Bit (if any) after addition for getting the outcome e.g. if 101 and 111 are added we get 1100(12 in decimal). Due to modulus addition is 1000(in decimal 8 or 2^3), therefore the result of addition will be 100(1100 − 1000 = 100). Removal of the carry from 1100 is equivalent to subtracting 1000 (i.e. 8 in decimal). That is why the result is 100 or 4 in decimal. This policy is applicable to all blocks irrespective of their sizes.

2.3   Example of the Scheme

The scheme under consideration is applicable to 729-bit input stream. To prove the scheme mathematically, we consider a bit-stream of 16 bits, 0110000101100010. To ensure odd number of bits in each block we have to add extra zeros in the given bit stream.

The Encryption Scheme

Considering Y = 000110000101100010 (Inclusion of two redundant zeros in the beginning)

Round 1: Block Size = 3, No. of Blocks = 6.

INPUT:

000	110	000	101	100	010
F1	F2	F3	F4	F5	F6

ITERATION 1:

000	**110**	000	101	100	010
F1	**F2**	F3	F4	F5	F6

(F1, F2) mod8, Alter F2.

ITERATION 2:

000	110	**110**	101	100	010
F1	F2	**F3**	F4	F5	F6

(F2, F3) mod8, Alter F3.

ITERATION 3:

000	110	110	**011**	100	010
F1	F2	F3	**F4**	F5	F6

(F3, F4) mod8, Alter F4.

ITERATION 4:

000	110	110	011	**111**	010
F1	F2	F3	F4	**F5**	F6

(F4, F5) mod8, Alter F5.

ITERATION 5:

000	110	110	011	111	**001**
F1	F2	F3	F4	F5	**F6**

(F5, F6) mod8, Alter F6.

Round 2: Block Size = 9, No. of Blocks = 2.

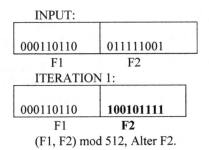

INPUT:

000110110	011111001
F1	F2

ITERATION 1:

000110110	**100101111**
F1	**F2**

(F1, F2) mod 512, Alter F2.

Thereby, we obtain the encrypted bit stream as Y' = 0110110100101111.

The Decryption Scheme

For decryption. 2's complement arithmetic has been followed to retrieve the plain text message in Y (in term of bits).

Round 1: Block Size = 9,
    No. of Blocks = 2.

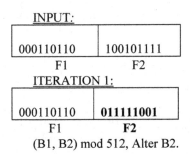

INPUT:

000110110	100101111
F1	F2

ITERATION 1:

000110110	**011111001**
F1	**F2**

(B1, B2) mod 512, Alter B2.

Round 2: Block Size = 3, No. of Blocks = 6.

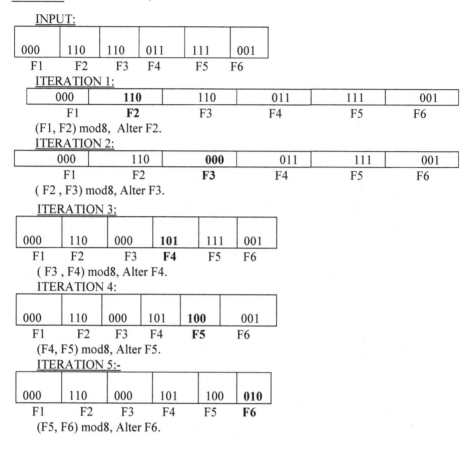

INPUT:

000	110	110	011	111	001
F1	F2	F3	F4	F5	F6

ITERATION 1:

000	**110**	110	011	111	001
F1	**F2**	F3	F4	F5	F6

(F1, F2) mod8, Alter F2.

ITERATION 2:

000	110	**000**	011	111	001
F1	F2	**F3**	F4	F5	F6

(F2 , F3) mod8, Alter F3.

ITERATION 3:

000	110	000	**101**	111	001
F1	F2	F3	**F4**	F5	F6

(F3 , F4) mod8, Alter F4.

ITERATION 4:

000	110	000	101	**100**	001
F1	F2	F3	F4	**F5**	F6

(F4, F5) mod8, Alter F5.

ITERATION 5:-

000	110	000	101	100	**010**
F1	F2	F3	F4	F5	**F6**

(F5, F6) mod8, Alter F6.

The Decrypted bit stream has been received as Y" = 000110000101100010. After discarding the redundant zeros from MSB we obtain 0110000101100010 which is identical with Input bit stream.

3   Flow Diagram of the Technique

Data bytes are fed into this cryptosystem and then blocks of equal bit size block is generated, then encryption and decryption is done simultaneously to check whether implementation is working or not. At last validation and testing is carried out to establish its feasibility which is given in details in Sect. 4 (Fig. 1).

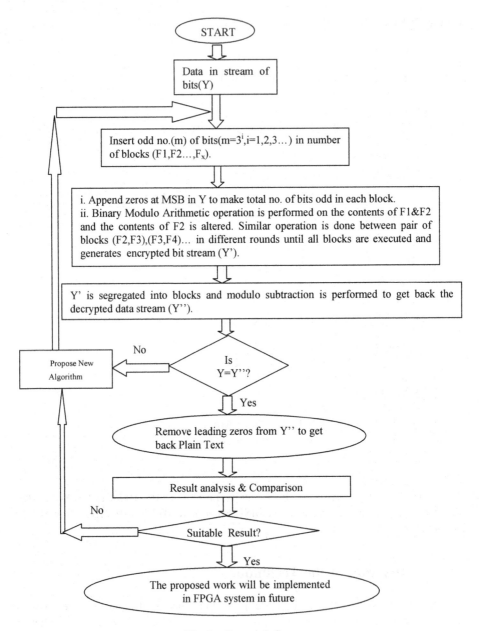

Fig. 1. Our work flow.

4   Results and Comparisons

The evenly distribution of character frequency of all the 256 ASCII characters, over the 0–255 region of the encrypted file of different algorithms are compared for validation and testing of the proposed algorithm.

We have applied our proposed Algorithm (MEDT) and RSA on Ten different files (exe, txt, doc, ping, jpg) for getting the plaintext and cipher text messages. For this article we have chosen one of those ten files for result analysis. Figures 2 and 3 demonstrates the frequencies of occurrence of all 256 ASCII characters in the source file, encrypted file with MEDT, and encrypted file with RSA. From frequency analysis it is clear that the characters in the encrypted file using MEDT are reasonably well distributed throughout the character space. Therefore our proposed Algorithm (MEDT) scheme may be analogous to RSA algorithm.

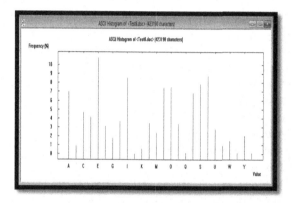

Fig. 2. Frequency diagram of source file

Our algorithm ensures better security against the source file and it also shows heterogeneity between the two files. As per the percentage occurrence of a particular character, the frequency distribution graph is drawn. That is it is not drawn on not the total number of occurrence.

We have performed homogeneity test of the source and encrypted file. For this purpose Chi-Square test has been performed. Table 1 and Fig. 4 shows the source file name, size and the corresponding Chi-Square values (using MEDT, RSA) for ten different files. Barring some exceptions we see that the as the file size increases Chi-Square value also increases proportionately. The high values prove that Chi-Square is highly significant at 1% level of significance. The degree of freedom (shown in Table 2) and in Fig. 5 of MEDT is 255 which is quite higher than that of the RSA.

Time Complexity is an important factor for every algorithm. So here we have compared the encryption and Decryption time for 10 different File Size using MEDT and RSA algorithm and plotted the graph for the same. Table 3 gives the encryption time analysis and Table 4 gives the decryption time analysis. Figures 6 and 7 illustrate

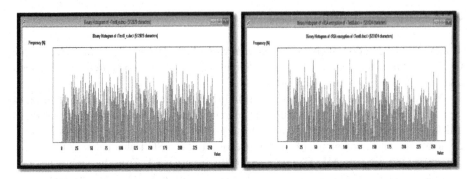

Fig. 3. Frequency diagram of RSA encrypted file and proposed technique encrypted file

Table 1. Indicates Chi Square value for MEDT algorithm and RSA algorithm

File size	File name	Chi Square value of MEDT	Chi Square values of RSA algorithm
15 kb	Out.exe	50865.846	22861.966
21 kb	Note.txt	50649.971	22861.966
51 kb	Resume.doc	49783.842	81858.947
102 kb	RoseDrawing.png	25862.820	23852.709
138 kb	Autmn.jpg	33215.645	23852.709
201 kb	StudyMaterial.txt	63309.245	22861.966
301 kb	Tool.exe	56233.193	22861.966
501 kb	Test8.doc	35776.117	39723.202
744 kb	NightSketch.jpeg	45461.436	23852.709
1 Mb	Cryptography.txt	22861.966	22861.966

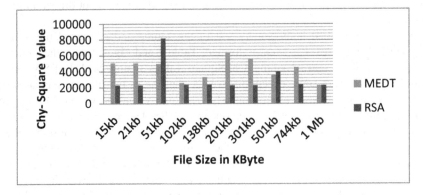

Fig. 4. Graphical representation of Chi-Square value for MEDT and RSA

Table 2. Degree of freedom of RSA and proposed technique

File size	File name	Degree of freedom MEDT	Degree of freedom RSA algorithm
15 kb	Out.exe	255	255
21 kb	Note.txt	255	255
51 kb	Resume.doc	255	195
102 kb	RoseDrawing.png	255	133
138 kb	Autmn.jpg	255	133
201 kb	StudyMaterial.txt	255	255
301 kb	Tool.exe	255	255
501 kb	Test8.doc	255	141
744 kb	NightSketch.jpeg	255	255
1 Mb	Cryptography.txt	255	255

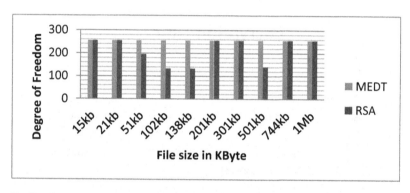

Fig. 5. Graphical representation of degree of freedom comparison between MEDT & RSA

Table 3. Encryption time of MEDT and RSA

Encryption time			
File size	File name	MEDT	RSA algorithm
15 kb	Out.exe	0.032 s	0.006 s
21 kb	Note.txt	0.028 s	0.010 s
51 kb	Resume.doc	0.054 s	0.022 s
102 kb	RoseDrawing.png	0.113 s	0.044 s
138 kb	Autmn.jpg	0.161 s	0.059 s
201 kb	StudyMaterial.txt	0.113 s	0.086 s
301 kb	Tool.exe	0.240 s	0.137 s
501 kb	Test8.doc	0.350 s	0.219 s
744 kb	NightSketch.jpeg	0.927 s	0.326 s
1 Mb	Cryptography.txt	1.320 s	0.444 s

Table 4. Encryption time of MEDT and RSA

Decryption time			
File size	File name	MEDT	RSA algorithm
15 kb	Out.exe	0.199 s	0.088 s
21 kb	Note.txt	0.123 s	0.141 s
51 kb	Resume.doc	0.220 s	0.315 s
102 kb	RoseDrawing.png	0.401 s	0.635 s
138 kb	Autmn.jpg	0.468 s	0.858 s
201 kb	StudyMaterial.txt	0.693 s	1.225 s
301 kb	Tool.exe	0.937 s	1.850 s
501 kb	Test8.doc	1.503 s	3.075 s
744 kb	NightSketch.jpeg	1.712 s	4.578 s
1 Mb	Cryptography.txt	2.364 s	6.328 s

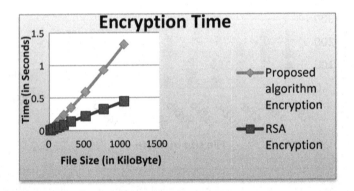

Fig. 6. Graphical representation of encryption time for the proposed algorithm (MEDT) & RSA

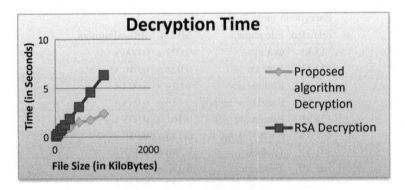

Fig. 7. Graphical representation of decryption time for the proposed algorithm (MEDT) & RSA

graphically the encryption and encryption time complexity respectively. The time taken to decrypt a file using MEDT Algorithm is very little compared to that using RSA.

5   Conclusion

The technique planned in this article takes little time to encipher and decipher irrespective of the high block length. The encrypted string will not generate any overhead bits. The scheme can be applied to any length of input stream which may enhance the security. Here each Block contains odd number of bits rather than even number of bits which may enhance security. The similar algorithms on Modular Arithmetic Techniques were based on considering even number of bits in every block to encipher and decipher data stream [4]. Hence our algorithm is a generalized algorithm. The scheme described here may be applicable to FPGA based embedded systems.

References

1. Guha, D., Basu, A.: An odd even block cipher based cryptosystem through modulo arithmetic technique (OEMAT). Int. J. Res. Eng. Technol. (IJRET) 2(11), 138–146 (2013). e-ISSN 2319-1163, p-ISSN 2321-7308
2. Guha, D., Chakraborty, R., Sinha, A.: A block cipher based cryptosystem through modified forward backward overlapped modulo arithmetic technique (MFBOMAT). Int. Organ. Sci. Res. J. Comput. Eng. (IOSRJCE) 13(1), 138–146 (2013). Article number 22, e-ISSN 2278-0661, p-ISSN 2278-8727
3. Chakraborty, R., Guha, D., Mandal, J.K.: A block cipher based cryptosystem through forward backward overlapped modulo arithmetic technique (FBOMAT). Int. J. Eng. Sci. Res. J. (IJESR) 2(5), 349–360 (2012). Article number 7, ISSN 2277-2685
4. Mandal, J.K., Sinha, S., Chakraborty, R.: A microprocessor-based block cipher through overlapped modulo arithmetic technique (OMAT). In: Proceedings of 12th International Conference of IEEE on Advanced Computing and Communications ADCOM-2004, 15–18 December, Ahmedabad, India, pp. 276–280 (2004)
5. Stallings, W.: Cryptography and Network Security: Principles and Practices, 3rd edn. Prentice Hall, Upper Saddle River (2003)
6. Kahate, A.: Cryptography and Network Security, 2nd edn. TMH, India (2009)
7. Forouzan, B.: Cryptography and Network Security, 4th edn. TMH, India (2010)
8. Cole, E.: Hiding in Plain Text. Wiley, Hoboken (2003)
9. Pachghare, V.K.: Cryptography and Information Security. Prentice-hall of India Pvt. Ltd, Delhi

Energy Efficient Secured Sharing of Intraoral Gingival Information in Digital Way (EESS-IGI)

Arindam Sarkar[1(✉)], Joydeep Dey[2], Anirban Bhowmik[3],
Jyotsna Kumar Mandal[4], and Sunil Karforma[5]

[1] Ramakrishna Mission Vidyamandira, Belur Math, Howrah 711202, India
arindam.vb@gmail.com
[2] M.U.C Women's College, The University of Burdwan,
Bardhaman 713104, India
joydeepmcabu@gmail.com
[3] Cyber Research and Training Institute, The University of Burdwan,
Bardhaman 713101, India
animca2008@gmail.com
[4] Department of Computer Science and Engineering, University of Kalyani,
Kalyani 741235, India
jkm.cse@gmail.com
[5] Department of Computer Science, The University of Burdwan,
Bardhaman 713104, India
dr.sunilkarforma@gmail.com

Abstract. This paper presents a novel cryptographic scheme for sharing intraoral information secretly where key is used to encrypt the secret Gingivitis image and then the secret is shared among 'n' number of experts. Periodontal diseases are almost a frequent disease in human body. The early stage of gingival inflammations with gum bleeding is called Gingivitis. If this disease is not diagnosed properly then it spreads to advanced Periodontotitis. Secured online transmission for such intraoral images is more significant factor in the advanced medicinal domain. An intraoral image is partially shared with 'n' number of recipients including patient for better expert opinions by applying encryption algorithm. While transmitting such vital images, the patients' confidential secrets are preserved in such a way that minimum 'k' number of recipients can only reconstruct without change of visual appearance. This scheme is valid for various types of Gingivitis with independent number of shares and threshold value. Different parametric tests have been done and results are compared with some existing classical techniques, which show comparable results for the proposed technique.

Keywords: Gingivitis · Secret sharing · Session key

© Springer Nature Singapore Pte Ltd. 2018
J. K. Mandal and D. Sinha (Eds.): CSI 2017, CCIS 836, pp. 584–599, 2018.
https://doi.org/10.1007/978-981-13-1343-1_49

1 Introduction

Protection of sensitive medical images is an important issue, at the time of transmission over Internet. Craniofacial expression reflects the good health of a person. Any sensitive data of the patients with periodontium diseases, needs to be tightly ciphered while transmitting over the Internet. Modern encryption algorithms [9–12] in the field of cryptography are better choice of solution which yields protected data communication. In the era of advanced medical domain, Gingivitis is an important dental disease which needs to be treated properly within the stipulated time frame. If Gingivitis left untreated, then it shall lead to Periodontitis and hence pulpal necrosis or permanent molar extraction. Besides these, there is a strong connection exists between periodontal disease with atherosclerosis and heart disease. The vital risk of clogged arteries and heart diseases are increased in such conditions with further worsen of such types Type I Cardio Vascular diseases (CVDs) [6]. Myocardial Infarctions are also linked with severe periodontal diseases that are caused due to blocked arteries. Periodontal diseases lead to premature birth of baby i.e. a woman with existing gum diseases during pregnancy period is highly probable to deliver baby too early, with infant bearing low BMI i.e. decreased Body Mass Index. Bacteria that contribute in gum disease may lead to lung infections; even it may worsen the existing lung conditions in case of hospitalized geriatric patients. Here the bacteria may go through lungs from the mouth to cause severe pneumonia attacks. Figure 1 shows an intraoral Gingivitis image

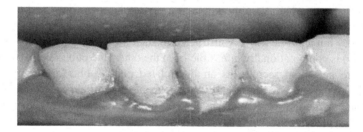

Fig. 1. Intraoral Gingivitis image

Food habits and life style of a person affects his oral hygiene. The food stuffs with higher calorie values like Yoghurt, dry fruits contribute in greater volume in advancing periodontal diseases. The connection between food values and Gingivitis is given in the following Figs. 2 and 3 shows Gingivitis affected intraoral image of a middle aged man.

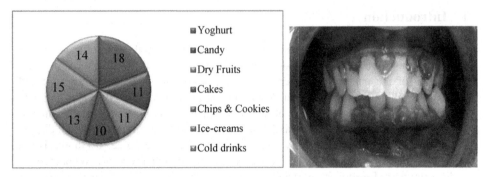

Fig. 2. Percentage of food stuffs contributing to Gingivitis   **Fig. 3.** Common Gingivitis attack.

Transmission of secret image is the most significant issue in cryptographic technique. In recent times wide ranges of techniques are developed to protect data and information from eavesdroppers [13–16]. These algorithms have their virtue and shortcomings. In encryption, a key specifies the particular transformation of plaintext into cipher text, or vice versa during decryption. Encryption algorithms which use the same key for both encryption and decryption are known as symmetric key algorithms. Asymmetric key algorithms use a pair of keys or keypair, a public key and a private one. Public keys are used for encryption or signature verification; private ones decrypt and sign [17]. The public key cryptography has two different keys but mathematically related to each other [1]. A public key and a private key was proposed by Whitfield Diffie and Martin Hellman in a ground breaking 1976 paper [2]. A public key is related to private key but a public key is constructed in such a way that calculation of one key (private key) is computationally infeasible from the other (the public key). But still both the keys are generated secretly as an interrelated pair. Public key cryptography is described as "the most revolutionary new concept in the field since polyalphabetic substitution emerged in the Renaissance" [3]. The public-key is freely distributed in a public-key cryptosystems, while its paired private key must remain secret. In a public-key encryption system, encryption is done by using public key while for decryption private or secret key is used. Being unsuccessful in finding such a system Diffie and Hellman showed that by presenting the Diffie-Hellman key exchange protocol, public-key cryptography was indeed possible a solution that is now widely use in secure communication to allow two parties to secretly agree on shared encryption key [4]. A widespread academic effort in finding a practical public-key encryption system was initiated due to Diffie and Hellman's publication, as a result in 1978 Ronald Rivest, Adi Shamir and Len Adleman design the technique which is known as RSA algorithm [5].

In this paper a secured technique has been proposed to manage the transmission of Gingivitis images through secretly transmitting the shares to different recipients along. The organization of this paper is as follows. Section 2 of this paper deals with the background and related work. Sections 3 and 4 represents the problem statement and the solution domain respectively. Proposed technique is discussed in Sect. 5. Experimental results are given in Sect. 6. Analysis regarding various aspects of the technique and results has been presented in Sect. 7. Conclusions with the future scopes are drawn in Sect. 8 and that of references at end.

2 Background and Related Work

The literal meaning of periodontal is "perio" means around and "dontal" means teeth. In simple words, periodontal disease is a type of gum disease with more gum swelling which may affect our jaw bones and related nerves and tissues. Bacterial biofilms are the major reason behind the damage of gums, cementum covering upon roots, alveolar nerves, periodontal ligaments, etc. Gingivitis is one of the most common infections occur in the craniofacial area. In United States, minimum 35% of adults aged 30 years and older have Periodontitis, as statistical data retrieved. About 22% suffer from Type I Gingivitis, and 13% belong to Type II Gingivitis [6].

Such a vital gingivitis disease needs proper medical diagnosis in appropriate time so that the patient gets exact medical opinion in terms of diagnosis, healing and recovery. For this online secured technique, various intraoral images are to be transmitted to several dentists and physicians for their expert opinion. Some related works listed below for secret image sharing over the Internet.

2.1 Shamir's Secret Sharing Scheme

Shamir's [7] Secret Sharing Scheme is based on (k, n) threshold based secret sharing technique. In this scheme a $(k - 1)$ degree polynomial is necessary. The polynomial function of order $(k - 1)$ is constructed as

$$f(x) = \left(p_0 + p_1 x + p_2 x^2 + p_3 x^3 + \cdots + p_{k-1} x^{k-1}\right) mod\, m$$

Where, p_0 is the secret and m is a prime number and all other coefficients are selected randomly from secret.

Each of the n shares is a pair (x_i, z_i) of numbers satisfying $f(x_i) = z_i$ and $x_i > 0$, $1 \leq i \leq n$ and $0 < x_1 < x_2 < x_3 < \ldots < x_k \leq m - 1$. Given any k shares, the polynomials are uniquely determined and hence the secret p_0 can be computed via Lagrange's interpolation.

2.2 Blakey's Secret Sharing Scheme

Blakey [8] used geometry to solve secret sharing problem. The secret message is a point in a k- dimensional space and n shares are affine hyper planes that intersect in this point. The set solution $y = (y_1, y_2, y_3 \ldots y_k)$ to an equation $p_1 y_1 + p_2 y_2 + p_3 y_3 + \cdots + p_k y_k = b$ forms an affine hyper plane. The secret the intersection point is obtained by finding the intersection of any k of these planes.

3   Problem Domain

There is an urge to diagnose and treat such Gingivitis with preservation of patients' confidentiality data. The positive materialization of this paper is the security of patient's medical data is preserved without any data leakage. The existing secret sharing system has several limitations. Some of them are listed below:

- In existing secret sharing technique, it is easier to share patients' private medical reports and images intentionally for the publicity, harassment and advertisement purpose without the legal consent of the patient.
- In many of the existing techniques, entire secret data is kept in a single channel. The secret data cannot be revealed if the channel or key is lost or corrupted.
- Misuse of data in terms of distortion in the images containing alveolar bones, and then tendency to deflect the curve of treatment. Hence probability of fake dental mediclaim and tooth patent policy re-imbursement is high.
- Insecured image transmission leads to inappropriate dental diagnosis and further ailment which may results to permanent teeth extraction.

4   Solution Domain

The limitations of existing secret sharing approach have been eliminated through proposed technique. The criteria based on which existing secret sharing approach is modified are:

- Data are secretly shared among n no. of recipients because treatment of such a significant gingivitis disease requires expert opinion from multiple experts. As, there is 'n' number of recipients, chance of lost or corruption of entire data due to corruption of medium or key is minimal.
- 'k' number of recipients must agree to reconstruct the original image which is minimum threshold.

5 Proposed Methodology

In this proposed method a mask is generated using *GenerateSecretMask*() method for generate the encrypted share of the secret image. After that Gingivitis affected image is ANDed with secret Mask to generate secret shares. A robust session key is generated through *SecretKeyGen*() method. This partially opened share gets encrypted using robust session key. Finally, these ciphered shares are individually transmitted to the n numbers of intended recipients by encrypted with recipient's public key.

The objective of this technique is to enhanced performance in terms of security at the time of transmission of Gingivitis intraoral image to follow up from different expertise dentists for exact specified treatment, even from various remote geographic zones.

Section 5.1 describes the Session key generation method and mask generation method is presented in Sect. 5.2

5.1 Session Key Generation

The Adhaar Card number (A) and the private key (P) of the patient is fed into RSA algorithm which generates an encrypted key. Now this encrypted key is passed through MD5 Hash generation function to produce a key of length 128 bits.

SecretKeyGen( ) **Algorithm**

Requirement: Two large prime numbers
Input: Patient's Aadhar Card no (A), Sender's private key (P)
Output: 128 bits key
Method:
{/*Encryption key generation*/}
    If (! *PrimeNo_Check*(*A*)) *Then*
      $A \leftarrow nearest\_CoPrime\_to(A)$
    End if
    $S = A \times P$
    $D(S) = (A-1) \times (P-1)$
    $L:$ An integer $,1 < L < D(S)$ such that $GCD(L, D(S)) = 1.$
    $K:$ An integer$, 1 < K < D(S)$ such that $L * K \equiv 1 \ (mod \ D(S))$
    $EncryptedKey = MD5 \ (L\ );$

5.2   Mask Generation

The objective of generation of mask is to hide the secret data from the unauthorized external access. The purpose of this algorithm is to raise the encryption complexities on the data by using different mathematical hardness. Here we are wrapping a protective security layer on the secret data before transmitting them online over the Internet. The main task of intruders present in the network is to steal the information while transmission, and then to use that information for unethical and unsocial works. An intruder sitting in the middle interface during the transmission can not reveal the wrapped up data hidden by applying this mask. Thus, only the minimum details are revealed in another format and the remaining architecture for hiding the data are kept unknown to the intruders. This mask generation algorithms takes two inputs number of shares (n) and threshold value (k). Depending upon the value of 'n' and 'k', the $mask[][n]$ matrix is calculated. The number of recipients i.e. 'n' and the minimum number of shares i.e. threshold value 'k' is put into the Mask Generator. The length of each masks can be calculated as to $n_{C_{n-k}}$.

A snapshot which contains a set of five share masks corresponding to three threshold values given in the following Table 1.

Table 1. Snapshots of shares

1	1	0	1	0	1	0	1	0	1	Share mask no. 1
0	1	1	1	1	1	1	0	0	0	Share mask no. 2
0	1	1	0	1	0	0	1	1	1	Share mask no. 3
1	0	0	1	0	0	1	1	1	0	Share mask no. 4
1	0	1	0	1	1	1	0	1	1	Share mask no. 5

Consider the following secret data as "**Prague1024**" then corresponding partially opened secret shares can be shown in the following Table 2.

Table 2. Snapshot of partially opened secret share

0	0	0	0	U	e	1	0	2	4	Share no. 1
0	r	A	G	0	0	0	0	2	4	Share no. 2
P	0	A	G	0	e	1	0	0	4	Share no. 3
P	r	0	G	U	0	1	0	4	0	Share no. 4
P	r	A	0	U	e	0	0	0	0	Share no. 5

Complete algorithm is illustrated as follows:

Proposed Algorithm

Requirement: Gingivitis affected intraoral image
Input: Patient's Aadhar Card no, Total no. of shares (n), no. of threshold (k)
Output: n number of secret shares of Gingivitis affected intraoral image.
Method: Encrypted   key   is   constructed   using $SecretKeyGen(\ )$
and $GenerateSecretMask(\ )$ is helps to generate secret mask. After that Gingivitis
affected image is ANDed with secret Mask to generate secret shares. This partially
opened shares gets encrypted using $SecretKeyGen(\ )$ and finally shares are
transmitted to the n numbers of intended recipients by encrypted with recipients
public key.

{/*Encryption key generation*/}
$\quad EncryptedKey[\ ]$
$\quad = SecretKeyGen$(Patient's Aadhar Card no, sender's private key)
{/*Secret Mask generation*/}
for $i = 1$ to $n_{C_{k-1}}$ **do**
$\quad$ **for** $j = 1$ to n **do**
$\quad\quad Mask[n_{C_{k-1}}][n] = GenerateSecretMask(\ );$
$\quad$ **End for**
End for
{/*ANDing of Gingivitis affected image with Secret Mask to generate secret
shares*/}
Set p=1, q=1
for $i = 1$ to n **do**
$\quad$ **for** $j = 1$ to $n_{C_{n-k}}$ **do**
$\quad\quad Share[i][j] = Mask[i][j]\ \&\ Image[p][q]$
$\quad\quad$ **increment** j, p, q
$\quad$ **End for**
$\quad$ **increment** i
End for
{/*Encryption of Partially open shares*/}
for $i = 1$ to n **do**
$\quad$ **for** $j = 1$ to $n_{C_{n-k}}$ **do**
$\quad\quad EncryptedShare[i][j] = Share[i][j]XOR\ EncryptedKey[j]$
$\quad\quad$ **increment** j
$\quad$ **End for**
$\quad$ **increment** i
$\quad EncryptedKey[\ ] = EncryptedKey[\ ] \gg j$
End for
{/*RSA Encryption of Encrypted shares with Recepient's Public key*/}
for $i = 1$ to n **do**
$\quad$ FinalShare[i]= $RSA\ (EncryptedShare[i], Recepient's publicKey[i])$
$\quad$ **increment** i
$\quad$ **End for**
Report n transmittable shares

6   Experimental Results

In this section result of the proposed technique is computed on different types of images having various sizes with extensive performance analysis. The comparative study among proposed techniques and the existing RSA, Triple-DES (168 bits), AES (128 bits) has been done based on twenty files by performing different types of experiment.

Statistical analysis of the NIST test suite has been performed to evaluate randomness of the proposed session key. These tests focused on a variety of different types of non-randomness that could exist in a sequence. Some tests are decomposable into a variety of subtests. Frequency (monobit) statistical test is performed for the proposed techniques along with existing and results of these tests compared and analyzed in Sect. 6.1. Twenty files of different size have been taken. Results are generated using proposed techniques, RSA, TDES (168 bits) and AES (128 bits) for all files. Using these results, comparison of encryption and decryption time presented in Sect. 6.2. Avalanche, Strict Avalanche effects and Bit independence has been done and presented in Sect. 6.3. Comparison based on Chi-Square values are presented in Sect. 6.4. Different image files have been taken to perform character frequency, entropy, floating frequency and autocorrelation test in Sect. 6.4.

6.1   Statistical Analysis

These tests focused on a variety of different types of non-randomness that could exist in a session key sequence. The objective of the test is to find proportion of zeroes and ones for the entire sequence which determine whether the number of ones and zeros in a sequence are approximately the same as would be expected for a truly random sequence. The test assesses the closeness of the fraction of ones to ½, that is, the number of ones and zeroes in a sequence should be about the same. In this experiment expected proportion for passing the test has been set to **0.972766**. Table 3 shows proportion of passing and uniformity of distribution.

Table 3. Proportion of passing and uniformity of distribution for frequency

Technique	Expected proportion	Observed proportion	Status for proportion of passing	P-value of P-values	Status for uniform/non-uniform distribution
Proposed	0.972766	0.985329	Success	2.835246e-03	Uniform
DES		0.979437	Success	3.122711e-10	Non-uniform
TDES		0.983333	Success	3.571386e-01	Uniform
AES (128)		0.984871	Success	3.915294e-07	Non-uniform
RSA		0.986667	Success	4.122711e-10	Non-uniform

From Table 3 it is seen that all proposed techniques along with existing technique passed the frequency (monobits) test successfully because observed proportion values of all the proposed techniques are grater than expected proportion value. It is also noticed that in case of proposed techniques, observed proportion for passing the test are quite comparable with existing DES, TDES, AES (128), RSA. It can be concluded that proposed techniques perform at par with existing benchmark technique.

6.2 Encryption/Decryption Time

Twenty image files of different sizes varying from $1,063$ bytes to $6,735,934$ bytes have been taken to generate the data containing various attributes for evaluation of the proposed technique. The encryption times (Enc.) and decryption times (Dec.) of different image files obtained using proposed and existing TDES, AES. Enc. varies from 15 ms to 674 ms for proposed, from 12 ms to 374 ms for AES, from 12 ms to 1379 ms for TDES. Dec. varies from 15 ms to 377 ms for proposed, from 15 ms to 399 ms for AES, from 15 ms to 1767 ms for TDES.

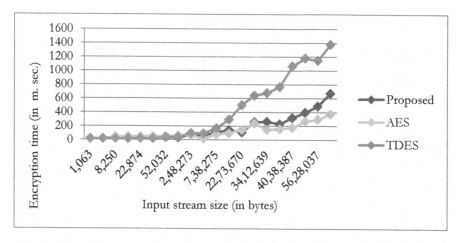

Fig. 4. Graphical representation of encryption time against the varying size of input files

Figure 4 and 5 shows the graphical representation of the relationship between the encryption times against the source files and the decryption times against the source files respectively for proposed, AES and TDES techniques. Enc. and Dec. for proposed and AES are near equal but much lower than that of TDES. In both the figures, the gradients of the curves for TDES are higher for larger source files.

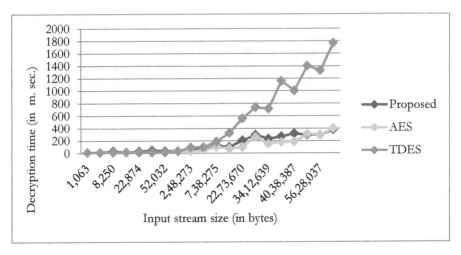

Fig. 5. Graphical representation of decryption time against the varying size of input files

6.3   Avalanche, Strict Avalanche and Bit Independence

Comparison between the source and encrypted byte has been made and changed of bits in encrypted bytes has been observed for a single bit change in the original message byte for the entire or a relative large number of bytes. To measure the Bit Independence concept, the correlation coefficient between the jth and k^{th} components of the output difference string is needed, which is called the Avalanche vector A^{e_i}. The higher and closer value to 1.0, the better Avalanche and Strict Avalanche is said to be satisfied. Twenty files of different sizes varying from 3216 bytes to $5,456,704$ bytes have been taken for Avalanche, Strict Avalanche and Bit Independence test. Average Avalanche values of proposed and existing RSA, TDES, AES are 0.9980800, 0.9999469, 0.9999142, and 0.9998914 respectively. Average Strict Avalanche values of proposed and existing RSA, TDES, AES are 0.9967630, 0.9996540, 0.9996324, 0.9996890 respectively shown in Table 4. Average Bit Independence values of proposed and existing RSA, TDES, AES are 0.7262960, 0.7211989, 0.7147735, and 0.7190952 respectively.

Table 4. Comparisons of average values of Avalanche, Strict Avalanche and Bit Independence

Techniques	Average values of		
	Avalanche	Strict Avalanche	Bit Independence
Proposed	0.9980800	0.9967630	0.7262960
RSA	0.9999469	0.9996540	0.7211989
TDES	0.9999142	0.9996324	0.7147735
AES	0.9998914	0.9996890	0.7190952

6.4   Analysis of Character Frequencies, Floating Frequencies and Autocorrelation

Program access both the original and encrypted files and stores the occurrence of each character in an array. The smoother or less curves in the spectrum of frequency distribution indicate that it is harder for a cryptanalyst to detect the original bytes which implies better degree of security. Well distributed floating frequencies are indicate the robustness of the encryption and finally Autocorrelation indicates goodness of the technique.

Figure 6 shows the spectrum of frequency distribution for the input source file. Figure 7 shows the spectrum of frequency distribution of encrypted image shares using proposed technique for the same input source file. It has been observed that frequencies are widely distributed in proposed encrypted file.

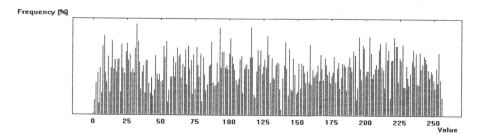

Fig. 6. Graphical representation of frequency distribution spectrum of the input source stream

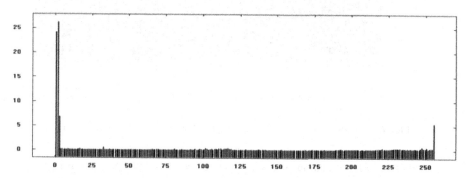

Fig. 7. Graphical representation of frequency distribution spectrum of the encrypted stream using proposed technique

Figure 8 shows the spectrum of floating frequencies for the input source stream. Figure 9 shows the spectrum of floating frequencies of encrypted file using proposed technique for the same input source file. From the figures it is observed that floating frequencies of proposed technique encrypted files indicates the high degree of security.

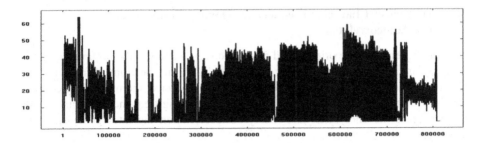

Fig. 8. Floating frequency of the input source file

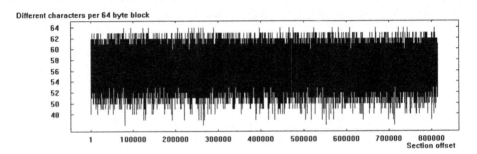

Fig. 9. Floating frequency of the encrypted file using proposed technique

Analysis of autocorrelation of twenty source files has been performed using proposed technique. Figure 10 shows the spectrum of autocorrelation of source file. Figure 11 shows the spectrum of autocorrelation of encrypted using proposed technique for the same input source file. From the figure it is observed that autocorrelation of proposed technique indicate the high degree of security.

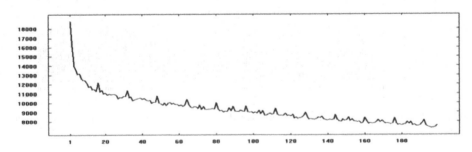

Fig. 10. Autocorrelation of the input source file

Number of characters that match

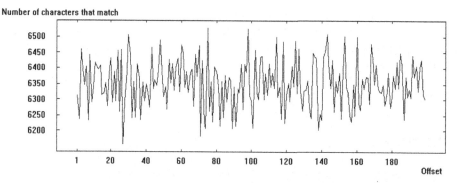

Fig. 11. Autocorrelation of the encrypted file using proposed technique

7   Analysis of Results

The technique is very simple and easy to implement in various high level language. The test results also show that the performance and security provided by the technique is good and comparable to standard technique. Since the encryption and decryption times are much lower, so processing speed is very high. The method takes minimum amount of resources which is greatly handle the resource constraints criteria of wireless communication. This method generates a large number of keys. No platform specific optimizations were done in the actual implementation, thus performance should be similar over varied implementation platform. The whole procedure is randomized, thus resulting in a unique process for a unique session, which makes it harder for a cryptanalyst to find a base to start with. This technique is applicable to ensure security in message transmission in any form and in any size in wireless communication.

Measures of central tendency, dispersion and Chi-Square value have been performed between the source and corresponding cipher streams generated using proposed technique. All measures indicate that the degree of non-homogeneity of the encrypted stream with respect to the source stream is good. In proposed technique it is observed that floating frequencies of encrypted files are indicates the high degree of security of proposed technique. The cipher stream generated through proposed technique is negligibly correlated with the source stream.

8   Conclusion and Future Scope

Proposed technique may effectively resist data correlation statistical attack. The technique generates an entirely different cipher stream with a small change in the key and technique totally fails to decrypt the cipher stream with a slightly different secret session key. It ensures that the technique has a grater key sensitivity. Encryption algorithm can work with any block length and thus not require padding, which result identical size of files both in original and encrypted file. So, proposed technique has no space overhead. Since the session key is used only once for each transmission, so there is a minimum time stamp which expires automatically at the end of each transmission of information. Thus the cryptanalyst may not be able guess the session key for that particular session.

Future scope of the proposed technique is to apply soft computing guided different metaheuristics tools to generate robust session key in this problem domain.

References

1. Cryptography key (cryptography). http://en.wikipedia.org/wiki/Key_. Accessed 06 Aug 2017
2. Diffie, W., Hellman, M.: Multi-user cryptographic techniques. In: Proceedings of the AFIPS, vol. 45, pp. 109–112, 8 June 1976
3. Kahn, D.: Cryptology goes public. Foreign Aff. **58**(1(Fall, 1979)), 141–159 (1979)
4. Diffie, W., Hellman, M.: New directions in cryptography. IEEE Trans. Inform. Theory **22**(6), 644–654 (1976)
5. Rivest, R., Shamir, A., Adleman, L.: A method for obtaining digital signatures and public-key cryptosystems. Commun. ACM **21**(2), 120–126 (1978). Previously released as an MIT Technical Memo in April 1977, and published in Martin Gardner's Scientific American Mathematical recreations column
6. Sfyroeras, G.S., Roussas, N., Saleptsis, V.G., Argyriou, C., Giannoukas, A.D.: Association between periodontal disease and stroke. J. Vasc. Surg. **55**(4), 1178–1184 (2012)
7. Shamir, A.: How to share a secret? Commun. ACM **22**(11), 612–613 (1979)
8. G.R. Blakley: Safeguarding cryptographic keys. In: Proceedings of AFIPS International Workshop on Managing Requirements Knowledge, p. 313 (1979)
9. Praveenkumar, P., Catherine Priya, P., Avila, J., et al.: Wirel. Pers. Commun. **97**, 5573–5595 (2017). https://doi.org/10.1007/s11277-017-4795-x. Springer, US. Print ISSN 0929-6212, Online ISSN 1572-834X
10. Anusudha, K., Venkateswaran, N., Valarmathi, J.: Multimed Tools Appl. **76**(2), 2911–2932 (2017). https://doi.org/10.1007/s11042-015-3213-1. Springer, US. Print ISSN 1380-7501, Online ISSN 1573-7721
11. Al-Haj, A., Mohammad, A., Amer, A.: J. Digit. Imaging **30**(1), 26–38 (2017). https://doi.org/10.1007/s10278-016-9901-1
12. Sarkar, A., Mandal, J.K.: Computational science guided soft computing based cryptographic technique using ant colony intelligence for wireless communication (ACICT). Int. J. Comput. Sci. Appl. (IJCSA) **4**(5), 61–73 (2014). https://doi.org/10.5121/ijcsa.2014.4505. ISSN 2200 - 0011
13. Sarkar, A., Mandal, J.K.: Intelligent soft computing based cryptographic technique using chaos synchronization for wireless communication (CSCT). Int. J. Ambient Syst. Appl. (IJASA) **2**(3), 11–20 (2014). https://doi.org/10.5121/ijasa.2014.2302. ISSN 2321 - 6344
14. Sarkar, A., Mandal, J.K.: Secured transmission through multi layer perceptron in wireless communication (STMLP). International Journal of Mobile Network Communications & Telematics (IJMNCT) **4**(4), 1–16 (2014). ISSN 1839 – 5678
15. Sarkar, A., Mandal, J.K.: Cryptanalysis of key exchange method using computational intelligence guided multilayer perceptron in wireless communication (CKEMLP). Adv. Comput. Intell. Int. J. (ACII) **1**(1), 1–9 (2014). ISSN 2317 – 4113

16. Sarkar, A., Mandal, J.K.: Neuro Genetic Key Based Recursive Modulo-2 Substitution Using Mutated Character for Online Wireless Communication (NGKRMSMC). Int. J. Comput. Sci. Inf. Technol. (IJCSITY) **1**(4), 49–59 (2014). ISSN 2320 - 8457
17. Sarkar, A., Chongder, J.: Cycle formation and hopfield network based key tuning and enciphering. In: Proceedings of the Third International Conference on Computing and Systems (ICCS-2016), 21–22 January 2016, Department of Computer Science, The University of Burdwan, WB, India, pp. 114–119 (2016). ISBN 978-93-85777-13-4

Digital Image Processing

A Novel Hierarchical Classification Scheme for Adaptive Quadtree Partitioning Based Fractal Image Coding

Utpal Nandi[1(✉)] and Jyotsna Kumar Mandal[2(✉)]

[1] Department of Computer Science, Vidyasagar University,
Paschim Medinipur, India
nandi.3utpal@gmail.com
[2] Department of Computer Science and Engineering,
University of Kalyani, Nadia, India
jkm.cse@gmail.com

Abstract. Fractal image coding becomes an efficient image coding method because of its very high rate of compression, low decoding time and resolution independent image decoding. However, a problem of known fractal coding techniques is its high encoding time. The technique partitions an image into sub-images (non-overlapping range and overlapping domain) and all ranges are compared with all possible domains to find the most similar domain that takes huge time to encode an image. In this paper, a new hierarchical classification scheme for fractal image coding has been proposed to address this issue that work on adaptive quadtree partitioning. It groups all the domains hierarchically into two levels and all ranges are only compared with domains of the same hierarchical class. The fractal image coding with proposed classification scheme and adaptive quadtree partitioning significantly reduces the encoding time than its counter parts without degradation of image quality and compression rate.

Keywords: Fractal image compression · Hierarchical classification scheme
PSNR · Adaptive quadtree partitioning

1 Introduction

Compression of image reduces its size and is very important before storing and communicating it over network. Fractal based image coding recently got attention for this task since it decodes image in resolution dependent way with very high compression rate and decoding speed is also very high. In the encoding process, the input image is divided into a number of domain and range and most similar domain must be searched for each range. The large number of comparisons between range and domain require huge time. The major limitation of fractal based coding is therefore its long encoding time. However, the domains can be classified to reduce the number of comparisons where each range is compared with only same class domains as range. There were varieties of schemes to meet this goal. The conventional classification presented by Fisher [1] grouped domains into 72 classes based on proportional average and variance of four quadrants of domains to reduce number of range-domain

© Springer Nature Singapore Pte Ltd. 2018
J. K. Mandal and D. Sinha (Eds.): CSI 2017, CCIS 836, pp. 603–615, 2018.
https://doi.org/10.1007/978-981-13-1343-1_50

comparisons. Xing et al. [2] improved the Fisher's classification scheme by grouping domains into 576 classes according to combinations of average and its variance in hierarchical way. Bhattacharya et al. [3] proposed a hierarchical classification scheme and reduced encoding time well. Jayamohan et al. [4] suggested a classification scheme depending on local fractal dimension using B+ tree. They [5] also did the same using AVL tree. Wang and Zheng [6] classified domains by applying pearson's correlation coefficient as similarity measure. Nandi and Mandal [7] proposed a fast classification strategy using 64 bit sub-image id. The existing classification schemes were specially designed for quadtree partitioning based fractal image coding. But, the quadtree partitioning divides image block into four equal quadrants without using image context and does not share self-similar portions of image. As a result, the quality of reconstructed fractal compressed image degrades significantly. To deal with this problem, adaptive quadtree partitioning [8, 9] can be applied where the partitioning is based on image context to share self-similar portions. However, there are few known classification schemes that fit with adaptive quadtree partitioning. Nandi and Mandal applied archetype classification scheme [10, 11] in adaptive quadtree partitioning based fractal image coding. But, the technique suffers from high encoding time. In this paper, a novel hierarchical classification scheme has been proposed for adaptive quadtree partitioning based fractal image coding that significantly reduces the encoding time and offers also better decoded image quality and compression ratio. The detail of adaptive quadtree partitioning is given in Sect. 2. The proposed hierarchical classification scheme is explained in Sect. 3. The fractal image coding with adaptive quadtree partitioning and proposed hierarchical classification scheme are discussed in Sect. 4. The performance analysis is done in Sect. 5. The comparative experimental results in terms of encoding time, reconstructed image quality (i.e. PSNR) and compression ratio are given and analyzed in Sect. 6. Final conclusions are made in Sect. 7 and references are given at end.

2   Adaptive Quadtree Partitioning Scheme

The adaptive quadtree partitioning splits image block based on its gray values to find structure that are similar with itself at different scale. Consider an $R \times C$ image block with left-top point (t_1, t_2) and $G_{i,j}$ is the gray value of point (i, j), $t_1 \leq i \leq t_1 + R - 1$, $t_2 \leq j \leq t_2 + C - 1$. It partitions image block (range/domain) into four unequal parts using three steps as shown in Fig. 1. In the first step, the scheme partitions the image block horizontally into upper and lower sub-images. It obtains the horizontal line (HL) for partitioning by Eq. 1 where the biased horizontal difference (BHD_i) of ith horizontal line is calculated in Eq. 2 for each horizontal line i, $t_1 \leq i \leq t_1 + R - 1$.

$$HL = MAX\ (BHD_i),\ Subject\ to\ t_1 \leq i \leq t_1 + R - 1 \tag{1}$$

$$BHD_i = MIN(i, R - i - 1) \left| \sum\nolimits_{j=t2}^{t2+C-1} G_{i,j} - \sum\nolimits_{j=t2}^{t2+C-1} G_{i+1,j} \right| \tag{2}$$

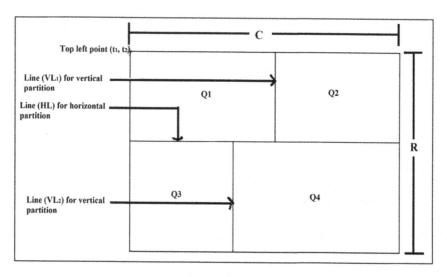

Fig. 1. The adaptive quadtree partitioning scheme

In the next step, the upper sub-image is divided vertically into left and right portions. The vertical line (VL_1) for partitioning is selected by using the Eq. 3 where the biased vertical difference ($BVD1_j$) of jth vertical line is calculated in Eq. 4 for each vertical line j, $t_2 \le j \le t_2 + V - 1$.

$$VL_1 = MAX\left(BVD1_j\right), \text{ Subject to } t_2 \le j \le t_2 + C - 1 \tag{3}$$

$$BVD1_j = MIN(j, C - j - 1)\left|\sum_{i=t1}^{HL-1} G_{i,j} - \sum_{i=t1}^{HL-1} G_{i,j+1}\right| \tag{4}$$

Finally, the lower sub-image is partitioned vertically into left and right portion. The scheme gets the vertical line (VL_2) for partitioning by using the Eq. 5 where the biased vertical differences ($BVD2_j$) of jth vertical line is evaluated in Eq. 6 for each vertical line j, $t_2 \le j \le t_2 + C - 1$.

$$VL_2 = MAX\left(BVD2_j\right), \text{ Subject to } t_2 \le j \le t_2 + C - 1 \tag{5}$$

$$BVD2_j = MIN(j, C - j - 1)\left|\sum_{i=HL}^{t1+R-1} G_{i,j} - \sum_{i=HL}^{t1+R-1} G_{i,j+1}\right| \tag{6}$$

3   Proposed Hierarchical Classification Scheme for Adaptive Quadtree Partitioning

The proposed Hierarchical classification scheme is designed for adaptive quadtree partitioning based fractal image coding. The steps of the classification scheme are given in algorithm 1. Initially, an input sub-image (range/domain) is taken as shown in Fig. 2

(a). Then, the sub-image is partitioned into four quadrants Q_1, Q_2, Q_3 and Q_4 (Fig. 2 (b)) using adaptive quadtree partitioning scheme. For each quadrant Q_i, $1 \leq i \leq 4$ obtain the sum of all the pixel values of Q_i as QS_i using Eq. 7 where n_j is the number of pixels and G_{i1}, G_{i2}, ...G_{inj} are the pixel values of Q_i.

$$QS_i = \sum\nolimits_{k=1}^{n_j} G_{ik} \tag{7}$$

There are 24 classes based on orientations of four quadrants Q_i, $1 \leq i \leq 4$. The appropriate class of first level is assigned to the sub-image based on its quadrant ordering. Then, each quadrant Q_i, $1 \leq i \leq 4$ is partitioned into four sub-quadrants Q_{i1}, Q_{i2}, Q_{i3} and Q_{i4} (Fig. 2 (c)) using adaptive quadtree partitioning scheme. Again, the calculation of sum of the pixel values as QS_{ij}, $1 \leq j \leq 4$, for each sub-quadrant Q_{ij}, $1 \leq i \leq 4$, are done using Eq. 8 where n_{ij} is the number of pixels and G_{ij1}, G_{ij2}, ... G_{ijnj} are the pixel values of Q_{ij}.

$$QS_{ij} = \sum\nolimits_{k=1}^{n_{ij}} G_{ijk} \tag{8}$$

Algorithm 1: The proposed Hierarchical classification scheme
Input: A sub-image (range/ domain)
Output: The class of the sub-image

---

1. *Input a sub-image (Figure 3 (a))*
2. *Partition the sub-image into four quadrants Q_1, Q_2, Q_3 and Q_4 using adaptive quadtree partitioning scheme. (Figure 3(b))*
3. *For each quadrant Q_i, $1 \leq i \leq 4$ obtain the sum of all the pixel values of Q_i as QS_i using equation 1 where n_j is the number of pixels and G_{i1}, G_{i2}, ...G_{inj} are the pixel values of Q_i.*
4. *There are 24 classes based on orientations of four quadrants Q_i, $1 \leq i \leq 4$. The appropriate class of first level is assigned to the sub-image based on its quadrant ordering.*
5. *Partition each quadrant Q_i, $1 \leq i \leq 4$ into four sub-quadrants Q_{i1}, Q_{i2}, Q_{i3} and Q_{i4} using adaptive quadtree partitioning scheme. (Figure 3 (c))*
6. *Again, calculate sum of the pixel values as QS_{ij}, $1 \leq j \leq 4$, for each sub-quadrant Q_{ij}, $1 \leq i \leq 4$, using equation 2 where n_{ij} is the number of pixels and G_{ij1}, G_{ij2}, ...G_{ijnj} are the pixel values of Q_{ij}.*
7. *There are 24 ordering of sub-quadrant Q_{i1}, Q_{i2}, Q_{i3} and Q_{i4} of each quadrant Q_i, $1 \leq i \leq 4$ and there are four such quadrants. Therefore, there are $24^4 = 331776$ classes in second level. The appropriate class of second level is assigned to the sub-image based on its sub-quadrant ordering.*
8. *Return sub-image class.*
9. *Stop.*

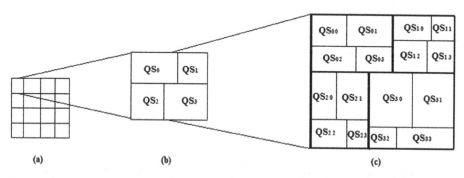

Fig. 2. Hierarchical decomposition of sub-image block to find its class (a) Input sub-images (b) First level classification using four quadrants (24 classes) (c) Second level classification using sixteen quadrants ($24^4 = 331776$ classes)

There are 24 ordering of sub-quadrant Q_{i1}, Q_{i2}, Q_{i3} and Q_{i4} of each quadrant Q_i, $1 \leq i \leq 4$ and there are four such quadrants. Therefore, there are $24^4 = 331776$ classes in second level. The appropriate class of second level is assigned to the sub-image based on its sub-quadrant ordering. Finally, the sub-image class is returned.

In adaptive quadtree partitioning, a range is compared with at least double size domain. If a similar domain is not found, the range is broken into four quadrants Q_i, $1 \leq i \leq 4$. The size of each quadrant may not be equal. If 2×2, 2×3 and 3×2 ranges are

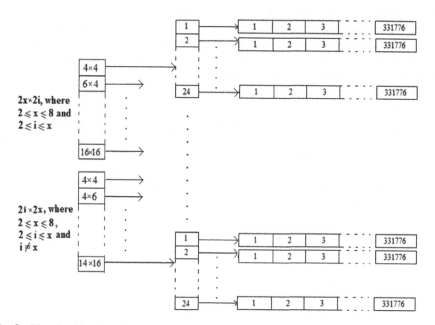

Fig. 3. The classification of domains based on domain-size, first level and second level classes

considered as minimum size ranges and 8×8 as maximum size range, then the possible quadrant sizes are $x \times i$, $2 \leq x \leq 8$, $2 \leq i \leq x$ and $i \times x$, $2 \leq x \leq 8$, $2 \leq i \leq x$, $x \neq i$. Therefore, the domain pool must contain domains of sizes $2x \times 2i$, $2 \leq x \leq 8$, $2 \leq i \leq x$ and $2i \times 2x$, $2 \leq x \leq 8$, $2 \leq i \leq x$, $x \neq i$. Initially, the domains are grouped based on their sizes (Fig. 3). Afterthat, these are classified into first level based on four quadrant pixel value sums and ultimately into second level based on sixteen quadrant pixel value sums. The domain is then kept in a list correspond to the second level class.

4   Fractal Image Coding with Adaptive Quadtree Partitioning and Proposed Hierarchical Classification Scheme

At the time of compression process, the coding technique splits the input image into a number of non-overlapping blocks of size 8×8 known as ranges (R_i). These ranges are included in the list of uncovered range. The input image is again partitioned into a number of overlapping blocks known as domains (D_i) where the size of domains are double than range. The coding technique applies adaptive quadtree partitioning scheme. Therefore, if an enough similar domain of an 8×8 range does not exist, it is further broken into four unequal sub-ranges. The possible ranges/sub-ranges sizes are $x \times i$, $2 \leq x \leq 8$, $2 \leq i \leq x$ and $i \times x$, $2 \leq x \leq 8$, $2 \leq i \leq x$, $x \neq i$. As a result, the sizes of domains are $2x \times 2i$, $2 \leq x \leq 8$, $2 \leq i \leq x$ and $2i \times 2x$, $2 \leq x \leq 8$, $2 \leq i \leq x$, $x \neq i$. The sizes of a range considered minimum are 2×2, 2×3 and 3×2 and the minimum size range is not broken further even no similar enough domain not found. The domains are classified by using proposed hierarchical classification scheme to reduce the number of comparisons between domain and range. After that, for each range (R_i), the technique detects its corresponding class (C_i) by using proposed hierarchical classification scheme and the range (R_i) is compared only with domains of class C_i and the domain that matches best with Ri is selected. If this domain is similar up to the certain threshold or the range size is minimum, the corresponding affine map is kept into the output compressed file and this range is removed from the list of uncovered range. Otherwise, the range is broken up into four unequal sub-ranges using adaptive quadtree partitioning scheme and these are included into the list of uncovered range. This process is continued until all ranges are covered. The final output compressed file contains a number of affine maps. At the time of decompression process, an arbitrary image is taken as input and affine maps are applied on it that produces another image. Now, this image acts as input and does the same. This is repeated for eight iterations and final decompressed image is produced. The technique is termed as Fractal image coding with adaptive quadtree partitioning and hierarchical classification scheme (FIC-AQP-HC).

A variant of FIC-AQP-HC has also been proposed. The technique is based on the concept that if a domain matches best with a large number of ranges of a class, then it has high chance to match again with other ranges also of that class and should give preference to it. To implement the idea, a counter is included with each domain. The counters of all domains are initially set to zero. The counter of a domain is incremented for each match with a range. The domains of each class are arranged in descending order based on counter. A range starts comparisons from the first domain of sorted same class domain list and ends searching as soon as a similar enough domain is found. As a result, it reduces further the number of comparisons between domain and range and termed as Fractal image coding with adaptive quadtree partitioning and modified hierarchical classification scheme (FIC-AQP-MHC).

5 Performance Analysis

In this section, the performances of conventional and proposed classification schemes are analyzed in terms of the number of comparisons between domain and range.

Let us consider the total number of domains and ranges of conventional classification are D_n and R_n respectively. The number of classes used in this scheme is 72. Therefore, the average number of domains per class is $\frac{D_n}{72}$ and the number of comparisons between domain and range is $\left(\frac{D_n}{72}\right)R_n$.

Now, the total number of domains and ranges of proposed hierarchical classification are considered as d_n and r_n respectively. The numbers of first and second levels classes used in this scheme are 24 and 244 respectively. As a result, the total number of classes is 245. Therefore, the average number of domains per class is $\frac{d_n}{24^5}$ and the number of comparisons between domain and range is $\left(\frac{d_n}{24^5}\right)r_n = \left(\frac{49D_n}{3\times24^5}\right)r_n$ since the possible domain sizes of conventional and proposed classifications are 3 and 49 respectively and $d_n = \left(\frac{49}{3}\right)D_n$. Hence, the proposed classification scheme reduces greatly number of domains and ranges as $R_n \approx r_n$ and $\left(\frac{49D_n}{3\times24^5}\right)r_n < \left(\frac{D_n}{72}\right)R_n$. However, the initial classification of the proposed classification scheme requires huge time. Again, the number of comparisons between domain and range of the proposed variant is less than or equal to the proposed scheme since it ends searching as soon as an enough similar domain is found.

6 Result and Analysis

Five gray scale image of size 256×256 [13] have been chosen for our experiment. The proposed FIC-AQP-HC and FIC-AQP-MHC are compared with existing Fractal Image Compression with Quadtree Partitioning and Fisher's conventional classification (FIC-QP-CC) [1], Fractal Image Compression with Adaptive Quadtree Partitioning and Fisher's conventional classification (FIC-AQP-CC) [8, 9], Fractal Image Compression with Adaptive Quadtree Partitioning and Archetype classification (FIC-AQP-AC) [10, 11] and Fractal Image Compression with Quadtree Partitioning and DWT (FIC-QP-DWT) [12] in terms of encoding time, reconstructed image quality (i.e. PSNR) and compression ratio with the help of statistical parameters mean and standard deviation. The compression ratio, PSNR, mean and standard deviation are obtained by using Eqs. 9, 10, 11 and 12 respectively.

$$\text{Compression ratio} = \frac{\text{compressed image size in bits}}{\text{Original image size in bytes}} \text{ bpp} \qquad (9)$$

$$\text{PSNR} = 20\log_{10}\left(\frac{255}{RMS}\right)\text{dB} \qquad (10)$$

$$\text{Mean}(\bar{x}) = \frac{1}{n}\sum_{i=0}^{n} x_i \qquad (11)$$

$$\text{Standard Deviation} = \sqrt{\frac{1}{n}\sum_{i=0}^{n}|(x_i - \bar{x})|^2} \qquad (12)$$

Table 1 contains the encoding time of all the examined techniques with its mean and standard deviation. The graphical representation of average encoding time of all the examined techniques is shown in Fig. 4. A significant reduction of encoding time is noticed in both the proposed techniques compare to others. Moreover, the proposed FIC-AQP-MHC is found faster than the proposed FIC-AQP-HC. Table 2 keeps the compression ratio with its mean and standard deviation of all examined techniques. Figure 5 illustrates the graphical representation of average compression ratio. The compression ratios of both the proposed techniques are same with FIC-AQP-CC and better than other examined techniques. The comparisons of reconstructed image quality in terms of PSNR including its mean and standard deviation are done in Table 3. The graphical representation of average PSNR is depicted in Fig. 6. For visual inspection, the original lena image is shown in Fig. 7 and the corresponding reconstructed images using all examined techniques are illustrated in Fig. 8. The average PSNRs of both the proposed techniques are better than FIC-QP-CC, same with FIC-AQP-CC and very close to FIC-AQP-AC for not only lena but also other four images.

Table 1. Encoding time in second

Image	FIC-QP-CC	FIC-AQP-CC	FIC-AQP-AC	FIC-QP-DWT	FIC-AQP-HC	FIC-AQP-MHC
Lena	0.22	0.36	0.34	0.17	0.16	0.16
Pepper	0.23	0.34	0.33	0.15	0.14	0.14
Boats	0.20	0.38	0.35	0.16	0.15	0.15
Cameraman	0.28	0.46	0.44	0.19	0.17	0.16
Baboon	0.23	0.33	0.32	0.20	0.16	0.15
Mean	0.232	0.374	0.356	0.174	0.156	0.152
Standard deviation	0.029	0.052	0.048	0.021	0.011	0.008

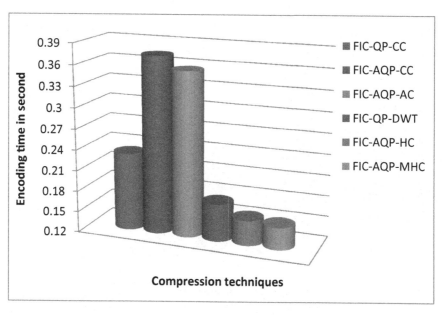

Fig. 4. The graphical representation of comparison of encoding time of fractal image compression techniques

Table 2. Compression ratio in bpp

Image	FIC-QP-CC	FIC-AQP-CC	FIC-AQP-AC	FIC-QP-DWT	FIC-AQP-HC	FIC-AQP-MHC
Lena	1.360	1.337	1.338	1.342	1.337	1.337
Pepper	1.026	1.003	1.003	1.005	1.003	1.003
Boats	1.119	1.094	1.098	1.122	1.094	1.094
Cameraman	1.278	1.242	1.241	1.254	1.242	1.242
Baboon	1.383	1.354	1.353	1.366	1.354	1.354
Mean	*1.233*	*1.206*	*1.207*	*1.218*	*1.206*	*1.206*
Standard deviation	*0.155*	*0.153*	*0.153*	*0.153*	*0.153*	*0.153*

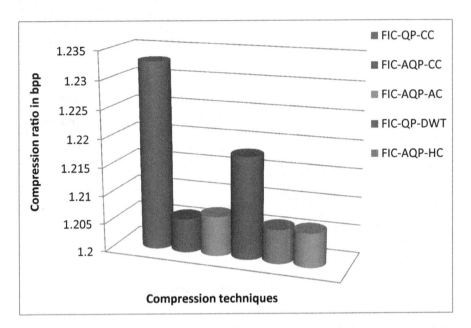

Fig. 5. The graphical representation of comparison of PSNR of fractal image compression techniques

Table 3. PSNR in dB

Image	FIC-QP-CC	FIC-AQP-CC	FIC-AQP-AC	FIC-QP-DWT	FIC-AQP-HC	FIC-AQP-MHC
Lena	28.90	29.31	29.36	28.86	29.31	29.31
Pepper	29.83	30.06	30.09	29.81	30.06	30.06
Boats	25.30	26.42	26.48	25.26	26.42	26.42
Cameraman	27.29	27.83	27.85	27.27	27.83	27.83
Baboon	20.11	21.58	21.59	20.10	21.58	21.58
Mean	*26.286*	*27.040*	*27.074*	*26.260*	*27.040*	*27.040*
Standard deviation	*3.857*	*3.358*	*3.367*	*3.851*	*3.358*	*3.358*

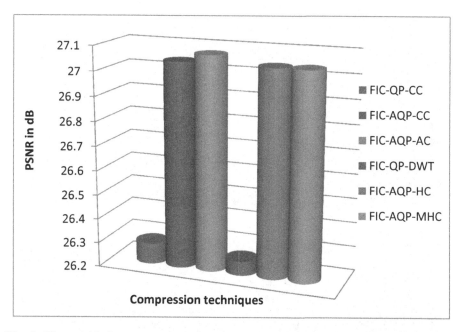

Fig. 6. The graphical representation of comparison of PSNR of fractal image compression techniques

Fig. 7. The original lena image

(a)   (b)

(c)   (d)

Fig. 8. The reconstructed images using all examined techniques (a) FIC-QP-CC (28.90 dB) (b) FIC-QP-DWT (28.86 dB) (c) FIC-AQP-AC (29.36 dB) (d) FIC-AQP-CC/FIC-AQP-HC/FIC-AQP-MHC (29.31 dB)

7   Conclusion

Both the proposed FIC-AQP-HC and FIC-AQP-MHC techniques applied hierarchical classification scheme into adaptive quadtree partitioning based fractal image coding and greatly reduces the encoding time than all other examined techniques. Moreover, the proposed FIC-AQP-MHC is faster than FIC-AQP-HC. The proposed techniques also have better compression ratio and reconstructed image quality. Further improvement of the compression ratio of the proposed techniques is possible by using loss-less coding to encode parameters of affine maps of compressed image.

References

1. Fisher, Y.: Fractal Image Compression: Theory and Application. Springer-Verlag, New York (1995). https://doi.org/10.1007/978-1-4612-2472-3
2. Xing, C., Ren, Y., Li, X.: A hierarchical classification matching scheme for fractal image compression. In: IEEE Congress on Image and Signal Processing. CISP 2008, 27–30 May, Sanya, Hainan, China, vol. 1, pp. 283–286 (2008)
3. Bhattacharya, N., Roy, S.K., Nandi, U., Banerjee, S.: Fractal image compression using hierarchical classification of sub-images. In: Proceedings of the 10th International Conference on Computer Vision Theory and Applications. VISAPP-15, 11–14 March, Berlin, Germany, pp. 46–53 (2015)
4. Jayamohan, M., Revathy, K.: Domain classification using B+ trees in fractal image compression. In: IEEE National Conference on Computing and Communication Systems (NCCCS), 21–22 November, Durgapur, India, pp. 1–5 (2012)
5. Jayamohan, M., Revathy, K.: An improved domain classification scheme based on local fractal dimension. Indian J. Comput. Sci. Eng. (IJCSE) 3(1), 138–145 (2012)
6. Wang, J., Zheng, N.: A novel fractal image compression scheme with block classification and sorting based on pearson's correlation coefficient. IEEE Trans. Image Process. 22(9), 3690–3702 (2013)
7. Nandi, U., Mandal, J.K.: Fractal image compression with quadtree partitioning and a new fast classification strategy. In: 3rd International Conference on Computer, Communication, Control and Information Technology (C3IT-2015), 7–8 February, Hooghly, West Bengal, India, pp. 1–4 (2015)
8. Nandi, U., Mandal, J.K.: Fractal image compression with adaptive quardtree portioning. In: International Conference on Signal, Image Processing and Patter Recognition (SIPP-2013), Chennai, India, pp. 289–296 (2013)
9. Nandi, U., Mandal, J.K.: Efficiency and capability of fractal image compression with adaptive quardtree partitioning. Int. J. Multimed. Appl. (IJMA) 5, 53–66 (2013)
10. Nandi, U., Mandal, J.K.: Fractal image compression with adaptive quardtree partitioning and archetype classification. In: IEEE International Conference on Research in Computational Intelligence and Communication Networks (ICRCICN 2015), Kolkata, West Bengal, India, pp. 56–60 (2015)
11. Nandi, U., Mandal, J.K.: Efficiency of adaptive fractal image compression with archetype classification and its modifications. Int. J. Comput. Appl. (IJCA) 38(2–3), 156–163 (2016)
12. Chetan, E., Sharma, E.D.: Fractal image compression using quad tree decomposition & DWT. Int. J. Sci. Eng. Res. (IJSER) 3(7), 112–116 (2015)
13. http://www.imagecompression.info/test_images

Multi-dimensional Encryption and Decryption Model for Grayscale Images to Secure the Images in Public Cloud Storage

D. Boopathy[(⊠)] and M. Sundaresan

Department of Information Technology,
Bharathiar University, Coimbatore, Tamilnadu, India
ndboopathy@gmail.com, bu.sundaresan@gmail.com

Abstract. Image encryption is a technique used to maintain the image confidentiality. Trust is needed to create and maintain in the cloud at the user and service provider end. The existing image encryption methods are using a map structure and s-box designs. While processing all the contents in cloud, it takes more resource and time to process. Directly, as part of the process it will make some delay in sending the image from user to cloud. Indirectly it will create the queue for next users; it will result in lack of cloud performance. This denotes that image encryption and decryption algorithms need to be redefined with lightweight approach for the cloud purpose with the same or improved security level. These things are taken into consideration in the proposed Multi-Dimensional Encryption and Decryption Method design. The proposed method is using the image pixel shuffling, image pixel reversing, image pixel reshuffling, and image pixel re-reversing concepts. The standard and non-standard grayscale images have been used for testing to analyze the performance and efficiency of proposed method.

Keywords: Image encryption · Decryption · Image security
Grayscale images · Cloud security

1 Introduction

"One picture is worth a thousand words", is a popular English saying which has been used since 1918, and a newspaper advertisement for the San Antonio Light [1]. The image conveys its information to the viewers without any loss. The viewers can simply understand the information of the picture without any caption, and such a strong impact has been made by the images for many years in the past. The digital era is also the continuation of the same concept and similar effects are implied in the image/ pictorial message. During the process some images must be safeguarded from the general viewers and unauthorized viewers in order to protect the confidential and sensitive contents. For that purpose the encryption standards' are applied on the images to maintain the confidentiality of the image and also to prevent that image from mishandling by the unauthorized and unidentified persons. In general, there are some existing encryption and decryption standards already in use. While coming to the

© Springer Nature Singapore Pte Ltd. 2018
J. K. Mandal and D. Sinha (Eds.): CSI 2017, CCIS 836, pp. 616–630, 2018.
https://doi.org/10.1007/978-981-13-1343-1_51

specific intention, the existing standards in use are not reliable due to their limitations, data processing technique and algorithm working architecture.

Once the images are stored or uploaded online then the users automatically lose their rights on those images. The online service providers are altering their policies in data handling also reformatted from time to time. Recently, a year ago one of the online service providers said, "Once the contents are uploaded or shared in their resources, those contents will be treated as property of their concern". This type of statements deters the users from sharing, sending and uploading their confidential images and sensitive images through online. These things evidently show that, while using the online encryption tools, the service provider will treat the images in the same way.

If the user uploads any image online for encryption, that image needs to be transferred from the user end to the service provider's end. That service provider's server may be geographically positioned in some other vicinity and in that place only the encryption and decryption will be take place. Once the user encrypts the data by using a specific service provider, then the user needs to decrypt that data by using that same service provider only but it may be done from anywhere because they are online. If the user is using the offline encryption tools, then the user needs to depend on that device for the encryption and decryption, but the user always must keep the device with him to perform either encryption or decryption whenever necessary.

The users' rights and privacy should not to be affected in online image encryption, and the users' image need to be encrypted within the users' country border limit. Moreover the encrypted images are needed to be kept back within users' country border limits and finally the user and their service provider need to maintain the trust between them are the most important highlighted requirements of the cloud service users. Taking all these things into consideration, the Secured Cloud Data Storage Prototype Model is designed whose model is explained in the following sections. The Multi-Dimensional Encryption and Decryption Method is one of the Secured Cloud data Storage Prototype Model's modules.

Section 2 reviews the related works concerning the encryption techniques to maintain the security of the data storage. Section 3 explains the proposed SCDSPM's methodology and Sect. 4 deliberates the different MDE&DPM algorithm's working methodology, MDE&DPM procedure; MDE&DPM Pseudo code and Testing file details. Section 5 represents the implementation, and experimental results and the features of the proposed method are also discussed here. Section 6 presents the conclusion derived from the findings, and the advantages of the proposed algorithm and finally its related future enhancements.

2 Literature Review

New image encryption design which utilizes one of the three dynamic chaotic [5] systems to shuffle the location of the image pixels and uses another one of the same three chaotic maps to mystify the association between the cipher image and the plain-image, thereby considerably increasing the resistance to attacks. To overcome this, sakthidasan et al. proposed the algorithm with the advantage of bigger key space, smaller iteration times and high security analysis such as key space analysis, statistical analysis and sensitivity analysis were carried out [2]. Navitha et al. proposed a very new and combined approach for DCT based image compression, pixel shuffling based encryption, decryption and steganography for real-time applications [3].

Quist et al. proposed the sets out method to contribute to the general body of knowledge in the area of cryptography application and by developing a cipher algorithm for image encryption of m*n size by shuffling the RGB pixel values. The algorithm ultimately makes it possible for encryption and decryption of the images based on the RGB pixel [4].

Junqin et al. proposed a permutation-substitution image encryption scheme based on generalized Arnold map. Only one round of permutation and one round of substitution are performed to get the desirable results. The generalized chaotic Arnold maps are applied to generate the pseudo-random sequences for the permutation and substitution [6].

Lohit et al. explored the implementation of AES in MATLAB on plaintext encryption and cipher text decryption. These results are superior to the similar software implementations of AES [7].

3 Secured Cloud Data Storage Prototype Model

The existing methods, updated algorithms using different concepts and implementation of existing algorithms are enough to handle the data encryption process in offline mode. While coming to the online mode, the existing methods require more time and utilize more resource to finish the encryption and decryption process. The geographically located data processing servers will raise the security breach issues and data transborder related issues. So, the data need to be encrypted before the data transferred from the user end to the server end. The proposed method considered all of these measures and provides the prototype model with different modules to overcome the data related storage, retrieval and encryption issues.

Figure 1 shows the Secured Cloud Data Storage Prototype Model (SCDSPM) [8, 9]. The Secured Cloud Data Storage Prototype Model contains four sub-modules; they are Authentication Authorization Resolving Module (AARM) [10, 11], Data Type Identification and Extension Validation Module (DTI&EVM) [12], Encryption and Decryption Gateway Module (E&DGM) [13–15] and Automatic Cloud Data Backup Module (ACDBM) [16]. This paper explains the third module of SCDSPM. This E&DGM is redefined with some modification and named in this paper as Multi-Dimensional Encryption and Decryption Model (MDE&DPM). Figure 2 shows the proposed Multi-Dimensional Encryption and Decryption Model (MDE&DPM).

4 Multi-dimensional Encryption and Decryption Model

The encryption is one of the methods to secure the confidential information. It prevents the unauthorized users to access or use that information. Nowadays, many types of existing encryption methods are available and most of them are in usage at present. But the standardizations are not available to follow any one method from the existing

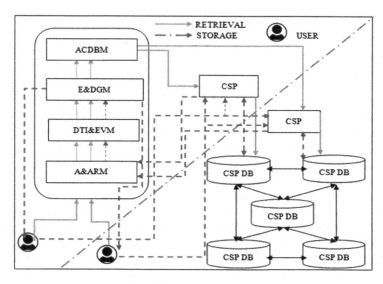

Fig. 1. Secure cloud data storage prototype model version

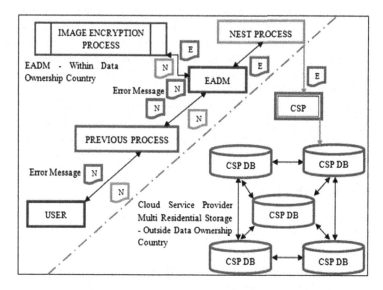

Fig. 2. Multi-dimensional encryption and decryption prototype method

methods. A few years back American whistle blower Edward Snowden reveals that "Many encryption services providing companies are fixed some back doors in their encryption algorithms to surveillance their users". In today's information technology era, most of the users are using online storage and also believing their service providers.

The online storage is now provided as a major service by most online service providers in different names. In online storage the data are transferred from user's country to another country (i.e. where the data server is located) and it is replicated to other data servers which are geographically located in different country locations. Moreover, following the standardized regulation on the online data is not possible due to the fact that data are widely spread around many servers in many different geographical locations. If any one of the geographically located servers might be hacked, if it happens then the data on that server are under critical problem. To avoid its related issues the user data must be controlled within the user's country boundary limit. For that the user's data must be encrypted within the user's country boundary limit before they are transferred into the cloud storage (i.e. online storage) with that country regulation. Using the new type of encryption method will avoid the user's data from superfluous risks. Each and every encryption and decryption logics must be unique from other methods. In that way, the proposing encryption algorithm is using new logic and it will lead to avoid the unconstitutional access, illicit usage and unlawful surveillance of the user's data by unauthorized persons.

The proposed Multi-Dimensional Encryption and Decryption Prototype Model (shown in Fig. 2) are presently concentrated on image format files only. This paper explains the proposed Multi-Dimensional Encryption and Decryption Prototype Model with tested standard and non-standard images and its related experimental results. It uses 512×512 pixel images for testing purposes. Currently it can be applied only on particular pixel size images. The encryption key concept of this proposed encryption method is a private key method. The private key of proposed model includes applied encryption algorithm type information, constant image pixel values with its related information and algorithm initialized server time details. Combined together, these things generate a private key at the time of encryption and that private key used to decrypt the image. In the proposed model the decryption key will be automatically prepared by the encryption algorithm at the time of image encryption. The user doesn't need to provide or generate the encryption key at the time of encryption.

4.1   MDE&DPM Algorithms

Multi-Dimensional Encryption and Decryption Prototype Model contains for methods different methods to encrypt and decrypt the image. The four methods are;

- Pixel Rearrange Algorithm (PRA)
- Pixel Reverse Rearrange Algorithm (PRRA)
- Pixel Shuffling Algorithm (PSA)
- Pixel Reverse Shuffling Algorithm (PRSA)

The above mentioned Fig. 3(a) and (b) methods are explained with the test case image which includes standard images and normal non-standard images.

4.2   Pixel Rearrange Algorithm

In Pixel Rearrange Algorithm the image pixels [17] are rearranged into different positions using the 4×4 matrix concept. The pixel values of the images are relocated

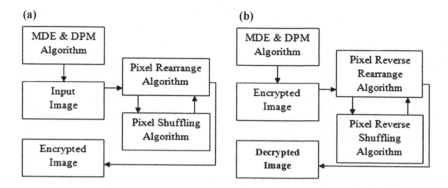

Fig. 3. (a) MDE&DPM encryption method (b) MDE&DPM decryption method

to other positions from their original position. Once the image pixels are relocated to another position, then they automatically reflect in the original structural content of the image. The Pixel Rearrange Algorithm is holding 4096 methods to rearrange the image pixels into a new position within the selected 4 × 4 matrix method. This algorithm is incorporated into the Pixel Shuffling Algorithm (PSA).

The Table 1(a) shows the image pixel value's location before applying Pixel Rearrange Algorithm (PRA). The Table 1(b) shows the image pixel value's location after applying Pixel Rearrange Algorithm (PRA).

Table 1. (a) before applying PRA, (b) after applying PRA

(a)

1	2	3	4	RN
5	6	7	8	RN
9	10	11	12	RN
13	14	15	16	RN
CN	CN	CN	CN	CN/RN

(b)

1	9	10	8	RN
16	2	7	11	RN
14	6	3	12	RN
5	15	13	4	RN
CN	CN	CN	CN	CN/RN

4.3   Pixel Reverse Rearrange Algorithm

The Pixel Reverse Rearrange Algorithm (PRRA) is a process going to take place on the Pixel Reverse Shuffling Algorithm (PRSA). This algorithm is used to reverse the Pixel Rearrange Algorithm's (PRA) relocated pixel values into their original position. It means the original structure content of an image will be given by this algorithm. The reversing method will use the rearrange method information from the decryption key.

The Table 2 (a) shows the pixel value's location before applying Pixel Reverse Rearrange Algorithm (PRRA). The Table 2 (b) shows the pixel value's location after applying Pixel Reverse Rearrange Algorithm (PRRA).

Table 2. (a) before applying PRRA, (b) after applying PRRA

(a)

1	9	10	8	RN
16	2	7	11	RN
14	6	3	12	RN
5	15	13	4	RN
CN	CN	CN	CN	CN/RN

(b)

1	2	3	4	RN
5	6	7	8	RN
9	10	11	12	RN
13	14	15	16	RN
CN	CN	CN	CN	CN/RN

4.4 Pixel Shuffling Algorithm

The Pixel Shuffling Algorithm (PSA) is used to shuffle the pixel values within the matrix value. This research work holding sixteen different types of pixel values shuffling methods. Within those different methods, one of the methods will be automatically (i.e. randomly) selected and applied by the Pixel Shuffling Algorithm (PSA), then the selected method results will be stored with the decryption key. In each and every pixel shuffling method, one of the value locations will be fixed as a constant to identify which shuffling method is used to shuffle the pixel values. Here the decryption key will be automatically generated by the PSA algorithm with PSA related information and that information will be use at the time of decryption.

Table 3. (a) before applying PRRA, (b) after applying PRRA

(a)

1	2	3	4	RN
5	6	7	8	RN
9	10	11	12	RN
13	14	15	16	RN
CN	CN	CN	CN	CN/RN

(b)

9	1	10	8	RN
16	2	11	7	RN
15	6	12	3	RN
5	14	13	4	RN
CN	CN	CN	CN	CN/RN

The Table 3 (a) shows the pixel value's location before applying Pixel Shuffling Algorithm (PSA). The Table 3 (b) shows the pixel value's location after applying Pixel Shuffling Algorithm (PSA). In the selected pixel shuffling method, the pixel value 14 fixed as a constant value to identify the shuffling method.

4.5 Pixel Reverse Shuffling Algorithm

The decryption key holds the used Pixel shuffling algorithm's information. By using that information only the pixel reverse shuffling algorithm will work. Once the Pixel Reverse Shuffling Algorithm (PRSA) gets the information from the decryption key, then it will apply that correlated reverse shuffling method on that shuffled image pixel values. Once the pixel values are reversed, then it needs to be processed with the Pixel

Reverse Rearrange Algorithm (PRRA). Then only the original structured content of the image will be constructed.

Table 4. (a) before applying PRRA, (b) after applying PRRA

(a)

9	1	10	8	RN
16	2	11	7	RN
15	6	12	3	RN
5	**14**	13	4	RN
CN	CN	CN	CN	CN/RN

(b)

1	2	3	4	RN
5	6	7	8	RN
9	10	11	12	RN
13	**14**	15	16	RN
CN	CN	CN	CN	CN/RN

The Table 4 (a) shows the pixel value's location before applying Pixel Reverse Shuffling Algorithm (PRSA). The Table 4 (b) shows the pixel value's location after applying Pixel Reverse Shuffling Algorithm (PRSA). By using that pixel value 14, which is fixed as constant value, is used to identify the shuffling method.

4.6   Procedure for Encryption

Step 1	Select the image to encrypt
Step 2	Read the image pixels and store them into a text file
Step 3	Apply the proposed algorithm's pixel rearrange method
Step 4	Then apply proposed algorithm's pixel shuffling method
Step 5	Then again apply proposed algorithm's pixel rearrange method
Step 6	Prepare the decryption key based on the algorithms information used on the image
Step 7	Convert the text file into an image file and store that converted image file
Step 8	Store that decryption key into a text file

4.7   Procedure for Decryption

Step 1	Select the image to decrypt
Step 2	Get the decryption key to decrypt the file
Step 3	Verify whether the decryption key is valid or not, then apply it to selecting the method
Step 4	Read the image pixels and store it into a text file
Step 5	Apply proposed algorithm's pixel reverse rearrange method
Step 6	Apply proposed algorithm's pixel reverse shuffling method
Step 7	Apply proposed algorithm's pixel reverse rearrange method
Step 8	Convert the text file into an image file and store that converted image file

624 D. Boopathy and M. Sundaresan

4.8 Encryption Pseudo Code

Get the image from the user
Store that image into an Object
Read the Object Pixel Values
Store that Object Pixel Values into a Text File
Get the Pixel Values from that Text File
Store that Pixel Values Text File as an Object
       Apply the Pixel Rearrange Algorithm on that Object
       Apply the Pixel Shuffling Algorithm on that Object
       Apply the Pixel Rearrange Algorithm on that Object
Prepare the Decryption Key with used algorithm method information
Convert the Pixel Values Text File into an Image File
Store that Image File into selected storage in selected format
Store that Image Decryption Key into the selected storage in desired format

4.9 Decryption Pseudo Code

Get the image from the user
Store that image into an Object
Get the Decryption Key to apply and decrypt the image
If the key got authenticated Then
       Forward the process to next step
Else
       Show an error message as key is invalid and STOP the process
Read the Object Pixel Values
Store that Object Pixel Values into a Text File
Get the Pixel Values from that Text File
Store that Pixel Values Text File as an Object
       Apply the Pixel Reverse Rearrange Algorithm on that Object
       Apply the Pixel Reverse Shuffling Algorithm on that Object
       Apply the Pixel Reverse Rearrange Algorithm on that Object
Convert the Pixel Values Text File into an Image File
Store that Image File into the selected storage in selected format

4.10 Test Files

Seven different standard images [18] are taken for testing purpose. Each testing file is 512 x 512 pixel method. The remaining details of the testing images are shown in the Table 5.

Table 5. Testing image details

Image Sl. No.	Test image name	Standard/normal image	Image size
1	Baboon	Standard image/Tiff format	258 KB
2	Cameraman	Standard image/Tiff format	256 KB
3	Lena	Standard image/Tiff format	260 KB
4	Pirate	Non-standard image/Tiff format	257 KB
5	Room	Non-standard image/Tiff format	258 KB
6	Peppers	Standard image/Tiff format	206 KB
7	House	Standard image/Tiff format	106 KB

5   Results and Discussion

The step by step working formation on image of the proposed encryption and decryption algorithm is applied on the baboon standard "TIFF" [19] format image and those step by step images are shown below. Figure 4 (a) – (d) shows the step by step encryption process results of the proposed algorithm and the Fig. 5 (a) – (d) shows the step by step decryption process results of the proposed algorithm.

Figure 4 (a) is the input image, Fig. 4 (b) is the first level output image, Fig. 4 (c) is the second level output image, and Fig. 4 (d) is the final level output image i.e., encrypted image. Similarly Fig. 5 (a) is the encrypted image, Fig. 5 (b) is the first level output image, Fig. 5 (c) is the second level output image, and Fig. 5 (d) is the final level output image i.e., decrypted image.

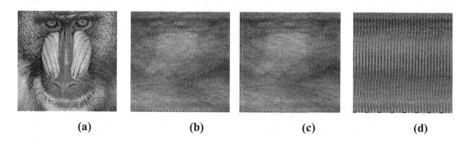

(a)   (b)   (c)   (d)

Fig. 4. (a) – (d) step by step encryption process of the proposed algorithm

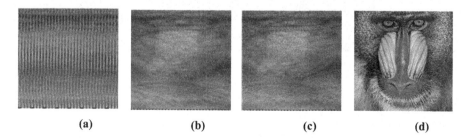

(a)   (b)   (c)   (d)

Fig. 5. Step by step decryption process of the proposed algorithm

Table 6. Comparison of histogram between input image, encrypted image and decrypted image

Sl. No.	Input Image	Encrypted Image	Decrypted Image
Test Image 1			
Test Image 1 Histogram			
Test Image 2			
Test Image 2 Histogram			
Test Image 3			
Test Image 3 Histogram			

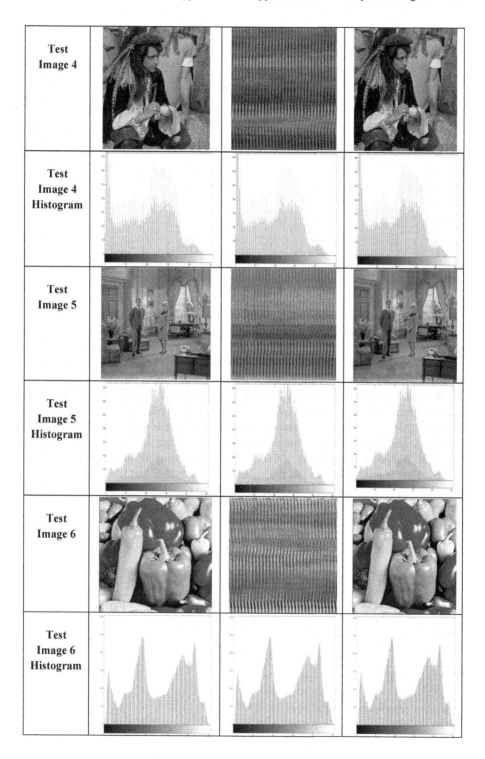

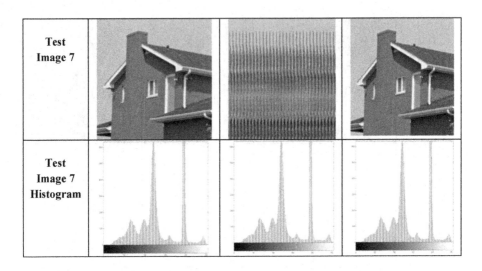

The seven different standard and non-standard images i.e. TIFF image file format [20] are tested in one of the proposed shuffling algorithm method. The seven different encrypted and decrypted images are shown in the Table 6. The Table 6 contains input image, encrypted image and decrypted images with its related histogram details.

The size of the images, isequal() function [21], PSNR Value [22] and MSE Rate [23] are taken into consideration as parameters and the input image, encrypted image and decrypted images are compared. This shows that there is no change is identified in processed images (i.e. input image to encrypted image and encrypted image to decrypted image-normal image). Table 7 shows that comparison between the tested images. Here the extra values are not added into the image and the image pixels are swapped and re-swapped by using the 4 × 4 matrix- based new logical method. So there is no difference figured out in the histogram of the encrypted images, when compared to the original and decrypted histogram [24] images.

Table 7. Comparison of size of the image, isequal() Function, PSNR value and MSE Rate between input image, encrypted image and decrypted image

Image name	Details		Size of the image	isequal () function	PSNR value	MSE rate
Test image 1	Input image vs	Encp img	258 KB	0	33.8481 dB	108.08
		Decp img	258 KB	1	Inf dB	0
Test image 2	Input image vs	Encp img	256 KB	0	34.7574 dB	87.66
		Decp img	256 KB	1	Inf dB	0
Test image 3	Input image vs	Encp img	260 KB	0	33.7661 dB	110.14
		Decp img	260 KB	1	Inf dB	0

(continued)

Table 7. (*continued*)

Image name	Details		Size of the image	isequal () function	PSNR value	MSE rate
Test image 4	Input image vs	Encp img	257 KB	0	33.7901 dB	109.53
		Decp img	257 KB	1	Inf dB	0
Test image 5	Input image vs	Encp img	258 KB	0	34.0635 dB	102.85
		Decp img	258 KB	1	Inf dB	0
Test image 6	Input image vs	Encp img	206 KB	0	35.1889 dB	79.37
		Decp img	206 KB	1	Inf dB	0
Test image 7	Input image vs	Encp img	106 KB	0	33.7953 dB	109.40
		Decp img	106 KB	1	Inf dB	0

kB=kilobytes, Encp Image = Encrypted Image, Decp Image = Decryption Image

6 Conclusion and Future Enhancements

The proposed Multi-Dimensional Encryption and Decryption Prototype Model The proposed Multi-Dimensional Encryption and Decryption Prototype Model were presently tested on grayscale type images. Seven different standard and non-standard images were tested to substantiate the algorithm's accuracy with the size of the images, SSIM Value, PSNR Value and MSE Rate parameters. Up-to now the proposed algorithm is working in the predictable way on that grayscale image. This working prototype model will be applied to the grayscale images to maintain its security with privacy. To the next level of the research work, the proposed algorithm will be going to apply to the color images and then the same parameters will be taken into consideration to verify the proposed algorithm's accuracy, performance and efficiency on that color image. The private key mechanism will be going to be added to image encryption to authenticate and authorize users to decrypt the encrypted image. If the proposed algorithm achieves the satisfied level in the color image encryption and decryption, then it will also be extended to the real time usage to maintain the user's image security and privacy on cloud storage.

References

1. https://en.wikipedia.org/wiki/A_picture_is_worth_a_thousand_words. Accessed 09 Aug 2017
2. Sakthidasan, K., Santhosh Krishna, B.V.: A new chaotic algorithm for image encryption and decryption of digital color images. Int. J. Inf. Educ. Technol. **1**(2), 137–141 (2011)
3. Agarwal, N., Sharma, H.: An efficient pixel-shuffling based approach to simultaneously perform image compression, encryption and steganography. IJCSMC **2**(5), 376–385 (2013)
4. Kester, Q.-A.: Image encryption based on the RGB PIXEL transposition and shuffling. Int. J. Comput. Netw. Inf. Secur. **7**, 43–50 (2013)

5. Desai, D., Prasad, A., Crasto, J.: Chaos-based system for image encryption. Int. J. Comput. Sci. Inf. Technol. **3**(4), 4809–4811 (2012)
6. Zhao, J., Guo, W., Ye, R.: A Chaos-based image encryption scheme using permutation-substitution architecture. Int. J. Comput. Trends Technol. **15**(4), 174–185 (2014)
7. Reddy, D.L.K.D.A.R., Jilani, S.A.K.: Implementation of 128-bit AES algorithm in MATLAB. Int. J. Eng. Trends Technol. (IJETT) **33**(3), 126–129 (2016)
8. Boopathy, D., Sundaresan, M.: Securing public data storage in cloud environment. In: 48th Annual Convention of Computer Society of India on ICT and Critical Infrastructure, Visakhapatnam, India, pp. 555–562 (2013)
9. Boopathy, D., Sundaresan, M.: Secured cloud data storage – prototype trust model for public cloud storage. In: International Conference on Information and Communication Technology for Sustainable Development, Ahmadabad, India, pp. 329–337 (2015)
10. Boopathy, D., Sundaresan, M.: Framework model and algorithm of request based one time passkey (ROTP) mechanism to authenticate cloud users in secured way. In: 3rd International Conference on Computing for Sustainable Global Development, New Delhi, India, pp. 5317–5322 (2016)
11. Boopathy, D., Sundaresan, M.: A framework for user authentication and authorization using request based one time passkey and user active session identification. Int. J. Comput. Appl. **172**(10), 18–23 (2017)
12. Boopathy, D., Sundaresan, M.: Data type identification and extension validator framework model for public cloud storage. In: Big Data Analytics - Proceedings of the 50th Annual Convention of Computer Society of India, New Delhi, India, pp. 533–541 (2014)
13. Boopathy, D., Sundaresan, M.: Data encryption framework model with watermark security for data storage in public cloud model. In: IEEE Eighth International Conference on Computing for Sustainable Global Development, New Delhi, India, pp. 1040–1044 (2014)
14. Boopathy, D., Sundaresan, M.: Enhanced encryption and decryption gateway model for cloud data security in cloud storage. In: Emerging ICT for Bridging the Future - 49th Annual Convention of Computer Society of India, Hyderabad, India, pp. 415–421 (2014)
15. Boopathy, D., Sundaresan, M.: Policy based data encryption mechanism framework model for data storage in public cloud service deployment model. In: Elsevier Fourth International Joint Conference on Advances in Computer Science, Haryana, India, pp. 423–429 (2013)
16. Boopathy, D., Sundaresan, M.: IDOCA and ODOCA – enhanced technique for secured cloud data storage. Int. J. Intell. Eng. Syst. **10**(06), 49–59 (2017)
17. https://en.wikipedia.org/wiki/Pixel. Accessed 05 Nov 2017
18. https://en.wikipedia.org/wiki/Standard_test_image. Accessed 05 Nov 2017
19. https://en.wikipedia.org/wiki/TIFF. Accessed 11 Nov 2017
20. https://en.wikipedia.org/wiki/Image_file_formats. Accessed 11 Nov 2017
21. http://in.mathworks.com/help/matlab/ref/isequal.html. Accessed 18 Nov 2017
22. https://en.wikipedia.org/wiki/Peak_signal-to-noise_ratio. Accessed 18 Nov 2017
23. https://en.wikipedia.org/wiki/Mean_squared_error. Accessed 18 Nov 2017
24. https://en.wikipedia.org/wiki/Histogram. Accessed 20 Nov 2017

Image Denoising Using Fractal Hierarchical Classification

Swalpa Kumar Roy[1], Nilavra Bhattacharya[2(✉)], Bhabatosh Chanda[3],
Bidyut B. Chaudhuri[4], and Soumitro Banerjee[5]

[1] Department of CSE, Jalpaiguri Government Engineering College, Jalpaiguri, India
swalpa@cse.jgec.ac.in
[2] School of Information, The University of Texas at Austin, Austin, USA
nilavra@ieee.org
[3] ECS Unit, Indian Statistical Institute, Kolkata, India
chanda@isical.ac.in
[4] CVPR Unit, Indian Statistical Institute, Kolkata, India
bbc@isical.ac.in
[5] DPS, Indian Institute of Science Education and Research, Mohanpur Campus,
Kolkata, India
soumitro@iiserkol.ac.in

Abstract. This paper proposes an efficient yet simple fractal-based image denoising technique. Denoising is carried out during fractal coding process. Hierarchical classification is used to increase encoding speed, and avoid a lot of futile mean-square-error (MSE) computations. Quadtree-based image partitioning using dynamic range and domain sizes is used to increase the degree of noise removal. Further denoising is achieved using pyramidal decoding, using non-arbitrary seed image, and additional post processing. Results from experiments show that our proposed scheme improves the structural similarity (SSIM) index of the Lenna image from 44% to 78% for low noise cases, and from 9% to 35% for high noise cases.

Keywords: Denoising · Fractal image coding · Image restoration

1 Introduction

Digital images are highly susceptible to contamination by noise during image acquisition and transmission. The commonest form of background noise found to corrupt digital images is Additive White Gaussian Noise (AWGN). AWGN can get into an image due to imperfect image-capturing device, insufficient illumination of the image subject during image capture, or due to transmission of the image over a noisy network. Background noise hampers both visual quality and object identification. Hence an efficient noise removal algorithm is required to remove or reduce its derogatory effects.

Linear filtering and smoothing operations are simple and popular methods for noise removal and image restoration. But their robustness is less, as they

© Springer Nature Singapore Pte Ltd. 2018
J. K. Mandal and D. Sinha (Eds.): CSI 2017, CCIS 836, pp. 631–645, 2018.
https://doi.org/10.1007/978-981-13-1343-1_52

hypothesize that the image consists of a stationary signal, formed through a linear system. However, real-world images are generally acquired using non-linear techniques, and the images have non-stationary statistical properties. The intensity distribution captured by the image acquiring device is a product of the illumination falling on the scene or object of interest, and its reflectance. Many non-linear and adaptive image denoising methods have been proposed which take these statistical variations into account, and therefore give better output image quality, while maintaining high frequency features of the input image [5,20].

In this paper, we examine the computational problem of estimating the original image f_{orig} from its noisy version f_{noisy}, corrupted by Gaussian noise. The problem may be defined as:

$$f_{noisy} = f_{orig} + G \tag{1}$$

where G is the additive white Gaussian noise. Noise removal, or denoising, is therefore the methodology of estimating the original signal f_{orig} from the noise-degraded signal f_{noisy}.

Proposed by Barnsley in 1988 [3], Fractal Image Compression (FIC) is a lossy image coding technique which exploits local self-similarities present in an image, and represents the image as a collection of affine transformations. Jacquin [13] presented the first automated and practical version of FIC, and it is known as the baseline fractal image compression (BFIC). BFIC uses Partitioned Iterated Function System (PIFS) to find matching image-patches without requiring human assistance. Recently Roy et al. [18] proposed a simple and efficient approximation of the scaling parameter which allows us to substitute to the expensive process of matrix multiplication with a simple division of two numbers. Hurtgen and Stiller [11] and Bhattacharya et al. [4] modified the Fishers method and obtained some improved performance. Since then, numerous FIC schemes have been proposed [7,9,23]. Apart from being an image compression technique, FIC has also been applied in various fields like image segmentation [6], image indexing and retrieval [17], image encryption [16], image authentication [15], and facial image recognition [21].

In this paper, we propose a fractal-coding based scheme for denoising an image corrupted by AWGN. Basic FIC theory is explained in Sect. 2. The proposed FIC based denoising scheme is discussed in Sect. 3. Experimental results of our scheme are shown in Sect. 4, and concluding discussions are presented in Sect. 5.

2   Fractal Coding

An Iterated Function System (IFS) is a collection of *contractive* affine transformations $\{w_i : \mathbb{R}^2 \to \mathbb{R}^2 | i = 1, \ldots, n\}$ which map the plane $\mathbb{R}^2$ to itself. This collection of transformations defines a *map*:

$$W(\cdot) = \bigcup_{i=1}^{n} w_i(\cdot) \tag{2}$$

A contractive map is one, which brings points closer together. Hutchinson [12] proved that if w_i for all i in an IFS be contractive, then W is contractive. If a contractive map is iterated from *any* initial point, it will always converge to a unique *fixed point*, which is called the *attractor* of the given contractive map. Given an input image S_0, we can apply W on it repeatedly in a feedback loop to obtain the fixed point x_W, which is the limit set:

$$x_W \equiv S_\infty = \lim_{n\to\infty} W^n(S_0) \tag{3}$$

where $W^p = W\{w^{p-1}(\cdot)\}$. Thus the attractor or the fixed point x_W of the map W is not dependent on the choice of S_0, and W alone can completely determine a unique image. This is called the *Contractive Mapping Fixed-Point Theorem* [1]. Also, if the error-difference between an original image f and the transformation of that image $W(f)$ is less than a certain threshold, the transform W is accepted as an equivalent representation of the image. This is the underlying concept of *Collage Theorem* [2]. FIC tries to find an IFS that maps an image onto itself. However, finding a single IFS that describes an entire image requires human intervention, and cannot be automated effectively. Jacquin [13] suggested that instead of finding transformations that describe a whole image, we can find transforms that apply only to portions of an image. These transformations are called Partitioned IFS (PIFS), which help to automate the encoding process.

2.1   Fractal Encoding

An image f is segmented into non-overlapping *range-blocks* R_i of size $r \times r$ and overlapping *domain-blocks* D_j of size $2r \times 2r$. The collection of all range blocks comprises the range pool R and the collection of all domain blocks comprises the domain pool D. Range blocks are smaller than domain blocks in order to make the transformations contractive. The domain pool is created by sliding a window of size $2r \times 2r$ from the top-left corner to the bottom-right corner of f with an integer step-size d in horizontal and vertical directions.

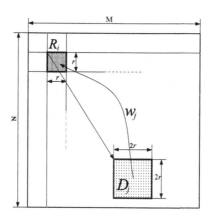

Fig. 1. Fractal encoding: mapping domains to ranges [11]

For each range block $R_i \in R$ an exhaustive search is carried out in the domain pool D to find a domain block D_j, such that D_j can be transformed "closely" to R_i. The contractive affine transformation w_j is then applied to D_j (Fig. 1). The optimal selection of w_j and D_j should ensure that the reconstructed image

$$g = W(D) = \bigcup_{j=1}^{n} w_j(D_j) \text{ (where } n = (M/r) \times (N/r)\text{): number of range blocks)}$$

has the minimum error-difference from the original image f. The transformation w_j and the location of the domain-block D_j comprise the *fractal code* of the range-block R_i. Fractal codes of all the range blocks collectively form the IFS of the image f. The contractive affine transform w_j is composed of a spatial transform and a grey level transform. The spatial transform is contractive, and it maps the spatial domain D_j (with size $2r \times 2r$) to the spatial range R_i (with size $r \times r$). The grey level transform G is of the form:

$$G(D'_j) = s_j \cdot D'_j + o_j \tag{4}$$

where D'_j is the spatially contracted domain block D_j to match the size of R_i it is mapping to (henceforth for brevity we use D_j to mean D'_j), s_j is the contrast or scaling factor, and o_j is the brightness or the offset of the transform. Using this definition, the FIC problem reduces to searching the domain pool D to find D_j, s_j and o_j for each R_i such that

$$E(R_i, D_j) < \varepsilon \tag{5}$$

where E is the error-metric between range block R_i and transformed domain block D_j, and ε is the target fidelity of the reconstructed image. A lot of image quality measures are available, but the mean square error (**MSE**) metric [8] is generally used as distortion criterion. So Eq. 5 becomes

$$\text{MSE}(R_i, D_j) = \|R_i - (s_j \cdot D_j + o_j)\|_2^2 < \varepsilon \tag{6}$$

where $\|\cdot\|_2$ is the two-norm.

2.2   Fractal Decoding

Fractal decoding is fast and recursive. An arbitrary initial "seed" image (typically a blank image) is chosen, and the encoded affine transforms are recursively applied on the image. By the principles of the *Contractive Mapping Fixed-Point Theorem* [1] and the *Collage Theorem* [2], the arbitrary image converges to the final decoded image within a few iterations.

3   Proposed Algorithm

In this section, we discuss the various components of our fast image denoising technique. Of the five components, "hierarchical classification", "optimal denoised image", and "non-arbitrary seed image" are our original contributions, while the rest have been adapted from their corresponding sources.

3.1   Fractal Image Denoising

Fractal coding exploits the presence of self-similarity in different magnification levels of an image. Fractal image denoising is based on the idea that since natural images contain self-similar structures, they can easily be approximated by contractive affine transformations. However, approximating random noisy components occurring in an image using such affine transforms is impossible [10].

Fractal coding and decoding schemes involve finding the scaling and offset parameters s_j and o_j for a given range R_i and a best matched domain D_j such that Eq. 6 is minimized. In order to store the parameters in the fractal file, they are quantized in the encoder and dequantized in the decoder. Hence post quantization of the parameters often leads to some degree of information loss as compared with pre-quantization [9]. Since noise is high degree of random information, this information is lost due to quantization, which aids the denoising process in fractal coding.

3.2   Hierarchical Classification

FIC is an asymmetric technology. Exhaustive searching of the domain pool to find matching block pairs is computationally intensive, and makes the encoding algorithm slower than most of the existing algorithms. A lot of research has gone into solving the lengthy encoding-time problem, and a popular solution is to perform domain pool classification [19, 26].

Fisher [9] proposed a classification scheme to illustrate the advantages of domain classification. A domain or range is partitioned into four quadrants. For each quadrant, values proportional to mean pixel intensity and to the variance of the pixel intensities are computed. Classes are identified based on the permutational orderings of these values.

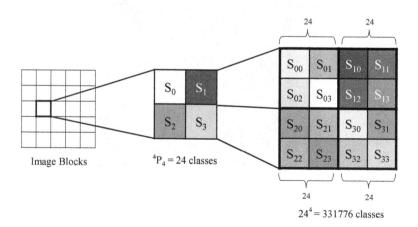

Fig. 2. Hierarchical classification.

The Hierarchical Classification scheme [4] is an improvement of Fisher's Mean-Variance classification scheme. A sub-image is divided into four quadrants (Fig. 2). Sum of pixel values (luminance) of each quadrant is calculated as S_0, S_1, S_2 and S_3. According to the ordering of the luminance sums, there are $^4P_4 = 24$ classes. This gives the Level - I classification. In Level - II, each quadrant is further subdivided into 4 sub-quadrants (sixteen subquadrants in total), and sum of pixel values over each sub-quadrant is calculated as S_{i0}, S_{i1}, S_{i2} and S_{i3} ($i = 0, 1, 2, 3$). Based on the ordering of S_{ij} in quadrant i, each quadrant gives 24 classes, totalling to $24^4 = 331776$ classes, as shown in Fig. 2.

Our proposed denoising technique incorporates the hierarchical classification scheme with the baseline FIC to speed up the encoding process in comparison to Baseline FIC.

3.3   Quadtree Partitioning

Some regions (range blocks) in an image can be defined well with domain range blocks, while some others are difficult. *Quadtree Partitioning* breaks up a range block into 4 equally sized sub-quadrants, when it cannot be approximated well enough by a domain block. The process repeats recursively, starting at the initial image and iterating until partitioned blocks are small enough to be approximated within some specified MSE threshold. Small blocks can be approximated better than large blocks because pixels within a small neighbourhood tend to show high correlation (Fig. 3).

Fig. 3. Quadtree partitioning with dynamic range sizes.

In our implementation, we have created domain pools of sizes 8×8 (D_{min}), 16×16 and 32×32 (D_{max}); corresponding range sizes are 4×4 (R_{min}), 8×8 and 16×16 (R_{max}) respectively. The program first tries with a 16×16 range block. If a suitable domain is found, an affine map is generated, else the range is quadtree partitioned into 4 smaller quadrants as range blocks, and domain blocks of appropriate size are searched for each of them. High detail areas are usually mapped by smaller ranges, while less-detailed areas are mapped by larger ones. The distance between two successive domains, called *domain step-size*, is set to 4 pixels in the default case.

3.4 Optimal Denoised Image

In our proposed technique, we obtain an optimal denoised image by averaging and post processing. Image decoding is done by iterating through the fractal code, where we approximate the i_{th} range block R^i_{apr} of kth approximate image from an arbitrary image using

$$R^i{}_{apr} = s \cdot \bar{D}^{k-1} + o \tag{7}$$

where $\bar{D}$ is obtained by averaging i.e. taking the mean value of every 2×2 pixel block of the $(k-1)^{th}$ image. Since noise is distributed randomly over the pixels, averaging the pixel values also averages the noise levels, resulting in low noise value. As ranges are encoded independently, the block boundaries may not be smooth. The human eye is sensitive to such discontinuities, however small. A post-processing step [9] has been applied to smooth-out the block boundaries and improve decoded image quality. The pixels at the block-boundaries are smoothed by a weighted average technique. The pixel values a and b (on either side of the block-boundary) are replaced by $w_1a + w_2b$ and $w_2a + w_1b$ respectively, with $w_1 + w_2 = 1$. For smallest ranges (4×4), the weights are $w_1 = 5/6$ and $w_2 = 1/6$, while for the larger ranges, the weights are $w_1 = 1/3$ and $w_2 = 2/3$. Though the weights are heuristic, they give satisfactory results (Fig. 7d).

3.5 Non-arbitrary Seed Image

Conventional fractal decoding uses an arbitrary seed image as the starting image of the recursive decoding process. For easy implementation, this image is chosen as a plain black image i.e. a matrix filled with zeroes. Since the first decoding iteration is dependant on the seed image, the plain black image may not always give the best results for denoising purposes. For images having self-similar structures, the final attractor image (fixed point) is not dependent on the choice of seed image. However, a noisy image has lots of random pixel intensity variations, and is therefore not very self similar. So for denoising, we have used some non-arbitrary noise free images as the starting seed image for fractal decoding (Fig. 4). The idea is to "help" the first decoding iteration by providing noise-free domains to map to ranges. Using these images we gained some small yet significant improvement in decoded image quality (Fig. 5).

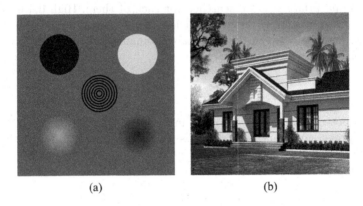

(a)   (b)

Fig. 4. Non-arbitrary noise-free seed images chosen to further improve denoised output.

4   Experimental Results

We tested our technique on seven benchmark 8-bit images (Aerial, Baboon, Boat, Bridge, Lenna, Man and Peppers) taken from the USC-SIPI Image Database. Image sizes are either 512×512 or 1024×1024. We have implemented the algorithm in C++ using OpenCV library, and have run the tests in Ubuntu 14.04 running on Intel i7 2630QM 2.0 GHz processor and 4GB DDR3 RAM. We compared the performance of our proposed technqiue to two popular adaptive image restoration schemes: Lee filter [14] and Bilateral filter [22]. For this comparison, we have run the tests on images − Lenna, Aerial, Baboon and Boat.

For all the images, varying levels of AWGN was incorporated by varying the standard deviation σ from 0.03 to 0.30. A higher σ means more noise. Below $\sigma = 0.03$, the image appeared practically noiseless, while above $\sigma = 0.30$, the image was not recognizable. Then each image was fractally encoded and decoded. The decoded image was compared to the noisy image and the original image.

We have measured the decoded image quality with respect to the original noise free image using Peak Signal to Noise Ratio (PSNR) and Structural Similarity Index (SSIM) [24, 25].

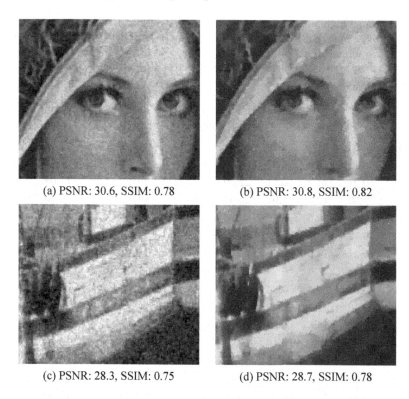

(a) PSNR: 30.6, SSIM: 0.78   (b) PSNR: 30.8, SSIM: 0.82

(c) PSNR: 28.3, SSIM: 0.75   (d) PSNR: 28.7, SSIM: 0.78

Fig. 5. Output after using (a, c) random seed image and (b, d) Fig. 4a as seed image, with AWGN $\sigma = 0.06$.

Figure 5 shows the output of denoising operation after using a random seed image versus using a noise-free seed image, as discussed in Sect. 3.5. Metric-wise the improvements are small. However to the human eye, object recognition and visual clarity is increased in Figs. 5b and d.

Table 1 lists the denoised image quality (in PSNR and SSIM) obtained using the proposed method, and comparares the results with that of Lee filter [14] and Bilateral filter [22]. Figures 6a and d show the comparison in the variation of noisy and denoised image quality with increase in image noise using PSNR and SSIM metrics, respectively, using the proposed denoising scheme. In both graphs, the denoised images have better quality than their noisy counterparts, indicating that denoising was indeed achieved. However, for the 'bridge' image, at very low levels of noise, our proposed scheme actually degraded the image quality.

Figures 6b, c, e and f show the comparison of our scheme with the Lee filter denoising method and the Bilateral filter method, for Aerial and Baboon images. Here again, our proposed scheme does degrade the image quality for very low noise levels. A possible explanation is that the fractal scheme acts more like a lossy compressor than an image restorator at these very low levels of noise. As

Table 1. Some highlights of experimental results obtained, showing denoised image quality (PSNR and SSIM) obtained using proposed denoising method, and comparing with Lee filter [14] and Bilateral filter [22]. Bold figures indicate cases where our proposed scheme performs the best denoising across varying noise values, compared to other methods.

Image	Sigma	Noisy image		Proposed method		Lee filter		Bilateral filter	
		PSNR	SSIM	PSNR	SSIM	PSNR	SSIM	PSNR	SSIM
Lenna	0.03	30.5	0.72	32.42	0.87	32.76	0.86	31.93	0.88
	0.12	18.6	0.22	**26.90**	0.58	**24.03**	0.43	**20.82**	0.26
	0.21	14.1	0.11	22.99	0.39	20.57	0.27	15.08	0.10
	0.30	11.7	0.07	20.51	0.29	18.63	0.20	12.16	0.06
Baboon	0.03	30.5	0.89	22.35	0.61	24.98	0.79	22.97	0.85
	0.12	18.5	0.47	21.88	0.55	21.42	0.53	18.77	0.41
	0.21	14.0	0.28	**20.21**	0.43	**19.15**	0.38	**14.38**	0.21
	0.30	11.6	0.18	18.76	0.34	17.76	0.30	11.74	0.13
Aerial	0.03	30.5	0.84	26.99	0.85	28.67	0.87	29.40	0.87
	0.12	18.7	0.40	**24.62**	0.67	**22.15**	0.54	**20.48**	0.33
	0.21	14.5	0.24	21.96	0.52	18.45	0.39	15.31	0.16
	0.30	12.0	0.16	19.71	0.41	16.32	0.29	12.46	0.11
Man	0.03	30.7	0.77	31.78	0.83	30.76	0.81	30.76	0.81
	0.12	19.0	0.25	22.84	0.41	21.19	0.30	21.19	0.30
	0.21	14.5	0.12	**19.44**	0.26	**15.48**	0.13	**15.48**	0.13
	0.30	12.0	0.08	17.32	0.19	12.44	0.08	12.44	0.08

noise levels gradually increase, our scheme starts performing well as a denoiser. When comparing to Lee filter, our scheme performs well for the baboon image, but not so well for the aerial image. It is interesting to note that Bilateral filtering actually degrades the image (according to the metrics) when noise level increases. An observation from the curves show that the proposed scheme performs best when σ is around 0.05. The downward slope is least around this region of the curve, and for baboon it even shows an upward trend.

Figures 7 and 8 show the actual output images of our proposed scheme compared with the noisy images, the images restored with Lee-filter and the images restored with Bilateral filter. The SSIM and PSNR values of each image, compared to the original, noise-free image is given below each image. Lee filter makes images look blurry. Bilateral filter makes the image look sharper, but noise particles are not effectively removed. Our scheme maintains the contrast and edges.

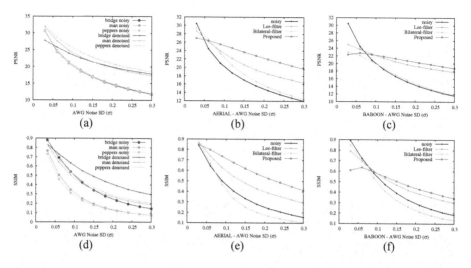

Fig. 6. (a) Comparison of level of restoration for different images using PSNR metric. (b) - (c) Comparison of performance of proposed method with Lee filter [14] and Bilateral filter [22] for Aerial and Baboon images using PSNR. (d) Comparison of level of restoration for different images using SSIM metric. (e) - (f) Comparison of performance of proposed method with Lee filter [14] and Bilateral filter [22] for Aerial and Baboon images using SSIM.

Size of range blocks chosen also influence the degree of denoising achieved. If only large range block sizes are chosen (like 32×32 or 64×64), then all noisy components disappear, but the quality of the output image is lowered as well. On the other hand, if only very small range blocks (like 2×2 or 4×4) are chosen, all the details from the noisy image will get approximated accurately, including the noisy components, thereby bringing back the noise in the decoded image, and leading to very little or no denoising This illustrates the importance of properly choosing the fractal encoding parameters for reducing noise. Our proposed scheme uses the quadtree partitioning scheme (Sect. 3.3), instead of using fixed size range blocks to tackle this situation. If the tolerance fidelity for a range block is exceeded, then it is partitioned into quadrants, and each quadrant is processed in a similar fashion as the parent block.

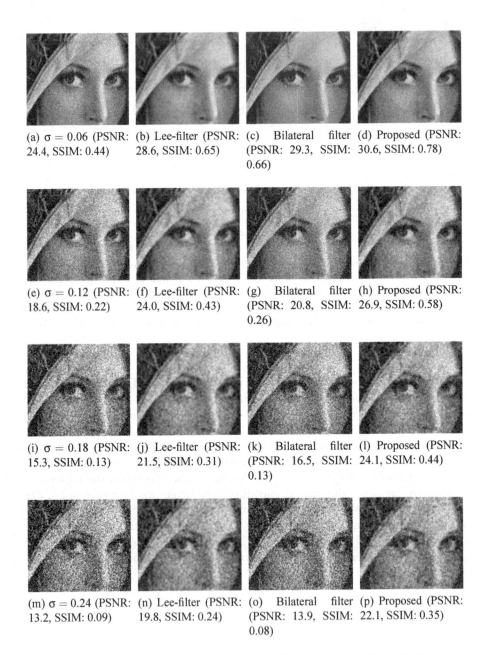

(a) σ = 0.06 (PSNR: 24.4, SSIM: 0.44)   (b) Lee-filter (PSNR: 28.6, SSIM: 0.65)   (c) Bilateral filter (PSNR: 29.3, SSIM: 0.66)   (d) Proposed (PSNR: 30.6, SSIM: 0.78)

(e) σ = 0.12 (PSNR: 18.6, SSIM: 0.22)   (f) Lee-filter (PSNR: 24.0, SSIM: 0.43)   (g) Bilateral filter (PSNR: 20.8, SSIM: 0.26)   (h) Proposed (PSNR: 26.9, SSIM: 0.58)

(i) σ = 0.18 (PSNR: 15.3, SSIM: 0.13)   (j) Lee-filter (PSNR: 21.5, SSIM: 0.31)   (k) Bilateral filter (PSNR: 16.5, SSIM: 0.13)   (l) Proposed (PSNR: 24.1, SSIM: 0.44)

(m) σ = 0.24 (PSNR: 13.2, SSIM: 0.09)   (n) Lee-filter (PSNR: 19.8, SSIM: 0.24)   (o) Bilateral filter (PSNR: 13.9, SSIM: 0.08)   (p) Proposed (PSNR: 22.1, SSIM: 0.35)

Fig. 7. Output for Lenna image. First column is the noisy image. Second column uses Lee filter [14]. Third column uses Bilateral Filter [22]. Fourth column has denoised image using proposed Fractal scheme.

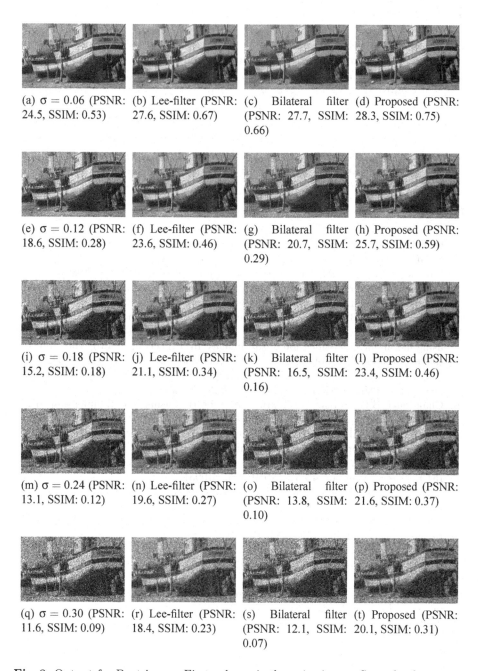

(a) σ = 0.06 (PSNR: 24.5, SSIM: 0.53)

(b) Lee-filter (PSNR: 27.6, SSIM: 0.67)

(c) Bilateral filter (PSNR: 27.7, SSIM: 0.66)

(d) Proposed (PSNR: 28.3, SSIM: 0.75)

(e) σ = 0.12 (PSNR: 18.6, SSIM: 0.28)

(f) Lee-filter (PSNR: 23.6, SSIM: 0.46)

(g) Bilateral filter (PSNR: 20.7, SSIM: 0.29)

(h) Proposed (PSNR: 25.7, SSIM: 0.59)

(i) σ = 0.18 (PSNR: 15.2, SSIM: 0.18)

(j) Lee-filter (PSNR: 21.1, SSIM: 0.34)

(k) Bilateral filter (PSNR: 16.5, SSIM: 0.16)

(l) Proposed (PSNR: 23.4, SSIM: 0.46)

(m) σ = 0.24 (PSNR: 13.1, SSIM: 0.12)

(n) Lee-filter (PSNR: 19.6, SSIM: 0.27)

(o) Bilateral filter (PSNR: 13.8, SSIM: 0.10)

(p) Proposed (PSNR: 21.6, SSIM: 0.37)

(q) σ = 0.30 (PSNR: 11.6, SSIM: 0.09)

(r) Lee-filter (PSNR: 18.4, SSIM: 0.23)

(s) Bilateral filter (PSNR: 12.1, SSIM: 0.07)

(t) Proposed (PSNR: 20.1, SSIM: 0.31)

Fig. 8. Output for Boat image. First column is the noisy image. Seoncd column uses Lee filter [14]. Third column uses Bilateral Filter [22]. Fourth column has denoised image using proposed Fractal scheme.

5   Conclusions

Our proposed fractal based denoising scheme has an advantage: as fractal transformations were primarily developed for image compression, our proposed scheme can also be optimized for performing image denoising and image compression simultaneously. Our scheme can remove noise effectively and also preserving edges, in order to reduce visual artifacts and distortions. The denoising is performed mainly during the fractal encoding process, where hierarchical classification has been employed to accelerate the encoder. Quadtree based image partitioning, pyramidal decoding and post processing has been used to enhance the degree of noise removal and improve the output image quality.

References

1. Banach, S.: Sur les opérations dans les ensembles abstraits et leur application aux équations intégrales. Fund. Math **3**(1), 133–181 (1922)
2. Barnsley, M.F.: Fractals Everywhere. Academic Press, Cambridge (1988)
3. Barnsley, M.F., Jacquin, A.E.: Application of recurrent iterated function systems to images. In: Visual Communications and Image Processing 1988. Third in a Series, pp. 122–131. International Society for Optics and Photonics (1988)
4. Bhattacharya, N., Roy, S.K., Nandi, U., Banerjee, S.: Fractal image compression using hierarchical classification of sub-images. In: Proceedings of the 10th International Conference on Computer Vision Theory and Applications, pp. 46–53 (2015)
5. Buades, A., Coll, B., Morel, J.M.: A review of image denoising algorithms, with a new one. Multiscale Model. Simul. **4**(2), 490–530 (2005)
6. Chaudhuri, B.B., Sarkar, N.: Texture segmentation using fractal dimension. IEEE Trans. Pattern Anal. Mach. Intell. **17**(1), 72–77 (1995)
7. Duh, D.J., Jeng, J., Chen, S.Y.: DCT based simple classification scheme for fractal image compression. Image Vis. Comput. **23**(13), 1115–1121 (2005)
8. Eskicioglu, A.M., Fisher, P.S.: Image quality measures and their performance. IEEE Trans. Commun. **43**(12), 2959–2965 (1995)
9. Fisher, Y. (ed.): Fractal Image Compression: Theory Appl. Springer, New York (1994)
10. Ghazel, M., Freeman, G.H., Vrscay, E.R.: Fractal image denoising. IEEE Trans. Image Process. **12**(12), 1560–1578 (2003)
11. Hürtgen, B., Stiller, C.: Fast hierarchical codebook search for fractal coding of still images. In: Berlin-DL tentative, pp. 397–408. International Society for Optics and Photonics (1993)
12. Hutchinson, J.E.: Fractals and self similarity. University of Melbourne. [Department of Mathematics] (1979)
13. Jacquin, A.E.: Image coding based on a fractal theory of iterated contractive image transformations. IEEE Trans. Image Process. **1**(1), 18–30 (1992)
14. Lee, J.S.: Digital image enhancement and noise filtering by use of local statistics. IEEE Trans. Pattern Anal. Mach. Intell. PAMI **2**(2), 165–168 (1980)
15. Lian, S.: Image authentication based on fractal features. Fractals **16**(04), 287–297 (2008)
16. Lin, K.T., Yeh, S.L.: Encrypting image by assembling the fractal-image addition method and the binary encoding method. Opt. Commun. **285**(9), 2335–2342 (2012)

17. Pi, M., Mandal, M.K., Basu, A.: Image retrieval based on histogram of fractal parameters. IEEE Trans. Multimedia **7**(4), 597–605 (2005)
18. Roy, S.K., Kumar, S., Chanda, B., Chaudhuri, B.B., Banerjee, S.: Fractal image compression using upper bound on scaling parameter. Chaos Solitons Fractals **106**, 16–22 (2018)
19. Saupe, D., Hamzaoui, R.: A review of the fractal image compression literature. ACM SIGGRAPH Comput. Graph. **28**(4), 268–276 (1994)
20. Shao, L., Yan, R., Li, X., Liu, Y.: From heuristic optimization to dictionary learning: a review and comprehensive comparison of image denoising algorithms. IEEE Trans. Cybern. **44**(7), 1001–1013 (2014)
21. Tang, X., Qu, C.: Facial image recognition based on fractal image encoding. Bell Labs Techn. J. **15**(1), 209–214 (2010)
22. Tomasi, C., Manduchi, R.: Bilateral filtering for gray and color images. In: Sixth International Conference on Computer Vision, pp. 839–846. IEEE (1998)
23. Wang, J., Zheng, N.: A novel fractal image compression scheme with block classification and sorting based on Pearson's correlation coefficient. IEEE Trans. Image Process. **22**, 3690–3702 (2013)
24. Wang, Z., Bovik, A.C.: Mean squared error: love it or leave it? A new look at signal fidelity measures. IEEE Sig. Process. Mag. **26**(1), 98–117 (2009)
25. Wang, Z., Bovik, A.C., Sheikh, H.R., Simoncelli, E.P.: Image quality assessment: from error visibility to structural similarity. IEEE Trans. Image Process. **13**(4), 600–612 (2004)
26. Wohlberg, B., De Jager, G.: A review of the fractal image coding literature. IEEE Trans. Image Process **8**(12), 1716–1729 (1999)

Optimal Geometric Active Contours: Application to Human Brain Segmentation

Ankur Biswas[1][(⊠)], Santi P. Maity[2], and Paritosh Bhattacharya[3]

[1] Tripura Institute of Technology, Narsingarh, Tripura, India
abiswas.tit@gmail.com
[2] IIEST, Shibpur, Howrah, West Bengal, India
spmaity@yahoo.com
[3] National Institute of Technology, Agartala, Tripura, India
pari76@rediffmail.com

Abstract. An efficient Segmentation of lateral ventricles plays a vital role in quantitatively analyzing the global and regional information in magnetic resonance imaging (MRI) of human brain. In this paper, a semi automatic segmentation methodology to support the study of efficient pathologies of the lateral ventricles along with white matter and gray matter of human brain is proposed. The segmentation is executed using an optimal geometric active contour with level set methods. A nominal anatomical knowledge is incorporated into the methodology in order to choose the most probable surfaces of the lateral ventricles of human brain, even if they are disconnected, and to eliminate addition of non ventricle cerebrospinal fluid (CSF) regions. The proposed segmentation method is applied to multislice MRI data and compared with region growing algorithms. The results Dice similarity coefficient 0.955, Jaccard similarity coefficient 0.815 demonstrates the reliability and efficiency.

Keywords: Magnetic resonance imaging (MRI) · Geometric active contour
Level set · Dice similarity coefficient · Jaccard similarity coefficient

1 Introduction

Image segmentation is a significant means used in image study and analysis in order to partition an image into disjoint regions, so that the regions correspond to the objects in the image. It is widely used in successful medical imaging tool. Magnetic resonance imaging (MRI) is a kind of more obtrusive way of imaging that has emerged as the method of choice for diagnosing a variety of human organs and tissue [1], which can provide a ideal, instinctual anatomical image for effectively analysis of human brain function and 3-D reconstruction to accurately segmentation, left ventricle and right ventricle. A perfect classification of brain images to lateral ventricles right and left (one for each hemisphere will facilitate computer aided disease diagnosis structurally, such as constriction of the foramina and cerebral aqueduct which means that they can become congested, by blood and may cause hemorrhagic stroke. Cerebrospinal fluid is recurrently produced by the choroid plexus inside the ventricles, any obstruction of hemorrhage leads to progressively more elevated pressure in the lateral ventricles that

© Springer Nature Singapore Pte Ltd. 2018
J. K. Mandal and D. Sinha (Eds.): CSI 2017, CCIS 836, pp. 646–657, 2018.
https://doi.org/10.1007/978-981-13-1343-1_53

commonly leads to hydrocephalus. Diseases of the lateral ventricles also include irritation in membranes (known as meningitis) and ventricles (known as ventriculitis) which are grounds of infection or the preamble of blood causing hemorrhage. Magnetic resonance imaging (MRI) has outdated the use of CT in research for detecting ventricles abnormality in psychiatric infirmity. Enlarged ventricles are reasons or effects of schizophrenia or disease like Alice in Wonderland yet requires some established facts. Enlarged ventricles are also established in organic dementia and already enlightened mostly in terms of environmental factors [2]. They have also been found to be enormously varied diverse between individuals and the percentage disparity in group averages in schizophrenia studies and described as "not a very reflective difference in the context of normal variation." [3].

Although there is a significant body of work for the segmentation methodology of the left ventricle of heart, there is less work for the joint segmentation of the both the lateral ventricles of human brain. Semi automated and Region growing algorithms are established as an effective approach for MR image segmentation [4, 5]. Active contour models like snakes [6, 7] and level sets [8–11] proved promising in variety of problems in medical image segmentation. Geometric active contour framework has been exposed as simple, efficient and fairly accurate [12, 13] but include a tendency to leak out in gaps of object edges due to existence of noise or indistinct boundaries. 3D snake was applied to segment the ventricle of heart requiring high level of user interaction in order to avoid the leakage of contour [14]. The main objective of this paper is to present a semi automatic segmentation method which is based on Active contour via level set method which will robustly and accurately extract the lateral ventricles, white matter and gray matter of the human brain to support the analysis of functional pathologies. The goal is to offer quantitative measures of the brain's function, including the thickness all over the ventricles, the internal volume and enlargement of temporal horns, and transependymal oedema that may be visible as high T2 signal on MRI. Data is attained in the form of multislice MRI. The resulting method will be free from clean up step as followed in segmentation algorithms like region growing that require filling holes and removing small connected components. The proposed technique is compared with previous segmentation methods in terms of region growing such as Connected Threshold [15], Confidence Connected [15], and Vector Confidence Connected [15]. The remainder of the paper is organized as follows: Sect. 2 provides the necessary background about previous work, covering aspects of region growing algorithm for MR imaging and interrelated work in lateral ventricle segmentation. While Sect. 3 illustrate the methodological outline of the proposed approach, Sect. 4 deals with various discussion on results of segmentation and Sect. 5 presents the conclusion with future scope of the methodology.

2   Previous Work

In this section several interactive and automatic methods using different region growing algorithm that have been developed to segment major anatomical structures of human brain are discussed.

2.1 Connected Threshold

In this technique, the criterion to include a pixel in a region is provided by the user as lower and upper threshold values which are used by the filter based on an interval of intensity values between lower and upper values. The inclusion criterion for a pixel is given by,

$$I(X) \in [\text{lower, upper}] \tag{1}$$

where I() is the image and X is the position of the picky neighbor pixel which is considered for addition in the region.

```
Algorithm 1:

   1. Set seed point using SetSeed()
   2. Adjust lower, upper threshold
   3. Preprocess Image using smoothing filter
   4. Include I(x) ∈ [lower, upper]
   5. Set intensity value included in the region with
      SetReplaceValue().
   6. Update()
   7. AddSeed() for multiple seeds
```

2.2 Confidence Connected

This region growing algorithm analyses the information of the current region in order to compute the mean, μ and standard deviation, σ and allows to perfectly specifying the threshold bounds. A constant value 'k' is taken as input from the user to multiply σ in order to define a range around μ and considered from the seed points, $\mu \pm k\sigma$. The inclusion criterion for a pixel is given by,

$$I(X) \in [\mu - k\sigma, \mu + k\sigma] \tag{2}$$

where I() is the image and X is the pixel being considered for addition in the region. k is the range of intensities called multiplier must be carefully selected than the number of iterations. In the first run the bounds are defined by the seed voxels specified, in the following iterations, μ and σ are estimated from the segmented points and the region growing is updated accordingly, iteration is the number of Iterations depend on the homogeneity of the intensities, INR is the Initial Neighborhood Radius, a region can be specified around each seed point "INR" from which the statistics are estimated.

```
Algorithm 2:

   1. Calculate µ,σ for intensity values of the pixels
      that are included in the region.
   2. Set  SetSeed(), k, iteration, INR
   3. µ ± kσ.
   4. Include I(x) ∈ [µ - kσ, µ + kσ ]
   5. Set intensity value inside the region with
      SetReplaceValue().
   6. Update()
   7. Repeat 3-6 until no more pixels are added or itera-
      tion.
```

2.3   Vector Confidence Connected

In this technique T1 and T2 image from the same person is loaded and combined to create a vector image. The execution is similar to Confidence Connected, and allows to completely specifying the threshold bounds based on the statistics estimated from the seed points. The main difference is that in this case Mahalanobis is used and not the intensity difference. It is a simplification of the previous approach to vectored images, for instance multi-spectral images or multi-parametric MRI. The neighboring voxel's intensity vector is within the implicitly specified bounds using the Mahalanobis distance,

$$\sqrt{(x - \mu)^T \Sigma^{-1} (x - \mu)} < k, \tag{3}$$

Where, μ is the mean of the vectors at the seed points, Σ is the covariance matrix and 'k' is a user specified constant.

3   Proposed Methodology

The proposed segmentation workflow is depicted in Fig. 1. The workflow consists of five major steps: 1. Initialize Active Contour – used to choose the region of interest (ROI), for segmentation to start. ROIs are regularly used to reduce the computer's workload by sinking the total number of pixels to consider, thus reducing the processing time. It can also be used to reduce the amount of different anatomical structure; when looking for lateral ventricles, the dataset to consider usually consist of the whole brain. If the region of interest is then determined to only encompass lateral ventricles, the other regions in the brain need not to be considered, thus eases the segmentation process. 2. ROI supersample - the selected ROI is re-sampled (supersampled) by a fixed factor in x, y and z voxels. There are two methods of interpolation, Linear interpolation (for better quality) and Nearest neighbour (for fast). This resampling is for reducing the noise and enhancing the boundaries of the ROI. 3. Adjust pre-segmentation parameters - the lower, upper threshold, smoothness values of thresholding function are set for segmentation to begin. 4. Initialize and configure the contour evolution equation – Contours on the image can be added for segmentation to begin and parameters are set for Region competition force that pushes the contour inwards or outwards and Curvature force that makes the contour boundary smoother and can prevent the contour's tendency of leaking into narrow objects. It also adjusts the stiffness of the snake. Level set method is utilized here for the ease of implementation of active contours. The method is implemented by 3D geodesic active contour method developed by [16] using ITK-SNAP [17]. The energy function, weighted combination of internal and external forces must be optimized. The internal forces and the external forces originate from the shape of the snake and image respectively. The solution can be obtained using techniques of variational calculus. The energy function is given by,

$$
\begin{aligned}
\text{Energy}_{\text{acm}} &= \int_0^1 \text{Energy}_{\text{acm}}(\mathbf{V}(q))dq \\
&= \int_0^1 \text{Energy}_{\text{internal}}(\mathbf{V}(q)) + \text{Energy}_{\text{image}}(\mathbf{V}(q)) + \text{Energy}_{\text{external}}(\mathbf{V}(q))dq
\end{aligned}
\tag{4}
$$

Where, $\text{E}_{\text{internal}}(\mathbf{V}(q))$ is the internal energy stands for smoothness or regularity along the curve that has two components (resisting to stretching and bending), $\text{Energy}_{\text{image}}(\mathbf{V}(q))$ is the image forces that guides the active contour towards the desired image properties (strong gradients) and $\text{Energy}_{\text{external}}(\mathbf{V}(q))$ is the external constraint force can be used to account for user-defined constraints, or prior knowledge on the structure to be recovered.

The internal energy is given by,

$$
\text{Energy}_{\text{internal}} = (\alpha(q)|\mathbf{V}'(q)|^2 + \beta(q)|\mathbf{V}''(q)|^2)/2
\tag{5}
$$

where the first-order term "membrane" term is the minimum energy when curve minimizes length, second-order term "thin plate" term is the minimum energy when curve is smooth, $\alpha(q)$ is the Region competition force, $\beta(q)$ is the Smoothnes (curvature) force.

5. Final step, Terminate the segmentation – it may requires some post-processing steps in order to extract and refine the boundaries of the ventricles and other anatomical structures.

The proposed approach is performed on datasets that comprise of T1-weighted brain MR images of MIDAS nac-hncma-atlas2013-Slicer4Version obtained from kitware. The main idea of the proposed method is to apply semi-automatic segmentation on MR Image of human to segment lateral ventricles. The sequence of intermediate steps of the proposed system is represented in Fig. 2.

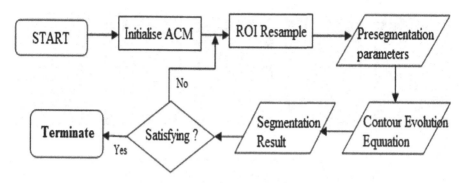

Fig. 1. Proposed segmentation workflow

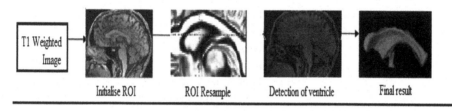

Fig. 2. Intermediate steps of the proposed methodology

4   Experimental Results

In this section the results of proposed approach are shown and compared with three other variants of region growing algorithms. The T1 weighted MRI brain scan is rescaled to the intensities [0, 255]. A preselected seed point in the lateral ventricle, (135, 145, 96) using Insight Software Consortium-SimpleITK. Result of ventricle segmentation seed point selection using three region growing algorithms and proposed method are shown in Fig. 3 with the locations and defining values for parameters used being presented in Table 1. And segmented results of ventricle, white matter, gray matter are shown in Fig. 4 with defining values for parameters used being tabulated in Table 2.

4.1   Evaluation

Comparison of segmented lateral ventricles obtained using proposed method (pink contours) and manual delineations (red contours) shown in Fig. 5. A comparison of segmentation accuracy of different tissues of brain obtained by different software package is also shown in Table 3.

The performance of the results obtained by proposed method was then evaluated by comparing the algorithm to the results of manual segmentation using volume-based metrics based on guidelines and the evaluation software by [19] are tabulated in

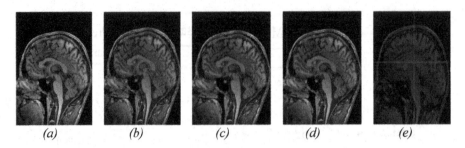

(a)   *(b)*   *(c)*   *(d)*   *(e)*

Fig. 3. Results of segmentation of lateral ventricle with predefined seed points using different scheme (a. original image, b. connected threshold, c. confidence connected, d. vector confidence connected, e. Proposed method)

Table 1. Parameters used for segmentation of ventricles of brain structure shown in Fig. 3

Segmentation type	Parameters	Value
Connected threshold	Lower threshold	100
	Upper threshold	170
Confidence connected	Iterations	0
	Multiplier	2
	Neighborhood radius	1
Vector confidence connected	Iterations	2
	Multiplier	4
Proposed method	Lower threshold	16
	Upper threshold	59
	Seeds	(20, 49, 29) (41, 49, 18)
	Region competition function	1
	Smoothing function	0.2

Table 4 and are presented in Fig. 6. Additionally, Jaccard index [20], Dice [21], hausdorff and surface distance (mean and max) are reported. Metrics are applied to binary valued volumes, so a metric computed on the ventricle for example considers only ventricle objects as foreground and everything else as background. The main metric is the Dice score, where the Dice score is in the interval [0, 1]. A perfect segmentation yields a Dice score of 1. In order to assess the efficiency of algorithm, average run time of several segmentations was considered as the segmentation time. The results of segmented lateral ventricle are compared to combined manual segmentation to obtain reference data that is closer to the "ground truth" and given a score for each case. In order to combine input from multiple observations two approaches, majority vote and the Simultaneous Truth and Performance Level Estimation (STAPLE) [22] are exploited.

Computational Complexity: Results obtained from the proposed approach was implemented on a Windows desktop with an Intel i3-CPU (2.93 GHz) and the user interface on Python environment. The average segmentation time is 10–15 s in addition

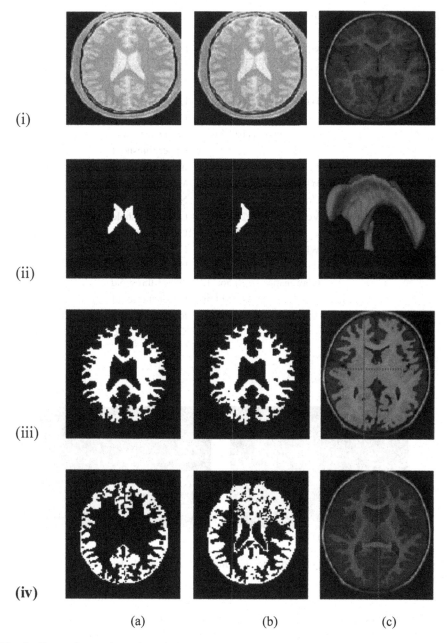

Fig. 4. Comparison of results of the major anatomical structures of human brain after segmentation of T1 weighted MRI, (i) original image on load, (ii) lateral ventricles (iii) white matter, (iv) gray matter: (a) connected threshold, (b) confidence connected, (c) proposed method.

654   A. Biswas et al.

Table 2. Parameters used for segmenting major anatomical structures of human brain on T1 weighted MRI shown in Fig. 4.

Segmentation type	Structure	Seed index	Parameters	Value
Connected threshold	Ventricle	(81,112)	Lower threshold	210
			Upper threshold	250
	White matter	(60,116)	Lower threshold	150
			Upper threshold	180
	Gray matter	(107,69)	Lower threshold	180
			Upper threshold	210
Confidence connected	Ventricle	(81,112)	Iterations	0
	White matter	(60,116)	Multiplier	2
	Gray matter	(107,69)	Neighborhood radius	1
Proposed method	Ventricle	(20,49,29) (41,49,18)	Lower threshold	89
			Upper threshold	125
	White matter	(48,60,91) (87,56,91)	Lower threshold	71
			Upper threshold	143
	Gray matter	(20,56,112) (110,13,48)	Lower threshold	13
			Upper threshold	62
			Region completion function	1
			Smoothing function	0.2

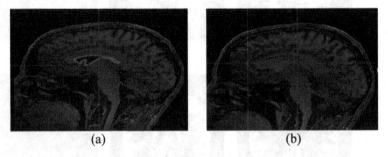

(a)   (b)

Fig. 5. Comparison of segmented lateral ventricles (a) manual delineations, (b) proposed method (semi-automatic)

to 50 s for initialization and setting parameters that results total segmentation time <60 s or 1 min for a single lateral ventricle in MRI image in 3D, which is considerably less than usual total time of manual segmentation which is approximately 30 min.

Table 3. Comparison of segmentation accuracy of SPM8, FSL and Brainsuite using Brainweb simulated MR images [18].

Structure	Software package	Dice	Jaccard
White matter	SPM8-Seg	0.92	0.86
	FSL	0.93	0.86
	Brainsuite	0.91	0.84
Gray matter	SPM8-Seg	0.90	0.83
	FSL 0.	0.92	0.85
	Brainsuite	0.80	0.68
CSF	SPM8-Seg	0.62	0.46
	FSL	0.74	0.6
	Brainsuite	0.46	0.31

Table 4. Comparison of different Quantitative segmentation results of the lateral ventricle on MR Image of human brain

Type	Dice	Jaccard	False_ negative	False_ positive	Hausdorff_ distance	Mean_ surfac_ distance	Max_ surfac_ distance
Manual1	0.938	0.883	0.083	0.040	2.121	0.101	2.828
Manual2	0.970	0.842	0.039	0.020	1.061	0.041	1.414
Proposed	0.955	0.815	0.021	0.067	3.354	0.021	1.000

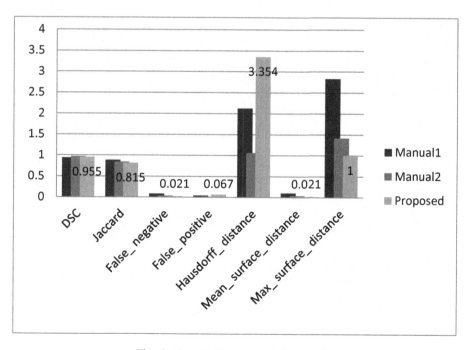

Fig. 6. Quantitative segmentation results

5 Conclusion and Future Scope

In this paper, a semi-automatic technique that is capable of detecting anatomical structure in MR images of human brain containing cerebral ventricles, White matter and Gray matter on MIDAS datasets [23]. The accuracy of the proposed algorithm in ventricle segmentation along with its little computational complexity demonstrates the efficiency. Another major advantage is its liberty from clean up step followed in low level segmentation algorithm. In addition, it does not require any input or initial assumptions like other methods such as number of iterations, multiplier, initial neighborhood radius, our method. Our result produces a 3D output that will make diagnosis of acute obstructive hydrocephalus and other diseases related to cerebral ventricles that can detected in terms of size and appearance more efficiently. This formulates the proposed technique more robust to a great extent and more general than other methods. The evaluation results indicate that semi-automatic approach significantly out-performs the approach of region growing that require initial parameters to set and lead to high computational complexities. These observations prove that the approach is adequate to discriminate the ventricles from other regions in T1-weighted MR images.

The proposed scheme can be easily extended to other organs mainly liver, breast to locate tumors, and to additional imaging modalities, such as US, CT and X-rays. On application to liver US or CT scan, it will facilitate computer aided disease diagnosis structurally, such as size of tumor in liver as well as brain for therapy, sizes of different renal calculi etc. The proposed methodology can also be applied to locate fractures on bones from medical images.

References

1. Filippi, M., et al.: MRI criteria for the diagnosis of multiple sclerosis: MAGNIMS consensus guidelines. Lancet Neurol. **15**(3), 292–303 (2016)
2. Peper, J.S., Brouwer, R.M., Boomsma, D.I., Kahn, R.S., Hulshoff Pol, H.E.: Genetic influences on human brain structure: a review of brain imaging studies in twins. Hum. Brain Mapp. **28**(6), 464–473 (2007)
3. Allen, J.S., Damasio, H., Grabowski, T.J.: Normal neuro anatomical variation in the human brain: an MRI-volumetric study. Am. J. Phys. Anthropol. **118**(4), 341–358 (2002)
4. Liu, T., Xu, H., Jin, W., Liu, Z., Zhao, Y., Tian, W.: Medical image segmentation based on a hybrid region-based active contour model. Comput. Math. Methods Med. **2014**, Article ID 890725, 10 p. (2014). https://doi.org/10.1155/2014/890725
5. Valverde, S., Oliver, A., et al.: Automated tissue segmentation of MR brain images in the presence of white matter lesions. Med. Image Anal. **35**, 446–457 (2017)
6. Kass, M., Witkin, A., Terzopoulos, D.: Snakes: active contour models. Int. J. Comput. Vis. **1**(4), 321–331 (1998)
7. Zhou, Y., Shi, W.R., Chen, W., et al.: Active contours driven by localizing region and edge-based intensity fitting energy with application to segmentation of the left ventricle in cardiac CT images. Neurocomputing **156**, 199–210 (2015)
8. Liu, Y., Captur, G., Moon, J.C., et al.: Distance regularized two level sets for segmentation of left and right ventricles from cine-MRI. Magn. Reson. Imaging **34**(5), 699–706 (2016)

9. Yang, C., Wu, W., Su, Y., Zhang, S.: Left ventricle segmentation via two-layer level sets with circular shape constraint. Magn. Reson. Imaging **38**, 202–213 (2017)

10. Osher, S., Sethian, J.A.: Fronts propagating with curvature-dependent speed: algorithms based on Hamilton-Jacobi formulations. J. Comput. Phys. **79**, 12–49 (1988)

11. Adalsteinsson, D., Sethian, J.A.: A fast level set method for propagating interfaces. J. Comput. Phys. **118**(2), 269–277 (1995)

12. Caselles, V., Kimmel, R., Sapiro, G.: Geodesic active contours. IJCV **22**(1), 61–79 (1997)

13. Goldenberg, R., Kimmel, R., Rivlin, E., Rudzsky, M.: Fast geodesic active contours. IEEE Trans. Image Process. **10**(10), 1467–1475 (2001)

14. Zhukov, L., Bao, Z., Guskov, I., Wood, J., Breen, D.: Dynamic deformable models for 3D MRI heart segmentation. Proc. SPIE Med. Imaging **2002**, 1398–1405 (2002)

15. Johnson, H.J., McCormick, M.M., Ibanez, L.: The Insight Softwar Consortium. The ITK Software Guide Book 2: Design and Functionality, 4th (edn.) (2017). https://itk.org/ITKSoftwareGuide/html/Book2/ITKSoftwareGuide-Book2.html

16. Caselles, V., Kimmel, R., Sapiro, G.: Geodesic active contours. Int. J. Comput. Vis. **22**(1), 61–79 (1997)

17. Yushkevich, P.A., et al.: User guided 3D active contour segmentation of anatomical structures: Significantly improved efficiency and reliability. Neuroimage **31**(3), 1116–1128 (2006)

18. Kazemi, K., Noorizadeh, N.: Quantitative comparison of SPM, FSL, and brainsuite for brain MR image segmentation. J. Biomed. Phys. Eng. **4**(1), 13 (2014)

19. Taha, A., Hanbury, A.: Metrics for evaluating 3D medical image segmentation: analysis, selection, and tool. BMC Med. Imaging **15**, 29 (2015)

20. Al-Faris, A.Q., Ngah, U.K., Isa, N.A.M., Shuaib, I.L.: MRI breast skin-line segmentation and removal using integration method of level set active contour and morphological thinning algorithms. J. Med. Sci. **12**(8), 286–291 (2012)

21. Cardenes, R., de Luis-Garcia, R., Bach-Cuadra, M.: A multidimensional segmentation evaluation for medical image data. Comput. Methods Programs Biomed. **96**(2), 108–124 (2009)

22. Warfield, S.K., Zou, K.H., Wells, W.M.: 'Simultaneous truth and performance level estimation (STAPLE): an algorithm for the validation of image segmentation'. IEEE Trans. Med. Imaging **23**(7), 903–921 (2004)

23. NLM: Imaging Methods Assessment and Reporting. http://hdl.handle.net/1926/586

Computational Intelligence

Classification of Library Resources in Recommender System Using Machine Learning Techniques

Snehalata B. Shirude[✉] and Satish R. Kolhe

School of Computer Sciences, NMU, Jalgaon, India
snehalata.shirude@gmail.com, srkolhe2000@gmail.com

Abstract. The objective of the proposed Library Recommender System is to make available efficient and quick use of library resources. The various tasks includes searching the appropriate book/s, research journal papers, and articles. Library recommender system filters library resources using content based and collaborative filtering approaches. To simplify and improve the results of recommendations, library resources are categorized referring to categories defined in Classification System 2012 defined by ACM. This classification is implemented using different machine learning techniques. This paper compares the results of different machine learning techniques and discusses about them.

Keywords: Library recommender system · Filtering · Classification
Ontology · Machine learning

1 Introduction

Great capacity of information, identifying interest/s of user implicitly are the problems motivated in improvement of recommender system for library users. Retrieval of relevant library records rendering to the importance of the user is one of the significant task in the improvement of recommender system for digital libraries. The objective of the proposed Library Recommender System is to make available library records such as appropriate books, research journal papers, and articles efficiently and quickly to members of library [33]. Since recommendation process requires to decide and act as per the perception, agent established architecture is appropriate to put forward the architecture of recommender system. Library recommender system filters library records using content based and collaborative filtering methods [20]. The filtering process requires library resources from dataset which is like picking out particular book/journal as per our interest from shelf of physical library. The classification of books, journal articles allow to arrange them which similar to the arrangement made in physical library. Classification of resources in library is made into 14 categories listed in CCS 2012 given by ACM. PU (Positive Unlabeled learning), NB (Naïve Bayes) classifier, k-NN (k-Nearest Neighbor), and decision tree are experimented [34]. Rough set rule generation (using Genetic, LEM - Learning from Examples Module, and

© Springer Nature Singapore Pte Ltd. 2018
J. K. Mandal and D. Sinha (Eds.): CSI 2017, CCIS 836, pp. 661–673, 2018.
https://doi.org/10.1007/978-981-13-1343-1_54

Covering) and LOOCV – Leave One out Cross Validation approaches builds a novel classifier.

2 Literature Study

The review of recommender systems for libraries gives various solutions [1]. The different aspects viz. methodology, techniques applied during the implementation of library recommender systems are considered [33]. It is analyzed that library domain requires to reach maximum recommendation performance in comparison with other domains such as news, music, tourism, etc. [12]. Some of the frameworks are seen using agent based approach [2–4]. The use of semantic web techniques and fuzzy linguistic modeling techniques reaches up to 50% precision, 70.66% recall and 58.19% f1 values [2]. These values suggests probability in more progresses. An intelligent agent which works as a tool to help students for searching a library is proposed. Pyramid collaborative filtering method and dominant distance method are used to compute the results. Classification of users is performed according to user's learning styles while filtering records [13]. A theoretical framework of multiagent based recommender system consisting of variety of agents is given [3]. The experiment is limited to software engineering ontology only. Porcel, Moreno and Herrera-Viedma proposed a recommender system for university digital libraries [2, 9]. Binary classification of resources is implemented by Lau et al. using k-NN [14]. Explicit feedback collection by asking users to give answers to questions is identified in some of the works. The performance improvement can be done implementing implicit feedback collection. In folksonomy, the similar users are clustered using tag based method [15]. KNN classification based on only title of the books is seen in location aware book recommendation system [17]. If more fields are added along with title, further improvement can be possible [33]. Need of implementation for effective searching, research guidance to library users is proposed in taxonomy of student driven library website [18]. The personal ontology generated for specific user is created in design of recommender system [19]. This gives intuition that the extensive use of ontology to retrieve weighted semantic similar keywords can improve the performance of recommender systems. To review it is clear that agent based approach, use of ontology, weight assignment, richer datasets are necessary to improve the performance of recommender system.

3 Library Resources Classification

This section describes about the proposed system, dataset preparation and design of different library resources classifier.

3.1 Proposed System

The architecture given in Fig. 1 describes the tasks to be performed in the library recommender system.

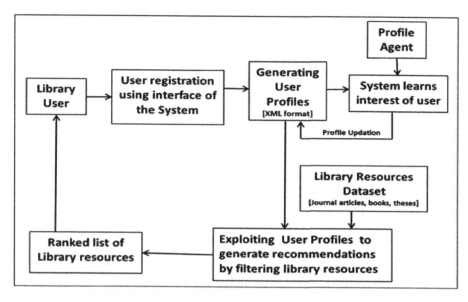

Fig. 1. Architecture of the proposed recommender system

Taxonomic architecture of recommender systems consists of profile generation & maintenance and profile exploitation as two important steps. Representing User profile, primary profile generation, profile learning method, significant response identification are important tasks to be performed in first step. Information filtering, user profile-item similarity computation, user profile matching, and profile revision technique are performed while second step [20]. In proposed system architecture, the library user has to register in the system to become member. System generates initial profile into XML format for each user. Profile agent obtains the interests of logged in user and provides it

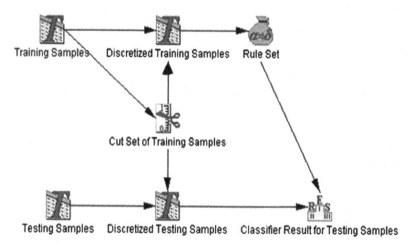

Fig. 2. Rough set rule extraction classifier for recommender system

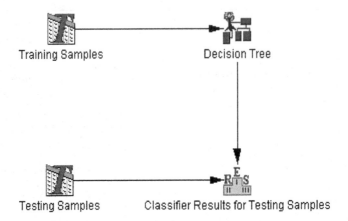

Fig. 3. Decision tree classifier for recommender system

to the system for updation of the profiles. There are library resources such as journal articles, books, theses into the dataset. The primary objective of the system is to offer the recommendations to active user as per the interests of that user. Therefore, by exploiting the active user profile, filtering is performed to generate the recommendations. Content based, collaborative and hybrid are three approaches for information filtering. In content based filtering, the interest of user is matched with all library resources in dataset. Collaborative filtering groups the similar user and accordingly the recommendations are provided [21]. The proposed system makes use of hybrid approach for filtering with content based and collaborative filtering techniques. Filtering practices similarity measures to find the closeness among the library resources and active user profile. Recommendations are provided to the active user via user interface in the form of ranked list of library resources.

3.2   Dataset Preparation

The dataset is created for the development of library recommender system as no benchmarking dataset is available [7, 23, 24]. It includes User Profiles, Library Resources, and ACM CCS 2012 as ontology.

User Profiles. User profiles are stored in XML format. One sample user is shown in following XML snippet.

<User ID="09"> <FirstName>Snehalata<FirstName>
<Lastname>Shirude</LastName><MemberType>Teacher</MemberType>
<Department>School of Computer Science
</Department><Course>Ph.D </Course><Subject>Computer
Science</Subject>
<EmailAddress>snehalata.shirude@gmail.com</EmailAddress>
<ResearchTopic>Development of Recommender System for Efficient Use of
Libraries</ResearchTopic> <PublishedWork></PublishedWork></User>

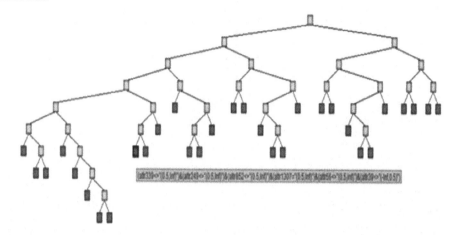

Fig. 4. Decision tree first fold for DT classifier for recommender system

The 25 numbers of users are considered for evaluation of the system.

Library Resources. The variety of books, journal articles and research articles are kept in XML layout. Major part of the library resources includes Computer Science related books and journal articles collected using Z39.50 protocol from Library of Congress, PHI, Laxmi Publications, Pearson education, Cambridge education and McGraw Hill Publications. Currently, there are around 705 different records added.

Ontology. Since no complete ontology is available for Computer Science, Computing Classification System 2012 defined by ACM is used as ontology [25]. SKOS format of ACM CCS 2012 is used. Concept, Broader, Narrower, Related, Preflabel, Altlabel, Hidden label are extracted to retrieve semantically related keywords.

3.3 Library Resources Classifier

Classification of library resources allows to increase recommendation performance [34]. The experiments are carried out on test data which contains 1463 input columns and single output bit. ACM CCS 2012 is used to generate these input features. A sample record is specified in Table 1.

Classifier Using Rough Set Rule Extraction. Rough set theory approach has found useful in many applications in the various areas [26]. Indiscernibility relation generation is the mathematical basis of rough set theory [27]. The indiscernibility relation of U (universe) is defined as $I(B) = \{(x, y) \in U \times U : f_a(x) = f_a(y), \forall a \in B\}$ where A is finite set of attributes with every attribute $a \in A$ having set of its values associated. Each attribute a determine a function $f_a : U \rightarrow V_a$. B is the subset of A. The indiscernibility relation is an equivalence relation. The approach assumes that any vague concept is replaced by a pair of precise concepts called the lower and upper approximation. The lower approximation $B_*(X)$ and upper approximation $B^*(X)$ over the X

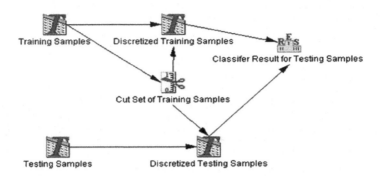

Fig. 5. k-NN classifier for recommender system

(subset of X) are defined as $B_*(X) = \{x \in U : B(x) \subseteq X\}$ and $B^*(X) = \{x \in U : B(x) \cap X \neq \emptyset\}$. The rough set can be characterized numerically as $\propto_B (X) = \frac{|B_*(X)|}{|B^*(X)|}$. The value of $\propto_B$ lies in between [0, 1]. The boundary region set $BN_B(X)$ is obtained as $BN_B(X) = \{x \in U : 0 < \mu_X^B(x) < 1$ where $\mu_X^B(x)$ is rough membership function giving value between [0, 1]. If boundary region comes out to be empty then X is crisp means exact with respect to B otherwise it is rough means inexact with respect to B. Rough set theory performs approximation of sets using these lower, upper, and boundary region conditions [28]. The attributes of each vector in defined set of library resources lies either of the set lower, upper, or boundary region with respect to vectors of categories in knowledgebase. A rough set based classifier designed for classifying library resources is given in Fig. 2.

Training and testing samples of library resources consists of 1463 attributes. The number of attributes is large enough which creates a low probability to properly recognize the new testing sample by matching its attribute value vector with the trained sample rows. Therefore, the value set reduction is performed by symbolic attribute value grouping as the attributes are symbolic. This technique reduces the cardinality of value sets of symbolic attributes. The computation involves use of clustering function defined as $c_a : V_a \rightarrow \{1, \ldots \ldots, m\}$, where $m \leq card(V_a)$ where V_a is the set of every attribute a in vector representing testing library resources. c is cut set calculated on V_a. Cut sets are generated by making partitions on V_a. Then the system generates the rule set. The rule sets are generated by using Genetic, LEM, and Covering methods [29]. These experiments are performed using RSRE Version 2.2 [33] using tenfold approach for each of the method. The.tab files are generated for testing and training library resources. The classes 'General and Reference', 'Social and professional topics' and 'Proper nouns: People, technologies, and companies' are not considered by the classifier as they are unrelated.

Classifier Using Decision Tree. Machine learning using decision tree is one of the most commonly used method for classification [30]. Tree is used as classification model. A decision tree is created by dividing the training records so that the resulting subsets are as pure as possible. A pure subset is one that contains only training examples of a single class. Divide and conquer strategy that recursively partitions the

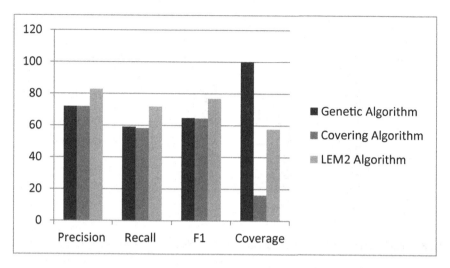

Fig. 6. Graph comparing precision, recall, and F1 values of RSRE classifier for recommender system

data to produce the tree is used while learning the tree. The best attribute is chosen while partitioning the data at the current node according to the values of the attribute. Impurity function is used to maximize the purity of partitioning process. Decision tree induction defines the stopping criteria of the recursion in such way that the procedure halts when all the training records in the existing data belong to similar class [31, 32]. The library resources classifier is designed using decision tree as shown in Fig. 3.

The decision tree is constructed by the decomposition of the training samples not larger than the predefined size. Then testing samples are classified using the decision

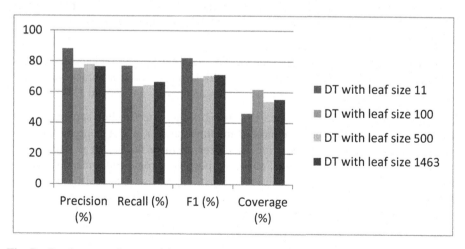

Fig. 7. Graph comparing precision, recall, and F1 values of decision tree classifier in recommender system

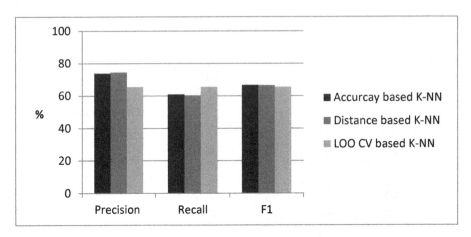

Fig. 8. Graph comparing precision, recall, and F1 values of k-NN classifier in recommender system

tree generated. To make the decomposition tree, the parameters "maximal size of leaf", "shortening ratio", and "discretization" are set. The experiments are performed for leaf sizes 11, 100, 500, and 1463 with shortening ratio 1.0 and discretization in leafs set to true using tenfold approach. The decision tree generated for first fold is shown in Fig. 4. It has generated 61 nodes when maximal leaf size is set to 11. Every internal node in the decision tree indicates it is a decision and leaf node indicates the decision to which category the library resource is classified.

In decision tree, at second level there are two branches. The first branch is entered matching the rule (attr339<>"(0.5, Inf)") and second branch is entered by matching the rule (attr339="(0.5, Inf)"). Likewise the rules are generated for all the nodes in decision tree. If any of the library resource is classified into fourth category the branch of tree ends with satisfying the rule for example: (attr339<>"(0.5,Inf)")&(attr249<>"(0.5, Inf)")&(attr852<>"(0.5,Inf)")&(attr1307<>"(0.5,Inf)")&(attr1339<>"(-Inf,0.5)")&(attr310<>"(-Inf,0.5)").

Classifier Using K-Nearest Neighbor. K-NN classifier [14] is implemented for 231 test library resources with the use RSRE 2.2 [29]. Distance based, accuracy based, hold out, tenfold, and leave one out cross validation techniques are applied [33] (Fig. 5).

Classifier Using Naïve Bayes. The PU learning occurs often in Web applications and text retrieval applications because most of the time the user is only concerned in Web pages or text documents of a specific topic. For example the tourist is interested in travel related pages, therefore travel pages are positive records and remaining one are negative. The PU learning approach is defined as: "Given a set P of positive documents that we are interested in, and a set U of unlabeled documents (the mixed set), which contains both positive documents and negative documents, we want to build a classifier using P and U that can identify positive documents in U or in a separate test set – in other words, we want to accurately classify positive and negative documents in U or in the test (or future) data set" [31]. Since this classification problem includes only

Table 1. A vector representing single library record

[Input]	[Output]
[3, 5, 0, 5, 0, 0, 2, 2, 3, 4, 0, 0, 0, 1, 6, 0,..., 3, 2, 0, 1]	[1]
[0, 7, 2, 9, 0, 0, 0, 1, 0, 0, 14, 0, 0, 1, 0,..., 0, 0, 5, 0]	[2]
[4, 2, 0, 5, 0, 0, 0, 2, 0, 0, 3, 0, 0, 6, 0, 3,..., 0, 0, 7, 0]	[3]
[9, 0, 1, 0, 2, 5, 0, 3, 0, 1, 0, 0, 7, 0, 0, 0,..., 1, 0, 0, 1]	[4]
[7, 4, 0, 3, 0, 5, 0, 2, 0, 0, 0, 0, 6, 0, 0, 3,..., 0, 4, 0, 2]	[5]
[6, 0, 1, 2, 1, 0, 11, 0, 0, 2, 0, 7, 0, 0, 1, 0,..., 0, 7, 3, 0]	[6]
[2, 0, 2, 0, 5, 0, 0, 1, 0, 0, 4, 7, 0, 0, 2, 0,..., 3, 1, 0, 1]	[7]
[0, 4, 2, 0, 2, 0, 1, 0, 0, 2, 0, 0, 0, 0, 0, 2,..., 0, 4, 0, 0]	[8]
[0, 1, 0, 7, 1, 0, 2, 0, 1, 0, 0, 7, 0, 0, 9, 0,..., 5, 0, 1, 2]	[9]
[5, 1, 2, 0, 0, 0, 1, 12, 0, 0, 11, 0, 1, 2, 2, 0,..., 0, 0, 0, 0]	[10]
[4, 0, 1, 0, 1, 2, 4, 1, 0, 0, 3, 0, 0, 1, 0, 1,..., 4, 2, 0, 6]	[11]

Table 2. Precision, recall, and F1 values for RSRE classifier for recommender system

Rough set rule extraction classifier

	Precision (%)	Recall (%)	F1 (%)	Coverage (%)
Genetic algorithm	71.96	59.09	64.72	100
Covering algorithm	71.88	58.30	64.38	16.10
LEM2 algorithm	82.76	71.80	76.90	57.80

Table 3. Precision, recall, and F1 values for decision tree classifier for recommender system

Decision tree classifier

	Precision (%)	Recall (%)	F1 (%)	Coverage (%)
DT with leaf size 11	88.05	76.90	82.10	46.10
DT with leaf size 100	75.43	63.80	69.13	61.70
DT with leaf size 500	77.89	64.50	70.57	53.90
DT with leaf size 1463	76.58	66.60	71.25	55.20

Table 4. Precision, recall, and F1 values for k-NN classifier for recommender system

When K is in range *1 to 100*

	Precision (%)	Recall (%)	F1 (%)
Accuracy based K-NN	73.78	60.91	66.60
Distance based K-NN	74.40	60.32	66.47
LOO CV based K-NN	65.52	65.52	65.52

Table 5. Summary of results for classification of library resources in recommender system

Machine learning technique	Precision (%)	Recall (%)	F1 (%)	Coverage (%)
Rough set rule extraction (Genetic 10 fold)	71.96	59.09	64.72	100
Rough set rule extraction (LEM 10 fold)	82.76	71.80	76.90	57.80
Rough set rule extraction (Covering 10 fold)	71.88	58.30	64.38	16.10
Decision tree (11 leaf nodes 10 fold)	88.05	76.90	82.10	46.10
Decision tree (100 leaf nodes 10 fold)	75.43	63.80	69.13	61.70
Decision tree (500 leaf nodes 10 fold)	77.89	64.50	70.57	53.90
Decision tree (1163 leaf nodes 10 fold)	76.58	66.60	71.25	55.20
K-nearest neighbor (Distance based 10 fold)	74.40	60.32	66.47	100
K-nearest neighbor (Accuracy based 10 fold)	73.78	60.91	66.60	100
K-nearest neighbor (LOOCV approach)	65.52	65.52	65.52	100
Naïve Bayes (PU learning approach)	**90.05**	**90.05**	**90.05**	**100**

positive records in the form of available library books and journal articles, the NB classifier is implemented using two iterations [34]. This classifier improved the classification accuracy up to 90.05% which is the maximum among all other methods tested [34].

4   Results and Discussion

Data set consisting of 25 users, 705 library resources and ACM CCS 2012 as ontology is used for evaluating the system. Results of classifiers given in Sect. 3 are given below:

The result summary of the Rough Set Rule Extraction classifier using three algorithms is given in Table 2. The graph in Fig. 6 performs the contrast between the outcomes specified by the procedures.

The average values of precision, recall, and F1 [35] for LEM2 in percentage are as 82.76, 71.80, and 76.90 respectively. The coverage is small but better than covering algorithm which is 0.578.

The results computed for all ten folds of Decision Tree Classifier are given in Table 3.

The graph in Fig. 7 gives the comparison between the results obtained for various leaf sizes in experiment of decision tree classifier. It is observed that the classifier cannot classify all 231 test library resources because the average coverage of the classifier is not more than 61.70%.

The experimental results by k-NN classifier are listed in Table 4 [33].

The graph given in Fig. 8 is plotted for comparison amongst these methods used by k-NN classifier.

The result for 231 library records is tested by k-NN classifier [33]. The performance of holdout approach is poor as compared to tenfold and LOO CV.

The performance is found better with the use of the other techniques. Table 5 provides the summary of the results obtained using various machine learning techniques. The Naïve Bayes Classifier improved the classification accuracy to 90.05% which is the maximum among all other methods tested [33, 34].

The comparison of this task performed in the development of proposed recommender system with [2, 9, 18] provides novel features like making use of ACM CCS 2012 as ontology, computation of semantic match, automatic update of interests to user profiles, and weight assignment to semantically related keywords.

5 Conclusion

Library recommender system offers results to the users after combining results using content based and collaborative approaches. The range of library resources proposed requirement of classifying and grouping them which look a lot like to the notion of keeping related library books/journals into the shared bookshelf. Machine learning techniques such as rough set rule extraction (genetic, LEM2, covering), decision tree (11 leaf nodes, 100 leaf nodes, 500 leaf nodes, 1463 leaf nodes), K-nearest neighbor (distance based, accuracy based), Naïve Bayes (PU learning approach) are experimented. Hold out, tenfold, leave one out cross validation techniques are applied. Tenfold and LOO CV approaches given better results as compared to hold out CV.

It is observed that the classification accuracy of RSRE using LEM2 algorithm is better than genetic and covering algorithms. But the classifier using LEM2 algorithm only covers 57.80% of the testing library resources samples. Considering the coverage the genetic algorithm proved better amongst the three algorithms such as genetic, LEM2, and Covering. The machine learning using the decision tree with 11 leaf nodes given classification accuracy 76.90% which is higher when compared with RSRE results but coverage is the problem with DT classifier. K-nearest neighbor classifier classified all the library resources with the classifier accuracy 65.52% using LOO CV approach. The results are improved further by using the PU learning approach. PU learning approach worked well as in the dataset negative documents do not exists. This approach is performed by designing Naïve Bayes classifier. Sample 100 records are tested out and 85.75% records are correctly identified. By adding these records into training data Naïve Bayes classifier improved results up to 90.05% accuracy which the better in all other approaches. The classes of the library resources are used to improve the task of providing recommendations. Generation of library resources to be recommended to the user requires filtering of relevant library resources from available ones.

References

1. Gottwald, S., Koch, T.: Recommender systems for libraries. In: ACM Recommender Systems 2011, Chicago (2011)
2. Morales-del-Castillo, J.M., Peis, E., Herrera-Viedma, E.: A filtering and recommender system for e-scholars. Int. J. Technol. Enhanced Learn. **2**(3), 227–240 (2010)
3. Pakdeetrakulwong, U., Wongthongtham, P.: State of the art of a multi-agent based recommender system for active software engineering ontology. Int. J. Digit. Inf. Wirel. Commun. (IJDIWC) **3**(4), 29–42 (2013)
4. Bedi, P., Vashisth, P.: Argumentation-enabled interest-based personalised recommender system. J. Exp. Theor. Artif. Intell. **27**(2), 199–226 (2015). http://www.springer.com/lncs. Accessed 21 Nov 2016
5. Heylighen, F., Bollen, J.: Hebbian algorithms for a digital library recommendation system. In: Proceedings of International Conference on Parallel Processing Workshops, 2002, pp. 439–446. IEEE (2002)
6. Huang, Z., Chung, W., Ong, T.H., Chen, H.: A graph-based recommender system for digital library. In: Proceedings of the 2nd ACM/IEEE-CS Joint Conference on Digital Libraries, pp. 65–73. ACM (2002)
7. Torres, R., McNee, S.M., Abel, M., Konstan, J.A., Riedl, J.: Enhancing digital libraries with TechLens+ . In: Proceedings of the 4th ACM/IEEE-CS Joint Conference on Digital Libraries, pp. 228–236. ACM (2004)
8. Zhang, M., Wang, W., Li, X.: A paper recommender for scientific literatures based on semantic concept similarity. In: Buchanan, G., Masoodian, M., Cunningham, S.J. (eds.) ICADL 2008. LNCS, vol. 5362, pp. 359–362. Springer, Heidelberg (2008). https://doi.org/10.1007/978-3-540-89533-6_44
9. Porcel, C., Moreno, J.M., Herrera-Viedma, E.: A multi-disciplinar recommender system to advice research resources in university digital libraries. Expert Syst. Appl. **36**(10), 12520–12528 (2009)
10. Kodakateri Pudhiyaveetil, A., Gauch, S., Luong, H., Eno, J.: Conceptual recommender system for CiteSeerX. In: Proceedings of the Third ACM Conference on Recommender Systems, pp. 241–244. ACM (2009)
11. Wang, C., Blei, D.M.: Collaborative topic modeling for recommending scientific articles. In: Proceedings of the 17th ACM SIGKDD International Conference on Knowledge Discovery and Data Mining, pp. 448–456. ACM (2011)
12. Bogers, T., Koolen, M., Cantador, I.: Workshop on new trends in content-based recommender systems: (CBRecSys 2014). In: Proceedings of the 8th ACM Conference on Recommender Systems, pp. 379–380. ACM (2014)
13. Yammine, K., Razek, M.A., Aïmeur, E., Frasson, C.: *Discovering intelligent agent*: a tool for helping students searching a library. In: Lester, J.C., Vicari, R.M., Paraguaçu, F. (eds.) ITS 2004. LNCS, vol. 3220, pp. 720–729. Springer, Heidelberg (2004). https://doi.org/10.1007/978-3-540-30139-4_68
14. Lau, S.B.-Y., Lee, C.-S., Singh, Y.P.: A folksonomy-based lightweight resource annotation metadata schema for personalized hypermedia learning resource delivery. Interact. Learn. Environ. **23**(1), 79–105 (2015)
15. Huang, C.-L., Yeh, P.-H., Lin, C.-W., Wu, D.-C.: Utilizing user tag-based interests in recommender systems for social resource sharing websites. Knowl.-Based Syst. **56**, 86–96 (2014)
16. Ghazanfar, M.A., Prügel-Bennett, A.: Leveraging clustering approaches to solve the gray-sheep users problem in recommender systems. Expert Syst. Appl. **41**(7), 3261–3275 (2014)

17. Chen, C.-M.: An intelligent mobile location-aware book recommendation system that enhances problem-based learning in libraries. Interact. Learn. Environ. **5**, 469–495 (2013)
18. Hulseberg, A., Monson, S.: Investigating student driven taxonomy for library website design. J. Electron. Res. Librariansh. **23**, 361–378 (2012)
19. Liao, I.-E., Hsu, W.C., Cheng, C.: A library recommender system based on PORE and collaborative filtering technique for English collections. Electron. Libr. **28**, 386–400 (2010)
20. Montaner, M., López, B., De La Rosa, J.L.: A taxonomy of recommender agents on the internet. Artif. Intell. Rev. **19**(4), 285–330 (2003)
21. Shirude, S.B., Kolhe, S.R.: Identifying subject area/s of user using n-Gram and Jaccard's similarity in profile agent of library recommender system. In: Proceedings of the 2014 International Conference on Information and Communication Technology for Competitive Strategies. ACM (2014)
22. Bobadilla, J., Ortega, F., Hernando, A., Gutiérrez, A.: Recommender systems survey. Knowl.-Based Syst. **46**, 109–132 (2013)
23. Ziegler, C.N.: Semantic web recommender systems. In: Lindner, W., Mesiti, M., Türker, C., Tzitzikas, Y., Vakali, A.I. (eds.) EDBT 2004. LNCS, vol. 3268, pp. 78–89. Springer, Heidelberg (2004). https://doi.org/10.1007/978-3-540-30192-9_8
24. Bird, S.: The ACL anthology reference corpus: a reference dataset for bibliographic research in computational linguistics (2008)
25. https://www.acm.org/about/class/2012/
26. Pawlak, Z.: Rough sets and intelligent data analysis. Inf. Sci. **147**(1), 1–12 (2002)
27. Pawlak, Z.: Rough set approach to knowledge-based decision support. Eur. J. Oper. Res. **99** (1), 48–57 (1997)
28. Komorowski, J., et al.: Rough sets: a tutorial. In: Rough Fuzzy Hybridization: A New Trend in Decision-Making, pp. 3–98 (1999)
29. Bazan, J.G., Nguyen, H.S., Nguyen, S.H., Synak, P., Wróblewski, J.: Rough set algorithms in classification problem. In: Polkowski, L., Tsumoto, S., Lin, T.Y. (eds.) Rough Set Methods and Applications, pp. 49–88. Physica, Heidelberg (2000). https://doi.org/10.1007/978-3-7908-1840-6_3
30. Quinlan, J.R.: Induction of decision trees. Mach. Learn. **1**(1), 81–106 (1986)
31. Liu, B.: Web Data Mining: Exploring Hyperlinks, Contents, and Usage Data. Springer, Heidelberg (2007). https://doi.org/10.1007/978-3-642-19460-3
32. Dumais, S., et al: Inductive learning algorithms and representations for text categorization. In: Proceedings of the Seventh International Conference on Information and Knowledge Management. ACM (1998)
33. Shirude, S.B., Kolhe, S.R.: Machine learning using k-nearest neighbor for library resources classification in agent-based library recommender system. In: Chakrabarti, A., Sharma, N., Balas, V.E. (eds.) Advances in Computing Applications, pp. 17–29. Springer, Singapore (2016). https://doi.org/10.1007/978-981-10-2630-0_2
34. Shirude, S.B., Kolhe, S.R.: Classifying library resources in library recommender agent using PU learning approach. In: International Conference on Data Mining and Advanced Computing (SAPIENCE). IEEE (2016)
35. Gunawardana, A., Shani, G.: A survey of accuracy evaluation metrics of recommendation tasks. J. Mach. Learn. Res. **10**, 2935–2962 (2009)

Fog-Based Hierarchical Search Optimization

Sudipta Sahana[1(✉)], Rajesh Bose[2], and Debabrata Sarddar[3]

[1] Department of CSE, JIS College of Engineering,
Kalyani, Nadia, West Bengal, India
ss.jisce@gmail.com
[2] Simplex Infrastructures Ltd. Data Center, Kolkata, India
bose.raj00028@gmail.com
[3] Department of Computer Science and Engineering, University of Kalyani,
Kalyani, Nadia, West Bengal, India
dsarddar@rediffmail.com

Abstract. In the modern world, information can comprise large amounts of data generated from personal and business use. Cloud computing provides an efficient way of handling those data. The introduction of Fog computing is a useful addition in the scenario of Cloud computing. Apart from data storing and processing, it offers various services to the users connected through the Internet. Fog computing along with cloud technology makes the task of data and information processing easier. It complements cloud computing in such a way that a major portion of data stored in cloud is taken away thus restoring the efficiency of the system. This paper focuses on search optimization in cloud with the help of fog technique. It not only considers the access to recent data but also deals with archival of the data. By separately dealing with recent and archived data, the proposed technique makes data retrieving more time efficient. Moreover it also reduces the complexities of copying data in a central server. The data can be retrieved directly from the cloud connected with Billboard Manager. Thus, this gives users a decentralized system.

Keywords: Fog computing · Search optimization · Decentralized system
Central server · Billboard Manager

1 Introduction

Fog computing also known as 'fogging', provides users the network facilities that is mobile and that works through a dense geographical distribution. The concept of fog computing has been introduced by CISCO. A large number of users who are connected with Internet of Things (IoT) via their devices can access the concerned service at the edge of networking [1]. First we discuss the CISCO's practices to offer various kinds of services to its customers. Here the customers are able to run different software application for their devices that they mostly used which includes routers, switches and IP video cameras. They can also develop and manage software on the CISCO IOx framework for the devices connected with the network. By providing the opportunity of applying new software it gives an open platform for the developer and makes the system more users friendly. With increasing users and devices the concerned

© Springer Nature Singapore Pte Ltd. 2018
J. K. Mandal and D. Sinha (Eds.): CSI 2017, CCIS 836, pp. 674–681, 2018.
https://doi.org/10.1007/978-981-13-1343-1_55

framework also calls for a secure connectivity interface. A multiusers multitasking operating system like Linux and CISCO IOS operating system are brought together under a single network system under the CISCO practice.

Though the cloud computing and fog computing are similar in terms of basic operations provided by them like resource computing, storing and accessing data and additionally various useful services to the end users. But there are some distinguishable features in the fog computing unlike the cloud. One such is the closer connectivity with the users by the means of a dense geographical distribution. Another thing that needs to be mentioned is the mobility in the services [2, 9].

In the current world where jobs are mostly service oriented maintaining records in the forms of data and information constitute a very important part. In the past few years cloud computing are providing an efficient environment for this task. The users can access the information stored in the internet on the basis of payment. Pay-as-you-go is a cloud model that supports data management in the private data center and makes web application and batch processing easier [3]. It is true that cloud computing makes data handling easier for both the individual and for business enterprises by reducing many complexities that were earlier required efficient data management but in some cases it also create obstacles for some specific program. For example, it removes the limitation in the front of resource computing and also optimizes the cost of network communication. Also the enterprises are not bound to fill all the details for storing resources. But this opens up problem for some applications to run, mostly those require access to all the nodes to fulfill delay requirement that is we are talking about latency sensitive application [2].

With the growing number of devices connected with the internet and cloud several shortcomings of cloud computing to meet the increasing needs of the users become more prominent. Modifications are demanded in the area of mobility, location sensitivity and for low latency.

Fog computing are designed to deal with all the above mentioned problems [1]. Fogging works at the edge of networking. Thus, the problem of location sensitivity and low latency is taken care of. In addition the quality of services (QOS) is improved by the improvement in the streaming and running real time application. Transportation, networking used in sensors and actuators, industrial automation are some examples of the application of fog computing. The newly introduced for computing is perfectly suitable for dealing with a large amount of data. Besides various other services like advertising, personal computing, running different applications are supported under the proposed program. Also the versatility of the system is ensured as it includes end users devices, diverse access points, routers, and switches.

Large, medium, small business enterprises are increasingly depended on the cloud computing for maintaining their confidential data. In connection with rapidly increasing data the security of the data become an important issue. On the security ground a well-known threat is that of data theft attack. And it is more dangerous when the attack is due to an inside malware. The surprising thing is that all the users are well aware of this threat but they have nothing to do for providing security to their data but only to rely on the cloud authorities to take proper steps. The traditional approaches of the cloud authorities such as authentication, audit control, authorization are unable to prevent the attack and provide proper security rather it intensified the problem by bringing more complications.

2 Related Work

In this section we consider various fogs computing related research works to get a clear idea in this regime and it will also help in our present work. The latency restriction and time lagging problem is looked after in [4]. A placement and migration methods are developed by Ottenwalder et al. In this paper there is an indication of optimal network utilization through the migration ahead of time. To reduce the required bandwidth for the migration technique the knowledge of complex event processing can be used. A thin line of distinction between the cloud and fog computing is also presented here. Fog devices used network intensive operators while cloud uses computationally intensive operators for the similar purpose. To minimize the cost of migration paths are chosen in such a way that uses network coverage as low as possible. But the aspect of workload mobility is not considered here. The fog technique considered here intended to do computational intensive task. Finding optimized size of network control information and also the network control policies are beyond the scope of this study.

Efficient dealing with customers query is the center of focus in the paper developed by Hong et al. [6]. Their proposed technique is based on prediction of future query of the consumers and takes advance step to avail the information at the intended location so that the customers can access those in the future. The events are present at their desired location as the system not only consider live event processing but also takes care of historical events. The processing of historical events is completed before the demand query made by the users and the live event processing starts at the time when the users arrive. Attention has also given to make the system competent with the speed of mobile users. In this regard the authors opt for activating pipeline processing based on parallel resources where processing is designed for the future locations in several time steps. Predictions have been made for each time steps and future locations are planned accordingly. When the final time arrived the system analyzes which prediction is closest to the current need, only that is selected and that event is returned to its users.

Zhu et al. discuss a method of combining the existing web optimizing technique with the knowledge of newly introduced fog computing [5]. With the earlier web optimizing technique time to tome adaptation of the users need was not possible. This dynamic issue can be addressed with the knowledge at the edge of networking that comes with the fog computing.

Cloud computing is also applicable for mobile devices connected with the internet. Various applications run on the devices generated a significant amount of data which can be stored in the cloud. In this mobile cloud computing network nodes are connected with each other to share the resources [8, 10]. When several nodes are connected in a local network then we have local cloud. Resources coming from different mobile devices are stored in the cloud, share resource and support their respective users.

A coordinating node is to be selected from those available in the local cloud system. This coordinator serves as a fog device. Architecture is suggested for sharing heterogeneous resources on the basis services for different utility needs in the paper [11]. Though the different type of resources can be classified on different scales like power, latency and bandwidth but in the paper the authors are more interested to take all the resources together and treat them equally under time resources. The methodology developed here is to consider all the utility function jointly by either taking the sum or product of the utility functions and build a suitable optimization technique based on approaches of convex optimization.

A different approach is found in the paper [7]. Apart from indicating the advantages of fog computing it also mentioned some reliability challenges that may come in future. For this, the authors first look into the reliability requirements that are presently lacking in cloud, smart grid, sensors and actuators and then suggested to adapt fog computing to meet these requirements. But at the same time the paper also reviewed the challenges in formulating fog based projects and also concluded that the fog paradigm alone cannot ensure a more reliable network for the increasing numbers of smart devices.

3 Proposed Work

In the cloud technology all the data stored in the internet are also copied to a centralized data center for the purpose of keeping a backup of the record and also to retrieve the data in case the data is lost from the local data center. But as more and more data are stored in a single data center the load increases beyond the capacity of the data center and the excess load can be resulted in the damage of the entire system. So, our present paper focuses on optimizing the load and decentralizing the data handling with the help of fog computing. Here cloud servers are employed along with fog technology to store dynamic information for several important sectors such as Blood bank status, festivals, current temperature, schools, Local newspaper, traffic update, colleges, hospitals, police stations, subdivisions, sports places of interest, block offices, Hospital seat availability, news archive, event and shows, history, location, political data, recruitment news, different schemes and contact number etc. There are pre-installed billboard managers for each zone and it is connected with the cloud. The archived information then stored here. Not only for different sectors but the "fog cloud" is also applicable for different category of services for a country or even for a state. These services can include Art & Culture, Youth & Sports, Defense, Commerce, Power & Energy Communication, Education, Environment & Forest, Finance & Taxes, Food & Public Distribution, Foreign Affairs, Social Development Governance & Administration, Information & Broadcasting, Health & Family Welfare, Housing, Home Affairs & Enforcement, Transport Industries, Infrastructure, Labour & Employment, Law & Justice, Rural, Science & Technology, Travel & Tourism, etc. Here billboard manager plays a very crucial role. For any purpose whether it is service specific or sector specific any cloud servers are connected with the billboard manager. For a better search process the billboard managers are connected in a distributed manner. The proposed system is able to maintain both the recent and previous record simultaneously. The recent data are stored in the region and the previous records are sent to the archived cloud. As a result the pressure on central data center is reduced. Also the data can be made easily available and accessible by reducing the network congestion. Instead of a central data center there is a fog supervisor to control all the connected fog cloud servers.

4 Communication Procedure

So far as the communication process is concerned it is designed to make as simple as possible and the one which is less time consuming. As mentioned earlier the nodes are connected with each other for sharing resources. Whenever any request or query comes from the users the connected nodes send the request to the zonal billboard manager. The task of processing the request is accomplished here. As the initial stage the type of resources requested are checked and further steps are executed as follows. BM here works very efficiently as instead of flooding all the packets of resources in the network it first examined whether the requested data are available in the fog cloud. If yes the packet consisting the data are forwarded to its users. Since only one packet consists of the intended resource is forwarded the entire communication process is free from unnecessary network congestion while processing any request (Fig. 1).

5 Algorithm and Flow Chart for Communication

Step 1: A user places a request for a resource at a particular node.

Step 2: The node transmits the request to the associated zonal Billboard Manager.

Step 3: The zonal Billboard Manager validates the request type.

Step 4: Following validation checks, the Billboard Manager looks up with its own connected Fog Cloud network to locate the resource, if available.

Step 5: In case the search does not yield positive results, the Billboard Manager forwards the request to associated Billboard Managers.

Step 6: The connected Billboard Managers process the request and forwards the same to their respective connected Fog Cloud networks.

Step 7: Fog Cloud networks that locate the requested resource respond with the relevant data to the destination node.

Step 8: In the event, any Billboard Manager can locate the data from within its own archive, the information is passed on to the Billboard Manager that initiated the request.

Step 9: The response is then forwarded to the user at the destination node.

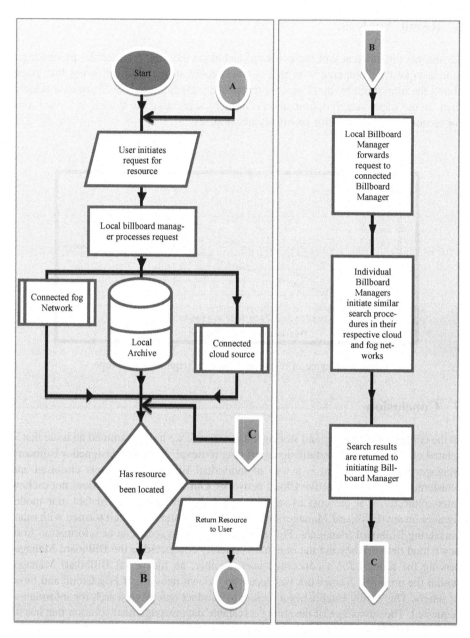

Fig. 1 Flow chart for communication

6 Result Analysis

To analyze the efficiency of the proposed technique the time required for processing a search request is compared with that of the traditional one. The following line graph shows the time taken by the 2 process (proposed and traditional) by 2 separate colored lines. In our paper search optimization is done by separating the storage in 2 parts- one for recent data and other for archived data (Fig. 2).

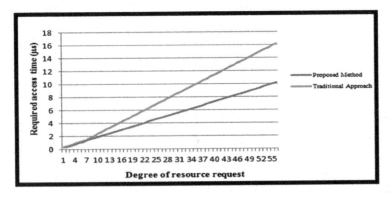

Fig. 2. Degree of resource request vs. required access time

7 Conclusion

In the context of managing and storing data on cloud, we have examined an issue that is related closely to speed and efficiency of data retrieval. We have designed a Billboard Manager-based model that is a web of individual Billboard Managers clustered and cloistered with their respective Cloud networks. Our model, however, does not eschew inter-connectivity at the cost of security and fast response times. In fact, our model focuses on any Billboard Manager being the central feature in a web formed with other partnering Billboard Managers. This enables any user to seek data or information from any Cloud network beyond the one that is directly connected to the Billboard Manager serving the request for a concerned user. Further, an individual Billboard Manager within the proposed framework has access to its own network of Fog Cloud and those of others. This firmly establishes a facility to conduct extensive search for information requested. The advantage of designing a scalable data management solution that has its roots embedded in Cloud and Fog computing is undeniable. Our research test reveals that the proposed method yields similar search results faster than traditional approach. In addition to this, our proposed method prepares the groundwork for future research on rationalizing and simplifying indexing of humongous volumes of data. This can be a significant advantage in cases where, for example, public utility services need to access data quickly and efficiently. A significant amount of time can be saved not only in the sphere of general services, but also in cases of emergency health services. Our proposed model offers an innovative approach wherein a Billboard Manager looks up its own archives before forwarding the request to other associated Billboard Managers and respective corresponding Cloud and Fog networks. Not only does it simplify the search mechanism, but it has the effect of speeding up the process of looking up for a resource anywhere within its network. As a consequence of this policy of searching for a requested resource, network congestion can be obviated to a great extent.

References

1. Bonomi, F.: Connected vehicles, the internet of things, and fog computing. In: The Eighth ACM International Workshop on Vehicular Inter-Networking (VANET), Las Vegas, USA (2011)
2. Bonomi, F., Milito, R., Zhu, J., Addepalli, S.: Fog computing and its role in the internet of things. In: Proceedings of the First Edition of the MCC Workshop on Mobile Cloud Computing, MCC 2012, pp. 13–16. ACM (2012)
3. Armbrust, M., et al.: A view of cloud computing. Commun. ACM 53(4), 50–58 (2010)
4. Ottenwalder, B., Koldehofe, B., Rothermel, K., Ramachandran, U.: MigCEP: operator migration for mobility driven distributed complex event processing. In: Proceedings of the 7th ACM International Conference on Distributed Event-based Systems, DEBS 2013, pp. 183–194. ACM (2013)
5. Zhu, J., Chan, D., Prabhu, M., Natarajan, P., Hu, H., Bonomi, F.: Improving web sites performance using edge servers in fog computing architecture. In: 2013 IEEE 7th International Symposium on Service Oriented System Engineering (SOSE), pp. 320–323, March 2013
6. Hong, K., Lillethun, D., Ramachandran, U., Ottenwälder, B., Koldehofe, B.: Mobile fog: a programming model for large-scale applications on the internet of things. In: Proceedings of the Second ACM SIGCOMM Workshop on Mobile Cloud Computing, MCC 2013, pp. 15–20. ACM (2013)
7. Madsen, H., Albeanu, G., Burtschy, B., Popentiu-Vladicescu, F.: Reliability in the utility computing era: towards reliable fog computing. In: 2013 20th International Conference on Systems, Signals and Image Processing (IWSSIP), pp. 43–46, July 2013
8. Nishio, T., Shinkuma, R., Takahashi, T., Mandayam, N.B.: Service-oriented heterogeneous resource sharing for optimizing service latency in mobile cloud. In: Proceedings of the First International Workshop on Mobile Cloud Computing and Networking, MobileCloud 2013, pp. 19–26. ACM (2013)
9. Sarddar, D., Bose, R., Sahana, S.: A novel approach on weight based optimized routing for mobile cloud computing. Braz. J. Sci. Technol. 2(1), 1–12 (2015)
10. Bose, R., Sahana, S., Sarddar, D.: An enhanced storage management scheme with search optimization for cloud data center. Int. J. Appl. Eng. Res. 10(12), 32141–32150 (2015)
11. Bose, R., Sahana, S., Sarddar, D.: An energy efficient dynamic schedule based server load balancing approach for cloud data center. Int. J. Future Gener. Commun. Netw. 8(3), 123–136 (2015)

A Novel Approach for Product Prediction Using Artificial Neural Networks

Soma Bandyopadhyay[1(✉)], S. S. Thakur[1(✉)], and
Jyotsna Kumar Mandal[2]

[1] MCKV Institute of Engineering, Howrah, West-Bengal, India
somabanmuk@yahoo.co.in, subroto_thakur@yahoo.com
[2] University of Kalyani, Nadia, West-Bengal, India
jkm.cse@gmail.com

Abstract. E-commerce business has grown at a rapid pace and buying products from E-commerce websites has become a very popular trend in modern society. Preferences of customers on various products can now be readily obtained online through various E-commerce Websites. As these E-commerce sites provide their customers with many choices they get in dilemma with this information and hence find it difficult to locate items of their interest. These E-commerce systems cannot offer one to one recommendation like a salesperson does and that's why customers are not able to choose products of their choice and hence there is a risk of losing loyal customers. Our main concern is to fulfill the needs of every customer and increase the product sales. Efficiently mining this information can generate useful data for providing personalized product recommendation services. Artificial neural network (ANN) is one of the preferred tool for data mining and it's a computational model based on biological neural networks, which consists of an interconnected group of neurons and it processes the information using a connection based approach. This paper presents a new approach using ANN that can be used to generate recommendations and help customers to satisfy their requirements. In this work the buying pattern of the students appearing for campus interviews has been taken into consideration and recommends the similar type of items to other student groups. The predicted values obtained by giving input data set and target (desired output) to ANN are quite satisfactory.

Keywords: Recommender system · E-commerce · Artificial neural network
Feed forward · Back propagation

1 Introduction

Electronic commerce (EC) recommendation system works in collaboration with end user application for which some new technologies are required in urgent basis e.g. web mining and artificial neural network [1]. The novel hybrid system EntreeC is a system which was used to recommend restaurant using knowledge-based recommendation and collaborative filtering. It was considered that personalized recommendation can be done more accurately if prediction algorithm is accurate based on user's preferences [2].

© Springer Nature Singapore Pte Ltd. 2018
J. K. Mandal and D. Sinha (Eds.): CSI 2017, CCIS 836, pp. 682–691, 2018.
https://doi.org/10.1007/978-981-13-1343-1_56

Creating and evaluating better prediction plays a significant role in recommendation research [3–5]. Improving the accuracy of any recommender system cannot be the only factor of recommendation. For evaluating recommendation system, a new user-centric direction was proposed [3]. A collaborative filter based recommendation system for movies was proposed where recommendations affect users' opinions of the items to be recommended and it is important to characterize and publish this information so that system designers and users can use the same for future recommendations [4]. Research on recommender system [6] focuses on the accuracy of prediction algorithms. The results of the said work have positive impact of diversification which is based on user experience. It was also observed that providing a diversified and non-personalized list of recommendations will result in better user experience. Although measuring algorithmic accuracy is an insufficient method to analyze the recommendation systems based on user experience [6].

Many recommendation techniques have been developed over a period of time such as collaborative filtering, content-based, and hybrid recommender systems [7]. In case of content-based systems user 'items' characteristics and ratings provided by the users has been used to generate useful recommendations and content-based online product recommendation system [8] was proposed. Amazon.com analyzed customers interest for recommending books [9]. Collaborative method provides best recommendations for known items for users with similar tastes provided sufficient user data is available [10]. Content based recommender system provides recommendation for items based on a comparison between user profile and items' content whereas, collaborative systems identify similar users and their preferences for generating useful recommendations.

Users' purchase patterns (e.g. ratings and items) [11–13] are used to find sequential pattern for doing analysis and for further recommendations to users [11]. If users have similar navigation patterns, then one can say that they have similar interests for some products [12, 13]. A system was proposed namely interior desire system (ISD) to assess potential customer's knowledge levels and their needs, and use this information to promote products for them which enhances the personalization strategy [14]. This is the ultimate goal for retaining customers which satisfies the needs of EC business [14].

2   Neural Network Preliminaries and Classification Approach

Artificial neural network (ANN) is a computational model which can analyze and process information analogous to human brain. Classification and prediction are two important aspects of artificial neural network (ANN) [15]. The input nodes of an ANN take the information from available dataset. An activation function is used which takes the summation of weighted input and produces the output of the neuron. A Multilayer Perceptron (MLP) with back propagation error is one of the mostly used algorithm [15], which is used for learning. The MLP Comprises of three major components namely input layer, hidden layer and output layer. The greatest advantage of ANN is its ability to use an arbitrary function that learns from observed data. Another important aspect is the choice of the model [16] which uses proper learning algorithm and in this case the robustness of the model is very important. The choice of the model depends on the available data and the application to be built. Any algorithm may work well with the correct parameters for training on a particular dataset. However, for selecting and tuning an algorithm on new data set a significant amount of experimentation [16] is required.

3 Proposed Work

This work presents a method to analyze customers' buying pattern which is based on artificial neural network model and it helps to predict potential customers' requirements in near future. In addition to this it predicts the future output i.e., the buying pattern of the future students keeping in mind the purchasing pattern of past students for item purchased during their campus interview and recommend the similar type of items to the students. For prediction, feed-forward and back-propagation algorithm have been applied where feed-forward algorithm is used to train the neural network (NN) and the weights are generated randomly for each neuron and the input is passed to it to obtain the final input to which the transfer function of ANN is to be applied. The paper is organized as follows. The flowchart of the proposed algorithm [17] is given in Sect. 3. Related algorithm is also explained in this section. In Sect. 4 the details of Implementation of the work using ANN is described. The Experimental Results are discussed in Sect. 5, followed by conclusion and future work.

Bayesian networks are used as a tool for real time recommendation for a grocery stored model with RFID systems [18]. Recommendation was done on the basis of long term and short term shopping goals in e-commerce site [19]. A recommendation system has been developed based upon customer reviews of various products on e-commerce data [20].

In this work students of different engineering colleges were targeted. Before the main survey, with 20 students a pilot study was done to make sure that the questions are clearly understood by respondents. The questionnaire was sent by e-mail or students were requested to participate in the survey. A google form was also designed and sent through e-mail to the targeted students. Some of the questionnaire were dropped as they were incomplete. A total of thousand usable responses were used in this research work. In this work the customers are of same age group and their purpose for purchasing is based on requirements for the campus interview they are going to face.

3.1 Flowchart of the Proposed Algorithm

See Fig. 1.

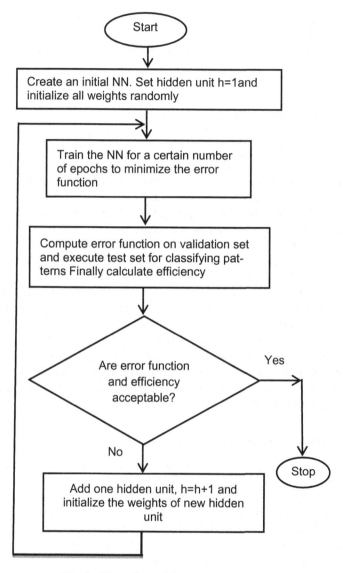

Fig. 1. Flow chart of the proposed algorithm

3.2 Steps to Build and Train the Network

Step 1: Create an initial neural network and set the hidden unit = 1. Initialize all weights randomly.

Step 2: Train the artificial neural network by training dataset for a certain number of epochs to minimize the error function.

Step 3: Compute error function on validation set and calculate the efficiency.

Step 4: Check whether error function and efficiency are acceptable or not.

Step 5: If acceptable then stop else add one hidden unit to the hidden layer and go to step 2.

4 Implementation of the Work Using ANN

In this work, a student survey was conducted to obtain the input dataset and target dataset. The input dataset was the products which the final year engineering students normally purchase before appearing campus interview. Here, the step function has been used as the input is in 0 and 1 form and so the output will also be in 0 and 1 form depending on threshold value. After applying the step function, the predicted output is obtained. But the output obtained is not optimized, so to optimize it, the back-propagation algorithm is applied. Firstly, the error is calculated by computing the difference between the predicted output and target dataset and then the weights for each neuron is updated. The feed-forward algorithm is again applied on the new updated weights and the inputs to obtain new set of predicted output dataset. This process continues until optimized predicted output is found. Based on the type of input dataset it may require to arrange the number of neurons and number of iterations for getting optimal results. In this work, only one hidden layer of neural network has been used. Multiple hidden layer neural network can also be implemented, if required for obtaining the desired results. For recommendation, association rule has been used which recommends the similar items to the future students depending on the items that are mostly bought by the students of previous batch.

4.1 Feed-Forward Neural Network

In ANN where corrections between the units do not form a loop is referred feed-forward neural network. In this case information moves forward from the input nodes to the output nodes through hidden nodes, if available. Based on weighted sum of inputs the computation is performed. Here, the weight of the connection determines the knowledge of the network. The calculated values are then used as new input values for the next layer. The process is repeated until it goes through all layers and finally provides the output. An activation function can be used which provides the output of a neuron to the output layer (Fig. 2).

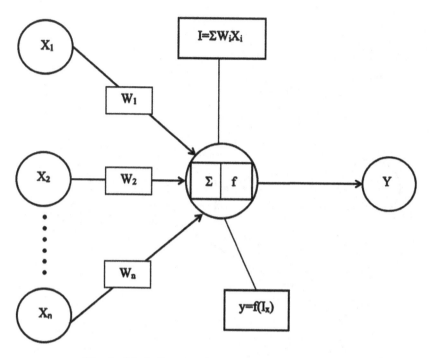

Fig. 2. Block diagram of feed-forward neural network

4.2 Back Propagation Algorithm

Once a batch of data is processed it requires calculating the contribution of error of each neuron and it can be done using back propagation method. The error obtained at output is returned back using the network. Additionally, it requires a known output for each input dataset, hence refers as supervised learning (Fig. 3).

4.3 Step Function

A step function is a function which is used by original perceptron. If the input sum is above a certain threshold its value is A_1 and if the input sum is below a certain threshold its value is A_0. The values used by the perceptron were $A_1 = 1$ and $A_0 = 0$. It is defined by

$f(v) = 1$, if $v \geq a$
$f(v) = 0$, otherwise

Here, a is called the threshold.

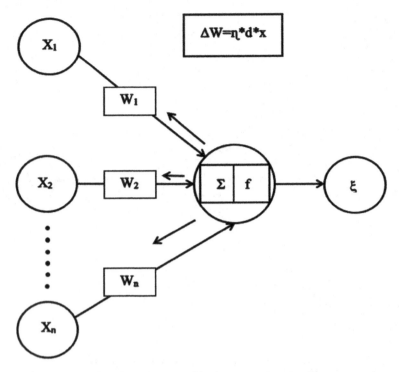

Fig. 3. Block diagram of back propagation algorithm

5 Experimental Results

In this work the purchasing data for campus interview of 1000 students of different engineering colleges were taken. It has been observed that they have purchased Shirt, Trouser, Salwar, Shoe, Socks, Watch, Tie, Belt, Blazer, Cosmetics etc. Artificial neural network was trained by the training set to build predictive models. Predicted output was compared with the target value. Target is the "correct" or desired value for the response associate to one input. This value was compared with the output (the response of the neural network) to guide the learning process involving the weight changes. After repeating this process for a sufficiently large number of training cycles the neural network will usually converge. In this work the error function ξ_{av} is defined as the mean-squared error.

$$e_i = d_i(n) - y_i(n) \tag{1}$$

$$\xi(n) = \frac{1}{2} \sum_{i \in Y} e_i^2(n) \tag{2}$$

$$\xi_{av} = \frac{1}{N} \sum_{n=1}^{N} \xi(n) \tag{3}$$

Where, i denotes i^{th} output unit, n indicates n^{th} iteration, Y denotes the number of output units, N indicates the total number of patterns, d_i and y_i denotes the desired output from i and actual output of neuron i respectively. Here, e_i denotes the error term for i^{th} output unit.

Table 1 shows the Input value, predicted output and actual output for 10 attributes. Figure 4 shows the graph depicting the difference between actual output and predicted output.

Table 1. Total number of different attributes for input, predicted outputs and actual output

Items	Attributes	Input(X)	Predicted O/P($\hat{Y}$)	Actual O/P(Y)	Error
1	Shirt	150	160	170	10
2	Trouser	132	140	150	5
3	Salwar	80	87	90	3
4	Shoe	55	41	50	9
5	Socks	43	32	40	8
6	Watch	13	15	10	1
7	Tie	32	27	25	8
8	Belt	18	9	15	6
9	Blazer	12	17	15	5
10	Cosmetics	45	50	52	2

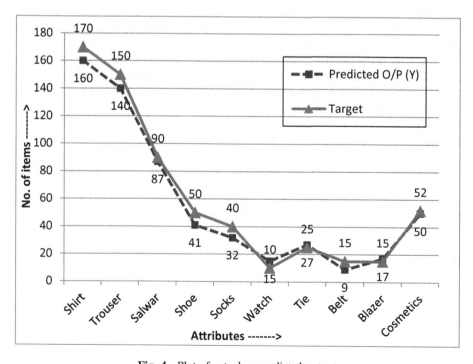

Fig. 4. Plot of actual vs predicted output

From Table 1. and the Graph of Fig. 4. it is clear that probability of purchasing shirt and trouser is maximum, while very few students have purchased blazer, watch, belt or tie. Prediction was done on the basis of purchasing pattern of students of one year. As in that dataset the total number of purchased watch, blazer and belt were low, the ANN predicted that in future this trend will continue.

6 Conclusion and Future Work

The challenges faced by organizations today is the dynamic and unpredictable business environment in which they have to operate. Customers' expectations are increasing as price and quality are concerned whereas manufacturers today no longer rely on cost advantages than their rivals. Instead it is good for the manufacturers to manage their supply chain efficiently and understand customer demands better. Neural networks are suitable for predicting time series because of learning from examples, without any need to add additional information that can add more confusion than prediction effects. Neural networks have good generalization capability but they are resistant to noise. On the other hand, it is not possible to determine exactly what a neural network learned and it is also hard to estimate possible prediction error. Whereas neural networks are successfully used for predicting time series data. They are ideal especially when there is no other description of the observed series. In this work, an architecture of neural network has been created that can predict the items that the student will buy in future for campus interview. Forecasting and prediction of future data can be possible by using historical data and neural network techniques. The same concept has been used to create a simple model for product prediction. To achieve this the data have been collected by conducting various online surveys. After data collection preprocessing of data has been done and the unwanted data has been removed. Then this dataset was used to train the neural network. Here the feed-forward network architecture has been used to perform training. After training and testing the performance of the model has been tested on the basis of Mean Square Error (MSE). In future this model can be used to predict output for other datasets but the accuracy of prediction may vary for different datasets.

Acknowledgment. The authors are thankful to Director, MCKVIE and Principal, MCKVIE, for providing the computer laboratories and other infrastructure to do the proposed work. The authors are also thankful to Ms. Aishwarya Chakraborty and Ms. Priya Agarwal students of CSE department of MCKVIE for collecting the required data for the proposed work.

References

1. Haines, W., Gervasio, M., Spaulding, A., Peintner, B.: Recommendations for end-user development. In: Proceedings of the ACM RecSys 2010 Workshop on User-Centric Evaluation of Recommender Systems and Their Interfaces (UCERSTI), Barcelona, Spain, pp. 42–49 (2010)
2. Burke, R.: Hybrid recommender systems: survey and experiments. User Model. User-Adap. Int. **12**, 331–370 (2002)

3. McNee, S., Riedl, J., Konstan, J.: Being accurate is not enough: how accuracy metrics have hurt recommender systems. In: 24th International Conference Human factors in computing systems, Montréal, Canada, pp. 1097–1101 (2006)

4. Cosley, D., Lam, S., Albert, I., Konstan, J., Riedl, J.: Is seeing believing?: how recommender system interfaces affect users' opinions. In: SIGCHI Conference on Human Factors in Computing Systems, Ft. Lauderdale, FL, pp. 585–592 (2003)

5. Ziegler, C., McNee, S., Konstan, J., Lausen, G.: Improving recommendation lists through topic diversificati. In: 14th International World Wide Web Conference, Chiba, Japan, pp. 22–32 (2005)

6. Knijnenburg, A.B.P., Willemsen, M.C., Gantner, Z., Soncu, H., Newell, C.: Explaining the user experience of recommender system. User Model. User-Adapt. Inter. **22**, 441–504 (2012)

7. Huang, Z., Chung, W., Chen, H.: A graph model for E commerce recommender systems. J. Am. Soc. Inform. Sci. Technol. **55**(3), 259–274 (2004)

8. Lee, Y.H., Hu, J.H., Cheng, T.H., Hsieh, Y.F.: A cost-sensitive technique for positive-example learning supporting content-based product recommendations in B-to-C e-commerce. Decis. Support Syst. **53**(1), 245–256 (2012)

9. Linden, G., Smith, B., York, J.: Amazon.com recommendations: item-to-item collaborative filtering. IEEE Internet Comput. **7**(1), 76–80 (2003)

10. Mooney, R.J., Roy, L.: Content-based book recommending using learning for text categorization. In: Proceedings of the 5th ACM Conference on Digital Libraries, San Antonio, pp. 195–240 (2000)

11. Choi, K., Yoo, D., Kim, G., Suh, Y.: A hybrid online-product recommendation system: combining implicit rating-based collaborative filtering and sequential pattern analysis. Electron. Commer. Res. Appl. **11**(4), 309–317 (2012)

12. Liu, Z.B., Qu, W.Y., Li, H.T., Xie, C.S.: A hybrid collaborative filtering recommendation mechanism for P2P networks. Future Gen. Comput. Syst. **26**(8), 1409–1417 (2010)

13. Wen, H., Fang, L., Guan, L.: A hybrid approach for personalized recommendation of news on the Web. Expert Syst. Appl. **39**(5), 5806–5814 (2012)

14. Chou, P.H., Li, P.H., Chen, K.K., Wua, M.J.: Integrating web mining and neural network for personalized e-commerce automatic service. Expert Syst. Appl. **37**, 2898–2910 (2010)

15. Safa, N.S., Ghani, N.A., Ismail, M.A.: An artificial neural network classification approach for improving accuracy of customer identification in e-commerce. Malays. J. Comput. Sci. **27**(3), 171–185 (2014)

16. Baha'addin, F.B.: Kurdistan engineering colleges and using of artificial neural network for knowledge representation in learning process. Int. J. Eng. Innov. Tech. **3**(6), 292–300 (2013)

17. Siddiquee, A.B., Mazumder, E.H., Kamruzzaman, S.M.: A Constructive Algorithm for Feedforward Neural Networks for Medical Diagnostic Reasoning (2010)

18. Cinicioglu, E.N., Shenoy, P.P.: A new heuristic for learning Bayesian networks from limited datasets: a real-time recommendation system application with RFID systems in grocery stores. Ann. Oper. Res. **244**, 1–21 (2012)

19. Jannach, D., Lerche, L., Jugovac, M.: Adaptation and evaluation of recommendations for short-term shopping goals. In: Proceedings of the 9th ACM Conference on Recommender Systems, Vienna, Austria, pp. 211–218 (2015)

20. Paul, D., Sarkar, S., Chelliah, M., Kalyan, C., Nadkarni, P.P.S.: Recommendation of high quality representative reviews in e-commerce. In: Proceedings of the Eleventh ACM Conference on Recommender Systems, Como, Italy, pp. 311–315 (2017)

PSO-GA Hybrid Approach in Image Encryption

Subhajit Das[1(✉)], Satyendra Nath Mandal[2], and Manas Shynal[3]

[1] Lakshya High School (H.S.), Haldia, West Bengal, India
subhajit.batom@gmail.com
[2] Kalyani Government Engineering College, Kalyani, Nadia, India
[3] Kalyani University, Kalyani, Nadia, India

Abstract. In this paper, a hybrid PSO-GA approach has been used to encrypt an image. The key is produced based on genetic and particle swarm optimization algorithm. The different numbers have been produced by genetic algorithm and elements of key set have been chosen based on particle swarm optimization. The encrypted image is constructed using the logical operation between image and key value. The effectiveness of the proposed algorithm has been proved based on number of tests applied between plain and cipher image. Finally, it has been observed that the algorithm has been given better result almost all tests.

Keywords: Particle swarm optimization · Genetic algorithm
Repetitive coding · Correlation coefficient · Information entropy analysis

1 Introduction

In the age of globalization security of information and image is a real challenge for the science and its development. This security is greatly achieved by Cryptography - the art of sending hidden message from one end to another end. Many newly developed scientific approaches have been used in the field of cryptography to make the subject most challenging to the researchers. Many branches of computing have been used to make cryptosystem more powerful in terms of efficiency, complexity etc. [1, 2].

Farshchi and Ebrahimi [3] have used chaos genetic algorithm and control parameter chaotic map to devolup a suitable color image encryption algorithm. They have generated four chaotic sequences from a 4D hyper chaos. It has been observed that their proposed scheme is quite suitable for real-time image encryption and transmission with increased encryption speed. Authors of "A novel image encryption algorithm using chaos and reversible cellular automata" [4] demonstrate an algorithm where intertwining logistic map used to generate a pseudorandom key stream. As the higher 4 bits of each pixel bits carry almost the information of an image they divide each pixel of input image into units of 4 bits. These units are permuted by pseudorandom key stream in confusion stage. And in diffusion stage, two-dimensional reversible cellular automata which are discrete dynamical systems are applied to iterate many rounds to achieve diffusion on bit-level.

A method of encrypting binary image have been proposed by Lee et al. [1]. In their proposed method, the binary image is used as a set of bit string and the bits are grouped

© Springer Nature Singapore Pte Ltd. 2018
J. K. Mandal and D. Sinha (Eds.): CSI 2017, CCIS 836, pp. 692–701, 2018.
https://doi.org/10.1007/978-981-13-1343-1_57

to form a block for encryption. A pseudorandom generator that generate a sequence of selected random pattern is used to make a scan pattern. The position of the bits in each block is changed according to the scanned pattern. This is followed by a flipping process in which for each x bit group, a value of x bits is randomly selected and an XOR operation is performed.

Kuppusamy and Thamodaran [11] developed Daubechies4 transform, particle swarm optimization and IQIM based image encryption scheme. With the help of particle swarm optimization High energy coefficients are selected encryption in dau-bechies4 transform. These high energy coefficients are selected as candidates for encryption. Shuffling of bits, coefficients and blocks are performed using Interweaving and Iteration method. The total encryption process is controlled by a symmetric key generated by a pseudo random process. This method gives strong cipher of the image, whose key length is significantly large. In 1995 James Kennedy and Russell C first described the concept of Particle Swarm Optimization (PSO) technique. This technique is used to explore the search space of a given problem to find the settings or parameters required to maximize a particular objective. Swarming habits by some kind of animals like birds and fish are the base of PSO concept.

In modern scientific research particle swarm optimization (PSO) has been shown to be effective in optimizing difficult multidimensional discontinuous problems in a variety of fields.

In this paper, a hybrid PSO-GA approach has been used to encrypt an image. A large integer number (N) have been taken as a key value. Prime numbers between 2 to N have been computed. All the elements are divided by 255 and the reminders are treated as particles. The frequency of occurrence of the particles in remainder set has been considered as position of each particle. The initial velocities of these particles have been considered as zero. The Crossover operation of Genetic Algorithm has been applied between two consecutive particles in remainder set and a set of number have been obtained-treated as a new generation. These set contains both prime and unprime numbers. Only prime numbers have been taken and these are divided by 255 and their remainder have been generated. The frequency of occurrence of each remainder in each generation has been considered as new velocity of each particle. New position of each particle has been updated by adding their previous position with their updated velocity. Probability value of each particle in each generation have been obtained by dividing their updated position with total number of particles-this is known as pbest. The particles having highest pbest treated as gbest, stored into final array and remove from initial particle set. This process has been carried out up to a specified number of generations and for each generation a particle has been stored into final array. All the elements stored into final array are converted into a bit stream by using repetitive coding method.

2 Proposed Method

The proposed algorithm has three parts as follows.

2.1   Key Generation

In the process of key generation a large integer number N (used as a key value) is arbitrarily selected. A Set of all prime numbers between 1 to N have been computed and considered as an initial population.

$$N \in \mathbb{N}, \mathbb{N} \text{ is a set of natural number}$$

$$\mathbb{P} = \{Pi | Pi \text{ is a prime } \& 1 \leq Pi \leq N \& 1 \leq i \leq m_1\}$$

Each element of the set has been converted into its equivalent binary value. We use 16 bit register to convert its equivalent binary number. Two Genetic algorithm tool crossover and mutation have been applied between every two consecutive element of the set to get a new set (C). From the new generated set only those are primes have been selected and considered as a new generation (S). This process has been continued to generate elements up to a specified generation's. Next an individual's remainder set is computed from every generation set (S).

16 bit binary representation of each P_i can be represented as

$$P_i = \{P_i(1), P_i(2), P_i(3), \ldots \ldots \ldots \ldots P_1(16)\} \quad \forall \quad i = 1, 2, \ldots, m1$$

So

$$P2i - 1 = P2i - 11, 2i - 12, P2i - 13, \ldots \ldots \ldots \ldots P2i - 116 \; \forall$$
$$i = 1, 2, \ldots, m/2$$

$$P_{2i} = \{P_{2i}(1), P_{2i}(2), P_{2i}(3), \ldots \ldots \ldots \ldots P_{2i}(16)\} \quad \forall \quad i = 1, 2, \ldots, m/2$$

Crossover between two elements results in

$$P^1_{2i-1} = \{P_{2i-1}(1), P_{2i-1}(2), P_{2i-1}(3), \ldots, P_{2i-1}(l), P_{2i}(l+1), P_{2i}(l+2) \ldots P_{2i}(16)\}$$
$$P^1_{2i} = \{P_{2i}(1), P_{2i}(2), P_{2i}(3), \ldots \ldots, P_{2i}(l), P_{2i-1}(l+1), P_{2i-1}(l+2) \ldots P_{2i-1}(16)\}$$

Where $1 \leq i \leq$ m/2 index l vary from 1 to 16.
C has been obtained after crossover between two consecutive elements.

$$C_1 = \{P^1_{2i-1}, P^1_{2i} | P^1_{2i-1}, P^1_{2i} = P_{2i-1} © P_{2i} \& 1 \leq i \leq m_1/2\}$$

© known as crossover between two numbers.

From new generated C1 only prime numbers have been taken and obtained a new generation S1.

$$S_1 = \{P^1_i | P^1_i \in C_1 \& P^1_i \text{ is prime } \& 1 \leq i \leq m_2 \& m_2 < m_1\}$$

Similar method has been used to generate up to a specified number of generations Sk

$$C_2 = \left\{ P^2_{2i-1}, P^2_{2i} | P^2_{2i-1}, P^2_{2i} = P^1_{2i-1} \copyright P^1_{2i} \,\&\, 1 \leq i \leq m_2/2 \right\}$$

$$S_2 = \left\{ P^2_i | P^2_i \in C_2 \,\&\, P^2_i \text{ is prime } \&\, 1 \leq i \leq m_3 \,\&\, m_3 < m_2 \right\}$$

. . . .

$$Sk = \left\{ PikPik \in Ck \,\&\, Pik \text{ is prime } \&\, 1 \leq i \leq mk+1 \,\&\, mk+1 < mk \right\}$$

All the elements of every generation have been combined to obtain a population $\mathbb{G}$. Where

$$\mathbb{G} = SjSj = \left\{ PijPij \in Cj \& Pij \text{ is prime } \&\, 1 \leq i \leq mj+1 \,\&\, 1 \leq j \leq k \right\}.$$

Every elements of $\mathbb{P}$ and each S_i is divided by 256 and its remainder is stored, value of each element of S_i is less than 256.

After generating the remainder set it becomes

$$\bar{\mathbb{P}} = \left\{ r_i | r_i = P_i - 256q_i, 1 \leq r_i \leq 255, 1 \leq i \leq m_1 \,\&\, q_i \in \mathbb{N} \right\}$$

$$\overline{S_k} = \left\{ r^k_i | r^k_i = P^k_i - 256q^k_i, 1 \leq r^k_i \leq 255, 1 \leq i \leq m_{k+1} \,\&\, q^k_i \in \mathbb{N} \right\}$$

$$\bar{\mathbb{G}} = \left\{ r^j_i | r^j_i = p^j_i - 256q^j_i, i = 1(1)m_{k+1}, j = 1(1)k, \,\&\, q^j_i \in \mathbb{N} \right\}$$

Image to be encrypted consist grey values between 1 to 255. Each grey value is considered as an individual particles. Collection of particles considered as

$$A = \left\{ x_i | 1 \leq i \leq 255 \right\}$$

Position (POS) of each particle has been initialized by considering the frequency of that particle in $\mathbb{P}$.

$$POS_{x_j} = \left\{ f^j_{r_i} | r_i = j, 1 \leq i \leq m_1, 1 \leq j \leq 255 \right\}$$

Velocity (VEL) of each particle in each generation has been considered as frequency of each particle in each generation.

$$VEL_{x^k_j} = \left\{ f^j_{r^k_i} | r^k_i = j \right\}$$

In every generation position and probability of each particle has been updated by

$$POS_{x^k_j} = POS_{x_j} + VEL_{x^k_j}$$

$$PROB_{x^k_j} = POS_{x^k_j} / m_{k+1}$$

Particles having maximum probability in each generation has been stored in to final array. Considered to repetition of particles have been allowed in final array. This process has been continued up to a specified number of generation and for each generation an element is stored info final array.

2.2   Coding

Elements stored into final array have been converted into a key stream using repetitive coding method. In this method 3D Coordinate of each endpoints (000, 001, 010, 011, 100, 101, 110, 111) of unit cube (Fig. 1) have been used to represent a key value .0 is represented by 000, 001, 010, 100 and 1 is represented by 011, 101, 110, 111 in a sequential manner (Fig. 2). First each elements of key value have been converted into its equivalent 8 bit binary number which is a sequence of 0 and 1. Then 0 and 1 is represented by upper mentioned bit strings in a clock wise sequential manner. Thus each 8 bit element of key value became a bit string of 24 bits so If any key value consists of n elements then total number of effective bits is 24n.

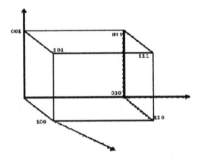

Fig. 1.   Repetition code based key generation model.

Let the key be 112.
8 bit representation of $112 = 01110000$
Using our proposed repetition coding method 112 becomes

$$000 \quad 011 \quad 101 \quad 110 \quad 001 \quad 010 \quad 100 \quad 000 = 24\,\text{bits}$$

Effective key stream $(\text{Ek}) =$
$$000 \quad 011 \quad 101 \quad 110 \quad 001 \quad 010 \quad 100 \quad 000 = 14,226,160$$

For a same key value more than one type of code can be generated by changing the initialization sequence of set "1" and "0".

2.3   Encryption and Decryption Method

An logical XOR operation have been performed between every element of final array with the every pixel of input image and encrypted image have been obtained. While decrypting one has to follow all the steps exactly in the reverse sequence to get back the original image.

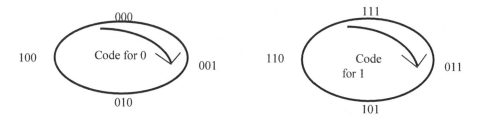

Fig. 2. Code generation for 0 and 1

3 Experimental Result

To test the performance of the proposed algorithm, it has been applied to some images encrypted images are furnished in Fig. 3.

	Lena	Babun	monalisa	flower
Plain image				
Cipherimage				

Fig. 3. Different images and its encrypted images.

4 Testing

4.1 Correlation Coefficient

Correlation Coefficient is an important parameter to determine the efficiency of image encryption algorithm. An image encryption algorithm is said to be good if characteristics of plain image hides from its cipher image. If correlation coefficient of a plain image and its corresponding cipher image is very low and very close to zero then it is said that plain image and its corresponding cipher image are completely different. To determine the value of correlation coefficient between plain image and its corresponding cipher image in our proposed algorithm we randomly select 2000 pairs of adjacent pixel in three dimension i.e. horizontal, vertical and diagonal from an image.

Then correlation coefficient of each pairs has been calculated using the following formulas.

$$D(x) = \frac{1}{N} \sum_{i=1}^{N} (x_i - E(x))2 \tag{1}$$

$$COV(x,y) = \frac{1}{N} \sum_{i=1}^{N} (x_i - E(x))(y_i - E(y)) \tag{2}$$

$$r = \frac{COV(x,y)}{\sqrt{D(x)}\sqrt{D(y)}} \tag{3}$$

Where x and y are grey-scale values of two adjacent pixels in the image. N is the total number of pixels [1, 4]. The correlation coefficients of horizontal, vertical and diagonal pixels of plain and encrypted images are shown in Table 1. These correlation analysis prove that the proposed encryption algorithm satisfy zero co-correlation.

Table 1. Correlation coefficient of two adjacent pixels in plain image.

Image name	Plain image			Encrypted image		
	Vertical	Horizontal	Diagonal	Vertical	Horizontal	Diagonal
Lena	0.9375	0.9693	0.9108	0.0055	0.0012	0.0035
Babun	0.9834	0.9824	0.9108	0.0008	0.0032	0.0027
Monalisa	0.9809	0.9792	0.966	0.0005	0.0045	0.0017
Flower	0.9544	0.9587	0.9287	0.0055	0.0011	0.0063

4.2 Information Entropy Analysis

The amount of information in an image which must be coded for by a compression algorithm is described by image entropy. Zero entropy means the image is perfectly flat and compressed to a relatively small size. An image has a great deal of contrast from one pixel to the next, has high entropy value and consequently cannot be compressed as much as low entropy images. Images having low entropy prove that it has very little contrast and runs of pixels with the same or similar DN values. Entropy of an image is defined as

$$H(n) = \sum p(n_i) \log_2 \frac{1}{p(n_i)} \tag{4}$$

The probability of the pixel value n_i is represented by $p(n_i)$. Theoretically, a true random system should generate 28 symbols with equal probability. Therefore, according to equation of H(n) entropy of the system will be H(n) = 8 [5]. Entropy value of plain image and its correspondent cipher image have been furnished in Table 2. The result proves that our proposed algorithm has the ability against entropy attack

Table 2. Entropy analysis of plain image and cipher image

Image name	Input image entropy	Encrypted image entropy
Lena	7.746	7.9953
Babun	7.4812	7.9957
Monalisa	7.4069	7.9938
Flower	7.2549	7.9744

4.3   Histogram Analysis

Distributions of image pixels at each intensity level are plotted in a graph known as histogram analysis. It is a good statistical characteristic of an image. An encryption algorithm is said to very good if its histogram of cipher image is very similar to the random image. As a result it is almost impossible for an attacker to determine the statistical nature of pixels of plain image from its corresponding cipher image. In Fig. 4 we furnished the histogram of plain image and its corresponding cipher image.

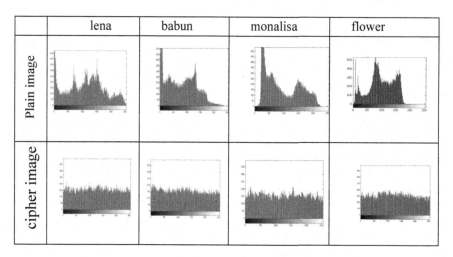

Fig. 4. Histogram of plain & encrypted images

4.4   Key Sensitivity Test

This test is carried out to describe how an encryption algorithm is sensitive towards the change in the key. For a good encryption algorithm, key value with only a single bit change from its original key value will not decrypt the cipher image. For a secure crypto system a large key sensitivity is required. Let C1 and C2 be the two cipher image has been obtained by applying our proposed algorithm with a single bit change in their key word. Table 3 shown their percentage of difference that proves our proposed crypto system is very sensitive to their key value. Figure 5 showed that if a single bit is changed in key value, original image cannot be obtained.

Table 3. The percentage of changed in key words

Image name	% of change if single bit change in key word
Lena	94.437
Babun	93.1882
Monalisa	93.7269
Flower	92.4186

plain image	decrypted image	Decrypted image (1 bit change key value)
		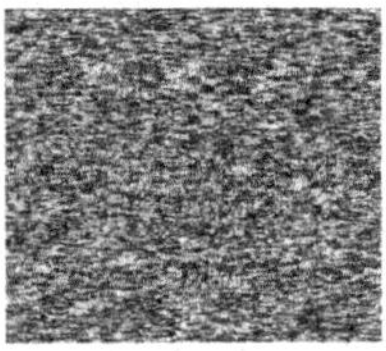

Fig. 5. Decrypted images with correct and wrong key values

5   Conclusion

In this paper, a hybrid image encryption and decryption algorithm based on PSO and GA has been proposed. The correlation coefficient of adjacent pixels of cipher image produced by our proposed algorithm prove it is highly resistive against any types of statistical attack and it also prove that proposed algorithm is very much effective for diffusion and confusion of pixels. Entropy value of every cipher image proves that information leakage is negligible. Encryption quality have been measured by calculating deviations of pixels that prove proposed algorithm has sufficient encryption quality. The NPCR and UACI values of all images are nearly 1 and are greater than 32 respectively. This shows the strength of the algorithm against differential attacks.

Acknowledgments. The authors would like to thank to the Department of Science & Technology, Government of West Bengal (Memo No.-20(Sanc.)/ST/P/S&T/Misc-9/2014 dated 16/05/2017) for funding this research work.

References

1. Lee, W., Chen, T., Lee, C.C.: Improvement of an encryption scheme for binary images. Pak. J. Inf. Technol. **2**, 191–200 (2003)
2. Zhang, W., Wong, K., Yu, H., Zhu, Z.: An image encryption scheme using reverse 2-dimensional chaotic map and dependent diffusion. Commun. Nonlinear Sci. Numer. Simulat. **18**, 2066–2080 (2013). Elsevier

3. Farshchi, S.M.R., Ebrahimi, I.D.: A novel encryption algorithm for transmitting secure data based on genetic hyper chaos map. In: 2011 International Conference on Computer Communication and Management. IACSIT Press, Singapore

4. Wang, X., Luan, D.: A novel image encryption algorithm using chaos and reversible cellular automata. Commun Nonlinear SciNumerSimulat. **18**, 3075–3085 (2013). Elsevier

5. Bhowmik, S., Acharyya, S.: Image cryptography: the genetic algorithm approach. In: IEEE International Conference on Computer Science and Automation Engineering (CSAE), pp. 223–227 (2011)

6. Pommer, A., Uhl, A.: Selective encryption of wavelet packet encoded image data: efficiency and security. Multimed. Syst. **9**(3), 279–287 (2003). Springer

7. Nichat, S.P., Sikchi, S.S.: Image encryption using hybrid genetic algorithm. Int. J. Adv. Res. Comput. Sci. Softw. Eng. (IJARCSSE). **3**(1) (2013). ISSN 2277 128X

8. Soni, A., Agrawal, S.: Using genetic algorithm for symmetric key generation in image encryption. Int. J. Adv. Res. Comput. Eng. Technol. (IJARCET) **1**(10), 137 (2012). ISSN 2278 – 1323

9. Chattopadhyay, D., Mondal, M.K., Nandi, D.: Symmetric key chaotic image encryption using circle map. Indian J. Sci. Technol. **4**(5), 593–599 (2011). ISSN 0974- 6846

10. Bhatt, V., Chandel, G.S.: Implementation of new advance image encryption algorithm to enhance security of multimedia component. Int. J. Adv. Technol. Eng. Res. **2**(4), 13–20 (2012). ISSN 2250-3536

11. Kuppusamy, K., Thamodaran, K.: Optimized partial image encryption scheme using PSO. In: Proceedings of the International Conference on Pattern Recognition, Informatics and Medical Engineering, 21–23 March 2012

12. EI-Fishawy, N.F., Ziad, O.M.A.: Quality of encryption measurement of bitmap images with RC6, MRC6, and Rijndeal block cipher algorithms. Int. J. Netw. Secur. **5**(3), 241–251 (2007)

13. Gray, R.: Entropy and Information Theory. Springer, Heidelberg (2010). https://doi.org/10.1007/978-1-4419-7970-4

14. Zeidon, I.E., Fouad, M.M., Salem, D.H.: Application of data encryption standard to bitmap and JPEG images. In: Proceedings Twentieth National Radio Science Congress (NRSC 2003), Egypt, pp. C16, March 2003

15. Chen, G.R., Mao, Y.B., et al.: A symmetric image encryption scheme based on 3D chaotic cat maps. Chaos, Solitons Fractals **21**, 749–761 (2004)

16. Gao, H., Zhang, Y., Liang, S., Li, D.: A new chaotic algorithm for image encryption. Chaos, Solitons Fractals **29**, 393–399 (2006). Elsevier

17. Kocarev, L., Jakimoski, G., Stojanovski, T., Parlitz, U.: From chaotic maps to encryption schemes. In: Proceedings of IEEE International Symposium on Circuits & Systems, vol. 4, pp. 514–517 (1998)

18. Kennedy, J., Eberhart, R.: Particle swarm optimization. In: Proceedings of the IEEE International Conference on Neural Networks, vol. 4, pp. 1942–1948 (1995). IEEE Press, Piscataway

A Modified Real-Coded Extended Line Crossover for Genetic Algorithm

Prabhash Kumar Singh[✉]

Department of Computer Science, Vidyasagar University,
Midnapore 721102, WB, India
singhg11@gmail.com

Abstract. The Genetic Algorithm (GA) is an evolutionary metaheuristic search technique built on the principle of natural selection and survival of the fittest. It follows the selection conducive to either maximize or minimize the fitness function. The crossover operator plays an important role and eventually, lots of crossover operators have been proposed. In this paper, a modified form of extended line crossover (m-RCELX) is proposed which is simple and efficient to solve the optimization problems especially the problems whose optimality lies at the boundary of its domain. Subsequently, to show the efficacy and viability of the proposed operator an assessment is done on the results obtained between the proposed operator and different pre-existing crossover operators. Furthermore, some statistical analysis is performed to show the potential and limitation of proposed work when compared with some state of art algorithms.

Keywords: Genetic Algorithm · Crossover · Optimization
Real Coded Genetic Algorithm · Extended line crossover

1 Introduction

Soft Computing methodologies help us to design and solve real life problems which are otherwise hard to formulate and compute mathematically. Among all Soft Computing algorithms, Evolutionary Algorithms became more prominent, especially Genetic Algorithm. The Genetic Algorithm is basically an optimization algorithm used to solve many optimization problems. Its efficacious applications can be found in the literature [1–4]. It is unbiased towards a locally optimal solution by approaching the global optimal through a random search and moving continuously towards a better search space. The Genetic Algorithm gets it main power from a crossover. Crossover is the most innovative operator available in the paradigm of GA that shares information between individuals by combining the feature of two or more individuals, the parents to create potentially better offspring. It is explicit in nature that during an exchange of genetic information among good individuals creates a possibility of generating even better individuals.

J. K. Mandal and D. Sinha (Eds.): CSI 2017, CCIS 836, pp. 702–716, 2018.
https://doi.org/10.1007/978-981-13-1343-1_58

A large number of researchers have focussed on this operator for improving the performance of GA [5–7]. Simultaneously in literature, it has been reported that numerous crossovers have been developed for Real-Coded Genetic Algorithms (RCGAs). Some of which is being reviewed here: Eshelman et al. [8] proposed a crossover operator (BLX-α) using the concept of interval schemata where an offspring solution is produced within the search space from the two selected parents based on a parameter α. Different experiments suggest putting the value of α at 0.5 to generate offsprings at equidistance from their parents. Deb et al. [9] announced a new crossover called Simulated Binary Crossover (SBX) by producing offspring close to its parents within search space. A couple of years later, Ono et al. [10] used an ellipsoidal probability distribution to create offsprings from three selected parents. This crossover produces an offspring with high probability between the first two selected parents whereas the second offspring is generated with low probability in the neighborhood of the selected parents. Deb et al. [11] developed a parent-centric crossover operator (PCX) which outclassed other comparative real coded crossover schemes found in the literature in finding the lowest optimum value for some of the test problems. Deep et al. [12] recommended a Laplace crossover (LX) using Laplace distribution as density function to symmetrically place the offsprings with respect to the locations of the parents. Another crossover, the boundary extended crossover was proposed by Yoon et al. [13] to eliminate any bias that may be present in any existing crossovers. A year later, Kuo et al. [14] used the reflection and expansion mechanism of Nelder-Mead's simplex method. Recently, Chuang et al. [15] too proposed a directed crossover called RGA-RDD in which a parallel structure coordinator is used to locate the global optimum.

Most of the pre-existing crossovers use the technique of either line-segment connection (SPX, UNDX, BLX) or distribution analysis of parent solutions (LX, SBX, PCX). In literature [5,16,17], it has been pointed out that although the reviewed crossovers could solve some applications successfully but may face difficulties when encountered some specific and stringent solutions. Also, these crossovers have an intrinsic bias towards the middle of the space. The concept of bias in crossover first appeared in [18] and thereafter have been studied extensively in [17,19]. Yoon et al. [13] put forward extended line, box and extended-box crossovers to show that extended-line crossovers have less bias towards the middle of the space. However, it is to be pointed while implementing GA, some restrictions are encountered due to existing machine system such as we had to have a finite number of population in comparison to the total range of the search space. The initial population may not represent a value from all the sections of the search space and hence it adds to the inefficiency of the algorithm to obtain global solution [16]. Moreover, it is to mention that sometimes the bias works well for the solution if it is towards the optimal solution and vice-versa. It is advisable to go with the unbiased operator if the spatial distribution of the considered problem is not known.

The remainder of this paper is organized as follows: In Sect. 2, two existing works are discussed. Subsequently, in Sect. 3 we systematically investigate the proposed Extended Line Crossover and its pseudocode by exploring its features. In Sect. 4, the CEC2005 testbed functions and its measuring parameters are presented. In Sects. 5 and 6, the experimental parameters and the performance of the proposed operator are discussed. Conclusively, in Sect. 7 some final remarks are presented on the performance of the proposed crossover.

2 Previous Work

2.1 Genetic Algorithm

Genetic Algorithm mimics the genetic evolutionary theory. It always exploits and explores the feasible solutions and tries to avoid premature convergence by iterating through loops of the different considered operator. A typical GA takes some random chromosomes to form a population and obtains its corresponding fitness function. The fitness values are analyzed for the selection to the next generation on the basis of "survival of the fittest". Next, the selected chromosomes go through crossover operator to produce an offspring by mixing parents. This approach signifies that the offspring generated from two better parents will yield better offsprings as it will combine gene of two fittest parents. It is controlled by crossover probability (p_c). The second important operator is the mutation which brings a diversity in the population. Few random chromosomes based on a distribution function within the search domain is added to the existing population. This operator helps to avoid premature convergence and is too guided by mutation probability (p_c). The p_m is generally kept low to avoid the formation of a high number of new chromosomes in the population which would further create an imbalance between the existing and new set of chromosomes. These operators are iterated for a pre-defined number of times to obtain the best parameters of the optimal solutions. The algorithm may be terminated after the iteration is completed or the desired optimal solution is achieved. The general procedure of Genetic Algorithm consists of the following steps: (as described in Fig. 1):

Step 1: Generate randomly a population of the initial feasible solutions
Step 2: Obtain the best fitness value for each chromosome
Step 3: Apply the selection operator to move the selected chromosomes to the next generation
Step 4: Apply crossover operator between the selected chromosomes to obtain new child chromosomes
Step 5: Apply mutation operator
Step 6: Combine new offsprings and chromosomes into the population
Step 5: If a terminating condition is met, return the best fitness value else go to step 2.

2.2 Extended Line Crossover

An extended line crossover is a recombination operator which generates offspring in a direction defined by its parent. The offspring produced more often lies

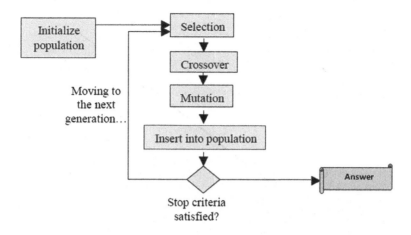

Fig. 1. Simple genetic algorithm

outside the area covered by its parents. Extended line recombination is applicable only to real coded variables. As shown in Fig. 2, if x, y are the parents to be crossover and l be the Euclidean distance between the parents, then, the new offsprings generated x', y' as given in Eqs. (1) and (2) would be at a distance αl away from either parent. Here α is the random number generated by some function. The extended crossover exploits the points on to the left and right of its parent respectively depending on the difference between them.

$$x' = x + \alpha l \tag{1}$$

$$y' = y + \alpha l \tag{2}$$

3   The Proposed Extended Line Crossver (m-RCELX)

A new technique is proposed to modify extended line crossover operator which uses a distribution function to generate a random number. It is not a parent centric crossover. Among the two offsprings produced, one increment and the other decrements with respect to its parent value (i.e. one will lie on to the left of its parent and the other will be at the right of its parent). Using the proposed technique, two offsprings $x'^{(1)} = (x_1'^{(1)}, x_2'^{(1)}, x_3'^{(1)}, ..., x_n'^{(1)})$ and $y'^{(1)} = (y_1'^{(1)}, y_2'^{(1)}, y_3'^{(1)}, ..., y_n'^{(1)})$ are generated from two parents $x^{(1)} = (x_1^{(1)}, x_2^{(1)}, x_3^{(1)}, ..., x_n^{(1)})$ and $y^{(1)} = (y_1^{(1)}, y_2^{(1)}, y_3^{(1)}, ..., y_n^{(1)})$ in the following way: Assume, $VarMax_i$ and $VarMin_i$ to be the range of the ith variable, such that

$$d_i = VarMax_i - VarMin_i \tag{3}$$

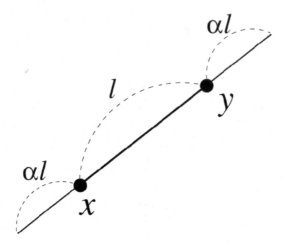

Fig. 2. Extended crossover

The offsprings obtained after reformulation of Eqs. (1) and (2) are given by the equations

$$x_i^{'(1)} = x_i^{(1)} + d_i\alpha_2 \tag{4}$$

$$y_i^{'(1)} = y_i^{(1)} + d_i\alpha_1 \tag{5}$$

where α_1 and α_2 are the random number obtained using the following distribution function:

$$\alpha_1 = (1 + r)^{\beta/d_i} - 1 \tag{6}$$

$$\alpha_2 = (1 + (1 - r))^{-\beta/d_i} - 1 \tag{7}$$

Here, r implies a random number between 0, 1 and β is given by

$$\beta = y_i^{(1)} - x_i^{(1)} \tag{8}$$

From Eqs. (6) and (7) it is clear that α_1 and α_2 are dependent on β, the difference in the distance of the ith variable. The values obtained from Eqs. (6) and (7) shows two contrasting behavior of α_1 and α_2 which are briefly discuss below:

(i) One offspring lies closer to its parent while other is at far away.

   As shown in Fig. 3, P_1, P_2, P_3, P_4 are the parents undergoing crossover. The offsprings O_1, O_2 is obtained after the crossover of parent P_1, P_2 and offspring O_3, O_4 is obtained after the crossover of parent P_3, P_4. The offspring O_1, O_2 generated are at greater distances from its parent P_1, P_2, since both the parents are farther away from each other, but offspring O_3, O_4 are relatively close to its parent P_3, P_4, as the distance between them is small. Subsequently, in each pair of the offspring, one offspring (O_2, O_3) lies closer to its parent while the other

(O_1, O_4) lies farther away from its parent. This enables the proposed crossover to efficiently converge to an optimal solution by continuously exploiting points which are nearer as well as farther away in the direction of its parents. Also, it helps to exploit the points aggressively as the problem converges. If at any time, the offspring generated lies outside the domain of the search problem, then the offspring will be restricted to its boundary. This helps to find the global optima at the boundary of the search domain, if any, lies at the boundary. So, it is quite evident from Fig. 3 that one offspring will be produced between $(VarMin_i, x_i^{(1)})$ and the other between $(y_i^{(1)}, VarMax_i)$.

(ii) α_1 always carry a positive value while α_2 carries a negative value.

In Fig. 4, a graph is plotted to show the distribution of α_1 and α_2 against the random number r keeping other parameters constant. Both α_1 and α_2 of Eqs. (6) and (7) respectively, are incrementing function, but α_1 increments positively where as α_2 increments negatively. When the crossover is done using Eqs. (4) and (5), the first offspring generated will always be on the right side of its parent where as second offspring will always be on left side of its parent. This helps to aggressively exploit points in both the direction along the line of the parent chromosomes.

To sum up, the procedure of the proposed operator (m-RCELX) along with Genetic Algorithm can be rewritten as:

Step-1: Generate a random initial population of size N in the given n-dimensional search space
Step-2: $i \leftarrow 1[i$ represents current generation]
Step-3: Obtain objective function value i.e. fitness value
Step-4: Apply selection operator
Step-5: Apply proposed crossover operator
    [**substep a**] For $j = 1, 2, ...n$
    [**substep b**] Compute r and β_j
    [**substep c**] Compute α_1 and α_2 as shown in Eqs. (6) and (7) respectively
    [**substep d**] Compute x_j and y_j as shown in Eqs. (4) and (5) respectively
Step-6: Apply mutation operator
Step-7: Recompute the fitness value
Step-8: Set $i \leftarrow i + 1$
Step-9: If the predefined stopping criteria fails, goto Step-4
Step-10: End

4   Test Problems

The performance of the proposed crossover as defined in the previous section is compared to a recent proposed direction based crossover operator (RGA-RDD) [15] in real coded environment of Genetic Algorithm. To do more analysis on different problem domain, the first 14 benchmark test problems from CEC2005

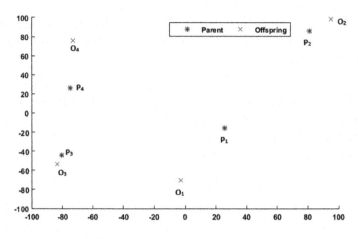

Fig. 3. Generation of offspring

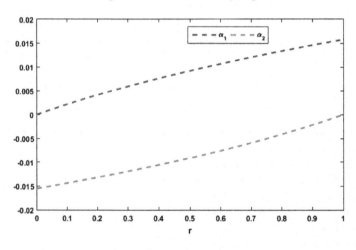

Fig. 4. r versus α

[20] have been selected. These benchmark functions are of various complexities and carry more than one local optimal solutions. These functions are elected because from the literature we can find that they give proper insight about the real coded optimization algorithms [21]. A brief elucidation of the given benchmark functions is given in Table 1. Some conditions for the experiment has to be laid to do a proper and fair evaluation. The dimension of the test functions are 10 with maximum number of function evaluations (MaxFEs) set to 10^5 iterations. Each benchmark function was executed for 25 runs and for every run the function error value $(f(x) - f(x_{opt}))$ was obtained. Also, the success rate and success performance, are recorded for performance measure as illustrated in [20].

Table 1. Benchmark function used

Function no.	Name	Properties
F_1	Shifted Sphere	Shifted; Separable
F_2	Shifted Schwefel's Problem 1.2	Shifted; Non-separable
F_3	Shifted Rotated High Conditioned Elliptic function	Shifted; Rotated; Non-Separable; High conditioning
F_4	Sifted Schwefel's Problem 1.2 with Noise in fitness	Shifted; Non-Separablen with Noise
F_5	Schwefel's Problem 2.6 with Global Optimum on Bounds	Non-Separable; Optimum at the boundary
F_6	Shifted Rosenbrock's Function	Shifted; Non-separable; Local optimum with narrow valley to global optimum
F_7	Shifted Rotated Griewank's Function without Bounds	Shifted; Rotated; Non-separable; No bounds for variables x
F_8	Shifted Rotated Ackley's Function with Global Optimum on Bounds	Shifted;Rotated; Optimum at boundary
F_9	Shifted Rastrigin's Function	Shifted; Separable; Local optimas number is huge
F_{10}	Shifted Rotated Rastrigin's Function	Shifted; Rotated; Non-separable; Local optima's number is huge
F_{11}	Shifted Rotated Weierstrass Function	Shifted; Rotated; Non-separable; Continuous but differentiable only on a set of points
F_{12}	Schwefel's Problem 2.13	Shifted; Non-separable;Scalable
F_{13}	Expanded Extended Griewank's plus Rosenbrock's Function (F8F2)	Multimodal; Non-separable; Shifted
F_{14}	Shifted Rotated Expanded Scaffer's F6	Shifted; Non-separable

5   Experimental Setup

Before implementing the proposed operator on the benchmark functions, the values of the parameters must be fixed. However, it is not an easy task especially when the problem deals with real coded parameters of the Genetic Algorithm. The test problems considered for experiment are of very diverse nature and therefore a common fixed value of the parameters for all the problems may not work. So, some random test was carried out with possible combinations to fix the final values of the parameters involved in these experiments. We cannot claim it to be the best settings for any problem, in particular, rather recommended to use as it has given continuously better results for the majority of the considered problems. The population size is ten times the dimension of the search space. The selection method used is Roulette wheel whereas mutation is done with uniform mutation. The value of p_c and p_m is 0.7 and 0.3 respectively. Also, all the algorithms that are executed for carrying out the experiments have the elite preserving property of 1. All the algorithms are implemented in Matlab on an intel core i5 2.6 GHz machine with 4 GB RAM on Windows platform.

6   Results and Discussion

6.1   Performance Analysis on CEC2005 Benchmark Functions

The results obtained after running the CEC2005 benchmark functions on the proposed algorithm is given in Tables 2 and 3. The table contains function error values of each function after $10^3; 10^4; 10^5$ iterations (FEs). The recorded average error values are sorted in an ascending order for the 25 independent runs. To give a clear picture, the 1st, 13th and last values are considered which is the best, median and worst values respectively of the test function. Also, the mean and standard deviation are taken into account for performance analysis. It is evident looking the results that the proposed technique m-RCELX is able to locate the global optimum for the benchmark problems F_1 and F_2 successfully with great accuracy. The function F_3 provides some hindrance due to its nature of non-separable and high conditioning but the function F_4, however being noisy, does not provide any obstacles to obtain the global optimum. As pointed in Sect. 3, the proposed crossover will be better for functions whose optimum points lies at the boundary, the function F_5 does have its global optimum value at the boundary for which the proposed crossover performs excellent and quickly obtains the global optimum. The m-RCELX performs brilliantly for the function F_6 in spite of narrow valleys from a local to the global optimum. The global optimum of the function F_7 lies outside its initialization boundary, in spite of that the m-RCELX is able to find a solution which is very close to the global optimum. But for the test function F_8 the proposed crossover fails to locate the global optimum due to its complex structure where a very sharp needle like point comes out of the valleys of local optimum points. But for the function F_9 where the local optima are huge, still it is able to find the global optimum. However, the function F_{10} which is the rotated version of F_9, creates an obstacle for the m-RCELX to find the desired optimum. The function F_{11} is multi-modal continuous but differentiable only on certain set of points. It also have many deep valleys of local optimum points providing difficulty to locate the global optimum. For function F_{12} it successfully locates the global optimum with great accuracy, which too is multi-modal and scalable but does not have deep valleys unlike F_{11}. The last two functions F_{13} and F_{14} are group of expanded functions. It could be found in the literature that these functions are hard to be computed by many optimization algorithms. However, for the function F_{13}, m-RCELX effectively finds a near solution but for function F_{14}, it fails to get hold of global optimum points.

Table 2. Error values of functions F_1–F_7 in 10 dimensions

FEs		F_1	F_2	F_3	F_4	F_5	F_6	F_7
1E3	Best	1.64E-05	1.96E-02	9.20E+04	3.63E-04	0.00E+00	1.15E+00	4.13E-02
	Median	9.85E-05	1.49E-01	2.50E+05	5.36E-01	3.64E-12	1.86E+01	2.81E-01
	Worst	7.67E-04	1.24E+00	1.44E+06	8.56E-01	3.64E-12	1.11E+02	5.05E-01
	Mean	2.41E-04	3.83E-01	3.86E+05	4.95E-01	2.76E-12	4.12E+01	2.74E-01
	Std	2.75E-04	4.63E-01	3.83E+05	3.21E-01	1.16E-12	4.28E+01	1.51E-01
1E4	Best	4.50E-25	3.66E-26	1.27E+03	2.50E-26	0.00E+00	2.48E-08	3.69E-02
	Median	1.54E-24	1.48E-25	4.93E+03	4.49E-26	3.64E-12	2.16E-04	2.57E-01
	Worst	1.15E-23	4.53E-25	9.04E+04	4.50E-25	3.64E-12	3.12E+01	5.05E-01
	Mean	2.98E-24	1.94E-25	1.59E+04	8.98E-26	2.76E-12	4.78E+00	2.62E-01
	Std	3.32E-24	1.28E-24	2.62E+04	1.23E-25	1.16E-12	1.01E+01	1.51E-01
1E5	Best	4.50E-25	3.66E-26	6.93E-03	2.50E-26	0.00E+00	1.45E-22	3.69E-02
	Median	1.54E-24	1.48E-25	1.48E+00	4.49E-26	3.64E-12	1.036E-20	2.57E-01
	Worst	1.15E-23	4.53E-25	1.40E+02	4.42E-25	3.64E-12	3.65E-20	5.05E-01
	Mean	2.98E-24	1.94E-25	3.25E+01	8.90E-26	2.76E-12	1.35E-20	2.62E-01
	Std	3.32E-24	1.28E-25	5.24E+01	1.21E-25	1.16E-12	1.23E-20	1.51E-01

Table 3. Error values of functions F_8–F_{14} in 10 dimensions

FEs		F_8	F_9	F_{10}	F_{11}	F_{12}	F_{13}	F_{14}
1E3	Best	2.02E+01	2.85E-05	1.59E+01	3.19E+00	6.89E-01	3.05E-02	3.37E+00
	Median	2.03E+01	3.11E-04	3.28E+01	6.42E+00	1.56E+03	3.63E-01	3.69E+00
	Worst	2.04E+01	1.69E-03	5.47E+01	1.01E+01	4.38E+04	1.09E+00	4.02E+00
	Mean	2.03E+01	5.64E-04	3.34E+01	6.58E+00	7.08E+03	4.05E-01	3.72E+00
	Std	7.52E-02	5.16E-04	1.22E+01	1.90E+00	1.09E+04	2.61E-01	2.54E-01
1E4	Best	2.01E+01	0.00E+00	1.59E+01	3.19E+00	1.37E-15	2.98E-02	3.36E+00
	Median	2.02E+01	0.00E+00	3.28E+01	6.42E+00	1.56E+03	3.10E-01	3.62E+00
	Worst	2.04E+01	2.84E-14	5.47E+01	1.00E+01	4.38E+04	5.71E-01	4.02E+00
	Mean	2.02E+01	8.53E-15	3.34E+01	6.57E+00	7.07E+03	3.11E-01	3.70E+01
	Std	8.98E-02	1.30E-14	1.22E+01	1.88E+00	1.09E+04	1.54E-01	2.63E-01
1E5	Best	2.01E+01	0.00E+00	1.59E+01	3.19E+00	3.31E-23	2.98E-02	3.36E+00
	Median	2.02E+01	0.00E+00	3.28E+01	6.42E+00	1.56E+03	3.10E-01	3.62E+00
	Worst	2.03E+01	2.84E-14	5.47E+01	1.00E+01	4.38E+04	5.71E-01	4.02E+00
	Mean	2.02E+01	8.53E-15	3.34E+01	6.57E+00	7.07E+03	3.11E-01	3.70E+00
	Std	7.75E-02	1.30E-14	1.22E+01	1.88E+00	1.09E+04	1.45E-01	2.63E-01

6.2   m-RCELX versus RGA-RDD

The proposed technique m-RCELX is further compared with a recent proposed alogrithm named RGA-RDD [15] with the mean value obtained after 25 independent runs of the individual benchmark problem (Table 1) at the end of FEs

1E3, 1E4 and 1E5. The mean value is considered since it will provide an overview on the efficiency of these algorithms on each run of the individual benchmark problem. It is noticeable from Tables 4 and 5 that m-RCELX in terms of obtaining the mean value among 25 independent runs performed significantly well for the functions F_1–F_4, F_6–F_9, F_{11} and F_{13} than the algorithm RGA-RDD. For the functons F_5, F_{10}, F_{12} and F_{14}, the RGA-RDD performed slightly better at the end of FEs 1E4 and 1E5. So, in view of the above comparisons it could be stated that m-RCELX outperforms RGA-RDD by performing excellent on most of the considered problems, however, RGA-RDD does perform better for few of the problems but the difference in result is very minimal.

Table 4. Comparison of mean value of functions F_1–F_7 in 10 dimensions

FEs	Algorithm	F_1	F_2	F_3	F_4	F_5	F_6	F_7
1E3	m-RCELX	2.41E-04	3.83E-01	3.86E+05	4.95E-01	1.82E-12	4.12E+01	2.74E-01
	RGA-RDD	1.73E+03	6.74E+03	5.46E+07	1.26E+04	4.68E+03	6.09E+07	7.27E+01
1E4	m-RCELX	2.98E-24	1.94E-25	1.59E+04	8.98E-26	1.82E-12	4.78E+00	2.62E-01
	RGA-RDD	4.45E-06	4.59E+00	4.88E+05	1.78E+02	7.83E-05	4.82E+01	4.95E-01
1E5	m-RCELX	2.98E-24	1.94E-25	3.25E+01	8.90E-26	1.82E-12	1.35E-20	2.62E-01
	RGA-RDD	4.09E-14	1.05E+03	3.50E+04	4.02E-10	0.00E+00	1.27E+00	4.65E-01

Table 5. Comparison of mean value of functions F_8–F_{14} in 10 dimensions

FEs	Algorithm	F_8	F_9	F_{10}	F_{11}	F_{12}	F_{13}	F_{14}
1E3	m-RCELX	2.03E+01	5.64E-04	3.34E+01	6.58E+00	3.55E+02	4.05E-01	3.72E+00
	RGA-RDD	2.07E+01	5.45E+01	7.80E+01	1.13E+01	2.38E+04	6.00E+00	4.39E+00
1E4	m-RCELX	2.02E+01	8.53E-15	3.34E+01	6.57E+00	3.47E+02	3.11E-01	3.70E+00
	RGA-RDD	2.05E+01	3.57E+00	1.95E+01	7.17E+00	9.21E+02	8.37E-01	3.64E+00
1E5	m-RCELX	2.02E+01	8.53E-15	3.34E+01	6.57E+00	3.47E+02	3.11E-01	3.70E+00
	RGA-RDD	2.03E+01	2.48E-13	1.86E+01	4.47E+00	3.90E+02	6.37E-01	3.23E+00

6.3   Performance Evaluation with Other Algorithms

For a rigorous comparison with the proposed m-RCELX algorithm, ten state of art algorithms are chosen: SPC-NX [29], L-SaDE [28], K-PCX [27], G-CMA-ES [26], EDA [25], DMS-L-PSO [21], DE [24], CoEVO [23], BLX-MA [22],RGA-RDD [15]. The idea of choosing these algorithms is due to the fact that from literature it could be seen that they had performed well on the CEC 2005 testbed functions as well as their optimization scheme is very much similar to the proposed scheme. To do a fair comparison, at first, the CEC 2005 test functions considered here are being divided into three sections of unimodal, solved multimodal and unsolved multimodal functions. The functions $F_1 - F_5$ are unimodal functions, F_6-F_7, F_9-F_{12} are the solved multimodal functions i.e. atleast one algorithm gave a successful run and the unsolved multimodal functions are F_8, F_{13}, F_{14} for which no single run was successful for any algorithm. As mentioned in [20], the data for statistical analysis were collected from the function error values of 25 runs at the end of n x 10^4 FEs, where n is the dimension. Then, the comparison results for different algorithms of different grouped functions are given in Tables 6 and 7. The table entries are Normalized Success Performance which is obtained after Success Performance FEs is divided by FEs required by the best algorithm to give a desired accuracy on the respective function (first row) and the number of successful runs (round brackets). Also, the Success Rate of each algorithms is shown for depth analysis. From Table 6, it could be seen that the proposed algorithm m-RCELX have excellent Success Rate and Success Performance than many state of art algorithms for the unimodal functions. The m-RCELX required very few FEs to obtain global optimum with the desired accuracy for all the unimodal functions except F_3. For functions F_1, F_2, F_4 and F_5, it took FEs almost equal to the best state of art algorithms but for function F_5 whose global optimum lies at the boundary, performed magnificently to locate the global optimum with desired accuracy by taking minimum number of FEs than all the comparative algorithms. In case of solved Multimodal functions (Table 7), the proposed algorithm behaved averagely with 37% success rate and performed well for functions F_6, F_9 and F_{12} giving significant success performance. For the function F_9, the proposed algorithm obtained the global optimum in least number of FEs in comparison with the comparative algorithms. So, it is quite conclusive from above that m-RCELX took very less number of FEs to attain global optimum for all those benchmark functions in which it run successfully at least once.

Table 6. Comparison of normalized success performance for unimodal functions

Algorithm	F_1	F_2	F_3	F_4	F_5	
	1000	2400	6500	2900	310	SR(%)
m-RCELX	1.5(25)	1.1(25)	-	1.1(25)	1.0(25)	80
RGA-RDD	10.0(25)	11.5(25)	-	20.8(25)	30.5(25)	80
SPC-NX	6.7(25)	12.9(25)	-	10.7(25)	129.4(25)	80
L-SaDE	10.0(25)	4.2(25)	8.0(16)	15.9(24)	-	72
K-PCX	1.0(25)	1.0(25)	-	19.7(21)	-	57
G-CMA-ES	1.6(25)	1.0(25)	1.0(25)	1.0(25)	19(25)	100
EDA	10.0(25)	4.6(25)	2.5(25)	4.1(25)	79.9(25)	100
DMS-L-PSO	12.0(25)	5.0(25)	1.8(25)	-	354(20)	76
DE	29.0(25)	19.2(25)	18.5(25)	17.9(25)	131.3(25)	100
CoEVO	23.0(25)	11.3(25)	6.8(25)	16.2(25)	-	80
BLX-MA	12.0(25)	15.4(25)	-	25.9(24)	-	59

Table 7. Comparison of normalized success performance for solved multimodal functions

Algorithm	F_6	F_7	F_9	F_{10}	F_{11}	F_{12}	
	7100	4700	700	5500	190000	8200	SR(%)
m-RCELX	1.2(25)	-	1.0(25)	-	-	2.9(5)	37
RGA-RDD	23.1(25)	-	60.6(25)	-	-	57.9(15)	43
SPC-NX	-	383(1)	-	-	5.8(1)	-	1
L-SaDE	6.9(25)	36.2(6)	24.3(25)	-	-	3.9(25)	54
K-PCX	1.0(22)	-	70.4(24)	1.0(22)	-	1.0(14)	55
G-CMA-ES	1.5(25)	1.0(25)	109.3(19)	1.2(23)	1.4(6)	4.0(22)	80
EDA	9.6(22)	404(1)	-	-	2.9(3)	4.3(10)	24
DMS-L-PSO	7.7(25)	126(4)	51(25)	-	-	6.6(19)	49
DE	6.6(24)	255(2)	257.4(11)	-	1.0(12)	8.8(19)	45
CoEVO	-	-	-	-	-	-	0
BLX-MA	-	-	138.4(18)	-	-	-	12

7   Conclusion

In this paper a new technique, called the modified real-coded Extended Line Crossover operator (m-RCELX), is introduced. It generates non-parent centric offspring away from its parent in either direction by continuously exploiting points in a real coded environment. For an analogical comparison, the m-RCELX algorithm have been applied on the first 14 functions of the CEC2005 testbed functions to get the global optimal value. The obtained value was compared with similar algorithm RGA-RDD to show the effectiveness of the proposed technique. Further to have a depth analysis of m-RCELX, it is compared by obtaining normalized Success Performance and Success Rate with ten chosen state of art algorithms found in literature. Based on the comparison and statistical simulations of the technique developed herein, the distinct features of m-RCELX are: (i) Required very minimal FEs to locate global optimum. (ii) Performed better than all the state of art algorithms for the unimodal function whose optimality lies at the boundary. It is expected that in future, the proposed modified Extended Line Crossover operator will show a great potential for further research based on this study in different fields of optimization.

References

1. Dyer, J.D., Hartfield, R.J., Dozier, G.V., Burkhalter, J.E.: Aerospace design optimization using a steady state real-coded genetic algorithm. Appl. Math. Comput. **218**, 4710–4730 (2012)
2. Yuan, Q., Qian, F., Du, W.: A hybrid genetic algorithm with the Baldwin effect. Inf. Sci. **180**, 640–652 (2010)

3. Hansen, N., Ostermeier, A.: Completely derandomized self-adaptation in evolution strategies. Evol. Comput. **9**, 159–195 (2001)
4. Singh, P., Mondal, S., Maiti, M.: A Hybridized chemotactic genetic algorithm for optimization. Comput. Sci. Syst. Biol. **9**(2), 45–50 (2016)
5. Beyer, H.G., Deb, K.: On self-adapting features in real-parameter evolutionary algorithms. IEEE Trans. Evol. Comput. **5**(3), 250–270 (2001)
6. Herrera, F., Lozano, M., Sánchez, A.M.: A taxonomy for the crossover operator for real-coded genetic algorithms: an experimental study. Int. J. Intell. Syst. **18**(3), 309–338 (2003)
7. Hervás-Martínez, C., Ortiz-Boyer, D.: Analizing the statistical features of CIXL2 crossover offspring. Soft Comput. **9**(4), 270–279 (2005)
8. Eshelman, L.J., Schaffer, D.: Real-coded genetic algorithms and interval-schemata. In: Proceedings of the Workshop on Foundations of Genetic Algorithms, Vail, CO, USA, pp. 187–202 (1993)
9. Deb, K., Agrawal, R.: Simulated binary crossover for continuous search space. Complex Syst. **9**, 115–148 (1995)
10. Ono, I., Kobayashi, S.: A real-coded genetic algorithm for functional optimization using unimodal normal distribution crossover. In: Proceedings of Seventh International Conference on Genetic Algorithms (ICGA-7), East Lansing, MI, USA, vol. 9, no. 4, pp. 246–253 (1997)
11. Deb, K., Anand, A., Joshi, D.: A computationally efficient evolutionary algorithm for real-parameter optimization. Evol. Comput. **10**, 371–395 (2002)
12. Deep, K., Thakur, M.: A new crossover operator for real coded genetic algorithms. Appl. Math. Comput. **188**, 895–911 (2007)
13. Yoon, Y., Kim, Y.H., Moraglio, A., Moon, B.R.: A theoretical and empirical study on unbiased boundary-extended crossover for real-valued representation. Inf. Sci. **183**, 48–65 (2012)
14. Kuo, H.C., Lin, C.H.: A directed genetic algorithm for global optimization. Appl. Math. Comput. **219**, 7348–7364 (2013)
15. Chuang, Y., Chen, C., Hwang, C.: A real-coded genetic algorithm with a direction-based crossover operator. Inf. Scie. **305**, 320–348 (2015)
16. Ono, I., Kita, H., Kobayashi, S.: A robust real-coded genetic algorithm using unimodal normal distribution crossover augmented by uniform crossover: effects of self-adaptation of crossover probabilities. In: Proceedings of the 1st Annual Conference on Genetic and Evolutionary Computation, vol. 1 pp. 496–503 (1999)
17. Tsutsi, S., Goldberg, D.E.: Search space boundary extension method in real-coded genetic algorithms. Inf. Sci. **133**, 229–247 (2001)
18. Eshelman, L.J., Mathias, K.E., Schaffer, J.D.: Crossover operator biases: exploiting the population distribution. In: Proceedings of the International Conference on Genetic Algorithms, pp. 354–361 (1997)
19. Yourim, Y., Yong-Hyuk, K.: The roles of crossover and mutation in real-coded genetic algorithms. In: Gao, S. (ed.) Bio-Inspired Computational Algorithms and Their Applications. InTech (2012). https://doi.org/10.5772/38236, http://www.intechopen.com/books/bio-inspired-computational-algorithms-and-their-applications/the-roles-of-crossover-and-mutation-in-real-coded-genetic-algorithms
20. Suganthan, P.N., et al.: Problem Definitions and Evaluation Criteria for the CEC 2005 Special Session on Real-Parameter Optimization. Nanyang Technological University, Technical report (2005). http://www.ntu.edu.sg/home/EPNSugan

21. Liang, J.J., Suganthan, P.N., Deb, K.: Novel composition test functions for numerical global optimization. In: IEEE Swarm Intelligence Symposium, Pasadena, CA, USA, pp. 68–75 (2005)
22. Molina, D., Herrera, F., Lozano, M.: Adaptive local search parameters for real-coded memetic algorithms. In: IEEE Congress on Evolutionary Computation, Edinburgh, UK, vol. 1, pp. 888–895 (2005)
23. Posik, P.: Real-parameter optimization using the mutation step co-evolution. In: IEEE Congress on Evolutionary Computation, Edinburgh, UK, vol. 1, pp. 872–879 (2005)
24. Ronkkonen, J., Kukkonen, S., Price, V.: Real-parameter optimization with differential evolution. In: IEEE Congress on Evolutionary Computation, Edinburgh, UK, vol. 1, pp. 506–513 (2005)
25. Yuan, B., Gallagher, M.: Experimental results for the special session on real-parameter optimization at CEC 2005: a simple, continuous EDA. In: IEEE Congress on Evolutionary Computation, Edinburgh, UK, vol. 2, pp. 1792–1799 (2005)
26. Auger, A., Hansen, N.: A restart CMA evolution strategy with increasing population size. In: IEEE Congress on Evolutionary Computation, Edinburgh, UK, vol. 2, pp. 1769–1776 (2005)
27. Sinha, A., Tiwari, S., Deb, K.: A population-based, steady-state procedure for real-parameter optimization. In: IEEE Congress on Evolutionary Computation, Edinburgh, UK, vol. 1, pp. 514–521 (2005)
28. Qin, A.K., Suganthan, N.: Self-adaptive differential evolution algorithm for numerical optimization. In: IEEE Congress on Evolutionary Computation, Edinburgh, UK, vol. 2, pp. 1758–1791 (2005)
29. Ballester, P.J., Stephenson, J., Carter, J.N., Gallagher, K.: Real-parameter optimization performance study on the CEC-2005 benchmark with SPC-PNX. In: IEEE Congress on Evolutionary Computation, Edinburgh, UK, vol. 1, pp. 498–505 (2005)

Interpretable Semantic Textual Similarity Using Lexical and Cosine Similarity

Goutam Majumder[1][(✉)], Partha Pakray[1], and David Eduardo Pinto Avendaño[2]

[1] Department of Computer Science and Engineering, National Institute of
Technology Mizoram, Aizawl, India
goutam.nita@gmail.com, parthapakray@gmail.com
[2] Facultad de Ciencias de la Computación, BUAP, Puebla, Mexico
davideduardopinto@gmail.com

Abstract. Transforming information in a digital way modifies the people views and their daily functioning. Social media is a key platform where people express their views regarding any event and it also plays an important role in daily activities. Digital marketing is an example of such digital transformation of information. In this present era, social channels use their personal information of the users to launch any product or tool. Digital Education plays a key role in transforming information in a digital way. In such cases, Natural Language Processing of people views and blog chatting plays an important role. Adding an explanatory layer is important for an Intelligent Tutoring System (ITS), where students interact with an application through natural language. This paper proposed a method, which will able to measure the interpretability between two sentences by rating the degree of semantic equivalence on a graded scale from 0 (not aligned) to 5 (semantically equivalent). The goal of the paper is not to add an interpretable layer but developed a method which can explain the similarities and differences between the two sentences. This task has been motivated by SemEval 2016 Task 2. The proposed method has been developed and tested over the headlines dataset. For the gold standard data, an accuracy of 0.64 for alignment type and score is reported.

Keywords: Semantic similarity · Word2Vec · WordNet
String similarity

1 Introduction

In Natural Language Processing (NLP), measuring semantic similarity score between text plays an important role for many application in NLP and its related areas. Applications such as text summarization (Aliguliyev 2009; Steinberger and Jezek 2004), Question Answering (QA) (Mohler et al. 2011), relevance feedback and text classification (Rocchio 1971), Word Sense Disambiguation (WSD) (Li et al. 2006), and extractive summarization (Salton et al. 1997) already reported as the use similarity score of text. Since its inception, the problem has seen a

© Springer Nature Singapore Pte Ltd. 2018
J. K. Mandal and D. Sinha (Eds.): CSI 2017, CCIS 836, pp. 717–732, 2018.
https://doi.org/10.1007/978-981-13-1343-1_59

large number of solutions in a relatively small amount of time. The central idea behind the most solution is that, the identification and alignment of semantically similar or related words across the two sentences and the aggregation of these similarities to generate an overall similarity (Islam and Inkpen 2008; Mihalcea et al. 2006; Šarić et al. 2012).

Semantic Textual Similarity (STS), also contributes for many semantic web applications like community extraction, ontology generation and entity disambiguation. It is also useful for Twitter Search application reported in (Salton et al. 1997), which requires the ability to accurately measure the semantic relatedness between concepts or entities. In Information Retrieval (IR), one of the main problems is to retrieve a set of documents and retrieving images by captions, which is semantically related to a given user query in a web search engine (Coelho et al. 2004).

The techniques used to solve this problem can be broadly classified into three groups. For the first group semantic similarity is estimated by defining a topological similarity, where ontologies are defined to determine the distance/similarity between the terms/concepts (Jiang and Conrath 1997). For the second category, methods are grouped as statistical/corpus based similarity measure. For this first a statistical method is developed and then similarity is estimated. For the third group different string similarity measures are used to computing the similarity between textual items.

In this paper, the goal is not only measuring a similarity score between the two text snippets but, also assigning a class label to it. From this similarity score and class label anyone will get a clearer idea, what type of information two text snippets are shared. Along with this an explanatory layer is also added by specifying a reason why texts are related/unrelated and this problem was first introduced by (Agirrea et al. 2015; Agirre et al. 2016). The final goal of any such method, which is able to explain the differences and commonalities between the two sentences. To understand this problem, let's consider the following two sentences: (a) US drone strike kills 5 militants in Pakistan (b) Drone strike kills four suspected militants in Pakistan.

The output of any such method would be something like the following: The two sentences talk about a blow with causalities in Pakistan, but they differs in two ways. In the first sentence, it is clearly mentioned about the blow done by a 'US drone' and clearly specifies whom it killed as 'militants'. But in the second sentence, it varies in causalities as four (4) not five (5) and simply mentioned about a 'Drone' not as specific as 'US drone'. It's also not clear about the causalities mentioned in second text as suspect militants.

To develop this method, we first identify the chunks/phrase among the sentences and aligned the chunks among the sentences. During the alignment of chunks, we also identify the relationships among the chunks. After that based on the relationship a similarity score between the chunks is measured. The details of the different relations and similarity score between the chunks are discussed in Sect. 2. This paper is organised as follows. The problem is defined in Sect. 2 and in Sect. 3 related work is reported. The preprocessing and development steps of the various modules is reported in Sect. 4. Performance of the system based on evaluation matrices is describes in Sect. 5. The conclusion and future task is reported in Sect. 6.

2   Defining the Problem

The Interpretable Semantic Textual Similarity (*i*STS) problem is divided into four (4) sub-tasks. The first task is to produce the parse trees for the sentences (i.e identify the chunks). Next task will be aligning the chunks of the sentences and third is assigning an alignment reasoning from a list of possible labels. Finally, relatedness/similarity score is measured between the aligned chunks. A list of all possible labels are already reported in (Agirrea et al. 2015):

1. Equivalent (EQUI) – the two chunks convey an equivalent meaning ("by chance", "accidentally")
2. Opposition (OPPO) – the two chunks convey an opposite meaning ("black cat", "white cat")
3. More General (SPE1) – this chunk conveys a more general meaning in first chunk than the other ("hot water", "water")
4. More Specific (SPE2) – this chunk conveys a more specific meaning than the other chunk ("Drone strike", "US drone strike")
5. Similar (SIMI) – the two chunks convey a similar meaning ("to accomplish", "to achieve")
6. Related (REL) – two chunks are somehow related ("car", "bus")
7. No Alignment (NOALI) – there are no chunks in the other sentence that are semantically similar to this chunk

To align chunks of the sentences boundary of each chunks and each of the tokens are considered and unrelated chunks are left unaligned. For this task, the similarity score is considered in a range of 0 to 5 and is divided into following ways:

5 – if the meaning of both chunks is equivalent
4 – if the meaning of both chunks are mostly equivalent, but differs by some unimportant details
3 – if chunks are roughly equivalent, but differs by some important information
2 – if chunks are share some details, but are not equivalent
1 – if chunks are not equivalent, but are from same topic
0 – (represents as NIL) if the meaning of the chunk is completely unrelated.

3   Related Work

Early work on adding an explanatory layer is an important task for a tutorial system, where Intelligent Tutoring System (ITS) interacts with the students through natural language. In most cases, applications have focused on problem–dependent and question-dependent knowledge (Aleven et al. 2001; Jordan et al.

2005). But some alternatives are also available on those are based on NLP techniques (Nielsen et al. 2009). Work reported in (Nielsen et al. 2009), which is coming from an educational domain and much more similar to textual entailment. They defined facets (words under some syntactic/semantic relation) in the response of a student answer (called hypothesis) was linked to a reference answer. The link would signal whether each facet in the response was entailed by the reference answer or not, but would not explicitly mark which parts of the reference answer caused the entailment. The initial motivation of this proposed method, is similar to the work reported in (Nielsen et al. 2009). As per our knowledge, we think interpretability is related to Natural Language Understanding (NLU) problem and especially useful in the field of ITS, we aligned all chunks of one sentence to another as well as providing labels to each alignment, which justifies why two texts are similar or not.

In natural language, finding the variability of semantic expression is a fundamental task for many NLP applications such as QA, Information Extraction (IE), text summarization and Machine Translation (MT). To develop such method the PASCAL Recognizing Textual Entailment (RTE) challenge was made a significant progress as recognising two text fragments as hypothesis (H) and text (T), whether the meaning of one text can be entailed from the other. Task was asked to tag each T–H pair as either True/False in addition with a confidence score between 0 and 1 (Dagan et al. 2006). The iSTS is not a directional task, it differs many ways. The proposed method is not only entailed the two text, it also adds reasoning, in the form of typed alignments between sentence segments, which also adds a score between 0 to 5.

This work is related to the field of NLU, which gives an explanatory layer is important, with applications in dialogue system, interactive system and educational system. For this task, it is important to determine when sentences or phrase 'mean the same thing'. One major obstacle to this research area is lack of annotated corpora. To minimise this gap, the Microsoft Research NLP group provide a corpus of several thousand paraphrase sentence pairs in (Dolan and Brockett 2005). To improve the effectiveness they release an annotated version of the 2006 PASCAL RTE development and test corpora (Brockett 2007). They identified two possible links between the word and phrase as 'SURE' and 'POSSIBLE'. As compare to this, we are not only align the word and phrases, but also labelled each alignment with a relation type and a similarity score.

In another similar effort (Ru et al. 2012), an annotated corpus (called the SIMILAR corpus) was developed, which fills an existing gap for text-to-text similarity by providing the judgements to the word-to-word similarity matrices. They proposed a protocol to annotate a set of 700 pair of sentences from Microsoft Research Paraphrase corpus and also give six (6) word-to-word semantic similarity relations such as 'CLOSE' (for similar words), 'RELATED' (for words those are related but not similar), 'CONTEXT' (words share same topic), 'KNOWLEDGE' (for the words from same domain knowledge), 'IDENTICAL' (words are identical in their raw form) and 'NONE' (for unmatched words). Further they use these semantic similarity information to get the text-to-text similarity. As similar to their work, we also identify nine (9) semantic relations to phrase-to-phrase matrices. But, along with the relations we also provide a similarity score by aligning the phrases.

We are inspired from SemEval 2015 Task 2[1], where *i*STS given as a pilot subtask with STS task. The initial goal of the task to check the STS system was able to explain why two sentences are related/unrelated, adding an explanatory layer to the similarity score (Agirrea et al. 2015). Further this pilot subtask has been extended in SemEval 2016 event, where it was updated into a standalone task[2]. The final goal of the interpretable system would be explained what are the differences and commonalities between two sentences. In 2015 it was restricted to 1:1 alignment of the chunks, but in 2016 this restriction was lifted and allow any number of alignments between the chunks (Agirre et al. 2016). Our intention to this task is a proposal of new method and improvement as compared with the methods reported in (Agirre et al. 2015; Lopez-Gazpio et al. 2016; Magnolini et al. 2016; Henry and Sands 2016).

4   System Description

In this section, we describe the required principal algorithm and the distinct modules for preprocessing of the dataset, chunking and alignment mechanism. We first pre-process the input sentences and then chunks of the sentences have been identified. Further, the chunks have been input to the alignment process, which will able to align the chunks based on relatedness/similarity score. Finally, a overall score has been measured and based on that a relationship label is assigned. Details of the proposed method has been discussed in subsequent sections. As best of our knowledge, the contribution to this work is designing a light and efficient algorithm for chunk alignment with reasoning and score.

4.1   Preprocessing

During pre–processing the following six stages have been carried out (i) name entity identification; (ii) lower case conversion; (iii) tokenisation; (iv) abbreviation normalisation; (v) part–of–speech (POS) tagging; and (vi) negation handling. Stanford Named Entity Recogniser (NER) (Finkel et al. 2005), have been used to recognise the named entities (NE) across the sentences. Further these set of NEs have been used for abbreviation normalisation. The lower case conversion is carried out after the tokenisation stage.

In the abbreviation normalization stage, the NEs have been considered and replaced with their full form. For this purpose WordNet 2.1 library[3] is used and to get the exact information of the words like 'US' and 'UK', the noun synsets

---

[1] http://alt.qcri.org/semeval2015/task2/.

[2] http://alt.qcri.org/semeval2016/task2/.

[3] https://wordnet.princeton.edu/wordnet/download/old-versions/.

have been considered and for this purpose a ready–made Java based library[4] of
WordNet is used.

After the abbreviation normalisation, POS of each tokens have been identified. We have to understand this, for any iSTS method, the first and most basic
task is chunking and to produce error free chunking POS tagging is one of the
fundamental tasks. Accuracy of the chunking module depends over the accuracy
of POS tagging task. So to choose one of the best available POS tagger, a testing
has been conducted on the following taggers (i) Apache OpenNLP 1.8.1[5] and
(ii) Stanford *bi-directional* English tagger (Toutanova et al. 2003). An example
of POS tagging using both of the library is listed in Table 1. Example taken
from headlines training dataset of SemEval 2016 Task2. This testing has been
conducted over a pair of 756 sentences of headlines dataset and based on these
POS tags it has been identified that POS tagging using Stanford *bi-directional*
English tagger has the higher accuracy over Apache OpenNLP library.

Table 1. Output of a part–of–speech tagging

Library	POS tags
Apache OpenNLP	Former_JJ Nazi_NNP death_NN camp_NN guard_JJ Demjanjuk_NNP dead_NN at_IN 91_CD
Stanford bi-directional English tagger	Former_JJ Nazi_JJ death_NN camp_NN guard_VBP Demjanjuk_NNP dead_JJ at_IN 91_CD

Finally, for negation handling, a list of negative word with antonyms have
been prepared and for this purpose SentiWordNet ver. 3.0[6] has been used.

4.2 Modules of the System

Before describing the system modules, we need to understand the importance of
each module those will be required to solve any iSTS problem. A flow of these
modules is depicted in Fig. 1.

Task of any iSTS method is divided into four modules such as (i) chunking of
the source and translation sentences; (ii) aligning the chunks of the sentences; (iii)
assigning a relation type to the aligned chunks from a list of available labels (discussed in Sect. 2); and (iv) measuring the similarity/relatedness score between
the aligned chunks.

---

[4] https://projects.csail.mit.edu/jwi/.
[5] https://opennlp.apache.org/download.html.
[6] http://sentiwordnet.isti.cnr.it/.

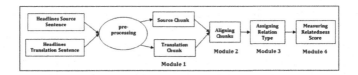

Fig. 1. Modules of the proposed method

Chunking. Chunking module consists of grouping the semantically correlated words of a sentence by means of phrases. For this task, *ixa–pipes–chunk* has been trained using the Apache OpenNLP 1.8.1 library. For this module, Stanford Dependency Parser (Klein and Manning 2003) has been used to linguistically process the source and translation sentences. Output of the parser, such as lower-cased token information, part–of–speech (POS) analysis and dependency structure has been recorded. Further this information has been used to implement the chunking module.

A set fo rules has been designed to fulfil the requirement of the gold standard chunks, those are available with the SemEval–2016 Task 2 training dataset. Based on these rules output of the Apache OpenNLP Chunker has been modified and rules are as follows:

1. Prepositional phrases followed by noun phrase are grouped together
2. Two nominal phrases are grouped together, if a consonant is found between the chunks
3. Another rules have been identified to unify noun phrases separated by punctuations
4. Symbols are ignored during the chunking module
5. If any prepositional phrase has fallen between two nominal phrase, then chunking has been done by considering the POS tags of the two noun tokens.

An example of a chunking module is illustrate in Table 2. The Apache OpenNLP Chunker has been categories the phrase into three groups, which is listed in the third row of Table 2. In this output, 'B' marks beginning of such phrases and 'I' means inner to the previous phrase and 'O' means others. After the chunking next part of the *i*STS method is aligning the chunks of two sentences.

Table 2. Stages of chunking module

Stages	Output of the modules
Sentence	Saudi women allowed to compete at Olympics
POS tags	JJ NNS VBD TO VB IN NNPS
OpenNLP Chunker	B-NP I-NP B-VP I-VP I-VP B-PP O
After adding rules	NP[Saudi women] VP[allowed to compete] PP[at Olympics]

Alignment Module. First a matrix (A) of dimension $M \times N$ has been initialised with all chunks of source text (S) against the all chunks of translation text (T), where M and N is the number of chunks in S and T respectively. For this alignment module, 1:M (Multi) alignment is considered, which means one chunk of S can be aligned with more than one chunk of T. Initially, we considered all chunks of S have been aligned with all chunks of T. By the imposing of following features set elimination has been done and final result of the alignment has been recorded into the another matrix called *alignedMatrix* (A_1).

1. Aligned chunk contains only one token, which is a symbol (, " $--$:' ') against a chunk of length greater than one is discarded from A.
2. The aligned noun phrase against verb phrase or vice versa has been eliminated from A.
3. Two chunks shares any common token has been kept in A.
4. After discarding all the stop word from a pair of aligned chunks, if any pair of token shares semantic relation like synonymy, antonymy, hypernymy, hyponymy, membership and part meronymy has been kept into A.
5. String matching between the aligned chunks
6. If condition (i–v) fails, cosine similarity between the two word vectors has been considered and a threshold value of 0.7 or above is considered for this purpose. Reason to such threshold value is discussed in Sect. 5.1.

An output of the alignment module is depicted in Fig. 2. First two lines are the inputs to the method as source (S) and translation (T) text and the next section is the list of tokens in S and T with token number. The last section i.e. alignment list the aligned chunks, which represents by token number and the last column of this section represents the alignment reasoning based on the features. The next task of iSTS method is assign a alignment type to the aligned chunks and if any chunks of S or T has been found unaligned (i.e. means no features have been satisfied), then those chunks will be labelled as 'NOALI' with aligned score of 0.

4.3   Alignment Reasoning

After alignment, a rule based classification algorithm has been designed to assign a relationship between the aligned chunks. All aligned pairs with the possible labels have been extracted from the training data set and these labels are reported in Sect. 2. Following features have been considered to measure a weight value and based on this value labels are assigned.

Named Entity Overlap. The Stanford Named Entity Recogniser (Finkel et al. 2005), has been considered to get the 3 classes (i.e. person, organisation and location) NEs between the aligned chunk. Then per-class NE overlap score is measured to assigning a class label as shown in Eq. 1:

$$OVLP_{score}(c_1, c_2) = \frac{2 \times |NE_1 \cap NE_2|}{|NE_1| + |NE_2|} \tag{1}$$

```
// Saudis to permit women to compete in Olympics (S)
// Saudi Women Allowed To Compete At Olympics (T)
<source>
1 Saudis :
2 to :
3 permit :
4 women :
5 to :
6 compete :
7 in :
8 Olympics :
</source>
<translation>
1 Saudi :
2 Women :
3 Allowed :
4 To :
5 Compete :
6 At :
7 Olympics :
</translation>
<alignment>
2 3 <==> 3 (vi)
4 <==> 1 2 (iii)
5 6 <==> 4 5 (v)
7 8 <==> 6 7 (iii)
1 <==> 1 2 (vi)
</alignment>
```

Fig. 2. Output of the alignment module

where c_1 and c_2 are the chunks of S and T. The overlapping score depends on number of NEs shared between c_1 and c_2.

Word Antonyms. Two aligned chunks in which an adjective from one is replaced by its antonym will have very similar structures (which indicates a good alignment). However, the sentences will have opposite meanings. This features is only considered to assign 'OPPO' means chunks are similar but shares opposite meaning. To do that POS of each token and antonym of that particular token is extracted. In the pre-processing stage a list antonyms has been prepared and to do that SentiWordNet is used.

Lexical Semantic Feature. To get the semantic information between the aligned chunks eight (8) knowledge based semantic measures have been used:

1. *Shortest Path*: Relatedness score is measured by counting the number of nodes between the word senses (for noun-noun and verb-verb POS pairs).
2. *Lesk Measure*: The relatedness score has been measured by the overlapping score of the words dictionary definitions (all pairs of POS) (Lesk 1986).
3. *LCH Similarity*: It considered the maximum WordNet similarity between the word senses by computing the shortest path (Leacock and Chodorow 1998) (for noun and verb POS).

4. *JCN Distance*: Measured by the notion of Information Content (IC), in the form of conditional probability between the instance of an child and parent synset (Jiang and Conrath 1997).
5. *WUP Similarity*: It measures the relatedness by considering the depths of two synsets between the WordNet taxonomies (Wu and Palmer 1994).
6. *LIN Similarity*: Measures the similarity between the word senses based on Information Content (IC) of the Least Common Subsumer (LCS) (Lin 1998).
7. *Resnik Score*: Same as (iv) and (vi), but differs in the way of measuring the IC value, in this case it is measued from an corpus (Resnik 1995).
8. *HSO Score*: Measures the similarity based on an assumption if two lexicalized concepts are semantically close and their synsets are connected by a path (Hirst and St-Onge 1998).

Cosine Similarity. Google pre–trained[7] Word2Vec model (of 300 dimension) is used to measures the cosine similarity between the two word vectors. Python implemented gensim (Rehurek and Sojka 2010) library is used to access the Google pre–trained Word2Vec model and to get the cosine similarity score between the vectors.

Along-with these set of features token overlap and chunk length is also considered to assign a class label. For the noun phrases, those has a digit or its word representation an extra pre–processing has been done before assigning a relation type. To understand this, consider two sentences as: (a) (*as source*) US drone strike kills **5** militants in Pakistan; (b) (*as translation*) – Drone strike kills **four** suspected militants in Pakistan. To align this, first 5 of the source has been translated to "five".

4.4   Alignment Score

Alignment scores are assigned as direct assignment between the aligned chunks or average similarity/relatedness score for each token (Karumuri et al. 2015). For the direct assignment 0 and 5 is assigned for 'NOALI' and 'EQUI' respectively. To measure the similarity score, method described by (Banjade et al. 2015), which is listed in Eq. 2.

$$chunkSim\,(c_1, c_2) = \frac{\sum_{i=1}^{n} max_{j=1}^{n} sim\,(w_i, w_j)}{min\,(n, m)} \tag{2}$$

where c_1 and c_2 are two aligned chunks, n and m are the number of token in c_1 and c_2 respectively. The similarity function between the words $sim\,(w_i, w_j)$ has been evaluated using lexical semantic similarity and cosine similarity, which is discussed in Sects. 4.3 and 4.4. An output of the proposed method combining Module 1 to 4 (see Fig. 1) has been depicted in Fig. 3.

---

[7] https://groups.google.com/forum/#!topic/word2vec-toolkit/z0Aw5powUco.

```
<sentence id="2" status="">
// Saudis to permit women to compete in Olympics
// Saudi Women Allowed To Compete At Olympics
<alignment>
......
......
2 3 <==> 3 // SIMI // 3 // to permit <==> Allowed
4 <==> 1 2 // SPE2 // 5 // women <==> Saudi Women
5 6 <==> 4 5 // EQUI // 5 // to compete <==> To Compete
7 8 <==> 6 7 // EQUI // 5 // in Olympics <==> At Olympics
1 <==> 0 // NOALI // 0 // Saudis <==> -not aligned-
</alignment>
</sentence>
```

Fig. 3. Output of alignment with type and score module

5   Excremental Results and Analysis

5.1   Analysis of Dataset

The dataset comprises of sentences from news headlines (Headlines) and image description (Images). The training dataset have 756 and 750 pair of sentence pairs in Headlines and Images dataset respectively. We have considered the Headlines dataset to developed the iSTS method. The test Headlines dataset comprises of 378 sentence pair. An statistics of the Headlines dataset w.r.t. total number of aligned chunks of each label type is shown in Table 3.

Table 3. Statistics of alignment types in training and test dataset

Type	Train	Test
EQUI	1323	686
FACT	29	0
NOALI	1792	869
OPPO	19	13
POL	4	2
REL	128	99
SIMI	324	158
SPE1	200	107
SPE2	193	108

Significance of Threshold 0.7 or Above. The proposed method have been developed using the training dataset and from the statistics shown in Table 3 it is clear that, 'EQUI' aligned type is the higher than other. The 'NOALI' alignment type is not consider, because it has a relatedness score as 0. We have trained the sentences of Headlines pair over the Google pre–trained Word2Vec model and the cosine similarity between the content words of source and translation sentences have been recorded. This process of assigning a relation type is continued till the last feature (cosine similarity see Sect. 4.4) that we used in this task.

Goal of the second and third module of the method is to get many 'EQUI' aligned type with a score of 5. So, whenever the algorithm has found that the corresponding tokens of the chunks are shared any semantic information, then cosine similarity score is extracted from the recorded data. We have scaled the cosine similarity score in seven (7) different ranges, which is depicted in Fig. 4. From the statistics shown in Fig. 4, it is clear that when system increase the threshold value by 0.1 the assigning of 'EQUI' type is reduces and which significantly improves the system performance. But, when the threshold value reach at 0.7 or above it remains unchanged and the total number of 'EQUI' labels, which is close to the actual count of the 'EQUI' label in training and test dataset.

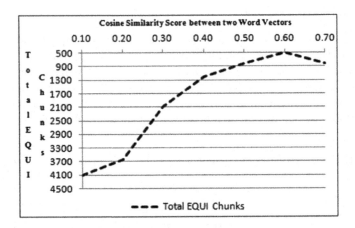

Fig. 4. Threshold scale from 0.1–0.7 vs assigned EQUI class

5.2   Result Analysis

System results have been evaluated using the script, which is publicly available with the dataset. It computes four distinct metrics: (i) **F1 Ali** (alignment correctness); (ii) **F1 Type** (alignment correctness with class label); (iii) **F1 Score** (alignment with score); and (iv) **F1 Type + Score** (alignment correctness with tag and relatedness score). The details about the evaluation matrix are described in (Agirrea et al. 2015).

Results on Training Data. Headlines training dataset comprises 750 pairs of sentences. The propose method has been developed using a rule based classification algorithm, which is based on a set of thirteen (13) features (discussed in Sect. 4.3). Results over the training dataset using system generated (sys) and gold standard (gs) chunks as shown in Table 4. Table 4 shows that system performance using the gs chunks are higher than the sys generated chunks.

Table 4. Results on training dataset

Chunks	Ali	Type	Score	Type + Score
gs	0.86	0.67	0.79	0.64
sys	0.84	0.64	0.76	0.62

Results on Test Data. Headlines test dataset was composed of 370 sentence pair and Table 5 illustrates the results using the proposed method and also compares the result against the baseline system.

Table 5. Results on headlines test dataset against the baseline features

GS	Ali	Type	Score	Type + Score
Baseline	0.84	0.59	0.78	0.62
Method	0.85	0.62	0.81	0.65
SYS	Ali	Type	Score	Type + Score
Baseline	0.74	0.55	0.72	0.60
Method	0.79	0.59	0.77	0.65

6 Conclusion and Future Work

From the result, it is clear that the proposed method has been outperform the baseline features and success of any *i*STS method is mainly depend on the chunking module. This method is developed and tested over the headlines dataset only. The *i*STS dataset composed of two other sets as image description and student answer. To work with image description dataset we need to pre–process the sentence pair in the other way that we did for headlines dataset. So, due to the time constraint we are not able submit the results on image description dataset. On the other side, the annotation guidelines are different for the student answer dataset. So for this task we didn't consider it. The final stage of any *i*STS method is adding an explanatory layer which, will take the alignment, relation type and score as an input and following that it generates the explanation and we left it for future work. Any *i*STS method plays important role for digital education, where a student can check his/her ability against a tutor answer. So we can conclude that, for digital transformation of any information STS plays an important role.

Acknowledgement. The work presented here falls under the Research Project Grant No. YSS/2015/000988 and supported by the Department of Science & Technology (DST) and Science and Engineering Research Board (SERB), Govt. of India. The authors would like to acknowledge the Department of Computer Science & Engineering, National Institute of Technology Mizoram, India for providing infrastructural facilities and support.

References

Agirre, E., Gonzalez-Agirre, A., Lopez-Gazpio, I., Maritxalar, M., Rigau, G., Uria, L.: UBC: cubes for English semantic textual similarity and supervised approaches for interpretable STS. In: Proceedings of the 9th International Workshop on Semantic Evaluation (SemEval 2015), Denver, Colorado, June, pp. 178–183. ACL (2015)

Agirre, E., Gonzalez-Agirre, A., Lopez-Gazpio, I., Maritxalar, M., Rigau, G., Uria, L.: SemEval-2016 task 2: interpretable semantic textual similarity. In: Proceedings of SemEval (SemEval 2016), San Diego, California, 16–17 June, pp. 512–524. ACL (2016)

Agirrea, E., Baneab, C., Cardiec, C., Cerd, D., Diabe, M., Gonzalez-Agirrea, A., Guof, W.,Lopez-Gazpioa, I., Maritxalara, M., Mihalceab, R., Rigaua, G., Uriaa, L., Wiebe, J.: SemEval-2015 task 2: semantic textual similarity, English, Spanish and pilot on interpretability. In: Proceedings of the 9th International Workshop on Semantic Evaluation (SemEval 2015), Denver, Colorado, June, pp. 252–263 (2015)

Aleven, V., Popescu, O., Koedinger, KR.: Pedagogical content knowledge in a tutorial dialogue system to support self-explanation. In: Papers of the AIED-2001 Workshop on Tutorial Dialogue Systems, pp. 59–70 (2001)

Aliguliyev, R.M.: A new sentence similarity measure and sentence based extractive technique for automatic text summarization. Expert Syst. Appl. **36**(4), 7764–7772 (2009)

Banjade, R., Niraula, N.B., Maharjan, N., Rus, V., Stefanescu, D., Lintean, M., Gautam, D.: NeRoSim: a system for measuring and interpreting semantic textual similarity. In: Proceedings of the 9th International Workshop on Semantic Evaluation (SemEval 2015), Denver, Colorado, 4–5 June, pp. 164–171. ACL (2015)

Brockett, C.: Aligning the RTE 2006 corpus. In: Microsoft Research Technical report MSR-TR-2007-77 (2007)

Coelho, A.S., Tatiana, A.S., Calado, P.P., Souza, L.V., Ribeiro-Neto, B., Muntz, R.: Image retrieval using multiple evidence ranking. IEEE Trans. Knowl. Data Eng. **16**(4), 408–417 (2004)

Dagan, I., Glickman, O., Magnini, B.: The PASCAL recognising textual entailment challenge. In: Quiñonero-Candela, J., Dagan, I., Magnini, B., d'Alché-Buc, F. (eds.) MLCW 2005. LNCS (LNAI), vol. 3944, pp. 177–190. Springer, Heidelberg (2006). https://doi.org/10.1007/11736790_9

Dolan, W.B., Brockett, C.: Automatically constructing a corpus of sentential paraphrases. In: Third International Workshop on Paraphrasing. Asia Federation of Natural Language Processing, January 2005

Finkel, JR., Grenager, T., Manning, C.: Incorporating non-local information into information extraction systems by Gibbs sampling. In: Proceedings of the 43rd Annual Meeting on Association for Computational Linguistics (ACL 2005), pp. 363–370, Stroudsburg, PA, USA, 25–30 June. ACL (2005)

Henry, S., Sands, A.: VRep at SemEval-2016 task 1 and task 2: a system for interpretable semantic similarity. In: Proceedings of the 10th International Workshop on Semantic Evaluation in Collocated in 15th Annual Conference of the North American Chapter of the Association for Computational Linguistics: Human Language Technologies (SemEval 2016), San Diego, California, 16–17 June, pp. 577–583. ACL (2016)

Hirst, G., St-Onge, D.: WordNet: an electronic lexical database chapter lexical chains as representations of context for the detection and correction of malapropisms, pp. 305–332. MIT Press, April 1998

Islam, A., Inkpen, D.: Semantic text similarity using corpus-based word similarity and string similarity. ACM Trans. Knowl. Discov. Data. **2**(2), 10:1–10:25 (2008)

Jiang, J.J., Conrath, D.W.: Semantic similarity based on corpus statistics and lexical taxonomy. In: Proceedings of International Conference Research on Computational Linguistics (ROCLING X) (1997)

Jordan, P.W., Makatchev, M., Pappuswamy, U., VanLehn, K., Albacete, P.: A natural language tutorial dialogue system for physics. In: Proceedings of the Nineteenth International Florida Artificial Intelligence Research Society Conference (FLAIRS 2006), Melbourne Beach, FL, United States, 11–13 May, pp. 521–526 (2005)

Karumuri, S., Vuggumudi, V.K.R., Chitirala, S.C.R.: UMDuluth-BlueTeam: SVCSTS -a multilingual and chunk level semantic similarity system. In: Proceedings of the 9th International Workshop on Semantic Evaluation (SemEval 2015), Denver, Colorado, USA, 4–5 June, pp. 107–110. Association for Computational Linguistic (2015)

Klein, D., Manning, C.D.: Accurate unlexicalized parsing. In: Proceedings of the 41st Annual Meeting on Association for Computational Linguistics, (ACL 2003), Sapporo, Japan, 7–12 July, vol. 1, pp. 423–430 (2003)

Leacock, C., Chodorow, M.: Combining local context and WordNet similarity for word sense identification. In: WordNet: An Electronic Lexical Database, chap. 13, pp. 265–283. MIT Press (1998)

Lesk, M.: Automatic sense disambiguation using machine readable dictionaries: how to tell a pine cone from an ice cream cone. In: Proceedings of the 5th Annual International Conference on Systems Documentation (SIGDOC 1986), pp. 24–26. ACM, New York, June 1986

Li, Y., McLean, D., Bandar, Z.A., O'shea, I.D., Crockett, K.: Sentence similarity based on semantic nets and corpus statistics. IEEE Trans. Knowl. Data Eng. **18**(8), 1138–1150 (2006)

Lin, D.: An information-theoretic definition of similarity. In: Proceedings of the Fifteenth International Conference on Machine Learning (ICML 1998), San Francisco, CA, USA, pp. 296–304. Morgan Kaufmann Publishers Inc. (1998)

Lopez-Gazpio, I., Eneko, A., Montse, M.: iUBC at SemEval-2016 task 2: RNNs and LSTMs for interpretable STS. In: Proceedings of International Workshop on Semantic Evaluation in Association with 15th Annual Conference of the North American Chapter of the Association for Computational Linguistics: Human Language Technologies (SemEval 2016), San Diego, California, 16–17 June, pp. 771–776 (2016)

Magnolini, S., Feltracco, A., Magnini, B.: FBK-HLT-NLP at SemEval-2016 Task 2: a multitask, deep learning approach for interpretable semantic textual similarity. In: Proceedings of the 10th International Workshop on Semantic Evaluation (SemEval 2016), San Diego, California, 16–17 June, pp. 783–789 (2016)

Mihalcea, R., Corley, C., Strapparava, C.: Corpus-based and knowledge-based measures of text semantic similarity. In: Proceedings of the 21st National Conference on Artificial Intelligence (AAAI 2006), Boston, Massachusetts, 16–20, July, vol. 1, pp. 775–780. AAAI Press (2006)

Mohler, M., Bunescu, R., Mihalcea, R.: Learning to grade short answer questions using semantic similarity measures and dependency graph alignments. In: Proceedings of the 49th Annual Meeting of the Association for Computational Linguistics: Human Language Technologies (HLT 2011), Stroudsburg, PA, USA, 19–24 June, vol. 1, pp. 752–762 (2011)

Nielsen, R.D., Ward, W., Martin, J.H.: Recognizing entailment in intelligent tutoring systems*. Nat. Lang. Eng. **15**(4), 479–501 (2009)

Rehurek, R., Sojka, P.: Software framework for topic modelling with large corpora. In: Proceedings of the LREC 2010 Workshop on New Challenges for NLP Frameworks, pp. 45–50. ELRA, May 2010

Resnik, P.: Using information content to evaluate semantic similarity in a taxonomy. In: Proceedings of the 14th International Joint Conference on Artificial Intelligence, (IJCAI 1995), San Francisco, CA, USA, 20–25 August, vol. 1, pp. 448–453. Morgan Kaufmann Publishers Inc. (1995)

Rocchio, J.J.: Relevance Feedback in Information Retrieval. Prentice-Hall, Englewood Cliffs (1971)

Ru, V., Lintean, M., Moldovan, C., Baggett, W., Niraula, N., Morgan, B.: The similar corpus: a resource to foster the qualitative understanding of semantic similarity of texts. In: Proceedings of Semantic Relations-II. Enhancing Resources and Applications. The 8th Language Resources and Evaluation Conference, (LREC 2012), 23–25 May 2012

Salton, G., Singhal, A., Mitra, M., Buckley, C.: Automatic text structuring and summarization. Inf. Process. Manag. Int. J. **33**(2), 193–207 (1997). Special issue: methods and tools for the automatic construction of hypertext

Steinberger, J., Jezek, K.: Using latent semantic analysis in text summarization and summary evaluation. In: Proceedings of 7th International Conference on Information Systems Implementation Modeling (ISIM 2004), Ostrava, CZ, pp. 93–100, April 2004

Toutanova, K., Klein, D., Manning, C.D., Singer, Y.: Feature-rich part-of-speech tagging with a cyclic dependency network. In: Proceedings of the 2003 Conference of the North American Chapter of the Association for Computational Linguistics on Human Language Technology (NAACL 2003), Edmonton, Canada, 27 May–01 June, vol. 1, pp. 173–180 (2003)

Šarić, F., Glavaš, G., Karan, M., Šnajder, J., Bašić, B.D.: TakeLab: systems for measuring semantic text similarity. In: Proceedings of the First Joint Conference on Lexical and Computational Semantics, vol. 1: Proceedings of the Main Conference and the Shared Task, vol. 2: Proceedings of the Sixth International Workshop on Semantic Evaluation (SemEval 2012), Stroudsburg, PA, USA, 7–8 July, pp. 441–448 (2012)

Wu, Z., Palmer, M.: Verbs semantics and lexical selection. In: Proceedings of the 32nd Annual Meeting on Association for Computational Linguistics (ACL 1994), Stroudsburg, PA, USA, 27–30 June, pp. 133–138 (1994)

Author Index

Printed in the United States
By Bookmasters